Improving
Reading
in
Every
Class

Ellen Lamar Thomas

reading consultant
university of chicago
laboratory school

H. Alan Robinson

professor of reading
hofstra university

Second Edition

Improving Reading in Every Class

a sourcebook for teachers

Allyn and Bacon, Inc.
Boston London Sydney

LIBRARY OF CONGRESS CATALOGING IN PUBLICATION DATA

Thomas, Ellen Lamar.
  Improving reading in every class.

  Includes bibliographies and index.
  1. Reading. I. Robinson, H. Alan, 1921–   joint
author. II. Title.
LB1050.T5 1977   428′.4   76-27734
ISBN 0–205–05590–7
Second printing . . . September, 1977

to
Helen M. Robinson
and Nila Banton Smith,
who believe in improving reading
in every class.

Contents

Foreword

For many years we have been hearing the softly spoken but never realized slogan "Every teacher, a teacher of reading." This book will make a genuine contribution toward reaching that goal.

One of the most distinctive features of the book is its scope. It suggests procedures not only for teaching the fundamental processes in reading, but procedures, also, for teaching reading in *all* of the high school subject areas. Four chapters present methods for teaching vocabulary, comprehension, rate, problem solving. The succeeding twelve chapters are devoted to practical classroom methods for teaching social studies, English, science, mathematics, industrial arts, typewriting and business education, foreign languages, home economics, music, library services, fine arts, and physical education, respectively. Thus, the teaching of reading in the whole gamut of high school subjects is covered. Just showing through practical examples and procedures how this can be done is a notable accomplishment in itself.

Another distinctive feature of this book is its practicality. The entire content is thoroughly practical and usable. Both elementary and secondary teachers, and more recently college teachers, are clamoring for how-to-do-it ideas and suggestions. They complain that their college courses, textbooks, extracurricular lectures, etc., deal chiefly with theory and research and that rarely are they given help in actual classroom procedures. Very few books in reading have been devoted exclusively to how-to-do-it suggestions and those that have been published are extremely limited in scope. The helps given in this book, in part, grew out of the experiences of teachers in the University of Chicago Laboratory School and were found to be useful and workable by them. Other ideas were gathered from various sources where those who had used them found them to be of practical value. Teachers will greet this veritable potpourri of usable classroom suggestions with enthusiasm.

A third characteristic which should contribute markedly to the usefulness of this volume is wide variety in the types of helps that are provided. There are motivating activities, teaching procedures, practice exercises, enrichment activities of many, many different kinds. There are examples of lessons, interviews on how to teach reading, directions to students, warnings in regard to "Do's and Don't's," etc. Tests of different reading abilities, both formal and informal, are suggested. Check lists, guide sheets, and work sheets for practice work are provided for the use of students. Certainly with such a wide variety of helps reading teachers and subject teachers should be able to assess needs, spark interest, and provide abundant practice in developing the necessary reading skills in their respective areas of teaching.

The references in this book are worthy of mention, both as to quality and number. While the authors devote their content to practical helps devoid of esoteric discourse on theory and research, the many references that they provide give evidence of their broad acquaintance with literature in the entire field of reading. Carefully selected references in the text and in bibliographies at ends of chapters provide enrichment reading for teachers and others who wish to have more background about topics treated in the book. Particularly noteworthy is the fact that in cases in which research is available, a practical help is reinforced by referring to a study which has indicated that the procedure suggested in the how-to-do-it help is the one that was found to be most effective.

In Chapter 1 the authors state, "We have been trailblazers in preparing this book." Indeed they have been trailblazers, and as such they deserve our high commendation.

Nila Banton Smith

Preface

We thank our readers for warmly receiving the first edition of *Improving Reading in Every Class,* where we suggested specific procedures for building reading improvement into the regular course work in a wide variety of subjects. We hoped to present procedures practical enough to be put to use in the classroom the next day. We offered how-to-do-it suggestions for reading as teachers go about everyday activities such as making assignments, helping students master key vocabulary or comprehend a chapter, formulating questions on reading selections, guiding students in solving problems, and encouraging wide reading. We suggested that these routine activities can be designed to "turn on" reading power in subject areas from English through physical education. Professional response to our book suggests that our efforts were useful.

The second edition includes new, extensive sections on upgrading the reading of students in English and social studies, two subjects where reading is critically important. The English section features a wide variety of possible aids for students "when their reading's a struggle"—classroom-tested procedures that have helped students to read and understand those selections they find difficult. We have devoted a section to the preparation of successful study guides in which we point out how solid reading assistance for students can be built right into their study guides. The social studies chapter offers a variety of ways to excite student interest and involvement in their social studies course content. Within this chapter we also report ways to help teachers cope with the dismaying range in reading achievement within a single classroom. An item, "Finding Out About Your Students Reading," suggests how teachers can learn, fairly easily, about their students' strengths and weaknesses in reading in order to plan a year of more successful learning. A section on upgrading the reading of difficult primary sources with the formidable roadblocks they place in the way of students concludes the social studies chapter.

The science chapter was expanded by reporting a physics teacher's successful venture in improving the reading of students who were giving their textbook a helter-skelter reading. An expanded vocabulary section now offers practical applications of the contributions of scholars of linguistics and semantics. Among these applications are ways to help students react critically to the tremendous power words have in influencing thought and actions. Our hearts are in this section—we consider alerting young people to "word power" a contribution to humanity's survival kit.

As in our first edition, techniques and procedures described were developed for various disciplines, then tested in classrooms at the University of Chicago Laboratory Schools, and at a number of other junior and senior high schools across the country. Obviously, adjustments are needed for different students, teachers, subjects, and situations.

Since our focus is on the subject classroom, our book emphasizes the developmental and corrective aspects of reading instruction rather than the remedial. The efforts of each classroom teacher can be most helpful in working with a severely retarded reader. These efforts should, of course, be supplemented with the help of a trained remedial reading teacher.

We believe our book is unique. We know of no other in which teachers in as great a variety of subject classrooms share their "success secrets" for extending and improving reading skills while at the same time teaching the regular course content—with important gains for students in this course work.

Without question *Improving Reading in Every Class* would not exist without the interest, efforts, and generous cooperation of certain members of the staff of the University of Chicago Laboratory School. Roy A. Larmee, former director, initiated a reading program that emphasized improving reading within the classroom, as well as remedial help for students, and Francis V. Lloyd and Willard J. Congreve, former administrators, assumed strong and inspiring leadership roles in extending the program. Donald O. Conway, associate director, and Betty Hollander, school examiner, have quietly supported the program in important ways.

This new edition contains an increased number of references to activities that have upgraded reading within the public schools. We express special thanks to Berenice Bragstadt, reading consultant of La Follette Senior High School, Madison, Wisconsin; and to Charles Carlson, social studies teacher at La Follette. Two other master teachers contributed ideas and inspiration: Emma LaPorte, formerly of New Trier High School, Winnetka, Illinois; and Margaret Hillman, formerly of St. Petersburg High School, St. Petersburg, Florida.

The University of Chicago internship program in the training of reading consultants provided help to the Laboratory School's reading consultant by furnishing the school with capable "assistant" reading consultants. A number of them assisted with the development of specific procedures and materials offered in the book; footnotes and, sometimes, introductory statements explain their contributions. General contributions were made by the following, who are now reading specialists in public school systems, independent schools, colleges, and universities: Eileen E. Bertellotti, Patricia Cookis, Camille Haegert, Joyce Ann Harris, Kathleen Jongsma, Margaret McAuliffe, and Dorothy Burr Woods.

We have dedicated this book to Helen M. Robinson and Nila Banton Smith, distinguished educators and our friends. We acknowledge with warm and deep appreciation their general contributions to our thinking and their specific contributions to this book. Any shortcomings in this book are in no way theirs but entirely our own.

We express most earnest thanks to two uncomplaining, capable, and conscientious secretaries—Nicky Barry of Hofstra University and Virginia Jacques in Chicago, who typed, proofread, copied, collated, and did many of the thankless tasks essential in preparing a manuscript for the publisher. Librarian Nancy Herb, of Hofstra, was tremendously helpful in finding current sources for this revision. Samuel Weintraub of the reading staff of the University of Buffalo was helpful with his patient answers to questions. Ruth Robinson, daughter of one of the authors, provided invaluable assistance with the mechanics of this edition.

The contributions of certain members of the faculty of the University of Chicago Laboratory School speak for themselves throughout the book. These dedicated teachers, striving to solve the reading problems of their students, made reading instruction an integral part of daily learning experiences. Francis V. Lloyd had this to say about the program when it was under his directorship: "Reading is taught in English class, over the cookstove in home economics, even on the basketball court." Laboratory School teachers made valued contributions to our new sections: Darlene McCampbell and Sophie Ravin in English; Earl Bell, Edgar Bernstein, Philip Montag, and Joel Surgal in social studies.

The passing of time, the availability of a reading consultant's services to teachers, and the turnover of faculty may alter the span and intensity of the reading effort at the Laboratory School. Many faculty members who were active in the projects reported here are now in other schools. There is no claim to having attained and maintained a model schoolwide reading program.

Through its reading program the Laboratory School has perhaps made its own contribution. A concept sprang to fuller life there and is reflected in this book: the concept of teachers in many different subjects being concerned with reading and skillful at improving it within their classrooms. The descriptions and results presented in this book are proof of the possibilities, and in some classrooms the reality, of fusing the teaching of reading skills with the teaching of course content.

E. L. T.
H. A. R.

1

HOW TO USE THIS BOOK

You may be a reading specialist, a classroom teacher, a curriculum specialist, a language arts consultant, a school administrator, or a college student planning to specialize in one of these fields. This book is written to help people in all those occupations.

If you are a reading or language arts specialist, you will find here approaches and devices that have worked for classroom teachers in helping their students read more competently in a number of subject areas, from English through physical education. You will find a great many insights about improving reading in chapters that talk right to the classroom teacher, free from reading "pedagese." And you will find the enthusiastic comments of subject teachers who talk about their reading effort: "It saves us time." "Students achieve better in the course all year."

If you are a classroom teacher, you will find procedures and devices for upgrading reading specific enough to try out in your classroom tomorrow. You do not need to be a reading expert. You will find suggestive answers to these questions: How can you improve the vocabularies of your students through their regular course work? How can you turn on reading power simply by the way you make a reading assignment? How can you equip your students with better techniques for mastering a textbook chapter? How can you give them more of the reading expertise they need for problem solving? You will find suggestions from classroom teachers who have successfully coped with the wide

1

range in reading achievement within their class groups, getting manageable books into the hands of not-so-able readers. And you will find possible ways of reaching unreached readers, generating their enthusiasm for reading—for life.

If you are a curriculum specialist, you already have a special interest in the weighty reading demands that different school courses—and different content within those courses—place upon the student reader, and in the varied skills and techniques students must acquire in order to meet these demands. You are probably interested in the specific and often sequential steps essential for developing these competencies. In this book you will meet subject teachers who do not ask, "Isn't reading the English teacher's job?" or "Why didn't students learn to read on a lower level?" These teachers are well aware that their students may meet patterns of writing never before encountered: the laboratory manual in science, the practice book in typewriting, a theorem in geometry, a recipe and a sewing pattern in homemaking, a musical example in music theory. They realize that perhaps some students have had no previous opportunity to learn to read these patterns of writing. You may wish to share with others the view of these teachers that the classroom is the ideal place to develop the specialized techniques that are essential for—and sometimes unique to— the particular subjects they teach.

If you are a school administrator, you will be interested in the possible procedures offered here for helping *all* the readers of a school, not only the retarded but the average and the highly gifted, to approach their potential. And you may wish to examine the procedures and instructional materials that grew out of a reading program aimed at involving teachers in subject classrooms.

If you are a student planning to enter one of the fields above, you will welcome insights into the heavy demands in reading which school courses impose on students. You may be interested in the ideal of a schoolwide developmental and corrective program aimed at meeting those demands. And you will welcome the practical how-to-do-its and why-do-its for helping students read better.

Development of the Procedures and Materials

We would like to share with you in the rest of this chapter how this book grew and why it has its present contents. We would like to suggest how to use the book to fullest advantage. And we offer you a subject-area index, which should help you find your way through the book and increase its usefulness.

Our book is in part a sharing of reading projects developed in the University of Chicago Laboratory School. There subject teachers and their reading consultant, working together, developed some new procedures and adapted known procedures to "new" disciplines. The units "just grew" (as they would in any school) whenever there were needs and teachers recognized those needs. Such projects, gathered into a book, form an "anthology." They are not intended to constitute a complete or balanced reading program. Some Laboratory School teachers, as do teachers elsewhere, observed in their students a special need for close, study-type reading. Hence you will find an emphasis on reading for information rather than for appreciation. Many Laboratory School teachers were already highly skilled in sparking a fervor for reading, in relating reading to exciting discoveries, and in developing more reflective, more critical readers. Teachers sought the consultant's help in giving students workaday skills for getting certain study-type reading jobs done. Mathematics teachers observed a need to improve textbook reading. They asked the consultant to help develop the comprehensive guidesheets for students that appear in Chapter 9. The home economics teacher and the consultant prepared materials to help students read recipes and sewing patterns. Projects were developed in areas where there were insufficient resources to meet the need at hand. We trust that this filling in of gaps is a contribution of our book and not a limitation. It is our special hope that the reader will find our "anthology" suggestive and will increase and multiply such materials, extending them into more and more disciplines.

For your convenience we repeat suggestions in one section that were used in another. We have tried to make each section a self-contained unit. You will not often need to leaf through the pages to locate related material. When strategies worked in one subject, we have not hesitated to repeat them in another. Our teachers exclaimed, as do teachers elsewhere, "My students can't read directions!" When a colorful notebook foldout helped shop students cope with complicated directions, we made another foldout to help science students handle the directions for laboratory procedures. Then we prepared one for typewriting classes. While all these foldouts *appear* similar, important differences tailor them for the different subjects.

Someone asked us, "Can you bottle the procedures that have worked successfully in one school and uncork them in another?" The experiences of others cannot offer routines to be followed explicitly in other classrooms. But successful experiences can offer ideas and guidelines. Obviously, the strategies, procedures, and materials in this book need to be adapted for older or younger students, for more capable or less capable readers, for particular situations, for a diversity of purposes. Since the Laboratory School has an academically somewhat favored student body, you will often need to adjust our ideas to fit your students' capabilities. We trust that the reader will make use of the aids most appropriate for each immediate situation, adjusting them as needed. We hope especially that teachers working in that area of special need, the inner-city classroom, will find here leads for effective approaches.

Throughout the book printed materials are addressed directly to students and are intended to be placed in their hands. Student materials have been marked with an asterisk (*) next to the page number so they can be quickly distinguished from materials directed to the instructor. You may wish to use these materials as they now appear if their level of difficulty is appropriate for your students. The student materials may be duplicated for classroom use after obtaining written permission from the publisher: Allyn and Bacon, Inc., 470 Atlantic Avenue, Boston, Massachusetts 02210. If the material contains matter that other publishers have permitted us to reproduce, it will be necessary for you to obtain reproduction permission from that company, as well (usually indicated in a credit line at the foot of a page or accompanying an illustration). You may wish to adjust or simplify the student materials or to use just parts of them. You have our permission to do this. Or they may serve simply as a source of ideas for your own class instruction. Certainly, extensive printed materials are not a must in giving reading guidance.

When printed materials for students are supplied in this book, they are intended only to supplement and reinforce instruction by the classroom teacher. We cannot emphasize too strongly that printed guidelines in themselves are not likely to effect much of a change in students' habits.

We have applied known insights about reading to the needs of students across a variety of disciplines—indeed, this is a major thrust of our book. We have tried to express these insights in plain English, to channel to classroom teachers know-how that has too often been the peculiar property of reading experts, and so to help reduce the lag between the lore of reading specialists and the practices that prevail in many classrooms.

The Subject-Area Index

The index at the back of this book is like other indexes in directing you to a great variety of topics. The subject-area index on pages 5–10 is different. The headings, as you will note, are various subject areas: English, mathematics, industrial arts, and others. It is placed in this introduction to guide you to all the parts of the book that offer help in improving reading in your particular subject.

You will ordinarily find under each subject heading—mathematics, for example—three subheadings. The first is *Specific Helps for These Classes*. Here you will find specialized strategies for mathematics or general approaches that have been tailored for mathematics. The second subheading is *General Aids for Improving Reading*. Index entries under this will guide you to broad background information on how to improve reading that you may relate to mathematics. You will sometimes find a third subheading, *See Also*. Here you are referred to approaches and techniques discussed in this book under other subject-area headings that are highly applicable to or suggestive for mathematics.

This subject-area index should be useful to a teacher looking for general aids for improving vocabulary, for example, in addition to any specific vocabulary techniques offered in the chapter devoted to that teacher's subject and to any related material discussed under another subject. The reading specialist, the language arts consultant, the curriculum consultant, or the college student preparing to specialize in one of these fields may wish to peruse the book from cover to cover. On occasion, however, any reader should find the subject-area index useful in meeting specific needs or in giving specific assistance to subject-matter teachers who are ready to help students fuse reading skills and course content.

We have been trailblazers in preparing the first edition of this book. It took courage for the writers, whose field is reading, to venture into areas like typewriting, music theory, and industrial arts. We hope you will find our efforts useful and that, with the addition of your own creative efforts, you will devise other still more effective ways of helping students reach their fullest potential in reading.

Subject-Area Index

English and Reading

Specific helps for these classes

General aids for improving reading

See also

Social Studies

Science

Homemaking

Music

Library

Comprehension, 101–193—especially 125–136, how to provide materials
that match the reading "reach" of students
Flexibility in rate of reading, 195–234

See also

Classroom libraries to turn on readers, 466–468, 563–571, 573–579
A classroom collection of reading resources, 296–305
Bringing the "right reader" and the "right reading" together, 305–310
Finding out about your students' reading, 278–283
Helps when reading is a struggle, 325–347
Helping students *want* to read, 284–296
Study guides that turn on reading power, 347–359

Art

Specific helps for these classes

Improving reading and selling reading, 563–571

General aids for improving reading

Vocabulary, 11–88
Word attack, 86–95
Comprehension, 101–183
Flexibility in rate of reading, 195–200, 208–234
Problem solving and topic development, 235–275

See also

How to upgrade reading directions, 460–466
Breaking the barrier of difficult concepts, 311–314

Physical Education

Specific helps for these classes

How coaches can get boys "hooked on books," 573–579

BUILDING VOCABULARY AND WORD ATTACK SKILLS

If you are a subject matter teacher and not a reading specialist, you may have little idea of what an important contribution you can make to improving the reading of your students. And in no area of reading are you likely to be more effective than in vocabulary.

You can give your students self-help techniques for improving their vocabularies through your regular class instruction—and you need not take additional class time. You can help them master new terms for their immediate course work as well as advance in reading ability. Special expertise in reading instruction is not needed.

Part of the content of the first and longest section of this chapter originated when the reading consultant promoted an idea exchange among University of Chicago Laboratory School teachers. She interviewed her colleagues in different subject classrooms, asking, "What are your favorite vocabulary development methods?" Then she added many ideas of her own and compiled all the ideas into a vocabulary reference guide. Through this booklet, the teachers shared with each other methods they had found effective.*

In the section "A Program for Vocabulary Development" we offer some answers to the following questions. We hope the answers are practical enough to try out in your classroom tomorrow.

1.   What are some principles to guide vocabulary growth?

2.   What are some characteristics of the "ideal product" of the vocabulary work in your class?

3.   How can you gain insights into each student's achievements and needs?

4.   What are some ways to motivate vocabulary improvement?

5.   How can you invest new words with meaning through experience?

6.   How can you encourage vocabulary growth through reading?

7.   How can you remove vocabulary obstacles before students read an assignment?

8.   How can students make full use of context to get at word meaning?

9.   How can students get vocabulary increments through frequently recurring word parts?

10. Is there a list of Greek and Latin word parts likely to help the student learn their English derivatives?

11. How can a teacher work with word origins to fix meanings in mind and stir interest?

12. What dictionary skills are vital to students if they are to continue their vocabulary growth independently?

13. What are some other ways to promote long-term, do-it-yourself vocabulary growth?

14. What is the "hidden consensus" of experts on the steps students should take when they meet a new word?

---

* The writers appreciate the contributions of the following teachers: science—Lestina Colby, Jerry Ferguson, A. J. Ferrantino, and Jan Housinger; social studies—Margaret Fallers, Dave Stameshkin, and Joel Surgal; mathematics—Paul Moulton and Richard Muelder; home economics—Dorothy Szymkowicz; typewriting—Faynelle Haehn; industrial arts—Herbert Pearson; foreign languages—Milton Finstein and Ruth Schroth; English—Sharon Calk, Sharon Feiman, Ruth Kaplan, Francis V. Lloyd, Darlene McCampbell, James McCampbell, Eunice McGuire, Emily Meyer, Carolyn Parker, Sue Phillips, Hope Rhinestone, Richard Scott, and Edith Tatel. Richard Scott was generous with his counsel when he served as chairman of the Laboratory School English Department. Special thanks go to his teachers for their lively ideas. Mr. Scott served as consultant for this section.

We fall far short in our vocabulary programs if our students learn only the meanings of words and not their tremendous power. In the second section in this chapter, "Danger: Words at Work," we suggest ways to help young people become aware—and wary—of the persuasive power of words and to react to words with critical reflection. We hope that work with "word power" will be a vital part of any vocabulary program.

Although background experiences as well as the semantic and syntactic aspects of language will usually help students figure out words they do not recognize immediately, some high school and college students need help in word attack skills. We offer in the third section of this chapter a five-part strategy to help students attack words that appear unfamiliar. The final section explains how to prepare a handy "instant word attack kit" with practice materials on appropriate levels.

A Program for Vocabulary Development

Rationale

General Principles

These principles, among others, can guide vocabulary growth in every classroom:

1. Direct and indirect experience: trips, TV, films, filmstrips, and models can enlarge the vocabularies of students and invest new words with meaning.

2. Wide reading accounts for much of the vocabulary growth of competent readers. Through reading they spend countless hours in a world of words. They meet new words repeatedly in similar and different settings, often with some increment of meaning at each encounter, and gradually incorporate them into their vocabularies. All teachers can encourage students to read widely and to approach their reading with a conscious effort to notice unfamiliar words and to make selected ones their own.

3. Direct attention to vocabulary should supplement vocabulary growth through reading. Research strongly suggests that planned instruction is superior to a casual or incidental approach.

4. Planned instruction can be built right into the regular course work and can yield returns in learning subject matter.

5. Teachers can remove obstacles from the reading road by first searching through assignments for "stopper" words and pre-teaching these to students.

6. Context clues can be a major self-help technique for students learning the vocabularies of many subjects. They should be given all possible help in learning to use context clues as an aid in getting at the meanings of unknown words. As students meet words in varying contexts, they should become aware

that words shift and change meaning and that the context of the moment determines the meaning of the moment.

7. Knowledge of frequently recurring prefixes, suffixes, and roots, when used in conjunction with context clues, can give students another important self-help technique to unlock the meanings of words.

8. Today's graduates are facing a new word explosion. Words not yet coined, emerging as a result of social, political, and scientific changes, will confront students after they leave our classrooms. Habits that will keep vocabulary growing after high school and college are therefore indispensable.

9. The young people we teach today belong to the most propagandized generation in history. Teachers in every classroom can bring home to students not only the meanings of words but also their persuasive power. Guiding young people to respond to words reflectively is a critical responsibility.

10. The overall goal of the vocabulary program is to sensitize students to all aspects of the English language and to instill in them the capacity to respond to language with perceptiveness and enthusiasm.

Characteristics of the "Ideal Graduate"

The "ideal product" of the vocabulary program has acquired many interests, attitudes, and competencies, such as those described below.

The student demonstrates a lasting enthusiasm for developing a superior vocabulary.

The student views vocabulary growth as a lifetime process and assumes the major responsibility for vocabulary development.

The student has been introduced to the "help-yourself" methods appropriate for personal vocabulary development, has practiced using these methods, and has built them permanently into reading and listening habits. These procedures will serve as lifetime tools for enriching word resources.

The student notices unfamiliar words encountered during varied reading and, through concious effort and the use of effective, individualized procedures, makes selected words permanently his or her own.

The student demonstrates alertness to the tremendous power of words —power to shape thoughts and influence actions. The student controls—is not controlled by—words.

Most importantly, the student delights in the precision, the power, and the artistry of words. "What is needed for all learning is interest.

A sense of excitement about words, a sense of wonder, and a feeling of pleasure—these are the essential ingredients in vocabulary development" (Deighton, 1959, p. 59).

This ideal will remain beyond the reach of many students. Accordingly, in almost all classrooms, teachers will want to give constant and abundant help with vocabulary development.

Diagnosing Vocabulary Strengths and Weaknesses

How can you diagnose the vocabulary achievements and needs of your students? As one teacher comments, "As a general rule, it's unsound to teach a poor reader *gargantuan* if he doesn't know *gigantic.*"

Standardized Tests

Your school may already have a vocabulary score on record for each of your students. However, you may want the results of more recent and more thoroughgoing testing, or you may want insights into their vocabulary strength in your subject area. The following tests offer some information about a student's vocabulary in a number of subject fields. It should be noted, however, that most standardized vocabulary tests have certain shortcomings: they measure the student's mastery of a word in terms of a single meaning; they test word power in an artificial situation, since the words are out of context; and they fail to measure some of the first goals of vocabulary learning, among them the student's enthusiasm for words and critical reaction to their power.

> *Diagnostic Reading Tests, Section 1: Vocabulary* (Mountain Home, North Carolina: The Committee on Diagnostic Reading Tests, Revised, 1967), intended for grades 7–13; two forms, A and B. This test yields scores in four subject fields: English, mathematics, science, and social studies. There are 200 words in all, 50 in each area. The complete test takes 40 minutes; each subject area, 10 minutes. Since the time limit may "contaminate" the vocabulary score with a speed factor, for some students and in certain circumstances it may be advisable to impose no time limit. Of course, disregarding the time limit converts the test into an informal diagnostic device as the norming of the test included the time factor.
>
> *California Achievement Tests: Reading—Vocabulary Section* (New York: CTB/McGraw-Hill, 1970 edition), Level 4 for

grades 6–9 and Level 5 for grades 9–12; two forms, A and B. The vocabulary section of this reading test yields information about four areas: English, social science, mathematics, and general. There are 90 words at Level 5 and 60 at Level 4, distributed equally among the four areas. A total of 12 minutes, or three minutes per area, is allowed for Level 4, while 16 minutes, or four minutes per area, is permitted for Level 5. The results per area provide only hints about specific vocabulary knowledge, since each subsection of the vocabulary test contains so few items. Dispensing with the time limits may be valuable for some students as indicated above, but remember the test then becomes an informal device for extremely rough screening.

Quick Check Using Course Materials

Using a passage typical of those students will be expected to read, or an actual coming assignment, you can make a quick check of each student's word power. Simply list key words from the passage, give their page locations, and add a headnote: "Do you know—or can you puzzle out—the meanings of these words as they are used in this passage?" You can use other quick self-made tests to assess mastery of the vocabulary techniques or the particular words that concern you at the moment. Such a test is described in the section "Context Clues" and in the section "Greek and Latin Word Parts" under "Don't Students Already Know Word Parts?"

Student Self-Appraisals

Students *live with* their own vocabularies—daily they experience their own strengths and shortcomings. Asking students the brief questions below, you can learn in minutes something about your students' insights into their vocabulary development and their habitual procedures.

For technical vocabulary in various subjects:

1. What do you do when you're studying an assignment and meet an important new technical term?

For general vocabulary:

1. Have you ever consciously done anything to build your vocabulary? If so, what methods have you used?

2. Are you using any of these methods at the present time? If so, which?

3. What do you do when you're reading and meet a word you don't know?

4. Would you like to be introduced to some effective ways to develop a superior vocabulary?

Almost invariably, students answer "yes" to question 4. Then through the entire year their response is likely to be positive when the teacher prefaces vocabulary instruction with, "We're having this vocabulary help because you requested it."

Motivating Vocabulary Study

Classroom teachers want students to learn the language of the subject—to master the specialized vocabulary. Tips for motivating students, easily adaptable to various subjects, are offered in Chapter 9 in the section "How to Master the Vocabulary of Mathematics," and in Chapter 14 in the section "Some Study Techniques for the Vocabulary of Music."

The Teacher's Vocabulary

A science teacher whose own command of words never fails to impress his classes tells how he "turns on" his students: "As my classes read their first selection of the year, Fabre's poetic nature study, 'The Courtship of the Scorpion,' someone is sure to misinterpret a word. I pull out my *own* list of words and the definitions *I* looked up when I read the selection for the first time. I let the class know that I, too, am a dedicated word collector. They realize the joy they missed in this poetic passage because they didn't attend to a word."

Vocabulary and Job Ability

A teacher might light the fire by reporting ideas adapted from an article, "Do You Know How Words Can Make You Rich?" (Winthrop, 1960, pp. 6–7):

> Did you know that big vocabularies and big paychecks seem
> to go right along together—and the same goes for small ones?
> More than any other factor studied, vocabulary appears to be
> related to money making success. That's the finding of the

Human Engineering Laboratory, a research institute which for years explored the factors that lead to getting ahead on the job.

They discovered that foremen had better vocabularies than the men who worked under them. Section managers had better vocabularies than foremen. And so on—up the ladder on the job—all the way to top executives, who had the top vocabulary scores.

Now school teachers in their classrooms did not conduct this study. It was conducted by down-to-earth, hardheaded investigators searching by scientific methods for the secrets of success.

Of course, we can't leap to the conclusion that a superior vocabulary guarantees promotions and a blue-chip bank account. Good work habits, responsibility, intelligence, and, of course, on-the-job "know-how" must go along with it.

Why does vocabulary contribute to on-the-job success? We *do our thinking* with words—*get our thoughts inside the minds of others* with words—*influence others* with words. Napoleon did not mention his armies when he said, "We rule men with words."

A Good Vocabulary Pays Off at School

A teacher might stir interest with thoughts like these:

What do you recite with at school? What do you write reports with? What goes down to represent you on your tests and exams? Words. When you turn on more word power, there's a plus for you on all of these.

College entrance personnel have found vocabulary to be one of the best predictors of college success. At the University of Illinois, entering students were given a 29-word vocabulary test. Their scores proved useful in predicting how they would fare for the next four years.

Word Power—A Personal Plus

This personal appeal may be persuasive:

Your word power is always with you in your personal life. Did you ever try to get very far away from your vocabulary?

Riches in your word bank are one form of social security.

What happens to self-confidence if you're talking to someone and the words you want won't come, if you falter and can't finish your thought? Most of us have had that experience. And we've all envied the people who make words behave, who have words right there when they want them.

Words Can Be CARE Packages

Since many young people have read and heard about alienation, thoughts like these may be persuasive:

> Words can be CARE packages. Through words we can enter into the thoughts and feelings of another. Then we can use encouraging words, understanding words, lifting words. The right words can bring us close to others so that they—and we— no longer feel alienated. This is the miracle of "mere" words.

Standardized Test Scores

Reporting standardized test scores *followed by an immediate program of action* can spur the vocabulary effort. Of course the dangers of "shock effect" to students whose scores are low are only too apparent, so student scores might be handed out in private envelopes with an optimistic, forward-looking interpretation: "You're mature enough to know where you stand, and then to respond as you think appropriate. There are ways to lift your vocabulary well above its present level."

Those with particularly low scores can be encouraged, "You'll have a score for comparison on another vocabulary test next spring. If you are not pleased today, you can start a constructive program and be one who is pleased next spring."

In a sensitive interpretation students can learn where they stand in the nation, in their own school and class, and in relation to norms desirable for entrance into different types of colleges. Suggestions for improvement should follow—*in the very same class period*. Reporting low scores often brings strong motivation rather than trauma when a program of action is launched immediately.

One teacher observed, "A report of vocabulary standings seems especially appropriate with high school juniors, who are concerned about their College Boards. The approach should be positive, designed to increase confidence: 'You can start an intensive, effective program.' "

Some teachers, alert to the danger of exposing a student's incompetency even in the most sensitively handled classwide interpretation, prefer to report rankings personally, inviting individuals to a conference.

Can Experience Enrich Vocabularies?

Experience, direct and indirect, can enlarge vocabularies and can richly invest new words with meaning. Students who appear not to be school-oriented and who make little or no effort to learn printed words will learn words when they *live* them. A field trip for junior high school students to an airport can give meaning to *beacon, ramp, dispatcher,* and *meteorologist.* The visit of a social studies class to a settlement house can give depth of meaning to *deprived area, immigrant, tenement, slum clearance,* and *social reform* (even for those who already reside in depressed areas). A tour of a dairy can give a science class an in-depth understanding of *pasteurization.* Of course, appropriate instruction on the new terms before and after such field trips helps refine and strengthen learning.

A high school or junior college teacher takes a shortcut in teaching *nautilus* when someone brings a many-chambered, spiral nautilus to class, in teaching *iridescence* when the class is shown iridescent sequins with their rainbow of shifting colors, in teaching *diaphanous* when students see a China silk scarf. A film focusing on problems of the desert can give *mirage, oasis,* and *irrigation* meaning as words *about* words can seldom do. A dramatic motion picture on Martin Luther King, Jr., can bring to life concepts like *boycott, sit-in, civil rights,* and *non-violence.*

Teachers often enlist the recall of student experience, encouraging sharing through discussion. With *charisma,* a teacher asks: "Do you know someone who has this quality? Have you felt the power of it?"

Teachers frequently bring words close to the lives of teenagers. Teachers enjoy teaching *sophomoric* to sophomores. *Irrepressible* is more easily retained when students consider, "What student in our class is irrepressible?"

An "imprint" of experience must exist, to some extent, in the reader's mind and back up the printed word before that word can take on meaning. What the student brings *to* those little marks on the printed page enables them to spring to life.

Does Wide Reading Increase Vocabulary?

Teachers sometimes ask, "How can I teach vocabulary to students who desperately need such help but are not very school-oriented? It seems as though they couldn't care less about new words." They also ask, "How can I help a classroom full of students improve in vocabulary when their vocabulary levels vary so greatly?"

Most of the vocabulary growth of capable readers is gained through their own reading. They have met new words repeatedly in a variety of context settings. Often a little bit of meaning brushes off each time, and gradually the word becomes a part of their vocabularies.

A teacher remarks, "When I find students who are deficient in vocabulary, I look first of all to their *reading habits*. If they are reluctant readers I try to start them reading—a magazine, if nothing else, at first. I consider this more important, as the initial step, than anything else." Teachers of subjects other than English often have a better opportunity to do this than the English teacher. Students' interests in particular subjects and their special liking for certain teachers are the "handles."

A young English teacher whose students came from homes in which there were few books used to feel twinges of guilt whenever she took time from the prescribed course to win her "I won't read-ers" to a new view of what is between the covers of a book. She stocked a corner of the classroom with fasten-your-seat-belt fiction, displayed bright magazines on a table, and brought *today* into the classroom through the daily paper. There was browsing time on Friday, a day when students were likely to have weekend hours ahead for reading. Soon some of her unreached boys were reaching for their first book —then for another—and another. An experienced teacher reassured her that she was surrounding nonverbal students with powerful verbal stimuli, influencing some of them to spend many hours in the world of words—working indirectly toward gains in vocabulary and comprehension. The experienced teacher pointed out that an artificial vocabulary push in class may add a few points to some students' scores on the next standardized test, but if they continue to view books as enemies, a year later those gains may be lost.

The young person who does not read widely, Levine pointed out, is "locked" into the few words that are used in conversation, in class discussions, and on television. He made this plea for "quantity" reading (Levine, 1972, pp. 578, 580):

> Of the half million words, less than 10,000 are used in daily conversation by most people. . . . Written language can thus be seen as a verbal bank storing the millions of concepts represented by the 95 percent of the words almost never used in oral language. If the student reads . . . daily in fiction and non-fiction, he [or she] will dip into this storehouse. . . . Words cannot be learned by the hundreds in any other way.

Of course the word resources of capable readers, too, will be enriched through many hours spent in reading. Top vocabularies usually go hand in hand with far-ranging reading interests.

Pre-Teaching "Stopper" Words

Teachers can take down the obstacle course *before* students read an assignment by pre-teaching selected words. They can search through the passage before-hand, pulling out "stopper" words, and then introduce these before students read the assignment. As the chill is taken off the reading, discouraged readers may take heart.

A mathematics teacher removes the obstacle of *coefficient* as a class approaches a passage on simplifying algebraic equations. A home economics teacher removes the word-block *colander* just before the class prepares spaghetti. An English teacher brings the *Odyssey* within reach by pre-teaching about the *imperturbable* Odysseus, the *stratagem* of the wooden horse, and the like—at the same time catching interest through intriguing snatches of plot. A social studies teacher clarifies *indulgence* before students read about the Reformation.

The following guidelines for pre-teaching "stopper" words are likely to prove useful:

1. Introduce the new word in context.   You might locate the word for the students in the coming passage or possibly project the page on a screen with an opaque projector. Lead students to make full use of any context clues to help them reason out the meaning.

2. Spotlight an easy root word within a long, forbidding word.   An extremely important service to students is simply to make them aware that long, forbidding words have parts. Left alone, some students meet a word like *imperturbable*, glance at the first few letters, and skip over the rest. It often helps to spotlight an easy root word within a difficult word. With *commutative*, mathematics teachers might ask, "What does commuter mean?" With *exponential*, they might ask, "Can you see a part you already know—one you've used many times?" A social studies teacher could direct attention to *total* in *totalitarian*. A science teacher can focus on the building blocks in *interplanetary*. A music teacher might point out *recite* in *recitative*.

Students will "see into" words quickly if, as they analyze words, you mark off root words on the board with vertical lines or highlight them with colored chalk.

extra|territorial|ity

inter**change**able

Now the words may be revealed as not so difficult after all.

3. Reduce difficult polysyllables to easy-to-manage syllables.   As numerous teachers will substantiate, many students slide over new and difficult words. How easily do you think you could learn *platyhelminthes* for biology class if you had not examined it syllable by syllable all the way to the end? For practical purposes some students seem unaware that syllables exist. They tend to glance at the first few letters of a difficult word and give up. Middles and endings of words thus receive only slight attention. Words of more than two or three syllables are, as one student expressed it, "just a mess of letters" (Bragstadt, 1975).

But a long, formidable polysyllable can be put on the board with its syllables marked off by vertical slashes, with accent marks, and perhaps with its phonetic spelling. The group can pronounce the word part by part with the teacher. They soon see that a word which looks as if it comes by the yard can be reduced to a number of short, easy-to-manage, pronounceable parts:

plat′|ē|hel|min′|thēz
an′|thro|po|log′|i|cal
en|vi′|ron|men′|tal|ist

It takes almost no time to slash the syllables apart with vertical slashes. And soon the students as they are reading silently should begin to break words down for themselves.

4. Call attention to accented syllables.   It will often be helpful to mark the stressed syllables with conspicuous accent marks. As you lead students through the pronunciation of a word, you can sharpen their awareness of the force of these marks.

As teachers follow guidelines 2–4, their students are learning to divide and conquer—to examine a difficult word for meaningful parts and to work through it syllable by syllable all the way to the end. As teachers direct attention to parts, they are helping to change the habits of those who did not really focus on new and difficult words.

5. Tap teen exerience.   Some new words or terms are made to order for tapping the experiences of teenagers. For example, a topic close to many young people is buying a first car. A teacher of typewriting relates new words to this experience as the terms *promissory note* and *collateral loan* are pre-taught. Now the new terms are likely to stick in mind.

6. Pre-teach multi-meaning terms.   Some words take off one meaning and put on another as students walk across the doorsill of a classroom! *Law* does so as they walk into science class, *between* and *point* as they walk into geometry, *role* as they walk into social studies. *Culture* can refer to an appreciation of the arts in English class and to tiny-celled organisms swimming around in a petri dish in biology! Such words often call for pre-teaching since the student often reacts, "That's easy; I already know that word!" Often, however, this student does not know the precise meaning called for in the particular field.

7. *Help ensure retention.*   Students should be helped to use all possible senses and strategies in attempting to retain new words. A mathematics teacher observes, "As a key word is pre-taught, my students see the word, say it, hear it, repeat it, and review it. Then in class sessions that follow, I use the word again and again—avoiding the use of pronouns."

8. *Help students move toward independence.*   On all levels teachers will want to give appropriate assistance with difficult terms. Sometimes teachers list crucial words as part of a study guide for a reading assignment, giving the page and line where these can be located in the context. They may pre-teach the most difficult words, while the others become the special responsibility of the students. Sometimes the students themselves help select the "stoppers" by culling the assignment. How to equip students with long-term *self-help* methods for dealing with difficult words is the subject of the rest of this section.

Context Clues

Many students do not rely on the language surrounding unknown words as sources of definition and clarification. Teachers often observe a tendency to read right on past unfamiliar words. Alerting students to the intelligent use of context encourages them to hunt for meaning instead of passing new words by without a try.

Few students, teachers report, make full use of context revelation. Few are aware of the existence of specific types of context clues. Almost without exception, students need help in judging when they can rely on context clues and when they should turn to the dictionary to find or verify the meaning. Extremes are noted. Some students consult the dictionary as a *first* resort with no regard for context. Others rely almost entirely on context and rarely turn to the dictionary. Obviously neither procedure is desirable in all situations. Many students need to understand that words shift and change meanings frequently and that the context of the moment determines the meaning of the moment.

Since context clues can be a tremendous help to students in learning the vocabularies of almost all their subjects, a strong case can be built for giving students all the help possible in the use of context clues:

1. Context is *the* major tool for students in vocabulary expansion. We can accelerate this growth by sharpening up their context clue power.

2. Students whose habit it was to half-glance at important new words can be led to zero in on these.

3. Judicious use of context clues is a long step toward independence in vocabulary growth—a real aid for getting at the meanings of new words during countless hours of reading in high school, in college, and in years thereafter. Used along with other vocabulary methods, it is a lifelong "help yourself" tool.

4. Overstress on reaching for the dictionary can be a deterrent to both vocabulary development and reading enjoyment. As one teacher comments, "It is neither possible nor desirable for students to deal meticulously with every new word. If we push students to look up *every* one, they may react negatively. One of my seventh graders was reading a circus story in which interest centered on the plot. When asked to underscore the words he did not know, he marked thirty-two!

   "I suggested, 'Come with the story for a conference.' Together we examined the words, deciding in each case whether context revealed enough meaning or whether the dictionary was called for. In the sentence, "The circus wagon was red, gold, and magenta,' the student had underlined *magenta*. Now he said, 'Oh, I guess it's a color.' In a fast-moving story in which interest centers on plot, 'a color' was probably enough. Painstakingly looking up all thirty-two words might have brought the reaction, 'I hate the dictionary! I hate words! I hate English! I hate reading!' "

Teacher-Made Tests

Using a passage students will actually be reading in the course, teachers can test students' facility with context clues by asking them to make an intelligent try at the meaning of underlined words. They might also be asked to explain how they arrived at each answer. The words selected should be important to the meaning of the passage, should be unknown, should have fairly revealing context, and should exemplify various kinds of context clues.

McCullough suggested a discussion following the test as a learning exercise. As the students talk over their answers, they are alerted to clues they missed. They become aware that there are clues of various types and conclude that context, while often limited in its revelation, frequently gives some suggestion of the meaning. Those who answered correctly are asked to share the ways they arrive at their answers. How-to-do-it suggestions from one student to another are sometimes more helpful than suggestions from the teacher (McCullough, 1945, p. 4). A test with ten parts, one for each type of clue explained on the following pages, will, as McCullough pointed out, suggest students' strengths and weaknesses in the various clues.

Students will have striking evidence of the usefulness of context clues if in Part 1 of the test the teacher first lists the words in isolation and asks the students to try to puzzle out their meaning without the aid of any clues. Next, in Part 2 each word is located in the reading selection and it becomes fair game to make use of every clue present. Not only does the teacher gain diagnostic insights, but the before-and-after contrast is a strong selling point with students for becoming eager clue-hunters.

One teacher says, "I probe orally, using our day-to-day course materials, observing the needs of individuals as they try out their powers of clue detection. Then I ask, 'What led you to the meaning?' Students experience delight when they work out meanings successfully."

Different Types of Context Clues

Students gain in context clue power when they become aware of specific types of clues and of the mental processes involved as they use all the hints at hand to reason out a strange word's meaning.* The following explanations of ten types of clues, with examples, should be suggestive to teachers as they clarify these clues for students and as they develop their own practice materials *using words of appropriate difficulty*. Overlap will be noted; clues rarely exist in pure form.

In explanations and discussions, students can be led to construe context broadly—to view the page as a "reader's paradise of clues"—to realize that in this paradise are clues not to be found in the words themselves: clues in the punctuation, word order, idea order, word groupings; clues in classes of words, sentence structure, paragraph structure; and signals in the possible intonation of an utterance that may give it an unexpected meaning. The students can learn to avail themselves of all these types of clues—to *draw on all their experience with the language* as an aid in discovering meaning.

The names of the ten types of clues are not important, and students should *definitely not have to learn a category system for context clues*. The purpose is

---

* Most of the types of context clues explained on these pages were first identified by McCullough (1945, pp. 1–5). Others have arrived at somewhat different classifications of contextual aids. The reader may wish to refer to Ames's broad classification (1966) and Quealy's (1969) summary of the classification schemes of major investigators.

to make the students generally context-conscious and to turn them into day-to-day context users.

1. Direct explanation clue. Sometimes writers realize full well that they have used a word the reader may not know. In that case they may provide an outright explanation of its meaning. They frequently try to tuck in a clear explanation:

> An *ecologist*, a scientist who specializes in the relationship between living things and their environment, is likely to have authoritative opinions on the problem of pollution versus man's survival.

The use of the appositive construction (with the word *or* and commas, or with commas alone) reveals to you beyond doubt that *ecologist* means *expert on environmental relationships*. There can be no question as to the meaning. Here is one type of context clue that will not let students down.

In the next example, *that is* indicates that the phrase it introduces is an explanation of the word *laser*:

> The development of the *laser*—that is, a device which concentrates high energies from radiation into a narrow, sharply focused beam of light—has practical applications in medicine.

Direct explanation clues are less obvious when they are not clearly marked by the appositive or by *that is* and when they are placed at a distance from the new word with a number of words intervening:

> Regardless of his many reforms and arguments, the senator was forced into a *cul-de-sac* by his opponents. What can a man —eminent senator or petty official—do to retrieve himself from a blind alley? (Adapted from Smith, 1961, p. 129.)

2. Experience clue. Often our own life experience—or our indirect experience through reading and other learning channels—provides the needed clue. We know from our own experience how people and things act or react in a given situation. Consequently, we can approximate the meaning. This clue yields high returns:

> Those first bewildering weeks, the thoughts of an entering college student drift back to high school where he was "in,"

knew everyone, and felt at home. A feeling of *nostalgia* sweeps over him.

3. *Mood or tone clue.* The author sets a mood—happy, somber, frightening, eerie. The meaning of the unknown word must harmonize:

> The *lugubrious* wails of the gypsies matched the dreary whistling of the wind in the all-but-deserted cemetery. (Strang, McCullough, and Traxler, 1967, p. 231.)

Since *lugubrious* reflects the mood of the sentence, the meanings *mournful, gloomy, dismal* readily come to mind.

Or the writer's mood might be ironic. In the example below, the writer intends the meaning of the word *nice* to be the direct opposite of what the words literally say. We sense the intonation:

> He isn't well-known for his fair play. He's a *nice* one to be talking to the team about good sportsmanship!

Here, of course, the word *nice* doesn't mean "pleasing" or "appropriate" at all. Quite the contrary—here it means "most inappropriate."

4. *Explanation through example.* Sometimes, when a writer uses a new word, the reader finds nearby an example that helps illuminate the meaning:

> In the course of evolutionary development certain human organs have *atrophied*. The appendix, for example, has wasted away from disuse.

> President Lincoln's attitude toward the fallen South was *magnanimous*—"with malice toward none, with charity for all."

> An occasional *respite* during a long evening of study is desirable. Ginnie often took a short breather between chapters or between assignments.

5. *Summary clue.* Here the new word appears to wrap up a whole situation. We can reason out the meaning because we know the circumstances the new word is summing up. Sometimes the situation that the word sums up is found before the unknown word:

> Pete Littlefield, our center, stands six feet three in his stocking feet and weighs an even 210 pounds. His teammates call him "Runt," an obvious *misnomer*.

Sometimes the situation the word sums up is found after the unknown word:

> The greatest effect of the Renaissance on education was a growing *secularization* in schools. More school curricula focused on man's expression of feelings toward the world in which he lived. Schools became interested in teaching about affairs of the world, not only about religious matters.

6. Synonym or restatement clue.   Here the reader infers the meaning of an unknown word because it repeats an idea expressed in known words nearby:

> Flooded with spotlights—the focus of all attention—the newly elected president began her year-long reign. She was the *cynosure* of all eyes for the rest of the evening.

Students quickly suggest "the focus of attention," "the center of interest." They should be cautioned, though, that synonyms are seldom exact equivalents and that when precision among shades of meaning is essential they will need a dictionary. The example below, from history, might send some students to the dictionary:

> Louis XIV kept his nobles constantly involved in rites and ceremonies and certain ways of doing things. Such *protocol* permitted him to keep them busily engaged while he ruled France without interference.

7. Comparison or contrast clue.   When a comparison clue is present, the readers get some suggestion of a new word's meaning because they compare it with a word or an idea already known:

> Peggy excels in basketball, photography, and music, and her older brother is even more *versatile.*

When a contrast clue is present, the meaning of the new word is obviously in contrast to an idea expressed in familiar words nearby:

> When the light brightens, the pupils of the eyes contract; when it grows darker, they *dilate.*

> They were as different as day and night. He was a lively conversationalist, with something to say on every subject, and she was reserved and *taciturn.*

8. *Familiar expression or language experience clue.* This clue requires a familiarity with common language patterns—expressions heard every day. In the example below, the reader, already well acquainted with the expression *take upon oneself,* has a strong clue to the meaning of *appropriate:*

> He took upon himself—yes, he *appropriated*—the entire responsibility for raising money for the class gift.

9. *Words in a series clue.* When reading words in a series, readers often get some idea of the meaning of a strange word because they know the general nature of the items being enumerated. In this example, one can easily gather that codlins and biffins are different types of apples:

> The apples had their places all around the room. They were *codlins*, and golden pippins, brown russets and scarlet crabs, *biffins*, nonpareils and queanings, big green bakers, pearmains, and red streaks. (Seibert and Crocker, 1958, p. 52.)

10. *Inference clue.* Listings of the various types of context clues often include the inference clue. Of course, this type overlaps all the foregoing types except direct explanation:

> Sharon told her roommate, "I'm through with blind dates forever. This one topped all! What a dull evening! I was bored every minute. The conversation was absolutely *vapid!*"

Making Full Use of Context Clues

Many teachers prefer to work with context only in natural situations, as students encounter new words in reading. Others prefer working initially with sentences that are contrived to "sell" the use of clues and that exemplify each type of clue. In either case the habitual examination of context, not the recall of specific types of clues or the drawing of fine distinctions in classification, is of course the objective.

Some teachers use practice exercises to help students become avid clue hunters. They share the following insights or draw them from students: "How have you become acquainted with a great number of the words you know? Not by looking them up or by word study under the supervision of a teacher, but through your own varied reading—meeting words again and again in clue-providing context. You are likely to make leaps and bounds in vocabulary growth by sharpening your context clue power. Before you reach for the dictionary, first ask yourself, 'What clues does context give?'"

text cont. pg. 33

WHAT IS YOUR CONTEXT CLUE POWER?

1. *Experience clue* (life experience, indirect experience through reading):
   Finally the moment of leaving home arrives. The unexplored world of college lies ahead. Almost every entering college student approaches life on campus with some *trepidation.*
   Your intelligent try at the meaning of *trepidation* in the light of context clues:

   _____

   _____

2. *Comparison or contrast clue:*
   Unlike his older brother, who could meet anyone from the president of a local community club to the President of the United States with ease, Bill was quite *gauche.*
   Your intelligent try at the meaning of *gauche:*

   _____

   _____

3. *Explanation through example clue:*
   Bob's reaction to the new girl was characterized by a strange *ambivalence*—faith conflicting with distrust.
   Your intelligent try at the meaning of *ambivalence:*

   _____

   _____

4. *Direct explanation:*
   The *exigency,* or emergency, that developed when the automatic pilot failed, forced astronaut John Glenn to neglect some of the experiments that had been planned and to take over manual control of the spacecraft for most of the second and third orbits.
   Your intelligent try at the meaning of *exigency:*

   _____

   _____

5. *Mood or tone clue:*
   The starchiness in his voice and the scowl on his face warned us that father was in a *captious* mood. Absolutely nothing suited him! Dinner was too late—the meat was too cold—the coffee was too hot!
   Your intelligent try at the meaning of *captious:*

   _____

   _____

Sentences 2–6 and 9 were contributed by Leitha Paulsen, Bloom Township High School, Chicago Heights, Illinois; and sentence 7, plus the first example of the summary clue above, by Edna Hoffman Evans, Phoenix College.

6. *Summary or restatement clue:*

The stories about Jackie, invented from bits and scraps of gossip and legend, soon developed into a "whispering campaign," and an innocent student became the victim of *calumny*.

Your intelligent try at the meaning of *calumny*:

_____

_____

7. *Synonym clue:*

Three times in succession the home team's players charged their opponent's line without gaining an inch of ground. The line proved *impregnable*. It could not be broken.

Your intelligent try at the meaning of *impregnable*:

_____

_____

8. *Familiar expression or language experience clue:*

In her eagerness to be elected, she fell over herself to impress the underclassmen—she made an *inordinate* effort.

Your intelligent try at the meaning of *inordinate*:

_____

_____

9. *Words-in-a-series clue:*

As a leader, he imposed his wishes on others. The Student Council members resented his finality, his decisiveness, his *peremptory* manner.

Your intelligent try at the meaning of *peremptory*:

_____

_____

10. *Inference clue* (overlaps almost all other types):

While driving his father's new car, Mike had a serious collision. Luckily, bystanders *corroborated* his statement that he had been driving carefully.

Your intelligent try at the meaning of *corroborate*:

_____

_____

Students may then read silently the first sentence of the exercise below. They are given a few moments to make an intelligent try at the meaning of the stimulus word. Students who already know the meaning are asked not to raise their hands. Volunteers offer their answers, which are checked or verified by the dictionary definition. Students who arrived at correct meanings share their "success secrets." There is some discussion of specific types of clues. The students understand that the sentences they are working with have exceptionally revealing context and have been contrived to clarify the different types of clues. Of course, the words should be matched to the level of the students. The preceding exercise is intended for capable upperclassmen.

Less Direct Clues

In the initial practice, obvious, clear-cut clues drive home the value of exploring context. In a second practice, students work with less direct clues. They come to realize that the meaning of an unknown word or words may not always be unlocked through the use of context. Frequently they will need to read beyond the sentence containing the unknown word or words, and even then they may be unable to obtain a precise meaning. Students are led to conclude that context often gives hints of the meanings of particular words, but that it may not clarify the whole of any meaning and infrequently reveals the nuance of meaning.

Missing or Misleading Clues

Students should become aware that context sometimes has nothing at all to reveal concerning a word's meaning and may, on occasion, even mislead the reader.

In the following example the context is a real fooler. Both the context of the word *noisome* and also its structure suggest the meaning *noisy*. Upon consulting a dictionary, however, students discover the meanings *offensive, distasteful, disgusting, ill-smelling.* The word *noisome,* they find to their surprise, is derived from the same root as *annoy* and is not related to *noise.*

For *livid,* in the second sentence, students often suggest the meaning *red* or *flushed.* In their own experience they have observed that people turn red with anger. They may be surprised to discover that the dictionary gives the meanings *lead color, ashen, pallid, ghastly.*

As one teacher sums it up, "Context is a magnificent help—*but beware!*"

DO CONTEXT CLUES ALWAYS WORK?

What does the context of the following sentences lead you to conclude? Is your conclusion correct in each case?

> Corbett had lived in this *noisome* slum for only two weeks, but he would never forget the screaming voices, the angry quarreling, and the fighting that made slum life so unbearable.*
>
> He was *livid* with rage.

Sometimes context provides no clues to the meaning of a word. What help can you get from the context in these sentences?

> One matter that was never discussed at our family dinners was Aunt Patricia's interest in *necromancy*. Even the slightest remark about it would send Uncle Calvin into a rage. And so, to insure peace, everyone suppressed his curiosity and carefully avoided the subject.†

---

* Richard Corbin, Marguerite Blough, and Howard Vander Beek, *Guide to Modern English for Grade Nine* (Chicago: Scott, Foresman and Company, 1960), p. 98.

† The second example is from Corbin et al., *Guide to Modern English, Upper Years* (Chicago: Scott, Foresman and Company, 1960), p. 104.

Meaning from Context in Natural Situations

Students proceed to reason out meanings in natural situations as the teacher directs attention to new words encountered in day-to-day study. Teachers may wish to stop at any opportune moment to help students probe for the meaning of a word or phrase in context. Paulsen (1962, p. 98) observed:

> As students move from contrived sentences to analyze words in paragraphs chosen from stories, clues become more subtle, and much practice is required. The dictionary comes into play as pronunciations are checked. There is also emphasis on using the dictionary to verify a context "guess," as well as much practice in fitting one of the many dictionary definitions to the particular context. As the work proceeds, attention is given to clues remote from the word to be defined. Clues may be in another part of the paragraph or even in another part of the selection.

Students may, considerably later in the passage, come upon details that help check the exactness of their first answers and perhaps commit themselves to the meaning they arrived at.

Attacking Assignment Words

Sarah Roody (1953) told how she worked with context clues in Rachel Carson's *The Sea Around Us:*

> One day the class walked in to find some difficult words on the board. "Why are all those words on the board?" demanded William suspiciously. "Do we have to learn them?"
>
> "If I were a gambler," replied the teacher, "I would bet a nickel that you will know most of them without even looking them up." William was doubtful—one of the words was *ichthyologist.*
>
> The teacher passed out a passage from *The Sea Around Us.* Written after each word on the board was the page and line where students could find it in context. The class was asked, "Read the paragraph containing *cachalot,* and try to guess what the word means." William made the discovery: "The book says 'the cachalot or sperm whale.' The definition is right here. You don't even have to guess."
>
> Next the students practiced the synonym-type clue, one of

the easiest types to guess. Then they proceeded to example clues. In one passage Rachel Carson uses the word *paradox* in referring to the fact that fragile creatures like the jelly fish and glass sponge are not crushed by the immense pressure of the deep water where they live. With a little assistance in the form of additional examples, most of the students were able to deduce that a paradox is "strange but true" or "it's impossible but it's a fact." Then the class turned to the dictionary for a more exact definition.

They moved on to more subtle clues—the use of one's own experience or knowledge, for example. Sea Scouts came closer than others to reasoning out the meaning of the word *sessile* in the context, "Barnacles are sessile." As the mental processes became more difficult, fewer students demonstrated ability to use the clues. (Roody, 1953, pp. 478–480.)

Students were impressed with at least two facts: hints of the meaning of strange words are often present to help them in their reading, and their guesses are not always correct.

Words in Context versus Words in Isolation

Students are sometimes sent to the dictionary with a list of words in isolation. They are to record and learn each word's meaning—but *which* of the meanings? Send a student to look up *abstract* in isolation, and he or she may be bewildered by a dozen different meanings.

Context is a tremendous help to students as they try to learn to *use* their new words. A sadder but wiser English teacher reports this classic how-*not*-to-do-it. She sent a class of seniors to the dictionary to look up the meanings of words on a list. They were to write original sentences for each. One of the words was *trite*. A student came up with, "The miners who have gone on strike are trite." He defended his answer staunchly, "I can prove it; the dictionary says it means *overworked!*" Another volunteered, "The bread is trite." "Why, it's right here—it says that *trite* means *stale*." One young lady offered, "The shoes I am wearing are trite." "But it says right here it means *worn out*." What an immense help it would have been to introduce *trite* to the class in this contextual setting: "Busy as a bee is a *trite* expression."

Figurative Language—Figure It Out!

Figurative expressions, which abound on the pages in English and social studies, may be stumbling-blocks for young readers. Their teachers, mature readers themselves, grasp these expressions so easily that they may be completely un-aware of the students' bewilderment. Consider the plight of the student who tries to interpret "our country, a melting pot" literally!

A student in social studies, one whose reading scores were average, lost out when she met the expression (it looks so easy!), "Egypt was the gift of the Nile." Puzzled, she sought her teacher. The teacher probed: "What was the relation-ship between the river and the country? How did the river, in a sense, *give* Egypt to the Egyptians? Then: "Just what did the river *give?* What did it supply?" The student thought it over: "It flooded and gave rich soil. It also gave water for irrigation. It gave a way of trade and transportation. It gave the people a country where they could live. Yes, I guess it did give Egypt to the Egyptians."

In many cases, students take in what the words actually *say*—and are lost: "our *shrinking* world," "*riding roughshod* over a veto," "*tongues* in trees," "*blind* justice," "*clothed in the garb* of justice," "*bring down* the house," "*fly in the face of* the opposition." Teachers can come to their rescue, alerting them to the control that context exerts over the meaning of individual words in figurative expressions, guiding them not to interpret these expressions literally, making them aware that they will frequently meet language that is figurative.

Words Are Like Chameleons

In one classroom the students had this experience with "chameleon" words:

> "Words are like chameleons. They change their color—their shade, too—to harmonize with their surroundings. You've already met the word *decimate*." The students recall the mean-ing *to destroy one out of ten*, a meaning close to the word's origin when the ancient Romans, by casting lots, marked for death every tenth man among soldiers guilty of cowardice.
>
> "But in the following sentence *decimate* changes its color to match different surroundings: 'The long years of warfare with the white man had *decimated* the thousands of Seminoles. Now there remained only a few survivors in the quiet live oak forests.' " The students quickly see that here *decimate* takes on a much stronger meaning than one in ten. For this context they suggest the meaning *destroy almost completely*.

Teachers Strive for a Delicate Balance

Teachers wants students to become aware as they work with context clues that context often supplies at least a hint of a word's meaning. On the other hand,

---

Do's and Don't's for Using Context

DO RELY ON CONTEXT CLUES

1. When you have an "unmissable clue" —a direct explanation.
2. When you have highly revealing clues and the meaning you arrive at definitely "clicks" with the rest of the passage.
3. When, in view of your purpose for reading the selection, you need only a general sense of the meaning.

DON'T RELY ON CONTEXT CLUES (TURN TO YOUR DICTIONARY)

1. When you require a precise meaning. It usually takes the dictionary to pin the meaning down.
2. When the word is a key word, one crucial to your understanding, and full comprehension is important to you.
3. When the clues suggest several possibilities—the meaning might be one of several—and you don't know which.
4. When you don't know the nearby words.
5. When you have encountered the word a number of times, realize that it is a common, useful one which you will meet again, and will want to master thoroughly for future reading.

---

they hope that students will realize that the meaning they arrive at through context is usually tentative or general and that the dictionary is indispensable and should usually be consulted to verify or reject a context guess that may have significance for further reading. Teachers will wish to emphasize frequently and strongly that no single context revelation will illuminate all future encounters with the word. They should help students recognize that many situations require the utmost precision of meaning, while for others a general meaning is sufficient. Teachers should guide students in making the distinction.

Students may wish to arrive at their own guidelines for using context clues. The table shows in capsule form a few that have already been generated.

Many students, as we have already noted, tend to slide over unfamiliar words. Teacher help with context clues should accustom students to zero in on important new words, to make the context reveal what meaning it can, and then to reach for the dictionary when appropriate. When they do this frequently and deliberately, they have added an important self-help skill to their repertory of vocabulary methods. And they may well be more intent on comprehending the meaning of the passage than they were in the past.

Activities to Teach, Enrich, and Motivate

Readers in search of class activities to sharpen up—and liven up—the use of context are referred to "Fun Fare for Vocabulary Growth" in Chapter 7.

Greek and Latin Word Parts

When we give students a working stock of common Greek and Latin word parts and teach them to use these in combination with context revelation, we are helping them acquire meanings of many related English words. And we are giving many of them a self-help technique through structural analysis—an added means of increasing their word power in an ongoing, lifelong process. Students with rich language backgrounds sometimes develop a fantastic affinity for words when they are introduced to this method. Students with meager vocabulary backgrounds can be helped to unlock a multitude of words that they meet in their daily reading assignments.

The social studies instructor who teaches the prefix *anti-* when, for example, students meet *antilabor*, gives them a key which will help them later to unlock *antitrust, antiwar, antislavery,* and *anti-imperialist.* The instructor who teaches the prefix *auto-* when students meet *autonomy* has already given them a grip on *automation, autocracy,* and *automaton.* The mathematics teacher who teaches each number prefix at the time it is needed gives students a hold on *pentagon, hexagon, octagon,* and the like—as well as on hosts of their mathematical and scientific relatives.

Nowhere do Greek and Latin word parts pay off more richly than in science. *Micro-* pays dividends in easier learning of *microscope, microbe, microorganism, micrometer. Hydro-* is a jackpot word part which pays off as the student meets *dehydrate, hydrosphere, hydrographic, hydraulics,* and many others. As one science teacher points out, "Breaking down words makes the vocabulary of science less awesome. The ability to find word parts and use them for meaning is a major vocabulary tool in science."

Don't Students Already Know Word Parts?

For an easy-to-make, easy-to-take informal test, list ten or so Greek or Latin word parts appropriate for your students' level. Use parts that should be part of their standard equipment for word analysis. Ask the students simply to write the meanings. The results may reveal surprising lacks.

Word Parts in Learning Situations

Teachers often use an inductive approach through which students discover the meaning of Greek or Latin parts as strange words confront them in their reading. When word analysis serves an immediate purpose, students seem to view it as practical and productive.

When science students come upon the suffix *-lysis* in words like *analysis*, *hydrolysis*, and *electrolysis*, the stage is set for learning a high-yield word part. They discover, "all those words mean 'breaking up' in some way." Now they have a handle on hosts of other words, among them *photolysis*, *thermolysis*, *autolysis*, and *biolysis*.

On noticing the classic anachronism in Shakespeare's *Julius Caesar*, when the clock strikes three although the ancient Romans had no striking clocks, an instructor of an honors class remarked, "That's an anachronism!" Students asked, "What's that?" The teacher wrote the word on the board and asked, "Do you notice a familiar part?" *Ana-* proved unfamiliar, but some students pointed out *chron-*. One explained, "That's in chronological!" Onto the board went a number of *chron-* words, each in a brief context:

> in *chronological* order
> a ship's *chronometer*
> a *chronic* ailment
> to *synchronize* the dancers' movements

The teacher probed, "Now what do you think *chron-* means?" Students responded, "Something about time."

Returning to the context in which the clock struck, a student contributed, "The Romans used sand or water clocks that didn't strike the hour." The class then arrived at the meaning of *anachronism* as placing a happening in some period of time where it doesn't belong.

One group of students was puzzled by the word *microcosm* in a poem. The teacher asked, "Is there a part you know?" The students quickly noticed *micro-*. "How many other words do you know that have that part?" As *microscope*, *microbe*, *microfilm*, and *microgroove* went up on the board, the meaning became apparent. An examination of the part *-cosm* suggested *cosmos* to a few. Someone suggested, "Does the word mean something like a very small universe?" With the aid of the context and some assistance from the teacher, the group arrived at the meaning, "a world in miniature." Then the teacher helped the students refine and extend the meaning.

The word *graphology* confronted a class. Students suggested other words containing *graph*, and these were splashed all over the board. *Logy* was easy—they had met it before. Someone quickly offered, "Oh, it's the study of writing!" Only a check with the dictionary, however, clarified the fact that it is a study of handwriting, particularly in regard to an expression of the writer's character.

From the foregoing examples a pattern for structural analysis emerges:

1. Students examine the word for familiar parts.

2. If they recognize a part as familiar but do not know its meaning, they try to think of other words in which the part appears, then try to reason out the meaning of the part.

3. Returning to the context, they combine contextual clues with structural clues to try to work out the word's meaning.

4. They check with the dictionary when necessary. With repeated success in the classroom, students should come to apply their techniques of structural analysis habitually.

"Selling" Word Part Study

A teacher might give a sales talk: "How would you like a method to help you to learn new words not one by one but several—even dozens—at a time. You may find this method your best vocabulary 'bargain.' Did you ever try to lift an unabridged dictionary—all 750,000 words? More than half of all those words entered our language from Greek and Latin. And, luckily, they did not come singly—they came in families. Learn one 'ancestor,' and you'll have a tool to help you learn an entire family of related English words.

"What a step ahead you make when you learn *poly!* You'll find 95 of its relatives in one small high school dictionary. What a giant stride you make when you learn *pseudo!* An unabridged dictionary actually lists 800 derivatives. Though many are technical, some are extremely useful."

Students then proceed to do the "bargain counter" practice that follows. They soon see how their knowledge of word parts can save them trips to the dictionary. You will notice that the words advance in difficulty, making it possible to discontinue the practice at the point where the words become too difficult for the student or the group involved.

Limitations in Using Word Parts

From the first, students should experience the limitations of word-part guessing. They should be prepared for deceptive combinations of letters—combinations that are foolers because they resemble a Greek or Latin word element but are completely unrelated.

text cont. pg. 44

A VOCABULARY "BARGAIN COUNTER"
(A Dozen or So for the Price of One)

If you know the Latin word part *mal-*, which means *bad, evil, ill,* or *wrong,* you have a clue to help you figure out the meaning of the English words below. Greek and Latin prefixes are often keys that help you unlock English word meanings.

Fold back the side of the paper giving the answer while you reason out the meaning of the *italicized* word from the context clues that are present together with the Latin part. Then unfold the paper and see if you arrived at the correct meaning.

Caution: Reasoning out word meanings from Greek and Latin parts usually yields no more than a general meaning. You will often need to check and refine your guess by consulting the dictionary.

Fold this side under

THE WORD IN CONTEXT AS YOU MIGHT MEET IT IN READING	THE MEANING
1. The child was placed in a foster home so that his parents could no longer *maltreat* him.	treat badly, roughly, unkindly, brutally
2. Damp towels that have mildewed are *malodorous*.	ill-smelling; having a bad odor
3. The doctor lost his license for *malpractice* of medicine.	wrong practice; injurious treatment or neglect of a patient
4. The *malefactor* was arrested, tried, and sentenced for his crime.	evil-doer; criminal
5. Because he threatened to sue the paper for libel, the *Weekly News* was careful not to *malign* him in a news story.	speak evil of falsely or maliciously; slander; defame
6. The villain gave the heroine a sinister, *malevolent* look.	showing ill-will; wishing evil to
7. Third period, Sue was troubled with a feeling of *malaise*, so she reported to the school nurse and received permission to leave school.	a vague, indefinite feeling of being ill
8. His staying home the day he had four tests, though he was perfectly well, was clearly a case of *malingering*.	pretending to be ill to avoid doing one's duty

9. Mary frets and fumes constantly. She never seems satisfied. She is a chronic *malcontent*.

   a *discontented* person seldom happy about prevailing conditions or circumstances

10. The city manager was removed from his job for *malfeasance* in office.

    wrongdoing or bad conduct in public affairs

11. The ancient Egyptians uttered a *malediction* against anyone who would ever open King Tut's tomb.

    a calling down of evil upon someone; a curse

12. The strange *malady* of Lady Madeline of Usher baffled her physicians.

    illness; disease

13. In sailboats in rough weather you may suffer from *mal de mer*.

    seasickness ("illness of the sea")

14. His *maladroit* reasoning lost him the decision in the debate.

    badly skilled in the use of mental faculties or of hands; clumsy; awkward (the opposite of *adroit*, which means quick or skillful)

15. Mrs. Malaprop, a "famous female" in Sheridan's comedy, *The Rivals,* was well known for her blunders with words. She cared more about her daughter Lydia's matrimonial success than about her intellectual success. Speaking of Lydia, she exclaimed, "I don't want any daughter of mine to be a progeny!"

    Such errors have come to be known as *malapropisms*.

    A *malapropism* is a word blunder in which the speaker mistakes one word for another word similar in sound. As you may know, Mrs. Malaprop confused *prodigy* (a child highly gifted intellectually) with *progeny* (offspring).

Do Word Parts Always Help You?

Sorry, the answer is no, not always. Some words, for example, contain the letters m-a-l when they do not form a Latin word part.

There's nothing necessarily *bad*, for example, about

> A *mallet*
> A *mallard* duck
> A *male*
> A chocolate *malt*.

In these words there is no connection at all between the letters m-a-l and the Latin word part, *mal-*, meaning bad, wrong, or evil.

A *possible check*: Ask yourself, "Does the meaning of the Greek or Latin word part 'click' with the rest of the sentence?"

Further limitations should be recognized:

1. Many prefixes (and some roots) have several distinct meanings. The prefix *de-* means away from or off in *decapitate*. It means down in *demean, debase,* and *degrade*. It means reverse the action in *defrost, decompose, devitalize,* and *depopulate*. And it isn't a prefix at all in *devotee!*

2. The Greek or Latin word element is often buried within the word and has changed in form across the centuries. "How," Courtney (1960, p. 43) asked, "can the student relate *perceive, receive, deception,* and *conception* to the Latin *capere* . . . without a knowledge of Latin or considerable guidance and explication on the part of the teacher?"

3. At best, reasoning from Greek or Latin usually yields only a general or partial meaning. It is rarely possible to add up the meanings of prefix, root, and suffix to arrive at a total precise meaning.

What to Do about Limitations

Make a thoughtful selection of word elements for instruction. Select those which are likely to unlock *useful* words, those which will act as "fast neutrons in the chain reaction of vocabulary development" (Deighton, 1959, p. 36).

Parts that have a single, invariant meaning (or closely related meanings) are likely to be most useful. Among these are *ante-, anti-, auto-, bene-, circum-, contra-, extra-, graph-, hetero-, homo-, inter-, intra-, mal-, micro-, mis-, multi-, neo-, non-, omni-, pan-, poly-, pseudo-, retro-, sub-, super-, syn-, tele-.*

When useful parts have more than one meaning, prepare the students for these variations by teaching the diverse meanings. They should know that *in* means *not* in *inhuman* and *into* in *inject*. They must try out meanings by returning to the context settings.

Select parts that students can readily recognize. Those buried in greatly altered form within a word are not likely to be helpful.

Prepare the students for deceptive combinations of letters—combinations identical with some Greek and Latin word parts, yet unrelated. The root *opt* in the words *optician, optical,* and *optics* refers to sight, but *optimist* and *option* are not their cousins (Gainsburg, 1967, 3, p. 115). One teacher suggests, "*Amo* in Latin means *like* or *love*. But love has little to do with an *ambush*, an *ambulance*, or *ambergris*! Try out a possible meaning for a word part in the surrounding context. Reject it if you can't tune it in."

Practice Work

All teachers—perhaps English teachers especially—may plan to work with Greek and Latin word parts. The following practices will suggest a few possible formats for exercises.

In the first exercise the student practices combining the root *phobia* with prefixes juniors and seniors are likely to find useful. In the second exercise students are asked to use the root *pseudo* along with context clues to figure out the definitions of words—an exercise adaptable for younger groups. The third brief exercise dealing with *acer* is also appropriate for juniors and seniors, but formats similar to it are successful and stimulating for most learners. The last exercise—featuring the prefix *auto*—is useful with a variety of individuals and groups. Its very nature permits flexibility of response.

PHOBIA—FEAR

We all have fears. When they are rational, these fears are often our friends, for they cause us to take steps to avert real danger.*

But there are people who have irrational, exaggerated, and persistent fears of one or many things. They may fear, for example, rain, bees, love, men, dolls, the sun, the color blue, pins, stillness, thirteen at the table, and cats (not always black).

Combine the prefixes below with the Greek word *phobia*, meaning *fear*, to fill the blanks below:

anthropo human beings
claustro something enclosed or confined
neo anything new
phobo fear
photo light
pyro fire
zoo animals

1. Would you linger in the shadows of a darkened hallway and panic on a sun-drenched beach? Then your personal neurosis, or nervous disorder, is _____.

2. You are a recluse. You live alone and try to avoid contact with other people. You are afflicted with _____.

3. Do you quake and quaver at a lighted candle, a fire in the fireplace, or even a purse-size box of matches? You are a victim of _____.

4. "Something old, *nothing* new!" is your watchword. Old styles, old familiar faces and places are to your liking. You have a morbid aversion to anything new. You suffer intensely from _____.

5. Is "Don't Fence Me In" your theme song? Do you have a dread of being physically hemmed in; of small, tight, enclosed spaces; of the crush of crowds? Then your excessive fear is _____.

6. Does a cuddly kitten or a soft, warm puppy send your pulses pounding? Do you quail and cower at a furry honey-bear? The cause of your jitters is _____.

7. The thing you fear is fear itself. You are deeply afraid of being afraid! You have a chronic case of _____.

* The lively explanation of phobias in Norman Lewis, *Word Power Made Easy*, suggested this exercise (Garden City, New York: Doubleday and Company, Permabooks, 1953), p. 251.

PSEUDO—FALSE

Using your knowledge of the Greek root, *pseudo*, plus context clues, fill in these blanks:

1. If one of your schoolmates is *pseudosophisticated*, does she really know her way around? _____

2. George Eliot, the English writer, was not really George at all but Mary Ann! George Eliot was the *pseudonym* used by Mary Ann Evans during the 1800s, a period when authorship was not socially approved for a woman. *Pseudonym* means a _____
   _____.

3. Phrenologists believe they can read your character and identify your mental abilities by studying the shape of your skull, but reputable anatomists consider phrenology a *pseudoscience*. A *pseudoscience* is a
   _____.

4. The Old Testament scholar was completely misled by some *pseudepigrapha* supposed to have been written by the prophet Isaiah. *Pseudepigrapha* (note the Greek word part *graph* meaning writing) means
   _____.

ARE YOU A "SHARPIE" WITH THESE?

ACER—SHARP, BITTER, HARSH, STINGING

1. The taste of vinegar is *acrid*. How does it taste? _____
   _____.

2. The discussion over the rival presidential hopefuls became *acrimonious*. What was the discussion like? _____
   _____.

3. Her apologies only *exacerbated* her friend's resentment. What was their effect? _____.

AUTO—SELF

The "ancestor" is the Greek prefix *auto*, meaning self. You name words that are "descendants." How many can you list?

_____	_____	_____
_____	_____	_____
_____	_____	_____
_____	_____	_____
_____	_____	_____
_____	_____	_____

Figure 2–1. *Vocabulary-building slip.*

Collector's Items

Students collect productive prefixes and roots and their derivatives on slips (see Figure 2–1) or in a vocabulary notebook. The teacher makes a "big deal" of starting the collection with some high-yield parts like *omni-*, *pan-*, or *auto-*. Students are encouraged to watch for derivatives in their reading. It may be advisable for the teacher to supply a basic list of parts.

Some Productive Greek and Latin Word Parts

The table gives a list of some Greek and Latin prefixes and roots likely to be useful in reasoning out word meanings. For the convenience of the teacher they have been roughly assigned to five levels increasing with respect to difficulty both of the parts themselves and also of the derived words. Of course, a teacher should draw freely from anywhere on the list when the moment is right for teaching a certain word part.

Level I

Latin Prefixes

PREFIX	MEANING	DERIVATIVES
ad	toward, to	adjoining, adhere
ante	before	ante meridiem, antechamber
circum	around	circumnavigate, circumference

dis	opposite of, away	dissatisfied, disarm, dismiss, disperse
in	in, into, not	insert, ineligible
inter	between, among	interscholastic, intervene
mis	wrong(ly), incorrect(ly)	misspell, miscalculate
non	not	nonresident, nonpartisan, nondescript
post	after	postdate, postscript
pre	before	premeditated, preface
pro	in favor of, forward, in place of	pro-British, protrude, pronoun
re	again, back	recur, regress
sub	under	subcellar, subordinate
trans	across	transatlantic, transcontinental

Latin Roots

aqua	water	aquaplane, aquarium
port	carry	portfolio, transport, portage
scrib, script	write	inscribe, scribble
spec(t)	look	inspect, spectator
vid, vis	see	video, vista, visible, vision
voc	call	vocal, vocation, convocation

Greek Prefixes and Roots

anti	against	antitoxin, antiwar, anti-inflation
graph, gram	writing, record	telegram, autograph
micro	small	microscope, microbe
phone	sound	telephone, dictaphone
scope	sight	telescope, microscope
tele	far	television, telegram

Level II

Number Prefixes*

LATIN	GREEK	MEANING	DERIVATIVES
uni	mono	one	unicellular, monologue, monopoly
du(o)	bi	two	duplicate, bilingual, biped
tri	tri	three	triplicate, triumvirate
quad(ri)	tetra	four	quadruplets, tetrameter, tetrachloride
quin(que)	pent(a)	five	quintet, pentagon
sex	hex(a)	six	sextet, hexagon
sept	hept(a)	seven	septet, heptagon
octo	octa	eight	octave, octagon
non(a)		nine	nonagon
dec(im)	dec(a)	ten	decimal, decade

---

* The lists of number prefixes and "prefix pairs" appear on pages 265 and 270 of Ward S. Miller, *Word Wealth Junior* (New York: Holt, Rinehart and Winston, 1962).

cent(i)	hect(o) hect(a)	one hundred	centipede, centennial, hectograph
mill(e) mill(i)	kilo	one thousand	millennium, kilometer
semi	hemi demi	half	semicircle, hemisphere demigod

Prefix Pairs

circum	peri	around	circumnavigate, perimeter
con, com, co	syn, sym	together, with	convention, cooperation, synchronize
lux, luc	photo	light	lucid, elucidate, photoelectric
magn(i)	mega	(very) large or great	magnate, megaphone
multi	poly	many	multimillionaire, polysyllabic, polygon
nov	neo	new	novice, neophyte
omni	pan	all	omniscient, Pan-American
prim	proto	first	primitive, prototype

super, ultra	hyper	over, above,
		  beyond,
		  excessive-
		  (ly)
			superfluous, ultrastylish, hypercritical

Latin Roots

ROOT	MEANING	DERIVATIVES
aud, audit	hear, listen to	auditorium, audience, audition
cap	take, hold	·captive, captivate
dic(t)	tell, speak	dictation, edict, dictator
fac	make, do	factory, manufacture, factotum
fid	faith, trust	fidelity, infidel
fract	break	fracture, infraction
mit(t), miss	send, sent	emit, remit, transmit, missive
ped, pod	foot	pedestrian, podium, tripod
rupt	break	interrupt, disrupt, eruption, rupture
spec, spic	look	spectator, conspicuous
ven, vent	come, coming	convention, intervene

Greek Roots

auto	self	autobiography, automatic
bio	life	biology, biochemistry
geo	earth	geography, geology
hydr	water	hydroplane, dehydrate
meter, metr	measure	thermometer, symmetry
ology	study of	biology, psychology

Level III

Latin Prefixes

PREFIX	MEANING	DERIVATIVES
a, ab	away, from, away from	aversion, abnormal, abduct, abdicate
bene	well, good	beneficiary, benefactor
contra, counter	against, opposed to	contradict, counterspy
de	down from, away from, reverse the action	descend, deplane, decapitate, depopulate
ex	out, out of, away from, formerly	exclude, expel, ex-president

Latin Roots

ROOT	MEANING	DERIVATIVES
acer, acr	sharp, bitter	acrid, acrimonious
amor	love	amorous, amour
carn	flesh	carnivorous, reincarnation, carnal
cogn	know	incognito, cognizance
cred	believe	credo, credulous, credible
crux, cruc	cross	crux, cruciform, excruciating
duc, duct	lead	induce, conducive, abduction
fort	strong	fortress, fortitude, forte
frater, fratri	brother	fraternity, fratricide
gen	race, birth, kind	Genesis, congenital, genocide
man, manu	hand	manicure, manual
mute	change	transmute, immutable
nihil	nothing	annihilate, nihilist
pac	peace	pacifist, pacifier
pli, plic	fold	implicate, pliable, complicity
sequ, secut	follow	sequence, consecutive, consequence
sol	alone	solo, solitary
son	sound	unison, resonant, sonorous
viv	live	revive, vivacious

Greek Roots

cardi	heart	cardiac, pericardium
derm	skin	epidermis, dermatology
path	feeling, disease	antipathy, apathy, pathology
phil	love	Anglophile, philanthropist
phob	fear	claustrophobia
pseudo	false	pseudoscience, pseudonym
psych	mind	psychology, psychosomatic
theo	god	theology, theist, atheist
zo	animal	zoo, zoology

Level IV

Latin Prefixes

PREFIX	MEANING	DERIVATIVES
inter	between, among	interscholastic, interpose
intra	within	intrascholastic, introspection
mal	bad	malady, malignant
per	through	perforate, permeate, perceptive

Latin Roots

ROOT	MEANING	DERIVATIVES
alter	other	alternate, alter ego, altruistic
ambul	walk	ambulatory, somnambulist
annu, enni	year	annals, millenium, perennial
corp, corpor	body	corporal, corpulent
culpa	blame	culprit, culpable
deus	god	deity, deify
equ	equal	equanimity, equable, equivocate
laud	praise	laud, laudable, laudatory
magn	great	magnify, magnate, magnitude
mort	death	mortal, post-mortem, mortuary
oner, onus	burden	onerous, onus
pater, patr	father	paternal, patrimony, patricide
plac, placa	please, appease	placate, implacable
string, strict	tighten	constrict, stringent, stricture
ten	hold	tenacious, tenets, tenable
tort	twist	distort, contort, extortion, tortuous
tract	draw, drag	tractor, tractable, extract
scien	know, knowledge	omniscient, science, prescient
terra	earth	terrain, terra firma, terrestrial
vert, vers	turn	divert, versatile, vertigo

Greek Roots

aster	star	astrology, asterisk
bibl	book	bibliography, bibliomania
caust, caut	burn	cauterize, caustic, holocaust
chrom	color	chromophotography, monochromatic
chron	time	chronological, synchronize
crat, cracy	power, rule	autocrat, democracy
dem	people	democracy, demagogue
gam	marriage	polygamy, bigamy, monogamy
miso, mis	hatred	misanthrope, misogamist, misogynist
nym	name	pseudonym, anonymous, acronym
ortho	straight, right, correct	orthodontist, orthodox, orthography
soph	wise	sophisticated, theosophy
tom	cut	appendectomy, epitome, microtome

Level V

Prefixes—Mostly Greek

PREFIX	MEANING	DERIVATIVES
a, an	not, without	asymmetrical, asocial, anarchy
ambi (Latin), amphi	both	ambidextrous, ambivalent, amphibious
dia	through	diagonal, diameter, diaphanous
dys	ill, bad	dysfunction, dyspepsia
epi	upon, above	epidermis, epitaph
eu	well, good	eulogy, euphonious, eugenics
hypo	under	hypodermic, hypoacidity
retro	backward	retrogress, retrorocket
se	away, apart	seclude, segregate, secede

Latin Roots

ROOT	MEANING	DERIVATIVES
caput	head	captain, per capita, decapitate
flagr	flame, fire	conflagration, flagrant
flu, flux	flowing	influx, superfluous, confluence
greg	flock, herd	congregate, gregarious
gress	go	progress, egress, digress
jac, jec	throw	projectile, eject
junct	join	junction, conjunction, adjunct
locu, loqu	speak	circumlocution, soliloquy, colloquial, loquacious, colloquy
nasc, nat	birth	nativity, renascence
pecc	fault	impeccable, peccadilloes
pend, pens	hang	dependent, pendant, impending
plen, plet	fill	replenish, plenary, deplete
preci	price	depreciate, deprecate
prim	first, early	primitive, primogeniture
pung, punct	point, prick	punctilious, pungent
quasi	as if, seemingly but not actually	quasi-official, quasi-intellectual
sanct	holy, sacred	sanctimonious, sacrosanct
sen	old	senior, senile
somn	sleep	somnolent, somniferous
tang, tact	touch	contact, tactile, tangible
verbum	word	verbal, verbose, verbiage

Greek Roots

ROOT	MEANING	DERIVATIVES
anthropo	man	anthropology, anthropoid
arch	chief, ruler	patriarch, archenemy
crypt	secret, hidden	cryptic, cryptogram, cryptography

dox	belief	orthodox, heterodox
gyn	woman	gynecology, gynarchy
hetero	different	heterogeneous, heteronym
homo	same	homogeneous, homonym
lith	stone	monolith, neolithic
mega	great	megaphone, megalomania
morph	form	amorphous, anthropomorphic
peter, petri	rock	petrify, petrology
pyr	fire	pyre, pyromania
thana	death	"Thanatopsis," euthanasia

Activities to Enrich Work with Word Parts

Readers in search of class activities to sharpen up—and liven up—the use of word parts are referred to "Fun Fare for Vocabulary Growth" in Chapter 7.

Word Origins Fix Meanings and Stir Interest

Work with Derivations Promotes Vocabulary Growth

Working with the origins of selected words, incidentally as students meet them in reading or in planned activities, has definite values:

1. A not-to-be-forgotten story, for example, the origin of *gerrymander* (below), may fix the meaning of a new word in mind more firmly than anything else.

2. The story of a word may give the word new overtones for the student and enrich and extend its meaning.

3. The romance and excitement of word origins can create word enthusiasts.

Social studies students are likely to remember *gerrymander* when they hear the lively story of Governor Gerry of Massachusetts during whose term an election district was drawn with fantastic boundaries—it was shaped like a salamander!

In any subject classroom, referring to a word's derivation may be helpful in strengthening retention of the meaning. A science student who learns the derivation of *equinox* (from the Latin *equi-*, equal, and *nox*, night) may more easily remember the meaning as the time when the day is equal to the night. A social studies student who learns the origin of *Pantheon* (from the Greek *pan-*, all, and *theos*, god) may more readily remember that this temple served the ancient Romans as a place to worship all their gods. A mathematics teacher might reinforce the meaning of *radius* through its Latin origin, the spoke of a wheel.

These two criteria should prove helpful in selecting words for derivation study: (1) If the objective is maximal vocabulary increment, the words selected should not, in general, be already well known to students. That *bonfire* was originally a fire of bones or funeral pyre catches interest and lends romance, but does not directly enlarge vocabulary. (2) The student should be able to form a ready association between the word's "story" and the current meaning.

Vivid and lasting mental pictures are likely to be formed when students discover:

—that *berserk* comes from an Old Norse warrior (or *berserkr*) who in
    battle worked himself into a frenzy, howled, and bit his shield.

—that *gamut* originally referred to the lowest note of the musical scale.
    If we "run the *gamut* of emotions," literally we run up or down
    the scale in a graded series of all the tones.

—that *pandemonium* means wild confusion, as if *all* Hell's *demons*
    were let loose at once.

—that *flamboyant* is derived from an Old French word meaning flame.

—that *shilly-shally* connotes all the irresolution in "Shall I? Shall I?"

—that *nonplus* derives from two Latin words meaning *not* and *more*.
    When you're nonplussed, you're at a loss as to what to say,
    think, or do, reduced to a state of "no-more-ness."

Students who become accustomed to noting the curious lore about deviation to be found within those brackets in the dictionary entry for a word have acquired one more permanently usable tool for vocabulary development. As we have noted, a story rich in associations often strongly reinforces retention of meaning.

Books on Derivation

The following books on derivation may be useful for browsing or reference. They are roughly classified by reading level:

Junior high school and up

Isaac Asimov. *Words from History*. Boston: Houghton Mifflin Company, 1968.

Isaac Asimov. *Words from the Myths*. Boston: Houghton Mifflin Company, 1969.

Charles W. Ferguson. *The Abecedarian Book*. Boston: Little, Brown and Company, 1964.

Colin Pickles and Lawrence Meynell. *The Beginning of Words: How English Grew*. New York: G. P. Putnam's Sons, 1971.

Picturesque Word Origins. Springfield, Mass.: G. and C. Merriam Company, 1933.

Bill Severn. *People Words*. New York: Ives Washburn, 1966.

Bill Severn. *Place Words*. New York: Ives Washburn, 1969.

Senior high school and up

Margaret S. Ernst. *More about Words*. New York: Alfred A. Knopf, 1951.

Margaret S. Ernst. *In a Word*. Drawings by James Thurber. Great Neck, N.Y.: Channel Press, 1954.

Charles Earle Funk. *Thereby Hangs a Tale*. New York: Harper and Row, 1972.

William and Mary Morris. *Dictionary of Word and Phrase Origins*, vols. 1, 2, and 3. New York: Harper and Row, 1962, 1969, 1972. (Offers more than 5,000 colorful and interesting stories.)

Nancy Caldwell Sorel. *Word People*. New York: American Heritage Press, 1970. (Offers profiles of 82 people whose names have become everyday words.)

Advanced high school and college

Wilfred Funk. *Word Origins and Their Romantic Stories*. New York: Grosset and Dunlap, 1950.

H. L. Mencken. *The American Language*, 4th ed. New York: Alfred A. Knopf, 1936.

C. T. Onions, ed. *Oxford Dictionary of English Etymology*. New York: Oxford University Press, 1966. (A standard source of information about the history of 38,000 words.)

Eric Partridge. *Name into Word*. London: Secker and Warburg, 1950. (A comprehensive reference on proper names that have become everyday words.)

Eric Partridge. *Origins: A Short Etymological Dictionary of Modern English*. London: Routledge and Kegan Paul, 1958. (A comprehensive dictionary of word origins useful for the teacher and for exceptionally advanced students.)

Activities to Enrich Work
with Word Origins

Some lively class activities on word origins will be found under "Fun Fare for Vocabulary Growth" in Chapter 7.

Dictionary Competency Is a Must

The "ideal product" of the dictionary program runs to the dictionary for the fun of learning about a word. When students learn to make appropriate and frequent use of the dictionary, they are strengthening their power to keep their vocabularies growing for life. To add the dictionary to their vocabulary tool kit, these three strategies (among others) are essential:

First, students cannot become independent in vocabulary development unless they know how to use the pronunciation key in a dictionary. If they cannot pronounce a difficult word, they learn it only vaguely, it easily slips from memory, and they cannot use it in speaking. They must learn how to translate pronunciation symbols into a spoken word—sounding out each syllable, then blending the syllables together into a whole word with the correct accent. Students require considerably more practice than you might think for full mastery of the pronunciation key.

Second, the dictionary usually confronts students with a choice of what may be a confusing array of meanings. They should not select the first one their eyes fall upon, nor the easiest, nor the shortest—but the one that is the best fit in the context setting. In one English class where the students were reading about the *providence* of an animal for its young, every student selected the religious meaning of the word.

Third, students often have *extreme* difficulty using a new word correctly. They need to be alerted to two priceless helps: (1) the dictionary's clear model sentences, and (2) the tiny boldface symbol, **syn.,** which guides them to a paragraph that discriminates among the word's synonyms and offers clear example sentences.

Obviously, thoroughgoing instruction in these skills is desirable during elementary and junior high school years. Students in high school and college find it difficult to admit they don't know how to use the dictionary; instruction in using the dictionary must then become subtle in approach.

Simplified Dictionaries Meet Individual Needs

To span the broad range in reading achievement among students on each grade level, a supply of multilevel dictionaries within each classroom is of utmost importance. College students who need help with dictionary skills may really learn how to use a dictionary if they practice on one intended for high school students. One teacher asks, "What is gained if a seventh-grader who is deficient in vocabulary looks up *inexorable* and finds the meaning given as *relentless?*" Such a student will need guidance in consulting a student dictionary within his reach.

Simplified dictionaries intended for students are listed below:

Harcourt Brace School Dictionary. New York: Harcourt Brace Jovanovich, 1972. Grades 4–8.

Holt Intermediate Dictionary. New York: Holt, Rinehart and Winston, 1967. Grades 4–9.

Macmillan School Dictionary. New York: Macmillan Company, 1974. Grades 4–6.

Macmillan Dictionary. New York: Macmillan Company, 1973. Grades 7–12.

Thorndike-Barnhart Intermediate Dictionary, 2nd ed. Glenview, Ill.: Scott, Foresman and Company, 1974, Grades 4–8.

Thorndike-Barnhart Advanced Dictionary, 2nd ed. Glenview, Ill.: Scott, Foresman and Company, 1974. Grades 9–12.

Webster's Intermediate Dictionary. New York: American Book Company, 1972. Grades 4–8.

Webster's New Student's Dictionary. New York: American Book Company, 1974. Grades 9–12.

Webster's New World Dictionary, basic school ed. Englewood Cliffs, N.J.: Prentice-Hall, 1971. Grades 4–8.

Webster's New World Dictionary, student's ed. Englewood Cliffs, N.J.: Prentice-Hall, 1971. Grades 9–12.

Dictionary Skills Important for Vocabulary Growth

Systematic and complete coverage of the skills below, among others, will benefit students:

Selected meaning

1. Select the meaning which is the best fit in light of the context. This includes recognizing the order in which meanings are arranged in the classroom dictionary and in other dictionaries, and using the information about parts of speech as an aid in selecting the appropriate meaning.

2. Learn that words have different meanings in different subject fields. Make use of such subject labels as *med., biol., bot., chem., astron., geol.,* and the like.

3. Use guide words to find entries quickly.

Figuring out pronunciation

1. Understand the pronunciation key of any dictionary, though the keys vary from one to another.

2. Understand how the dictionary respells words to show pronunciation.

3. Know how syllable division is indicated.

4. Understand accent—primary and secondary.

5. Know how to blend the syllables together into a word with the correct accent.

Interpreting the information on derivation

1. Know its location in the dictionary.

2. Appreciate the interest, adventure, romance, and humor to be found within the brackets in the entry for a word.

3. Understand the meanings of the abbreviations which convey information about derivation.

4. Become aware of the value of studying derivations as an aid in retaining word meanings.

Using the information about synonyms

1. Know that the notation **syn** in a word entry signals an enumeration and explanation of the word's synonyms.

2. Value and use the explanation of the nuances of meaning among those synonyms.

"What Is Your P.Q.?"

Many students—even top readers—do not know how to use the dictionary's pronunciation key. Many use it carelessly or not at all. In every classroom, teachers will find natural situations that are just right for helping students acquire this essential skill.

When students are having difficulty pronouncing new words, one classroom teacher prepares a ditto with the heading, "What Is Your P.Q.?" (Pronunciation Quotient). Then the teacher sets out to send that "P.Q." upward:

> "We've all felt embarrassed when, in a conversation, we've
> groped for a word, then faltered and trailed off because we

couldn't pronounce it. Where can you find help in pronouncing a word that has a surprise twist in it—for instance, *d - e - v - o - t - e - e?*" (The word is printed on the ditto in a snatch of context.) The students, classroom dictionaries ready, respond that the pronunciation is "fenced in" by parentheses just after the word in the dictionary.

"Please copy on your paper all the signs and marks that tell you how to pronounce *d - e - v - o - t - e - e.*" The students record after the word on the ditto the phonetic entry:

a *devotee* of sports   (dev′ ə tē′)

"How can you be *positive* about how to pronounce each sound?" The students suggest the pronunciation key. Then the teacher "walks them through" the process of sounding out each syllable.

Many students are likely to need help with the schwa sound (ə). The teacher points out, "This is one of the most frequent sounds in English—it occurs in *thousands* of words. Learn it, and you'll save yourself countless future trips to the pronunciation key."

Students, surprisingly, may not understand the force of accent. Then they need an explanation: "Stress *most* strongly the syllable with the heavy accent mark. Stress *less* strongly— but still stress—the syllable with the lighter accent mark." Now the students try to pronounce *devotee,* accenting the syllables correctly. They might tap out the syllables on their desks with a pencil, the teacher explaining: "It's like a drumbeat—the heavy beat on the syllable with the heavy accent, and the lighter beat on the syllable with the lighter accent." Finally, they blend the syllables together into a whole word with the correct accents. The teacher suggests, "Now say it again and again until you're comfortable forming the sounds."

All this for the word *devotee!* But now the students have an important new vocabulary tool, one that will enable them to pronounce difficult new words always. More "handle-with-care" words follow on the ditto, words whose pronunciation may be a surprise—words like *circuitous, scion, respite.* For the students, the pay-off of this work on pronunciation is finding that they can pronounce the "word champ" of the English language in "Fun Fare for Vocabulary Growth" in Chapter 7.

Students should understand that the symbols in pronunciation keys differ from one dictionary to another and should definitely have practice using dictionaries with different sets of symbols.

Can You Tune in on the Right Meaning?

Students often lose their way among the confusing array of meanings the dictionary offers for a word they have met in reading. There will be natural opportunities in classrooms to help them "tune in" on the right meaning.

The teacher might point out: "You see that in your dictionary the meanings of each word are numbered: 1, 2, 3, 4, 5, and so on. In what order do you think these meanings are given?" The students usually suggest, "The most common meaning first."

"In some dictionaries, your classroom dictionary, for example," the teacher helps out, "that is indeed the practice. In other widely used dictionaries, though, it's the *oldest meaning* in use today, not the most common meaning, that is given first. And this oldest meaning may not be the one you, for today's reading, are after at all!

"Just how *can* you select the right meaning from among those numbered in the dictionary entry?" The students suggest, "Choose the one that fits in with the thought."

The teacher goes on, "Yes, you tune one of those numbered meanings into the context. It's *like doing fine tuning on your radio dial.* You move the pointer along the dial, turning it carefully to the different numbers until one number brings in what you want exactly right."

The students now practice "fine tuning," using the example: "Some salespeople become impatient when they wait on *nice* people" (adapted from Witty and Grotberg, 1960, p. 67).

The dictionary entry for the word *nice* holds a surprise—two of its meanings are almost exact opposites! Of course, the students "tune in" on meaning number 6 (from *Thorndike-Barnhart High School Dictionary*, fifth edition. Copyright © 1968 by Scott, Foresman and Company. Reprinted by permission).

---

nice (nīs), *adj.*, **nic er, nic est.** **1.** pleasing; agreeable; satisfactory: *a nice face.* **2.** thoughtful; kind: *He was nice to us.* **3.** exact; precise; discriminating: *a nice ear for music.* **4.** minute; fine; subtle: *a nice distinction.* **5.** delicately skillful; requiring care, skill, or tact: *a nice problem.* **6.** exacting; particular; hard to please; fastidious; dainty: *nice in his eating.* **7.** proper; suitable. **8.** scrupulous: *too nice for a politician.* **9.** *Archaic.* modest; reserved. **10.** refined; cultured: *a nice accent.* [< OF *nice* silly < L *nescius* ignorant < *ne-* not + *scire* know] **—nice′ly,** *adv.* **—nice′-ness,** *n.* **—Syn. 1.** gratifying, enjoyable. **3.** accurate.

Other Ways to Promote Long-term, Do-It-Yourself Vocabulary Growth

A vocabulary program should help students become self-motivated, self-guided, and self-directed—knowing ways to help themselves and assuming responsibility for their own progress. Otherwise they are left dependent, and their vocabulary growth will probably come to a standstill after high school and college.

Daily in subject classrooms, teachers want students to develop on-their-own competence in mastering the technical terms of the course. Tips adaptable to almost any subject are offered in Chapter 9 in the section, "How to Master the Vocabulary of Mathematics." Students report that two of the techniques offered are extremely helpful: the "divided page" and the "most powerful study technique." More tips are offered in Chapter 14 in the section, "Some Study Techniques for the Vocabulary of Music."

A personal word collection can be one means of encouraging students in any classroom to take the responsibility for their own vocabulary growth. One teacher reports, "My students lament, 'We look up new words but don't retain them.' I find this the right moment to launch word-collecting. It catches on if I suggest some starting words and make a big deal of the collections."

Launching the Word Collections

Students often respond to an enthusiastic sendoff:

"Here's a method that can lift your vocabulary well above its present level. It's tailored to your individual preferences. *You* decide the words you want and need. You collect them when time's available and not when it isn't. You set your own goals and move toward them as you wish to. You make the new words yours—to *stay*.

You'll be a better, faster reader with more word power. Suppose you're reading this sentence and don't know *anomaly*: "Mark Twain's philosophical despair was only an *anomaly*." What happens to your comprehension? In this case, context doesn't help. You may lose the meaning of the entire passage. What happens to your speed? From perhaps 300 words per minute it may drop to *no* words per minute. You may go backward and forward several times as you struggle, through rereading, to wrest the meaning from the total context. Each new word you learn helps take down the obstacle course.

"The method is wide reading, meeting new words, and collecting certain ones with a personal word collection. Small word slips (or a note pad) go with you everywhere in a convenient kit. When you find a word that's worth col-

```
┌─────────────────────────────────────────────────────────────┐
│                      VOCABULARY SLIP                          │
│                                                               │
│  New word ___POIGNANT_____  │
│                                                               │
│  Pronunciation __Poin'yənt  or  Poin'ənt_____    │
│                                                               │
│  Sentence in which you found it used __Lincoln's memories of his │
│  lost Anne Rutledge were always poignant._____    │
│                                                               │
│  Derivation (if helpful) __From O.F. poindre, to pierce____   │
│                                                               │
│  Meaning _piercing with a stab of emotion; piercing one's__   │
│  heart with emotion; painfully moving; touching_____    │
│                                                               │
│  Your example of its use __The story of the child without a__ │
│  home at Christmas time was poignant._____     │
│                                                               │
└─────────────────────────────────────────────────────────────┘
```

Figure 2–2.   Vocabulary slip.

lecting, you record it and the sentence in which you found it used. When convenient, look up and record the meaning that fits that context. Record the pronunciation *if* it gives you trouble—and the derivation *if* it helps you remember the meaning."

In one classroom the word kits, homemade from small manila envelopes, are in school colors and trimmed with a colorful sticker of the school pennant. The word slips, too, are colorful—printed on blue, pink, green, and canary ditto paper.

"Where can you find your new words? [The class suggests textbooks, words teachers and students use in class, personal reading, conversation, TV.] Listen to TV with a pencil and your vocabulary slips, and highly articulate national leaders and news analysts will supply words for your vocabulary.

"You may not want to break your train of thought to fill out a slip when reading. In that case, check the word in the margin, or make a light pencil dot, and record it later. If you don't own the book, use a bookmark to write down words you plan to work on later, together with their page locations.

"A dictionary should be near whenever you read or study. When you meet a new word important to you, try to reason out its meaning from context clues nearby or from familiar parts. If you can't do so, or if you need a more exact meaning, use your dictionary.

[Students urgently need criteria for word selection.] "You can't collect all the unfamiliar words you meet. Which ones are worth collecting? [Class discusses.] Not *syzygy* or *zyzzogeton*, which you'll probably never see again, but words you've seen several times and think you'll see again—words with an aura of familiarity—perhaps *taciturn, paragon, scintillate.* [Possibilities on an easier

```
┌─────────────────────────────────────────────────┐
│ ┌─────────────────────────────────────────────┐ │
│ │                                             │ │
│ │        SOCIAL STUDIES VOCABULARY TERM       │ │
│ │                                             │ │
│ │                                             │ │
│ │   Term_____      │ │
│ │                                             │ │
│ │   Definition_____      │ │
│ │                                             │ │
│ │        _____     │ │
│ └─────────────────────────────────────────────┘ │
└─────────────────────────────────────────────────┘
```

Figure 2–3. *Example of content area vocabulary slip.*

level: *nocturnal, agile, affluent.*] Chances are you'll run across these a dozen, two dozen, perhaps countless times more.

"A word is likely to be worth collecting if you find it in live contexts—on TV, or in a book, magazine, or newspaper intended for the general reader. You can be confident this word should be deposited in your word bank.

"Collect 'personal words,' words of special usefulness to you. Is it probable that some of you will need different words from those others need? [Class discusses.] Future nurses, businessmen, astronauts need extensive and quite different collections of technical words.

"You'll want to be on the lookout for vivid, expressive words with your own conversation and writing in mind. These need not be ostentatious.

"Through your word collection you literally *write your own vocabulary builder* along the lines of your own interests, uncluttered with words of no use to you.

"You'll probably want to strengthen your technical vocabularies in different subjects—science, social studies, math, business or technical courses, music—by collecting highly important 'official' terms. A simple word slip like the accompanying one, adapted for social studies, is a handy means of recording special terms for special study.

"Has it occurred to you that you have two vocabularies—*passive* and *active?* [Students talk these over.] Your active vocabulary consists of words you have on call for speaking and writing. Your passive vocabulary includes less familiar words, those you recognize and understand in reading but do not use in your own expression. Your passive vocabulary is considerably larger than your active —perhaps three or four times as large. It's far more difficult to add a word to your active vocabulary than merely to recognize it when you meet it in reading.

"But if you wish to be more fluent in expressing yourself, certain words— those you'll really have occasion to use—will be worth this extra effort. You'll want to practice using these words by making up sentences of your own. Take care, though, when you make up the sentences. It may be extremely difficult to use a new word with precision. An appropriate dictionary or synonym book offers clear model sentences. In the dictionary entry, the notation **syn.** guides you to the nuance of meaning. Your teacher, too, is here to guide you.

"You may wish to set a quota—one, two, three, even five new words each day. [Class discusses this.] Or you may prefer to collect your words whenever your reading lends itself. Or you may set a weekly or monthly quota.

"This is an odd-moment method. You can build vocabulary waiting for a friend, riding in a car, waiting for a bus. You can prop word slips on the sink and learn words while doing the dishes. Such spaced reviews give stronger reinforcement than a single too-long session. When you feel confident that a word is permanently yours, you retire the slip from pocketbook or pocket and file it alphabetically in a file box. Even your 'retired' words should be reviewed occasionally, perhaps every month or so.

"Again, your word kit goes with you everywhere—to class, to the library, to the bus stop, to your home for TV or personal reading. *You* are in the driver's seat. Choose the words that interest you—select your own convenient time—set your own goals."

During the next few days, the teacher suggests starter words, and the students bring in their finds and share them. The teacher continues to make a big deal of the collections—and so do the students!

Helping Students Retain Their New Words

When the collections have had a chance to grow some, the teacher offers some tips on how to retain the words.

"Students say, 'I've collected a hundred words but I can't remember them.' It takes reviews to clinch retention. You've already printed the word at the top of the word slip. Now play solitaire. Cover the meaning and look at the word. Ask yourself the meaning. Try to express it not by rote but with full appreciation of its content. Or test yourself the other way by covering the word and looking at the meaning. Ask yourself the new word. Separate your word slips into an I-do-know and an I-don't-know pile.

"You can put new words on instant call through powerful retention techniques. Why not use triple-strength learning? If you learn words with your eyes alone, you're using just one-third of your possible learning channels. Why not employ all-out VAK learning—Visual, Auditory, and Kinesthetic?

1. Use your eyes as you *see* and reread the word and definition.

2. *Say* the word—aloud or in a whisper. This is powerful reinforcement. And *saying* the word helps it slide into your speaking and writing.

3. Strengthen learning with your ears as you *hear* yourself say it.

4. Add kinesthetic (muscular) learning as you *write* out the word and definition with, perhaps, an illustrative sentence.

"Do occasional self-testing. Pull ten or twenty word slips at random from your collection and play solitaire by writing meanings of words. You may want to write sentences using the words.

"You can have imaginary conversations with yourself in which you practice using each new word. You could write an imaginative account of some happening and work into it as many new words as you can within reason. At the first real life opportunity, really *use* your new words in your own conversation and writing."

Students Set Their Own Goals

One teacher reports: "Collecting words is like keeping a diary— you start off with good intentions. Using the form in the following exercise, my students make a voluntary commitment to themselves—a definite number of new words to be collected. They fill out two copies, one to keep and the other to hand in. Students who want me to 'nudge' them to keep their commitment add a note to this effect on my copy. I record in my record book each student's pledge and the requests for prodding. I 'nudge' the students through conferences and class announcements. Short-term goals are more effective than long-term with younger and less enterprising students. These students need their enthusiasm periodically rekindled. Frequently the 'Best Word of the Day' might be chosen, the honors going to a word exceptionally useful for other students."

Activities to Stimulate Word Collecting

Bookmarks for New Words

A physics teacher, one with a broad personal interest in students, observed in his classes a need for general vocabulary improvement. So he designed an attractive bookmark as a stimulus. He suggested: "You may not want to break your train of thought to look up a word while reading for enjoyment. Just jot the word in one of the numbered spaces on this bookmark, with its page location. Then look up the word whenever you want to" (Kimmel, 1975). Bookmarks proved contagious. Another class designed its own, with space for both the words and their meanings.

text cont. pg. 69

SET YOUR OWN GOALS FOR VOCABULARY

Only you can set goals for yourself! Only you can move toward them!

If you've decided to start a personal word collection, please set goals for yourself as suggested below. You'll want to consider your test score, your own judgment as to what you need, and any suggestions from your teacher.

The goals you set today are only tentative. You may wish to change them as you make progress. Your goals should be realistic. Planning more than you can possibly attain brings only disappointment.

Your teacher will confer with you about your goals.

TO IMPROVE VOCABULARY	PLANNED	FINISHED
1. How many words do you plan to have in your personal word collection (and really learn) before the end of this month?	_____	_____
2. Have you decided to collect a definite number of words each day? Each week? If so, what is your quota?	_____	_____
3. Some students prefer not to set a daily or weekly quota but to collect their new words whenever the reading they are doing at the moment lends itself. If this is your decision, indicate by checking here: _____		

Extra Mileage out of Words

Students will want to get extra mileage* out of their words. While working with *altruistic*, they can also jot on their word slips and quickly learn *altruist, altruism*, and *altruistically*. While working with *tenacious*, they can jot down and quickly learn *tenacity*, and *tenaciously*—even *pertinacious* and *pertinacity*.

They may wish to collect synonyms, too, on their word slips. While they are collecting *neophyte*, they may find it defined as *beginner, novice, tyro*. Now they can quickly pick up the additional word *tyro*.

Bring Twilight Words out into Daylight

This convincing invitation to collect "twilight words" is slightly adapted from Dale and O'Rourke (1971, p. 8):

> The best source of new words is the "twilight zone" of your own vocabulary. There you have hundreds, perhaps thousands of almost-known words. They may need only a nudge to become your own. Why not bring them from the twilight zone of confusion and partial knowledge into the broad daylight of clear understanding? You can probably increase your vocabulary by 10 percent by bringing hazy words into sharp focus.

Examples of "twilight words" for a capable high school upperclassman might be *nostalgia, nonchalant, blasé, vicissitudes, incongruous*, and *iridescent*.

Dale and O'Rourke (1971, p. 21) drove home the twilight word concept by asking students to indicate on a list of selected words how well they already know each word:

+ means: I know it well. I use it.
✔ means: I know it somewhat.
— means: I've seen it or heard of it.
O means: I've never heard of it.

From then on, students are likely to be on the lookout for twilight words and eagerly nudge them into their vocabularies.

Authority for the Moment

Students select from their collections words they consider especially useful to the class, make themselves authorities on these words, and become the "au-

---

* The phrase, "more mileage out of words," belongs to Witty and Grotberg, 1960, p. 31.

thority for the moment." *The* "authority" announces the word, explains the derivation (if helpful), uses the word in a sentence, and then challenges someone to give the meaning. Students often refine their knowledge of a word and devise sentences painstakingly when they are to be the "authority."

A teacher comments, "After a student has finished, I have seen others snatch his or her word slip and eagerly copy the information for their own collections." For review, students sometimes print words on flash cards and flash these at each other (Kaplan, 1970).

Testimonials of VIPs

Upperclass students who have used word collecting to their advantage can give "testimonials" to younger students. A popular senior class president who had worked intensively on vocabulary from his sophomore year visited classes and shared the methods he had used to lift his vocabulary from ordinary to superior. He exhibited his own collection of word slips, which had reached shoebox proportions.

Word-Calling Game

Students exchange collections and call the words to each other, counting the number of correct responses as the score. They are aware that words have more than one meaning and that their partner is supposed to give the meaning that fits the context recorded on the word slip.

Teacher Testing

Some students may want the stimulus of testing by their teacher. At the student's request, the teacher pulls ten or twenty slips at random from the student's collection and asks her or him to write the meaning and perhaps an illustrative sentence. Students are encouraged to study their collections until they feel confident, then announce that they are ready for the test. Success experiences build confidence in word collecting.

Voluntary versus Compulsory Word Collections

Some teachers who once made collecting words compulsory have dropped the requirement. "When the work is assignment-like, many students react negatively. They abandon the method the minute the year ends and they escape the requirement."

Other teachers express a different view: "We can't expect students to be enthusiastic until they try the method and see the results. Until junior year in high school, when there's a strong vested interest in PSATs ahead for some students, they need to be pushed. Word collecting should be required on at least one grade level. Some students appreciate the discipline."

Still other teachers suggest sectioning off a group deficient in vocabulary, dismissing the others to some other project, and giving word collecting a persuasive sendoff.

Whatever the conditions of collection, the word slips for many students are a constant stimulus to be alert for new words and to consciously attend to their meanings. These students are moving toward independence, recognizing that no one can give them a readymade vocabulary, taking the responsibility for their own collecting, being responsible for retention.

The "Hidden Consensus" on Vocabulary Building

In the preceding discussion of vocabulary building we have considered a number of procedures for vocabulary improvement: using context clues, unlocking new words through Greek and Latin word parts, associating the current meaning with the derivation, consulting the dictionary, recording and reviewing

---

How to Crack Down on a Word

1. *Always search the context for clues first.*
   Through the context you may catch overtones of meaning. As you do so, you may develop a psychological "set" toward the word—you may "lay the first layer of cement for fixing the term in your vocabulary."
2. *Examine the word for familiar parts.*
   Take the word apart if you can. It may help to sound it out as best you can. Do you recognize any part? Guess all you can from any part you recognize. "When you *do* note a familiar section, your gain is usually great. You develop a strong 'set' toward the word."
3. *Reach for the dictionary,* if Steps 1 and 2 haven't yielded all the meaning you want.
   Now here is where your vocabulary can improve dramatically. Recall any guess you made from context. Now verify or reject your guess. This order of things gives you full benefit of the mental set you created by previously trying to deduce the meaning. "The more correct your guess proves to be, the more likely you are to remember the meaning. Nevertheless, if your guess is ridiculously wrong, you may find yourself less likely to forget the word than if you had not guessed at all."
   As you learn the meaning, try to associate the word with its derivation. The derivation is often rich with unforgettable associations.
4. *Record the word,* if it is one you wish to collect to work on further, on a word slip or in your vocabulary notebook.

The quoted material is from Shaw (1955, pp. 290–300).

---

words through a personal word collection. With which of these procedures should the student react when he meets an unfamiliar word? Under what circumstances? In what order?

According to Johnson (1962), there is a "hidden consensus" among vocabulary experts on the strategy on the preceding page. Students may, on occasion, stop after Step 1 or Step 2 or Step 3. If examining context clues and word parts yields all the meaning they need for present purposes, they should proceed no further. Shaw (1955, pp. 290–303) made the strategy inviting to students— makes them want to try it.

Vocabulary work offers an opportunity for a great variety of word play activities, activities that through a lighter approach reinforce vocabulary learnings. The reader will find an assortment of these in the section "Fun Fare for Vocabulary Growth" in Chapter 7.

DANGER: WORDS AT WORK

Teachers in every classroom will want their students to learn not only the meaning of words but also their tremendous power.

More words are bombarding our young people—for good or ill—than have bombarded any other generation in history. Our vocabulary programs fall far short if our students learn only the meanings of words and not their tremendous power to control thoughts and actions.

Hayakawa (1972, pp. 14–17) reminds us of the effect of this Niagara of words on Mr. T. C. Mits* (*The Celebrated Man in the Street*):

> From the moment he switches on an early-morning news broadcast until he falls asleep at night over a novel or magazine, or in front of his television, he is, like all other people living in modern, civilized conditions, swimming in words. Newspaper editors, politicians, salesmen, disc jockeys, columnists, luncheon-club speakers, and clergymen; colleagues at work, friends, relatives, wife and children; market reports, direct-mail advertising, books, and billboards—all are assailing him with words all day long. . . .
>   . . . There are few occasions on which Mr. Mits thinks about language as such. . . . Like most people, he takes words as much

---

* Lillian and Hugh Lieber of Long Island University christened Mr. Mits.

for granted as the air he breathes, and he gives them about as much thought. . . .

. . . Mr. Mits is profoundly involved in the words he absorbs daily. . . . Words—the way he uses them and the way he takes them when spoken by others—largely shape his beliefs, his prejudices, his ideals, his aspirations. They constitute the moral and intellectual atmosphere in which he lives—in short, his semantic environment.

Cooperation through the use of language, Hayakawa indicated, is the fundamental mechanism of human survival: "Human fitness to survive means the ability to talk and write and listen and read in ways that increase the chances for you and fellow-members of your species to survive together."

Should We Stop with Teaching Word Meanings?

Perhaps Mr. T. C. Mits, so oblivious to the words around him yet so susceptible to their influence, is a graduate of one of our high schools, All too often, students learn only the *meanings* of words. The study of words stops there. Any study of the *power* of words to control their thoughts and actions is delayed until college.

In this section the authors share a number of "collector's items" for teaching the persuasive power of language. They are intended for use in English, social studies, science, mathematics—in fact, in any classroom. They are related to two aspects of the broad field of critical reading: *awareness of the power of connotations* and *alertness to the dangers of abstractions*. The authors have drawn ideas and inspiration from S. I. Hayakawa's latest edition of *Language in Thought and Action* and from Richard D. Altick's *Preface to Critical Reading*. Somehow insights from these classics have not filtered into a number of secondary school classrooms. The authors also express their appreciation to the social studies department of Evanston Township High School, Illinois, for ideas and inspiration from their *Unit on Clear Thinking*, and to the same department of Thornton Township High School, Harvey, Illinois, for their *Introduction to Clear Thinking*.

Readers will surely be interested in many additional aspects of critical reading and may wish to prepare broad critical reading units. They will find the following sources rewarding:

Altick, Richard D. *Preface to Critical Reading*, 5th ed. New York: Holt, Rinehart and Winston, 1969.
Black, Max. *Critical Thinking*. Englewood Cliffs, N.J.: Prentice-Hall, 1952.

Chase, Stuart. *Guides to Straight Thinking with Thirteen Common Fallacies.* New York: Harper and Row, 1956.

Chase, Stuart. *The Tyranny of Words.* New York: Harcourt, Brace and Company, 1959.

Chase, Stuart, and Marian T. Chase. *Power of Words.* New York: Harcourt, Brace and Company, 1954.

Hacking, Ian. *A Concise Introduction to Logic.* New York: Random House, 1971.

Hayakawa, S. I. *Language in Thought and Action,* 3rd ed. New York: Harcourt Brace Jovanovich, 1972.

Ruby, Lionel. *The Art of Making Sense: A Guide to Logical Thinking,* 2nd ed. Philadelphia: J. B. Lippincott Company, 1968.

Werkmeister, W. H. *An Introduction to Critical Thinking,* rev. ed. Lincoln, Neb.: Johnsen Publishing Company, 1957.

While practice exercises for students are included on later pages, work with word power can be built right into the regular course work. *Guiding students to respond to words critically in genuine reading situations is ideal.*

Are Words in Charge of You?

Students can share—discuss—read—or hear in comments from their teacher some of these ideas:

> Are you in charge of words, or are words in charge of you? All day long—almost every waking hour—you are assailed by words. From the television screen, from newspapers and magazines, from advertising spreads, from books, from billboards, others intend their words to control your thoughts and actions—sometimes for your good, sometimes for their own.
>
> If you lived under a totalitarian regime, every word you would see and hear on crucial issues would be selected for you by others. Every word, every comma would be controlled. But in a democracy you are exposed to words expressing many different viewpoints. It is your privilege in a democracy—and your tremendous responsibility—to select *which* words you wish to influence your thoughts and actions.
>
> The more thoughtfully you respond to words and the more clearly you think, the more powerful the influence you'll have in human affairs and the greater the good you can accomplish:*

---

* According to *Introduction to Clear Thinking* (Harvey, Ill.: Thornton Township High School Social Studies Department), p. 22.

Connotations Exert Subtle Thought Control

Many students consider the dictionary definition the "last word" about a word. They are not aware that many words have *connotations* as well as *denotations* and that these connotations *suggest* much that goes beyond their explicit or primary meanings.* Nor are they aware that words are often used in an effort to convince us of something by connotation alone, that a word's connotations —without one scrap of evidence or one iota of logic—can impel us to some course of thought or action or as strongly repel us.

Words Can Make Us Support Angels and Fight Devils

Students will no longer consider the dictionary definition the "last word" about a word if they share, discuss, hear, and work with these ideas, ideas familiar to their teachers but all too often quite new to secondary school students:

> Some words have a favorable connotation, or aura, for us. The very words alone tend to arouse our approval. Like good angels, they seem to wear a halo. *Brotherhood, democracy,* and *humanitarian* wear halos for most of us. Other words have an unfavorable connotation. All by themselves, they tend to arouse our disapproval. It seems as if they wear a pair of horns. *Communist, un-American,* and *revolutionary* wear horns for many people.
>
> Words with horns and halos tend to *stop thought* and *turn on feeling*. Writers sometimes use them to try to induce us— on the basis of the words alone, not on the basis of the evidence —to support their particular angels or to fight their particular devils. One writer may call someone who fights for the Arab cause "a crusader for sacred rights"; another may call the same fighter "a terrorist who maims and mutilates." How differently we react, and are intended to react, to these words!
>
> It is easy for all of us to give in to an instant emotional impulse. It is infinitely more satisfying to turn on critical reflection.

---

* The denotation of *home*, of course, is a place where one lives with one's family. Its connotation, for many, is a place of warmth, comfort, and security.

Can You Call Your Thoughts Your Own?

Students may want to talk this over: "How *can* you call your thoughts your own?" They are likely to come up with some of these suggestions:

> We need to think, "Wait a minute! Are these words helping me think through a difficult question?" We need to say to ourselves, "I'll delay reacting until I consider the effect the writer intends the words to have." Then we need to decide whether or not we care to be so influenced. We need to hold firmly to our privilege of weighing the pros and cons. Then, after examining all sides of the question, we can arrive at our own informed opinion.

There's Much To Believe In

Students should not be left with the impression that the power of words to turn on emotions is solely a force for evil. They might discuss ideas like these, borrowed from Altick (1963, pp. xxi, 24, 120–121):

> Used in one way, they [words] are a means of spreading and intensifying the basest sort of prejudice and bigotry; used in another, they are a means of stirring the human spirit to heights of nobility and courage. . . . Mankind would never have risen from barbarism had there not constantly been men—poets, orators, preachers—to stir it to action. . . .
>
> Training in critical reading would be of little use if it led you merely to substitute cynical disbelief for uncritical belief. . . . It is the healthiest possible sign if you have lost faith in false gods. But believing nothing is as little to be desired as believing everything. . . . It is infinitely more satisfying to be able to separate the true from the false—to establish positive critical standards by which you may detect what is good and credible and sincere in what men write.

It is natural, commented Gainsburg (1967, 2, p. 267), for writers to try to influence their readers with word power:

> When a writer feels strongly about some subject, it is entirely natural for him to want his readers to feel as he does. Therefore he employs terms that are likely to influence the reader in one direction or another, to be sympathetic to his side

and to resent the other. He may be quite sincere and honest about his feeling and belief, but you, as the reader, have the right to *know* that he is trying to persuade you to his way of thinking. You need to realize the writer's purpose in writing. Then you can put the emotional appeals aside in your mind, and base your judgment on the facts and the evidence, not on the words of persuasion.

As we have mentioned, work with connotations can be built right into the regular course work in any subject classroom. Guiding students to respond reflectively in genuine reading situations from day to day is ideal. The following practice exercises should be suggestive to teachers who are working in natural situations or who wish to develop their own practice materials, using words of appropriate difficulty. They might also become part of broad units on critical reading.

Abstract Terms Flash Warning Signals

Many students are unaware that abstract terms present dangers, that they can lead us into unsound judgments and unwise actions, and that we should see such terms as flashing red warning signals.

A teacher might elicit, share, discuss, and work with background understandings like these:

A *concrete* term stands for something that actually exists in the material world—it represents something we can touch or see or hear. In contrast, an *abstract* term is something thought of apart from any real object—it stands for something we cannot touch or see or hear. *Sugar,* of course, is a concrete term—*sweetness,* an abstract term.

Justice, democracy, courage, honor, and *brotherhood* are all abstract terms. Of course, we could not do without these terms. They represent some of our finest ideals and aspirations. Yet words like these can also confuse our thinking.

An abstract term refers to something that "isn't there at all." We cannot take an abstraction in our hands, as you can your concrete looseleaf notebook, bring it near, and examine it closely. There is no such "thing" as *justice*—there are only *just* practices, and in a given situation what two people view as just may be quite dissimilar. Both the Israelis and the Arabs plead for a *just* settlement of their conflicts, yet how different is the settlement each has in mind as just! Both the United

text cont. pg. 82

"GOOD GUYS" OR "BAD GUYS"?

Writers often use words with strong favorable or unfavorable connotations to refer to their own heroes or villains. They want *their* heroes and villains to become *your* heroes and villains, too. They seem to feel that emotionally charged words will have a stronger influence than words that give evidence for their views.

Some of the words below are "good guys." They are sometimes used to persuade you to support the person or cause referred to. Others are "bad guys." They are often used to influence you against some person or cause.

Which of the words below do you think are "good guys" *for most Americans* and might be used to influence readers in favor of some person or cause, and which are "bad guys"? Make two columns. Head one column "Good Guys" and one "Bad Guys." Then place each word in the appropriate column.

As you read and as you listen to television, be on the lookout for "good guys" and "bad guys." Perhaps they are being used in a subtle attempt at thought control.

100% American	idealist	crusader
humanitarian	middle-of-the-roader	opportunist
wild-eyed fanatic	fence-sitter	aggressor
radical	atheist	dictator
Communist sympathizer	founding fathers	terrorist
do-gooder	statesman	revolutionary
defender of sacred rights	dedicated public servant	patriot
agitator	bureaucrat	fuddy-duddy
mother	power-happy officeholder	flag-waver
rabble-rouser	one who is un-American	egghead
bloated profiteer	die-hard reactionary	Good Samaritan

WHAT IS THE CONNOTATION—
FOR YOU?

Most students, indeed many people among the educated public, are unaware that words may have two types of connotations: personal and general.* Your *personal* connotation—let's say for the word *teacher*—is the cumulative result of all your own experiences with the word *teacher* and with living teachers, or it may have resulted from a single striking experience with one living teacher. *Your* reaction to the word *teacher* may, therefore, be quite

---

* The ideas about personal and general connotations are from Richard D. Altick, *Preface to Critical Reading*, 5th ed. (New York: Holt, Rinehart and Winston, 1969), pp. 4–5.

different from that of a friend of yours. A word's *general* connotation, on the other hand, is the flavor it has for most people, the associations surrounding the word that, for most people, are much the same. Associations with the term *national honor*, for instance, are favorable for most Americans.

We need to be conscious of the instant personal reaction we have to some of the words we meet in reading. And we need to be on guard against letting this control our response to whatever the word refers to.

Think about each of the terms below. Some may have a personal connotation for you. Do some spontaneously call up positive feelings? Negative feelings? Mixed feelings? Are some of them neutral words for you? Can you figure out the why of some of your reactions? Label each word below with one of these symbols:*

Positive   +
Negative   —
Mixed   + —
Neutral   0

_____ American way of life
_____ law and order
_____ the Establishment
_____ national honor
_____ the Pentagon
_____ police brutality
_____ black power
_____ police officer
_____ liberated woman
_____ hawk
_____ dove
_____ power to the people
_____ military-industrial complex
_____ draft-evader
_____ conscientious objector
_____ economic equality
_____ Wall Street
_____ minority group
_____ giant corporation
_____ liberal
_____ conservative
_____ male chauvinist
_____ America First
_____ hippie
_____ square
_____ pro-abortionist

_____ Stars and Stripes
_____ Hammer and Sickle
_____ welfare state
_____ racial integration
_____ peace
_____ member of the working class
_____ free enterprise
_____ part of a Communist plan
_____ capitalist
_____ communist
_____ Women's Lib
_____ un-American
_____ welfare recipient
_____ minority candidate
_____ Jew
_____ AFL-CIO
_____ hillbilly
_____ Southerner
_____ demonstrator
_____ Afro-American
_____ brotherhood
_____ the American heritage
_____ John Bircher
_____ patriot
_____ fair play
_____ rights of the people

---

* This activity is adapted from W. Royce Adams, *How to Read the Humanities* (Glenview, Ill.: Scott, Foresman and Company, 1969), p. 39.

Because connotations are so often personal, it is certain that not all of you in the class marked these terms in the same way. The term *the Establishment*, for example, may call up strong and decidedly different—often clashing—reactions.

Now select several terms to which you had a particularly strong positive or negative reaction. Try to figure out why you reacted so strongly. Make some jottings about why.

WHICH WORDS WEAR HORNS OR HALOS?

Search out in the media quotations in which certain words "wear horns" and are meant to turn you against a person, a political party, an institution, a belief, a course of action. Copy or encircle these "horn" words. You might look for these in newspaper stories and editorials, television newscasts and editorials, or political speeches.

Now take the horns off. Rewrite the quotations removing all the emotion-packed words and substituting neutral words. What is the difference in the impact?

Next, search out quotations in which certain words "wear halos" and are intended to win you to some belief or course of action. Indicate the "halo words." Ads supporting a political candidate or supporting some cause related to business or labor unions should provide good hunting.

Then take off the halos. Rewrite the quotations removing all the emotion-packed words and substituting neutral words. What is the difference in the impact?

We might add that *there is nothing wrong with a writer's using emotional words unless the words are used as a substitute for presentation of evidence for the writer's opinions.* . . . If the writer calls someone an extortionist but gives no facts to prove that person is an extortionist, the writer is guilty of . . . misuse of emotional words.*

Did the writers of the passages you have just worked with present evidence for their views?

PUT ON HORNS AND HALOS†

Fill in on the left a word or expression that "wears horns" and on the right one that "wears a halo." For *police officer* you might fill in on the left "sadistic persecutor of the poor" and on the right "noble protector of the masses."

---

* Adapted from *Unit on Clear Thinking* (Evanston, Ill.: Evanston Township High School Social Studies Department), p. 17.

† Idea for this activity is from *Introduction to Clear Thinking* (Harvey, Ill.: Thornton Township High School Social Studies Department), p. 12.

UNFAVORABLE CONNOTATION	NEUTRAL	FAVORABLE CONNOTATION
_____	teen-ager	_____
_____	soldier	_____
_____	striker	_____
_____	member of a minority	_____
_____	receiver of welfare	_____
_____	payments	_____

States and the Soviet Union regard themselves as democracies, yet their "democratic" practices are so divergent that each repudiates the other as a democracy. And in our own Congress there are constant debates over what is "just" or "democratic."

Wait a Minute!   What Does This Really Mean?

 Young people are likely to become more reflective readers when their instructor elicits, shares, and discusses with them comments and conclusions like these:

> High-level abstractions are often used, consciously or un-consciously, to confuse and befuddle us (Hayakawa, 1972, p. 160). When writers urge us to support something they associ-ate with "national honor," we need to think, "Wait a minute! That term can get me in trouble! It might refer to the just claim of a powerful nation, or it might also cover up an oppres-sive act against a small and unprotected nation." We need to ask, "Just what does that term mean to the person who is using it? Just what is that person proposing in terms of specific ac-tions or behavior? Is what the writers are advocating as fair and pleasing as the term appears on paper? If I probe what the writers *really* mean, will I respond quite differently from the way I would have reacted on first impulse?"
>
> Such delayed reactions, observed Hayakawa (1972, p. 174), are a sign of adulthood.

Ask "Logically Prior Questions"

Students should delay reacting, Engle and Longstreet (1972, p. 151) suggested, until they have asked *logically prior questions*, questions which must be asked and answered before a reasonable conclusion can be reached. They use as an example *law and order*:

> If the statement is made, "I want law and order," before a positive value of "good" can be assigned to it, one must know in what context and according to what criteria law and order would be used. There is considerable law and order in a dic-tatorship as well as in a democracy. Furthermore, law and order may be more valuable in one situation than in another. Students could be asked to think of situations in which law

and order would not be very valuable. Some examples are: (a) when minorities are oppressed; (b) when constitutional rights are curtailed by the enactment of a law; (c) when in-class creativity is discouraged; or (d) when necessary change is stifled.

Abstract Terms Hide Differences

Hayakawa's abstraction ladder is, of course, well known to our readers. Its message, though, will be quite new to most secondary school students. The rungs of the ladder, you recall, ascend from the concrete-object level to extremely high levels of abstractions. With each rung, the terms become increasingly "cover-all" terms as differences are disregarded.

On the lowest rung of Hayakawa's ladder is the concrete object, Bessie, a living, breathing cow that we can actually see and hear and touch. Then the rungs ascend through "Bessie," the cow's name, the word-symbol that represents this particular cow, with all this cow's individual characteristics—through the general term *cow*, which covers all the differences among individual cows —through the term *livestock*, which swallows up the differences among horses, cows, and sheep—through the term, *farm assets*, which groups together cows, barns, and tractors—through *asset*—until finally the ladder ascends to the term *wealth* on the uppermost rung, a term that is on a very high level of abstraction indeed. The reader who would like a more detailed explanation of the process of abstracting is referred to Hayakawa (1972, p. 153).

Hayakawa's message is that abstract terms *cover up differences*. We might bring the abstraction ladder close to students' lives by considering with them how the abstract term *teen-ager* covers up differences. On the bottom rung are Tom, Sharon, Jeannie, and Bob, all very much alive teen-agers, all different, indeed unique. On a higher rung is the abstract term *teen-ager*, and, oh, what a multiplicity of differences in appearance, personality, mannerisms, and behavior that term covers up!

"The Little Man That Wasn't There"

Borrowing from Hayakawa (1972, pp. 167, 185), teachers might share thoughts like these and elicit them from students:

> The words *teen-ager, capitalist, Jew, Policeman,* and *politician* are, of course, abstractions. They tend to conceal the differences within a group—thus they can contribute to much prejudice and to serious mistakes in judgment and action.

3. "teen-ager"

3. The abstract term "teen-ager" is a cover-all term, which obviously leaves out characteristics peculiar to individual teen-agers. What a multitude of differences in appearance, mannerisms, and behavior this term covers up!

2. "Tom"

2. The *word* "Tom" is the word we use to stand for the living, breathing teen-ager below. But the word is not the thing—it merely stands for the thing.

1.

1. On the lowest rung is the concrete, very much alive teen-ager, Tom, whom we can actually see, hear, and touch. He has many individual, indeed unique, characteristics. There's nothing in the universe exactly like Tom.

Figure 2–4.   *Teen-Ager's Abstraction Ladder. Its message: Abstract terms cover up differences! (Based on S. I. Hayakawa's abstraction ladder in* Language in Thought and Action, *1972, p. 153.)*

We sometimes react to such terms as if all members of the group are identical—as if every person in the group has characteristics associated with that group and no other characteristics. But the "typical" *teen-ager, capitalist, Jew, policeman,* and *politician* is, as Hayakawa pointed out, "the little man who isn't there."

One teen-ager who is in serious trouble with the law is not identical with most teen-agers. There is a device to remind us of this. It is simply to flag group terms in our mind's eye with index numbers: teen-ager[1], teen-ager[2], teen-ager[3], and so on. These little numbers remind us to be aware of *differences* as well as similarities and to say to ourselves. "Teen-ager[1] is not teen-ager[2] or teen-ager[3]. He or she is an individual. It's only fair to judge this individual as one."

By silently adding index numbers to group terms as we meet them in reading, we can form the habit of considering the *differences* within groups as well as the similarities: "Republican[1] is not Republican[2] or Republican[3]," "Politician[1] is not Politician[2] or Politician[3]."

In classrooms where these numbers have been used to "flag" group terms, the expressions "the little man who isn't there" and "teacher[1] is not teacher[2]" are likely to become "in" among the students and to be heard frequently in class discussions.

Climb Down the Abstraction Ladder

Classes can discuss, develop, hear, and digest cautions like these:

Sometimes we need to climb down that abstraction ladder and put our feet solidly on the ground!

Suppose a candidate for political office holds forth: "We must protect our sacred heritage, the American way of life" (Altick, 1960, p. 28).

One listener (a factory machine operator) may react: "Good stuff! American way of life—high wages, profits of big business limited by taxation, monopolies forbidden, labor unions protected by law, equal opportunity for all, nobody too rich, nobody too poor . . . I'll vote for him!"

A second listener (the owner of a small factory) may react: "My sentiments exactly! American way of life—government keeps its hands off business, no excess profits tax, labor unions kept in hand by restrictive laws. If a man has the brains and the aggressiveness he can make a million dollars and it'll be his own . . . I'll vote for him!"

Clearly, one of those voters is going to feel let down after this candidate takes office!

When we hear or read "high-rung-of-the-ladder" abstractions, we need to ask, "*Just what does the candidate mean in the world of experience? What stand does he or she take on specific issues? Just what specific things does he or she propose to do? When I know the answers, will I still want to support the candidate?*"

Work with abstractions, as with connotations, can be built right into the regular work in any classroom. Guiding students in genuine reading situations is ideal. The following practice exercises are intended to be suggestive to teachers who are working in natural situations or who wish to develop their own practice materials, using words of appropriate difficulty. They might also become part of broad units on critical reading.

HOW TO HELP STUDENTS ATTACK SEEMINGLY UNFAMILIAR WORDS

Can a teacher in a subject classroom help students build the "first story" of the reading structure? Here is a five-part strategy to help them attack words that appear to be strange.

"You can't built a second story without a first story!"

Vocabulary, comprehension, and rates of reading are the upper stories of the reading structure. Some students on the secondary level, generally the less able readers, lack a solidly built first story—the all-important base of word recognition. These students need tools for attacking words as a means of recognizing them. You can supply some of these tools, and help them catch up in reading, in the regular work of your course using the regular course materials, with worthwhile gains for students in their course work besides.

What Is Word Attack?

Students recognize on sight some of the words they meet in reading. Others they must attack for clues that reveal their sound and meaning. Readers can attack words in three ways: Through context clues, through phonic analysis, and through structural analysis. In *context analysis*, they use clues present in the language surrounding the words as a source of identification. In *phonic*

text cont. pg. 89

A BAD CASE OF "ABSTRACTIONITIS"

As you read or listen, be on the lookout for writers or speakers who have a bad case of "abstractionitis." Find clippings or quotations in which the writers remain high on the rungs of the abstraction ladder. They never climb down, plant their feet on the ground, and tell us what they are talking about in terms of specific actions and behavior in the everyday world. Share your findings with the class.

CLIMB DOWN THE ABSTRACTION LADDER

Now try bringing some abstractions down to earth yourself. After you've struggled to do this, you'll be more alert to abstractions that lack down-to-earth substance in the writings of others. You'll be more inclined to ask, "What does the writer *really* mean?"

Write explanations for five of the abstract terms below.* Climb down the abstraction ladder to solid ground by including specific examples of practices and behavior that can be observed in the everyday world:

patriotism	corruption
fair play	honor
injustice	good sportsmanship
popularity	intolerance
	equal opportunity

WHAT PICTURES FLASH INTO MIND?

Abstract terms often call *personal pictures* into our minds—pictures that result from our own experiences. We are all in danger of "seeing" abstractions in terms of these strong personal associations. Your reaction and mine to the word *disciplinarian* may differ greatly. One of us may recall a teacher who disciplined through coldness, sternness, and repression. Another may recall one whose classes were at their best because of the teacher's fairness, humor, understanding, and wisdom.

We should be aware—and wary—of these "instant" pictures. Because of them we tend to "see" abstractions in concrete, personal, and often misleading terms. We should delay reacting while we do some probing: "Just

---

* Idea for this activity from *Introduction to Clear Thinking* (Thornton Township), p. 16.

what is really behind this word in the mind of the writer? Should my response be different from my first impulse?"

It's a fascinating game to examine the mental images that flash into our minds when we meet certain words.* Study your reaction to five of the words below (or words of your own choice) *to which you react strongly.* Ask yourself: (1) What picture is thrown on the screen of my mind? (2) What in my memory are the personal associations and experiences that cause me to see this picture? Make jottings about these associations.

disciplinarian	mother
counselor	boss
police officer	welfare recipient
alcoholic	principal
liberated woman	father
coach	member of a minority group

---

* Idea for this activity from Altick, *Preface to Critical Reading*, 4th ed., pp. 11, 16.

analysis they associate sounds with letters and blend these sounds into words. In *structural analysis* they attack words by analyzing their meaningful parts—roots, inflectional endings, prefixes, and suffixes—and use these parts as aids in recognizing the words.

What is the difference between learning to *recognize* a word and *learning* a new vocabulary word? Why not just teach vocabulary? In the act of *recognizing* a word, the student identifies before him on the page a word whose mean- is already known to him—a word already in his speaking-listening vocabulary. He comes to recognize in printed form a word he can already say or understand when he hears it. In *learning* a new vocabulary word, he learns a word whose meaning is unknown to him.

A boy may have met the words *chassis, ignition,* and *carburetor* many times through his ears, may have spoken them many times, and may know their meanings better than his teacher—yet he may never have seen them in their printed form. Helping him to read these words will involve word recognition learning. In contrast, the word *philatelist* may be completely unknown to him. It will call for vocabulary learning, which includes work on both meaning and word attack.

Students' Word Attack Needs

A pupil may disclose word attack needs while doing incidental oral reading, through what he does when he meets a word that appears to be a stranger. If he so misreads a word that it makes no sense in the context, he may have failed to note context clues—an immensely important aid to word recognition. If he is blocked by the sound of *qu* in *quintet, au* in *authentic,* or *g* in *gesture,* he has revealed certain phonic needs. If he makes no effort to sound out a polysyllabic word like *communication* by easy-to-manage syllables, he may have revealed the need for a working knowledge of syllable division. If he is a "half-glancer" —if he glances at the first few letters of *internationalization,* for example, and then gives up, when analyzing its parts would have brought recognition— clearly he should have tools for structural analysis.

You might make quick jottings of a student's needs on a card with his name: "needs to examine context," "needs *qu,*" "needs soft *g,*" "needs syllable division." Or you might prefer the form in Figure 2–5, filling in the first two columns at the moment, then later analyzing the student's errors and filling in the third column.* Some teachers make a "Needs-at-a-Glance Chart" listing

---

* The authors are grateful to Nila Banton Smith for this suggestion gleaned from notes taken during one of her lectures at New York University, 1951.

Pete Westcott

THE WORD WAS	HE SAID	APPARENTLY NEEDS HELP
soldier	solder	to examine letter patterns in context
advisability	adwi— (He gave up)	to scrutinize middles and endings of words
gnarled	gn-narled	silent g
fugitive	fugitive ↑hard g	hard and soft g

Figure 2–5.   *Needs chart.*

essential word attack skills across the top and the students' names down the side. A glance down the chart quickly reveals the skills needed by the class or a subgroup. A glance across reveals skills needed by an individual.

Teachers may have occasion to explore needs more thoroughly. They may wish to consider the following tests or to use parts of them as patterns as they create their own tests.

Diagnostic Reading Tests, Section IV, Word Attack; Part I, Oral; Part II, Silent; Grades 7–13 (Mountain Home, North Carolina: Committee on Diagnostic Reading Tests, Inc., 1967).

California Phonics Survey; Grades 7–12 and college (Monterey, California; California Test Bureau, 1962).

Diagnostic Tests in *Tactics in Reading*, books A and B, intended for junior high, and books 1 and 2, intended for senior high (Glenview, Ill.: Scott, Foresman and Company, 1972, 1973; 1965, 1967).

Upper Grade Survey Test, Forms A and B (Glenview, Illinois: Scott, Foresman and Company, 1967).

Strengthen Word Attack Skills

Teachers often say, "My students slide over unfamiliar words without a try at them."

Opportunities to encourage systematic word analysis abound in classrooms. You may not realize as you capitalize on these opportunities from day to day that you are helping to build crucially important techniques into your students' on-their-own habits for as long as they live.

Students are frequently told that whenever they meet an unknown word they should immediately reach for their dictionary. But if they reach for it too soon, they will be overlooking other *highly effective*, often speedier means of coping with that word. Rather, they should be equipped with a five-pronged tool for word attack. The authors are indebted to Joseph C. Gainsburg (1967) for a number of ideas used in this approach.

1. *Train readers to search the surrounding context for clues.* Context examination will be the most important single aid for readers if they do not recognize a word at sight. To some students the word *lubrication*, if observed in isolation, will appear to be a totally strange word form. The context, however—if they are led to examine it—will probably be a giveaway: "Jack drove the car to the filling station for an oil change and lubrication" (Niles et al., 1965, p. 13). Now they may react, "Oh, it's lubrication!"

The suggestion, "Read to the end of the sentence or paragraph to see if you can identify the word" will encourage the attitude and habit of seeking meaning. As Stauffer (1969) observes, you will be focusing attention sharply on these questions: "What is the writer trying to say? What words would you, the student, use to say the same thing?" You will be inviting the student to reconstruct the author's ideas and to think.

Students, he notes, have had many experiences doing the same thing when communicating orally: "Often when two people are having a conversation, a speaker hesitates on a word and, before he can supply it and finish his idea, the listener has supplied it for him. How does the listener know what word to supply? He does so because he is listening intently and has grasped the speaker's ideas. So, with his attention focused on meaning, he is ready to . . . supply the word. It is this same intentness on meaning that should characterize the circumstance in which a pupil reads on and uses printed language-context clues to word recognition. . . ." Referring to the printed page as a "reading detective's paradise of clues," he points out, "Every word, every word order; each idea, each idea order; every line, sentence, paragraph, and page; all punctuation; all mechanics—all aid the knowing reader in his search for understanding (Stauffer, 1969, p. 304).

Context clues to the word's identity should *always* be tried first. Holding meaning clues in mind, the student should then (if he needs to) proceed to use the aids in Steps 2–5, which follow.

2. *Have students examine words for meaningful parts.* A word like *unconstitutionality* may appear endless to some students. Word that have picked up a number of prefixes and suffixes may frighten students out of all proportion to their difficulty. An extremely important service teachers can perform for some readers is simply to make them aware that long, forbidding words have parts. Much can be accomplished as needs become apparent in genuine reading situations—and it takes just minutes.

Left alone, some readers come upon a word like *inadvisability*, glance at the first few letters, and skip over the rest. These students can be led to spot an easy, familiar root word—here, *advise*—in a long word that appears to be unfamiliar. Once they do so, the puzzle of the "new" word may be solved.

If *unproductively* should be a block for some readers, you might inquire, "Can you see a word within a word—a root word—in this word?" printing it on the chalkboard. With guidance, students will mentally snip off the *un-* and the *-ive* and the *-ly*, discovering *product*—and then note the effect of the prefixes and suffixes. When they mentally reassemble the parts and return to the context, they have very likely solved the word.

If the word *diplomatically* is a stumbling block, you may wish to print it on the board, asking, "Is there a part you know?" Students may respond, "Oh, diplomat!" They now perceive the long word *diplomatically* as an easy word which has two suffixes tail-ending it. Only its length made it appear forbidding.

As other words come up as reading hurdles, these can go onto the chalkboard. "Can you strip this one down to its root word?" (*vaporization, immunization, longitudinal, consolidate*). "Can you see into this word—how it's built up?" (*incontestable, supersonic*).

Of course, word-part analysis presupposes some familiarity with frequently recurring prefixes and suffixes. As you guide each analysis, you will be adding to your students' working stock of these.

"Can you take this apart—break it into its building blocks?" (*interplanetary, circumpolar, transcontinental, extraterritorial, prediagnosis*).

Students will see into words quickly if, as you analyze them, you mark off the root word on the board with vertical lines

im | measur | able

or highlight it with colored chalk

im<u>practical</u>ity
re<u>forest</u>ation

With each analysis you are building a working knowledge of common affixes— their identities, their meanings, their variations in meaning.

There are dangers lurking in asking students to find the small word in the large word. They may discover the small word *ailment* in *derailment*. They will usually escape these dangers if they are told to look for the *root word* within the word. The root word, in turn, may be clarified as the part that carries the main load of the meaning—the base of the word to which other parts (prefixes, suffixes, and inflectional endings) are added. Prefixes may be clarified as added beginning parts that modify the meaning and suffixes as added ending parts that modify the meaning.

Once a trial word has been arrived at through part-by-part analysis, students should return to the context setting and check whether this word fits in. Those trained to do so will quickly reject *ailment* as the root word in *derailment* when reading about "the derailment of a crack commuter train."

3. Lead pupils to work out, syllable by syllable, the pronunciation of words that seem forbidding. The readings in your course will confront your students with many polysyllabic words. Once they reduce these to a series of short, easy-to-manage syllables, they may exclaim, "Oh, I know that word after all!" Demonstrating that at the chalkboard often takes just moments. If students are ready to give up before *authentic*, you might suggest, "Attack it syllable by syllable," writing it on the board

au | then | tic

You might point to each syllable, encouraging them to try to give its sound. Recalling the context, "an authentic portrait," some are likely to exclaim, "Oh, authentic!"

If students fail to recognize *unanimous* in "a *unanimous* vote," this, too, might go onto the board in syllables

u | nan | i | mous

You might expose one syllable, then another, from left to right, with an index card. As students recall the context, recognition may dawn.

If *quizzical* is a bar to understanding, it, too, might go up on the board in syllables

quiz | zi | cal

and then be exposed part by part with an index card. Your students' scrutiny of the syllables—their discovery of the meaning-carrying part *quiz*—plus the clues they find in the context, "The *quizzical* look on his face reflected his uncertainty," should combine to help them identify the word.

Often the student's sounding out of the word yields only an approximate pronunciation, but this is frequently enough to bring recognition if the word is already in the student's speaking-listening vocabulary.

Your guidance of students in making a syllable-by-syllable analysis will be changing the habits of the "half-glancers"—training these readers to work through a word, part by part, when they need to, all the way to the end. They will be learning that it is often possible when reading on their own to divide and conquer. Of course, students should gradually advance in the direction of on-their-own competency in using both structure clues and sound clues.

4. *Help students develop a shift-the-accent strategy.* Students should be aware that if their first try at pronouncing the word doesn't yield a word that fits the context, they can sometimes get a breakthrough by shifting the accent to another syllable.

A student meeting the word *notation* might pronounce it "NO-tə-shun"— and be left bewildered. But if he has a working knowledge of accent, he might try shifting the accent, "no-TA-shun," and quickly recognize the word. The teacher's reminder, "Try shifting the accent," may help.

A student blocked by the word *project* in "a *project* to reclaim the swampland," might misread the word as "prə-JEKT" and lose out on the meaning. Here again, if he is alert to the possibility of a shift of accent, he may try accenting another syllable and recognize the word as "PROJ-ekt."

As you write important terms on the board and mark off their syllables, you will often want to decorate the stressed syllable(s) with conspicuous accent marks—primary and, if necessary, secondary (perhaps in colored chalk). As you lead students through the pronunciation, you can sharpen their awareness of the force of these marks.

5. *Train students to turn to the dictionary when appropriate.* In the word attack tool kit, the dictionary ranks second in importance only to context. When you help the student make use of this tool, you are strengthening his or her power to read and learn independently—for life. The student will need the following skills and understandings:

a. The dictionary is a check on the meaning and pronunciation of a word the reader has tentatively arrived at through word-attack skills. And it is the place to turn if, after applying these skills, the word still resists analysis.

b. "Because the dictionary can't talk, special symbols are used to show in print the sounds of English" (Niles et al., 1965, 1, p. 40). The reader must translate these symbols into a spoken word, sounding out each syllable, then blending the syllables together into a whole word with the appropriate accent. Students may require considerably more practice than you may realize for full mastery of the use of the pronunciation key.

c. The dictionary usually offers a *choice* of a number of definitions. Students should not select the first one their eyes light on, as students·are likely to do—or the easiest—or the shortest—but should search for the best fit in view of the context. Day-to-day practice

A FIVE-PART STRATEGY FOR WORD ATTACK

1. *Launch your attack by searching the word's context for clues.*
   Crack down on the word instead of reading right on past it without a try. Context is likely to be your most important single aid.
2. *Look for word-part clues.*
   Take the word apart if you can. Do you recognize any part—a root? a prefix? a suffix? an inflectional ending? Words that at first look difficult can often be broken down into well-known building blocks. Considering the context again, do you now recognize the word?
3. *Work through the word, syllable by syllable. "Divide and conquer."*
   Try to sound out the word by easy-to-manage syllables. A long word is simply short syllables strung together. Is it familiar after all? Recalling context, have you now "solved" the word?
4. *Try a shift in pronunciation.*
   If you have not yet arrived at a word you know, attack it again by seeing if a change—perhaps in syllable division or accent—gives you a breakthrough. Again, does the word you have worked out click with the context?
5. *Reach for the dictionary.*
   If after Steps 1–4 the word still defies you, you have a never-failing tool. Now is the time to turn to your dictionary.

tied in with live reading situations is usually required before students habitually select the meaning that fits into the context setting.

The skilled reader does not click off these steps one at a time in the order given. Steps 2 and 3 are not sequential but all mixed in. It may be desirable to use any combination of the first four steps almost simultaneously. If one method fails to work, the reader attacks with another.

CAN ANYONE WITH MY BACKGROUND LEARN TO TEACH PHONICS?

An instant word attack kit can help a classroom teacher answer "yes" to that question.

A young English teacher observed in her seventh-graders a need for phonic and structural skills. She asked the reading consultant, "Can anyone with my background learn to teach phonics?" The consultant prepared an "instant word attack kit," placing at her fingertips insights on how to teach phonics and a generous supply of practice material.

Spend an evening or two with the scissors and some phonics workbooks and you can add such a kit to your classroom resources. Cover a spacious carton with bright construction or adhesive-backed paper. Put two or three dozen manila folders in the carton.

In the first folder go tests to explore the needs of students. The second is to contain charts or profiles to record the needs of individuals. Next come folders, in alphabetical order, for each of many different phonic and structural elements and skills—hard and soft *c*, the diphthong *oi*, the schwa, silent consonants, syllable division, accent, diacritical marks, and many others. Each folder is stocked with practice exercises cut from workbooks on various grade levels, with each exercise coded by grade level in the upper left-hand corner. The folders of the English teacher were stocked with exercises on all levels from 4 through 9.

When economy matters, the pages of a few workbooks will go a long way when classified in a file of this type. You will need two copies of each workbook so that the reverse side of each page can be included.

As a timesaver, the kit is great. If a student or group is having trouble with the sounds of *c*, for example, you can find within seconds practice work on just the right level. Of course practice work is timely when the need has just been demonstrated in a live reading situation and when the student is ready to use the skill for an immediate job. The file supplies material before motivation cools.

But how can a teacher with no training or experience in teaching reading learn quickly how to teach phonics? The box itself teaches the teacher. Place the teacher's manuals for the workbooks in the box behind the manila folders. In the upper right-hand corner of each practice page from a workbook record the initials of the corresponding manual. A teacher who doesn't know how to teach hard and soft *c* can refer to the manual from the practice exercise and receive sound instruction. To provide general background for the English teacher mentioned, Anna D. Cordts, *Phonics for the Reading Teacher* (New York: Holt, Rinehart and Winston, 1965) was added to the kit.

When working with a group whose members have a common need, you may refer to the kit, then ditto your own practice materials; or you may wish to project a workbook page on a screen before the group with an opaque projector. When working with an individual, you can place the practice page in a plastic envelope, and the student can write on the plastic surface with a china marker. Thus the materials are reusable. You may wish to turn to the teacher's manuals for insights, then create your own instructional materials, using subject matter of compelling interest to students. Your self-made materials can be filed in the appropriate folder, thus enriching the resources of the kit.

In the English class for which the word attack kit was created, each student had an individual folder. If the teacher observed a special need, the student was likely to find a note in the folder guiding him or her to an appropriate practice exercise. Sometimes the practice exercise served as filler. A student could work on it the first time she or he completed the class work ahead of the others. Since students were accustomed to working in laboratory-type kits, no stigma was attached.

If you plan to stock such a file, you may wish to consider appropriate levels of the following books and workbooks. Pages that look juvenile can be rejected.

Useful Books and Workbooks

Hargrave, Rowena, and Leila Armstrong. *Building Reading Skills.* New York: McCormick-Mathers Publishing Company, 1970–1971.

Kottmeyer, William, and Kay Ware. *Conquests in Reading.* St. Louis: Webster Publishing Company, 1968.

Kottmeyer, William, and Kay Ware. *The Magic World of Dr. Spello,* 2nd ed. St. Louis: Webster Publishing Company, 1968.

Monroe, Marion, A. Sterl Artley, and Helen M. Robinson. *Basic Reading Skills,* 2nd ed. Glenview, Ill.: Scott, Foresman and Company, 1970.

Niles, Olive S., Dorothy K. Bracken, Mildred A. Dougherty, and Robert F. Kinder. *Tactics in Reading,* Books 1 and 2. Chicago: Scott, Foresman and Company, 1965.

Roberts, Clyde. *Word Attack.* New York: Harcourt, Brace and World, 1956.

Rudd, Josephine. *Word Attack Manual.* Cambridge, Mass.: Educators Publishing Service, 1961.

Smith, Nila Banton. *Be a Better Reader,* 3rd ed., Books 1, 2, and 3. Englewood Cliffs, N.J.: Prentice-Hall, 1969–1970.

Wolfe, Josephine B. *Merrill Phonics Skilltext.* Columbus: Charles E. Merrill Company, 1973.

A teacher inexperienced in teaching phonics may be at a loss as to how to label the manila folders with all the essential phonic and structural skills. The workbooks just enumerated, or their teacher's manuals, offer lists of skills. In stocking a folder with diagnostic materials, a teacher may wish to consider some of the tests listed in the section, "How to Help Students Attack Seemingly Unfamiliar Words."

With an instant word attack kit, the task of learning to teach phonics need not be overwhelming. By following the simple, clearly stated, this-is-how-to-do-it procedures in the teacher's manuals, you can add one skill at a time to your word attack lore.

Bibliography

Altick, Richard D. *Preface to Critical Reading*, 5th ed. New York: Holt, Rinehart, and Winston, 1969.

Bortnick, Robert, and Genevieve S. Lopardo. "An Instructional Application of the Cloze Procedure." *Journal of Reading*, 16, no. 4 (1973): 296–300.

Botel, Morton. "What Linguistics Says to This Teacher of Reading and Spelling." *Reading Teacher*, 18, no. 3 (1964): 188–193.

Dale, Edgar, and Joseph O'Rourke. *Techniques of Teaching Vocabulary*. Palo Alto: Field Educational Publications, 1971.

Doemel, Nancy J. "Vocabulary for Slow Learners." *English Journal*, 59, no. 1 (1970): 78.

Goldfield, Ben. "Semantics: An Aid to Comprehension." *Journal of Reading*, 16, no. 4 (1973): 310–313.

Goodman, Kenneth S. "Reading: A Psycholinguistic Guessing Game." *Journal of the Reading Specialist*, 6, no. 4 (1967): 126–135.

Goodman, Kenneth S. "Behind the Eye: What Happens in Reading." In *Reading: Process and Program*, edited by Kenneth S. Goodman and Olive S. Niles. Champaign, Ill.: National Council of Teachers of English, 1970, pp. 3–38.

Greene, Amsel. *Word Clues*. New York: Harper and Row, 1962.

Introduction to Clear Thinking. Harvey, Ill.: Thornton Township High School Social Studies Department.

McCullough, Constance M. "Linguistics, Psychology, and the Teaching of Reading." *Elementary English*, 44, no. 4 (1967): 353–362.

Miller, Clyde R. "How to Detect Propaganda." *Propaganda Analysis*, 1, no. 2 (1937): 1–4.

Niles, Olive S., and Margaret J. Early. "Adjusting to Individual Differences in English." In *Teaching Reading in High School: Selected Articles*, edited by Robert Karlin. Indianapolis: Bobbs-Merrill Company, 1969.

Overstreet, Harry A. *The Mature Mind*. New York: W. W. Norton and Company, 1959.

Petty, Walter T., Curtis P. Herold, and Earline Stoll. *The State of Knowledge about the Teaching of Vocabulary*. Champaign, Ill.: National Council of Teachers of English, 1968.

Robinson, H. Alan. *Teaching Reading and Study Strategies: The Content Areas*. Boston: Allyn and Bacon, 1975.

Shepherd, David L. *Comprehensive High School Reading Methods*. Columbus: Charles E. Merrill, 1973.

Sherbourne, Julie F. *Toward Reading Comprehension*. Boston: D. C. Heath and Company, 1958, pp. 44–74.

Smith, E. Brooks, Kenneth S. Goodman, and Robert Meredith. *Language and Thinking in the Elementary School*. New York: Holt, Rinehart and Winston, 1970.

Smith, Frank. *Understanding Reading: A Psycholinguistic Analysis of Reading and Learning to Read*. New York: Holt, Rinehart and Winston, 1971.

Spache, George D., and Evelyn B. Spache. "Building Sight and Meaning Vocabulary." In *Reading in the Elementary School*, George D. Spache and Evelyn B. Spache. Boston: Allyn and Bacon, 1973, pp. 511–541.

Unit on Clear Thinking. Evanston, Ill.: Evanston Township High School Social Studies Department.

References

Adams, W. Royce. *How to Read the Humanities*. Glenview, Ill.: Scott, Foresman and Company, 1969.

Altick, Richard D. *Preface to Critical Reading*, 4th ed. New York: Holt, Rinehart and Winston, 1963.

Ames, W. S. "The Development of a Classification Scheme of Contextual Aids." *Reading Research Quarterly*, 2 (Fall 1966): 57–82.

Bragstadt, Berenice, reading consultant at La Follette Senior High School, Madison, Wisconsin, in remarks to Ellen Thomas, May 1975.

Courtney, Brother Leonard, F.S.C. "Methods and Materials for Teaching Word Perception in Grades Ten Through Fourteen." In *Sequential Development of Reading Abilities*, Supplementary Educational Monographs No. 90, edited by Helen M. Robinson. Chicago: University of Chicago Press, 1960.

Dale, Edgar. *The Word Game: Improving Communications*. Bloomington, Ind.: Phi Delta Kappa Educational Foundation, 1975.

Dale, Edgar, and Joseph O'Rourke. *Techniques of Teaching Vocabulary*. Palo Alto: Field Educational Publications, 1971.

Deighton, Lee C. *Vocabulary Development in the Classroom*. New York: Teachers College Press, Columbia University, 1959.

Engle, Shirley H., and Wilma S. Longstreet. *A Digest for Social Education in the Open Curriculum*. New York: Harper and Row, 1972.

Gainsburg, Joseph C. *Advanced Skills in Reading*, Books 1, 2, and 3, teacher's annotated ed. New York: Macmillan Company, 1967.

Hayakawa, S. I. *Language in Thought and Action*, 3rd ed. New York: Harcourt Brace Jovanovich, 1972.

Johnson, Harry W. "The Hidden Consensus in Vocabulary Development." In *Problems, Programs, and Projects in College-Adult Reading,* National Reading Conference, 11th Yearbook, edited by Emery Bliesmer and Ralph Staiger. Fort Worth: Christian University Press, 1962, pp. 105–112.

Kaplan, Ruth, former University of Chicago Laboratory School English teacher, in remarks to Ellen Thomas, May 1970.

Kimmel, Richard, former University of Chicago Laboratory School physics teacher, in remarks to Ellen Thomas, July 1975.

Levine, Isidore. "Quantity Reading: An Introduction." *Journal of Reading,* 15 (May 1972).

McCullough, Constance. "The Recognition of Context Clues in Reading." *Elementary English Review,* 22 (January 1945): 1–5.

Niles, Olive S., Dorothy K. Bracken, Mildred A. Dougherty, and Robert F. Kinder. *Guidebook for Tactics in Reading,* levels 1 and 2 (2 vols.) Chicago: Scott, Foresman and Company, 1961, 1964.

Paulsen, Leitha. "Testing and Teaching the Bright Underachiever in Grades Nine Through Fourteen." In *The Underachiever in Reading,* Supplementary Educational Monographs No. 92, edited by H. Alan Robinson. Chicago: University of Chicago Press, 1962.

Quealy, Roger J. "Senior High School Students' Use of Contextual Aids in Reading." *Reading Research Quarterly,* 4 (Summer 1969): 512–533.

Roody, Sarah I. "Clues in Context: A Reading Project on New Words." *Clearing House,* 27 (April 1953): 478–480.

Seibert, Louise C., and Lester G. Crocker. *Skills and Techniques for Reading French.* New York: Harper and Row, 1958, pp. 44–56.

Shaw, Philip B. *Effective Reading and Learning.* New York: Thomas Y. Crowell Company, 1955, chapters 5 and 6.

Smith, Donald E. P. "Vocabulary Development: Context Clues." In *Learning to Learn,* edited by Donald E. P. Smith. New York: Harcourt, Brace and World, 1961, pp. 125–131.

Stauffer, Russell G. *Teaching Reading as a Thinking Process.* New York: Harper and Row, 1969.

Strang, Ruth, Constance M. McCullough, and Arthur E. Traxler. *The Improvement of Reading,* 4th ed. New York: McGraw-Hill Book Company, 1967.

Thorndike-Barnhart High School Dictionary. Glenview, Ill.: Scott, Foresman and Company, 1968.

Unit on Clear Thinking. Evanston, Ill.: Evanston Township High School Social Studies Department.

Winthrop, Morton. "Do You Know How Words Can Make You Rich?" *This Week,* 29 (October 30, 1960): 6–7.

Witty, Paul, and Edith Grotberg. *Developing Your Vocabulary.* Chicago: Science Research Associates, 1960.

IMPROVING COMPREHENSION

You can upgrade your students' reading comprehension in any classroom where reading is required. You can do this as you go about the everyday activities of the course—as you make the assignment, as you select materials, as you help students master a textbook chapter, as you formulate questions on their reading selections. These routine activities can be designed to turn on reading power.

You can improve students' comprehension by the way you make a reading assignment. In the first section of this chapter we suggest six ingredients for an assignment that should help poor readers crack a difficult passage and should enable capable readers to comprehend it even better.

Of course any progress in comprehension comes to a standstill when the reading is years beyond the reach of students or else so easy for them that they merely mark time. But is it possible and practical to guide individual students to materials which are on their reading levels? Can differentiated materials be supplied within a subject area classroom so that students can work at their own instructional levels? In the second section of this chapter, presented in interview form, classroom teachers of the University of Chicago Laboratory School offer some pragmatic answers to such questions.

Some powerful reading techniques for mastering a textbook chapter are brought together in the third section. You will find comprehensive guidesheets addressed directly to the student. These suggest procedures specific enough for students to try out as they work on a chapter tonight. Students who in the past have been making a "whip-through" of difficult reading should now have a clear conception of what the thorough study of a textbook chapter demands.

The everyday classroom activity of asking students questions on their reading selections can also turn on reading power. In the section "Questions Can Develop Comprehension," we focus on some of the thought-getting processes that seem to be involved in comprehension. We also offer sample questions designed to help students acquire a more complete collection of mastered abilities.

The final unit, "Finding the Key Thought," focuses on one specific and important aspect of comprehension. A rationale is presented for the teaching of key thought or main idea with emphasis on instructional procedures to be used by any classroom teacher.

Other sections in this book offer crucial reading for anyone concerned with comprehension. "When Their Reading's a Struggle" in Chapter 7 offers a variety of ways to help troubled readers handle reading that would otherwise have overcome them. "Study Guides to Turn on Reading Power" in the same chapter suggests how to build solid reading help for students right into a study guide. You will also find sections in Chapter 6 worthwhile: "Helping Students Want to Read" and "You Can Have a Silent Reading Teacher in Your Classroom."

TURN ON READING POWER THROUGH ASSIGNMENTS

How many reading assignments will you make
in a teaching lifetime? Each one of these can
help toward better reading.

You can increase the reading power of your students by the way you make your assignments. You do not need formal training or experience in teaching reading in order to do this.

"Homework for tomorrow" is often the most unpopular announcement of the day. The assignment often appears to be overtime work with only one purpose: to deprive students of precious free time. It is viewed as the unfinished business that casts its gloom over activities more to their liking (Rivlin, 1948, pp. 175–176).

However, the assignment can be designed to change resisting readers into enthusiastic readers. It can help discouraged students who "just can't get it" approach their reading with new hope and purpose, and it can enable some of them to handle an assignment that would otherwise have been beyond them.

An effective assignment can salvage countless working hours for students, hours which otherwise would have been wasted in clumsy, inefficient study. Students spend a total of thousands of hours over their books in a school year; effective assignments can help ensure that these hours will be spent productively.

Such assignments are not likely to be made at the end of the class period. Time and thought—both *well rewarded*—go into making an assignment that turns on reading power.

To help toward better reading, an assignment should have several of the components listed below. Not all of these, however, are called for in all assignments. Factors to be considered as an assignment is planned include the interest pull of the selection itself, the preparation the students already have in terms of past experience, the reading skills they have at their command, and other factors. There will be much overlap among the components:

1. Capturing interest.

2. Relating the reading to students' past experience or providing a background of experience.

3. Helping students have a purpose for their reading.

4. Helping them know *how* to read to accomplish their purpose.

5. Pre-teaching vocabulary and concepts that would otherwise block their understanding.

6. Providing, when appropriate and possible, reading materials on a suitable variety of levels.

We will be concerned here with only the first four components. We have already suggested methods of removing vocabulary roadblocks *before* the students read an assignment. And we will stress later the priceless benefits for students when it is possible to provide materials which span their reading levels. Here it is sufficient simply to point out that Components 5 and 6, too, are often vital if the assignment is to increase reading power.

Component 1—Capturing Interest

An important component of a student's reading readiness for an assignment is interest caught up beforehand—anticipation—zest for the reading. When groups of poor readers were asked, "What makes reading easy?" they answered, "Interest" (Strang, 1965).

Giving a Preview

In one English class Poe's "The Pit and the Pendulum" would have been beyond the reach of many students. The opening was obscure, the setting far away and long ago, the vocabulary beyond them. Was there a way of saving the story? The teacher decided to provide a thumbnail background on the Spanish Inquisition and its extreme cruelty to heretics, then to tell the class the first part of the story—with dramatic flourish:

> Once upon a time an innocent prisoner was condemned—for his religious beliefs—to die by the cruelest tortures of the Spanish Inquisition. After the strain of the long trial, the prisoner fainted. Black-robed figures carried him unconscious —down—down—down—far below the surface of the earth, into a dungeon where the mind of man had excelled itself in devising fiendish implements of torture. When he regained consciousness, he examined his surroundings. On the walls were grotesque carvings—figures of imps and demons—and on the ceiling was the figure of Father Time, pictured, as usual, with a scythe.
>
> Suddenly he observed something startling about the figure. Father Time's scythe was a pendulum—in motion! The sharp blade was descending inch by inch—and he lay, bound securely, *directly in its path.* Now the full meaning of his sentence was clear. He was to die by the cruelest of all tortures, mental torture; for his was to be the anguish of watching death approach by slow degrees.
>
> *Down—down—steadily—steadily down.* Hours passed—perhaps days—he had no way of knowing; and still the pendulum descended. Nearer and nearer—*still nearer and nearer,* until he could feel the rush of the swift blade as it swept past.
>
> Now the blade, as it passed, cut the folds of his garment. One more stroke *and it would reach his heart. Can the fiendish torturers be stopped? Will the prisoner be saved?* If you want to know what happens, read Poe's story, "The Pit and the Pendulum," for tomorrow.

Many of the students could now enjoy Poe's story. A special Poe collection had been trundled on a cart from the library into the classroom. Next day the teacher gave exciting previews of "The Tell-Tale Heart," "The Oblong Box," "Ligeia," and other short stories. These previews took just minutes. That night every Poe book in the classroom went home with a student.

Teachers can often capitalize on the fiction writer's (or the biographer's) narrative hook, telling or reading a selection up to a point where the audience becomes captive. Similarly, they can search nonfiction assignments for attention-catching content to intrigue the students before they begin reading.

Never a Dull Moment in Zinch Valley

In one social studies class, an aura of mystery surrounds the first assignment (Bernstein, 1970). Each student is handed a dittoed sheet, on it, only this:

> A group of ten people enters and settles in Zinch Valley. Write an essay answering the following questions:
>
> 1. What are the immediate and long-range problems these people face?
> 2. What are the solutions these people bring to bear on both the immediate and the long-range problems?

That's all! No other information is provided.

But in class there will be an opportunity for questions. For the last thirty minutes of that period, and those thirty minutes only, students may ask questions. They may have *all* the information they can pull out of their teacher in thirty minutes.

Questions come pell-mell: "How did they arrive—by jet plane?" "Did they bring guns?" [The students soon begin to realize that they are dealing with very ancient times.] "Where did this happen?" [In the Middle East—Egypt through Mesopotamia.] "When?" [The late upper Paleolithic Age.] "What's the climate of the valley?" "Are there mountains?" "What are the resources?" "What can these people do?" "What do they bring with them in the way of equipment?" [The students are led to understand that clues to these answers have already been given—that the dating clue is the one to research further to discover what prehistoric man of that time and place could do.] "Are they male or female?" "Any children?" "How old?" [Answer: Five males, five females, nine between ages 10 and 45, a mother, a father, one small child.]

The session is lively and the time is up too soon. No more questions are permitted. The students are provoked and frustrated, yet challenged. Of course it is "permitted" to learn more about Zinch Valley through reading! Some of the students react, "I don't *need* all the answers from you—I can find out for myself." A list of readings spanning the reading levels within the class is provided; this includes everything from easy adventure stories of a Stone Age family menaced by cold, hunger, and wild beasts to advanced scholarly discourses. What happened in Zinch Valley, the wellspring of some of man's first painting, sculpture, music, and complex social patterns, becomes a thrilling chapter in the upward march of human progress. (Years later, students return from college or from jobs and ask the teacher, "How's Zinch Valley?")

Component 2—Using or Providing a Background of Experience

Students learn more easily when a new concept or fact is related to some previous learning. Seemingly remote times and happenings can come close when they are made to touch the students' own experiences.

Long-ago Lyrics Touch Today

The lyrics of the sixteenth century might seem to be moldering in the dust of four hundred years. But one teacher (Parker, 1939, pp. 462–463) called them "the popular songs of the sixteenth century" and compared them with our popular songs. The students listed the ten most popular songs of today, then ten old-timers that had survived for years. The question arose, "What makes a song survive?" The class reached these conclusions: universality of theme, simplicity, beauty of words, sweetness of tune. In every class "Stardust" headed the list of older songs still popular. Its theme of thwarted love, the students decided, was general enough to have wide appeal.

They compared "Who Is Sylvia?" and "Come Live With Me and Be My Love" with their own popular songs. The class studied the characteristics of the age which these earlier songs embodied, then studied our age as reflected in song.

The teacher reports: "They developed a feeling of 'hail-fellow-well-met' for the sixteenth century. Next day they dug into Shakespeare's sonnets and were eager to get to the drama to see what it shows about the people and ideas of an age so rich in both."

Nonreading Resources Provide Background

It is often of great benefit in strengthening the reading power of students for an assignment not only to relate the new learning to their previous experience but also to provide them with background experience. You have probably noticed in your own experience as a reader how much easier it is to grasp the content of a selection if the subject matter is at least slightly familiar. The background information you acquire, for example, simply from watching a TV program often helps you take hold of a selection about a subject otherwise unfamiliar and read that selection with greater ease, interest, involvement, comprehension, and speed.

Paradoxically, the use of nonreading resources often leads to better reading. Poor readers can get crucial background through excursions, television, films, filmstrips, projected pictures, records and tape recordings, models, interviews, and talks by classroom visitors. Then, with their backgrounds strengthened, they can often "stretch" and handle readings that would otherwise have been too difficult. Of course, teachers can maximize the dividends for students from these nonverbal experiences through preliminary discussion, through pre-teaching crucial terms and concepts, through assigning questions to be held in mind during the experience and answered, and through follow-up.

Nonreading Experiences Help with Vocabulary

Difficult key terms and concepts can often be handled more easily after students have met them through a nonverbal experience. Industrial arts teachers might strengthen their students for reading about mass production through a fascinating film on how a car is born. As the students view it, it is as if they are *on* an assembly line watching. They see the line, "like a giant river," absorbing 15,000 parts and giving birth to a precision machine which rolls off the line and is driven away. Now terms like *mass production, conveyor belt, quality control, division of labor, high output techniques,* and *specialization,* which might otherwise have been lifeless letters on the printed page, come alive with meaning.

Nonreading Experiences Step Up Comprehension

Social studies teachers have used the film *The Twisted Cross* (1956) to make difficult readings on Hitler's Germany more comprehensible. The students have front seats at dramatic events from the conquest of Austria to the death of Hitler; they hear voices and meet people from this period of the past. Students who are less verbally oriented have a chance to get important background learnings from sound and pictures *before* they learn from words. After this experience poor readers can sometimes crack a difficult reading assignment, and capable readers can comprehend it better (Fallers and Surgal, 1970).

Slides offer another means of bringing difficult reading matter more nearly within reach. When rigorous readings on population genetics confronted a class in biology, slides on blood typings helped some of the under-par readers to work their way through the chapter. These slides were viewable again and again, as often as needed. Slides on cell theory, on the cell and its parts, on the life cycle of a plant, and on photosynthesis have helped students grasp other difficult chapters.

Filmstrips Offer Special Opportunities

Filmstrips offer opportunities for strengthening reading, especially if their captions are read aloud. The captions expose students to the stimulus of the printed word, an advantage not offered by films, television, or recordings. Here is an opportunity for synchronizing *hearing* a new word with *seeing* it—a coordination conducive to acquiring vocabulary. A filmstrip on *Air Masses and Weather Fronts* (1966) is an example. The students' recognition or understanding of an unfamiliar key term, such as *cyclone* or *anticyclone*, is made possible by the heard word as the caption is read aloud. They have the opportunity to form a visual image of the printed term *cyclone*, to "photograph" it with the mind's eye, and they will be more likely to understand it when they meet it in the readings they will soon be doing on the subject of weather. Good readers in the class can be called on to read the captions aloud. Captions that present difficulties or call for special emphasis can be read aloud by the teacher.

Nonreading Experiences Stimulate Wide Reading

Nonreading experiences can be used to bring about more extensive reading. One class (Flickinger, 1970) became interested in the problem, "How can we help the friendly organizations of our community? How can they help us?" Seeing and doing preceded reading. There were excursions to the Red Cross, International House, the YMCA, and other organizations. The students collected quantities of pamphlet materials. Their living experiences made them more active, more involved, and more extensive readers.

Lead-Ins Strengthen Background

Of course the use of excursions, films, and filmstrips is not always practical as a means of strengthening the background of students for an assignment. Some teachers write a clear, easy-to-grasp lead-in to the selection assigned, ditto it, and hand it to the students. This lead-in is a preview that can close gaps in background, provide a thumbnail sketch of the content, intrigue the student with promise of what is to come, raise interesting questions, and give direction to the reading. When high school seniors are confronted with a college-level treatise by Adam Smith on his *laissez-faire* economic doctrines, such a lead-in helps them grapple with—and grasp—this difficult assignment.

Similarly, a social studies teacher (Flickinger, 1970) helps her students step right into historical fiction:

> We use the reading of fiction to enrich a period. In order to be objective, textbook writers often drain all the life out of a period. Fiction writers put it back in. To less competent readers, the plots and characters of *Uncle Tom's Cabin* may seem as confusing as Tolstoy's. So I wrote an easy preview, making the two plots perfectly clear, introducing the student to each of the many characters, and intriguing him with promise of dramatic situations. With this introduction, some of those less capable can work their way through a book that would have been unreadable. Some teachers give such introductions orally.

Component 3—Helping Students Have a Purpose

Suppose students go into an assignment with no real purpose. They may have been told only, "Read the next ten pages." What are they to do? There are many different purposes for reading. Are they to try to remember the details? Read just for the general impression? Learn the author's viewpoint? Weigh the arguments? Search out certain relevant information? Read for pure enjoyment? If students are told only to read the next ten pages, they may run their eyes aimlessly over the pages, taking in little, their purpose only to get the assignment over with and close the book as quickly as possible.

Contrast their reading with that of other students who have a real, immediate, clear-cut purpose. Now the reading has sharp focus. These students weigh everything they read in terms of their purpose, and as they do so their reading becomes an active thinking process rather than a passive covering of words (Howland et al., 1943, p. 7). They understand what they are supposed to know and be able to do when they complete the reading, and as they close their books they are *far* more likely to know and be able to do it.

Purpose-Questions Give Direction

Among the various ways teachers can encourage their students to read purposefully are: 1) providing them with purpose-questions, 2) and helping them formulate their own purpose-questions.

Of course, these two are not dichotomous—purpose-questions for a given assignment will often include both teacher-given and student-formulated questions. Nor do students necessarily advance as they progress through school from all teacher-given to all self-formulated questions. With appropriate guidance, students should formulate questions close to their concerns and then read to find the answers, from their earliest years of schooling. And during their higher education—even in graduate school, if they attend—few of their professors will wish to abdicate their own responsibility for guiding their students' reading by raising important questions. At every level, instructors are likely to recognize a dual responsibility: to provide purpose-questions centered around the needs and concerns of their students, and to help students formulate their own important purpose-questions. Gradually, however, students should become more and more independent of teacher-given purposes and should read more and more often for important purposes of their own.

The following guidelines are suggestive for preparing purpose-questions:

Purpose-questions should guide students to not-to-be-missed learnings.   As you sit at your desk starting to plan a reading assignment, you may wish to ask, "What are the learnings students simply must take away from this reading?" And then, "What purpose-questions will guide them unerringly to these?"

Purpose-questions should lead to learnings close to the needs and concerns of students.   You may wish to ask not only, "What do I consider crucial?" but also, "What do my students want to know?"

A science teacher about to teach the storage battery, Rivlin (1948, p. 192) observed, might limit preparation to listing facts considered basic. Or the teacher might concentrate on this question, "If I were a seventeen-year-old, what would I *want* to know about storage batteries?" He or she might reflect, "What contact have my students had with storage batteries? What difficulties? What experiences in using them?" The teacher's mind will doubtless run to the portable batteries of transistor radios and record players, flashlights, and automobiles.

Chances are, Rivlin commented, the students will get as much factual information about storage batteries when the topic is presented from the students' point of view as they will from a more formal presentation. And they will gain more than mere knowledge if their interest in science is aroused and if they learn that the science classroom is a place to ask questions and to try to answer them.

Questions should stress the implications of the topic for the student rather than the mere development of a logical thought pattern. This principle applies only to pivotal questions. So long as the basic problem is vital to the students, enough interest will probably be generated to carry the class over minor questions that contribute to the major one (Rivlin 1948, p. 199).

Pivotal questions should be broad enough. Pivotal questions should be inclusive enough to require a grasp of the essential content yet specific enough so readers know clearly what they are after. When questions demand *only* directly stated details, the student may skim the assignment for bits and pieces of information and lose out on broad understandings.

A social studies teacher (Association of Teachers of Social Studies, 1967, p. 58) might ask, "Where would you have preferred to live in ancient Greece —in Athens or in Sparta? Why?" This is clearly a broad coverage question. The student must read to compare the schools, social institutions, government, architecture, religion, ideals and values, and so on, of these two ancient cities and then choose between prosperous, culturally brilliant, democratic Athens and austere, self-disciplined, totalitarian Sparta.

Minor questions may also be essential. Minor questions may be indispensable in order to enable the student to handle the major, pivotal questions. Higher-level thinking usually rests solidly on a foundation of facts—the student cannot build a second story without a first story. As instructors plan the guiding questions for an assignment, they will often need to formulate sub-questions to help students "pull out" the underlying facts. Students will then be better equipped to answer pivotal questions that require inferences or drawing conclusions based on these facts.

*A **study guide** may prove helpful.* A printed study guide that provides the students with pivotal and, often, minor questions can be a most effective device for improving reading comprehension. In a major study with 1,456 social studies students (Washburne, 1929), the effectiveness of approaching reading with questions versus approaching it without questions was explored. Providing preliminary questions brought *decided* gains in comprehension. In another study (Holmes, 1931), students who approached their reading with questions performed better on answering the preliminary questions and performed as well when additional questions were given on other parts of the passage. They showed better immediate retention on tests immediately after the reading as well as better long-term retention as demonstrated on tests two weeks later.

A well-formulated question asked *before* students read a selection can help develop comprehension. If the same question is not asked until *after* the students have completed the reading (unless they return to the passage and analyze it), comprehension is tested but is not likely to be developed (Niles, 1963, p. 2).

The following ideas for devising interesting purpose-questions, along with the illustrative examples, may be suggestive to the creative teacher. There will be much overlap.

Purpose-questions can make a striking statement. A pivotal question can take the form of a provocative statement—one that catches attention, appeals to curiosity, or demands analysis. Sometimes there is a believe-it-or-not quality.

> Instead of "Read the next ten pages about Franklin D. Roosevelt," a teacher gives out two dittoed quotations. One praises him extravagantly. The other condemns him as an arch-villain of recent history. This statement sets the student's purpose for reading: "He was one of the most loved and most despised men in our history. Read to find out why and what you think of him." (Adapted from Kenworthy, 1966, p. 203.)

> An ancient Greek, one of the characters you have met in the *Odyssey*, steps out of the past and into your city today. Compare his life then and now, and write his reactions to his new "life style." Take your choice from among the characters you have met in the epic. (Meyer, 1964.)

> The first toy automobile costs $10,000. The next ten thousand sell for $1.00 each. Explain. (Association of Teachers of Social Studies, 1967, p. 56.)

> Suppose tomorrow the earth suddenly stopped rotating on its axis. How would all of us be affected? (Adapted from Association of Teachers of Social Studies, 1967, p. 56.)

Colorful phrasing can be used to stir the imagination of students. This is a perfectly clear and adequate question: "Why did Japan fear Russian expansion in Korea?" But this question gives the student a more vivid picture of the situation. "Why was Korea called a dagger pointing at the heart of Japan?" (adapted from Association of Teachers of Social Studies, 1967, p. 42).

Of course, effective questioning is more than pulling a novelty out of a bag of tricks, and motivation should be more than momentary. Ideally, purpose-questions should be a sustaining force throughout the reading.

Purpose-questions can set a challenging task. Students are unlikely to drift aimlessly through their reading when the assignment sets a task they find challenging. When students in a Spanish class were reading the epic *Araucana*, the teacher took on the class in a debate:

> For tomorrow you'll be reading how the conquistadores enslaved the Incas and put to death their great chief Atahualpa. Which side was in the right? Tomorrow I'll take the side of the conquistadores. *You* come prepared to plead the case of the Incas. Look for evidence in your reading that the Incas were grievously wronged.

Now the students' reading became an active search for points to use in the debate rather than a passive translating of words (LaPorte, 1970).

The student vaguely assigned to "look up medieval castles" may read with wandering attention because the goal is only to read the lesson. Contrast such performance with that of the student who is set this task: "Read to compare castle life with modern apartment living" (Niles, 1963, p. 2).

Nominations to a Classroom Hall of Fame sometimes stimulate reading with real purpose:

> Select a living scientist to nominate for a Classroom Hall of Fame in biology. You must limit yourself to one. Prepare a strong campaign talk supporting your nomination. The class will select five scientists from among all those nominated.

Clashing quotations may set the stage for a challenging task (Association of Teachers of Social Studies, 1967, pp. 144–146):

> Social studies students are given conflicting quotations about the causes of the War of 1812. On a dittoed assignment sheet excerpts from Canadian history textbooks and U.S. history textbooks are juxtaposed. The students read to interpret different viewpoints, to analyze source materials, to search out evidence, and finally to prepare their own well-supported statement on the causes of the War of 1812.

Purpose-questions can bring the reading close to students. We learn best when we apply new knowledge to concrete situations close to ourselves. Questions can be formulated to help students relate to the reading matter, identify with it, perceive its significance for their own lives, and read it with real purpose.

The following question is perfectly clear and definite: "What future developments are predicted for automation?" But this one brings reading about automation closer to students: "What changes is automation likely to bring in the lives of students in this class—in *your* life—during the next quarter of a century?"

This question, too, is adequate: "Suggest some reasons that women have a greater life expectancy than men." This one, though, is more exciting: 'According to life expectancy tables, you girls in the class—Sharon, Judy, Peggy—have the prospect of living about seven years longer than the boys. Can you find out some possible reasons?"

Purpose-questions personalize a problem. Questions can lead students to see themselves *in* the problem situation:

Make a list of some of your own traits that you think are in-
herited, and list the members of your family who have the
same traits. Make another list of characteristics you have acquired during your lifetime. (Jacobson et al., 1964, p. 208.)

Many people would not cross a picket line. Would you? Explain. (Association of Teachers of Social Studies, 1967, p. 56.)

How can you as a teen-ager and a nonvoter take action against
pollution? (Bell, 1970.)

Would you favor having your political party engage in gerrymandering if it had the opportunity? (Sanders, 1966, p. 5.)

What fault would you find with railroads if you were (1) a
truck garden farmer near a large city, (2) an employee of an
industrial plant on the Eastern seaboard, (3) one of those who
had invested their life savings in railroad bonds in order to provide a steady income for old age, only to find that these bonds
depreciate in value and yield? (Rivlin, 1948, p. 217.)

A classwide public opinion poll can bring instant involvement of every student in a problem-solving situation. The students examine some live controversial question, or they are confronted with sharply conflicting statements,
and they are then polled on their opinions:

Should our nation increase its appropriation for underdevel-
oped nations?

Space probes are extremely costly in manpower, money, and
material resources. Do you think these projects should be
continued?

After wide reading and discussion to arrive at an informed opinion, the students are polled again to determine how many have changed their views
(adapted from Association of Teachers of Social Studies, 1967, pp. 37, 63).

Questions can lead students to play roles.   Role playing can help students to get
inside the minds of other people—to feel as they feel or have felt, and to think
as they think or have thought (Kenworthy, 1966, p. 119). Questions can
encourage role playing:

Pretend that you are a bystander who sees Monseigneur's carriage run over the child in *A Tale of Two Cities.* What do you
think your feelings would be toward Monseigneur?

Assume the role of Galileo as you are interviewed by a classmate. The interviewer is likely to ask you about your pioneer

> use of the telescope, your discoveries while studying the skies, your use of the modern experimental method, your clash with Rome, your trial by the Inquisition, your enduring contribution to mankind.

Students dramatize the operation of the General Assembly of the United Nations. First, they study its operation and some of the issues facing it. Next, an agenda is chosen, and each student is assigned to play the part of the representative of a certain nation. One young man researches this question: "How is your nation likely to react to these issues?" He tries to play his role accurately while taking part in the actual debate (adapted from Sanders, 1966, p. 83).

Purpose-questions can create a "you-are-there" effect. Through questions, students can be encouraged to experience through their imaginations what is far away and long ago:

> If you could have foreseen the results of the French Revolution, would you have joined the crowd at the storming of the Bastille? (Association of Teachers of Social Studies, 1967, p. 54.)

> Karl Marx wrote that during the heyday of the Industrial Revolution family ties were reduced to "a mere money relation." Was his observation sound? In what ways can *you* interact with your family today, in contrast to someone your age in, say, England in 1848? (Surgal, 1970.)

> Would you rather be a lord during the Middle Ages or yourself today? (Association of Teachers of Social Studies, 1967, p. 53.)

> If you had been the senator from your state after World War I, would you have voted to ratify the Treaty of Versailles? (Association of Teachers of Social Studies, 1967, p. 56.)

> If you were living in Philadelphia in 1800, why might you want to move west? (Kenworthy, 1966, p. 98.)

Students Should Formulate
Their Own Purposes

We have discussed teacher-formulated questions at some length, for as has been noted, instructors often need to guide the reading of students in important directions. But of course they will not wish to leave students dependent on teacher-given questions. Being told what to look for is not the way a person learns during adulthood. Seeing questions that demand answers and then searching out solutions through reading is behavior that will prove useful to students for the rest of their lives.

There is no timetable for advancing down the road to independence. Students should be involved in planning with their teacher and in asking questions as soon as and as much as possible—from their earliest years at school through college—gradually becoming more and more skillful at formulating important purposes of their own. They should also become adept at holding several purposes in mind simultaneously. Research on the learning process supports this move toward independence; students learn best when they select problems of vital interest and importance to themselves, then probe for the answers themselves rather than being presented with "gift-wrapped" answers (Kenworthy, 1966, p. 217).

As a step toward independence, an instructor might pose a broad purpose-question for a class or group while encouraging the students to formulate other questions of their own.

> Before we can form an intelligent opinion about aid to under-developed countries, we should understand why there are strongly conflicting opinions in both the Senate and the House of Representatives. Your textbook will help by giving arguments for and against this aid. As you read, try to decide whether Congress acted wisely when it recently cut the appropriation for this aid. Can you think of some other questions you'll want to have in mind as you read this assignment?

Sometimes, after surveying the pages assigned, the students themselves set up an outline of what they want to look for while reading. This outline is duplicated and supplied to each class member as a study guide.

Students who have been assigned an important chapter to master thoroughly should acquire the ability to preview the chapter, get a general view of what it's all about, then decide for themselves, "What should I look for when I go back and read this chapter carefully? What important questions will be answered?" Suggestions for helping students set their own purposes for reading a chapter are offered in "You Can Upgrade Students' Textbook Reading," a section that comes later in this chapter.

Setting the Stage for
Student-Formulated Questions

The stage can be set for students to formulate their own purposes for reading by putting them into a situation that stirs interest and provokes questions— some exciting observations, an experiment, an excursion, a fascinating travelogue, a filmstrip, an exhibit or a visitor in the classroom. The teacher might then ask, "What are some things you would like to learn about this scientific phenomenon / country / period / person?"

One instructor (Podendorf, 1970) took some young science students out onto the school grounds to see a crabapple tree in bloom. Around the trunk close to the ground was a conspicuous scar. The teacher asked, "What do you think caused that scar?"

The students thought this over. "A dog chewed it!" "Insects ate it!" "A wire was too tight!"

The instructor remarked, "I happen to know that that tree has roots of one variety and the trunk, branches, and leaves of another!"

The class had heard of grafting. Perhaps it was that! One student commented, "I've seen a tree with two different kinds of apples!"

The instructor added, "I've seen one with seven different kinds!"

The students were full of questions. "Why is grafting done?" "How?" "When?" "Does it always work?" "Can all plants be grafted?" Then with guidance they arrived at other questions. "Are there different kinds of grafting?" "How are these done?" "What determines the success or failure of grafting?"

Questions like these can go on the chalkboard and become a master list. The class has now developed its own study guide, which can be dittoed and handed to each student.

In a class of advanced students, a science teacher (Colby, 1965) dissected an earthworm, provoked many questions, refused to answer any, and turned the students into human question marks. The students asked, "What are those fibers?" "What is that white cord?" "Why is that organ a different color?" "What is that large swelling?" "Why is the front end darker?" "Where can we learn about this?" Impelled by their own purpose-questions, the students dug into the reading and covered references far beyond the assignment.

Component 4—Helping Students Accomplish Their Purpose

It is not unusual for superior teachers to make assignments involving the components discussed thus far. They excite the interest of their students, bring the reading close to their experience, and help them read with purpose. Far less frequently, though, do an instructor's assignments involve the fourth component: helping students know *how to read* the assignment.

Haven't Students Already Acquired the Necessary Skills?

Most students develop their reading procedures by trial and error, and the errors are many and costly. They may lack strategies for handling specialized patterns of writing that confront them in their courses. And they may need more effective general approaches. Some read the crucial content of a difficult chapter with the "once over lightly" approach suitable for a light novel. Then they close the book, having gained at best only a smattering of information. Others read a light novel as ploddingly as they would a textbook chapter. Many are not aware that the various parts of a passage may not all be of equal value for their present purpose. Somewhere along the way they have picked up the idea that it is a sin to scan or skim. Time-saving, productive reading techniques and approaches, tailored to the learning task at hand, are awaiting all these readers. But only if they are guided are they likely to discover them.

A teacher intent on bringing about reading success can do three things:

1. Learn, often through observation, which skills students already have.

2. Examine the assignment to learn precisely what skills they must have in order to complete it.

3. Tie in instruction in those skills in which students are deficient, thus removing roadblocks.

This question is bound to come to mind: "How can an instructor find time for this?" Students' study can be extremely wasteful if unguided. Instead of draining time, reading guidance stretches time. It removes obstacles to learning that would have blocked students day after day all through the year.

When Can Reading Guidance Be Given?

Like other skills, reading skills are best learned in a functional setting, ideally in the very situation in which they will be used. Marked improvement in these skills should follow when this improvement is considered a worthwhile objective of classroom activities. Guidance in reading may be appropriate at the following times:

1. As the assignment is given, a few minutes can be spent discussing the best method of reading it. Brief pointers may be enough. If the students have time to start the assignment in class, they will have the added advantage of applying the suggestions—under the eye and with the help of their teacher—before the pointers grow cold.

2. Guided open-book practice can develop and strengthen reading techniques. Moments of need during the class hour may offer an opportune time. Sometimes only a brief while need be spent.

"Let's turn to our textbooks and . . ." can be a frequent suggestion of teachers (Kenworthy, 1966, p. 104).

3. It may be profitable to spend most of a class period in a how-to-read-it session, "walking" students through the model reading of a passage. Students read passages silently for specific purposes. Then they discuss and analyze. The subject matter content thus covered is likely to be thoroughly mastered; in addition, students are likely to acquire effective techniques for their permanent use.

4. Sometimes, when the rest of the class is occupied with some other activity, the instructor may wish to work with a group in need of certain skills.

5. Help can be given to students during an individual conference or during a supervised study period as the teacher moves around the room.

6. Most promising for truly far-reaching results, many teachers view assignments as an integral part of their students' school experience rather than as overtime work, and they plan these assignments to cover longer periods of time. An entire class period—sometimes two or three periods—can then be spent on making the assignment. The time available makes possible an excellent sendoff on reading procedures—with important benefits for students. The students work on these long-term assignments in class, in workshops, in laboratories, and in the library, under the watchful eye of their instructor, who now has a chance to observe their blocks in reading and can go into action to remove them.

What Students Are Likely to Need Reading Guidance?

Students have a special need for help on certain grade levels and in certain situations:

1. Students need a great deal of help during junior high school years. Instruction offered at this time may enable them to succeed—and survive—during the school years that lie ahead.

2. The first year of high school is a crucial year for many students.

3. Students who are beginning a new course are especially receptive to help. If help is given during the first few weeks, many will be more successful in their course work all through the year.

4. A "how to use your textbook" session is appropriate just after students receive new textbooks.

5. There is a special need for help whenever the writing pattern of the assignment demands special techniques that students may have had no previous opportunity to learn.

6. Slow learners have a constant need to read and study under the supervision and with the assistance of the teacher.

Meeting Observed Needs

The following pages offer ideas for developing two or three representative abilities. They are intended merely to suggest possibilities. Concerned teachers will plan their own reading guidance to meet needs they see in students. The subject-area index in Chapter 2 and the general index at the back of this book can guide instructors to procedures others have found effective for teaching some of the specialized techniques called for in most school courses. Chapter 5, "Reading Skills for Problem Solving," offers leads for giving students expertise for making investigations. Leads to specific methods, adaptable for all levels are offered in *Reading, Grades 7, 8, and 9* (Curriculum Bulletin No. 11. New York: Board of Education of the City of New York, 1959); in Joseph C. Gainsburg, *Advanced Skills in Reading*, Books 1, 2, and 3, teacher's annotated ed. (New York: Macmillan Company, 1967); and elsewhere.

Rapid Reading for Background Information

The ability to read fairly rapidly for background information is called for in many subjects. Students who attack all reading with a slow, intensive approach will find themselves spending impossible amounts of time. Broad coverage is especially essential in social studies, for in this field depth of understanding demands extensive reading. The need for rapid coverage continues, and may even intensify, in adulthood. Much of the content of a person's professional reading, of popular magazines and newspapers, of many biographies and of novels, can and should be covered rapidly.

Some students have the impression that all their study demands concentration on details—that it is almost a sin to cover anything rapidly. They need guidance not only on how but also on when to do rapid, broad coverage reading.

Suppose the students' purpose is to get a general picture of what a tropical rain forest is like—its beauty, its lush vegetation, its dangers. The teacher might suggest, "Read this selection rapidly for a general impression—just to catch the feel of being in the forest, not to remember all the details."

Then the instructor might ask, "How do you think you should do this type of reading?" With guidance, the students might suggest that they move right along, picking up main thoughts, learning all they can from the pictures, not slowing down to try to learn details, looking up unknown words only if these block getting the gist, pressing on to learn the general drift.

The instructor might also call attention to the fact that previewing is a speed device—that through previewing one can often get an instant view of the general content. He or she might point out that introductory paragraphs often announce what is to come, that concluding paragraphs often wrap it up, and that topical headings (and sometimes topic sentences) helpfully yield the big points covered.

Before these pointers grow cold, the students might read the selection in class. All year long this particular in-class practice might serve as a referent as the teacher suggests reading other selections "as we did the one about the rain forest."

Students who have always been "one-pace plodders" are learning at last that different approaches to reading exist. Once they have acquired rapid reading techniques, just a word or two at the time the assignment is made should be enough to remind them to shift gears into this type of reading:

> Read this account of a southern plantation owner about the life of the Negro on his plantation. Then read *Up from Slavery* to see how a slave himself looked at those years. Read fairly rapidly—just to get the gist of these contrasting viewpoints.

> In reading this fast-moving adventure story your purpose is enjoyment. Fairly rapid reading is suitable for "The Most Dangerous Game."

Ultimately, students should be able to look over a selection, consider their purpose and what they already know about the subject, and then answer for themselves, "Is this something I can read rapidly, or should I read it slowly and carefully?"

If the assignment is an informational book to be covered rapidly for background information, you may wish to share with students the pointers in "Can PQ4R Help You Read Supplementary Books?" later in this chapter.

High-Speed Scanning for Specific Information

Students may lack the useful skill of scanning columns or pages for specific information. They sometimes plod doggedly down the page, line by line, when all they are after is a brief passage related to their problem. What a drag, when they should be doing efficient reference reading! Specific suggestions for developing scanning techniques are offered in Chapter 4, "Developing Flexibility in Reading Rate."

After students have been introduced to scanning procedures, just a word from the instructor at the time the assignment is made will nudge them to apply their new techniques. A science teacher reminded the class when assigning the question, "Can we control our blushing?"

> Scan these pages quickly, looking for clues, until you *think* you've found your information. Then *slow way down* to see whether you've really located what you're after. If you have, settle down to read carefully.

Ordinarily, scanning is neither difficult nor time-consuming to teach. Students quickly recognize its value and put it to work in reference reading in order to cut through masses of extraneous information.

Close, Intensive Reading

Much of this book is devoted to helping students acquire techniques for the close, intensive reading frequently demanded in their school courses. The subject-area index and the general index will guide readers to helps that may serve their needs. The section "You Can Upgrade Students' Textbook Reading," later in this chapter, offers students help in mastering the crucial content of a textbook chapter. Concerned teachers will draw on various sources and develop their own procedures.

Tips for close, intensive reading can sometimes be elicited from students, then combined with the expertise of the instructor to evolve the final guidelines. The instructor might ask the class, "Suppose you want to master the content of this passage thoroughly without a word of help or explanation from your teacher. How would you go about reading it?" With their attention focused on how they would read ideally, the students themselves often come up with some highly practical pointers.

Students will need first their instructor's how-to-do-it guidance, then frequent when-to reminders:

> These three pages of science assigned for tomorrow may be the equivalent of fifty pages of a novel for English. Read to trace

the path of blood as it moves from your heart back to your heart, and try to remember its course.

Do tomorrow's reading slowly and thoroughly—to learn the disagreements that almost wrecked the Constitutional Convention and how each one of these was settled.

Read this chapter on the Reconstruction period slowly and thoughtfully and find questions still troubling Americans today which are the aftermath of the "Brothers' War."

Shifting Approaches and Techniques
Within an Assignment

Students will not necessarily select a single reading approach, then continue it without deviation until they have completed a passage. On the contrary, they will frequently need to shift their approach within the assignment. Their teacher's reminders will help them make this internal adjustment.

Students who have been assigned a chapter on the Civil War might be advised to adjust their speed and method:

You can read fairly rapidly these easy, interesting, story-type pages on Abe Lincoln's young manhood. But slow way down and read closely to learn and remember the provisions of the Thirteenth, Fourteenth, and Fifteenth Amendments in the same chapter.

Science students beginning a chapter on "Fish and Fishlike Vertebrates" might be reminded:

You can read this interesting narrative introduction about an invasion of lamprey eels into the Great Lakes fairly fast. Then reduce your speed for the closely packed body of the chapter. Speed up again for the easy paragraphs on sport fishing as a hobby.

Independence in Selecting Reading
Procedures

"Use this technique here . . . this one here . . . this one here" can be suggested to maturing readers from day to day. But as with setting a purpose, students should be led more and more to select for themselves the appropriate approach. Their life need is to be able to set their own purposes, then read in the appropriate manner to accomplish these purposes. A question like this is a step in the direction of independence:

> We have talked over the purpose of this assignment. How do you think you should read to accomplish this purpose?

Then on, even closer to independence:

> What do you think it is important to find out from this reading? What will be the best method of reading in order to find this out?

Students will need many experiences, under guidance, in setting their purposes and selecting their approach. The long-term goal is the development of mature readers who are competent to survey the reading ahead, consider their purposes, judge the difficulty, and then decide on and use the approach to the passage—and the shifting of approaches within the passage—called for. The ideal of the "finished reader" who has reading competencies for all purposes is likely, however, to remain beyond complete attainment in secondary and even college classrooms. Bringing the ideal closer will be a continuing concern.

Gaining Maturity in Reading

If teachers were to list the characteristics of the ideal graduate, they would probably include maturity in reading. Some of the student's learning takes place in school—more of it outside school. Perhaps the most important contribution of teaching and learning in the classroom is to further this out-of-school learning. As nearly as possible we should be teaching what will transfer to the out-of-school situation during the next half-century or more of the student's life. Those who adopt this view are likely to regard as one important measure of the success of their course the degree to which their students learn to learn with decreasing guidance. They are likely to assign a high priority to turning on reading power.

GIVE THEM SOMETHING THEY CAN READ!

In some classrooms there's a single book for everyone, and it's the survival of the fittest. Not so, though, in the classes of the teachers interviewed here.*

Give them something they can read! The right books placed in the hands of not-so-able readers may be a promising hope for their progress.

When poor readers are confronted with reading materials that are years beyond their reach all through the school day, they simply cannot cope; they are deprived of the opportunity to practice and may fall farther, even hopelessly, behind. But when they are guided to books suitable in ease of reading, they have a fair chance to complete their assigned readings successfully. Hours of beneficial reading practice (along with real learning in the subject) may follow.

Handicapped readers have probably experienced hundreds of failures. They go to class day after day already defeated, full of insecurities, knowing in advance they will probably not be able to read the pages assigned. Fear may take over and add a serious emotional block to other obstacles in reading. But reading on appropriate levels can make it possible to experience desperately needed success. Lost readers are sometimes contemplating dropping out of school. Reading matter that is "right" can help them take hold and renew their efforts. It can help make school a center for success instead of a place for failure.

Negative attitudes often lead to behavior problems and are difficult to change once formed. Such attitudes are less likely to develop if, from the first weeks of a new course, a teacher can get "manageable" materials into the hands of the student.

The self-confidence of young people is a precious attribute and a generative force in much future achievement. But self-confidence can be devastated if day after day they are directed to perform impossible tasks. "It's heartbreaking," a school librarian commented, "to see students take home heavy books at night

---

* The following University of Chicago Laboratory School teachers answered interview questions: social studies—Edgar Bernstein, Margaret Fallers, Alice Flickinger, Philip Montag, and Joel Surgal; science—Jerry Ferguson and Murray Hozinsky; mathematics—Paul Moulton; library—Mary Biblo, Sylvia Marantz, and Winfred Poole; English—Emily Meyer. John Patrick, social studies, and Richard Smith, science—former Laboratory School teachers—also contributed comments.

and bring them back next day unread because they were years beyond them."
Confidence is nurtured, however, when teachers and librarians make possible
day-to-day reading successes.

A student's self-concept determines much of his or her behavior, including
reading behavior. Young people who view themselves as individuals who
cannot read tend to fulfill their own expectations. Their self-concepts may be
altered by experiences of success and approval in and through reading. They
may do an about-face in their attitudes toward their own learning potential.

Appropriate Materials

It is a familiar cry that students should have materials appropriate for their
reading achievement—that poor readers should have something they can cope
with and that top readers should be challenged so that they can reach their full
potential. But is it really practical to make these adjustments in the classroom?
On the next few pages teachers, librarians, and the reading consultant of the
University of Chicago Laboratory School, in response to interview questions,
share their efforts at adjusting materials, with the thought that their suggestions
may help others find more effective methods or prompt them to share methods
they have found effective.* The goal of adjusting materials throughout the
school has not yet been attained. There will be much for us to do tomorrow.

It should be added that merely providing suitable materials will not solve
problems of retarded readers. Instruction in reading skills in subject classrooms
and through the school's reading services should complement adjustments in
materials.

Question.   Is it practical to try to match the "reading reach" of students
      and their materials?

Answer.   "I couldn't operate without it. It's hardly a matter of choice!
      I see Ron, who can read only around seventh-grade level seated be-
      side Dave, who can read at the college level. Six-year spans, or more,
      within one classroom confront me daily."

Question.   How can you get some insights into what each student can
      and cannot read successfully?

Answer.   A social studies teacher answers, "Early in the year I jot each
      student's reading test scores after his or her name in my record book.
      This is a first step in getting acquainted. Daily these scores give me a

---

* Some of the teachers' comments appeared in Ellen Lamar Thomas and Philip Montag, "A Social
Studies Department Talks Back," *Journal of Reading*, 9 (October 1966), pp. 22–28.

suggestion of the student's reading power and remind me to make adjustments. Sometimes I add a self-made test that checks the student's comprehension and speed when using actual course materials."

The reading consultant adds, "I've had a quiet drive to report the wide reading range we have on each grade level to teachers in our school in the hope that some will make adjustments. A personalized reading score kit is placed in the hands of the teachers on request. In the kit is a card for each student, with all the test scores (from the guidance department's spring testing) that throw light on reading strengths and weaknesses. I've tried to make the cards so handy, so convenient, that teachers cannot resist using them. Appropriate cautions go along with the kit. Teachers are aware that the scores offer only a hint of the level at which the student can handle most materials and that no student should be considered locked forever on a certain level. They recognize, too, that a student's reading power often varies greatly from one subject to another.

"Teachers and librarians are also given class reading placement sheets. These show at a glance the spread of reading scores within each class—from freshman through senior—and the distribution of students scoring on each grade level. As teachers plan reading lists, these spread sheets serve as a reminder to offer enough choices and enough copies at the upper and lower extremes."

Question.   Can textbooks on varying difficulty-levels within a class help solve the problem of the reading range?

Answer.   A social studies teacher sees this analogy: "Suppose you were given a book in third-year Russian (which you could not read), informed that it would be your textbook for the coming year, assigned the first chapter, and notified that an important test was coming Friday. That's the plight of the seriously handicapped reader! And it's just as important to give top-notch readers books to stretch on."

Question.   Some say it's difficult to bring a class together using multilevel textbooks and almost impossible to find textbooks on different levels yet parallel in organization and content.

Answer.   A teacher of United States history commented:* "At first we thought that having different textbooks would be unwieldy. Now we find them intensely practical. As our students start each unit, they are given guidesheets so that they can approach their reading with broad questions and problems. Although textbooks of varying difficulties are

---

* John Patrick, former University of Chicago Laboratory School social studies teacher, in remarks to Ellen Thomas, October 1964. For this edition, the authors have updated the titles of some of the textbooks mentioned. Teachers will wish to select a gradation of textbooks carefully with a view to difficulty and parallel content.

not strictly parallel in content, such broad topics as the discovery of the New World, life in the colonies, the making of the Constitution, the opening of the West, and the Industrial Revolution can be found in almost all the books.

"For our junior high school level American history course, we found four quality textbooks that span the reading levels within the classes: Reich and Biller, *Building the American Nation* (New York: Harcourt Brace Jovanovich, 1969) can be handled by most of our less competent readers. Bragdon and McCutchen, *History of a Free People* (New York: Macmillan Company, 1973) challenges the best. For in-between readers there are Casner and Gabriel, *Story of the American Nation* (New York: Harcourt Brace Jovanovich, 1967) and Leinwand, *The Pageant of American History* (Boston: Allyn and Bacon, 1975). We stock a number of copies of each of these in both the classroom and the school library.

"Making multilevel reference lists looked formidable to us—at first. Now we prepare them quickly and simply. We save time all year by using the authors' initials to designate the books. These initials soon became familiar to students. Reich and Biller is simply *RB*; Leinwand is *L*.

"Here are some typical guiding questions. The students can find the answers in any of the books listed:

1. What were the grievances of the colonists against British policies—grievances that caused a growing storm of opposition?

2. Why were these grievances not resolved peacefully?

3. What part did each of these play in starting the American Revolution: Sugar Act, Quartering Act, Stamp Act, Sons of Liberty, Samuel Adams, Committees of Correspondence, Boston Tea Party?

"This easily prepared reference list accompanies these questions:

Pp. 156–167 in RB   [Students of fifth-grade reading level and up could handle this one.]

Pp. 50–64 in L   [These are suitable for readers of seventh- and
Pp. 116–134 in CG   eighth-grade reading levels and up.]

Pp. 32–49 in BM   [This would challenge a reader on eleventh- or twelfth-grade level.]

"How are students guided to books they can handle successfully? Of course, no notation of the difficulty of a book appears on the students' reading list. But, when students come into class the first few days they find on their desks a text that I have carefully selected on the basis of reading achievement as suggested by reading scores and my observation. Chances are each student will have success with this book and will search it out and use it for future assignments."

An experienced teacher, however, expressed the view that the use of several textbooks within one class may create problems: "Some teachers find it difficult to handle a class using several textbooks. There may be confusion for both teacher and students. These teachers miss the security, the stabilizing values, the unifying values of using a single textbook. It may be preferable for these teachers to select a textbook most of the class can read and then challenge the top readers and provide for the poorest through a wide range of supplementary readings."

In some schools teachers cannot influence the choice of textbooks they will be working with from day to day. New teachers coming into the school simply "inherit" a textbook. The realistic question, then, becomes how to use this textbook to best advantage:

Question. Do you have any suggestions for counteracting the disadvantages of a single textbook?

Answer. A biology teacher answers, "Although a single textbook may be prescribed for all the students in a class, they need not necessarily feel locked into this one book. We keep a number of easier-to-read textbooks on a reserve shelf in the school library. Students who are thrown by the explanation of mitosis in a more advanced textbook, *Modern Cell Biology,* by William D. McElroy and Carl P. Swanson (Englewood Cliffs, N.J.: Prentice-Hall, 1968), may be able to grasp the simpler explanation in *Biological Science, an Ecological Approach,* BSCS Green Version (Chicago: Rand McNally and Company, 1973). Now, having acquired some background understandings of the terms and processes, perhaps they can extend themselves and digest the corresponding passage in their own textbook. If not, they are still ahead in what they have learned about mitosis from the easier book."

A mathematics teacher echoes the preceding suggestion: "One reading assignment for all is the prevailing practice in mathematics class. But must this be so? When students cannot grasp the explanations in their own textbook, it is possible to guide them to similar material in a textbook easier to read. They can then return to their own textbook and make another try. They are likely to find two explanations clearer than a single explanation."

The reading consultant adds: "It is often desirable for students to arrange readings in this easy-to-difficult sequence—to select a relatively easy source in order to get background orientation to the topic. Broadening background information is a major factor in increasing power of comprehension. Once students have strengthened their backgrounds, they may be able to stretch and handle more difficult reading. I watched a student whose 'textbook' was the *Iliad* accomplish this the other day. At first he was lost trying to work his way through the page-long Homeric similes, the obscure references to myths, the galaxies of major and minor gods and goddesses. Then he was guided to a first-quality simplified *Iliad*. After becoming acquainted with the gods and heroes in the simplified version, picking up the plot threads, and being captured by dramatic situations, the student could now return to the original *Iliad* and work his way through."

Question. Is it practical to span the reading levels of students through their supplementary readings?

Answer. A science teacher (R. Smith, 1965) whose classes were soon to study reptiles said to himself, "Surely, with all the books on reptiles, there should be something everyone can read about this exciting subject." Then he began to search out the materials. "I turned through the card catalogue, then assembled a reserve shelf of promising books. The guidesheet below (Figure 3–1) was provided for each student. Of course, no notation of the reading difficulty of a book appeared on the student's book list."

The reading consultant adds: "Reading lists can lure readers with attractive paperbacks, slim and trim enough to invite the hand of a reluctant reader. Some of the teen-tested titles listed in *Hooked on Books* by Daniel L. Fader and Morton H. Shaevitz (New York: Berkley Publishing Corporation, 1968) might be considered. Short pamphlets, perhaps from the library's vertical file, may offer quick rewards to poor readers—a sense of accomplishment as they easily reach the last page. Easy-to-grasp booklets with a disarming comic book format are available on certain subjects from firms like General Motors and General Electric. Popular magazines and newspapers offer live content related to every subject on the students' schedules. A clipping-file, growing from year to year, can become a rich classroom resource."

A science teacher comments: "I find long-term problem solving units an opportunity to keep a sharp eye for students who are overwhelmed by a book and to guide them to one that *they* can overwhelm. The students often study the background of a problem together, then

Figure 3–1. *Through the reading list on the following page a science teacher provides something everyone in the class can read. He meets the needs of the poorest readers and challenges the best.*

GUIDING QUESTIONS FOR THE STUDY OF REPTILES

THESE
BROAD
QUESTIONS
ARE
ANSWERABLE
IF THE STUDENT
CONSULTS
ONE OR MORE
OF THE BOOKS
LISTED.

1. List some characteristics which distinguish reptiles from other verte-brates.

2. What four groups of venomous snakes are found in North America?

3. What arguments can you give for the conservation of snakes, especially the nonpoisonous species?

4. Describe the methods used by various snakes in capturing their prey.

5. What are the benefits of many snakes and lizards to man?

6. What characteristics distinguish snakes from lizards?

7. Where do most reptiles make their homes?

8. What do they eat?

9. Which reptiles are good pets?

10. What reptiles live in my part of the United States?

REFERENCES

THIS IS ON
JUNIOR
HIGH
SCHOOL
READING
LEVEL.

THIS IS RIGHT
FOR A
STUDENT
WITH
HIGH SCHOOL
READING
ABILITY.

A STUDENT
WITH
GRADE 4–5
READING
ABILITY
COULD HANDLE
THIS ONE.

A STUDENT
WITH
GRADE 4–6
READING
ABILITY
COULD
HANDLE
THIS ONE.

THIS IS
FOR
STUDENTS
WITH
COLLEGE-
LEVEL
READING
ABILITY.

Carr - *Reptiles*

Danforth - - - - - - - - - - - - - - - - *What You Should Know About Snakes*

Ditmars - - - - - - - - - - - - - - - - *Fieldbook of North American Snakes*

Ditmars - - - - - - - - - - - - - - - - *Reptiles of the World*

Ditmars - - - - - - - - - - - - - - - - *Reptiles of North America*

Hecht - - - - - - - - - - - - - - - - - *All About Snakes*

Hylander - - - - - - - - - - - - - - - *Animals in Armor*

Otto and Towle - - - - - - - - - - - *Modern Biology*, Chapter 37, "The Reptiles"

Parker - - - - - - - - - - - - - - - - - *Reptiles and Animals of Yesterday*

Pope - - - - - - - - - - - - - - - - - - *The Reptile World*

Schmidt and Davis - - - - - - - - - *Fieldbook of Snakes of North America and Canada*

Storer and Usinger - - - - - - - - *General Biology*, Chapter 33, "Class Reptilia"

Zim - - - - - - - - - - - - - - - - - - *Reptiles and Amphibians, A Guide to Familiar American Species* they divide it into sub-topics and do individual and group research, using a great diversity of reading and nonreading resources. Under my eye and with my help, they 'research' their sub-topics in the classroom and in the school library. I have appropriate books in mind and ready to offer the less able readers."

Question. Suppose a core of readings seems desirable for commonality of experience, and almost everyone in the class can handle these. What can be done for a very few handicapped readers?

Answer. A social studies teacher suggests, "In our unit on the early colonial period in Africa, we have a core of readings, all of which are beyond the poorest readers. I make certain that there 'happens to be' a need for special investigations of related topics. These topics are right in difficulty and interest for the handicapped readers, who are guided in conference to references they can handle. They share their findings with the others in the class. Through class discussions, slides, and the opaque projector, the 'special investigators' get some of the information they missed through not completing the assigned readings. They do not feel that they are second-class citizens. Instead, they seem to like being exempt from the regular assignment in order to pursue a bit of original 'research.' Particularly good readers, too, can be used as 'specialists.' Knowing they are to serve as resource persons for the class, they often read far beyond my expectations in order to make themselves the 'teacher of the moment.' "

Question. What about books to be read for enjoyment?

Answer. An English teacher sees a special opportunity: "English teachers have an extremely wide selection of books to choose from. Our list of novels includes a gradation of difficulty levels, almost chromatic, from *Sounder,* within the reach of our least able readers, to *Giants in the Earth,* a challenge to the best. Our lists of suggested vacation books span all the levels."

Question. What about school librarians as a help in matching materials?

Answer. A librarian contrasts how *not to* and *how to* enlist the librarians: "Librarians are asking—no, they are *begging*—to work with teachers to plan for the benefit of students. The students cannot possibly lose, and the possibilities of gain are limitless.

"First let me give you an example of how *not* to give an assignment. I will use a recent, actual example.

"A question or problem is passed out to students. A list of sources to help solve this problem is also distributed. The teachers have . . . checked to see whether the students are all equipped to read at least some of these sources—or have they? One thing is sure—they have not checked to see whether any of these sources are in our library.

We don't even know what they and their class are up to. I think you know what happens next. The first few students through the library doors grab off the shelves whatever books we do have on the list, regardless of whether these are the best books for them. The rest of the students find nothing and are frustrated and discouraged before they begin, or they are forced to go all over the town looking.

"Other fine books on the subject, which we may have waiting to be catalogued, will never be used. Books already on our shelves but not on the list may be searched out by the brighter or more persistent students or may not be found at all. And, of course, all our efforts to learn the reading abilities and interests of the students so that we can help each to find the materials on his level cannot be used. By the time some student passes the assignment on to a librarian, it is usually too late to do much.

"But let's leave this dismal picture—it is one that I have viewed, with variations, too many times—and move to a brighter and more productive one. Let me paint for you the bright, encouraging picture of the kinds of projects we feel are productive and successful, partly at least because the librarian and the teacher worked together.

"The first step, planning the assignment, is usually done in the teacher's mind. But once the assignment begins to take shape, the teacher is already thinking in terms of materials, and this point is where we like to start our part of the job. Teacher and librarian, working with the class's reading profile in mind, can begin to discuss what the students can profitably use to solve the problem the teacher will pose. If students help with part or all of the planning, the questions remain the same: Will we need to make a special search for easier-to-read materials to have enough for the less able readers? How about some filmstrips or slides for the less verbally oriented students?" [Adapted from Marantz, 1969, pp. 123–124. How librarians can have quick access to the reading levels of individuals and can use class reading profiles to advantage is discussed in Chapter 15.]

"Now that the materials are being made ready, it is time for a decision on how to give the assignment so that each student can find the materials best suited for solving the problem. Sometimes we have found it wise to bring the materials into the classroom where the teacher or the librarian can work with the students individually to guide them to their best sources. Sometimes, instead of or in addition to this, the librarian will prepare a bibliography with annotations, not only of what the materials cover but also with such key words as *readable, popular treatment, scholarly,* and *highly technical* to help students find books on their reading levels in that subject. [Marantz, 1969, p. 124.] Often a special collection is assembled in the library for this particular assignment. Then when the students rush through the library doors, they find a well and suitably stocked reserve shelf.

"Our ideal assignment concludes with a joint evaluation by teacher and librarian (and usually students, who are—in our school—quite free with their opinions). Here is where we discover that we need more copies of a book which so many found just right; or that a few poor readers never did find anything they could use to solve the problem, a condition indicating a need for easier-to-read books or perhaps a different kind of problem if there are similar poor readers next time. . . ." [Marantz, 1969, pp. 124–125.]

The possibilities just mentioned—the increase in students' potential for succeeding in their assignments as a result of the librarian's services—suggest the desirability of having more than one librarian. If services like these are not available in a school, it may be that the librarian is serving an overload of students.

Question.   Aren't poor readers extremely sensitive about their handicap? How can they be guided to easier materials in such a way that they don't appear different from the others?

Answer.   Here are some observations of teachers and librarians:

"Poor readers are nearly all sensitive. Guidance to easier materials must be done quietly, constructively, and understandingly. We may do more harm than good if they feel exposed as poor readers."

"Of course, a book should not offend through a juvenile appearance, and there should be no notation of its difficulty."

"Some students do not seem to need much guidance. When given a list of readings and freedom of choice, they select books suitable in difficulty."

Quiet guidance can often be offered with positive comments about the book. It is not necessary to specify that the book is easy. Thus, "All these books are excellent. This one has some good points that may be useful to you. Why not look it over and see if you like it?" Or, "How about trying this one? It really covers that assignment. I think you'll find all the answers you need right here."

Readers may need to be warned away from too rigorous books with "You may want to read this as background before you read this." Or, "Maybe that one's a little too difficult. I know students in college who could not read that book." And, "You can take this one now if you wish, but you'll enjoy it much more in a year or two."

One teacher who notices that a student has checked out a book that is too difficult has another one quietly ready next day.

A frank discussion may be desirable with certain students: "You need to improve your reading. We are trying to meet it by starting with less difficult materials and then advancing. Many people have this problem. You have the ability to become a good reader."

A realistic teacher cautions, "No teacher should be discouraged when the ideal of individual guidance of students is always beyond reach. In large classes and in the press of things, the individual word of guidance to a student is often impossible."

Question. Isn't there danger of providing poor readers with easy materials and then leaving them so that they never stretch their reading ability?

Answer. The reading consultant observed, "At first, materials for a retarded reader should be selected to guarantee success. Relatively easy materials help to overcome a failure mind set. Books a year or two below the student's reading level may be appropriate at first. However, we should not overlook the importance of keen interest in empowering students to stretch and read material seemingly beyond them. If we can find topics vital to students, they may be able to handle surprisingly difficult reading. Of course, it is desirable to challenge students with more difficult reading as rapidly as possible. The ideal is a sequence of increasingly difficult reading experiences with the students held to all they can do. Teachers will experience deep satisfaction when, as time passes, they see some of their poor readers advance to more difficult materials."

Question. In summing up, then, it *is* possible for a teacher to provide materials for students reading on a wide range of levels?

Answer. "Let no one give teachers the impression that doing this is easy. Years of searching go into this! Two of our teachers spent two summers searching for appropriate materials. Experience is essential for teachers to develop a feel for the difficulty of materials. The right reading for the right reader is an ideal to work toward, a little at a time. No teacher should be discouraged when attainment of the ideal all at once is not possible."

Question. Of course, readings matched to students can make them more comfortable and help them acquire subject matter learnings. But how can appropriate readings help build reading power?

Answer. The reading consultant answered, "The world of words has never been the world of the poor readers. When a teacher guides them to a book right for them in difficulty and interest, they may, for the first time, spend many hours in the world of printed words. As they read, they meet words in similar and different settings, often with a little increment of meaning at each encounter, and gradually incorporate the words into their vocabularies. Their reading practice tends to strengthen their comprehension. Speed is developed at the easy end of the reading spectrum. As students read easy, interesting material for pleasure and information, many of them increase their speed. Fast moving, narrative-style biographies and exciting novels, including historical novels and science fiction, may be effective speed builders."

Staggering sums are required to reclaim students who leave the doors of schools without reading power and without earning power. The efforts of teachers to renew the hope and confidence of young people and to make progress possible through individualizing their reading materials is an investment in *prevention*.

YOU CAN UPGRADE STUDENTS' TEXTBOOK READING

> *Teachers ask, "How can I improve my students' reading of their textbooks when I've had no training or experience in teaching reading?" The PQ4R procedure, in which any teacher can instruct his students, incorporates some powerful study-reading procedures.*

Perhaps nowhere in all their years at school have students had help in developing an efficient approach to textbook reading. The waste of study hours, the unfulfilled potential, are appalling. Dividends can be tremendous if streamlined habits are developed, starting at least as early as the seventh grade, and proceeding through the college and university years.

A notebook section for students explaining how to use the PQ4R study procedure follows this introduction. The guidelines for students are intended to supplement something far more important—instruction in the application of PQR4 by the classroom teacher. Classroom teachers with no formal training in teaching reading have used such procedures to upgrade textbook reading. They have changed helter-skelter readers into more systematic readers. They have changed overly conscientious readers who tried to retain everything on the page into "differentiating" readers, better able to select out what is important to remember. They have transformed students who used to dream their way through the chapter into alert, participating readers.

A journalism teacher (Brasler, 1971) whose students were making a whip-through of their textbook reading sought the school's reading consultant. Together they served up PQ4R in attractive format, a handy booklet with its cover in school colors, and the consultant briefed the teacher in giving classes reading guidance. The teacher reports: "Instead of blank stares, there are now excited, informed class discussions. The change in retention of important content has been dramatic. Several students have exclaimed, 'This thing really works!' I know this sounds too good to be true, but this is exactly what happened."

PQ4R is a package of techniques that should be effective in improving the reading of chapter-length materials when the student's purpose is thorough understanding of the content. It should help the student comprehend better, concentrate better, and retain better. The steps in the procedure are: Preview, Question, Read, Reflect, Recite, and Review. As explained in the opening pages of the students' guidelines it is a variation of the SQ3R approach designed by Francis P. Robinson at Ohio State University and based on many years of experimentation with students. (The steps in Dr. Robinson's original approach are Survey, Question, Read, Recite, and Review.) In presenting PQ4R here, the writers have leaned heavily on his classic book, *Effective Study* (New York: Harper and Row, 1961), on *Learning to Learn,* edited by Donald E. P. Smith (New York: Harcourt, Brace and World, 1961), and on Thomas F. Staton, *How to Study* (Montgomery, Alabama, Box 6133, 1968). *How to Study* is an excellent little guide—inviting, clear, and readable—to put into the hands of students.

PQ4R Upgrades Reading in Many Subjects

PQ4R is applicable to reading informational chapters in science, health, history, civics, contemporary problems, geography, sociology, economics, philosophy, journalism, homemaking, vocational education and industrial arts, business law, accounting, music appreciation, music history, music harmony, art appreciation, art history, and other courses—and in English when the chapters are expository. It is adaptable to expository passages in mathematics, to informational passages in a second language, and to articles in periodicals.

PQ4R Meets a Special Need in English Classes

Many English teachers recognize proficiency in reading informational prose as one of the life needs of students. These instructors are aware that a student's success in almost every course at school is related to ability to do expository reading. They want graduates to be well equipped to continue their education through reading, to leave school proficient in grasping the content of informational books, of expository writing in popular periodicals and in journals related to their trade or profession. They are likely to assign a high priority to instructing students in the reading of "practical" prose.

Top Honor Students May Need PQ4R

Left to their own devices, what do students do when they open a book to study the chapter assigned for tomorrow? All too often they have no response other than plunging in and plodding through. They may "preview" the chapter by estimating its thickness between their thumb and forefinger! Then on they plod—from the first line on the first page to the last line on the last. Good, now they're through! Often, their only review technique is a passive rereading.

Extreme cases? Studies of prospective Phi Beta Kappas at the University of Pennsylvania and of top honor students at Ohio State (Danskin and Burnett, 1952; Preston and Tufts, 1948) revealed the study methods of many to be quite inefficient. Their A's appeared to be the result of their superior scholastic aptitude—*not* their superior study habits. In another investigation (Moe and Nania, 1959) junior high school students whose grades on their report cards were top ranking proved quite deficient in their approach to chapter-length materials.

PQ4R Saves Time for Class and Teacher

A science teacher (Ferguson, 1970) who instructed his students in PQ4R during the opening weeks of school was asked, "How can you manage to spare the time from science?" He answered, "I can't afford *not* to spare it. Ultimately it gives us more time. Students come better prepared all year."

How to Teach PQ4R

Since old study habits are deeply ingrained in most students, practice under supervision is essential in order to build improved working techniques into their permanent habits. Simply reading printed guidelines or listening while the teacher talks about study methods is likely to fall short of effecting a permanent change in habits (Stordahl and Christenson, 1956). But in teaching followed by practice, skills can be brought closer to a top level of efficiency.

Students Should Recognize a Personal Need

Obviously, for full advantage, "how to study" sessions should be offered early in the course. But this is a time when students do not always recognize a personal need. To create a sense of need during the first few days, one science instructor simply assigned a representative section of a chapter for reading in class or at home—then, before there was any classwork on the content, he asked questions of the type students would be expected to answer all year. The shallowness of their reading was brought home to many students when they discovered that they knew far less than they needed to know about what they had read (Ferguson, 1970). The stage was then set for a "how to read it" session.

A Send-Off Demonstration

Early in the school year a chemistry teacher and a reading consultant planned a team sendoff for PQ4R. Using the chapter just assigned, the reading consultant suggested general procedures for previewing, formulating questions, reading to find the answers, and the like. After the consultant had explained each step, the chemistry teacher demonstrated how that step would be applied in studying the chapter assigned. *Students are quickly turned off if they get the impression that PQ4R is slow and labored.* The chemistry teacher's run-through left the impression of an efficient, smoothly operating system of study.

Success Can Sell PQ4R

Initial successes with PQ4R encourage students to continue using the method when studying on their own. One teacher deliberately plans striking "before and after" quiz results. To create a sense of need, the teacher quizzes students on their reading of an assigned passage *before* introducing PQ4R. For some students the results are a disaster. PQ4R procedures are then demonstrated with another passage, guiding students through a model reading. Finally the teacher has them close their books and take a quiz on the material just covered. Most of the students are delighted to discover how well the new procedures have worked for them.

Research Results Stir Interest

The findings of research studies in which parts of PQ4R were tested can catch the interest of students. A group of sophomores at the University of Michigan practiced techniques for previewing a selection in sociology. Matched partners did not receive such practice. When the two groups were tested on their reading of a selection, the group with the advantage of the preview practice read 24 percent faster than the control group and with the same degree of comprehension (McClusky, 1934). Research results with other steps of PQ4R can be used as selling points with students.

Use PQ4R Flexibly

PQ4R is by no means a lock-step system of study. Modifications are likely to be desirable from one subject to another, from one passage to another, and from one student to another. Individuals should be encouraged to make their own adaptations and to use the approach that works best *for them.* As they approach each assigned chapter, they should ask such questions as, "Did the instructor make any comments that would suggest a special way of approaching this chapter?" "Is my purpose in reading it to gain a thorough understanding or only a general impression?"

Practice the Individual Steps

PQ4R consists of a number of proved study techniques packaged into a step-by-step approach. Instruction on the individual steps is often advisable before practice with the total approach is attempted. Possible ways to work with each separate step and then to coordinate the steps into a smooth sequential operation are now offered.

How to Practice the Preview Step

(See pages 151–154 of the guidesheets for students.)

Ask teachers, "Do your students preview the chapters you assign?" They will probably answer, "My students just plunge in and read."

A study by Perry (1959) with 1,500 freshmen at Harvard supported this observation. A chapter in social studies was assigned to the freshmen, who were directed to study the chapter as if they would have two hours to complete it. After 22 minutes, the students were interrupted and asked to make a brief statement telling what the chapter was all about. Only 150 out of 1500 had done any exploring beyond the page on which they were reading—and many of these had looked ahead only to estimate the length of the chapter! And only 15 students could give a general view of where the chapter was going.

How-to-Do-Its from Students

A teacher might guide students to make their own discoveries about the techniques and values of previewing: "How does an author help you to learn in just minutes what this chapter will contain? What are all the different means an author uses to clue you in quickly on what you'll find in the chapter?" "Can you suggest a technique for previewing based on the use of the author's clues?" "What are some advantages of making an advance survey of each chapter?"

Assignment Time Right
for Preview Practice

One instructor selects a chapter ideally structured for students' preview practice and suggests, "Let's practice the preview technique on the chapter assigned for tonight's reading. When you've finished, you should be able to answer these two questions: What, in general, is the content of the chapter? and What big points will be discussed? You may need about _____ minutes." (As students are first introduced to the preview technique, time allotments should be generous and flexible.)

As the students finish their examination of the chapter the instructor asks, "What did you find to be the general subject matter?" or "What broad problems will be explored?" Then the teacher asks, "What aspects of the subject will be discussed? Can you possibly give them in order?" As students name the big topics they have gleaned from major chapter division headings and subheadings, the teacher records these on the chalkboard, indenting to indicate levels of subordination and revealing to the class that in this well-structured chapter they have neatly discovered the author's "hidden" outline. The students perceive that they now have a map to guide them during their thorough reading.

Since many of the chapters students will need to preview are not so ideally structured as those a teacher might select during this instructional step, it is desirable later to practice with materials that present difficulties.

Can You Find the Hidden Outline?

To reinforce the awareness that previewing often reveals the author's plan of organization, the instructor might suggest, "We've discovered that an author's major chapter division headings and sub-headings sometimes fall into an outline. Can you find the hidden outline in the chapter assigned for tomorrow?"

"How Much Can You Learn
in Just _____ Minutes?"

As students become adept in using preview techniques, a time limit can be imposed to jolt some of them out of unnecessarily sluggish habits. "How much can you learn about the content of this chapter (or article) in just ＿＿＿ minutes? Use your new preview techniques to hit the high spots of organized prose."

Previewing—An Automatic First Step

As the next few chapters are assigned, students might quickly preview them in class, linking their background information and experience to the chapter, hitting the high spots of organized prose, getting a view of what lies ahead. Brief previews under guidance should be continued until previewing becomes an automatic first step in studying a chapter.

Practice on Everything

Students should be encouraged to practice widely and thus perfect their new techniques. "Preview *everything you read* (except fiction) before you do your more thorough reading. Preview chapters in your textbook for this and other classes. Preview magazine and newspaper articles for your personal reading. Make the Preview Step your lifetime habit. You're likely to do your reading *better and faster* for having previewed."

How to Practice the Question Step

(See pages 151–156 of the students' guidesheets.)

In a study with 1,456 students the effectiveness of approaching reading with questions versus without questions was explored (Washburne, 1929). The effects of four different placements of questions were also compared: (1) all questions just before the reading, (2) all questions just after the reading, (3) each question just before the paragraph(s) in which it was answered in the selection, and (4) each question just after the part of the selection in which it was answered. Two of these placements brought decided gains in comprehension: all questions just before the selection, and each question just before the part of the selection in which it was answered.

Students should capitalize on their awareness of strategic question placement to increase their own comprehension. Where can they get their questions? They can formulate some of them simply by shifting the topical heading of each section into a question.

In-Class Practice Turning Headings into Questions

Many students read headings passively as more or less nonmeaningful phrases. However, if students try to formulate a question from a heading, they are forced to focus on its meaning. They have made a desirable shift in mind set at the beginning, starting each section with an immediate questioning attitude, pausing to ask, "Why are we going into this?" (Robinson, 1961, pp. 33–34).

If the author has provided specific headings that disclose the gist of the section, it will be simple to recast them as questions. This should take just a few moments. (See examples in the students' notebook section.) During their first experience with the Question (Q) Step, students should work with headings that facilitate the shift to a question. They should then try headings less ideal if their textbook includes them—vague, general, or very brief headings that do not reveal specific content. A few minutes of the assignment time for several days is well invested in converting some headings of the next day's assignment into questions.

Depth Questions and Surface Questions

Donald E. P. Smith of the University of Michigan's Reading Service stressed the importance of asking depth questions in addition to surface questions. He gave an example from social studies (Smith, 1961, p. 25). As students read the heading "Hitler's Rise to Power," they might think of the surface questions, "Who was Hitler? How did he rise to power? When?" It may, however, require a depth question to direct attention toward the more significant ideas of the author: "What generalizations for our own time can we make—in other words, are there certain conditions which in *any* society would threaten the democratic process?" Students will need special guidance in moving beyond factual questions and probing "between the lines and beyond the lines" of their textbook.

Practicing the Q Step

For added reinforcement of the Q Step, students might be asked to fill in a table like that in Figure 3–2 during their reading of an assigned chapter.

HEADING FROM YOUR TEXTBOOK	QUESTIONS WITH WHICH YOU APPROACHED YOUR READING OF THE SECTION

Figure 3–2.   *Q Step table. (Adapted from Ralph C. Preston and Morton Botel. How to Study. Chicago: Science Research Associates, 1974, p. 25.)*

"What Questions Would Your Instructor Ask on This?"

One teacher (Hillman, 1971) projects a headed section of the assigned chapter on a screen, then suggests to the class, "Pretend you are the teacher. What questions would you ask the class on this section? Of course you want your questions to get at the important content." With help, students arrive at questions tailored to the content, and at depth as well as surface levels.

Next they are told, "Now you're no longer the teacher. You're *you*, the student. Now *really learn* the answers to your questions. Then close your book and write the answers." (Books are to be closed to discourage rote copying.)

"Now that's the way you should study—formulating questions, then reading to learn the answers."

As the students perfect the Q Step they discover that their next tests and examinations hold fewer surprises. They now formulate questions so skillfully that they can often predict some of their test questions.

"Won't I Overlook Important Content?"

Students may wonder, "If I read to find the answer to an overall question suggested by the topic heading, won't I overlook important content?" The following advice, which appears on the students' guidesheets, will need emphasis: Read to find the answer to your question *and other important content.* You'll need to continue questioning—to add questions and perhaps to adjust your questions *all the while* you're reading. Turn topic sentences into questions. Turn the heading for a series of steps or a list into questions: "Just what are the steps in mitosis?" "Just what phyla are listed here?" Turn key concepts and terms into questions: "Just what *is* a theory?"

Especially with questions that call for details, care must be taken lest students scan for the bits and pieces that answer the questions and bypass all the rest of the passage.

How to Practice the Read Step

(See pages 156–157 of the students' guidesheets.)

Some students have no conception of what a rigorous passage demands. For years they have made a whip-through of demanding reading. A teacher can walk students through a model reading of a difficult passage. In the process, students—some of them for the first time—experience digging into difficult sentences, reading and rereading a passage until they get a breakthrough, pausing to think something through: "Do I understand?" "What is the evidence for this?" "Can I make a generalization here?"

The reader will notice, in the students' notebook section, that an added R —for reflect—is built right into the Read Step. PQ4R is not intended to overstress the memory level of learning to the neglect of higher intellectual processes. Information that is worth remembering is a *foundation* for higher-level thought. As Sanders (1966) observed, "The memory category is indispensable on all levels of thinking. The more important and useful knowledge a student possesses, the better his chances for success in other categories of thought."

How to Practice the Recite Step

(See pages 157–159 of the students' guidesheets.)

Students sometimes say, "I've read that chapter twice, but I still can't remember it." These students may have failed to firm up their learning through recitation. They are likely to retain better when they ask themselves, as they complete each section of the chapter, "Just what have I read here?"

The Steps Should Become a Smooth
Operation

Guidance will be needed in coordinating the Question, Read, and Recite Steps
into a smooth operation. Students are advised on their guidesheets to work
through the chapter, carrying out the Question, Read, and Recite Steps in
order, one headed section at a time. Guided practice—in which they actually
perform these steps in sequence, converting the heading into a question, reading to find the answer, then reciting to themselves the essential information—
is important in entrenching PQ4R.

Making Notes and Marking Books

A number of quick, labor-saving methods of making notes or marking the
book (if the student owns the book) are offered to students in their printed
guidelines. Too often, notemaking amounts to labored and absentminded
copying. Indeed, notemaking often *operates against learning*. Some students
actually copy a sentence without ever having read it for meaning, thinking,
"I'll copy this now and learn it later"—if indeed they are thinking at all. Notemaking becomes merely a mechanical note*taking* of every sentence or so. Similarly, students underline without really reading the content (Robinson, 1961,
p. 38).

One teacher holds a session on "How to Make Important Points Flag You,"
projecting examples on a screen before the class. Facsimiles of actual textbook
pages are prepared as models of various marking or notemaking techniques:
selective underlining, "mini notes" in the margin, marginal numerals, and
others. The instructor also shows on the screen model notes made in labor-
saving personal shorthand. Tips are offered about the use of these techniques,
and the pros and cons of each are discussed. Many students are intrigued by the
prospect of developing their own personal shorthand, a shortcut suggested in
the students' notebook section.

How to Practice the Review Step

(See pages 163–165 of the students' guidesheets.)

Having worked through the chapter section by section, questioning, reading,
and reciting on the content, the student now returns—in the Review Step—
to the total chapter.

Students who have no idea what thorough study involves may be inclined to leave out the Review Step, thinking, "All that for an assignment!" Demonstrating the deft review of a chapter should impress them with the fact that a skillful review—provided the preceding steps have been properly carried out —is not wearisome restudy but rather a relatively quick *overlearning* step that clinches retention. Of course the Review Step, too, should be an intensely active process, with the student looking away from the page and reciting and bringing every possible learning channel to bear.

In one classroom large wall placards depicting the "curve of forgetting" (see students' notebook section) serve as daily reminders to students to space out their reviews to best advantage.

Instructors often lament, "Many students read their textbooks like a novel." Obviously, instruction on the various parts of the PQ4R process—previewing, questioning, self-reciting, involving multisensory channels, notemaking, spacing out reviews—discourages the impression that "he who runs may read" a textbook chapter.

PQ4R for Supplementary Books

The steps discussed above and the guidesheets that follow deal specifically with the reading of single textbook chapters. There is also much value in students' learning how to apply PQ4R to supplementary books of an informational nature. Obviously, when students are searching for information in a number of books, they can't spend the amount of time they expend in the careful, intensive study of one textbook chapter. On later pages you will find tips directed toward the student on how to adapt PQ4R to the reading of supplementary books.

Practice with PQ4R Should Be Realistic

We have mentioned that not all textbook chapters are ideally written to facilitate study with PQ4R. Practice should be realistic. While the students' first experiences should be planned with chapters well structured for PQ4R, they should move on to passages that are not ideal, then on to material that confronts them with real difficulties.

PQ4R Needs Reinforcement

PQ4R should be reinforced as needed over the weeks and months that follow its introduction. A particular technique from the package of skills can be suggested at the time of an assignment: "Your cover card will help you check this diagram to see if you've really grasped its parts and labels."

Students may need encouragement during a period of readjustment in which the newly adopted techniques seem difficult and awkward. Learning experts draw analogies with sports. Swimmers who change their strokes to reduce water resistance feel clumsy at first, but with practice they improve in speed and power and streamline their performance.

Of course, printed guidesheets for students are not a do-it-yourself kit—in themselves, they are not likely to produce much of a change in habits. The ones that follow are intended as a supplement to the teacher's instruction, as a permanent reference for students, and as a constant reminder to *practice* PQ4R.

Adopting Parts of PQ4R

A number of effective techniques have been clustered in PQ4R. Some teachers report that it is difficult to get students to use the complete cluster. The authors, however, have not found it at all difficult to get almost all students to immediately try out, and then adopt, two or three of the techniques. If students adopt only the Preview Step and the practice of self-recitation, for example, they will have acquired two tools broadly applicable in study. If they adopt the whole package, they will have acquired a most effective study method for the thorough mastery of a textbook chapter.

A Lifetime Tool

Through PQ4R, teachers can give their students a lifetime tool for better learning. As one educator (Congreve, 1965) observes, "Knowledge is growing and changing so rapidly that much of the education we give students today will go out of date several times within their lifetimes. They will need to update the education we give them—for their careers. They will need to reeducate themselves for careers not yet in existence. What can we give them more useful than power in reading?"

STUDY BETTER AND FASTER WITH HIGHER-LEVEL STUDY SKILLS*

From time to time you'll be given tips in class to help you keep on top of your assignments. You can put these to work to get the maximum results from every moment you spend in studying.

CAPITALIZE ON SCIENTIFIC LEARNING

Psychologists at top universities have experimented for years to find out how students learn most easily and well. Certain principles of learning are now well known. Procedures based on such principles are called "higher-level study skills." Through these, you can learn more readily, remember longer, and conserve your study time. You'll want to cultivate techniques like these as you enter higher-level courses.

DEVELOP HIGHER-LEVEL SKILLS

Of course, effective study methods aren't inherent—they're acquired. *You can develop these skills.* Some students with extraordinary ability achieve little. Others with less ability achieve much. What makes the difference? Often, it's knowing how to study.

After all, teachers don't grade a student's intellect but the quality of work done. It's important to make the most of your capabilities. Higher-level study skills can help you do this.†

THREE THINGS TO DO

You'll be introduced to higher-level study skills in class with your teacher and through a series of guidesheets. There are three things for you to do:

1. Make the most of tips from your instructor.
2. Study the guidesheets that follow, then file them in your notebook for reference.
3. And especially—without which there will be no value for you, now or ever—*practice* your higher-level study skills from here on.

FAIR EXCHANGE?

One learning expert comments, "You'll probably put forth more effort every hour you spend studying than you have in the past. Are you willing to do this—and finish the job with *more learned and more remembered* in the process? Scientific study procedures have enabled thousands of students to

---

* The term "higher-level study skills" belongs to Francis P. Robinson and is used in his *Effective Study*, 4th ed. (New York: Harper and Row, 1970).

† Ralph C. Preston and Morton Botel, *How to Study* (Chicago: Science Research Associates, 1974), pp. 2, 3.

do that very thing: swap extra effort for better performance—and perhaps more free time. Fair exchange?"*

STEP UP YOUR STUDYING WITH PQ4R

PQ4R is a package of study techniques. It can help you comprehend more difficult material, cut through what is less important and find main points, concentrate better, remember longer, and have a lifetime tool for better learning.

It is a variation of a study approach originated during a war-time crisis when a highly select group of young men had to be rushed through training courses. Although they had been selected for high intelligence and top records at school, their study methods proved extremely inefficient. Dr. Francis Robinson, an authority on the psychology of learning, was called in. Drawing on the results of years of experiments with students, he designed scientific procedures to streamline their study. (The steps in Dr. Robinson's original approach are Survey, Question, Read, Recite, and Review, or SQ3R.)

The steps in PQ4R are **Preview, Question, Read, Reflect, Recite,** and **Review.** It should help you get solid results when your goal is thorough learning and retention of the content of a chapter.

Of course, you'll want to vary any study system from one textbook to another and even from one passage to another. As you approach each reading assignment, you'll want to ask yourself such questions as, "Did the teacher make any remarks that would suggest a special approach to this chapter?" "Is my purpose here a detailed understanding of the content or only a general impression?" You'll want to use the new method flexibly, adjust it to your needs and preferences, and add effective ways of your own.

You'll find on the next pages some powerful study techniques for mastering a textbook chapter.

A HIGHER-LEVEL APPROACH TO READING A CHAPTER

Suppose it's 7:30 tonight. You've watched the news, had dinner, and now you're starting your assignment—the reading of a difficult chapter. How should you handle the job and learn and remember the maximum amount in the process?

No one should expect to comprehend difficult new material in a single reading, not the most gifted student nor even a scholar with special aptitude in the subject. So, first of all, plan to do more than a once-over-lightly reading.

---

* Thomas F. Staton, *How to Study* (Montgomery, Alabama, P.O. Box 6133, 1968), preface.

PREVIEW TO LOOK OVER THE TERRAIN

You would hardly plunge in blindly and try to cross rugged terrain if you could have in advance an accurate map of the region. When you plunge into a difficult chapter and "just read," you are trying to work your way through rugged territory without a map.

Spend a few minutes in an advance survey of the chapter to get a general view of what lies ahead.

1. *Hit the "high spots" of well-organized informational writing.*

   a. *Examine the title.*

   This in an instant should clue you in on the general content. Speculate, as you read it, about just what the chapter may have to offer.

   b. *Read the introductory paragraphs thoroughly.*

**ONCE
OVER
LIGHTLY**

   Here the author usually "announces" the general content, raises broad problems to be explored, conveniently briefs you on what's ahead. How does the content link up with what you've been studying?

   c. *Now skim the body of the chapter.*

   As you do so, hit the headlines. What aspects of the general subject does the chapter zero in on?

   > Sometimes authors flash signals of their major thought-divisions in conspicuous headings. While textbooks vary, these headings are often set off with space and in large letters. You'll usually find no more than four or five of these within one chapter. Leaf through the chapter to locate these "announcements" to you from the author of the big chapter divisions under the title.
   >
   > Now take each of the big chapter divisions as a unit and look for signals of what it contains. You will often find sub-headings at the side of the printed column clearly announcing the sub-topics. These stand out; they are frequently printed in a dark type called **boldface**. Perhaps there will be five or six of these sub-headings. Pause to reflect on each of these, and try to predict the content of the passage that follows it.*
   >
   > You may find that you have discovered the authors' hidden outline; i.e., that is, their chapter division headings, and under them the side headings, fall into an

---

* Gilbert C. Wrenn and Luella Cole, *Reading Rapidly and Well* (Stanford: Stanford University Press, 1954), p. 11.

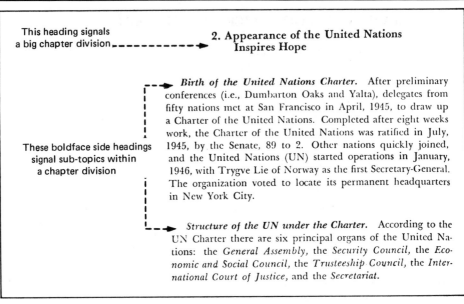

This heading signals
a big chapter division ⟶ 2. Appearance of the United Nations
Inspires Hope

⟶ *Birth of the United Nations Charter.* After preliminary conferences (i.e., Dumbarton Oaks and Yalta), delegates from fifty nations met at San Francisco in April, 1945, to draw up a Charter of the United Nations. Completed after eight weeks work, the Charter of the United Nations was ratified in July, 1945, by the Senate, 89 to 2. Other nations quickly joined, and the United Nations (UN) started operations in January, 1946, with Trygve Lie of Norway as the first Secretary-General. The organization voted to locate its permanent headquarters in New York City.

These boldface side headings signal sub-topics within a chapter division

⟶ *Structure of the UN under the Charter.* According to the UN Charter there are six principal organs of the United Nations: the *General Assembly,* the *Security Council,* the *Economic and Social Council,* the *Trusteeship Council,* the *International Court of Justice,* and the *Secretariat.*

Figure 3–3. *Using headings. (Text material from Samuel Steinberg,* The United States, Story of a Free People. *Boston: Allyn and Bacon, Inc., 1963, pp. 587–588.)*

outline. Of course, finding the hidden outline makes the chapter content easier to grasp. Now you have your map of the conspicuous features of the territory.

You may wish to examine the first and perhaps the last sentences of paragraphs. Topic sentences are often located here. In chapters that lack headings, topic sentences frequently announce aspects under the general subject.

Look over graphic aids—photos, charts, graphs, art, and so on. Each one is saying to you, "This is clearing up something important." It actually costs the publisher several times as much to use a graphic aid as it does to use ordinary print. The publisher includes one, you may be sure, only to drive home something of special importance.

d. *Read the concluding paragraphs.*

In their last moments with you, the authors often wrap up important content—review major principles and concepts explored in the chapter—drive home what they want most of all to leave with the reader. By reading the summary or conclusion *first,* you may learn important content to look for when you go back to do your thorough reading.

e. *You'll find exceptions!*

You'll find exceptions to much that's been said here. Introductions may fail to introduce all important areas, and conclusions may fail to wrap it all up. Topic sentences aren't always first or last—or even present—in all paragraphs. You may need to preview flexibly—running your eyes over the pages, following one promising lead after another.

2. *Ask yourself, "What do I already know about this?"*

Summon up your background information—your own ideas and experiences on the subject. You'll grasp new concepts better if they click with something you already know.

3. *Questions should come to mind as you preview.*

Ask yourself constantly, "What can I expect to learn from this chapter? What should I look for when I go back and read it more carefully?" If you own the book, try jotting in the margin questions you'll want to answer during your thorough reading. If the book is not yours, you might jot your questions on slips from a memo pad and place them between the related pages.

You will often find self-check questions at the end of chapters. These are a giveaway of points the authors themselves consider important. Look these over as you preview.

4. *Skillful previewing will not be instant.*

As with any skill development, you'll improve your survey techniques with practice.

5. *How long will it take?*

That varies with individual students, their purposes, and the difficulty of the chapter. You should be able to work through a long, difficult chapter in ten or fifteen minutes. An easier chapter may take no more than five.

Why preview?

1. *You've taken the chill off the reading.*

You have a general view of what it's all about and where it's going.

2. *Main points should now stand out.*

If with no advance survey you just begin reading with the very first line and plod on through, you may find yourself lost among the details— you may have missed out on the main points completely.

3. *Details should now fall into place in relation to the whole.*

Now you should retain them with less effort.

4. *Now you should intensify your concentration.*

You'll be more alert when you know what to look for.

Don't conclude that previewing is time consuming. It's the first step in an approach which when practiced and perfected should enable you to pack 60 seconds of faster, firmer learning into every minute of study.

QUESTION

Now that you've previewed, you're ready for your in-depth reading of the chapter.

In this step, you work through the chapter mastering one manageable section at a time. A section marked off with a boldface or italic side heading is likely to be a manageable amount for thorough study. Of course, the length of the section you work with need not be rigid. A headed section has the advantage of being a fairly comprehensive thought unit. But if the headed section continues over several pages or is extremely difficult, you may wish to work with the content in smaller bites.*

Carrying out the steps Question, Read, and Recite in order, you now read and master one section before going on to the next.

Read with a questioning mind set. This should help you crack the most difficult chapter. While you were previewing, you may have jotted down some questions. As you probe more deeply by thorough reading, further questions should come to mind. You constantly ask questions as you read along.

 More than one thousand college students took part in an experiment. Those who approached reading selections with *questions* showed decided gains in comprehension.† In another experiment students who approached reading selections with questions showed better *immediate retention* on tests just after their reading—and better *long-term retention* on tests two weeks later.‡

1. *Convert section headings into questions.* In the heavy black headings the author is shouting, "I'm presenting you with these headings as clear clues to major points. Shift them into questions and you'll be guided to the main ideas."

> Suppose a section has the boldface heading, **Results of the Scientific Process.** Quickly shift this into the question, "*What are* the results of the scientific process?" Suppose a section is headed, **The Difference Between a Physical and a Chemical Change.** Change that heading

* Donald E. P. Smith, ed., *Learning to Learn* (New York: Harcourt, Brace and World, 1961), p. 31.

† John N. Washburne, "The Use of Questions in Social Science Material," *Journal of Educational Psychology*, 20 (May 1929): 321–359.

‡ Eleanor Holmes, "Reading Guided by Questions versus Careful Reading and Rereading without Questions," *School Review*, 39 (May 1931): 361–371.

into the question, "*What is* the difference between a physical and a chemical change?"

Some headings are quite general, **Systems of Classification,** for example. You might formulate the general question, "What are the important points here about systems of classification?" Better still, skim the content, then tailor a question to the information you find there. You may discover that the section deals with early and modern classification systems and formulate this question, "What systems of classification have been devised?"

2. *You'll often find hidden questions* in the topic or key sentences of paragraphs. There's one quickly apparent in the topic sentence, "Linnaeus used Latin as the language of plant classification for several reasons." Rephrase it quickly: "What are the reasons why Linnaeus chose Latin?" There's a hidden question in this topic sentence, "Any system of classifying living things brings up problems." The question is obvious: "What problems are involved in systems of classification?"

3. *If headings and topic sentences are missing or elusive, skim the content itself.* Glance through the content as you ask, "What question was the author trying to answer when he wrote this?" Zeroing in on the first few sentences of a paragraph will often suggest the question.

4. *Ask depth questions as well as surface questions.* Dr. Donald Smith of the University of Michigan's Reading Service pointed out that the questions suggested by a textbook heading may be surface questions—so you may need to ask deeper, more probing questions to penetrate to the really significant ideas of the author.*

Smith gave an example from social studies. As you read the topic heading, **Hitler's Rise to Power,** you might think of the surface questions, "Who was Hitler? How did he rise to power? When?" It will, however, require a depth question to direct your attention toward the more significant ideas of the author: "What generalizations for our own time can we make—in other words, are there certain conditions which in any society would threaten the democratic process?"

5. *Be a human question mark!* Read to find the answer to your question *and* other important content. You'll need to continue questioning, to add questions, and perhaps to adjust your questions all the while you're reading. Turn topic sentences into questions. Turn the headings of a series of steps or a list into questions—"Just what are the steps in mitosis?" "Just what phyla are listed here?" Turn key concepts and terms into questions—"Just what *is* a theory?" You may be wondering, "If I read to find the answer to an overall question suggested by the boldface heading, won't I overlook important content?" Take care not to skim for bits and pieces of the passage and bypass the rest.

---

* Smith, *Learning to Learn*, p. 25.

Why the Q Step?

1. *Try it if you can't decide what's important.* Since the author announces important thought divisions in chapter division headings and boldface side headings, questions formulated from these headings should help you cut through what's less important to the main points.

2. *Try it if you can't concentrate.* Now your reading becomes an active search for answers.

3. *Try it if you want a powerful tool for independent learning.* As you perfect your skill in formulating your own questions, you become less dependent on teacher-given questions, and gain a lifetime tool for independent learning.

> A PASSAGE THAT WOULD HAVE BEEN A "STOPPER"
> FOR YOU MAY BE EASY TO GRASP IF APPROACHED
> WITH A QUESTION.

READ—AND REFLECT

The Read Step has an added R built right in, and this added R is *Reflect.*

Is reflective thinking built right into the way you operate in reading? Do you constantly read between and beyond the lines? Do you weigh and consider, explore implications, draw conclusions, speculate and wonder?

Reading and reflecting should be simultaneous and inseparable.

After you've previewed, you're ready for close, intensive reading of the section of the chapter. You may be reading for a depth of comprehension never before demanded.

1. *Go in with a question!* We have noted the plus values of approaching your reading with questions. A questioning mind set is a powerful aid to concentration. Holding questions in the forefront of your mind you

THINK

read, searching intently instead of dreaming through the assignment.
   Now read to find the answer to your question and other important content.

2. *If full comprehension is important, read to "pull out" the meaning of each sentence.* New concepts are often built on full understanding of preceding ones. Keep at it until you get a breakthrough.

   When it's rough going, think over each sentence to be sure the meaning is clear to you. Try not to go on to the next sentence until you fully understand the one before.

   The meaning of difficult parts will frequently escape you. Expect this! Successful students read difficult passages again and again. A passage that blocked you at first may become clear with a third or fourth reading.

3. *Reduce speed for dense passages.* Even your instructors with their broad backgrounds and long experience in reading in their subjects,

find that they must read difficult new material slowly. Reduce your own speed for passages that deliver a heavy load of ideas and information.

Vary your approach and tempo as needed within a single section of a chapter. Within an otherwise fact-packed chapter in science you may, for example, come upon an interesting vignette of a great discovery in science or a short narrative sketch of the life story of a scientist. Speed up appropriately for this comparatively easy content.

4. *Complete stops are often called for.* In some situations a reading-straight-on pattern will be appropriate. You may wish to read in this way when you are covering light narrative material or when all you want to gain is a general impression of the content of a chapter. But in difficult material, when your goal is comprehending fully, you will need stop-and-go reading. Part of the time you will read standing still! Thought time is needed in addition to reading time.

Read, then stop to ask, "Do I understand?" or "Can I give an example?" Stop to reflect: "What is the basic *why* of this?" "What outcome do I predict in view of this?" "Can I make a generalization here?" "How does this apply in the world outside of class?" Constantly question the written word: "What is the evidence that supports this?" Challenge the author. Stop to ask not just, "Why is this true?" but, "Is it indeed true?"

Part of your reading time should be visualizing time. When the content lends itself, try to form a mental picture of what you've just read.

If an illustration is lacking, you may wish to sketch one of your own. Making your own sketch helps you really *see*—brings what you've read into sharp focus.

5. *Graphic aids may give you instant insights.* "Read" graphic materials as thoroughly as you read words. Drawings, diagrams, and the like save you reading time. A single diagram may make hundreds of words instantly clear.

Preview—Question—Read—Reflect—and now:

RECITE

How can you "firm up" your learning? You can use the most powerful study technique known to psychologists. This is the technique of self-recitation.*

1. *Ask yourself, "Just what have I read?"* In the Recite Step, ask yourself as you complete a section, "Just what have I read here?" Without looking at the print, check to see if you can recite to yourself the main points

---

* Walter Pauk, *How to Study in College* (Boston: Houghton Mifflin Company, 1962), p. 25.

Figure 3–4. *Cover card.*

TALK TO YOURSELF

and the important sub-points. Put the ideas into actual words—*your own words.*

If you can't do this, that's your cue to reread appropriate parts. No need to reread it all. Skip the parts you can recall.

The Reading Study Center at Cornell University is nationally known for the solid gains it gets for college students. These students are advised to keep the print out of sight at least 50 percent of the time they're studying, to look away from the book or cover it with their hand or with a card.

When college students at Cornell, in repeated experiments, spent *one minute* in recalling the content of a passage just read, they nearly doubled retention.*

2. *You may find a cover card convenient.* A cover card is an index card of the size you find convenient, perhaps 5 × 8. Use it to conceal parts of your textbook or notes as you recite important content to yourself (See Figure 3–4).

3. *Turn on triple-strength learning.* As you recite to yourself, you can turn on triple-strength learning. If you learn with your eyes alone, you're using just one-third of your sensory channels for mastering the printed page. Why not use all-out VAK learning—Visual plus Auditory plus Kinesthetic?

---

* Pauk, *How to Study in College*, p. 76.

Use your eyes in study, then add your ears and muscles:
See it!
Say it!
Hear it!
Draw it or write it!*

a. Use your eyes as you *see* the printed words. You have now brought your visual memory into play.

b. *Say* what you're learning, aloud or in a whisper. Now you've added kinesthetic (muscular) learning as you involve the muscles of your throat, lips, and tongue.

c. Strengthen learning with your *ears* as you hear yourself say it. Now you've brought to bear your auditory memory.

d. Add *kinesthetic learning* again as you make more jottings or draw a sketch. Here you've involved your motor memory.

"See it! Say it! Hear it! Draw or write it!" is a four-way reinforcement. The variety itself helps you recall. The change of pace—eyes, voice, ears, pencil—keeps you alert and increases your "intake."

4. *You are not being urged to memorize; in fact, you are being urged* not *to memorize.* Your textbooks may be condensations of broad fields of knowledge or distillations of centuries of experiment and observation and may well deserve your thoughtful study.

> *SELF-RECITATION IS ALL-OUT, ACTIVE STUDY. YOU'RE CHANGING HALF-LEARNED TO FULLY LEARNED MATERIAL.*

Make important points "flag" you

You'll probably want to make the highlights *stand out in some way* so that you won't have to reread the entire chapter when you return to review important points later on.

1. *Select what you want to remember.* There are more than 500 facts and ideas crowded into some textbook chapters. You simply can't remember all of these. The first step in retention is selecting out what is important to remember.

   Facts given to illustrate a concept are usually less important than the concept itself. On the other hand, some facts and examples, once remembered, help you retain the concept.

2. *Delay marking or making notes until the end of a section.* Having

---

* George J. Dudycha, *Learn More with Less Effort* (New York: Harper and Row, 1957), p. 96.

selected out the significant information, your next step is to mark the book or make notes.

Some students plunge into a chapter and mark or make notes immediately. They mark or copy whatever their eyes first glimpse on the page. It's probably best to delay marking or making notes until you've read to the end of a headed section. Why? Only when you have encountered all the ideas in the section can you see their relationships, and only then can you judge their relative importance.

3. *The change of pace as you mark your book or make notes is a definite plus in study.*

    The rapid succession with which ideas come crowding in one after another during reading tends to block your learning because of retroactive interference.* The break as you mark the book or make notes interrupts this rapid flow of ideas and provides "fixating" time for the ideas to make an impression.

4. *Take your choice of marking and notemaking methods.* Techniques like those below—any one or a combination—will enable you to spot the high points immediately when you review them later on. And you should collect a fringe benefit—pencil work has a "no-doze" effect.

    If the book is yours to mark, the following marking methods—your preference—are likely to be useful:

    a. *Quick marginal lines.* This is a high-speed marking method; much speedier than underlining, it's the quickest marking method of all. Draw a *solid* vertical line down the margin (just to the left of the column of print) next to a *major point* which you wish to stand out. Carefully mark the exact extent of the part you've selected as important. Since your markings should show relative importance, use a broken line to mark an important *sub-point*. Using light pencil makes it possible for you to reconsider and perhaps revise your markings later.

    b. *Underline to show relative importance.* You might underline main ideas with a *solid* line and important details with a broken line.

    _____ = main idea

    _ _ _ _ _ _ _ _ _ = important detail

    Be selective. Underline not more than 15 or 20 percent of the passage. When you underline too much, none of the ideas flag you as outstanding, and the task of learning such a mass of detail looks overwhelming. If you find you need to underline several successive lines, just enclose them in brackets as a time-saver.

    c. *Use see-through color accents.* Use color if you like, but use it sparingly. Because of the ease with which color accents can be applied,

---

* H. F. Spitzer, "Studies in Retention," *Journal of Educational Psychology*, 30 (December 1939): 641–656.

there's a tendency to become "color happy" and over-accent. You might accent main points with one color, sub-points with another.

d. *Make marginal mini-notes—brief jottings of key words or cue phrases.* Key words or phrases that call to mind main points can be jotted near the far edge of the left margin of your book. Key words that suggest sub-points can be jotted below these, set in a little.

   When you review the passage later, you can use these cue words to trigger your recall of the important points.

e. *Use marginal numerals.* As you read a paragraph or longer unit, you might place numerals in the margin beside points to be remembered. You might use *a*'s and *b*'s, set under these, to indicate sub-points. For example, a paragraph that gives several different causes of an event in a series might lend itself to numerals placed in the margin.

f. *Make asterisks.* An asterisk (*) can guide your eye to an idea of supreme importance—the major idea of a chapter, for example, or an underlying principle or concept.

g. *Use marginal question marks.* A question mark in the margin can indicate a statement you question or with which you disagree.

h. *A check mark can remind you, "Check this out!"* Use a check mark to indicate something you don't understand and plan to check with your instructor later.

i. *"Capsulate" important content.* A capsule summary of a concept, principle, or other crucial content can be jotted in the book itself, perhaps in the upper or lower margin. If you don't own the book, you can use a small slip of paper and place it between the related pages.

j. *Where do your ideas come in?* Of course, you'll want to make notes on your *own* observations, impressions, and conclusions. You might jot these in the margin, marking them with your initials or the word ME with a circle around it, or else place your own ideas in brackets.*

If the book is not yours to mark, the following notemaking methods are appropriate:

a. *Make quick, labor saving notes or make an outline.* A shorthand of your own will save you time as long as you use the same abbreviations consistently. You can soon develop a personal "notehand" something like this:

about	= abt
be	= b
before	= bf

* Many of the ideas about marking a book were suggested by Walter Pauk, *How to Study in College*, 2nd ed. (Boston: Houghton Mifflin Company, 1974), pp. 153–159.

no	= n
are	= r
point	= pt
development	= dev
observation	= obsrv
environment	= env
hypothesis	= hypth
evolution	= evol

Notetaking sometimes amounts to absentmindedly copying the book. Don't take notes—*make* notes. Rephrase the content when possible.

How complete should your notes be? This varies with the person and the purpose. Enough for *you* to recall as much of the content as you need.

Again, it's probably best to delay making notes (or outlining) until you've read to the end of a section. Only then can you judge the relationships of the ideas and decide on their relative importance.

b. *Memo slips can be useful.* If the book is not yours to mark, you can easily jot your notes on a small memo pad and insert the slips between the related pages of the book.

When you've finished studying a chapter, remove the slips from your book. Otherwise your book will bulge with these inserts. Clip them together in order, label an envelope with the title of the chapter, and place these envelopes in order as "pockets" in your notebook.*

c. *You can convert the Q Step into a quick, efficient way of making notes.*† As you formulate questions during the Q Step, you might jot these on slips from a memo pad and keep them between the related pages of your textbook. As you come upon the answers during your thorough reading, jot them on the slips, too.

d. *The divided page is sometimes handy.* Make a dividing line down a page in your notebook. In the *Question* column to the left, record the question you formulated during the Q Step, or some other important question. In the *Answer* column to the right, jot quick notes that call to mind the answer.‡

The divided page, you'll find, is handy when review time comes. The dividing line makes it possible to conceal the answers completely as you check your understanding later.

The divided page is convenient for recording important new terms and their meanings. Mark the end of each unit, perhaps with

---

* Illa Podendorf, former University of Chicago Laboratory School science teacher, in remarks to Ellen Thomas, November 1970.
† Horace Judson, *The Techniques of Reading* (New York: Harcourt, Brace and Company, 1954), p. 159.
‡ Preston and Botel, *How to Study*, p. 25.

a double line. Now when you want to go back and check on the new words you've studied in a certain unit, you'll know exactly where to find them.

e. *The divided notebook offers all the space you need.* You may prefer the divided notebook to the divided page. Open your looseleaf notebook so it lies flat on the desk before you. On the left-hand page, record the questions you formulated during the Q Step. Just across, in a corresponding position on the right-hand page, jot notes that call to mind the answer. Check your memory later by folding the right-hand half of the notebook underneath so that the questions are exposed and the answers out of sight.

You may wish to leave extra space between your questions for making class notes on related discussions and lectures.

f. *What about your own brainstorming?* What of your own reflections, your own interpretations, your own evaluations? If it's a case of inserting your own ideas right into notes you are making from other sources, you should enclose your own ideas inside of brackets. Or you might jot your own reflections on slips from a memo pad, mark them with your initials or with the word ME and place them between related pages of the chapter.

> WHY MAKE JOTTINGS? NOW YOU'VE INVOLVED MOTOR MEMORY—IN MANY STUDENTS ONE OF THE STRONGEST LEARNING CHANNELS OF ALL. IF YOU WERE TO DO NOTHING MORE THAN RECORD YOUR NOTES, THEN LOSE THEM FOREVER, YOU WOULD STILL BE AHEAD. THE MUSCULAR ACT OF WRITING, IN AND OF ITSELF, WOULD HAVE STRENGTHENED YOUR LEARNING.

REVIEW

Unless you learn for the future, a lot of hard work goes by the board. More than three thousand students read a passage with no review. Within two weeks they had lost 80 percent and retained only 20 percent of what they had at first remembered. But when these same students carried out a review step just after their reading, the figures were reversed. They retained 80 percent and lost just 20 percent!*

1. *Regain the broad view of the chapter.* You have just completed a close, intensive reading by applying Question, Read, Reflect, and Recite to sections of a chapter. You've been concentrating on sections—even on bits and pieces, like the meaning of a single key term. As you've focused on each part, you may have lost the broad chapter plan.

ONE MORE TIME

---

* Spitzer, "Studies in Retention," pp. 642–648.

To regain the broad view, turn through the chapter in a final run-through. Try to recite its broad organization and to recall its big thought divisions. You've attended to the little pieces of the jigsaw. Now look once more at the total picture. Here you're focusing once more on what you learned in your preview.

2. *Then check on the important sub-points.* Work through the chapter once again, checking your understanding of the content just below each topic heading. Your cover card may be useful again. Reread parts you have forgotten.

3. *Once more turn on triple-strength learning: eyes, ears, muscles. Use* your *eyes* to reread selectively. *Say* things aloud and *hear* yourself. *Write* down cue phrases, little jottings of the key words in ideas you want to remember.

4. *Use the memory aid of overlearning.* Learning for the future requires overlearning. A football player learns to take his man out in a run around left end. Then he goes over and over the play until he over-learns it. He does this so that there will be no forgetting or confusion. An actor memorizes lines well enough to deliver them without error. Then he or she continues to go over them until they are automatic.*

   Learning experts say, "Minimal learning is not enough. When you can say, 'I have learned this material,' you may need to spend perhaps one-fourth the original time overlearning it." In one study, students who overlearned a vocabulary lesson remembered *four times as much* after four weeks had passed.

5. *You can retain longer through spaced reviews.* You can remember longer simply by the way you place your reviews. You can place your first review to minimize forgetting.

   Suppose you read an assignment today. When will forgetting take its greatest toll? The greatest loss will be within one day. Arrange your first review to check this drop. Place it from 12 to 24 hours after you study. Reinforce immediately, and you will remember *much* longer.

   A study expert† pointed out the "curve of forgetting" to military officers returning to academic study after being out of school for several years.‡

   The first student studied one hour on September 30, and six weeks later retained very little (see Figure 3–5).

   The second student studied only thirty minutes on September 30 but spaced out reviews—fifteen minutes on October 1, and ten minutes

---

* Richard Kalish, *Making the Most of College* (Belmont, Calif.: Wadsworth Publishing Company, 1959), p. 119.

† Thomas F. Staton, a study expert, has contributed a number of the ideas used in several sections of this book.

‡ Staton, *How to Study*, pp. 58, 59. The drawings to illustrate the "Curve of Forgetting" are reproduced from page 59 with Dr. Staton's generous permission.

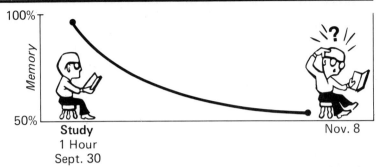

Figure 3–5. *Curve of forgetting. (Drawing reproduced by permission of Dr. Thomas F. Staton.)*

Figure 3–6. *Spaced review. (Drawing reproduced by permission of Dr. Thomas F. Staton.)*

more on October 8. On November 8 it took this student just a five-minute review to bring back the vital information—with 100 percent mastery (see Figure 3–6).

Both students studied just one hour, but the one who spaced out the review had far better retention.

A SUMMING UP

In the Preview Step you're concerned with the entire chapter, surveying it for the total picture. Then you work through the chapter, one manageable section at a time, completing the Question, Read, Reflect, and Recite Steps in order, one right after another. In the Review Step you're concerned with the entire chapter again, as you regain the broad view.

THAT IS PQ4R

Is it cumbersome? It was a method of fast, efficient study at Maxwell Air Base and elsewhere during a wartime crisis.

Will there be difficulties applying PQ4R? Poorly organized material is likely to present difficulties. But poorly written material makes strategies that facilitate reading even more essential.

What do we have in PQ4R? An approach to help you comprehend better, concentrate better, retain better, and have a powerful tool for more efficient learning—useful in reading *any* informational selection.

It's a cluster of techniques and skills. If you incorporate into your permanent habits just two or three of these techniques, you should upgrade your study. If you adopt the whole package—or a close adaptation of it—you will have acquired a powerful study approach for the thorough mastery of a textbook chapter.

CAN PQ4R HELP YOU READ SUPPLEMENTARY BOOKS?

Often your reading assignment is not a single textbook chapter. It may be an informational book or perhaps several books. Suppose your instructor has suggested, "Just read this rapidly for general background."

If you attack your extensive supplementary readings with the slow, intensive approach you use in studying your textbooks, you'll find yourself spending impossible amounts of time. PQ4R, adapted somewhat as follows, should help you get *what you're after faster* when you're reading supplementary books for general background:*

*Consider why the assignment
was made*

Did your instructor make any comments about the *why* of this assignment? These may dictate a special approach. A teacher may suggest, "This book offers a point of view about the role of large corporations quite different from that in your textbook." Then you'll want to approach your reading with the question, "Just what *is* this different viewpoint?" Make the most of any suggestions from your instructor.

While your teacher's comments may suggest a special emphasis and way of approach, some or all of the following general suggestions should prove useful.

Preview the book

Provide yourself, first of all, with a "map" of the book. Through the preface, you can often discover the author's viewpoint. Through the table of contents, you have at a glance a concise listing of the major topics.

Skim the opening chapter. Sometimes this chapter takes the form of an introduction—a look ahead at what is coming in the book. Here the authors may tell you what they're going to tell you.

Skim the concluding chapter. This is sometimes a summary chapter—a look back. Here the authors may tell you what they've told you. The final

---

* In preparing this explanation, the writers have leaned on the insights of Francis P. Robinson, *Effective Study*, 3rd ed., pp. 39–40.

chapter is often highly concentrated. It's the writers' *last opportunity* with you, the audience. So here they often wrap up the big ideas, drive home the points and conclusions they want most of all to leave with you.

Go *in with a question*

This time, you've been assigned an entire book as supplementary reading. You're probably not expected to read for minor details but for major points or "chapter points." Your teacher may have alerted you to important content to look for.

Converting *chapter titles* into questions may be an effective technique for guiding you to broad "chapter points." So will shifting into questions the conspicuous headings of *big* chapter divisions.

In Harry A. Overstreet's *The Mature Mind*, the first section of the book is headed "The Maturity Concept," and within that section the first chapter has the title "Psychological Foundations." A broad question with which to approach that chapter quickly comes to mind: "*What are* the psychological foundations of the maturity concept?" Chapter 2 is headed "Criteria of Maturity." Shift that into a question, "*What are* the criteria or standards for measuring maturity?" Chapter 3 is entitled "Two Old Theories and a New One." Convert that title into the question, "What are two old theories about maturity and what is the new theory?" Questions like these will guide you to the big ideas of chapters.

You'll probably want to jot down your questions as an aid in keeping them in mind.

Read and reflect

Working through the book one chapter at a time, you'll approach your reading with a broad "chapter question," "chapter division questions," or questions your teacher or the class has posed. Since you're reading just for major points, you can build up more speed on this type of reading.

You may want to give *certain spots within the chapter* your special attention. Beginnings and endings are often strategic spots within expository chapters. The introductory and concluding paragraphs are likely to give you an idea of the general chapter content. The beginnings of paragraphs frequently carry a heavy load of meaning. You'll often find topic sentences located here.

As always, reading and reflecting should be intermingled as you wonder about something—ask *why*—weigh a statement—argue with the author—and apply what you're reading to the world outside the classroom.

You'll probably want to make some quick notes on the answers to your questions.

Recite

In your in-depth reading of your textbook, you took small "bites"—perhaps you worked with a headed section, a fairly short section marked off with a boldface or italic side heading. Since you're now reading just for main ideas, you can probably take larger bites. The ends of chapters or of *long* chapter divisions are usually good places to stop for evaluation.*

Look away from the book or cover your notes while you try to recall the answers to your broad questions. Reread, if you need to, to call something back to mind.

Review

You've just worked through the book chapter by chapter. You may now need to call back to mind the book's total plan or broad view.

Turn through your notes, checking to see if you can answer each question with your notes covered. A run-through of the book as a whole should "firm up" your learning.

SUMMING UP

1. Consider *why* you're reading.

2. Preview the book.

3. Approach with *broad* questions.

4. Read for major points.

5. Recite.

6. Review.

---

* Robinson, *Effective Study*, 3rd ed., p. 40.

QUESTIONS CAN DEVELOP
COMPREHENSION

Using the regular course materials, every teacher can turn on comprehension power through the everyday classroom activity of asking questions.

Just what is comprehension? According to Nila Banton Smith (1963, p. 257), "Comprehension is a big, blanket term that covers a whole area of thought-getting processes in reading."

We help students grow in comprehension when we set purposes and create the right mental set for the reading task at hand and when we elicit their thoughtful reaction to the passage. The questions we ask from day to day in subject classrooms can accomplish all three of these objectives: purposes, mental set, and thoughtful reaction.

Since we can help develop comprehension more effectively if we have some idea of what it embraces, some of the thought-getting processes that seem to be involved in comprehension are listed below:*

1. Grasping directly stated details or facts.

2. Understanding main ideas.

3. Grasping the sequence of time, place, ideas, events, or steps.

4. Understanding and following directions.

5. Grasping implied meanings and drawing inferences.

6. Understanding character (emotional reactions, motives, personal traits) and setting.

---

* The writers have based this list of processes (with the exception of the added area of evaluation) on Helen K. Smith's enumeration of comprehension skills in Chapter 4, "Sequence in Comprehension" in *Sequential Development of Reading Abilities*, edited by Helen M. Robinson (Chicago: University of Chicago Press, 1960), pp. 51ff. Other investigators who have explored the mental processes involved in comprehension have come up with somewhat different lists. For other analyses the reader may wish to consult Frederick B. Davis "Research in Comprehension in Reading," in *Reading Research Quarterly*, 3, no. 4 (1968): 499–545; and Richard Rystrom "Toward Defining Comprehension: A Second Report," in *Journal of Reading Behavior*, 2, no. 2 (1970). Sanders's classification of classroom questions (based on Benjamin S. Bloom's categories of thinking) and his rich offering of clarifying examples is of related interest (Morris M. Sanders, *Classroom Questions: What Kinds?* New York: Harper and Row, 1966). Some researchers see comprehension not as composed of discrete skills but as a rather unitary reasoning process. You will find this view expressed in Robert L. Thorndike, "Reading as Reasoning," in *Reading Research Quarterly* 9, no. 2 (1973–1974): 135–147.

7. Sensing relationships of time, place, cause and effect, events, and characters.

8. Anticipating outcomes.

9. Recognizing the author's tone, mood, and intent.

10. Understanding and drawing comparisons and contrasts.

11. Drawing conclusions or making generalizations.

12. Making evaluations.

One of the authors confesses that during her years as an English teacher she regarded reading comprehension as esoteric—an indefinable something beyond her powers to teach and requiring the training and experience of a reading specialist. She was not aware that she was already building comprehension in many ways from day to day in her classroom—and that she could do infinitely more. Classroom teachers who examine Smith's enumeration and the classifications of other investigators should appreciate more fully what they are already doing to achieve better comprehension. And they may respond, "But we can do more!" as the enumeration calls to mind specific needs they have observed in their students. They can then plot a strategy to add to their students' working stock of competencies and they will be sensitive to constant opportunities.

How can a classroom teacher encourage the development of comprehension essential for reading competence in a subject? This can be done daily, using the regular course materials, formulating questions intended to elicit the use of thought processes—questions probing for information that won't yield itself without use of the desired response. Upon observing a deficiency in one of the aspects of comprehension an instructor can deliberately plan a question strategy to force the practice of the desired response. At times the questions can be supplied as guides for students in advance of their reading. At other times questions can be raised in the course of class discussions.

Students Need All the Competencies

To grow toward maturity in reading, students need wide experience in using the full spectrum of comprehension processes. All too often, however, there is overemphasis in classrooms on the memory aspects—on just-plain-fact questions. When Helen K. Smith (1965, p. 14) analyzed the questions asked by instructors on tests and examinations, she discovered a preponderance of questions requiring no more than factual information. She reported, further, that the questions teachers asked when assigning reading and making out examinations were strong determiners of the manner in which their students read. If we are content, she observed, that students read merely to remember a body of factual information, then we will concentrate on factual questions: "Ask for details—get back details." If, on the other hand, we are committed to helping them handle ideas, cope with relationships, make critical evaluations, then we must compose our questions carefully with these higher purposes in mind (H. Smith, 1960).

The comprehension processes enumerated above are in a sense a hierarchy, advancing as they do from tasks that involve reading for literal meanings (tasks 1–4 on the list are often literal), in which students read what is actually printed in the lines, to beyond-the-literal responses (tasks 5–12), in which they read "between and beyond the lines." Most higher-level thinking rests solidly upon a basis of factual information. As instructors plan guiding questions to accompany assigned reading, they may want to devise questions to help students pull out the underlying facts. With these at their command, students should then be better prepared to proceed to depth questions—ones that require them to grasp implications, draw conclusions, make generalizations, arrive at evaluations. Before students can respond to the penetrating question, "What purely personal motives of Pericles can you infer from what he said in the Funeral Oration?" clearly they must have on call considerable factual information about Pericles and must have grasped the literal content of the Funeral Oration.

Sanders (1966, p. 21) viewed facts in this perspective: "For the most part, facts should serve as a means to an end rather than as ends in themselves. When a teacher approaches a new unit, he should ask himself: 'What are the most important generalizations that deserve to be emphasized? What facts are necessary to develop these generalizations?' "

While well-formulated questions encourage both breadth and depth of comprehension, *skillful questioning alone is clearly not enough.* Comprehension is "taught not caught." If students are having difficulty coping with implications, conclusions, and generalizations, instruction and class discussion can focus here. Guided open-book practice in which students analyze how to arrive at the answer to a question is a highly rewarding practice. "Let's turn to the passage and . . ." can be a frequent suggestion of teachers (Kenworthy, 1966, p. 104).

The rest of this section of the chapter consists of examples of questions classified according to the thought-getting process they foster and is intended to encourage the development of comprehension in various disciplines. Each question attempts to throw a searchlight on one aspect of comprehension. You will undoubtedly find these examples suggestive, will improve on some, and will generate a host of your own in keeping with the needs of students and the materials they are reading. Many of the questions are not purely one type or another—there will be much overlap. Questions classified under one discipline may prove suggestive for another.

Questions Encouraging Specific Comprehension Processes

Grasping Directly Stated Details or Facts

All reading subjects

After introductory work with paragraphs, students practice with paragraphs in which the main idea sentence has various locations in the paragraph and is supported by clear-cut details. They are directed: Mark the sentence that gives the main idea, and number the details that support it.

Possibilities for introductory work with paragraphs will be found in "Finding the Key Thought" later in this chapter. Highly practical ideas for working with the main idea and details of paragraphs are offered in Joseph C. Gainsburg, *Advanced Skills in Reading*, Books 1, 2, and 3, teacher's annotated edition (New York: Macmillan Company, 1967).

Students might analyze paragraphs with the aid of simple diagrams in keeping with the structure of each paragraph. They might be asked to record the

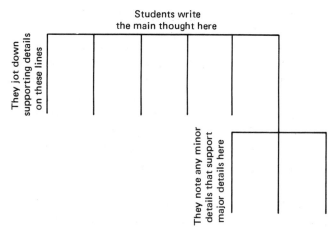

Figure 3–7.　*(Adapted from Ruth Strang, in lecture to class in methods of teaching secondary school reading, University of Chicago, Summer 1965.)*

main idea and the details of appropriate paragraphs on a framework like that in Figure 3–7.

In paragraphs in which the main idea is expressed at the beginning, students are asked to anticipate what lies ahead in the rest of the paragraph. They discover that the main idea sentence often provides a strong clue about what is to follow: supporting details, a clarifying example or two, an explanation or reasons, details of a comparison or contrast, a series of steps in time order, the steps in a process. They experience being able to grasp the details with less effort once they foresee the trend of the paragraph.

They are asked, for example, to predict the contents of a paragraph starting with the topic sentence: "The Gregorian calendar is now used in almost every civilized country because of its great accuracy." From the moment they read the topic sentence with the phrase "because of its great accuracy," their minds are set to expect the reason or explanation for this great accuracy. They now know what to look for. Consequently they read the paragraph with greater understanding (Gainsburg, 1967, p. 232).

English

We've already observed that Holden Caulfield has difficulty communicating. Can you find more evidence for this in the chapter? (Ravin, 1975.)

What details create a mood of melancholy in the opening paragraphs of "The Fall of the House of Usher?"

Would you like (a character in the story) for your friend? What has the author done or had the character do to make you like or dislike him? (Adapted from Strang et al., 1961, p. 135.)

Illustrate this scene from the story. First, make quick jottings of details that the author has used to help you "see" the scene.

Social studies

Read this account of the life of John F. Kennedy. Notice how new paragraphs introduce new events in his life or important aspects of it. Make brief notes (just a word or two) that give the gist of the event or, if you own the book, jot a word or two in the margin.

Science

What conditions are probably necessary for a tornado to form?

What are catalysts? What are their unusual properties? (Biological Sciences Curriculum Study, 1968, p. 145.)

Can you find in this passage evidence that supports the author's statement that some present-day land areas were once covered by the ocean?

Mathematics

In the initial reading of a word problem, students should read to size up the problem situation and ask, "What am I to find here?" The next step involves grasping directly stated details: "What facts are given? What information is already supplied me in the problem?"

Art

Draw this character just as she is portrayed in this story. First, jot down the details the author uses to help you "see" her.

Understanding the Main Idea

All reading subjects

After introductory work, students are asked, "Can you find the main idea of this passage? Look for the point the paragraph makes; the broadest, most significant message of the author; the idea the author wants most of all to drive home and leave with you."

After being introduced to the paragraph patterns below (and others), students, upon meeting these types in expository materials, might be asked, "What pattern that we have studied does this paragraph follow?"

1. A paragraph whose main idea is supported—or is proved to be true —by the details.

2. A paragraph whose main idea is explained or made clear by the details or by an illustrative example.

3. A paragraph in which the author leads you through a process of reasoning until you arrive at a conclusion that logically follows. In a paragraph of this type, the last sentence is often the general conclusion toward which a series of details, a line of argument, or a chain of reasoning has led.

English

Read to find out why this selection has the title "The Most Dangerous Game?"

What is a good title for this section? Be sure your title is a good wrap-up of what the passage contains and is broad enough to cover its content.

Write a telegram of ten words or less conveying the broadest, most significant information in this paragraph.

Science

Read the procedures you will follow in this laboratory experiment. Give the purpose of the experiment in a sentence or two.

Mathematics

Students' initial readings of a word problem, before they pull out the data and plan their attack, involve grasping the main idea. Students can be directed: "First, read the problem thoroughly, asking, 'What is this all about?' Size up the problem situation. Read it again, if necessary, asking, 'What am I to find here?' "

Art

An art history class studying twentieth century art, including Marc Chagall's efforts to reinterpret Jewish and Hebrew folklore in terms of the twentieth century, had this assignment: "Within the next week, will all of you examine this book about Chagall and sum up in one sentence what he is trying to do." (Erickson, 1971.)

Grasping the Sequence of Ideas, Events, or Steps

English

Briefly describe the Emperor Jones at the beginning of the story. Then describe him toward the close. List in order the people, things, and events that caused the character to change during the story. (Strang et al., 1961, p. 135.)

This sequence of steps from the passage is scrambled. Unscramble it by placing the steps in correct order.

Social studies

How does a bill introduced in Congress become a law?

Read this selection about the territorial growth of the United States. Note the important events in order, associating them with their dates, and thinking how each event led to the next one.

Science

Trace an "excited electron" from the chlorophyll molecule in photosynthesis until it is added to oxygen during respiration. (Biological Sciences Curriculum Study, 1968, p. 211.)

Jot down brief notes (a word or two) that call to mind each step in the life cycle of the gypsy moth or jot in the margin a word or two that sums up each step. Then look away and try to recall the steps. Are your steps in order?

What changes take place in the fatty nutrients of a hamburger as they travel through your digestive tract?

Study the process of refining petroleum through use of a fractionating tower. Shift your attention to the diagram whenever you are referred there. After reading a sentence explaining a step in the process, look at the diagram and try to picture the step as taking place. Continue to read, referring to the diagram after reading each step. Finally, try to express all the steps in your own words without looking at the diagram. (Adapted from N. Smith, 5, 1960, p. 101.)

Mathematics

Read through this explanation of the derivation of a formula. See whether you can follow the reasoning that leads to its final form (Strang et al., 1961, p. 165.)

Understanding and Following Directions

Science

What procedure do you follow to focus your microscope on an object?

Mathematics

Study this explanation for finding the square root. Make brief jottings in your own words of the steps you'll take in reaching the solution. Then work a problem, carrying out this process step by step.

Photography

Study these directions on the can for mixing a gallon of developer. They must be followed 100 percent in order for you to have a usable product. To be sure you understand, write out in your own words a list of things to be done. Before mixing the developer, check your list with the teacher. (Erickson, 1971.)

Crafts

You'll soon be doing soldering. To be sure you understand, jot down the steps in the process in your own words. The order in which you carry out the steps is crucial. Are your steps in the correct order?

Grasping Implied Meanings or Drawing Inferences

English

Young Gareth took certain vows when he became a knight. What were these vows, and what do they reveal to you about the values of his day?

What truth about the inner lives of all of us does Hawthorne suggest in "The Minister's Black Veil"?

Social studies

What can you learn about the customs, values, and ideals of the Athenians from Pericles' Funeral Oration? (Surgal, 1971.)

What purely personal motives of Pericles can you infer from what he said in the Funeral Oration? (Surgal, 1971.)

Science

From the characteristics of the bill of this bird, what do you infer about its eating habits?

Mathematics

In a student's initial readings of a word problem, she or he should size up the problem situation and ask, "What am I to find here?" and "What facts are already given?" The next step involves an inference: "Read the problem through once more, asking, 'What processes will I use?' and/or 'What formulas will I need?' "

Understanding Character (Emotional Reactions, Motives, Personal Traits) and Setting

English

What motive do you think prompted George's action toward Lennie? Imagine what your reactions would be if you were in his situation.

Often fiction writers tell you without telling you. Instead of revealing outright a character's innermost emotions, they challenge you to use your imagination. An author provides hints through the character's actions, conversation, and the details of appearance. Can you find in this passage a subtle revelation of the rookie catcher's true feelings toward the coach?

Often in a story we know full well what type of person a character is although the authors never once mentioned a personal trait. Instead they revealed traits *indirectly* through the character's words and actions and through the reactions of others toward the character. How much can you discover about Jerry's character in this passage from "A Mother in Manville"?

Sometimes authors, in the opening of a story, tell you outright where and when the action will occur. Other times they provide subtle clues, and you must *infer* the setting. In this story can you find such clues and identify the setting?

Imagine yourself in Brutus' place when he heard Caesar say, "And you, too, Brutus!" How do you think he felt?

Sensing Relationships of Time, Place, Cause and Effect, Events, and Characters

Social studies

You are living in the days of the Crusaders. Why will you go on a Crusade if you are (1) a parish priest, (2) a knight, (3) a scholar, (4) a king? (Surgal, 1971.)

What are some of the causes or explanations of the wide

variations in the distribution of income and wealth in the United States? What evils result from the disparities in income distribution? (Association of Teachers of Social Studies, 1967, p. 153.)

History is the record of a chain of causes and effects. Read the passage to answer this question: "What causes led to the purchase of the Louisiana Territory, and how did it in turn become a cause with its own effects on our national growth?" (Adapted from N. Smith, 5, 1960, p. 66.)

You'll be reading about the Northwest Ordinance of 1787. Many people consider 1787 one of the half-dozen most important dates in the entire course of American history. Why is it so important? (Kenworthy, 1966, p. 96.)

If you were living in Philadelphia in 1800, why might you want to move west? (Kenworthy, 1966, p. 98.)

Does political patronage cause bad government, or does bad government produce political patronage? (Wesley and Wronski, 1964, p. 356.)

Science

If you drop a needle carefully upon the surface of water, it will float. Can you explain why?

The sun can still be seen after it is really below the horizon. Why?

What will happen to the water line of a boat when it moves from salt water into fresh water? Why does this happen? (Jacobson et al., 1964, p. 317.)

What were two important consequences of the formation of the atmospheric ozone layer? (Biological Sciences Curriculum Study, 1968, p. 199.)

Anticipating Outcomes

English

After the murder of Duncan, who will stand the strain of guilt better—Macbeth or Lady Macbeth?

You know this character—his disposition, his feelings, and his motives. What action do you anticipate? (Strang et al., p. 138.)

Authors often plant clues that lead the "sharp" reader to anticipate coming events. At the tournament, what foreshadows a romance between Ivanhoe and Rowena?

Read up to the last chapter of the book. Then stop and try to predict the outcome.

Social studies

What changes is automation likely to bring in *your* life during the next quarter of a century?

Science

What do you think we will use for energy when coal and oil are exhausted? (Jacobson et al., 1964, p. 54.)

You know about this theory. What can we expect in a certain situation on the basis of it?

Mathematics

Estimate the answer to this word problem. Ask yourself, "What would a reasonable answer be?" Make a good guess based on thoughtful consideration of the data.

When the proof of a theorem is on the page before you, complete with every step, try to resist the temptation to be a mere spectator. Use two index cards to conceal the proof supplied you by the authors. Cover the Statements with one card and the Reasons with the other. Read the statement of the theorem, examine the diagram, and search out what you're to prove and what's already given. With the first Statement concealed, ask yourself, "What will the author's first statement be?" Formulate your considered guess. Then lift your card and see if you predicted correctly. Next ask yourself, "What will the authors give as a reason?" Formulate your answer. Lift your card and check. Continue through the sequence of Statements and Reasons, lowering your card step by step. (Moulton, 1968.)

Recognizing the Author's Tone, Mood, and Intent

All reading subjects

It is well to ask, "What is the writer's purpose? Does he or she have a hidden motive? Does the writer want to win your support in behalf of some policy or practice? Will your uncritical acceptance of his or her point of view result in financial gain?" What might be the intent of the following writers: (1) the president of the National Association of Manufacturers writing about a proposed law to curb the activity of labor unions in politics; (2) the president of the United Auto Workers writing about the same subject. (Altick, 1956, p. 181.)

Read these two newspaper accounts that give sharply contrasting viewpoints of the same event. What is each writer's intent? Can you find emotionally charged words used by each to sway you to a viewpoint? Underline these words.

Are the writers unbiased reporters or do their own personal beliefs show through in this selection? If so, how? Are they trying to influence you to accept their viewpoint?

English

Sometimes writers say one thing, but the meaning they intend to convey is exactly the opposite. The ordinary meaning of the words they use are the opposite of the thought in mind. This writer is using *irony*. Can you find an example in the passage?

Zero in on opening sentences. Here the author often plants clues from which you can infer, through reading just a few sentences, the mood of the story. Will the mood of this story be (1) lighthearted, (2) humorous, (3) serious, (4) foreboding? What clues reveal this?

Understanding and Drawing Comparisons and Contrasts

English

Who would be a better husband—King Arthur or Sir Lancelot? Why?

Who would be a better wife—Guinevere or Elaine? Why?

Social studies

In what ways does Soviet communism follow and in what ways does it depart from the plan for an ideal communist society described by Karl Marx? (Sanders, 1966, p. 54.)

Where would you have preferred to live in ancient Greece—in Athens or in Sparta? (Association of Teachers of Social Studies, 1967, p. 58.)

Science

Compare the telephone transmitter to the human ear, listing the similarities. (Jacobson et al., 1964, p. 361.)

Compare the earth and the moon as an ideal base for astronomical observations.

What is the difference between a "young" river and an "old" river in terms of erosion features? (N. Smith, 4, 1963, p. 93.)

Drawing Conclusions; Making Generalizations

All reading subjects

This sample question from social studies is easily adaptable to other subjects: A teacher (Sanders, 1966, p. 15) supplied three examples of conflict of interest in passages to be studied by the class. He explained that the meaning of the concept could be determined from the three examples of the operation of the concept which he presented. After giving some time for studying the examples and composing the definitions, the teacher asked that some of them be read to the class. The one chosen by the class as the best was assigned to be remembered. The assignment for the following day was to find in the newspapers examples of the operation of conflict of interest or to make up plausible examples.

Students might examine a well-founded conclusion drawn by the writer, then search out the facts given in the passage to consider whether they warrant this conclusion. They might also examine a false conclusion and decide whether the data in the passage support it.

Social studies

Why is our city located here rather than forty miles north or south? Who decides where to put a city? The class might study the early location of various cities, then generalize in answer to the question, "What determines the location of cities?" (Flickinger, 1970.)

Does your reading support the generalization that the world's advanced civilizations have not developed in the tropics?

Have certain conditions in recent history led to the rise of dictators? If so, what do they appear to be?

Science

What general rule can you make concerning the effect of heat upon molecules?

What conclusion can you draw from the report of this experiment?

Making Evaluations

All reading subjects

After reading several descriptions of an event that is subject to controversy, such as a race riot, the teacher might ask, "Which report of this incident is most reliable?" Before the students undertake to answer such a question, they should set up standards for judging whether an observation statement is reliable. (Sanders, 1966, p. 25.)

English

Is Thoreau relevant? Do his thoughts about how to live ring true to you today?

Social studies

Would you favor having your political party engage in gerrymandering if it had the opportunity? Support your view. (Sanders, 1966, p. 5.)

Were the great industrial figures of the late nineteenth century robber barons or industrial statesmen? (Bailey, 1961, p. 106.)

What are some important differences between education in the Soviet Union and education in the United States? Are there some features which you think the United States should adopt in its system of public education? If so, what are they? Are there some features which, in your opinion, should not be incorporated? Explain.

Science

Should we try to engineer man's heredity? If so, what kinds of people should we be engineering for? Should we be meddling at all?

FINDING THE KEY THOUGHT

An example of teaching procedures in helping students learn to work with a cluster of thought-getting processes.

As we have indicated, the art of questioning is a powerful tool in helping to develop comprehension. In addition, the instructor should be aware of specific teaching strategies for specific comprehension processes. Too often we appear to follow the course of practice makes perfect: if a student can't recognize the main idea or key thought, provide more exercises until the ability is mastered. For many students, such a procedure only succeeds in causing further frustration and failure. We need to analyze an important aspect of comprehension and attempt to delineate the thought-getting processes needed to accomplish that type of comprehension. This section of the comprehension chapter attempts to do just that with one major comprehension aspect, key thought or main idea.

Finding or grasping the main idea or key thought is *not* essential for all types of reading or for all purposes. Sometimes we overgeneralize and overemphasize its significance. For example, if we need to read to bake some cookies, there is no reason to search out a main idea—it already exists in the mind of the reader; here, specific details in appropriate sequence with emphasis on how-to-do-it is the goal.

On the other hand, finding the key thought is often important, and many students from grade 7 through graduate school are sometimes unsure of themselves in this area. The following material is but slightly adapted from H. Alan Robinson's original material (1961).

The concept of a cluster of skills grew out of the belief that students should not be asked to find the main idea before getting a great deal of practice in learning how to read for details. The ability to recognize and formulate main ideas calls for a decided degree of reading and thinking maturity. In the final analysis, in order to deal with main ideas or key thoughts, a student must be able to recognize important or key words in sentences, understand basic organizational patterns of written material, draw conclusions, and make inferences.

Step One: Key Words in a Sentence

The technique of sending a telegram (Hovious, 1938, p. 163) is used to establish the concept of key words as the most important words. Students quickly observe that "Arrival Kennedy nine Wednesday evening" is a statement of the most important words in the sentence, "I shall arrive at John F. Kennedy International Airport in New York at nine o'clock on Wednesday evening." (Dependent upon background experience, some students may need to include *Airport* and/or *New York* as key words.)

Students should soon move from telegrams to looking at sentences taken from conversation. A typical sentence might be, "Please be very careful that you do not damage the brand new desks." When asked to underline the key words, most students will underline "do not damage" or "not damage" "brand new desks." Once proficiency is established at this level, and students are beginning to realize that they are finding the main ideas of sentences, much more practice should be initiated using sentences from content area materials. Some students who find it difficult to let go of details may need the individual attention of the instructor for a while. Other students might be given more complex sentences to figure out. During this step, however, all sentences should be isolated and should not be presented as parts of paragraphs.

Step Two: Key Sentence in a Paragraph

In this step students first learn to be concerned with fewer key words when sentences are treated together in a paragraph unit. They learn this through the experience of underlining key words in the sentences of short paragraphs. For example:

> A school performs many services for the residents of a community. It offers instructional services for school-age children during the day and, often, courses for adults in the evening. It provides a meeting place for community organizations. It also serves as an active cultural center, as plays, concerts, and lectures are often scheduled.

In this paragraph the sentences are so closely linked that it is unnecessary to keep repeating the subject when searching for key words in each sentence. The pronoun *it* replaces the subject *a school*. Most students soon realize that they are primarily concerned with verbs and their objects once the subject is established.

The paragraphs presented in this step, at this point in time, should be well structured, containing definite key sentences mainly as first or last sentences. One or two of the paragraphs may contain key sentences placed in other parts of the paragraph.

Students are asked to list the key ideas (groups of key words) they have found in the paragraph. For example, this list might have been written about the paragraph on school services:

school performs many services

offers instructional services

provides meeting place

serves as cultural center

Students learn to add up the key ideas and decide whether or not one of them represents an overall idea. In the paragraph above, it happens to be contained in the first sentence. Here the overall or main idea is contained in a key sentence at the beginning.

Here is another example. The task is a little more difficult because some of the sentences in the paragraph contain two key ideas. Students learn to treat these ideas as separate units in their search for the key sentence:

> Everyone saluted as the flag was slowly raised. A smartly dressed woman cracked a champagne bottle across the ship's prow and named it *Sea Hawk*. The order was given, and the *Sea Hawk* started down the ways. A new ship was launched.

Everyone saluted + flag raised + woman cracked bottle across ship's prow + named it + order given + started down ways = new ship launched. Obviously, the key sentence is the last sentence in the paragraph. Key idea + key idea + key idea = the overall or main idea contained in the key sentence.

Look at this example:

> Animals have interesting habits. One of the habits of some animals is to use nature's medicines when they are ill. Deer may eat twigs and the very tender bark of trees. Cats and dogs may eat grass when they are not feeling up to par. Bears often eat different kinds of roots and berries.

Deer eat twigs and tender bark + cats and dogs eat grass + bears eat roots and berries = some animals use nature's medicine when ill. The first sentence in the paragraph serves only an introductory purpose. It may be introducing a series of paragraphs that will deal with interesting habits of animals. It is not, of course, the main idea of this particular paragraph. Hence in this case the key sentence is the second sentence in the paragraph. Some students need much assistance with this kind of directed teaching-practice to establish the fact that it is not necessarily just the broadest statement in a paragraph which expresses the main idea (when one is present), but *the broadest, most significant* statement, very often a conclusion that the other key ideas support.

Step Three: Main Thought in a Paragraph

After students have completed a great deal of successful guided practice in working with paragraphs containing key sentences in a variety of positions, they should be ready for this next step. At this time they can be presented with a paragraph like the one below:

> We visited the seals frolicking in the water. Then we paid a visit to the colorful birds in the big new birdhouse. After that we stopped for a Coke and hot dog. Before going home we spent a lot of time watching the funny monkeys.

The students are again asked to find key ideas. Visited seals + paid visits to birds + stopped for Coke and hot dog + spent time watching monkeys = ? At this point numerous students will point out that there is no *stated* overall idea.

Students must now make inferences, for the author does not state the key thought in a sentence of the paragraph. The student must look at all key ideas and determine the main idea of the paragraph. In this easy paragraph most students, of course, will agree that the key thought is "we visited the zoo" or something similar. Further paragraphs should present more difficult material and should be intermingled with paragraphs that contain key sentences. The most important part of this step is having the student decide whether the main idea is or is not stated by the author. We don't believe students ever learn to make inferences well through deductive teaching techniques. They must be placed in the position of successful induction.

When students have mastered the basic ideas in this three-step cluster of skills using carefully structured materials, normal textbook material should provide application and reinforcement. Students soon become aware of the fact that paragraphs that are parts of chapters in books don't always stand by themselves. One main or key thought may be carried through a number of paragraphs without repetition in each paragraph. Often students will decide on the key thought by noting part of a main idea stated by the author and adding to it through their own reasoning. For instance:

> It is not only radio that has given them a great deal of help. Ballistics experts can tell whether or not a bullet was fired from a particular gun by examining the bullet under a microscope. Chemists help solve crimes by analyzing blood, dust,

cloth, and other materials. Photographers, also, are used in
helping police solve crimes. Often photographs, especially
when enlarged, reveal clues that the human eye overlooked.

Obviously, in the paragraph above, the key thought is something like "various
people and things help police solve crimes." Clues can be found in the paragraph, but the reader can also arrive at the key thought through reasoning and
the context that preceded this paragraph. Certainly a preceding paragraph, or
several, dealt with radio as it helps police solve crimes.

The following worksheet is an example of the kind of teaching-practice
material that can be developed for working with the "key thought cluster."
This worksheet was prepared for students who could proceed quickly through
the concepts and for whom this lesson was by way of review and evaluation.
It contains examples of the three steps in the key thought cluster. Instructors
can develop a variety of worksheets—those just with examples of sentences in
which to find key words for step one, those just containing paragraphs where
the key sentence is at the beginning of the paragraph, worksheets with the
gamut of paragraph structures.

Most important of all, certainly as each new step is begun, is to provide a
series of experiences that will make learning *successful*. The challenge of more
difficult material is of tremendous significance *after* students feel they have mastered the basic tools and can use them to explore ideas.

WORKSHEET: Finding the Key Thought

NAME _____

CLASS PERIOD _____ DATE _____

SENTENCES

1. Please be very careful that you do not damage the brand new desks.

2. Bob Johnson and Ann Magee were candidates for President of the Student Council.

3. If I were you, I should report to the office not later than 10:00 this morning.

4. The prize fight took place in Madison Square Garden on Wednesday, September 10.

5. The hurricane destroyed many of the farms and crops, such as wheat, corn, and rye.

PARAGRAPHS

A. A school performs many services for the residents of a community. It offers instructional services for school-age children during the day and, often, courses for adults in the evening. It provides a meeting place for community organizations. It also serves as an active cultural center, as plays, concerts, and lectures are often scheduled.

B. Everyone saluted as the flag was slowly raised. A smartly dressed woman cracked a champagne bottle across the ship's prow and named it *Sea Hawk*. The order was given, and the *Sea Hawk* started down the ways. A new ship was launched.

C. Animals have interesting habits. One of the habits of some animals is to use nature's medicines when they are ill. Deer may eat twigs and the very tender bark of trees. Cats and dogs may eat grass when they are not feeling up to par. Bears often eat different kinds of roots and berries.

D. We visited the seals frolicking in the water. Then we paid a visit to the colorful birds in the big new birdhouse. After that we stopped for a Coke and hot dog. Before going home we spent a lot of time watching the funny monkeys.

Bibliography

Association of Teachers of Social Studies of the City of New York. "The Art of Questioning." Chapter 3 in *Handbook for Social Studies Teaching*. New York: Holt, Rinehart and Winston, 1967.

Davis, Frederick B. "Research in Comprehension in Reading." *Reading Research Quarterly*, 3, no. 4 (1968): 499–545.

Dudycha, George J. *Learn More with Less Effort*. New York: Harper and Row, 1957.

Herber, Harold L. *Teaching Reading in Content Areas*. Englewood Cliffs, N.J.: Prentice-Hall, 1970.

Herber, Harold L., and Joan B. Nelson. "Questioning Is Not the Answer." *Journal of Reading*, 18, no. 7 (1975): 512–517.

Herber, Harold L., and P. L. Sanders, eds. *Research in Reading in the Content Areas: First Year Report*. Syracuse: Reading and Language Arts Center, 1969.

Kalish, Richard. *Making the Most of College*. Belmont, Calif.: Wadsworth Publishing Company, 1959.

Lewenstein, Morris R. *Teaching Social Studies in Junior and Senior High Schools*. Chicago: Rand McNally and Company, 1963.

Pauk, Walter. *How to Study in College*, 2nd ed. Boston: Houghton Mifflin Company, 1974.

Rivlin, Harry N. "Using the Question as an Aid to Learning." Chapter 7 in *Teaching Adolescents in Secondary Schools*, 2nd ed. New York: Appleton-Century-Crofts, 1961.

Robinson, Francis P. *Effective Study*, 4th ed. New York: Harper and Row, 1970.

Robinson, H. Alan. *Teaching Reading and Study Strategies: The Content Areas*. Boston: Allyn and Bacon, 1975.

Rothkopf, E. Z. "Learning from Written Instructive Materials: An Exploration of the Control of Inspection Behavior by Test-Like Events." *American Educational Research Journal*, 3, no. 4 (1966): 241–249.

Rystrom, Richard. "Toward Defining Comprehension: A Second Report." *Journal of Reading Behavior*, 2, no. 2 (1970): 144–157.

Shepherd, David L. *Comprehensive High School Reading Methods*. Columbus: Charles E. Merrill Publishing Company, 1973, chapter 4.

Staton, Thomas B. *How to Learn Faster and Better*. Montgomery, Ala.: Box 6133, 1968.

Thorndike, Robert L. " 'Reading as Reasoning.' " *Reading Research Quarterly*, 9, no. 2 (1973–1974): 135–147.

Weaver, Wendell W., and Albert J. Kingston. "Questioning in Content Reading." *Journal of Reading*, 2, no. 2 (1967): 140–143.

Weintraub, Samuel. "The Question as an Aid in Reading." *The Reading Teacher,* 22, no. 8 (1969): 751–755.

Wheat, Thomas E., and Rose M. Edmond. "The Concept of Comprehension: An Analysis." *Journal of Reading,* 18, no. 7 (1975): 523–527.

References

Air Masses and Weather Fronts. Understanding Weather and Climates filmstrip series. Chicago: Society for Visual Education, 1966.

Altick, Richard D. *Preface to Critical Reading.* New York: Holt, Rinehart and Winston, 1956.

Association of Teachers of Social Studies of the City of New York. *Handbook for Social Studies Teaching.* New York: Holt, Rinehart and Winston, 1967.

Bailey, Thomas A. *The American Pageant Quiz Book.* Boston: D. C. Heath and Company, 1961.

Bell, Earl, University of Chicago Laboratory School social studies teacher, in remarks to Ellen Thomas, April 1970.

Bernstein, Edgar, University of Chicago Laboratory School social studies teacher, in remarks to Ellen Thomas, August 1970.

Biological Sciences Curriculum Study. *Biological Science: Molecules to Man,* rev. ed. Boston: Houghton Mifflin Company, 1968.

Brasler, Wayne, University of Chicago Laboratory School journalism teacher, in remarks to Ellen Thomas, November 1971.

Colby, Lestina, former University of Chicago Laboratory School science teacher, in remarks to Ellen Thomas, October 1965.

Congreve, Willard J., former University of Chicago Laboratory High School principal, in remarks to Ellen Thomas, September 1965.

Danskin, D. G., and C. W. Burnett. "Study Techniques of Those Superior Students." *Personnel and Guidance Journal,* 31 (December 1952): 181–186.

Erickson, Robert, University of Chicago Laboratory School art teacher, in remarks to Ellen Thomas, May 1971.

Fallers, Margaret, and Joel Surgal, University of Chicago Laboratory School social studies teachers, in remarks to Ellen Thomas, April 1970.

Ferguson, Jerry, University of Chicago Laboratory School science teacher, in remarks to Ellen Thomas, September 1970.

Flickinger, Alice, University of Chicago Laboratory School social studies teacher, in remarks to Ellen Thomas, September, November 1970.

Gainsburg, Joseph C. *Advanced Reading Skills,* Book 2. New York: Macmillan Company, 1967.

Hillman, Margaret, former St. Petersburg High School Reading Clinic director, in remarks to Ellen Thomas, April 1971.

Holmes, Eleanor. "Reading Guided by Questions versus Careful Reading and Rereading without Questions." *School Review*, 39 (May 1931): 361–371.

Hovious, Carol. *Flying the Printways*. Boston: D. C. Heath and Company, 1938.

Howland, Hazel P., Lawrence L. Jarvie, and Leo F. Smith. *How to Read in Science and Technology*. New York: Harper and Brothers, 1943.

Jacobson, Willard J., Robert N. King, Louise E. Killie, and Richard D. Konicek. *Broadening Worlds of Science*. New York: American Book Company, 1964.

Kenworthy, Leonard S. *Guide to Social Studies Teaching in Secondary Schools*. Belmont, Calif.: Wadsworth Publishing Company, 1966.

LaPorte, Emma, former New Trier High School (Winnetka, Illinois) Spanish teacher, in remarks to Ellen Thomas, May 1970.

Marantz, Sylvia. "A Hot Issue for a Cool Librarian." In *Fusing Reading Skills and Content*, edited by H. Alan Robinson and Ellen Lamar Thomas. Newark, Del.: International Reading Association, 1969.

McClusky, H. Y. "An Experiment on the Influence of Preliminary Skimming on Reading." *Journal of Educational Psychology*, 25 (October 1934): 521–529.

Meyer, Emily, former University of Chicago Laboratory School English teacher, in remarks to Ellen Thomas, October 1964.

Moe, Iver L., and Frank Nania. "Reading Deficiencies among Able Pupils." *Journal of Developmental Reading*, 3 (Autumn 1959): 11–26.

Moulton, Paul, former University of Chicago Laboratory School mathematics teacher, in remarks to Ellen Thomas, May 1968.

Niles, Olive S. "Help Students Set a Purpose for Reading." *English High Lights*, 20 (April-May 1963): 2.

Parker, Carolyn. "Shakespeare in Swing Time" *Clearing House*, 13 (April 1939): 462–463.

Perry, William G., Jr. "Students' Use and Misuse of Reading Skills: A Report to a Faculty." *Harvard Educational Review*, 29 (Summer 1959): 193–200.

Podendorf, Illa, former University of Chicago Laboratory School science teacher, in remarks to Ellen Thomas, May 1970.

Preston, Ralph C., and Morton Botel. *How to Study*. Chicago: Science Research Associates, 1974.

Preston, Ralph C., and E. N. Tufts. "The Reading Habits of Superior College Students." *Journal of Experimental Education*, 16 (March 1948): 196–202.

Ravin, Sophie, University of Chicago Laboratory School English teacher, in remarks to Ellen Thomas, July 1975.

Rivlin, Harry N. *Teaching Adolescents in Secondary School*. New York: Appleton-Century-Crofts, 1948.

Robinson, Francis P. *Effective Study*, 3rd ed. New York: Harper and Row, 1961.

Robinson, H. Alan. "A Cluster of Skills: Especially for Junior High School." *The Reading Teacher*, 15 (September 1961): 25–28.

Sanders, Norris M. *Classroom Questions: What Kinds?* New York: Harper and Row, 1966.

Smith, Donald E. P., ed. *Learning to Learn*. New York: Harcourt, Brace and World, 1961.

Smith, Helen K., in lecture to class in methods of teaching secondary school reading, University of Chicago, 1960.

Smith, Helen K. "Responses for Good and Poor Readers When Asked to Read for Different Purposes." Doctoral dissertation abstract, University of Chicago, 1965.

Smith, Nila Banton. *Be a Better Reader*, Book 5. Englewood Cliffs, N.J.: Prentice-Hall, 1960.

Smith, Nila Banton. *Be a Better Reader*, 2nd ed., Book 4. Englewood Cliffs, N.J.: Prentice-Hall, 1963.

Smith, Nila Banton. *Reading Instruction for Today's Children*. Englewood Cliffs, N.J.: Prentice-Hall, 1963.

Smith, Richard, former University of Chicago Laboratory School biology teacher, in remarks to Ellen Thomas, January 1965.

Stordahl, K. E., and C. M. Christenson. "The Effect of Study Techniques on Comprehension and Retention." *Journal of Educational Research*, 49 (April 1956): 561–570.

Strang, Ruth, in lecture to class in the teaching of secondary school reading, University of Chicago, summer 1965.

Strang, Ruth, Constance M. McCullough and Arthur E. Traxler. *The Improvement of Reading*. New York: McGraw-Hill Book Company, 1961.

Surgal, Joel, University of Chicago Laboratory School social studies teacher, in remarks to Ellen Thomas, October 1970, May 1971.

Twisted Cross, The. NBC film. Champaign, Ill.: Visual Aids, University of Illinois, 1956.

Washburne, John N. "The Use of Questions in Social Science Material." *Journal of Educational Psychology*, 20 (May 1929): 321–329.

Wesley, Edgar B., and Stanley P. Wronski. *Teaching Social Studies in High Schools*. Boston: D. C. Heath and Company, 1964.

DEVELOPING FLEXIBILITY
IN READING RATE

This chapter presents a rationale concerning rates of reading together with practical insights for developing rate adjustment through the day-to-day work of classes. Procedures for getting at the real needs of students are followed by specific how-to-do-it suggestions for helping students acquire and use a full range of reading rates.

These are times when speed reading programs often appear to be promoted as panaceas for the ills of retarded readers, and when fantastic speeds are encouraged in inappropriate situations. Perhaps the rationale and suggestions presented here will help as support for school administrators and instructors who are under pressure to alter basically sound programs, and for parents and students who are selecting among a number of possible reading improvement programs.

We, therefore, again offer a set of questions followed by answers which we trust will provide some sound and practical solutions:

1. What is a sound rationale concerning rates of reading?

2. How can you acquire insights about student attainments and needs
    in rate adjustment?

3. What is an appropriate sequence for developing rate adjustment?

4. How do you drive home the concept of flexibility of rate of reading?

5. How can you help students acquire appropriate rates of reading?

6. How can you help students reach the goal of independence in adjustment?

Developing Flexibility in Reading Rate

Rationale

General Beliefs about Reading Rates

1. The efficient reader demonstrates flexibility, adjusting rate to the reading task at hand.

2. While speed in many situations is highly desirable, constant speed is not a characteristic of a highly skilled, purposeful reader.

3. It is desirable for each student to acquire reading rates along a continuum from slow and careful to very rapid reading, to develop techniques of scanning and skimming, and to learn to identify the situations for which each is appropriate.

4. As teachers work with the approaches suitable for reading about the causes of World War II, for following the steps in an experiment, for reading dense analytical passages in mathematics, or for understanding the universality of an essay by Emerson, they are building training in rate adjustment into the daily work of their classes.

5. Students need much guidance in using the appropriate approach—at first. They should move in the direction of independence as they learn to select the approach with less guidance from their instructors. The long-range goal is independence, with the students proficient in selecting for themselves the suitable approach.

6. It is possible and highly desirable to increase the speed of many students on certain types of reading matter and in certain situations.

7. Students whose habits are overly conscientious when the situation does not demand close reading should be encouraged and assisted to increase their reading rates appropriately.

8. Students within a single class may differ markedly in the speed attainable. Rate of thinking and, hence, rate of comprehension appear to be factors that influence the speed an individual may achieve (Buswell, 1951). Nothing is accomplished when students cover the pages faster than they can assimilate the

ideas. Personal tempo may play a role (Mitchell, 1953). Some students who are below average in rates of reading may already be reading well up to their capacities, even straining beyond. Some who are above average may be far below their potentials (DeBoer and Dallman, 1970, p. 240).

9. A number of students need help in acquiring a close, careful, reflective approach to reading. Teachers often observe that some students tend to read rapidly and superficially in inappropriate situations. Standardized test scores frequently confirm this observation. And, indeed, there is a danger in overemphasizing rapid reading with today's young people, who belong to the most propagandized generation in history. The maturing student reader must often "pierce to the basic truth or falseness of any piece of writing . . ." by reading it with searching questions—weighing authority, detecting weak links in a chain of reasoning (Altick, 1969, p. 313). The problems of today's bewildered and bewildering world call very often for deeply reflective reading.

10. Master teachers of literature deepen awareness of writing as a form of art. Despite the assertions of some speed reading businesses, we believe that encouraging students to read great works of literature at excessive speeds might be compared to training them to run through an art gallery and boast, "I ran past Van Gogh's *The Starry Night* in five seconds."

11. Many students who read slowly do so because they are blocked by deficiencies in basic skills. Inadequacies in word analysis may be the roadblock. Precision instruction by a patient instructor may be required to release this brake on flexibility of rate. Or when vocabulary is meager, reading may be an obstacle course. Students can hardly profit from covering a page rapidly if they do not know the meaning of the words. Instruction in skills of comprehension may be necessary before speed can be increased. Until students have the substructure of essential skills, pressuring them to build faster rates of reading may be futile and probably harmful.

12. When interfering factors are no longer present, increased flexibility in rates of reading often follows without special training. On the other hand, directed guidance through classroom instruction and practice is in order and often highly desirable.

Characteristics of the Ideal Graduate

The ideal product of the reading program evidences these understandings and abilities with respect to rates of reading:

1. The student has acquired the concept of rate adjustment.

2. The student has acquired reading rates along a continuum from

slow and careful to rapid reading and has developed techniques of scanning and skimming.

3. The student demonstrates the ability to identify the reading situation where each approach is appropriate.

4. The student has built rate adjustment into permanent habits, shifting in view of three considerations: difficulty of the material, the purpose at the moment, and familiarity with the subject matter.

Attainments and Needs in Rate Adjustment

Diagnostic insights are an important first step in helping students acquire and use a full range of reading rates. Sub-scores on rate from standardized survey tests offer useful insights. Observation, students' self-appraisals, and teacher-made tests are desirable supplements.

Standardized Tests

A great many schools have available the results of standardized reading tests. Many tests have rate-of-reading sections. Should such results not be available or should you wish to supplement the results with another standardized test, the test below should be helpful. It is easily administered and scored:

> *Cooperative Reading Test*; Cooperative Test Division, Educational Testing Service; Lower Level intended for grades 9–12; Upper Level intended for superior students in grades 11 and 12 and for college freshmen and sophomores; two forms:
>
> The Cooperative Reading Test offers sub-scores in vocabulary, level (power) of comprehension, and speed of comprehension. The score on level of comprehension is based on the number of answers correct. The score on speed of comprehension is a function of both the number correct and the number completed. The content of this test is primarily fairly difficult study material. The speed score gives you some indication of the speed with which the student can handle reading matter of this type.

Of course a low speed score combined with a high comprehension score suggests the need for the student to increase the rate of reading study-type material.

A high speed score combined with a low comprehension score suggests the need to adjust speed downward for closer, more reflective reading.

Standardized Test Scores Leave Unanswered Questions

Most standardized tests yield a single rate of reading score based on the student's performance with only the type of material represented by the test items. We may be left completely in the dark about the following:

Is the student aware of the need for rate adjustment?

Can the student scan a mass of material for specific information?

Can the student skim a passage for the general drift?

Can the student speed up appropriately for *easy* informational material?

Can the student attain high speeds on easy, fast-moving fiction?

Is the student able to shift to slow rates when demanded by the type of study material?

Classroom Observation

Observation from day to day often helps identify students whose needs are urgent:

Does the student consistently finish in-class reading tasks among the last in the group?

When all the student is seeking from a passage is a single bit of information, does he or she start at the beginning and read ploddingly line by line?

Does the student fail to adjust rate in other situations?

Does the student do the work thoroughly and well but fail to finish on tests over course content as well as on standardized tests?

Does the student shy away from long recreational books because they take too long to finish?

Does the student speed through in-depth study assignments in math, science, or other subjects with minimal comprehension?

Student Self-Appraisals

Using the following question one instructor gets some idea in just minutes whether students have acquired the concept of rate adjustment and can identify some of the factors involved: "Do you use the same rate of reading in most of your assignments? If you shift your rate, what considerations cause you to do so?"

Conferences, too, offer the teacher opportunities to discover whether the student realizes the necessity for variations in rate and can identify the types of situations that require the different rates.

Teacher-Made Tests

Teachers can use informal tests to get at the specific needs of individuals. Brief tests like the four suggested below might be used to explore whether each student has these rates in his "collection." Each of the four tests can be given in 10 to 15 minutes:

1. Thorough reading approach for study materials.

2. Rapid rate for easy fiction.

3. Skimming rate.

4. Scanning rate.

A graph of all four scores (Figure 4–1) might be used as an eloquent message to students. Students who performed all four reading tasks at much the same rate can see clearly that they are in special need of rate adjustment.

1. Exploring rate of reading study material

Students are asked to read an actual passage from their course materials—one on which close, careful reading is appropriate. Directions are carefully worded to elicit the use of thorough reading *if* students have this approach in their repertoires: "Read the passage carefully and accurately. Be sure you grasp its main ideas and also its details. You will be asked to answer questions on these when you finish reading. Use the method of reading which will enable you to achieve maximum comprehension."

As the students read, the instructor writes on the board the elapsed seconds, changing the figure every 5 seconds. Students look up and copy the figure as soon as they finish reading—*before* they answer the questions. The short-answer comprehension questions follow. The student's rate in words per minute and comprehension (in a percentage score) are recorded on the graph. (*Note:*

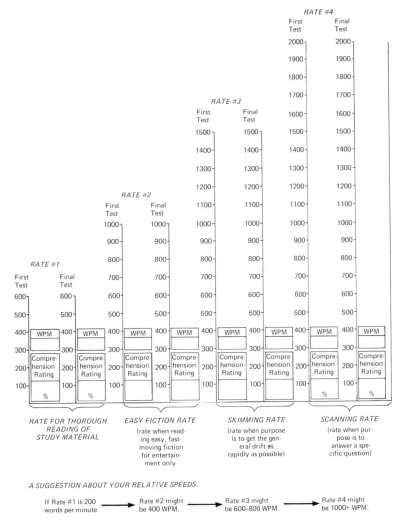

Figure 4–1. *Rate adjustment graph.*

Words in the passage divided by elapsed seconds multiplied by 60 = words per minute.)

Sample test

Instructions to the teacher. Each student should have a pencil and paper. The teacher should give the following directions, making sure they are perfectly clear:

> Please write your name and class period (or class title) in the upper right-hand corner of your paper. Then number from 1 to 10. When the starting signal is given, read the selection that

follows. Read *very* carefully and accurately. Be sure you understand and remember the information given. You will be asked to answer questions after reading. Use the method of reading which will enable you to achieve maximum comprehension, and take the time you need for this.

While you are reading, I will be holding up numbers on a placard. The minute you finish, look up, notice the number, and write it near the top of your paper. *After you have recorded the number,* you will be asked to write the answers to some questions.

When you are told to start, turn the page and begin immediately. WAIT FOR THE SIGNAL.

Now read the selection carefully.

You find out how fast your heart beats by taking your pulse. When you do this, you count the number of pulsations per minute in the walls of the artery.

In some people the heart beats much faster than in others. For some the rate is as low as 50 beats per minute or even less, and for others as high as 90. The average is about 72, although the rate varies with age and sex. In newborn babies the heart beats about 140 times per minute. It slows down to 85 in youth and to around 72 in the average adult. In old age the rate varies between 70 and 80. The rate for girls and women runs about 5 beats faster than for men.

Just as a small clock ticks faster than a large one, so a small heart beats faster than a large one. In some animals the heart beats at an astonishing rate. An elephant's heart chugs away at a rate of only 20 beats a minute, while the heart of a mouse beats 700 times a minute.

REST, EXERCISE, AND RATE OF HEARTBEAT

Your heart beats most slowly when you are lying down, because it does not have to pump blood uphill from your feet and legs. When you sit up, it goes about 4 beats a minute faster. When you stand up, it speeds up another 10 to 14 beats.

Exercise makes the heart beat faster. After a long swim or run, it may take an hour or more for the heart to slow down to normal. The more efficient the heart is, the more quickly it returns to normal after exercise. Proper athletic training should speed up the rate of recovery.

Trained athletes often have the slowest resting heart rates. Some famous runners have a pulse rate of 40 to 60 per minute, which may speed up very little during exercise.*

Now look up! Record near the top of your paper the number your instructor is holding up before the class.

Now go ahead to the next page!

---

* Thomas Gordon Lawrence, Jessie Williams Clemensen, and R. Will Burnett, *Your Health and Safety* (New York: Harcourt Brace Jovanovich, 1963), pp. 63–64. Reprinted with permission.

Below are ten True or False statements. Read each one carefully. Then write *True* or *False* after the appropriate number on your paper. **Do not turn back to the selection.**

1. The average number of heartbeats per minute is about 72.

2. The heart rate for men is about 5 beats per minute faster than for women.

3. When you take your pulse, you count the number of pulsations per minute in the walls of a vein.

4. We can conclude from the passage that the hearts of young children beat more rapidly than those of newborn babies.

5. We can conclude from the passage that the heart of a tiger beats faster than the heart of a kitten.

6. We can conclude from the passage that your heart as you are working on this test· is probably beating faster than it did before you first awakened in bed this morning.

7. After a long swim or run, the heart may take an hour or more to slow down to normal.

8. The more efficient the heart is, the more quickly it returns to normal after exercise.

9. Trained athletes often have the most rapid resting heart rates.

10. The hearts of some famous runners may speed up very little during exercise.

2. *Exploring rate of reading easy, fast-paced fiction*

The teacher searches out an easy, interesting, fast-moving story to be read for entertainment, one with exceptionally interesting opening pages. Directions are intended to encourage the use of the rate at which the student customarily reads this type of material, not an "artificial" rate stepped up temporarily under the pressure of the testing situation.

> Read at your usual rate—the rate at which you ordinarily do reading of this type. Again—read at your *usual* rate. It is important not to skim the story or lose the thought. When I say *stop*, mark with a light pencil the word you are reading.

At the end of three minutes (or possibly five) the students are to count the number of words read, divide by three (or five), and note their score in words per minute.

As a check on comprehension, each student writes a paragraph summing up the story as far as he or she read. The teacher quickly sorts the papers into three piles: good, fair, and poor. Each student's comprehension rating as well as the score in words per minute is recorded on the graph.

No sample test is provided here, for the instructor can best provide the somewhat lengthy material needed from readings planned as part of the course.

3. *Exploring rate of skimming*

The instructor selects, preferably from the actual course materials, a passage that lends itself particularly well to skimming for the general content. In the passage chosen, it is possible for the reader to get the gist readily through examining the introductory paragraph(s), the first or last sentences of the paragraphs in the body, and the conclusion.

The instructions are intended to elicit the technique of gist-skimming if the student has acquired this ability: "Your purpose as you approach this selection is only to catch the general drift. All you need is a general impression of what it is about. Approach it in the best way for getting the gist of the content just as rapidly as you possibly can. Get the drift in any way you can from the passage."

At five-second intervals the teacher records on the board the elapsed seconds. Students look up and copy their time before they answer the question. As a comprehension check, students write the gist of the passage in a brief paragraph. The teacher rates the papers by sorting them as explained in the fiction test and records the comprehension rating as well as words per minute. (*Note:* Words in the passage divided by elapsed seconds multiplied by 60 = words per minute.)

No sample test is provided here, for the instructor will want to provide a fairly long selection from readings that are a part of the course.

4. *Exploring rate of scanning*

A brief test of scanning may be useful in distinguishing students who can flash their eyes quickly down a page and find a single piece of information from those who invariably plod line by line down the page. The directions for such a test. should be worded expressly to elicit the technique of scanning for a single fact if the student has acquired this ability (see example under "Sample Test," below).

The instructor records the elapsed seconds on the board, this time changing the figure every second or two since some students may already be high-speed scanners. Students look up and copy the figure as soon as they have finished—*before* they write the answer. The student's "words scanned per minute" score, which is recorded on the graph, may be derived by this formula:

$$\frac{60}{\text{seconds elapsed}} \times \begin{array}{l}\text{number of words} \\ \text{the student must} \\ \text{cover before} \\ \text{reaching the item} \\ \text{to be found}\end{array} = \begin{array}{l}\text{words} \\ \text{scanned per} \\ \text{minute}\end{array}$$

If the test includes only one scanning question, the student's comprehension score (also recorded on the graph) is 100 percent if the answer was found. It is, of course, zero if it was missed.

The instructor who administers such a test can quickly detect students who lack techniques of scanning. The successful scanners will look up quickly while the others are laboriously reading the entire passage.·

Sample test

Instructions to the teacher. Each student should have pencil and paper. The instructor should give the following directions, making sure they are perfectly clear.

> Please write your name and class period (or class title) in the upper righthand corner of your paper. Your purpose in reading the selection on the next page will be to answer a single question. You do not need to notice any other information. First, fix in mind this question: *How many members are on the board of directors that manages the Federal Deposit Insurance Corporation?*

While you are reading, your teacher will be holding up numbers on a placard. The minute you find the answer to the question, look up, notice the number, and write it near the top of your paper. *Then* write the answer to the question.

When you are told to start, turn the page and begin immediately. WAIT FOR THE SIGNAL. Remember the question: *How many members are on the board of directors that manages the corporation?* **You may begin.**

THE FEDERAL DEPOSIT INSURANCE CORPORATION

The Federal Deposit Insurance Corporation was organized under authority of section 12B of the Federal Reserve Act, approved June 16, 1933. The chief purpose of the Corporation is to insure the deposits of all banks entitled to that benefit under the law. The major functions of the Corporation are to reimburse the depositors of insured banks closed without adequate provision having been made to pay claims of their depositors; to act as receiver for all national banks placed in receivership and for State banks placed in receivership when appointed receiver by State authorities; and to prevent the continuance or development of unsafe and unsound banking practices. In protecting depositors the Corporation may also make loans to or purchase assets from the insured banks when such loans or purchases will facilitate a merger or consolidation and will reduce the probable loss to the Corporation. The Corporation is also authorized to make such loans or purchase of assets in order to prevent the closing of an insured bank or to reopen a closed insured bank when the Corporation considers the continued operation of such bank is essential to provide adequate banking service in the community.

Management of the Corporation is vested in a board of directors of three members. The President appoints two members for terms of six years, by and with the advice and consent of the Senate. The third member is the Comptroller of the currency. One of the appointive members is made chairman of the board of directors, and not more than two members of the board may belong to the same political party.

No appropriations are made by Congress to the Corporation. Its entire income consists of assessments on insured banks at the annual rate of one-twelfth of one percent of their total deposits on selected base days, less authorized deductions and income from investments. The Corporation is authorized to borrow from the Treasury funds not exceeding $3,000,000,000 outstanding at any time.*

Now look up! Record near the top of your paper the number your teacher is holding up before the class.

Now write the answer to the question on your paper.

---

* Abstracted from *United States Government Organization Manual 1959–1960*, pp. 386–387. Reprinted by permission from *Improve Your Reading Ability* by Arthur W. Heilman (Columbus, Ohio: Charles E. Merrill Books, Inc., 1962), p. 97.

Students Set Their Own Goals

Interpreting the rate adjustment graph (Figure 4–1) with its graphic comparison of the four rates drives home the concept of rate adjustment and accents individual attainments and needs. The bars labeled "Final Test" provide space for recording improved scores on "matching" tests later—after appropriate help has been given.

Rewarding gains should follow when students are encouraged to set their own specific goals, then move toward them under their own momentum. The interpretation of diagnostic findings should leave the student with clearly defined aims in mind: "I need to read study material more slowly to get the thought of the passage," or "I need to read fiction faster and yet get the amount of comprehension I want," or "I need to speed up my scanning since my purpose is just to find a specific detail."

Developing Rate Adjustment

Instructors concerned with encouraging the use of a full repertory of reading rates may find the following sequence useful. In many instances the steps may come out of sequence or may be concurrent:

1. A first step is acquiring insights into the attainments and needs of the students.

2. The concept of rate adjustment should be introduced and driven home.

3. Appropriate guidance in acquiring the full range of rates should be provided.

4. Much teacher guidance in identifying the approach suitable for different reading situations is necessary—at first. Day-to-day assignments offer abundant opportunities.

5. Students should identify the suitable approach for an assignment with gradually decreasing guidance from the instructor.

6. The long-range goal is independence—with the students proficient in selecting for themselves the appropriate approach.

Driving Home the Concept of Rate Adjustment

It cannot be assumed that students in high school or college have already acquired the concept of rate adjustment. With seemingly fantastic reading speeds in the national spotlight, it is not surprising that some students view speed as the be-all and end-all. In science, where reading rates must usually be slow, some teachers report that many students read the text and other materials as though they were reading a novel. At the other extreme, overconscientious students may think, "It's a sin to skim or skip," so they may read a Perry Mason mystery at a very slow pace.

Opportunities in Course Materials

Abundant opportunities for introducing and reinforcing the concept of rate adjustment present themselves from day to day as instructors work with subject area materials. Teachers encourage rate adjustment as they lead students to search the context for clues that illuminate the meaning of a difficult new word, to scrutinize the word for familiar parts, and to reach for the dictionary whenever essential. They are helping to build rate adjustment into students' lifetime habits when they work with the reading approaches suitable for a lyric poem, a historical document, obscure passages in an essay, a scientific treatise, a fast-paced short story, a theorem in geometry, a sewing pattern, the directions for a shop project.

A Lively Exercise Introduces the Concept

The following exercise, "Can You Adjust Your Reading Rate to the Task at Hand?" has proved highly effective in introducing the concept of rate adjustment. The teacher elicits from or shares with students the insights on the first few pages of the exercise. The students then complete the practice exercise, sizing up various reading tasks and making a deliberate choice of approach. Lively discussion of their decisions follows. Students are aware that there is not always a "right" answer, that reading rates are highly individual and suited to particular purposes.

Internal Rate Adjustment

The frequent need for *internal* rate adjustment, for shifts of rate within a single reading task, should be brought home to students. A placard with the following "speed signals" was displayed in one class as a constant reminder:

Reduce speed signals

1. Unfamiliar terms.
2. Difficult sentence or paragraph structure.

text cont. pg. 215

CAN YOU ADJUST YOUR READING RATE
TO THE TASK AT HAND?

If someone asked you, "What is your speed in reading?" you would know that this person does NOT know much about reading.

You should have not a single rate but *several different rates*. Reading everything fast is a sign of a poor reader. The good reader develops *flexibility* instead of constant speed.

1. Shift from one rate and method to another in view of these considerations:
    a. Your purpose
       Why are you reading this material?
       —to get just the gist of an easy selection
       —to learn, point by point, a specific process or a detailed sequence
       —to find one particular point in a selection you've already read
       —to entertain yourself with light, easy reading
    b. What is the *difficulty* of the material for you?
       —the selection is easy
       —it is rough going
    c. How *familiar* are you with the subject matter?
       —you already have broad background on the topic
       —it is "new terrain"
2. You should have in your "collection" of rates the following approaches:

APPROACH	HOW FAST	WHEN TO USE
Scanning, not a true reading rate—just glancing until you find what you want	*Maybe* 1500 or more words per minute (rate is an individual matter)	—when glancing down columns to find a single piece of information
Skimming (previewing or overviewing), not a true reading rate—just getting the gist of the article, hitting the high points	*Maybe* 800–1000 words per minute	—to get the general content of an article, "what it's all about"
Actual Reading Rates		
1. **Very rapid**	*Maybe* 400 words per minute	—for light, easy, fast-moving fiction (entertainment reading)
2. **Rapid**	*Maybe* 350 words per minute	—for fairly easy materials —when you want only the more important facts, ideas

| 3. **Average** | *Perhaps* 250 words per minute | —for magazine articles such as *Scientific American;* some chapters in social studies; some travel books; some novels like *My Antonia* or *Cry the Beloved Country.* |
| 4. **Slow and careful** | From 250 words per minute—all the way down to a *slow* 50 words per minute or *even slower* | —for difficult concepts and vocabulary
—for thorough reading of technical material
—for retaining every detail
—for weighing the truth of difficult reading (Here *"thought time"* is needed in addition to reading time.) |

INTERNAL RATE ADJUSTMENT

You may need to *shift* from one rate (and approach) to another *within a single chapter* of a textbook or within an article.

Example: Chapter on "Fish and Fishlike Vertebrates" in *Modern Biology:*

	PURPOSE	APPROACH
1. Beginning of chapter (happens to be an easy, interesting, narrative opening)	—to get introduced to the contents of chapter	Fairly fast
2. A section in the middle (steps in a specific process)	—to retain the details of the step-by-step process of digestion in the fish	Slow and careful
3. End of chapter (easy paragraphs, sport fishing as a hobby)	—to get the high points about sport fishing	Fairly rapid

There are *other factors* which influence rate. The *speed attainable is not the same* for each person.

1. Temperament—some people, by nature, are just plain FAST in almost everything and, of course, some are just plain SLOW!

2. Intelligence.

. . . so, do not work for *indiscriminate speed* in reading; rather, work for *flexibility of rate*.

Adjust your approach to the demands of different types of reading tasks!

PRACTICE SHEET—WHAT APPROACH WILL YOU TAKE?

Remember: Your purpose
Difficulty of the material for you
Your familiarity with material

DELIBERATE CHOICE OF APPROACH

1. Scanning
2. Skimming
3. Actual reading
   a. very rapid reading
   b. rapid reading
   c. average reading
   d. slow and careful reading

Suppose you are to read the materials described below for the purposes as stated.

Think over the considerations listed above, then select your approach. Of course, practice in setting your approach by examining the actual material you're to read is essential, and your course will provide such practice soon. This practice exercise is just to alert you to the considerations which should control your reading rates.

TYPE AND DIFFI-CULTY OF READING MATERIAL	YOUR PURPOSE IN READING IT	ESTIMATE THE APPROACH FOR YOU
1. The chapter on Reconstruction after the Civil War in a social studies textbook.	Your instructor has announced that thorough understanding and retention are expected. There is to be a test on the details.	
2. A light, fast-moving Perry Mason story, *The Case of the Borrowed Brunette*.	You are reading only to pass time pleasantly.	
3. A chapter on "The Chemical Basis of Life" in a science textbook.	You want to retain the main ideas and all the important details in this chapter.	

4. Your science teacher has assigned the problem, "What are the factors which influence the climate of any area of the earth's surface?"

   You want to look through various books to locate the parts that offer material which you will read carefully later.

5. A health insurance policy that you are considering for yourself.

   You want to understand the exact extent of the coverage provided under the terms of the policy.

6. An interesting adventure story in a magazine.

   Your only purpose is entertainment.

7. A *Reader's Digest* article.

   You would like to find out the general content before deciding whether you want to read the article.

8. An encyclopedia article on the life of President Franklin D. Roosevelt.

   You want to learn what college President Roosevelt attended.

9. The various essays on friendship by Emerson, Aristotle, and Bacon. The rhetorical patterns are complex. Some of the concepts are abstract and difficult to comprehend.

   You are reading for ideas that will guide your own thoughts and actions in your relationships with your own friends.

10. The chapter on American colonial life in a social studies textbook.

    Your teacher has explained that you are to get an overall picture of what it was like to live in colonial times. You are expected to gain from your reading just a general impression, not specific facts.

11. A feature article, "The Latin Pot Comes to the Boil," discussing unrest in Latin America, in the magazine section of the Sunday newspaper.

    You want to broaden your general information.

12. The section of Plato's *Symposium* dealing with Platonic love. Concepts are abstract and difficult to grasp. "Thought time" is required.	You would like to understand fully what Platonic love means.
13. News stories of local interest in your daily paper.	You wish to keep informed about what is happening in your city.
14. One of Shakspeare's sonnets that "defines" enduring love.	You want to grasp Shakespeare's ideas about the experience of a love that lasts. As you read, you will be comparing Shakespeare's experiences with your own.
15. A chapter in a social studies textbook containing easy, interesting material on Abe Lincoln's young manhood and also more difficult material on the provisions of the Thirteenth, Fourteenth, and Fifteenth Amendments.	You want just a general impression of Abe Lincoln's young manhood. On the other hand, you want long term retention of the provisions of the three amendments.

3. Difficult concepts.

4. Detailed technical materials, especially those on which you have scant background.

5. Difficult and detailed directions.

6. Material on which you want detailed retention.

7. Material with a diagram, requiring constant shifting from text to diagram.

8. Material you wish to weigh carefully.

9. Material that requires "visualizing time."

10. Artistic writing which invites your lingering.

Increase speed signals

1. Simple materials with few ideas new to you.

2. Examples and illustrations unnecessary for understanding.

3. Detailed explanation and elaboration which you do not need.

4. Ideas which are restatements of previous ones.

5. Material from which you want only the most important ideas and facts.*

Student groups might formulate and display on a placard their own speed signals, adapted to the materials of the course at hand. It is also helpful for internal rate adjustment to have students read a common selection within which varying rates are appropriate, and then discuss the selection. They should indicate where and why the variations in rate were needed as they discuss the material with their classmates (DeBoer and Dallman, 1970, p. 243).

ACQUIRING APPROPRIATE READING RATES

We have discussed developing the awareness that expert readers have rates at their command that move along a continuum from slow to fast, as well as techniques of scanning and skimming, and that they vary the approach accord-

---

* These lists of signals are adapted from pages iv–70 of *Developing Reading Competence* by John K. Wilcox and others (Denver: Communication Foundation, 1961).

ing to the reading situation. Though developing this awareness is clearly an important step, it is not to be assumed that students will *acquire* this complete set of rates or bring them to peak efficiency without further instruction.

Scanning

Developing Techniques of Scanning

Teachers and librarians often note students plodding line by line down a long column or page when all they actually want is a single bit of information. These students are surprised to learn that the date of an event, for example, can be located without reading every word—that, with practice, they can search out a given fact or figure from 15,000 or 20,000 words in a minute or two! (Spache and Berg, 1966, pp. 53–54). Countless opportunities to help students acquire or perfect scanning techniques arise in day-to-day course work as students need to scan for answers to live questions—a fact they need for a certain assignment, a statement that will prove or disprove a point, a quotation they wish to locate. Their scanning techniques will prove invaluable while they are doing research for a discussion, a report, or a paper.

How can students acquire highly efficient techniques of scanning for particular information? A progression through increasingly difficult levels of scanning appears to be desirable.

Level 1. Scanning for a bit of information that stands out easily—the date of a historic discovery in science, or the university with which a noted author was affiliated.
Level 2. Scanning for an answer that is worded like the question.
Level 3. Scanning for an answer that is worded differently from the question.

Spache and Spache (1973, pp. 406–407) identified three steps involved in scanning: (1) knowing clearly what is being sought and the form in which it is likely to appear; (2) looking swiftly over the page, list, or column, expecting the fact to stand out from the rest of the page; and (3) verifying the answer when it is found by reading it carefully.

Alerting students to conspicuous signposts of the book can markedly increase their speed in scanning. These include chapter titles, headings of major chapter divisions, and boldface or italic section headings. These signposts suggest whether the section at hand may yield students what they are seeking or whether they can speed on past that section. Within a section, topic or concluding sentences sometimes suggest whether a certain paragraph is a promising or an unpromising hunting ground. By noting these signals, students can often rapidly bypass whole sections or chapters. Use of the index is another shortcut in scanning.

Scanning Using Classroom Materials

An instructor might share insights like the following, or elicit them from students, when a long unit on the planet Mars, for example, confronts students with the necessity for frequent scanning. The students scan for the answers to questions stated in their assignment, using the regular materials of the unit. The instructor might suggest:

> You will often need to use a text or reference book to search out a single fact, the answer to a single question, or one aspect of your topic. High speed scanning can *save you time* in study. You can learn to crack the printed page, moving your eyes down the page swiftly to the heart of what you want.
>
> First, fix in mind exactly what you're looking for. Hold this in the forefront of your mind. Flash your eyes down the page for this information *only*.
>
> Suppose you're looking for the date of *Viking I*'s space probe of Mars. How should you move your eyes in scanning? Perhaps there is no one best way. Some top-speed scanners suggest a vertical sweep right down the middle of the page or column. Others prefer a zigzag pattern every five or six lines. Still others suggest that a regular pattern may make you think of your eyes instead of the meaning and that it may be preferable just to "float" down the page in a relaxed way without a definite pattern. Running your index finger down the page ahead of your eyes may help your concentration. You might try these different techniques and see which works best for you.
>
> Once you've found lines in the passage that may yield what you're seeking, stop scanning instantly. Shift gears into careful reading as you weigh whether you've really found what you're after.

First level of scanning

For your assignment on Mars you are concerned with the question, "On what date did Viking I actually touch down on Mars?"

There are three levels of scanning. Level One is easy and very rapid. Here you're looking for one particular item—a proper name, a number, or a word or phrase—that stands out easily. In the part of the passage that answers this question, what is likely to stand out? [Possibilities appear to be the numerals in the date itself, the words "*Viking I*," or the words *touch down*, and the students suggest these.]

You'll sweep down the page—alert every second for the date and the target words—rejecting everything else! When you think you may have found your information, shift to careful reading in order to make sure.

Start to scan when I give the signal. When you've located the information look up.

The instructor observes which students finish quickly and which ones are plugging along down the page, obviously deficient in scanning. Those who scanned most successfully tell the class how they arrived at the answer first.

Students are intrigued by the possibility of reaching spectacular speeds in the easier levels of scanning and respond well to knowing their attainments. A teacher can devise a time chart for each practice by counting or estimating the number of words the students must cover before they reach the target information, dividing by the number of seconds, then multiplying by 60. If they must scan 500 words before locating what they are after, the time chart looks like this:

If you finished in:	*Your scanning rate was:*
10 seconds	3000 wpm
15	2000
20	1500
25	1200
30	1000
and so on	

Using a stopwatch the teacher records the elapsed seconds on the board. Students look up as soon as they have finished and record their scanning rate.

Second level of scanning

Level Two of scanning is still easy and rapid. Here you're scanning for an answer worded like your question. Try it with this question: "What is the temperature range in summer at the Martian equator?" In what form is the answer likely to appear? What may flag you? [The students suggest the words *temperature, summer,* and *equator*. Someone also suggests the degree symbol (°), F for Fahrenheit, or C for centigrade.]

Those are your targets. Good scanners concentrate; their attention is unwavering. Take the attitude of expecting what

you want to stand out from the rest. Find what you think to
be the answer. Then slow way down! Check to make certain
you've found it, then look up!

Again a time chart may be used to impress students with the rates attainable.
Higher rates will come with practice. It is desirable for students to perfect their
techniques with Levels One and Two before advancing to Level Three.

Third level of scanning

Level Three is considerably more difficult. You'll need Level
Three to answer a question such as, "What climate are the
first Earthmen likely to find near the Martian equator?"

Now the answer is worded differently from the question.
The word *climate* may not appear on the pages at all. But climate involves a number of sub-topics. What words are you
likely to find as signals that you're close to information about
the climate? [Individuals may suggest *temperature, seasons,
rainfall, humidity, winds.*]

You can really see why Level Three of scanning is the most
exacting. You are scanning for any idea related to climate. You
must have a mind set for ideas rather than for key words.
Your scanning rate will now be much slower. [The group now
locates and shares such answers as "average temperature,
32° F," "seasons similar to Earth's but longer," "no rainfall."
The top scanners in the group share their success secrets.]

Obviously, when you're on your own you will not always
know which of the three levels of scanning will be called for.
Today we clued you in, in advance. In practice, take a moment
before you begin scanning to reflect on the possible 'formats'
your answers are likely to take.

A time chart may be used. Students should expect their rate on Level Three
to be considerably slower than on Levels One and Two.

Classroom Opportunities for Practice

Sharpen up your scanning.   As opportunities arise in class from day to day,
students are reminded that here is a chance to sharpen up their new techniques
of scanning. The occasion might be verifying a statement, finding a quotation,
supporting a line of argument, locating a new word in context.

Chapter titles are signals.   Students scan the chapter titles in the table of
contents to find one that appears to offer help with a special problem.

The index—a speed device.   Students practice using the index to learn the page location for an item, then scan the page to find the information. They may compete to locate it first.

Which source is promising?   Students who need information for a current assignment are supplied with a number of possible resource materials. They are encouraged to use their new scanning techniques to decide, within a few minutes, which of the sources promises to be useful. A time limit might be imposed.

Key or topic sentences are signals.   Students practice using key or topic sentences as an aid in scanning. They scan a selection for the sentence that signals the desired information, then scan within the paragraph to find the information.

Skimming

Getting the Gist of Informational Writing

A skill extremely useful in study and personal reading is skimming for the general drift of a passage. Teachers observe that students do not just grow into this skill, that much is to be gained from demonstration, instruction, and practice.

After observing the need for proficiency in skimming for the drift of a passage, a teacher might select from the course materials a chapter or selection that lends itself almost ideally to developing this technique. The introductory paragraph(s) announce the content, boldface or italic headings announce important thought divisions, topic sentences carry key ideas, and the conclusion is a general summing up.

For days in advance, the instructor might advertise the coming lessons on high-speed skimming, catching the interest of students. Then when the day arrives the teacher says:

> Today you'll be learning how to do high-speed skimming. It will be convenient to make a distinction between *preview* skimming (a rapid coverage to learn the general content before reading), and *overview* skimming (a quick coverage to get the drift when no second reading is intended). Though the purposes differ, the techniques involved are much the same. Both preview and overview skimming should save time for you in both study and personal reading.
>
> President Kennedy is said to have "read" three books a day and to have whipped through newspaper and magazine materials at extremely high rates. He pointed out that at these rates he was doing overview skimming—hitting the high spots.

He knew where the strategic spots were located, those likely to yield the general content. He was familiar with the structure of well organized factual writing, and he turned this knowledge into speed. (President Kennedy followed his rapid survey with a more careful reading when appropriate.)

Once you've learned, as he did, to get the gist very quickly, you'll want to preview-skim almost everything you read—chapters assigned in your textbooks, newspaper and magazine content, almost everything but fiction.

How do you skim for the drift of a selection? First, you examine the title. This is often a concise label of the content. Examine the subtitle if there is one. With magazine and newspaper feature articles, you'll sometimes find a little blurb about the content. This is often gist-packed and should be read carefully.

Next, read the introduction carefully, a paragraph or two or three to see if you can get the gist. Here the authors often announce the content—tell you what they're going to tell you—conveniently brief you on what's ahead.

Be sure to hit the headings within the selection. Do you see any in this passage? [Students note the italicized or boldface sub-headings that mark off sections of the selection.] These signal thought divisions and announce or suggest the content of each coming section.

Where within each paragraph will you look for key ideas? [Students suggest the first, and, less frequently, the last sentence.] First and last sentences often carry a heavy load of meaning. Words in italics or boldface also flag you down for important content.

Look over the diagrams and pictures—often worth many words.

Last, read the concluding paragraph or two. What do you think writers might do in their conclusion? It's their last chance with the reader. Here they often wrap up or summarize the big ideas—drive home what they want most of all to leave with you.

You'll find exceptions to all that's been said. Introductions may fail to announce, and conclusions may fail to wrap up. Topic sentences may not always be first or last—or even present at all—in paragraphs. Your skimming techniques cannot be rigid. A flexible floating down the page or through a paragraph following one promising lead or another is often desirable.

When you're finished, take your preview test. You may be surprised and delighted at how much you've learned from just a preview.

Students now skim the selection (untimed during the learning stage), then take a preview test of five or ten short-answer questions, all readily answerable if they have examined the strategic spots. Good scores help sell the worth of the new technique. Since speed rather than perfectionist attention to detail is being encouraged, 80 percent is considered a commendable score. The instructor deliberately plans an encouraging success experience.

The class is asked, "What possible uses do you think you might make of skimming?" With some guidance, students arrive at these uses:

1. You'll study better and faster if you preview-skim chapters you're going to study at school before your thorough reading.

2. Skim to learn how the author has organized the material.

3. Skim chapters and articles when all you want is a general impression.

4. Skim a chapter or article to decide whether you want to read it at all.

5. Skim to see whether, in view of your purpose, the entire selection or just parts should be read. What a saving of time to bypass irrelevant parts!

6. Skim to see if a passage or a book is relevant to a research problem.

7. Skim when you wish to learn only the writer's opinion or point of view on a given question.

8. Review-skim.

Students discuss: "Are there possible dangers in skimming? What cautions would you add?" They may suggest: It is important not to substitute hitting the high spots when you want in-depth comprehension of the entire selection. A complete reading is often necessary to clarify concepts or learn how the writers support their points. Content which you wish to weigh carefully or artistic expression which you wish to savor does not lend itself to light skimming.

The point that selections are not always perfectly structured for skimming should be strongly emphasized. Students should move on from well-structured material to prose that does not lend itself ideally to skimming, then on to material that confronts them with real difficulties.

High-Speed Skimming for Top Executives

One instructor sparks enthusiasm with this selling point: "You've just learned a technique corporation executives often learn in speed courses. Top executives at General Electric have been trained to skim first—then use a slower rate when needed—to get through the load of reading matter on their desks. They have learned, many of them, to skim their daily correspondence and the reports they receive, before reading carefully. They find that much of the load requires no more than skimming. Communications that *do* require a second reading are covered more rapidly and efficiently because they were skimmed first.

"Skim all printed matter—except fiction—before you do anything else. Skim your daily paper and your weekly news magazine. You'll be surprised how soon you can get so much from deft skimming that much of your reading, like that of the top executives, will require only this."

Skimming a Book

Students sometimes ask, "How can you skim an informational book?" The following procedure should give a quick grasp of the general content. After this sampling readers may conclude that the overview is all they want. If not, they will read the book more efficiently for having previewed:

1. Examine the title, and the subtitle if there is one. These are often the author's labels of the content.

2. Read the publisher's blurb on the jacket. This is dense with information—gist-packed.

3. Examine the preface and other introductory material. Here you will often find a statement of the purpose and scope of the book.

4. The table of contents may be closely packed with major topics. When read continuously, the chapter titles may offer a concise summary of the book's content.

5. Skimming a book is in many respects an expansion of skimming a short selection. The opening chapter corresponds to the opening paragraphs of a short selection. It is often somewhat general and announces the overall content.

6. As students leaf through subsequent chapters, they will discover that introductory and concluding paragraphs are often "strategic spots."

7. The concluding chapter is frequently highly concentrated. It is the writers' last chance with the reader. Here they often wrap up their big ideas—drive home what they want most of all to leave with their readers.

You will find exceptions to these guidelines. There is no intent to prescribe rigid procedures.

Activities for Skimming Practice

What can you learn in one minute?   Using an unexplored textbook chapter or magazine article, students are set this task: "How much can you learn about the content of this chapter (or article) in just one minute? Use your skimming techniques to hit the high spots of well organized prose."

Do you want to read this?   Using a magazine, students are given this task: "Skim this article, using your new techniques, to see whether you want to read it at all. What a time-saver in personal reading to make this quick appraisal, then reject an uninviting selection!" (Students should be prepared to offer reasons for rejection or acceptance.)

What's his point of view?   Using the editorial page, students practice skimming editorials solely to learn the writer's opinion or point of view. They discuss this question: "Suppose you wish to learn the stand of the writer of this editorial on U.S. foreign policy. That's all you want—just to learn the editorial viewpoint. Where do you think you might zero in as you do this type of skimming?" (The group may suggest examining the editorial's conclusion. Here the writer may stress the point he or she wants most to leave with the reader. The introduction, too, may reveal the viewpoint.)

The same type of activity might also be conducted with modern and "classical" essays.

Can you skim a news story?   Students are led to observe that straight news stories require a different technique of skimming. Here the headlines, the subheads, and the "lead" yield the essence. The lead is dense with the answers to key questions—the five *w*'s and sometimes *h*: who? what? when? where? why? how? The content of the rest of the news story tapers off in importance. Against a time limit, students skim the headlines, the subheads, and the lead for the gist of front page stories.

Rapid and Moderately Rapid Reading

Students like Martha urgently need their teachers' guidance in acquiring rapid rates of reading. Her parents reported to an English teacher, "She studies until twelve and one each night—and most of the weekend, too. Her grades are good, but she sacrifices relaxation and friendship. Her interests are math and science. She's done so much slow reading in these fields that now she reads the lightest novel, even the comics, slowly."

Students who have an absorbing interest in science or math, students who concentrate on nonfiction to the neglect of fiction, and students who are over-conscientious are likely to be slow readers.

How can instructors help these students attain higher rates of reading? Instructors can (1) encourage practice with highly interesting material read for less exacting purposes, (2) give assignments that call for the general impression, (3) provide timed practice exercises, and (4) use instruments to force more rapid reading.

Practice with Highly Interesting Material

Much practice with easy, highly interesting material, read for less exacting purposes, is a natural, effective means of increasing rates. The material should be lower than the student's instructional level and should present no vocabulary or comprehension blocks. The student should be pulled along by intense interest.

Browsing sessions offer classroom teachers an opportunity to influence book selections. Exciting, fast-moving fiction and narrative-style biographies, rather than books like *War and Peace*, are appropriate for students who need to increase their rates. Librarians, too, can guide students to fast-moving books which match their interests.

Have students graph their rates of reading easy material, so they can observe day-to-day improvement. This should spur them on to greater efforts. Many students respond well to the "alarm clock graph" and the "ten-page graph," later in this chapter.

Reading for the General Impression

Making assignments that call for the general impression—cutting down, for the time being, the number of demands for detailed information—should be of special value to readers in need of speed. Directing attention to the role played by introductions and conclusions, headings, topic sentences, and to the technique (when appropriate) of hitting the meaning-carrying words and slighting those less important should help these students get a quick grasp of important content.

Tests on the content of a selection should be keyed to reading purposes. Exhorting speed on a selection and then quizzing students on the details is unfair. The type of question that encourages rapid reading calls for a general reaction to the passage. Noting details, unless they are very obvious, calls for a slower rate of reading.

The reader will find helps for students on how to do rapid reading for general background in "Turn On Reading Power Through Assignments" in Chapter 3.

Timed Practice Exercises

Timed practice is suitable for students whose vocabulary and comprehension are already adequate. Groups or individuals read short selections under a time limit, then answer comprehension questions. Under pressure, students often discard unnecessarily sluggish habits. Selections intended for rapid reading should include few unfamiliar words.

Asking for rapid identification of the main ideas of paragraphs, without intent to note details, might go hand in hand with the study of paragraph patterns in writing. After students have made an intensive study of paragraphs of cause and effect, comparison and contrast, problem and solution, and the like, the main ideas should stand out and be more quickly grasped.

Whatever the exercise, from the first the students should have concrete evidence of progress. By starting with easy material, the instructor should deliberately plan encouraging successes. Graphing improvement spurs continued effort.

Reading Pacers

While pacers produced by different manufacturers vary, with all pacers a cover, a bar, or a beam of light moves down the page, pressuring the student to increase his rate. A dial controls the speed of the descending occluder or light beam.

Pacer training is motivational for most students and profitable for many as long as vocabulary and comprehension are already adequate. If not, until such inhibiting factors are removed, forcing such training may be harmful. In one reading laboratory a young man was in tears about his performance on the pacer. He was being forced to "read" faster and faster when he did not know the meanings of the words on the page.

When no blocks are present, remediation in the area of rates of reading is rapid as compared with vocabulary and comprehension. Reading clinicians comment, "Pure rate cases are the easiest and show the most rapid improvement of all remedial problems." They caution, though, "When a severe emotional problem is present, imposing an added pressure through rate training is usually inadvisable."

Controlled Reading Techniques

In addition to the functions of the pacer, controlled reading devices force specific left-to-right eye movements. Such techniques are used in connection with films or filmstrips. Probably the most popular of these techniques is the filmstrip approach used in the Controlled Reader (for four to fifteen students) or the Controlled Reader Jr. (for one to three students) produced by EDL-McGraw-Hill. Taylor and Frackenpohl (1968, p. 38) caution that students should be grouped for such training on the basis of reading achievement levels and rate of reading with comprehension.

Rapid Reading Activities
Without Instruments

Easy fiction speedway. Here's an adaptation of an idea that Spache and Berg (1966, p. 91) suggested for readers who dally over easy fiction: "If a light novel of 200 pages would ordinarily take you five hours to read, set a four-hour time limit. That's about 25 pages every half hour. Mark every twenty-fifth page through the book with a paper clip, to drive toward. Check yourself at these points to see if you're up to schedule. If you find yourself lagging, attempt to catch up the next 25 pages. On your next book, try to top your performance by setting an even shorter time limit."

What can you gain in an hour? Strang (1965) made this suggestion for con-conscientious students overly careful in reading light fiction: "Assume that you have just an hour to spend in reading a light popular book which you have heard mentioned frequently and are eager to read. See how much you can get from this short contact." Students report in class what they have gleaned. They often surprise themselves.

With dreamers who need to call back wandering thoughts, she adapted this idea to appropriate sections of textbooks: "See how much you can gain from this section in ten minutes."

Supersonic reading. Strang (1965) also told about one instructor who held "supersonic" speed sessions—two each week, each only ten minutes long. Students read easy, interesting fiction for one minute, then counted the words read and recorded the count on a file card. During each timing they tried to break their records of the minute before. Even these short sessions proved helpful when reinforced with much fiction reading outside of class. The average increase was 200 words per minute.

Alarm clock graph. Students are advised, "The reading material best suited for developing your speed is probably easy, fast-moving fiction read for enjoyment. One secret is forcing yourself beyond your usual rate. Soon the increased rate should become a comfortable rate for you."

Unless the next book a student reads corresponds in words per page and in difficulty, she or he will need to start a new graph.

ALARM CLOCK GRAPH
(For Home Practice)

Reading material best suited for speed practice is easy, interesting fiction read for pleasure. Set aside an hour (or half-hour) each day if possible for rate practice at home. Set your alarm clock to ring at the end of an hour (or half-hour), count the number of pages read, chart the results below, then try each day to better the record of the day before.

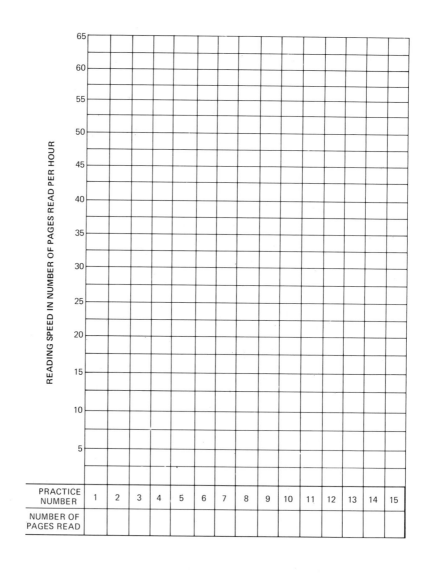

PRACTICE NUMBER	1	2	3	4	5	6	7	8	9	10	11	12	13	14	15
NUMBER OF PAGES READ															

READING SPEED IN NUMBER OF PAGES READ PER HOUR

Ten-page graph. The student notes the starting time, beginning on an even minute, then reads ten pages of the fiction book and records the time on the graph. He or she then reads ten more pages, trying to cut down the time. The student may wish to count ahead ten pages and mark the "finish line" with a paper clip to drive toward. Daily practice is desirable.

Busy students may prefer the "ten-page graph" to the "alarm clock graph," for though it may be difficult to set aside a full hour, they can often manage the time required to read ten pages.

"Countdown."* The reading material for "Countdown" should be light, fast novels, teen materials, books of short stories, books about sports, and the like— not school-assigned material. Students read one page and record their time, then read the next page and, setting a time limit, try to increase their rates. They chart the results on a graph, gradually decreasing the time limit as they proceed.

This activity is especially inviting to busy students. Although they may find it difficult to free an hour or even a half hour for rate practice, they can usually find time to read a page, then try to break their record on the following page.

Push-card pacer. Some students may find it helpful to improvise a reading pacer with an ordinary 4 × 6 card, using it somewhat as follows:

1. Students place the card *above* the line to be read. They then move it down the page, forcing themselves to keep ahead. Or they may prefer to place the card just *below* the line to be read, exposing the reading matter line by line and "chasing" the card down the page.

2. Students push the card down the page more rapidly than they think they can comprehend. They may be surprised at the speed attainable without loss of comprehension.

3. This suggestion is given: "You now have a lifetime 'portable reading pacer.' If you really want to pick up speed, use it with easy newspaper and magazine content and light, fast-moving books."

Some students find the push-card distracting and respond negatively. Others quickly become accustomed to it.

Two-readings procedure. Judson (1963, pp. 82–83) suggested a series of speed practice sessions using materials from day to day reading. The reader pushes strenuously just fifteen minutes at a stretch, no more than once a day and no less than three times a week.

---

* This activity is adapted from George Hillocks, Bernard J. McCabe, and James F. McCampbell, *The Dynamics of English Instruction, Grades 7–12* (New York: Random House, 1971), p. 395.

text cont. pg. 231

TEN-PAGE GRAPH

The reading material best suited for developing your speed of reading is easy, interesting, fast-moving fiction read for pleasure. Read ten pages of your book. Record the time this takes. Then read ten more pages trying to improve the first record and *pushing* yourself to read faster than seems comfortable for you. One secret of increasing your reading speed is *forcing* yourself beyond your usual rate. Soon the new increased rate should become comfortable for you.

1. Preview the selection quickly.

2. Then do a first reading, using a push-card if you like, dangerously beyond your comfortable rate. Recite to yourself what you have learned.

3. Then read the selection again, more slowly, to discover what you missed on your first reading.

4. Do not hesitate to push yourself dangerously on your first reading. You can always pick up on the second reading anything you missed.

5. With practice you will miss less and less on your first reading until finally, on many occasions, only one reading will be necessary.

Slow, Careful Reading

As teachers work with the approaches suitable for reading the propositions underlying a theory in science, the precise parts of a mathematical equation, a sonnet, or the directions in typewriting, they are encouraging habits of close, intensive reading.

Much of this book is devoted to helping students develop the thorough reading constantly demanded in school courses. The subject-area index in Chapter 1 will guide subject teachers to strategies others have found effective. Procedures for helping students do thorough reading of an informational chapter are offered in "You Can Upgrade Students' Textbook Reading" in Chapter 3.

INDEPENDENCE IN RATE ADJUSTMENT

We have mentioned steps (often concurrent) for building rate adjustment into students' permanent habits:

1. Diagnosing attainments and needs.

2. Introducing the concept of rate adjustment.

3. Developing the full range of rates.

4. Guiding students in selecting the suitable approach.

5. Eliciting the suitable approach from students—with less instructor guidance.

6. Achieving independence in using the appropriate approach.

We have considered in detail steps 1, 2, and 3. Now let us move on to the ultimate objective: guiding students to full independence in the use of suitable approaches.

Rate adjustment is likely to come for the majority of students only with guided practice in actual course materials. It is in their day-to-day assignments that they can experience reading rates in action.

One of the foremost causes of ineffective rate of reading, McKim (1963, p. 341) stressed, is the absence of clear purpose. And, conversely, she listed as the first and fundamental step toward rate adjustment *ensuring that students know the purposes for which they are reading and discussing with the group how they will read to achieve these purposes.* Ways and means of accomplishing this are considered in detail in "Turn on Reading Power Through Assignments" in Chapter 3. An instructor might profitably suggest the following at the time a reading assignment is made:

> In reading this fast-moving short story, the purpose is enjoyment. What rate do you think is appropriate for "The Most Dangerous Game"?

> All you need is a general impression of this chapter. How will you read for the general content?

> There are many books for you on the library table. How could you skim so as to find those that will be most helpful to your group? (McKim, 1963.)

> We have talked over the purpose of this assignment. How do you think you should read to accomplish this purpose?

> What do you think it's important to find out from this reading? What will be the best method of reading in order to find this out?

Ultimately, students should be able to deliberate and decide for themselves the appropriate approach for the material and purpose at hand.

No teacher should be discouraged when the majority of students move slowly and gradually toward rate adjustment. Training to achieve it must be a continuing instructional concern through the school years. Such training is given not only directly as discussed in this chapter but through many indirect ways: vocabulary instruction, help with comprehension, stress on purpose, work with the structure of prose and with patterns of writing, and the improvement of study habits. Strang (1965) cited as one of the most important insights gained in her long and distinguished career: "Generally effective instruction in reading is a means of improving speed. A good reading program will have speed as a byproduct."

But the direct teaching of rate adjustment as a concomitant of purposeful reading is a decided plus factor. Instructors who work actively with rate adjustment are helping students acquire a strategy that conditions to a large degree their success in high school and college, efficient informational reading in adulthood, and lifelong enjoyment in personal reading. Rate adjustment is one of the hallmarks of the mature reader.

Bibliography

Fiddler, Jerry B. "Contemplative Reading: A Neglected Dimension of Flexibility." *Journal of Reading*, 16, no. 8 (1973): 622–626.

Grob, James A. "Reading Rate and Study-Time Demands on Secondary Students." *Journal of Reading*, 13, no. 4 (1970): 285–288 ff.

Karlin, Robert. *Teaching Reading in High School*, 2nd ed. Indianapolis: Bobbs-Merrill Company, 1972, chapter 9.

McConkie, George W., Keith Raynor, and Steven J. Wilson. "Experimental Manipulation of Reading Strategies." *Journal of Educational Psychology*, 65 (1973): 1–8.

Robinson, H. Alan. *Teaching Reading and Study Strategies: The Content Areas.* Boston: Allyn and Bacon, 1975, pp. 190–92.

References

Altick, Richard D. *Preface to Critical Reading*, 5th ed. New York: Holt, Rinehart and Winston, 1969.

Buswell, Guy T. "Relationship between Rate of Thinking and Rate of Reading." *School Review*, 59 (September 1951): 339–346.

DeBoer, John J., and Martha Dallman. *The Teaching of Reading*, 3rd ed. New York: Holt, Rinehart and Winston, 1970.

Judson, Horace. *The Techniques of Reading*. New York: Harcourt, Brace and World, 1963.

McKim, Margaret G. *Guiding Growth in Reading*. New York: Macmillan Company, 1963.

Mitchell, June Frary. "Prediction of Increase in Silent Reading Rate." *Clinical Studies in Reading II*, Supplementary Educational Monographs No. 77. Chicago: University of Chicago Press, 1953.

Spache, George D., and Paul C. Berg. *The Art of Efficient Reading*. New York: Macmillan Company, 1966.

Spache, George D., and Evelyn B. Spache. *Reading in the Elementary School*, 3rd ed. Boston: Allyn and Bacon, 1973.

Strang, Ruth, in class lecture on the teaching of secondary school reading, University of Chicago, summer 1965.

Taylor, Stanford E., and Helen Frackenpohl. *Controlled Reading*, teacher's guide. Huntington, N.Y.: Educational Development Laboratories, 1968.

READING SKILLS FOR PROBLEM SOLVING AND TOPIC DEVELOPMENT

With knowledge exploding in almost every field, the answers of today can—and may—become obsolete tomorrow. For the closing years of the twentieth century, the student must have resources for searching out current answers. Teachers whose subjects call for such reading tasks are concerned that students gain this kind of expertise.

This chapter offers for your consideration a number of helps for students as they face investigative tasks. And it alerts the teacher to the many and complex skills students must have in order to attack problems through reading.

We hope you will find the following questions suggestive and the answers pragmatic, as you consider ways to strengthen students for their problem-solving tasks.*

1. Do students know how to narrow the problem to manageable proportions and to state it precisely?

2. Do the students know how to set up reading targets?

---

* The interest of Laboratory School teachers and their insights into students' needs were a contribution to this chapter. In science, these teachers include: Department Chairman Ernest Poll, Murray Hozinsky, Judith Keane, Barbara Wehr, and also Jerry Ferguson, A. J. Ferrantino and Hiroshi Kanno, formerly of the school. In social studies, they include Earl Bell and former Laboratory School teacher, Gerald Marker. Ernest Poll was generous with time and help when asked a multitude of questions by the writers.

3. Can they locate books and other sources of the desired information?

4. Can students use a table of contents and an index as aids in locating the sought-for information?

5. Can students scan a passage for information that bears upon the problem?

6. Do they discriminate between what is relevant to the problem and what is irrelevant?

7. Do students evaluate what they read—selecting or rejecting after a critical appraisal?

8. Can students make notes efficiently from a number of scattered sources?

9. Can students bring the information they have collected into an orderly presentation of their own?

10. Do students keep an open mind for later evidence that may modify their solution to the problem?

Urgent Need for Problem-Solving Skills

We have acquired more knowledge in the last twenty-five years than in the preceding thousand years. With human knowledge growing and changing at this fantastic pace, the advanced information of today may appear primitive tomorrow. Today the successful student must have on call resources for searching out the current information. Among these resources is a complete collection of reading skills for solving a problem or investigating a topic.

We can no longer regard a single textbook as containing a course in science or social studies. Many courses are now centered around problem solving. Indeed, students' success in almost all subjects and on all levels is becoming more and more dependent on ability to search out answers independently. And of course the problem-solving skills are at the heart of independent study, an important new direction.

Haven't Students Already Acquired
These Skills?

Haven't students in secondary schools and colleges already developed the reading skills they need for making an investigation? Instruction in these skills is not often given in depth as part of the elementary school program in fundamentals of reading. Nor is it generally offered in secondary school English or reading courses. Indeed, the responsibility for these skills is a no-man's land. The result? Students are often assigned problems that involve complex skills of reference reading, then left to explore these problems largely unassisted.

Isn't a Compelling Interest in the Problem Enough?

If the teacher can arouse students' curiosity—create a compelling purpose for reading—involve them in their very own thing, isn't that enough? Certainly it would be difficult to overstress the drive generated when students are caught up with interest in a problem of immense significance to them. But are students led, simply by virtue of the task set, to develop the most rapid, the most labor-saving, the most effective problem-solving techniques? Left to their own devices, poor students often develop deficiencies that disable them as they try to attack most of their school subjects, and capable students have at their command only those skills which they have picked up haphazardly along the way.

When students already possessed with interest in an exciting problem have the added advantage of their teacher's guidance in the most effective techniques, an ideal situation is created. The immediate need motivates students to learn the facilitating skill. They are likely to react, "That's a real short cut!" Their satisfaction leads to continued use of the skill and to its reinforcement.

How Can You Take Time from Your Regular Class Work?

One science teacher (Hozinsky, 1970) whose course is problem oriented accompanies his students to the school library, where he guides them in the skills they need for problem solving. If he is asked, "How can you find the time?" he answers, "I can't afford not to find it. The problem-solving jobs are at the heart of the study of science. During a school year my classes spend thousands of 'student hours' in problem solving. I want these hours well spent, so I take down the obstacle course. I *spend* the time—to *regain* it later as students search out information more rapidly and intelligently and with considerably less supervision."

Teachers should (1) learn what skills their students already possess, (2) analyze an assignment to learn exactly what skills students must have in order to complete it, and (3) tie into instruction the needed skills, thus removing roadblocks. An instructor who develops reading skills for problem solving helps prevent discouragement and frustration and sustains student interest in study and in school. Such an instructor prepares students for tasks demanded in almost every subject and in every level. And the instructor is developing skills essential for solving life problems after the courses at school are over. Can the school afford to leave these vital skills—these basic, imperative tools of learning—to the students' fumbling efforts to develop them on their own?

What Is Required of Students?

Scholarly adults whose use of reading tools has become second nature may not be fully aware of the weighty demands that solving a problem or developing a topic imposes upon the student. But how does the task appear to the student? If the problem or topic is complex, the student may need to narrow it to manageable proportions, then analyze it into component aspects before beginning a search for material. The student may have to decide among thousands of books and periodicals. It may be important to consult specialized and unfamiliar sources. Once a promising book is in hand, the student must select what is relevant to the problem and reject what is irrelevant and must know how to make notes efficiently on widely scattered information. Finally, all this information must be organized into a unified, orderly presentation.

The rest of this section calls attention to some of the specific and often sequential steps essential for the broad problem-solving tasks just mentioned. For a heightened awareness of all that is involved, the writers are indebted to *Reading, Grades 7, 8, 9: A Teacher's Guide to Curriculum Planning*, Curriculum Bulletin No. 11 (New York: Board of Education of the City of New York, 1957). The reader in search of a comprehensive list of skills combined with practical how-to-do-it suggestions may wish to consult this timeless bulletin.

Many Skills Can Be Taught in Minutes

The skills and strategies given here need not, by sheer weight of numbers, be overwhelming. They should be approached with the question, "Which of these skills do my students need in order to complete this particular assignment?" Many reference skills can be taught with just a few brief pointers. In minutes, students can be introduced to such useful reference aids as the encyclopedia's most recent yearbook or its priceless index volume. In a short time, students can learn to use the *Reader's Guide to Periodical Literature* and can have this tool at their command through *years* of reference reading. Many skills and understandings enumerated here are accompanied by instructional suggestions. In other cases, selected references are offered to the reader.

Students' day-to-day reports, their talks to the class, their research papers, their projects that combine laboratory investigation with reading to find out what others have discovered—all stand to improve as students become accomplished users of the tools of reference reading.

Can Students Narrow the Problem and State It Precisely?

Let us suppose that a class or a group expressed interest in making a study of the planet Mars. The teacher suggested, "You could spend *lifetimes* studying Mars. What do you want to find out about Mars? Are you interested in its distance? Its motion? A recent space probe? A future space probe? The mysterious canals?"

It appeared, after a discussion, that the interest of the students centered around the topic, "What will the first visitors from Earth find on Mars?" The teacher pointed out that Mars is a vast expanse from icy polar caps to equatorial deserts. The students concluded that further limitation was in order. They decided to assume that the first Earthlings would make their landing somewhere in the equatorial region of Mars. The topic they finally decided on was "What are we likely to find on Mars if we land near the equator?"

"You'll find a tie-in," the teacher added, "between limiting your topic, as you have just done, and skillful reference reading. By narrowing your subject, you've put on 'reading blinders.' Your blinders will help you focus on what is related and shut out what is unrelated. For example, you'll reject as unrelated —at least to your specific problem—passages about the surface features of Mars *away from the equator,* the change of seasons away from the equator, and about perils to humans in the Martian polar areas. You'll examine thoroughly passages about the mysterious blue-green areas of Mars to check whether these extend to the equator."

Can Students Set Up Reading Targets?

*A Complex Problem or Topic
Requires Breakdown*

Obviously a simple problem or topic requires little analysis before students begin searching for information. Students may be looking for the answer to a single question, for instance, "What is the usual direction of travel of a tornado?" A complex problem, however, requires breakdown into its component aspects. When the problem is broad, preparing in advance a framework of questions—setting up, insofar as possible, specific reading targets—will help locate the information.

A Class Sets Up Reading Targets

We have imagined a class or a group selecting as a major project the problem, "What are the first visitors from Earth likely to find on Mars if they land near the equator?" (For purposes of illustration, a complex problem has been selected. Many of the problems students explore will be much more limited.)

The instructor suggests, "You've selected your broad problem. Now try to think of everything you'd like to learn about it. Break it down into sub-topics. These will become your reading targets—the specific information you'll search for during your investigation. Now what *are* some of the things you want to find out?"

As the students offer suggestions, someone writes them on the board:

**What the First Visitors from Earth Are
Likely to Find on Mars Near the Equator**

Your reading targets:

1. How will the terrain appear?

2. Are they likely to observe signs of life? Plants? Animals?

3. How will the sky appear?

4. Will they find water? Bodies of water?

5. What will the temperature be?

6. Will they find any canals?

7. Will they find any plants?

8. What are the perils to man's survival? What life support systems will they need?

9. What about the climate? Does it rain?

10. What will the pull of gravity be? Its effect on walking?

11. Does Mars have a moon?

12. What kind of soil?

13. What about the atmosphere? Can they breathe?

14. What about the seasons?

Obviously, here is an outpouring of major and minor topics in chaotic order. The teacher suggests, "Will it be any easier to read for the answers if we group together topics that are related?" The students consider the *why* of this: the convenience of approaching their reading with grouped together questions when related bits of information are found close together in a certain section of a book. With guidance, the class perceives that their broad problem falls into several major subdivisions: surface features, atmosphere, climate, possibility of life, perils to survival, and others. These main topics go up on the chalkboard, with plenty of space to insert sub-topics later:

**What the First Visitors from Earth Are
Likely to Find on Mars Near the Equator**

Your reading targets:

    I.   Surface features

   II.   Atmosphere

  III.   Weather

  IV.   Features of sky

   V.   Force of gravity

  VI.   Life forms (if any)

 VII.   Perils to human survival

The class is now helped to perceive how the sub-topics in which they expressed interest drop into slots under the main topics. As they sort and arrange these, they refine some and add others.

**What the First Visitors from Earth Are
Likely to Find on Mars Near the Equator**

Your reading targets:

    I.   Surface features
        A.   Terrain
        B.   Materials
        C.   Canals (if any)

   II.   Atmosphere
        A.   Composition
        B.   Pressure

  III.   Weather
        A.   Seasonal variation
        B.   Daily variation

IV. Features of sky
    A. Appearance of solar system and stars
    B. Appearance of moon(s)

 V. Force of gravity
    A. Comparison with Earth
    B. Effect on weight
    C. Effect on movement

VI. Life forms (if any)
    A. Plant life
    B. Animal life

VII. Perils to human survival
    A. Specific problems, e.g., oxygen
    B. Life support systems needed

"Of course this list of target information," the teacher comments, "is incomplete and tentative. You'll modify it as you do your reading. You'll run across important sub-topics you haven't thought of. You may find a discussion of possible hot springs on Mars and decide to add the sub-topic "hot spots" under the heading Surface Features. You may find yourself reading about the shortage of water vapor and decide to add the sub-topic "humidity" under the main topic Atmosphere. You may decide to drop out one of your topics or sub-topics. You'll be *constantly revising your target outline* as you do your research reading."

Simple Problems or Topics Require Simpler Reading Targets

As has been noted, a simple problem or topic calls for little analysis before the students begin reference reading. They may be searching for the answer to a single question, "What are the signs of an approaching tornado?" and their reports, oral or written, may be quite brief.

   Many problems explored by students involve far fewer aspects than the one on Mars. A class was interested in investigating the supply of water they use each day. At the suggestion, "Try to think of everything you'd like to find out about it," the students brought up these questions:

Where does it come from?

How pure is it?

How much does it take to supply us?

Is there enough?

How is it purified?

How is it brought to our homes?

Is there enough for the future?

The teacher continued, "Can you sort out these topics? Bring together the ones that are related? Arrange them in logical order?" The class worked out this simple framework:

Our Water Supply

Your reading targets:

I.   Where the water supply comes from

II.   How it is brought to our homes

III.   How it is purified

IV.   How pure it is

V.   How adequate the supply is
     A.   How much our community needs
     B.   Whether the supply is sufficient for now
     C.   Whether it is sufficient for the future

Target Outlines Take Shape during Reading

With many investigations students will have no idea how they will organize their information until they are well into the reading. Sometimes their target outline will not shape up until they have almost finished their reading.

A social studies class became interested in how they, although nonvoters, could take action against air pollution (Bell, 1970). Class members, divided into five committees, set out to gather facts. Each committee approached the reading with one of the broad questions below:

What federal, state, and city laws to control pollution are now on the books?

Which industries must take preventive measures?

What procedures has the government taken in the past to control air pollution?

What are the scientific reasons for air pollution?

What scientific measures are used to estimate the degree of pollution?

It was during the process of reading that many of the sub-topics to be included in each committee's report emerged.

Why Reading Targets?

Students might think about and discuss the why of reading targets. With guidance, they will arrive at some of the plus values in the table below.

Why Set Up Reading Targets?

---

1. You'll find reading targets a speed device. You'll get what you're after faster. The key words in your topics and sub-topics will now serve as clue words for locating your information. These will speed you to appropriate books and chapters and, within a chapter, to the target information.
2. Some students stop searching before they have fully explored a problem—discovering too late that they have omitted crucial information. Clearly, your target plan, with its thoughtful advance listing of topics, will do much to ensure complete coverage.
3. Some students include in their reports information that is unrelated, that is off target. Your target plan is an advance lineup of really relevant topics. It's easy to be lured by catchy but unimportant content. When you set up specific targets, you will not be sidetracked by what is dramatic and spectacular yet really insignificant in relation to your problem.
4. Now you'll approach your reading with a mind full of questions. A questioning mind set should greatly increase both your reading comprehension and your retention of the information.
5. Your reading targets should step up your concentration. You'll be more alert when your reading is an active search for answers.

Can Students Locate Books and Other Sources?

Whenever individuals either during their years in school or thereafter want to attack a problem by means of reading, one of the first tasks they face is that of locating relevant information. Locational skills, as Gainsburg observed, are better taught than caught. Without teacher help, students often wander like lost souls among the thousands of books and periodicals in the library. With teacher help they can be equipped with the basic tools, the keys that open up for lifelong use the endless resources that await them there (New York Board of Education, 1957, p. 40).

The following check list of questions is intended to sharpen awareness of the many locational skills involved in problem solving. In preparing the sections on the card catalog and the *Reader's Guide*, the writers have drawn some helpful suggestions from Martin Rossoff's *Using Your High School Library*, an excellent guidebook for students (New York: The H. W. Wilson Company, 1964).

The reader may wish to consult the following sources of instructional methods:*

Boyd, Jessie, et al. *Books, Libraries and You*. New York: Scribner, 1967.

Buttle, Faye J. *Steps to Beginning Research*. Provo, Utah: Extension Publications, Division of Continuing Education, Brigham Young University, 1967.

Cleary, Florence D. *Discovering Books and Libraries: A Handbook for Upper Elementary and High School Grades*. New York: H. W. Wilson Company, 1966.

Kranyik, Robert. *How to Teach Study Skills*. Englewood Cliffs, N.J.: Prentice-Hall, 1963.

Lubans, John, Jr. *Educating the Library User*. New York: R. R. Bowker Company, 1974.

Rossoff, Martin. *The Library in High School Teaching*, 2nd ed. New York: H. W. Wilson Company, 1961.

Rossoff, Martin. *Using Your High School Library*, 2nd ed. New York: H. W. Wilson Company, 1964.

Shankmann, Florence V. *How to Teach Reference and Research Skills*. Englewood Cliffs, N.J.: Prentice-Hall, 1963.

Moments of Need Are Often Enough

Teaching locational skills need not place a heavy drain on time. Many of these skills can be taught in minutes at the time students need them, yet they can save students countless hours later as they search out information more efficiently. The school librarian can be a strong ally, available to visit classes or work with groups in the library. Again a checklist of skills need not seem overwhelming if approached with the question, "Which of these skills do students need *right now* in order to complete their coming assignments?"

---

* List compiled with the assistance of Sara Fenwick, former Associate Professor, Graduate Library School, University of Chicago.

A CHECKLIST OF LOCATIONAL SKILLS FOR PROBLEM
SOLVING OR TOPIC DEVELOPMENT

_____ 1. Are the students generally oriented to the library?

   _____ a. Do they know its floor plan—charging desk, card catalog, information (or vertical) file, magazines and newspapers, microfilm, microfiche, films, tapes, recordings, pictures, and the like?

   _____ b. Do they know where reference books, fiction, nonfiction, bibliographies, and special collections are placed on the shelves?

   _____ c. Have they observed printed placards above the bookshelves, announcing that books on certain subjects are housed below: Aeronautics, Astronomy, Biology, Mammals, Birds, Geography, Roman History, Greek History, European History, Economics, Drama, and many others?

_____ 2. Can students use the card catalog to learn what materials the library has to offer on a particular subject and where they can locate these?

   _____ a. When confronted with what might be a bewildering array of wooden trays, do they find their way by means of their alphabetical labels?

   _____ b. Are they aware that, although they may not know of a single piece of material or book on a given subject or of a single author who has written about it, the subject card will guide them to materials that bear upon the problem?

      _____ (1) Do they realize that knowing the subject under which to look is not always obvious—that they will wish to ask themselves thoughtfully, "*Just what key word* will lead to the appropriate information?"

      _____ (2) Do they know that they may need to cast about in their minds for every possible related topic? If the topic is "What are the first visitors from Earth likely to find on Mars?" they may find it rewarding to look not only under Mars but also in other catalog drawers under such subject headings as Solar System and even Astronautics.

      _____ (3) Are they aware that a specific subject may require search under a *broader* classification? If, again, the subject is Mars, they may turn up rewarding sources by consulting the subject card Planets.

      _____ (4) Do they follow the recommended sequence of first thinking of the most precise subject heading, then working their way to broader or more inclusive subject headings? Would they proceed, if necessary, from Mars to Planets to Solar System to Astronomy?

      _____ (5) Are they aware that they may find a valuable added resource in the cross-reference or "see also" card? They may find one of these placed in the card catalog just following the last card under Mars (see Figure 5–1). This cross-reference card is saying, "You've looked through all the cards under Mars. If you still need material, why not try the additional subject headings below?"

_____ (6) Do they realize that often there is no sure way of knowing which key word will lead to the information they are after? An expert (Rossoff, 1964, p. 22) offered this suggestion: "Locating the appropriate key word is a matter of trial and error. If you don't find what you're looking for under one subject, try another. Keep trying every possibility until you have exhausted them all."

_____ (7) Do they understand that determining the key word is crucial in investigating a topic? Do they persist until they get a breakthrough?

_____ (8) Are they aware that a subject card in the card catalog may point the way to a list of carefully selected books on the subject (see Figure 5–2)?

_____ c. As they go along, do they compile a working bibliography? When a book looks promising, do they make a 3 × 5 bibliography card (see Figure 5–3)? Do they save a great deal of time later by taking down all the essential information *at once?*

_____ (1) Are the items they take down on the card *the same* and *in the same order* as those they will need for the final bibliography? Will they compile a final bibliography with speed and ease because they have made out these cards with care?

_____ (2) Do they accurately record the call number—the "address" where the book can be found on the shelf?

_____ d. For quick access to a particular card they may want while doing their research, do they arrange the cards in a pack alphabetically by the last name of the author?

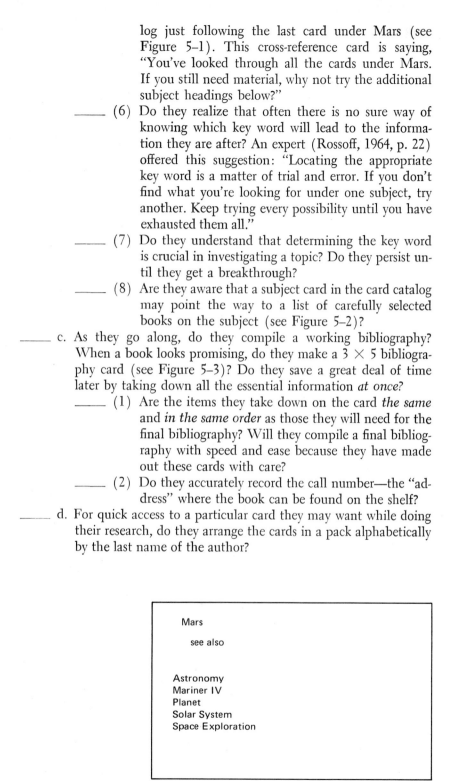

Mars

    see also

Astronomy
Mariner IV
Planet
Solar System
Space Exploration

Figure 5–1. *Cross-reference card.*

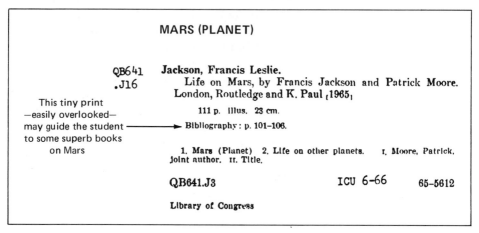

MARS (PLANET)

QB641
.J16

This tiny print
—easily overlooked—
may guide the student ────────▶
to some superb books
on Mars

Jackson, Francis Leslie.
  Life on Mars, by Francis Jackson and Patrick Moore.
London, Routledge and K. Paul ₍1965₎

  111 p. illus. 23 cm.

  Bibliography : p. 101–106.

  1. Mars (Planet) 2. Life on other planets. ɪ. Moore, Patrick.
Joint author. ɪɪ. Title.

QB641.J3   ICU 6–66   65–5612

Library of Congress

Figure 5–2.   Bibliographic aid.

QB 43
.2
.I 52

Inglis, Stuart J., *Planets, Stars
and Galaxies*. New York: Wiley,
John & Sons, Inc., 1972

Figure 5–3.   Sample bibliography card for a book.

_____ 3. Do they know the broad classifications of the Dewey Decimal or Library of Congress systems? Can they use the call number to locate a book quickly?

_____ 4. Can they use an encyclopedia to full advantage?

    _____ a. Do they appreciate the encyclopedia as a possible starting point, sometimes the ideal starting point in making an investigation? Are they aware that it may offer a quick overview of their subject—that they can base more detailed study on this helpful orientation? Do they know that once they have strengthened their background through this general introduction, they may be able to advance to more difficult, more technical material and comprehend reading matter that would otherwise have been beyond them?

    _____ b. Can they draw quickly and efficiently from the vast fund of human knowledge stored up in an encyclopedia? Do they value the index as a guide to easy finding? Do they often make use of the index first?

Figure 5–4. *Index entry on Mars. (Reprinted by permission from the* Encyclopaedia Britannica, *15th ed., Micropaedia. Chicago: Encyclopaedia Britannica, Inc., 1975, p. 644.)*

Figure 5–5. *Index entry on Mariner IV. (Reprinted by permission from* The World Book Encyclopedia, *Index Volume. Chicago: Field Enterprises Educational Corporation, 1976, p. 590.)*

_____ (1) Are they aware that the information they are seeking may be scattered here and there among hundreds of articles and that the index is the *only sure way* to locate this scattered information?

_____ (2) Do they realize that, by overlooking the index, crucial information on the topic may be lost? Suppose they need the astonishing evidence about Mars revealed by *Mariner IV.* If they look for *Mariner IV* in the "M" volume, these findings will elude them—they will find no article on that subject. If, however, they look in the index under *Mariner IV,* they will find references to scattered articles with crucial information.

_____ (3) Do they know where to find the index, this "key to maximum usefulness" of the encyclopedia—usually not in the last pages of each volume but in a separate volume? Have they ever actually held an index volume in their hands and availed themselves of its direction?

_____ (4) Since the arrangement of an index entry and the symbols used may differ from one encyclopedia to another, do they consult the simple, clear directions that precede each index?

_____ (5) Can they correctly interpret a "see" cross reference? Do they understand that a "see" reference corresponds not to an encyclopedia article with that name but to *another subject heading in the index* where the desired information may be found?

_____ (6) Do they take full advantage of the "see also" cross references? Do they understand that these send them to index entries for related material and that the related information may prove to be not only useful, but actually more helpful in solving their own particular problems?

_____ c. Do they use the guide words at the top of each encyclopedia page to locate an article quickly?

_____ d. Are they alert to the cross-references at the close of an encyclopedia article as clues to added information (see Figure 5–7)?

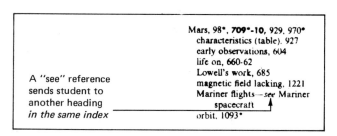

Figure 5–6.   A "see" reference. (Reprinted by permission from The Harper Encyclopedia of Science, Vol. 2. New York: Harper & Row, Publishers, 1967, p. 1343).

Figure 5–7.   Cross-reference information. (Reprinted from the Encyclopedia Americana by permission of the publishers, Grolier Incorporated, New York.)

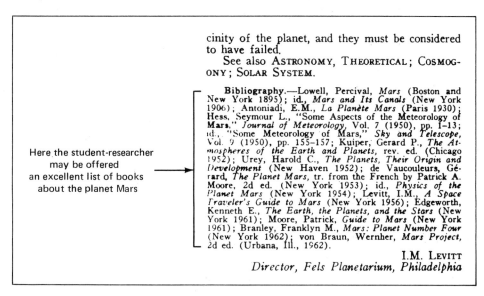

Here the student-researcher may be offered an excellent list of books about the planet Mars

cinity of the planet, and they must be considered to have failed.

See also ASTRONOMY, THEORETICAL; COSMOGONY; SOLAR SYSTEM.

Bibliography.—Lowell, Percival, *Mars* (Boston and New York 1895); id., *Mars and Its Canals* (New York 1906); Antoniadi, E.M., *La Planète Mars* (Paris 1930); Hess, Seymour L., "Some Aspects of the Meteorology of Mars," *Journal of Meteorology*, Vol. 7 (1950), pp. 1–13; id., "Some Meteorology of Mars," *Sky and Telescope*, Vol. 9 (1950), pp. 155–157; Kuiper, Gerard P., *The Atmospheres of the Earth and Planets*, rev. ed. (Chicago 1952); Urey, Harold C., *The Planets, Their Origin and Development* (New Haven 1952); de Vaucouleurs, Gérard, *The Planet Mars*, tr. from the French by Patrick A. Moore, 2d ed. (New York 1953); id., *Physics of the Planet Mars* (New York 1954); Levitt, I.M., *A Space Traveler's Guide to Mars* (New York 1956); Edgeworth, Kenneth E., *The Earth, the Planets, and the Stars* (New York 1961); Moore, Patrick, *Guide to Mars* (New York 1961); Branley, Franklyn M., *Mars: Planet Number Four* (New York 1962); von Braun, Wernher, *Mars Project*, 2d ed. (Urbana, Ill., 1962).

I.M. LEVITT
Director, Fels Planetarium, Philadelphia

Figure 5–8. *Bibliography in encyclopedia article. (Reprinted from the* Encyclopedia Americana *by permission of the publishers, Grolier Incorporated, New York.)*

The current yearbook of a science encyclopedia offers a "quick update" on Mars

Mars **66** 125–126; **67** 118; **68** 243–245
  atmosphere **67** 300–301; **68** 243
  carbon dioxide and nitrogen **68** 243–244
  craters **68** 244–245
  detection of atmosphere **66** 384
  escape and origin of gases **68** 244
  extraterrestrial life **67** 163
  Mariner probe **66** 383–385
  possibility of life **68** 245
  water and polar ice caps **68** 244

Figure 5–9. *Yearbook information. (From* McGraw-Hill Yearbook of Science and Technology, *p. 442. Copyright McGraw-Hill Book Company, 1974. Used with permission of McGraw-Hill Book Company.)*

_____ e. Are they aware that the expert who wrote the encyclopedia article may offer at its conclusion a bibliography of selected references (see Figure 5–8) and that such a list may be a good starting point in locating books on the subject?

_____ f. Do they realize that certain information in the most recent set of encyclopedias may already be outdated—that the recent touch-down of a spacecraft on the surface of Mars may have exploded theories widely held just months ago? Do they know that once each year many encyclopedias are updated by means of a yearbook? Have they ever actually held a yearbook, examined its contents, and availed themselves of its index to update their information on some current topic?

_____ g. Do they know of the existence of encyclopedias in specialized fields, for example, *International Encyclopedia of the Social Sciences* and *The McGraw-Hill Encyclopedia of Science and Technology?* When appropriate, do they consult these for more detailed, more technical information?

The following list is intended to be suggestive rather than exhaustive.

Art

Encyclopedia of the Arts. New York: Meredith Press, 1966.

Literature

Cassell's Encyclopedia of World Literature. New York: William Morrow and Company, 1973.

Music

Milton Cross New Encyclopedia of the Great Composers and Their Music. New York: Doubleday and Company, 1969.

Science

General: *The McGraw-Hill Encyclopedia of Science and Technology.* New York: McGraw-Hill Book Company, 1971.

Biology: *The Larousse Encyclopedia of Animal Life.* New York: McGraw-Hill Book Company, 1967.

Encyclopedia of the Biological Sciences. New York: Van Nostrand Reinhold, 1970.

Chemistry: *Encyclopedia of Chemistry.* New York: Van Nostrand Reinhold, 1973.

Physics: *Encyclopedia of Physics.* New York: Van Nostrand Reinhold, 1974.

Social studies

General: *International Encyclopedia of the Social Sciences.* New York: Macmillan Company, 1968.

American history: *An Encyclopedia of American History*. New York: Harper and Row, 1970.

World history: *Encyclopedia of World History*, 5th ed. Boston: Houghton Mifflin Company, 1972.

Sports

The Encyclopedia of Sports, 5th ed. Cranbury, N.J.: A. S. Barnes and Company, 1974.

_____ 5. Do they know which of their needs in reference reading will be served by other general library tools—almanacs, atlases, gazetteers, *Who's Who*, dictionaries, biographical dictionaries, and others?

_____ 6. Do they avail themselves of valuable source materials in specialized fields —science, social studies, music, and others—whenever they need these to complete an investigation?

Encyclopedias of specialized knowledge—example: *International Encyclopedia of the Social Sciences.*

Dictionaries of terms in specialized fields—example: *Harvard Dictionary of Music.*

Biographical dictionaries—examples: *American Men of Science, World Who's Who in Science.*

Trade books on specialized topics.

Scholarly research papers and abstracts of scholarly papers.

_____ 7. In an age when knowledge is changing and increasing at a furious pace, are they alert for ways to search out the latest information?

_____ a. Do they realize that publishing an ordinary book may take from six months to a year, a reference book even longer, and that consequently books cannot offer them the most recent information? Do they view periodicals, issued more frequently, as a promising source of up-to-the-minute information? Have they discovered that the *Reader's Guide to Periodical Literature* will help locate information on the subject in *thousands* of magazine and newspaper articles?

_____ (1) Do they appreciate the recency of the latest *Reader's Guide?* Are they aware that through the green paperback supplements they are offered a guide to periodicals which is updated as often as twice a month?

_____ (2) Are they aware that the crucial problem in finding articles related to a problem is determining the subject heading under which these will be listed—that the heading Mars may lead to rewarding articles, and also the heading Space Flight to Mars?

_____ (3) Are they aware that the specific information they seek may require search under a broader subject— that to locate certain information about a Mars probe they may need to look under the more inclusive term, Space Probe?

_____ (4) Can they read an entry in the *Reader's Guide* (Figure 5–10) correctly and completely, interpreting all the abbreviations and all the numerals (volume, date, page number)?

_____ (5) Are they alert to the value of the "see also" cross-reference (see Figure 5–11) in directing them to subject headings other than the one they originally looked under?

_____ (6) When searching for the latest information, do they begin with the latest green paperback supplement and work back into the earlier issues—compiling, as they go along, a working list of articles to be consulted?

_____ (7) For each promising article, do they make a 3 × 5 bibliography card—with the facts the same and in the same order as they will need them for their bibliography (see Figure 5–12)?

_____ (8) Do they understand that magazine and newspaper references are often of value when recency is *not* the consideration and that the *Reader's Guide* is the key which unlocks the vast storehouse of information in periodicals of the past?

_____ b. Are they aware that there are "reader's guides" in various specialized areas—social studies, science, art, music, education, and other fields—and that these will unlock the contents of thousands of specialized articles? (Example: *Social Science and Humanities Index, New York Times Index*)

_____ c. Do they consult the Information (or Vertical) File as another promising source of current information? Have they ever explored its large drawers, often well stocked with pamphlets and clippings?

_____ d. Are they aware of other possible sources of current information, such as:
New York Times Index (available on microfilm).

LIFE on Mars
    Are we alone in the cosmos? R. Jastrow. il
    Natur Hist 83:62-5 Je '74

Figure 5–10.   Reader's Guide *entry. (Reprinted by permission from* Reader's Guide to Periodical Literature, LXXIV, *New York: The H. W. Wilson Company, 1975, p. 638.)*

This cross-reference clues the students in to other promising headings →

MARS (planet)
Day the dam burst. D. E. Thomsen. il Sci
N 106:250-1 O 19 '74
Earth's neighbors yield surprises. il U.S.
News 76:44-5 Ap 15 '74
Occultations of Mars and Saturn. il Sky &
Tel 47:346-7 My '74
Update on Mars: clues about the early solar
system. W. D. Metz. il Science 183:187-9
Ja 18 '74
    See also
Life on Mars
Space flight to Mars
Space vehicles—Landing systems—Mars

Atmosphere
Martian climate: an empirical test of possible gross variations. T. Owen. bibl Science 183:763-4 F 22 '74

Photographs
Photographs of a recent Martian dust storm.
Sky & Tel 47:168-9 Mr '74
Roundup of amateur photographs of Mars. il
Sky & Tel 47:341-4 My '74

Photographs from space
Mars 5 photos show erosion patterns. il
Aviation W 100:16-17 Ap 1 '74

Surface
Carbon dioxide hydrate and floods on Mars.
D. J. Milton. bibl il Science 183:654-6 F
15 '74
Explanation of floods on Mars. il Chemistry
47:21-2 Je '74
Mars through the eyes of geologists; round
table discussion; ed by B. Konvalov. M. M.
Markov; P. N. Kropotkin; A. Sukhanov.
Space World K-9-129:27-9 S '74
Mountains of Mars. C. Sagan. il Sci & Pub
Affairs 30:42-6 Mr '74
Wind tunnel simulations of light and dark
streaks on Mars. R. Greeley and others.
bibl il Science 183:847-9 Mr 1 '74

Figure 5–11.   *Cross-reference in* Reader's Guide.
(Reprinted by permission from Reader's
Guide to Periodical Literature, *LXXIV.
New York: The H. W. Wilson
Company, 1975, p. 674.)*

Jastrow, R., "Are We Alone in the
Cosmos?" Natural History,
June, '74, pp. 62-65.

Figure 5–12.   *Sample bibliography card for periodical
article.*

> Encyclopedia yearbooks, recording major increments to knowl-
> edge within the past year.
> Almanacs and political handbooks:
> *Information Please Almanac.*
> *World Almanac.*
> *Statesman's Year Book.*

_____ e. Do students turn to indexes of other media for possible assistance, such as:

> *Library of Congress Catalog: Motion Pictures and Filmstrips,*
> 1948 to date.
> *Multi-Media Review Index.* Ann Arbor, Michigan: Pierian Press,
> 1970 to date (annual).
> *Schwann Record and Tape Guide.* Boston: W. Schwann Com-
> pany, 1949 to date (monthly).

_____ f. As they move from one library tool to another, do they compile
their own working bibliography, making a note of those references that look most promising?

_____ 8. Do the students select readings on an appropriate difficulty level?

We have mentioned the encyclopedia as the source of a quick overview
of a topic and a promising starting point in an investigation. This strengthening of background information can be extremely valuable to less able
readers. An inconspicuous word of guidance from the teacher can often
ensure the right encyclopedia for the right student and help to reduce discouragement and frustration.

The following annotations of encyclopedias commonly found in school
libraries may be useful:

The New Book of Knowledge. New York: Grolier, 1972. With the former
subtitle *The Children's Encyclopedia* deleted, *The New Book of Knowledge,* outstanding in attractiveness and readability, is now intended for a
wide range of users up to the age when they are ready for an adult encyclopedia. An outstanding feature is the attempt in the opening section to
motivate the student's reading further about a topic. In many of the articles, the reading difficulty advances within the article. The first few paragraphs convey information in short, simple sentences and easy vocabulary,
and subsequent paragraphs add more elaborate concepts. The style of
writing captures interest; illustrations are lavish. The field of social studies
is especially well covered. The articles are within the reach of grade-school
readers. Instructors working with less able teen-age readers will welcome
The New Book of Knowledge.

The World Book Encyclopedia. Chicago: Field Enterprises Educational
Corporation, 1974. Intended for students reading at grade 4 and up, the
World Book offers high-interest reading matter that many poor secondary-
school readers can grasp. In many articles, the reading difficulty advances
within the article. Handicapped readers can often handle the opening

section, which is approximately fourth-grade level. Bibliographies are well chosen.

Compton's Encyclopedia. Chicago: Encyclopaedia Britannica, 1976. Intended for upper elementary and secondary school use, *Compton's* offers readable material within the reach of many less able high school readers. The abundant full-color pictures with their easy captions appeal to under-par readers. Many articles conclude with graded bibliographies.

Britannica Junior. Chicago: Encyclopedia Britannica, 1973. This set, designed for pupils in grades 4–8, will also serve older students whose reading ability is not up to grade level.

Collier's Encyclopedia. New York: Crowell Collier and Macmillan Educational Corporation, 1975. This encyclopedia offers articles appropriate for many students in junior and senior high school as well as in college. An "in-between" encyclopedia, *Collier's* is more advanced than the "juveniles" but less advanced than the *Americana*. Each article begins with a brief explanation. After that, the material gradually increases in sophistication. The style is popular, clear, and direct. Graded bibliographies are grouped together in the last volume.

Encyclopedia International. New York: Grolier, 1976. This, too, is an "in-between" encyclopedia, designed primarily for the high school or college student but appropriate also for many capable junior high school readers. The articles are usually short; the style popular, clear, and concise; the illustrations abundant.

Encyclopedia Americana. New York: Americana Corporation, 1976. The coverage is broader and the information more detailed than in the sets previously mentioned. Capable high school and college readers will use this encyclopedia to advantage.

Encyclopaedia Britannica. Chicago: Encyclopaedia Britannica, 1974. This, of course, is an advanced encyclopedia with contributions written by eminent scholars. Capable high school and college readers can use it to advantage.

_____ 9. Are students aware that in reference reading it may be desirable to arrange readings in an easy to difficult sequence?

    _____ a. When appropriate, do they first select a relatively easy source to get a general orientation to a subject? Do they realize that broadening one's background information is a *major factor* in increasing power of comprehension and that once they have strengthened their backgrounds, they may be able to stretch and handle reading matter otherwise beyond their reach?

        _____ (1) Do they recognize that the encyclopedia is sometimes the ideal place to get this easy introduction,

this instant background—and that if they are planning to consult several encyclopedias, a desirable
sequence is from easy to more difficult—perhaps the
World Book, then *Collier's*, then *Americana?*

_____ (2) When appropriate, do they arrange the sequence of
their magazine reading from popular to scholarly—
first, for instance, a readable article for laymen in
Science Digest, then a more learned and technical
article in *Scientific American* or *Science?*

Can Students Use the Table of Contents and Index as Aids?

Suppose students have narrowed their problem and have stated it precisely,
have analyzed it into its component aspects and set up reading targets, and have
found some reference materials that look promising. They now each hold a
book in hand.

How can they find out whether the book really contains the information
they seek? Do they thumb through it haphazardly, examining many pages
unnecessarily? Or do they take advantage of two ready aids—the table of contents and the index—to help them learn what the book has to offer?

_____ a. Do they turn to the table of contents (See Figure 5–13) for an
outline—a concise, sequential listing of the major subject divisions covered in the book and the page where they can find the
beginning of a certain section?

_____ b. Do they use the index for instantly finding the precise page
where they will find a specific item from among the thousands
of words in the book? Do they view it as the *sure way* to find all
the help the book has to offer on a topic no matter how widely
it is scattered? Are they aware that if they should overlook consulting the index, they may miss the facts they are after?

_____ (1) Are they skillful at determining key words to help
find the information?

_____ (a) Are they aware that to dig out *all* the
help the book has to offer, they may need
to use more than one key word? (Examples: Mars, Viking 1)

_____ (b) Do they realize that the index may not
list the exact term they have in mind
and that they may have to look under a
synonym? Are they skillful at coming up
with possible synonyms?

Contents

Figure 5–13. *Table of contents. (Francis Jackson and*
              Patrick Moore, reprinted from Life on
              Mars. *By permission of W. W. Norton*
              & Company, Inc. and Routledge and
              Kegan Paul Ltd. Copyright © 1965 by
              Francis Jackson and Patrick Moore.)

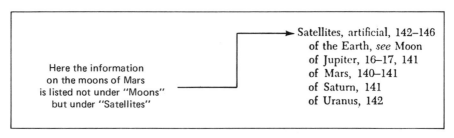

Figure 5–14.   *Index entry. (Reprinted by permission from* An Introduction to Astronomy *by Charles M. Huffer, Frederick E. Trinklein, and Mark Bunge. New York: Holt, Rinehart and Winston, Inc., 1967, p. 379.)*

_____ (c) Are they aware that they may need to think of a term broader and more inclusive than the one that first comes to mind and that they may need to look under *several* such broad terms?

_____ (2) Since the arrangement of an entry and the abbreviations and symbols used may differ from one index to another, do they consult, when necessary, the simple, clear directions that ordinarily precede the index?

_____ (3) Can they read the entry correctly and completely—the abbreviations and symbols? The punctuation marks?

_____ (4) Do they take advantage of the "see also" cross-references? When they need to, do they "squeeze out" from the index entry all references it offers on the topic?

_____ (5) Do they understand that a "see" cross-reference is a detour sign that sends them from a heading under which *no* references are listed to another index heading where exactly what they want may be found?

_____ c. Do they discard from their working bibliography, cards for books that offer them no useful information on their subject?

Papers, Oral Reports, and
Class Discussions All Gain

A teacher (Hozinsky, 1970) who builds help with locational skills into the day-to-day course work in natural science, has this comment: "I guide my students

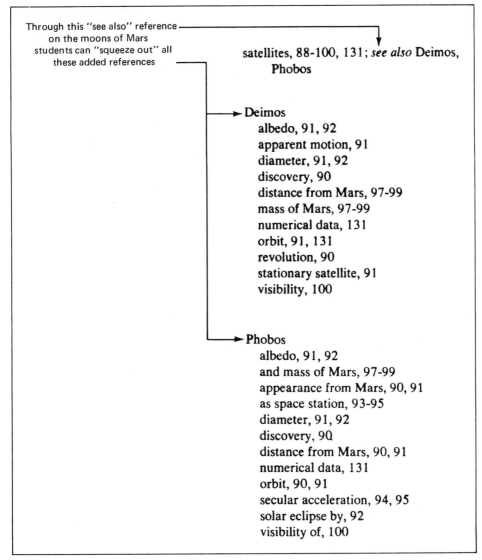

Through this "see also" reference on the moons of Mars students can "squeeze out" all these added references

satellites, 88-100, 131; *see also* Deimos, Phobos

Deimos
albedo, 91, 92
apparent motion, 91
diameter, 91, 92
discovery, 90
distance from Mars, 97-99
mass of Mars, 97-99
numerical data, 131
orbit, 91, 131
revolution, 90
stationary satellite, 91
visibility, 100

Phobos
albedo, 91, 92
and mass of Mars, 97-99
appearance from Mars, 90, 91
as space station, 93-95
diameter, 91, 92
discovery, 90
distance from Mars, 90, 91
numerical data, 131
orbit, 90, 91
secular acceleration, 94, 95
solar eclipse by, 92
visibility of, 100

Figure 5–15. *"See also" reference in index. (Reprinted by permission from* Mars *by Robert Richardson and Chesley Bonestell. New York: Harcourt Brace Jovanovich, Inc., 1964, pp. 147, 145, 149.)*

in using the *Reader's Guide*—the index of a book—the card catalog—an encyclopedia yearbook—the specialized reference works of science—at the moment when they are caught up with the desire to solve an exciting problem and will get immediate results through using the new skill. Their papers, their oral reports, their class discussions all gain as they become increasingly at home among the reference tools of science."

Can Students Scan a Passage for Information?

Let us imagine that the students have located a book, have it on the desk before them, and have turned to a passage that has information that will be useful. All they want from these pages is the particular content that throws light upon the problem.

Many students have no approach other than starting at the first word of the passage and plodding through it line after line, page after page. They will add a valuable reference skill to their collection when they learn the technique of scanning for specific information. Here are some "trade secrets" of successful scanners:

Have your reading targets clearly in mind before you begin your scanning. Cement in mind all the elements of the question, both main topics and sub-topics.

Watch for "highway signs." Your author has put up conspicuous highway signs for much the same reason the road department builds these in unfamiliar country. Among these signposts are chapter division headings, often in large capital letters, and side headings, often in heavy (boldface) or italic type. Such headings often announce the content of the section that follows. Some of these headings are saying, "This is promising hunting ground—you'll find what you're after here." Other headings are saying, "Speed right on past this section—there's nothing for you here."

If, for instance, you're searching for information on "What are the first visitors from Earth likely to find on Mars?" you can flash right on past a section headed *Motion of the Planet.* You'll slow down, though, and digest a section with the heading *Is There Life on Mars?*

Zero in on paragraph openings. The opening sentences of expository or explanatory paragraphs frequently flash signals as you look through a passage for specific information. You can often hop down the page, alighting on the first sentence or two of each paragraph, gathering up the gist of the paragraph quickly. Opening sentences may tell you, "Reader, slow down for this paragraph and search it carefully." Or they may say, "Bypass this paragraph—it isn't related to your problem."

Let's take an example. Suppose you're intent on finding just what temperatures the first Earthpeople are likely to find near the equator on Mars. You'll speed right past the first paragraph in Figure 5–16, but you'll zero in on the second.

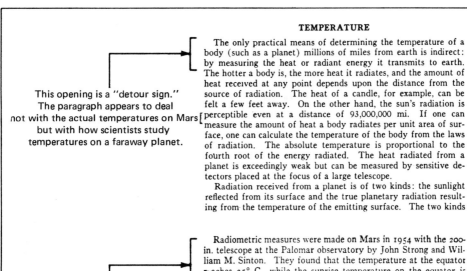

TEMPERATURE

The only practical means of determining the temperature of a body (such as a planet) millions of miles from earth is indirect: by measuring the heat or radiant energy it transmits to earth. The hotter a body is, the more heat it radiates, and the amount of heat received at any point depends upon the distance from the source of radiation. The heat of a candle, for example, can be felt a few feet away. On the other hand, the sun's radiation is perceptible even at a distance of 93,000,000 mi. If one can measure the amount of heat a body radiates per unit area of surface, one can calculate the temperature of the body from the laws of radiation. The absolute temperature is proportional to the fourth root of the energy radiated. The heat radiated from a planet is exceedingly weak but can be measured by sensitive detectors placed at the focus of a large telescope.

Radiation received from a planet is of two kinds: the sunlight reflected from its surface and the true planetary radiation resulting from the temperature of the emitting surface. The two kinds

This opening is a "detour sign." The paragraph appears to deal not with the actual temperatures on Mars but with how scientists study temperatures on a faraway planet.

Radiometric measures were made on Mars in 1954 with the 200-in. telescope at the Palomar observatory by John Strong and William M. Sinton. They found that the temperature at the equator reaches 25° C., while the sunrise temperature on the equator is at least as low as −50° C. They also found that the maximum temperature occurs about 12:30 P.M., instead of about 3:00 P.M., as on Earth. This slight lag, they concluded, results mainly from thermal conduction into the ground. This "greenhouse effect" is produced by the blanketing effect of water vapour and carbon dioxide in the Martian atmosphere, and is consistent with the theory that the surface of the planet is covered with dust. They estimated the average night-time temperature as −70° C.

These opening sentences flag you. They say, "Here's what you're after: the actual temperatures on Mars."

Figure 5–16. *Scanning signals. (Reprinted by permission from the* Encyclopaedia Britannica, *Vol. 14, article "Mars." Chicago: Encyclopaedia Britannica, Inc., 1963, p. 959.)*

Examine summary paragraphs at the close of chapters. Here the author often wraps up the main points he has made in the chapter. If, judging from the summary, the chapter appears to offer what you're after, you may wish to turn back to the more detailed discussion.

Opportunities to help students scan for answers to immediate questions arise in day-to-day course work. A progression through increasingly difficult levels of scanning is desirable:

Level 1. Scanning for a bit of information that stands out easily—the date of some historic discovery about Mars, the university with which a certain scientist was affiliated.

Level 2. Scanning for an answer that is worded like the question.

Level 3. Scanning for an answer that is worded differently from the question.

Using Scanning Techniques
for the Unit on Mars

A teacher may share insights like the following, or elicit them from students, when a long unit like the one on Mars confronts the student with the necessity for frequent scanning. The students scan to find answers to questions from the current assignment.

"You will often need to use a book to search out a single fact, the answer to a single question, or one aspect of your topic. High speed scanning can *save you time* in study. You can learn to crack the printed page, moving your eyes down the page swiftly to the heart of what you want.

"First, fix in mind exactly what you're looking for. Hold this in the forefront of your mind. Flash your eyes down the page for this information only.

"Once you've found lines in the passage that *may* yield what you're seeking, stop scanning instantly. Shift gears into careful reading as you weigh whether you've *really* found what you're after."

What a teacher might do and say in helping students become skillful scanners on all three levels mentioned above is suggested in the section on scanning in Chapter 4, pages 217–219.

Can Students Discriminate Between
Relevant and Irrelevant?

(*Note:* The suggestions given previously for practicing the technique of scanning are also applicable here.)

"Students often need to sharpen up their selectivity," teachers observe. "In reports and discussions, they waste their time and that of the class offering unrelated information. At the same time, they fail to include vital information."

The instructor's special guidance in selecting passages that are really relevant to the problem at hand should help students become discriminating reference readers. Suppose, for example, students are working on the question, "What *terrain* are the first Earthlings likely to find if they land near the Martian equator?" They will need to hold in mind that precise question—to resist the lure of information that is fascinating but has no real bearing on the problem.

The pages before them may offer a confusing choice of diverse information:

the cratered surface

origin of the craters

the intense wildness and loneliness

a desperate shortage of water

a hushed, deathly silence

the expanses of dusty "desert"

the color and type of soil

the curving surface and nearness of the horizon

bright white polar caps

"blue-green" areas

components of the atmosphere

severity of the conditions for living things

and other information

They should learn to concentrate on a precise topic (the *terrain* of Mars at the equator), to reject unrelated information (the polar caps, which are not near the equator), and to resist vivid and dramatic but irrelevant information (the eeriness of the Martian landscape).

Do Students Select or Reject After Critical Evaluation?

The critical reading skills in the accompanying checklist are vital to students in deciding which information contributes soundly to the solution of a problem.

CHECKLIST ON CRITICAL EVALUATION

_____ 1. Do the students note the recency of the copyright date? Are they aware that since the *Mariner VIII* picture-taking probe made startling revelations about the terrain of Mars, they must search out sources with a publishing date recent enough to include these findings?

_____ 2. Do they thoughtfully appraise the qualifications of the writer or investigator whose findings are reported?

_____ 3. Do they constantly ask, "What is the evidence that supports this statement? Is it soundly supported or is it just opinion—pure speculation passed off as fact?" What is the evidence, for example, for the statement that hot springs may provide water on Mars and warm the temperature?

_____ 4. Do they consider whether the statements made stem from emotion, bias, or a desire for sensationalism? As they probe the "great canal mystery," are they aware that the conclusion that intelligent Martians survived by building waterways carrying water from melting polar caps may have over-intrigued a popular writer?

_____ 5. Do they weigh the writer's conclusions, inferences, and generalizations? What about the mysterious blue-green areas of Mars with their seasonal changes? Does the theory that they are advancing and retreating tracts of vegetation appear to be well supported?

_____ 6. Do they resist the impulse to accept the first plausible solution to the problem? Do they suspend judgment—asking, for example, "Are there alternative hypotheses about the changing appearance of these blue-green 'tracts of vegetation'?"

_____ 7. Do they accumulate sufficient information? What about those widely debated canals? Do they explore deeply enough to learn that the closeup photographs of *Mariner VI* and *VII* revealed no sign of them? Do they weigh the conclusion that optical illusion may have created "canals" as the human eye joins up disconnected spots and streaks into canal-like lines?

_____ 8. Do they read widely, looking for and welcoming different points of view? Do they understand how to proceed when the viewpoints of authorities are in conflict?

Teachers working with processes of logical thinking may wish to consult the following sources:

Altick, Richard D. *Preface to Critical Reading,* 5th ed. New York: Holt, Rinehart and Winston, 1969.

Bilsky, Manuel. *Patterns of Argument: A Provision of Logic and Effective Argument.* New York: Holt, Rinehart and Winston, 1963.

Hayakawa, Samuel I. *Language in Thought and Action,* 3rd ed. New York: Harcourt, Brace and World, 1972.

Purtill, Richard L. *Logical Thinking.* New York: Harper and Row Publishers, 1972.

Ruby, Lionel, and Robert E. Yarber. *The Art of Making Sense,* 3rd ed. New York: J. B. Lippincott, 1974.

Sund, Robert B., and Leslie W. Trowbridge. *Teaching Science by Inquiry in the Secondary School,* 2nd ed. Columbus: Charles E. Merrill Books, 1973.

Washton, Nathan S. *Teaching Science Creatively in the Secondary Schools.* Philadelphia: W. B. Saunders Company, 1967.

Werkmeister, William H. *An Introduction to Critical Thinking.* Lincoln, Neb.: Johnsen Publishing Company, 1957.

Zahner, Louis, Arthur L. Mullin, and Arnold Lazarus. *The English Language.* New York: Harcourt, Brace and World, 1966.

Can Students Make Notes Efficiently
from Scattered Sources?

Let us imagine students at the stage where, with promising reference materials piled on the desk before them, they have located in one of these some highly important information. They want to make notes on this and include it in their reports or papers. Here, for many students, is a critical point in the research-study process.

All too often, adequate preparation in the making of notes, if offered at all, is delayed until the final year of high school, when a major research paper is assigned in English. Yet on every secondary level, assignments in the content subjects confront students with the necessity for frequent notemaking. Left to devise their own notemaking systems, many students are handicapped for years by methods that are helter-skelter.

Motivating and Teaching Notemaking

Let us picture a teacher holding a sendoff session when the problem requires notemaking from scattered sources, offering students some of the following insights and eliciting insights from students.

"As you do your reading on Mars, you'll want to take down important information. Of course you'll be making notes on all the different aspects of your problem. Have you considered the simple device of topical note cards? You'll complete your project better and *much faster* if you use these." The teacher projects the card in Figure 5–17 on a screen.

"Suppose you reach for a card and begin jotting notes on several different aspects of your subject at random on that single card." The teacher goes on. "This student's notes could hardly be more confused if they had been mixed up with a Mixmaster! Notes on seven different aspects of the Mars problem are jotted on that single card!

"Notes that you *scramble* as you take them, as this student has done, must be painfully *un*scrambled later—at the cost of adding *greatly* to your research time. Later you must reread and reconsider your notes, one by one, and thoughtfully assign each note to its proper classification.

"Instead, why not sort out your notes *as you do your reading*—reaching for a separate card whenever you make a note on a new sub-topic? You'll find this a most effective speed device in study."

The teacher projects on a screen the topical note cards in Figure 5–18 and Figure 5–19. Of course the "pattern" cards should be appropriate for the student's purpose, level of advancement, and the time to be allotted to the project.

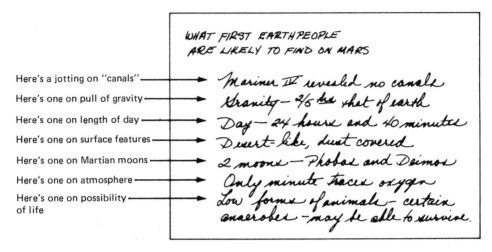

Here's a jotting on "canals"——▶   *Mariner IV revealed no canals*

Here's one on pull of gravity——▶   *Gravity— 2/5 ths that of earth*

Here's one on length of day——▶   *Day— 24 hours and 40 minutes*

Here's one on surface features——▶   *Desert-like, dust covered*

Here's one on Martian moons——▶   *2 moons— Phobos and Deimos*

Here's one on atmosphere——▶   *Only minute traces oxygen*

Here's one on possibility
of life——▶   *Low forms of animals— certain anaerobes —may be able to survive.*

Figure 5–17.   *Note card with badly scrambled jottings.*

Make a note of
the subtopic here.

     Make a note(s) <u>on a single aspect</u> of your topic and
<u>from a single source</u> here.

Make a condensed note of your
source here--author's last
name, a shortened title, and
the page(s) where you found
the information. (You already
have the complete data on your
bibliography card.) OR you
might number each bibliography
card and write just the corresponding number here.

You might want to record
here a cross reference to
information noted else-
where. ("See also"
another of your note
cards.)

Figure 5–18.   *Note card for a single sub-topic.*

"Through your topical note cards, you've saved yourself time, trouble, and bother—simply by sorting out and classifying your notes as you go along!

"You'll find it greatly to your advantage to make notes *on only one aspect of your topic* and *from a single source* on each card." (Students may need to think about and discuss the *why* of this.) "Later you can re-sort, regroup, and rearrange all the bits of information conveniently without the wasted effort of

Only notes
on
one topic
and from one source
will go on
each card

CLIMATE- TEMPERATURE

Colder than earth

At 7 A.M. on equator during Martian
summer — -60°F.

At high noon — higher than 80°F.

Gallant, *Exploring Planets,*
pp. 56-57.

POSSIBILITY OF LIFE — ANIMAL

In experiments, certain new forms- with
little need for oxygen or water-grew and
survived in an environment which
simulated that of Mars.

Unlikely higher forms of animal life, as
we know it, could exist in cold, and,
oxygenless world.

Wright and Richardson, "Mars,"
Encyclopedia Britannica, p. 954

SURFACE FEATURES- TERRAIN

Believed to be flat or rolling,
Mariner IV revealed cratered surface
nothing in *Mariner IV* photos suggests
valleys, ocean-basins, continents,
may be eroded mountain chains.

Michaux, *Handbook of Physical
Properties of Mars,* p. 115.

Figure 5–19.   Sample note cards.

recopying. You can shuffle and reshuffle your cards with complete freedom as you contemplate different ways of organizing your material for your final presentation. You can easily add a new note on a topic or throw away notes you've taken which later prove to be worthless.

"As you're making the note, decide on an identifying topic label, one that closely fits the information on the card." (Students may want to think about and discuss the value.) "You can often pick up labels from the topics and sub-topics in your target outline—those reading goals you set up before you begin reading. Print this heading in the upper left-hand corner of the card.

"It's handy to write on one side of the card only. Later you can spread out a number of cards on the desk before you while you're working and have in full view all the information you've gathered on a topic.

"Keep your cards arranged in alphabetical order according to their topic labels. Insert each new card at its appropriate place in your packet. Now you can quickly locate any card you want."

Use Your Own Words—Unless

"It's generally advisable to take down the author's thoughts in your own words. You may wish, though, to record the writer's *exact* words under certain circumstances:

1. If you think your paraphrasing will alter the original meaning.

2. If you wish to quote directly a writer who has expressed an idea more vividly, persuasively, or compactly than you could express it.

3. If you wish to quote an authority directly to reinforce an argument.

"Some students crowd and clutter their note cards by recording identical information two or three times. Be alert to recognize repetition when it's disguised in different phrasing."

Where Do Your Own Ideas Come In?

"Where do *your* ideas come in during all this reading? What about your own observations, impressions, and conclusions? Of course you'll want to make notes on your own interpretations. If it's a case of interjecting your own ideas into notes you are making from another source, enclose your own ideas inside brackets. If you use separate cards to record your own ideas, flag these cards in some way so that you recognize *yourself* as the source. You might write the

"CANALS"

No trace of canals in *Mariner 4* pictures. Most astronomers don't report seeing them.

Terrain has craters and ridges. I tend to share view that "canals" may be optical illusion — the eye may connect these geographical features up into continuous lines.

(ME) But why, then, are "canals" clearest in early spring?

Figure 5–20. *Note card with student's reflections.*

word *me* with a circle around it—or your initials—in the lower corner where you usually make a note of the published source. Place the cards with your own reflections *with* related material from published sources" (Leslie et al., 1968, pp. 212–213).

In summing up, the students might review and discuss values of the topical note cards. Among the other plus factors, they are likely to mention the values below:

WHY USE TOPICAL NOTE CARDS?

---

1. If your assignment is a written report, you'll now find much of the task of organizing already done. Your paragraphing will be much easier. You've already grouped together all the bits of information on each sub-topic. You can locate these sets of related facts quickly.

2. If your report is to be oral, you'll probably talk from notes, and you'll want to recast the notes on your cards into an outline. Here again, you'll find much of the assembly job already done.

Can Students Bring Their Notes Together into an Orderly Presentation?

After collecting their notes, students may be at a loss in bringing them together into the final report or paper. Although assignments that call for presenting the results of reference reading are routine in many courses, the student's preparation is often too little and too late.

The guidelines below direct attention to steps students must take as they transform their notes into the final presentation. For more thorough coverage, the reader may wish to refer to Leslie et al. (1968) and Perrin (1972).

Instructors will wish to adapt these procedures to the level of advancement of their students, ensuring early mastery of appropriate skills.

Tips for Transforming Notes into Your Final Presentation

Let us now picture a teacher helping students prepare their final reports or papers, using the chalkboard to work out tentative and final outlines. "You will often be called upon to present your library research findings in the form of a paper or report. To do so, you must bring many bits and pieces into a unified, orderly statement.

"The notes you have made on cards are not yet in their final sequence, and you have probably made slight attempt to show levels of subordination. If you have used the one-note-on-a-single-card system so there is not much overlapping, you can now sort, group, and arrange topics, sub-topics, and sub-sub-topics conveniently without the wasted effort of recopying. You can shuffle and reshuffle your cards until you are satisfied with the final arrangement. The following suggestions are likely to be helpful."

First, you have already grouped your note cards by topics. Now *look through your notes to identify the main topics under your general problem.* These will become the "highest value headings" in your outline. You already know the identity of some of these main topics from your original reading targets and your topical note cards. Should other main topics now be added in the light of all your reading?

Second, *in what order should these main topics be discussed in your final presentation?* Arrange them in the order you decide on, leaving plenty of space to insert sub-topics. Number these main topics with Roman numerals:

What the First Visitors from Earth Are Likely to Find on Mars Near the Equator

    I.   Surface features

   II.   Features of sky

  III.   Force of gravity

  IV.   Atmosphere

V.   Weather

VI. Life forms (if any)

VII. Perils to human survival

Third, *working with one main topic at a time, look through your note cards for points that develop, explain, or support that topic.* These, of course, will become sub-topics in your outline. Arrange these sub-topics in the order in which you plan to discuss them. Label them with capital letters, as you would in any outline. As you work with the main topic "Surface Features," for example, you may decide that you will discuss four sub-topics in this order:

I.   Surface features

    A.   Terrain

    B.   Soil

    C.   "Hot spots" (?)

    D.   Canals

Working on down to the main topic "Life Forms," you conclude that the logical sub-topics are definitely "Plant Life" and "Animal Life." You will now identify subordinate points that drop into slots under these sub-topics. Number these with Arabic numerals, as in the usual outline:

VI. Life forms

    A.   Plant life
        1.   Possible types
        2.   "Hot spots" favorable to other types?

    B.   Animal life
        1.   Experiments simulating the Martian environment
        2.   Higher forms possible?

Fourth, *don't start writing too soon.* The organizing you are doing calls for strenuous logical thinking. Do not try to hurry this! Weigh the alternatives carefully, then make your decision. Do not hesitate to change your mind (Brewton et al., 1962). Your final outline may appear something like this:

What the First Visitors from Earth Are
Likely to Find on Mars Near the Equator

I.   Surface features
    A.   Terrain
    B.   Soil

         1. Type
         2. Color
    C. "Hot spots" (?)
    D. Canals
         1. Proof of advanced life?
         2. Natural features?
         3. Optical illusion?

II. Features of sky
    A. Appearance of solar system and stars
    B. Sun
         1. Length of day
         2. Length of year
    C. Moons
         1. Deimos
         2. Phobos

III. Force of gravity
    A. Comparison with Earth
    B. Effect on weight
    C. Effect on movement

IV. Atmosphere
    A. Composition
    B. Pressure
    C. Humidity
    D. Color of sky
    E. Cloud formations
         1. Yellow clouds
         2. Bluish-white clouds

V. Weather
    A. Seasonal variation
    B. Daily variation

VI. Life forms
    A. Plant life
         1. Possible types
         2. "Hot spots" favorable to other types?
    B. Animal life
         1. Experiments simulating Martian environment
         2. Higher forms possible?

VII. Perils to human survival
    A. Insufficient oxygen
    B. Intense cold
    C. Ultraviolet radiation
    D. Life-support systems needed

Fifth, with your note cards now arranged in the order in which you plan to present your information, *write your rough draft* (or prepare the notes for your talk), using your outline and note cards as guides.

And last! At this stage you'll be extremely thankful for those bibliography cards on which you took down the essential facts about your reference sources in the exact order in which you'll need them for your bibliography. Now you can quickly *convert these cards into your final bibliography.*

Do Students Keep an Open Mind for Later Evidence?

Students should of course regard their final reports as something less than "final." In the closing years of the twentieth century, solutions in the field of science, social studies, and other areas may not long remain solutions. Unmanned landings with equipment for life-detection and, not too far in the future, the first manned vehicle that touches down on the red planet, may disprove much that the student has searched out so carefully about the planet Mars.

Bibliography

Burmeister, Lou E. *Reading Strategies for Secondary School Teachers*. Reading, Mass.: Addison-Welsey Publishing Company, 1974, chapters 9 and 11.

Goldsmith, Stephanie. *Library Tools: Reader's Guide to Periodical Literature*. Chicago: Independent Learning Project, Laboratory Schools, University of Chicago, 1969.

McKee, Paul. *The Teaching of Reading in the Elementary School*. Boston: Houghton Mifflin Company, 1948, pp. 425–530.

New York Board of Education. *Reading, Grades 7, 8, 9—A Teacher's Guide to Curriculum Planning*. Curriculum Bulletin No. 11. New York: Board of Education, 1957, pp. 30–51.

Sanacore, Joseph. "Locating Information: The Process Method." *Journal of Reading*, 18, no. 3 (1974): 231–233.

Smith, Donald E. P., ed. *Learning to Learn*. New York: Harcourt, Brace and World, 1961.

Spache, George D., and Paul C. Berg. *The Art of Efficient Reading*, 2nd ed. New York: Macmillan Company, 1966.

References

Bell, Earl, University of Chicago Laboratory School social studies teacher, in remarks to Ellen Thomas, May 1970.

Brewton, John E., R. Stanley Peterson, B. Jo Kinnick, and Lois McMullan. *Using Good English*, grade 12. River Forest, Ill.: Laidlaw Brothers Publishers, 1962, pp. 134–155.

Hozinsky, Murray, University of Chicago Laboratory School science teacher, in remarks to Ellen Thomas, May 1970.

Leslie, Louis A., Roy W. Poe, Charles E. Zoubek, and James Deese. *Gregg Notehand*, 2nd ed. New York: Gregg Division, McGraw-Hill Book Company, 1968.

New York Board of Education. *Reading, Grades 7, 8, 9—A Teacher's Guide to Curriculum Planning*. Curriculum Bulletin No. 11. New York: Board of Education, 1957.

Perrin, Porter G. *Writer's Guide and Index to English*, 5th ed. Chicago: Scott, Foresman and Company, 1972.

Rossoff, Martin. *Using Your High School Library*, 2nd ed. New York: H. W. Wilson Company, 1964.

SOCIAL STUDIES

"How can I teach social studies when many of my students can't read well?" This chapter will suggest a number of ways classroom teachers can help their students read with greater success in social studies.

How can teachers easily find out something about the reading of their students? How can they learn what may be blocking some of their non-performers? The first topic in this chapter suggests practical procedures for exploring their students' strengths and shortcomings for handling readings in the course, procedures that in a teacher's busy schedule require little time.

That plaguing problem of no interest on the part of some students—what are some possible ways to combat it? In the next section, "Helping Students *Want* to Read," we offer suggestions for exciting the interest of students, pulling them into the reading, helping them really want to find answers.

Teachers are likely to find among their students a dismaying range in reading achievement. Giving all those students the same reading materials is like giving them all size nine shoes and expecting them to wear them! (Robinson, 1958). How can teachers have on call reading materials their limited readers can succeed with, reading materials their most competent readers can grow on? In the third section, "You Can Have a Silent Reading Teacher in Your Classroom," we suggest ways a teacher can develop a full range of classroom reading resources. Then how can they bring the "right reader" and the "right reading" together? In the same section we report how teachers have accomplished this in actual classrooms.

Those abstract concepts that crowd the pages of social studies reading—how can you break the barrier? In the following section we offer procedures for helping students grapple with—and grasp—elusive concepts.

Last, we offer a number of suggestions for upgrading the reading of primary sources—eyewitness accounts, excerpts from diaries, texts of speeches, and the like. Originally intended for mature adult readers, primary sources may place formidable roadblocks in the way of today's young people. We also include some specific how-to-do-its, "Ten Tips for Reading Primary Sources," intended for students.

This social studies section is not a complete package. Since many reading needs in social studies are identical with needs in English, we urge you to consider Chapter 7 on English a vital part of this chapter. There you will find important ways to help students "when their reading's a struggle." You will also find a section on "Study Guides to Turn on Reading Power." Those interested in helping students understand the contents of an important textbook chapter may wish to turn to "You Can Upgrade Students' Textbook Reading" in Chapter 3. For other procedures for social studies, we refer you to the Subject-Area Index in Chapter 1.

We share the reflection of a master teacher of social studies at the University of Chicago Laboratory School (Flickinger, 1970), whose teaching from day to day was evidence of her belief in reading as one of the most productive activities of her students: "To misread a telephone book is to get a wrong number. To misread on social issues is to get a wrong world."

FINDING OUT ABOUT YOUR STUDENTS' READING

How can you learn, fairly easily, something about your students' strengths in reading and the blocks in their way—to plan a year of more successful learning?

"How can I learn whether my students are able to handle readings I am considering?" "How can I learn which students should be challenged with rigorous reading?" "How can I find out the range in reading power within my classes?" "How can I get insights into what may be blocking one of my non-performers?" "How can I find time for this?" Numerous teachers have come to the authors with these questions.*

In this section we have tried, above all, to offer practical procedures, procedures that in a teacher's busy schedule require little time. They should prove

---

* For additional detailed suggestions about assessing students' abilities, consult Robinson, 1975, chapter 2.

useful with a single student who troubles you or with all your students. Even one of these procedures should yield useful information. Obviously, you will value diagnostic insights most during the opening weeks of school. Insights gained then will help you plan a year's successful learning.

Standardized Reading Scores Offer Some Insights

Your school may have standardized reading test scores that are yours for the asking. One instructor (Flickinger, 1969) searches out these scores even before she meets her first classes:

> During planning week I spend an hour jotting reading scores after each name in my class record book. This is a first step toward getting acquainted. Daily the scores give me a suggestion of each student's reading power. Daily they remind me of the wide range within the class. Daily they nudge me to make adjustments for individuals and *prevent* failure.

Standardized reading scores often include subscores in vocabulary, comprehension, and speed. While group survey tests yield only rough insights about individuals, the subscores suggest possible strengths and weaknesses. The teacher who sees that Ted, who is having difficulty, has a low score in comprehension will reflect, "It looks as if he may have difficulty here. Now I need to find out more."

You may wish to have further interpretation in terms of the reading range within a class, for example, to have percentiles explained in terms of grade levels. The reading specialist of a school or system may be available to assist you. This specialist can also assist in matching reading materials to groups and individuals.

Time required to jot down the scores: perhaps an hour. The dividends for you: hints about your students' strengths in reading and the blocks in their way.

Students' Insights Can Be Revealing

Year after year young people live with their own reading strengths and shortcomings. Their requests for help can be revealing. In one classroom the instructor probes for the students' insights through a simple checklist:

> Students return to school in September thinking, "This year I'll really study." I capitalize on these good intentions by hav-

ing them indicate on a checklist the type of help they need
in order to have a good year. I do this *after* they have had a
chance to sample some of the course materials.

Then all year I use the students' own requests for help as
"motivators." I preface the help: "We're having this work
with vocabulary because you requested it" or "You asked
for comprehension help, so here it is" or "These tips on making
notes were one of your requests." These motivators work like
magic for me—the students take full advantage of help they
themselves have "ordered." Of course students do not always
appraise themselves accurately. Their answers should be combined with other insights.

The questionnaire that follows suggests possible items for a checklist.
*Estimated time to make a checklist: perhaps an hour—or just use ours. Time
required to give it: about ten minutes. The dividends for you: a student's-eye-
view into his needs, the rapport that comes with caring about students' requests.*

Give Your Own Homemade Test

How can you learn how well your students can handle the actual course
materials? Here standardized reading tests yield only limited information.
Ordinarily the words on a standardized test are not specialized terms from the
field of social studies. And the comprehension section usually includes only a
few passages with social studies content.

You can, however, make your own "homemade" test and assess your students' competencies in reading their course materials. Just select two or three
pages of representative difficulty. If all your students have copies of the book,
you don't even need to duplicate the passage. Then ask questions probing for
whatever competencies you wish to investigate. You might ask: "Please study
this passage right here in class just as you would ordinarily read such material.
A little later, you will have some questions. You may make notes on the important ideas, and you may use these as you answer your questions. You'll have
_____ minutes."

Students who do not complete the passage within the time allotted should
note on their papers the point where they stopped. All who finish should enter
in an upper corner the elapsed time, the figure they see on the board when they
look up after completing the reading. (While the class is working, the instructor records the elapsed minutes on the board, changing the number every
half minute.)

The check-up on comprehension can be quite simple (or as elaborate as

text cont. pg. 282

WHAT STUDY TIPS WILL HELP YOU HAVE
A GOOD YEAR?

Name	*Period*	*Date*

What kind of study tips will help you have a good year?

Students often mention the factors below as playing a part in their achievement. Please check the factors that you think will help you. Your teacher will consider your requests carefully and use this information to help you have a good year.

Check Your
Requests Here

1. I often need help in understanding the meanings of words. (   )

2. I often need help in comprehending the readings. (   )

3. I need help because it takes me so long to read my assignments. (   )

4. I need to be able to tell the difference between what is important and what is unimportant as I am reading. (   )

5. I should like to have help in taking notes when I read an assignment. (   )

6. I need help in bringing ideas I have gained from reading together into a final paper or oral report. (   )

7. I need to become really interested in what I am reading. (   )

8. I am not aware of difficulties. (   )

What else can you think of that will help you have a good year? Please write your requests below.

_____

_____

_____

_____

_____

_____

you wish). It should begin with one free response question: "What, in the main, did the author say?" or "Just write a summary of the main points." You may wish to ask questions of the type you will actually be asking in future assignments. Since difficulty with writing can block responses of the essay type, you may consider it advisable to include some short answer questions.

If you wish to explore vocabulary strengths, you can list key words and their locations on the board or underline them in a dittoed passage and ask: "What do these words mean as they are used in the passage?" Here the student is permitted to refer back to the selection.

All students should hand you their notes. The quality of jottings on their note sheets, their answers to the questions, their elapsed reading time, plus your observations while they are studying should provide you with valuable insights.

1. Can individual students discriminate between main ideas and subordinate material?

2. Can they take notes?

3. Can they sum up the results of their reading?

4. How rapidly do they read such material?

5. Are the students' vocabularies equal to the passage?

6. Can they handle material of this difficulty, or does it appear to be beyond them?

Care must be taken lest students regard this important diagnostic test as "just another quiz." They should feel that their teachers are sincerely interested and eager to help. The purpose of the test should be made quite clear: "We'll use this information to help you have a good year."

Of course, an informal test can, if the instructor wishes, yield more specific information. Once constructed, such a test may be usable for years. You may want to ask questions that involve skills you know will be important for the year's work, skills like grasping the main idea, retaining details, seeing relationships, making inferences and generalizations, detecting bias, and other skills essential for coming assignments. Test papers can be returned to the students and used as a springboard for sessions on how to read and study. It is probably best not to assign a grade to these papers but simply to note strengths and shortcomings. A reading specialist may be available to assist in preparing and interpreting this more comprehensive test.

You may wish to consider another procedure for judging the suitability of materials for students, the cloze procedure, explained later in this chapter under "You Can Have a Silent Reading Teacher in Your Classroom."

Readers in search of patterns to follow in making informal tests will find these in abundance in Ruth J. Viox, *Evaluating Reading and Study Skills in the Secondary Classroom* (Newark, Del.: International Reading Association, 1968). Ralph C. Preston and his colleagues offer practical suggestions in *Guiding the Social Studies Reading of High School Students* (Washington, D.C.: National Council foɪ the Social Studies, 1963).

Students Send Out Telltale Signals

As students carry on reading activities from day to day, you may detect these and other distress signals (from a comprehensive list compiled by Eileen Sargent, Marquette University):

1. Some students are eager to avoid reading, turning to other activities on the slightest pretext.

2. They are among the first to finish reading but can recall little.

3. They are always the last to finish reading an assignment.

Of course, each student's contribution in class and the quality of his or her writings based on reading are two more important "revealers." And finding out about students' reading is an ongoing process as they change and improve all through the year. What happens each day in the classroom is an opportunity for further insights.

Teachers sometimes ask: "How can I know when students have unfulfilled potential and when they are already reading about as well as we should expect them to?" Be alert from day to day for students who comprehend what they *hear* better than what they *see* on the printed page. Clearly, those students have learning potential that is not coming through in reading. Be alert, too, for those who perform considerably better in school subjects that do not require much reading. They, also, may have unfulfilled potential.

Time required: hardly any time at all—you would be observing your students anyway.

To sum up, we have mentioned four ways to explore reading competencies, equally useful if you want insights about a single student or about all your students. What will be the dividends? A greater sensitivity to the needs of students and insights to help you plan a year of more successful learning.

HELPING STUDENTS WANT TO READ

*That plaguing problem of no interest—here
are some possible ways to combat it.*

How can we help students *want* to read in social studies? Mindy, sitting in the back row with her head in her hands and her book upside down, may not see the value of what is between those covers. In this section we offer possible ways to interest the Mindys in our classrooms, to pull them into reading, to help them really want to find answers.

Experienced teachers observe how strong interest helps students dig out the meaning of difficult material, how it pulls them along and speeds up their reading, what wonders it does for concentration. Just let a student have trouble with a motorbike, then give him or her the *Honda Repair and Tune-up Guide*, and you may find this student digging out the meaning of quite difficult passages.

For this section we have collected a wide choice of possible types of motivators and a great variety of examples—knowing what a diversity of teaching styles exists in social studies classrooms. We hope they will be helpful to teachers, especially those less experienced who have not already developed their own motivators. Many of the examples are not purely one type or the other; there will be much overlapping.

Instructors may feel a special need to motivate reading as students use primary sources in making investigations or as they encounter the excerpts from primary sources that are appearing more and more often in textbooks. All through their years in school, these students have used reading materials designed by skilled writers to appeal to young people and to ease their way in reading. Primary source materials, intended for adult readers, may confront young people with special difficulties.

Of course interest alone will not solve the problems of all troubled readers. Other procedures for helping them are offered in the first five chapters. Few of these are likely to succeed, though, without interest.

While the motivators below may not be as exciting as the *Honda Repair and Tune-Up Guide*, you will undoubtedly find some of them suggestive.

Motivator Number 1

Motivator Number 1 is an intangible. This motivator is inspiring young people to investigate the experience of past generations of human beings and to apply this knowledge to the understanding of problems of their own world.

It is giving them "a link with past human experience to help them feel that their own relatively short span of life may have meaning of its own in relation to the generations past and to their contemporary experience (Krug, 1969, p. 59). The young person who enters the field of social studies teaching is probably already disposed to use Motivator Number 1.

Clashing Interpretations May Send Students into Reading

Interpretations of history and of historical figures sometimes clash head on. These clashes may interest students and stimulate them to dig into the past through reading. In a course on the American frontier, the teacher in the example below sends students digging into eyewitness accounts and other original sources (Carlson, 1975):

> Two differing interpretations of Jesse James give me an opportunity. Using the opaque projector, I first project a dime-novel-type lithograph of Jesse in which he appears as a gallant Robin Hood. I comment: "Jesse James was like Robin Hood—generous, great-hearted. He was just misunderstood and persecuted! Of course, we all know how a coward shot Jesse in the back. . . ." and so on.
>
> Next I project a picture of Jesse as a cold, steely-eyed criminal and comment: "Jesse James was a wild animal who deserved exactly what he got. He was a psychopathic killer. . . ." and so on.
>
> "Now let's go on a search for truth. *Which* picture is closer to the true Jesse?"

Here is another head-on collision:

> The great industrial figures of the late nineteenth century are sometimes called "robber barons" and sometimes called "industrial statesmen" (Bailey, 1961, p. 106). Read to try to decide which is the more accurate picture. Were they robbers who grasped at immense wealth and reaped it with ruthless disregard for others? Or were they men who realized the importance of capital for the nation's growth, used their leadership in the public interest, and brought our country immeasurable benefits? What is a fair-minded conclusion?

Believe-It-or-Nots Stir Interest

Questions that have a "believe-it-or-not" quality provoke curiosity. They fly in the face of what students have heard or what they would expect. Such questions invite students to read in order to explain the unexplainable:

> Henry Bragdon, historian, wrote: "The Emancipation Proclamation did not free a single slave." Is his statement true? Explain your answer.

> Manufacturing the automobile you ride in takes 300 products that come from 56 nations! Read to find out what some of these products are and from what faraway lands they come (adapted from Kenworthy, 1969, p. 499).

"Purposeful Projects" Involve Students

In an enthusiastic new look at an old technique, Sartain (1973) recommended the "purposeful project involvement approach." We sum up his article here:

> You can lead students to reading, but you can't make them read? Many students in today's schools are not convinced that book learning has much value for them. But there is *one* subject that appeals to *all* students. What is this miraculous motivator? Why, driver education, of course! Here instead of purposeless readings and busy work, the assigned readings contribute directly to the attainment of competencies the students know to be immediately useful.
>
> We can make students just as enthusiastic—well, almost as enthusiastic—about reading in other subject fields as they are in driver education. We can do so if we break away from the pedantically subject-centered approach to secondary teaching and adopt a *purposeful project involvement approach*.
>
> We need first to observe what is important in the everyday lives of our young people, to observe their behaviors and listen to their conversations to determine their major frustrations, their strongest desires, their peer values, their social activities, and their family concerns. Consider what these young people would do with their time if they were not required to attend school. Then make a list of projects that can be carried out in school to satisfy some of their needs as growing human beings. You may find them almost as eager to engage in a community

survey of opinions or conditions or in trying to solve the problems of an area of economic blight as they are to take driver
training.

Launch the project in some striking way—a bulletin board
with captioned illustrations, a film, a class discussion, a field
trip. As interest intensifies, ask whether the students would
like to engage in a related activity, or wait until the project
idea comes from them. Engage the youngsters in step-by-step
planning of what they want to do. Invite them to itemize types
of information they need. This can lead to the listing of sources
—people and references—followed by individual and committee efforts to locate, read, share, and use the information.
Voilà! Your students are purposefully involved in reading in
order to complete a project that is *important to them.* Plan
with the class the form the final project will take—a display;
a program at school; a publication for students, parents, interested citizens, or community leaders; a radio or TV program;
a program at a shopping center. Divide the class into committees to work on parts of the investigation. Guide the students
to reading materials they are comfortable with. Introduce the
reading and study skills they need to gain the information they
must have for their activity. Arrange and carry out the final
presentation as planned.

Young people, Sartain reminded us, learn when they *want* to learn.

This inner-city class caught fire (as reported on the ABC TV program
"Make a Wish," April 27, 1975):

The students redesigned their own community as the ideal
community of the future. They transformed its residences,
recreational centers, transportation—even set up its government. They "tried on" roles like building inspector and mayor.
They "plugged in" to reading to find solutions to problems.
They emerged with important insights: "Environment happens because people make it that way," and "Each individual has a responsibility toward his city to make it what it
should be."

Add "Now" Appeal

It is often possible to inject "now" into questions about the happenings between the covers of history books. These examples link up the far away and
long ago with the here and now:

Compare the songs of the Westward Movement with songs
that reflect life today, and show how the characteristics of each
age are reflected in song.

Who was braver—the crew of *Apollo Eleven* or the crews
on the *Nina, Pinta,* and *Santa Maria?*" (Shaftel, 1972, p. 4).

"Inflammables" Can Light the Fire

"Inflammables" is the term Engle and Longstreet (1972, p. 100) use for highly
provocative questions—questions intended to elicit strong reaction. Some of
them fly in the face of time-honored ideas. They need not, though, encourage
cynical or iconoclastic attitudes. Instead, with a guiding hand present, they
can generate thoughtful reading and discussion:

> As the students study the moods and problems of Revolu-
> tionary days, they become aware that the American patriots
> rebelled against British "law and order." They consider this
> question: When, if ever, is it just to use violent protest to se-
> cure one's right? (Adapted from Shaftel, 1972, p. 34).

> The students will be reading conflicting sources about the
> Founding Fathers, who drew up the Constitution. According
> to one view, they were men dedicated to the highest principles
> of human liberty and to creating a republic that would pre-
> serve these principles enduringly. According to another view,
> they were the "Funding Fathers," men of property who met
> to create a document that would permit them, without inter-
> ference, to enjoy that wealth—some of it black men held in
> bondage. The students are asked: "Read to find evidence.
> What is your conclusion?"

Controversial Issues Spark Interest

Issues students are seeing in the day's headlines and hearing hotly debated can
ignite their interest. Here is one way *any* live issue can quickly come alive in
the classroom (adapted from Association of Teachers of Social Studies, 1967,
pp. 37, 63):

> A class public opinion poll is conducted on some live ques-
> tion—it might be a heated election campaign or some issue
> like the part our nation should play in solving the world's food

problems. Through the poll, each student is instantly involved in a problem-solving situation. The students consider, "What more do we need to know?" and set up an outline of what they want to look for. After reading and discussion to arrive at an informed opinion, a follow-up poll is taken to determine how many have changed their views.

"Read about pollution in the next chapter," a class might be told. Two clashing classroom visitors, though, are more likely to lead to an in-depth exploration:

> The public relations representative of a public utility company, one charged with polluting the community's land, air, and water, visits the class and presents her viewpoint. Then the spokesman for a militant environmentalist group takes "equal time" to present his view. The students ask: "Can I decide this question until I get more information?" They read to decide what position the facts support.

Use "Puzzle Appeal"

Situations that leave the student puzzled may motivate reading in order to solve the puzzle:

> The United States has the highest output of goods and services for its people and the highest standard of living anywhere in the world. Yet for many Americans in Appalachia poverty is a way of life. How can this contrast exist? How can such a fabulously rich nation have such a large impoverished area?

In geography, the assignment might have been "Read the next chapter." But the "mystery" below was more intriguing to students (Kenworthy, 1969, p. 89):

> After a class had studied communities in various parts of the world, the teacher brought to class a stack of colorful scenes from some "mystery land." The captions had been cut away. The students were to decide what part of the world these exotic scenes represented. They searched the pictures for clues, then decided "It's some part of Southeast Asia." Actually it was Indonesia. Then the class proceeded to study two communities there—one a village and one a large city.

Tap Young People's Social Caring

Many of today's young people feel genuine concern about social problems. We can make this a more informed concern, help channel it into constructive action, and tap it as a stimulus to reading. Tasks like the following (developed by the Social Studies Department, La Follette Senior High School, Madison, Wisconsin) appeal to social caring and may inspire young people to help finish "the unfinished business of democracy:"

> Members of minority groups in the community—an Indian, a Puerto Rican, a black—are invited to talk about what it means to be in their minority group in America today. They touch off extensive reading by the students, who now see the problems in human terms and care about finding solutions.

Students do their best learning, studies indicate, when the task stimulates them emotionally as well as intellectually (Kenworthy, 1969, p. 68). Questions that might have been coldly factual can be written so that they have an emotional aura:

> Why in our city, where some of the world's greatest doctors practice, where some of the greatest hospitals are located, and where the latest medical knowledge is available, do many of our citizens have little or no health care? What is the situation? What is being done? What is proposed? What are the merits of the proposals? The demerits?

As with many of the other "motivators" in this section, the appeal to social caring engages initial interest. But lest there be only an exchange of intense but flimsily supported opinions, the instructor must soon shift the focus to a reasoned study through "scientific" questions.* Often the students themselves, with the teacher contributing, formulate specific questions. They usually work harder to find answers to their own questions than they work at questions the teacher hands them all neatly prepackaged. Students and teacher, working together, suggest possible sources of information. Both the questions and the sources can be dittoed. Then in an organized investigation, individuals and committees—emotion aside—locate, read, and share information on different aspects of the problem.

When students have learned to put their analytical skills to work and reject instant answers, when they can walk into supercharged emotional situations and be dispassionate, social studies teachers have achieved one of their first objectives (Bell, 1975).

---

* James A. Banks suggests excellent ways to do this in *Teaching Strategies for the Social Studies* (Reading, Mass.: Addison-Wesley Publishing Company, 1973), pp. 117–121.

Give a Mini-Preview

You can catch students' interest and set the stage for a coming assignment through a mini-preview. A mini-preview that has proved extremely successful with students is found under "Never a Dull Moment in Zinch Valley" in Chapter 3.

Previews are crucial, Krug believes, when the readings at hand are documents, letters, speeches, and other original sources. In his view, presenting a document in its historical setting is *the most important condition for the effective use of the document*. He discussed, as an example, Lincoln's moving farewell to his friends in Springfield. The teacher would do well, he suggested, to precede this farewell with a brief but dramatically delivered lecture. Here is the background Krug suggested (1969, pp. 55–56):

> Soon after his election, Abraham Lincoln realized quite clearly the tasks that lay before him. . . . During the crucial months before his inauguration, the President-elect remained at his home in Springfield. . . . Not wanting to infringe on the authority of President Buchanan, he was reluctant to offer solutions to the slavery crisis. Helplessly he watched the Union being split asunder by secession. Almost daily he received warnings that the Copperheads . . . would prevent his inauguration even if it meant his assassination.
>
> Disregarding these warnings and forebodings, Abraham Lincoln decided to go to Washington by the longest possible route, taking twelve days, in order to see as many people as he could. . . . He was eager to talk and listen to the people of the North who had elected him to the highest office in the land. Surrounded by a handful of friends, Lincoln arrived at the railroad station in Springfield to board his train. The day was cold and damp; the skies were overcast, and a steady, bone-chilling drizzle fell. Mr. Lincoln wore a black coat, a top hat, and a shawl over his shoulders. Around the rear platform of the train stood a wet and rather gloomy crowd of friends who had come to bid farewell to their illustrious native son, the man they knew and loved so well.
>
> Mr. Lincoln mounted the platform.

Now, with the class in a mood of expectation, the teacher could read the moving farewell, bringing out the sadness and drama of the occasion.

One teacher (Surgal, 1975) considers Elizabeth Barrett Browning's "The Cry of the Children" his most successful preview. Written in the heat of her distress that children of four and five were living lives without hope in mines and factories, this poem—read dramatically—sends students into readings on the abuses of the Industrial Revolution. In the same instructor's course on urban studies, Wilfred Owen's "A Fable: How the Cities Solve Their Transportation Problem" really sends his students into readings on urban planning alive with questions.

Visual aids can greatly increase the interest of a preview. Classes might hear: "Tomorrow we'll discuss the Depression. Study about it in your textbook." Or, instead, they might become eyewitnesses (adapted from Shaftel, 1972, p. 96):

> Few records convey the human anguish of the Depression as strongly as do Dorothea Lange's photographs, available in anthology form. An opaque projector could display these strikingly, while the teacher gives a running commentary.

Colorful Phrasings Catch Interest

Lively language excites the imagination. This question is clear and adequate: "Why did the colonists react strongly to Thomas Paine's *Common Sense?*" This one, though, creates more interest (Casner and Gabriel, 1967, p. 5):

> Why was Thomas Paine's pamphlet *Common Sense* like a spark dropped into a keg of gunpowder?

Inject "You-Appeal"

Injecting "you" into a question adds interest. Now there is more personal involvement:

> How old will you be in the year 2000? Here are some readings with some startling predictions about what the United States may be like in that year. If these predictions come true, what do you think you will *like* about life in the year 2000? What do you think you will *not like?*

> Imagine that you are a Pilgrim. Your colony needs more settlers. Write a letter to a friend in London persuading him or her to sail to the Plymouth Colony. (Shaftel, 1972, p. 11.)

> Write a story, a skit, or a page in an imaginary diary about what it was like to live one day as a member of Columbus' crew on his flagship, the *Santa Maria.*

Striking Statements Stimulate Reading

Striking statements *ask* for analysis—invite inquiry to find out more. In one classroom the teacher sometimes makes a preposterous statement, one *sure* to provoke controversy or one that flies in the face of the truth. He challenges the protesting students: "Then prove me wrong!" To do so, they dig into primary sources (Carlson, 1975).

> In a course on Western civilization: "Hitler *cannot* be blamed for Nazi Germany."

> "All Indians are alike!"

The statements below appeal to curiosity:

> Some people believe that the Dred Scott decision is the "most disastrous opinion the Supreme Court has ever issued." Why would anyone believe this? What is your opinion of this decision? (Shaftel, 1972, p. 62.)

> When Harriet Beecher Stowe, author of *Uncle Tom's Cabin*, was introduced to President Lincoln in 1862, he remarked, "So this is the little lady who made this big war." Was Lincoln justified in saying this?

Set a Challenging Task

Students are unlikely to read "just to get it over with"—or not to read at all—if the reading is tied in with tasks they find challenging.

An instructor whose students were to read eyewitness accounts of the Spanish conquest of the Incas sparked interest by taking on the class in a debate:

> For tomorrow you'll be reading how the conquistadores enslaved the Incas and put to death their great chief Atahualpa. Which side was in the right? Tomorrow *I'll* take the side of the conquistadores. *You* come prepared to plead the case of the Incas. As you read, look for evidence that the Incas suffered great wrongs.

Interviewing relatives and friends is exciting, especially when the issue is explosive. Vehement opinions may send students into reading:

Ask adults you know—relatives, neighbors, friends—what they think when they hear "handgun control" (or some other controversial figure or issue). They will probably respond with sharply conflicting views. What information do you need in order to make up your mind intelligently? Read to arrive at an informed opinion.

Make a Tie-Up with Today's Problems

Although much that is between the covers of history books may seem eons away from today's students, there can be a tie-in with today's world and its problems in almost all social studies subjects. In each example below, a class is led to see a problem from the past in terms of a present problem:

> Many Northerners broke the Fugitive Slave Law. Read these sources about runaway slaves and about sympathizers in the North who aided their escape. Then try to decide if *you* would have broken this law and helped a runaway to freedom. Would you have hidden a runaway slave in your home? Would you break a law you considered wrong today, for instance, a law about draft regulations?

> You'll be reading how the early Puritans banished Roger Williams into the wilderness of Rhode Island for his "obnoxious heresies." Should we take similar action against some of our most militant radicals today? (Banks, 1973, p. 120.)

Create a "You-Are-There" Effect

The pages of history are crowded with the dilemmas faced by past generations. Many present opportunities for some form of role-playing. Here is a possible way for students to relive some of those dilemmas.

> *Before* the students read about one of the great dilemmas of the past—it might be President Truman's order to drop the atomic bomb—the instructor says, "Think quietly about this dilemma, then jot down what you think *you* would have done and *why*." Then, before the students make their decision, the instructor dramatically conveys President Truman weighing the pros and cons of using "the most terrible weapon the world has ever seen." Another dilemma might be a Northerner trying to decide whether to break the Fugitive Slave Law and

hide a runaway in his home. After a discussion, the students
may read with greater interest since they themselves have felt
the painful dilemma.

Especially with younger students and those interested in dramatics, questions like the ones below throw students into roles and put them inside someone else's shoes. The student may reflect: "Do I need more information? What was it like to be in this situation? What did this person think and feel? What would that individual do and say?" Such questions may send the student to eyewitness accounts, including diaries and biographies, to historical novels, and to textbooks:

> Prepare a short dramatization on the differing attitudes of the patriots and the loyalists in 1775. Play the role of a son who has come to tell his father, still loyal to England, that he has decided to fight in General Washington's army. A classmate will play your father, who pleads with you to stop and consider the consequences of what you plan to do (adapted from Casner and Gabriel, 1967, p. 53).

> Play the role of Robert E. Lee in great conflict, debating within himself whether he should join the forces of the Union or those of the Confederacy (Kenworthy, 1969, p. 98).

In the example below, students read widely in order to play their role accurately in a present-day clash of interests (MacKinnon, Bazan, and Carlson):

> Classes planned "U.N. Days" when they would dramatize the operation of the General Assembly. With other issues, Arab-Israeli problems were on the agenda. One student was to play the role of the delegate from Israel; another, the delegate from an Arab country. For weeks they researched their positions in order to play their roles realistically when they debated before the U.N.

The Most Striking Send-Off?

As you plan an assignment, you might ask, "How can I introduce this reading in the most striking way?" A group of reading "hold-outs" responded to this send-off (Social Studies Department, La Follette Senior High School, Madison, Wisconsin):

> A parole officer and some young ex-prisoners under his guidance visited the class. They talked about the influences that

lead young people to crime, about whether the penal system discourages crime or fosters it, and about the need for change as they saw it. Their visit touched off weeks of reading about young people and crime.

Capable readers, too, respond to striking send-offs. In assigning readings about inflation, a class might have no send-off other than, "Read pages 457 to 463." On the other hand, the teacher might take a tip from Dick Cavett:*

> Holding up a realistic facsimile of a dollar bill, the teacher calls it the dollar of 1946. Picking up the scissors, he snips away two inches. Now, in terms of what it will buy, it is the dollar of 1956. Snipping one-half inch more, he holds up the dollar of 1966. Snipping off still more, he has left in his hand the two-inch dollar of today. He snips once more at the dollar and holds in his hand a one-half inch stub. That, barring the unpredictable, will be the dollar of the year 2000 if prices rise at 6 percent a year (*U.S. News and World Report*).
>
> By this time, hands are likely to be waving: "*Why* has the dollar dwindled?" "What are the effects on us?" "How can we control this?"

We have shared a number of ideas for arousing the interest of students. More than just motivators, they should help young people leap over some of their reading barriers.

This momentum may be lost, however, if as the students begin their reading, they open book after book only to be confronted with difficulties. In the next section we talk about the good results for students when we bring the right reading matter and the motivated student close together.

YOU CAN HAVE A SILENT READING TEACHER IN YOUR CLASSROOM

> *You'll work to build this important classroom resource for social studies teaching. Then it will be working for you—to bring your students more successful reading experiences.*

You can have a silent reading teacher in your classroom, daily helping your students toward reading success. This silent teacher is a collection of reading resources that are right for your students. You can have on hand—to draw on

---

* Dick Cavett snipped away parts of a dollar bill to introduce an interview on the subject of inflation on his ABC television show.

daily—reading materials most of your students can succeed with, reading materials students can grow on. Building such a collection need not be overwhelming, instead, it should make the task of teaching much *less* overwhelming.

How can the right reading resources be a silent reading teacher? The world of printed words has never been the world of troubled readers. But when they are guided to books right for them in difficulty and interest, even poor readers may spend many hours in the world of printed words. They meet new words repeatedly in similar and different settings, often with a little increment of meaning at each encounter, and gradually incorporate some of these into their vocabularies. The reading practice helps to strengthen their comprehension. Easy, exciting readings pull them along quickly and tend to increase reading speed.

A classroom reading collection will benefit your competent readers, too. Challenging books will stretch their reading power.

Such a collection is built up over a period of time—one item and then another. Each item, as it is added, becomes an instant asset. That one item can mean a successful reading experience for some student. Beginning teachers are especially likely to want to start collecting reading resources. With time, their collection can become an invaluable classroom resource to draw on through future years.

Of course, appropriate materials alone cannot solve the problems of all troubled readers. For those who are seriously behind, instruction from a remedial reading teacher may also be needed. Remedial teacher and classroom teacher will then work hand in hand. The remedial teacher cannot succeed those few hours a week spent with a handicapped reader unless the classroom teacher provides continuing practice with appropriate materials.

In classrooms where more innovative practices prevail—case studies, court cases, activities that stress decision making, build-your-own-curriculum unit books, multimedia kits—and in more traditional classrooms, supportive reading resources can be of tremendous value.

Teachers of subjects other than social studies need not rest content with materials chosen for the average reader in the class. Reading resources differing as widely as do the reading capabilities within the classroom are available in almost every subject area.

A Roomful of Reading Facilitators

A Textbook to "Match" the Reader?

Let's imagine that a class of juniors studying United States history has the following reading range:

	Probably read most materials
Number of students	*about as well as the average*
2 / /	4th grader or below
3 / / /	5th or 6th grader
4 / / / /	7th or 8th grader
5 / / / / /	9th or 10th grader
9 / / / / / / / / /	11th grader
6 / / / / / /	12th grader
4 / / / /	first-year college student

How does it seem to place in the hands of each of these students the same once-and-for-all textbook, a textbook chosen to match the average reader in the class? And how does it seem to assign to each student, day after day, the same pages? According to the reading profile, fourteen of the students may find the textbook beyond them (though some can read it with help), while ten may be able to handle more advanced material.

During the first few days in American history courses, classes often study the great voyages of discovery and the daring explorers who risked their lives on unknown oceans to find the New World. Must some of the students become lost readers on this very first assignment? And from then on, must they lose the opportunity to practice reading and perhaps end the year even farther behind than they began it?

Publishers are offering more and more textbooks to meet the needs of less capable readers. If some of these books are on hand in a classroom (or in the library), they can supplement—or even supplant—for certain students that single textbook. Several sets of four or five quality textbooks, several copies of each, could span the reading levels of the class whose profile appears here. Reich, Strickland, and Biller, *Building the United States*, offers 5th and 6th-grade-level readers hope of success. Schwartz and O'Connor, *The New Exploring American History*, does the same for 6th- and 7th-grade-level readers. Wood et al., *America: Its People and Values*, is a match for junior-high-school-level readers. Todd and Curti, *Rise of the American Nation*, is appropriate for 11th-graders who are reading around their grade level. Of course, books should be available to extend the reach of the superior readers. Hofstadter et al., *The American Republic*, will challenge the most accelerated on the profile. Such a gradation of textbooks can be available for students to reach for during their work periods in class and to check out for overnight and weekend use. The reading specialist may be available and may be called on—especially by less experienced teachers—to appraise the reading and interest levels of textbooks, to estimate the reading range within a class, and to help match up the two.

How do you hold a class together when the students are using several different textbooks? How do you make reading assignments in all these different books? How do you guide each student to the book that is on the right level of difficulty? We suggest some possible answers under "Supplanting That Single Textbook" later in this chapter.

We should not fail to add another view about the use of multilevel textbooks. Many experienced teachers value the unifying effect upon the class of a single textbook. They want classes to have common reading experiences, and they believe these lead to more productive discussions. And many less experienced teachers cling to the security of a single textbook. They are not comfortable at the possibility of confusion in the class when the students are working with several different textbooks. For these reasons, some teachers prefer to place a single basic textbook in the hands of all the students, even though they must give considerable help to some in reading this book. In this case it becomes imperative to select a basic textbook most of the class can read. And it becomes a responsibility to the advanced readers, who might otherwise mark time in reading the entire year, to challenge them with advanced supplementary materials.

The Right Reading Matter in the Reading Corner

Giving the students all the same reading materials is a little like giving all the patients waiting in a doctor's office the same prescription. A classroom reading corner can help supplant or supplement one book for all with the right book for each:

> "In my track-three classes," reports a concerned teacher (Bell, 1975), "my students and I stockpiled the classroom. We created our own little learning world. There wasn't much money to buy materials, but we brought in armloads. Biographies and historical fiction we trundled in from the library. The colorful, lavishly illustrated *American Heritage*, brought from the library, was useful. The students brought in the local papers, and I brought in top national newspapers and news magazines. I asked the students to look around their homes. I know this sounds unreal, but they found copies of *National Geographic*, *Life*, even useful textbooks, brought these in, then let us keep them. We got a great library out of their homes! Oh, yes, I collect books of original documents, and I brought these in. I got my name on the mailing list for catalogs of free and low-cost publications from government agencies.* Pamphlets on every contemporary problem were avail-

---

* Write to the Superintendent of Documents, Government Printing Office, Washington, D.C., for a biweekly annotated list of publications and for the U.S. Government Printing Office Monthly Catalog.

able—some beautifully done. I got on the mailing list of historical societies. When we overflowed the bookshelves, my boys built larger ones in shop. One day I walked into class and found that two big husky football players had grabbed the same book and were fighting over it. Though I had failed, obviously, in teaching the cool, analytical approach to problems of the social studies scholar, I had my reward."

Inexperienced teachers may not be aware that trade books, many already awaiting them on the shelves of their school libraries, offer reading related to almost every conceivable social studies unit. Unlike textbooks, *trade books* are not designed for day-to-day lessons but are published primarily for the general public. Already available by the thousands, more trade books are appearing all the time. Many are on easy reading levels. A reader with fourth- or fifth grade reading power can find success with some of the books in the Landmark Series, published by Random House, or the First Book and Focus Book Series, published by Franklin Watts. Trade books have special appeal to social studies teachers who like to create their own units. The quality varies greatly, so it is well to examine individual books carefully.

Some teachers—during a unit—give intriguing thumbnail sketches of the content, then spread the books out invitingly on a reading table. If the students are studying the age of exploration, *Courageous Companions* might be there— the stirring story of a lad who with courage undaunted sailed with Magellan and shared the perils of his crew. As the class goes on to other units, historical events *live* and so do men of long ago—through the reading corner. The pages in the textbook on the American Revolution may not be stirring. But in Julia M. Carson's *Son of Thunder: Patrick Henry*, the student lives through those thrilling and turbulent days. George Washington Carver may be dealt with in two or three lifeless lines in the textbook. But in Florence Crannell Means's *Carvers' George,* he becomes a living, breathing person—the former slave who, years later, crowned with honors, met the world's great in his plain old clothes.

Talented juvenile writers produce these trade books. Representing widely varying levels of reading difficulty, they offer at least a partial answer to the problem of that dismaying range in reading levels on the profile.

Slim, trim books are on the table to invite the reading "hold-outs." They want a book that feels thin between their thumb and forefinger. In the past they have lost the battle in working their way through books. Now they want to see the end from the beginning. Lavish illustrations invite the "hold-out"— they are well aware how much they can learn from illustrations.

Fiction abounds in the reading corner. "Writers of textbooks," one teacher comments (Flickinger, 1970), "drain all the life out of a period. Writers of fiction put it back in." Compare a capable reader's reaction to the textbook's passing mention of the slave trade to experiencing the living agony of young Hwesuhunu chained down in the dark hold of a slave ship in Courlander's moving novel *The African*. Compare the student's reaction to reading about the Okies on the pages of the textbook to living with the Joad family through "black blizzards" and black despair in *The Grapes of Wrath*. Eyewitness accounts bring the past to life, too. Capable readers live D-Day through the eyes of brave men who landed on the coast of Normandy through reading *The Longest Day*.

Many social studies teachers are welcoming the new "build-your-own-curriculum" unit books, designed for use with single units as teachers put together the course that they believe best serves their students' needs. The titles cover a wide variety of key subjects—some historical, many contemporary. Readable and inviting as these books are, if the entire class is using a single set, then every student is handed a book on the same reading level. In that event, what valuable supportive materials a classroom reading corner can offer!

In some schools books for the reading corner are yours for the trundling—a cartful from the school library can remain in the classroom during the weeks a unit is under study. If it does not seem practical for the library to make books available to classrooms on extended loan, colorful, attractive books related to the unit can be spread out on tables in the library. The students can make their selections, check out books they want, and bring them back to the classroom.

We can dream, though, that some marvelous books remain in the classroom permanently—books like *April Morning, Shane, Geronimo, My Story, True Grit, The Little House on the Prairie, Autobiography of Lincoln Steffens, Giants in the Earth*—right there, always available, where hands will reach for them. Perhaps the teacher has done some "scrounging" in used book stores, at sidewalk sales, at rummage sales. Windfalls may have come from students' parents. Books for a classroom are sometimes made possible by a fund from the department budget. To add resources to the school library, teachers may be able to interest community civic organizations in donating books or the money to buy them. They can also investigate the possibility of government funds, for example, under programs like NDEA and ESEA.

Simple checkout systems for classroom libraries are explained in the industrial arts and fine arts sections of this book (chapters 10 and 16). Students sometimes serve as librarians.

We have not mentioned reference books likely to be standard in social studies classrooms: a dictionary, atlases, and *World Almanac*, perhaps an encyclopedia. By now, as you see, books have overflowed the students' reading corner. Reading is all around them.

A Clipping Bank To Draw From

Here is a classroom resource that costs just pennies and a few dabs of paste! It's a clipping bank of news stories and articles—some easy, some challenging —stored in a file or perhaps a bright-covered box. Scissors near, you scan magazines and newspapers for clippings related to your units. A few snips with the scissors, a dab of paste to mount them, and into the bank they go. Your students, too, are on the lookout. What a rich collection could be accumulated for a unit, for example, on young people and crime! Students can mount and file the clippings.

The *Reader's Digest* and the easier *Reader's Digest Skillbuilders* offer short articles, many on popular social studies subjects. Supplied with a bright construction paper cover, these can go into the bank. *News for You* (Syracuse, N.Y.: New Readers Press), an adult newspaper in interest and format, can supply clippings from 3rd- to 5th-grade reading level. *Scholastic Search* (reading levels 4 to 6), *Junior Scholastic* (6 to 8), and *Senior Scholastic** (8 to 12) offer rich "deposits" about America and the world your students live in. So do *Know Your World* and *You and Your World*, described in the next paragraph. Place the clippings in topical folders in a no-cost file—it can be a carton covered with construction paper. There they are ready for instant retrieval.

Something Everyone Can Read—in the Paper

Today's headlines can invite students to reach for reading. Two student newspapers, *Know Your World* and *You and Your World* (Columbus, Ohio: Xerox Education Publications), purchasable with NDEA and ESEA funds, are designed to have an impact on students. The news is presented with strong visual appeal and is written so students can relate to it. *Know Your World* is intended for students ages ten to sixteen—those reading at 2nd- to 3rd-grade levels can read this inviting paper. *You and Your World* is for students age fourteen and older; it is within the grasp of those on 3rd- to 5th-grade reading levels.

Parents may be glad to send in, when they have finished reading them, copies of periodicals they subscribe to, glad to have them put to good use, for instance, *Holiday, Travel, National Geographic, U.S. News and World Report, Time, National Review, Newsweek,* the *New York Times,* the *Christian Science Monitor,* foreign newspapers. A request to parents may bring you a windfall.

One instructor (Bell, 1975) helps lower-track readers "climb up" a gradation of newspapers:

---

* Published by Scholastic Magazines, New York, N.Y.

Each student becomes a specialist on a continuing news story or on some area of the world that catches his or her interest. I start the student on an easy-level newspaper. Later when he or she is hooked and ready, I hand out one that is more difficult. Students can sometimes advance from the local paper, around sixth-grade level, to the student weeklies of the *Christian Science Monitor* or the *New York Times*. Incidentally, it's great for these students when the teacher coordinates the newspaper with TV—a presidential news conference, for example—and next day the class has an analysis of it.

A Pamphlet Collection, Giftwrapped

Pamphlets and brochures, ordered by students, can come to your classroom giftwrapped. The federal government' can contribute, from its countless low-cost publications, a series of leaflets on American Indian life, a pamphlet on every one of the world's countries, and materials on every contemporary problem. You can order catalogs of Government Printing Office publications from the Superintendent of Documents, Washington, D.C. Manufacturers and businesses will supply countless other printed materials of interest to social studies classes. The John Hancock Life Insurance Company will send *Story of the Pilgrims, Presidents of the United States*, and *Flags of the United States of America*. General Motors offers *The Automobile Story* and other publications. State tourist bureaus offer booklets, like *Hawaii, the Aloha State* and *Come Swing Through Minnesota*. Chambers of Commerce and tourist bureaus will send pamphlets about their communities—size, productivity, and historic sites. Canadian province tourist bureaus also publish educational brochures. Travel agencies and foreign embassies offer colorful booklets on their lands. When students order these materials themselves, they watch the mails for their arrival, examine them eagerly when they arrive, and regard them as theirs in a special way.

Teachers Turn Author

When published materials are not exactly what they want, many a teacher turns author. You can create materials exactly to your liking. Sometimes you need only to select and bring together a few parts of a passage that originally was too long and complex for your students. Sometimes you need only to bring together short passages from several different sources. Other times you may write a short, easy-to-read digest of crucial points in a unit and supply this as alternate reading to far-below-average readers. Or you may occasionally simplify an entire article or chapter, although lowering the reading level appropriately may call for the help of a reading consultant. In the Social Studies Department at La Follette Senior High School (Madison, Wisconsin), three teachers of the course in western civilization lightened the task of rewriting materials. All wished to use some eyewitness accounts of the Nuremberg trials from Davidson's *Trial of the Germans.* They divided up the accounts, and each rewrote a share, lowering the reading level.

A Plus When Students Turn Author

There can be a definite *plus* for below-grade readers when a student turns author. The words a student will use are usually fairly simple, the sentences short, the concepts within reach. A student-author file can be a growing repository of easy-to-read materials.

Too often, projects over which students have spent many hours—dramatizations, imaginary diaries, reports of field trips, interviews with community figures, reviews of books—have their brief day in class and are then returned to the writers. Instead, these could go into a student-author file to be preserved for the use of future classes. The classes of La Follette High that used eyewitness accounts to research the Nuremberg trials took the roles of lawyers and of those accused of war crimes, then in class enacted the proceedings in a full-dress "trial" (Carlson, 1975). The student-lawyer's defense of Rudolf Hess, for example, might deserve to be preserved among the student writings. The report of an interview, for instance, on *"What It's Like to Be a Policeman,"* would be an interesting item for the collection. Young authors feel a sense of worth as their creations are selected for the student-author file—to be used through the years by future classes.

One of the author's classes compiled their writings into a class magazine and placed it in the school library, where students could check it out. It went home—almost nightly—in some student's book bag.

Estimating the Difficulty Level

How can classroom teachers estimate the difficulty level of reading materials as an aid in matching them to students? Teachers of long experience develop a "feel" for this. It may be helpful to use one of several readability formulas, provided one realizes that the resulting grade-level equivalent for a given piece of writing is an extremely rough estimate. Most formulas consider vocabulary (based on frequency of usage), number of syllables, and sentence length as the major ingredients of readability. Obviously, there are a number of other important semantic and syntactic considerations not measured by a formula. Also formulas can assess only the sample passages used for computation of grade equivalent, and any given text is probably uneven in levels of complexity. For a rapid idea of readability, recognizing its roughness and inconsistency, readers might turn to a handy graph in Edward Fry's "A Readability Formula That Saves Time," *Journal of Reading*, vol. 11 (April 1968): 513–516, 575–578.

Readers might be inclined, however, to turn to another procedure for judging the suitability of materials for readers—the cloze readability procedure developed by John Bormuth (1968). Unlike the Fry formula, it tests actual performance of students on the materials in question. Using a passage (or passages from a graded series of books), the tester deletes every fifth word and replaces it by underlined blanks. Without a time limit, the students are to write in each blank the word they think was deleted. The passage should be at least 250 words long and should contain exactly 50 blanks. Students' responses are scored correct when they match the words deleted exactly. If a student's score falls between 44 and 57 percent, the materials are judged suitable for use in an instructional situation (with ordinary help from the teacher). If students fill in more than 57 correctly, they can probably read the selection independently with ease and comprehension. The most critical task is selecting a passage that accurately represents the difficulty of the book. The procedures recommended should be followed exactly. For essential information, the reader is referred to Bormuth's article (1968).

Certainly the classroom reading collection we have described develops slowly. Never complete, it remains an ideal to work toward. Over a period of time you add to the collection—a few copies of a new textbook, some interesting original records, a thin book for the reading hold-out, a windfall of magazines from a parent, an article snipped for the clipping bank, a passage you've rewritten, an outstanding piece of student writing. Then the reading collection that you have worked for will be *working for you*—a silent reading teacher in your classroom daily contributing to habitual and successful reading.

In writing the preceding pages, the writers drew both ideas and stimulus from R. Murray Thomas and Dale L. Brubaker, "Reading Materials," *Decisions in Teaching Elementary Social Studies* (Belmont, Calif.: Wadsworth Publishing Company, 1971), Chapter 10. Thomas and Brubaker are convinced that classrooms with matched-to-students reading resources are both possible and practical—indeed, that it is difficult to operate without them.

Bring the "Right Reader" and the "Right Reading" Together

When new teachers come into a school system, they may "inherit" a single textbook and observe in the classrooms around them the practice of placing that textbook in the hands of every student. But as they look over their class-rooms, they are likely to see Ted, who can barely handle material on a sixth-grade level, sitting next to Teresa, who can easily do college reading. Here they have a dilemma and a challenge. Must their students have a single text-book as their steady fare? It may well take years to build up rich supplementary resources. And even with a classroom and a school library stocked with a full range of materials, there remains the question of how to bring the right reader and the right reading together.

Here are some ways teachers have tried to work out solutions in actual class-rooms. You will of course, be evaluating their procedures. Since all the methods probably leave some problems unsolved, let us call them "efforts." We hope that in an area where solutions are so urgently needed, readers of this book will share ways they have found successful.

Effort 1: Creating Units with Something Everyone Can Read

In classrooms where a single textbook is used, some teachers work out a com-promise. They use that textbook for some units in the year's program, giving some students more than ordinary help in reading. Then they create their own units on contemporary problems and work these in with the historical units. Teachers' guides to textbooks suggest tie-ins between the events of history and the problems of today.

During the contemporary units teachers make a special effort to give each student reading practice on an appropriate level. For a unit on, let's say, "Dis-sent—Is It Part of the Democratic Process?" they assemble and help the students locate a variety of multilevel materials: magazines, newspapers, clip-pings, and absorbing biographies and fiction through which the student can feel personally the problem of dissent.

Moving among the students, the teacher guides the selection of materials. To a poor reader: "This book has some good material for you," or "Maybe that one's too difficult. This one really covers the material." To an able reader: "This book is excellent—it will stretch your reading ability."

Many social studies teachers are welcoming the build-your-own-curriculum unit books now being published—books or booklets designed for use with single units. These cover a wide variety of key subjects, both historical and modern. Their titles and contents should be suggestive as teachers create their own units. The titles offered by one publisher (Scott, Foresman) in 1975 included *Crime and Safety, Can Earth Survive?, Struggle for Change, Who Governs?, Buyers Beware, Getting Jobs, Neighborhoods, Suburbs, Who Needs School?, Housing Conflicts, You've Been Arrested,* and *What About Tomorrow?*

How one teacher prepared a unit study guide with broad study questions and with references that offered something *everyone in the class* could read and grow on is shared under "Guiding Questions to the Study of Reptiles" in "Give Them Something They Can Read" in Chapter 3.

Effort 2: A Gradation of Books on the Reserve Shelf

In one school where a single "average" textbook is placed in the hands of all world history students, the teacher sees to it that students are not locked into this book and this book only. The teacher places on the library reserve shelf several copies each of three or four supplementary textbooks. On that shelf extremely limited readers, those as low as fifth-grade level, can reach for, then read successfully Reich, Krug, and Biller, *Building the Modern World*. Top readers can find and extend their reading reach on Crane Brinton et al., *Civilization in the West*. In-betweeners, those reading around their grade level, can find their "match" in Wallbank and Schrier, *Living World History*. The use of several books differing in organization is made possible by supplying guide-sheets with broad questions and problems and citing page references.

Students who check out an easier book do not feel a stigma. During the opening week of school teachers tell their classes that the books are on reserve and encourage students to seek out the books in order to compare different historians' interpretations. The least secure readers are guided with a quiet word, to the easiest alternate book. Students often find their own levels. The labels "readable," "average," and "mature" are on the books to guide them in their choices. The books may be read in the library during the students' open periods, checked out for overnight use, or brought to class for work periods. Copies of quality textbooks formerly used in the class might become part of the gradation on the reserve shelf.

Effort 3: Jotting Down a "Starter" Reference

During the course of a unit, students often work on some individual or group activity, ideally one in which they pursue some strong personal interest. One way to introduce reading matter would be for each student to write his or her name and the activity on an index card (Strang et al., 1961, pp. 148–149). Before the students go to the library to investigate their problems, the librarian and the teacher, having reading achievement in mind, jot on each card one appropriate reference. Now students have something "right" to start with. After they have drawn information from that source, they can use the card catalog, the *Reader's Guide,* the microfilm index, the *Social Science and Humanities Index,* and other sources to locate additional information.

School librarians appreciate this card system. It serves to alert them in advance to the topics students will be exploring so that they can make a special search for the right materials. And the librarians have a better background for talking with students about individual problems.

Effort 4: Publishers Offer Possible Solutions

Publishers' efforts to help solve the problem of widely differing reading capabilities within a classroom include offering "coordinated" textbook editions—two textbooks varying considerably in reading difficulty designed to be used in a single class. An example intended for junior high school is Henry F. Graff, *The Free and the Brave,* 2nd ed. (Chicago: Rand McNally and Company, 1972) and *The Free and the Brave,* Diamond ed., simplified and intended for students with reading difficulties. These books are identical in organization and scope and in illustrations and page format, even to the material covered on a certain page and in a certain paragraph.

In addition, publishers are offering more and more easy-to-read materials. They are breaking with the traditional textbook in offering, as a substitute for a single volume, a series of attractive, colorful, magazine-like paperbacks that have strong visual impact. A series of perhaps four of these covers the content of the usual course: American history, American problems, world history, western civilization, geography, urban studies. High in interest yet low in reading level, these promise to be a contribution toward solving the problems of many who have reading difficulties. Troubled readers may find paperbacks lavishly illustrated and inviting, while they are intimidated and defeated in advance by the tome-like textbook with which they have failed so often. An example of a program in this new format is the Spectra Program, which includes the *Promise of America* series (Chicago: Scott, Foresman and Company). Of course, when easy-to-read materials are placed in the hands of an entire class, it becomes a responsibility to the advanced readers to challenge them with advanced supplementary materials.

Effort 5: Enlisting "Right-Hand Angels"

School librarians, in our experience, are "right-hand angels" in matching materials and students. Here is one way it can work. The teacher informs the librarian that a class will soon be researching a problem—it might be, "What should be our policy toward Cuba?" Ten students are reading around grade level, six are above, six below, and three will need quite easy reading. The librarian helps locate a full range of materials, then places them on reserve for this class as a special collection. Now when the students rush through the library doors to get "something on Cuba," they find a well and suitably stocked collection. When a full range is available, students often find their own levels.

School librarians are "right-hand angels," too, in preparing supplementary booklists. The subject might be the debatable, "Does the Penal System Discourage Crime or Foster It?" The teacher shares with the librarian the reading range of the class, and the librarian prepares for student use a matching bibliography, labeling each book for its difficulty. Here is one possible set of labels: *very easy, easy, easy to average, average, average to mature, mature*. The following set of labels probably accomplishes the same purpose but omits the suggestion of easy: *readable, highly interesting, popular treatment, average difficulty, mature presentation, scholarly, academic, highly technical*. Difficulty labels provide built-in reading guidance and greatly enhance the value of the booklists librarians prepare for teachers and students.

Effort 6: Supplanting That Single Textbook

In one junior high, a group of teachers finally decided to try to use in the classroom "mini-sets" of four or five quality textbooks spanning the reading levels of the class. They made this decision with great hesitation. Would the books be parallel in organization and content? How could they make assignments in all these different books? How could they guide each student to a book she or he could handle successfully? How could they bring the class together when the students were using different textbooks? How they answered these questions and decided that differentiated textbooks were not only practical but were something they couldn't do without is shared under "Give Them Something They Can Read" in Chapter 3.

Again, the use of several books differing somewhat in organization was made possible by supplying guidesheets with broad questions and problems, with page references. Sometimes, during work periods, instructors would place a broad guiding question on the chalkboard together with page references for each of the different textbooks.

Incidentally, how can each student be guided to a book he or she can handle successfully? One teacher (Patrick, 1964) suggests an answer: "When students come into class after the first few days, they find on their desks a textbook I have carefully selected for each of them on the basis of reading scores and my own observation. Chances are they will have success with this book and will search it out and use it for future assignments."

Effort 7: Keeping a Sharp Eye During Work Periods

Long-term study units offer a special opportunity, especially when students spend full periods working in library or classroom under their watchful, helpful teacher. "I have appropriate books in mind," one teacher comments (Hozinsky, 1970), "and ready to offer to less able readers. I keep a sharp eye for students who are overwhelmed by books and guide them to one that *they* can overwhelm. I keep a sharp eye, too, for gifted readers who are 'underwhelmed,' and I guide them to books to stretch on." Of course, students can be reminded to appraise for themselves a book's appropriateness, to ask themselves as they pick up a book: "Is this the right difficulty for me?" and then to dip into the book to sample its difficulty.

"During work periods in the library," another teacher remarks (Carlson, 1975), "I can *really individualize* the levels of materials students use. And during these same periods they are constantly learning how to retrieve information on their own. The *Reader's Guide*, the social science indexes, the *Congressional Record* index, the microfilm index, the pamphlet index, and others —all become their right-hand tools."

Of course, students will need skills for investigating *life* problems on their own long after their school courses are over. Hand in hand with all the reading guidance mentioned in this section, they will move from more guidance to less —closer to independence in searching out appropriate materials and conducting inquiries. All of Chapter 5 is devoted to developing lifelong find-it-yourself skills.

On these pages, we have talked about multilevel resources as a means of providing readings right in difficulty for every reader. Of course, there are other plusses. As the students search through a variety of materials for answers, they will find different interpretations of the same historical events. No longer can they believe that the right answer is divinely revealed in the textbook on certain specified pages. They will develop the attitude that questions are open to a systematic search in all the sources available, that this search yields at best only a tentative answer, that there is rarely a total and final answer in social studies, and that the search for truth—the approximate truth—goes on.

THOSE DIFFICULT CONCEPTS—
BREAKING THE BARRIER

When concepts are elusive, here are ten tips for helping students grapple with—and really *grasp—those abstractions.*

Can we assume students will grasp important concepts as they are reading—that the passage itself will make the concepts clear? Preston investigated how well seventy-nine high school juniors, above average in intelligence, mastered ten key terms they had met in their textbook. Since they were capable students, their instructors had not considered it necessary to work on these terms. The students could explain an average of *just three* in ten. One student defined *arbitration* as "cheating against the government." One defined *moratorium* as "a place of death, such as a funeral parlor" (Preston, 1969, p. 22).

Why are some social studies concepts stumbling blocks for students? Many of the concepts—*laissez-faire*, for instance—are on high rungs of the abstraction ladder, and the higher the rung, the more difficult it is for the student to see the concept. We cannot show a physical object to help a student grasp *laissez-faire*. We cannot throw *laissez-faire* on a screen before the class. We cannot teach a single event or situation and make the concept clear. We cannot give the student a pat synonym or settle for a scholarly definition. The student who reels off a definition may not comprehend the concept at all.

The ten procedures below may prove suggestive in breaking the concept barrier.* They are not intended as a lock-step sequence or even necessarily as a sequence. Instead, they are procedures that may be useful somewhere along the line—before reading, along with reading, or during activities and discussions—after students are motivated and always in natural situations. Of course, not every procedure will be called for with every concept:

1. The instructor uses the term for the concept *(laissez-faire)* and perhaps asks the students to repeat it, stressing the pronunciation if necessary.

2. Ask yourself, "Is there a way to use *show* along with *tell* in teaching this concept?" In military and industrial training, models,

---

* Jack R. Fraenkel offers a table for attaining concepts. We have used it to guide our thinking and have incorporated, adapted, and elaborated some of the steps for teaching concepts that he suggests in *Helping Students Think and Value: Strategies for Teaching the Social Studies* (Englewood Cliffs, N.J.: Prentice-Hall, 1973), pp. 198–204. Fraenkel, in turn, adapted the table from Hilda Taba, Mary C. Durkin, Jack R. Fraenkel, and Anthony H. McNaughton, *A Teacher's Handbook to Elementary Social Studies: An Inductive Approach* (Reading, Mass.: Addison-Wesley Publishing Company, 1971), p. 71.

filmstrips, drawings, diagrams, and charts are even more effective in teaching concepts than direct observation or involvement. Suppose the concept the students are to grasp is *assembly-line production*. Suppose we try to *tell* about it: "It's a moving table a product is placed on, and as the table is moved rapidly through various areas of the factory, different groups of workers add something or make some change in the product as it passes by in a series of stages until it reaches its final form." How much more quickly students will grasp this concept if we show a set of animated transparencies or a short film loop! (Banks with Clegg, 1973, pp. 87, 88).

3. One way or another—through having the students read, listen, or view an object or a representation—the teacher conveys or elicits the information, "This is an example of (the concept)," and, "This is also an example."

4. One way or another—again, through having students read, listen, or view an object or a representation—the teacher conveys or elicits the information, "This is *not* an example" and "This is *not* an example either." Non-examples of *assembly-line production* might include a local jeweler repairing a watch or a shoemaker resoling a pair of shoes (Banks with Clegg, 1973, p. 87). As a general rule, negative examples should follow a number of positive examples and should be fewer. Now the students are sharpening their awareness of the essential elements which all the examples of the concept have in common but which the non-examples lack.

5. At some point the teacher might ask, "What characteristics does (the concept) have that make it possible for you to identify it?" Now the class can try to identify the major characteristics that all the examples have in common. These might go onto the board for all to see.

6. The teacher might ask, "Can you tell what the concept is?" Now the students analyze the meaning of the concept, (*exploitation*, for example) working out a definition that includes its essential attributes. The teacher has formulated a good definition in advance and has in mind the major attributes.

7. A concept more readily springs to life when, as students discuss the concept, the examples are close to their own lives. The concept of *subsidy*, for instance, may come alive when one example cited is the student activity fund's subsidizing their school newspaper. The concept of *revolution* takes on fuller meaning when one example is the revolution in teen-age dress. The concept

constitution becomes more real when a copy of the Student Government Constitution is brought into class and examined. *Detente* can be applied to the relaxing of strained relations between two opposing school factions; *culture* to consensus among members of the youth culture. Many other concepts, among them *social action, social responsibility, enforcement, compromise,* and *dissent,* can be brought to life through firsthand examples.

8. To broaden and deepen students' understanding of a concept, instructors can later spotlight more complex or unusual examples. They might ask, "Is this an example of *civil disobedience?*" These later examples involve new attributes that expand the definition.

9. At an appropriate time the teacher asks, "Can you find examples of your own?" Now the students might search out and bring to class their own examples.

10. The instructor will wish to avoid concentrating the learning of a concept into a single, short, intensive session. Spaced-out learning will result in firmer learning and retention.

In the procedure above, the learning proceeds inductively. Students examine examples and non-examples, then discover for themselves the defining characteristics of the concept. If teachers find it is necessary to work deductively with some students at some times, they provide the definition of the concept and its key attributes at the outset. Then as examples and non-examples come up (at first mostly examples), they raise the question: "Is this an example of *conflict of interest?* Why or why not?" Later the students suggest their own examples.

Here is how the understanding of a concept—in this case *intervention*—might develop in a natural situation (Fraenkel, 1973, p. 261):

> Suppose that a student argues that the intervention by the United States into the affairs of another nation is often justified. Other students disagree, arguing that such intervention is never justified. . . . The first task of the teacher is to help students analyze and arrive at a clear definition of the term *intervention.*
>
> The teacher can ask students for *examples* of intervention. Was the sending of troops by the United States to the Dominican Republic in 1965 an example of intervention? What about Russia's sending tanks and troops into Hungary in 1956? Or India's sending of troops into East Pakistan in 1972? Are such efforts as the Marshall Plan or the Truman Doctrine examples? The Peace Corps? The activities of medical missionaries such as Albert Schweitzer or Tom Dooley? How

about the actions of the United Nations in the Congo in 1960?
What about the expansion of U.S. business interests into other
countries? The teacher can also ask students for the defining
characteristics of intervention (e.g., must a nation actually
send troops into another country for an action to be considered intervention?).

. . . Students are encouraged to differentiate between examples and non-examples of the concept and to identify the
essential characteristics which the examples of the concept
possess. . . . Students can be helped to pin down the meaning
of *intervention* as they compare and contrast examples of actions that represent intervention with examples of similar actions that do not represent intervention.

When the meaning of intervention is clear, . . . the question
of consequences needs to be pursued. The teacher's task at this
point is to encourage students to consider where a given policy
might lead.

Certainly, not every procedure among the ten above is called for with every
concept. Instructors can use as many as necessary—or all of them—to help
students grapple with and really grasp elusive concepts.

HELPING STUDENTS READ
PRIMARY SOURCES

*Original source materials may confront students
with real difficulties. Here are procedures to
help them read these materials more effectively
and, in the process, become competent in handling them independently.*

With today's emphasis on inquiry-centered learning, we are finding more and
more primary source materials included in textbooks and selected for student
reading as teachers design their own courses. Among the materials now offered
are "inquiry kits" containing a collection of primary sources for investigating
a particular historical topic or social issue. These materials may place formidable and perhaps unsuspected roadblocks in the way of students.

All through their reading experience at school, students have been accustomed to reading materials prepared by skillful writers who have used appeals
to catch and hold their attention and devices to ease their way in reading. Suddenly the reading includes eyewitness accounts, letters, diaries, texts of speeches,

biographical sketches, newspaper accounts, official papers, and business and legal records. These communications were, of course, intended for mature adult readers; their writers did not have a youthful audience in mind.

Through their school years, students have become accustomed to having study helps built into their readings—introductions announcing the content of the selection, conspicuous headings for each new section, boldface or italic type signaling key terms, summaries. Suddenly they miss these signals. Now they may find, instead, a long, forbidding block of print. Now they must work their way through adult-level reading without supports to which they have been accustomed.

Still other obstacles may lie in their way. Not only are they confronted with adult vocabulary, they may also encounter words and phrasings not in current use, legal phraseology, archaic spellings. As today's students read the Pocahontas story, they may well be puzzled when Chief Powhatan is described as covered with *rarowcun* skins with young *wenches* seated on either side. And they may be puzzled that an Indian in the wilds is surrounded with *grim courtiers* (Robinson, 1975).

Still another concern comes to mind. An instructor may want an entire class to read some document that is a historical landmark. Yet with the diversity of reading levels within the classroom, some find it *far* beyond their reach—unless they have reading guidance.

What can you do to help students read difficult primary sources and, in the process, develop their own competencies? First, give the document a *lift-off*, placing it in its historical setting for the class, making it exciting fare. Make sure students know exactly what to look for as they are reading. Often we can do this by eliciting or supplying questions that guide them to the heart of the content. While planning the assignment, you can ask yourself, "What will the trouble spots be?" Then you can give "preventive instruction" so that barriers fall in advance of the reading.

You can walk students through the opening of a difficult document. Perhaps they can then walk alone through the rest of the passage. If it is appropriate, read the opening aloud expressively. Reading aloud may create momentum— and power—so the student can read on alone. As you and your students start the document together, you can help break the "bygone days" barrier—you can supply the meanings for archaic expressions or guide students in working out their meanings, thus making the style and language more familiar. If you ditto a difficult document, you can place the meanings of difficult words in brackets after the word or perhaps in footnotes. By providing these instant meanings, you remove obstacles to students' grasp of the document and, at the same time, help their vocabularies grow.

You can guide students to focus on graphic source materials: photographs,

paintings, cartoons, diagrams, charts, and maps. For years they may have reacted to graphic materials with "Good! Here's a part I can skip!" Now you can
throw a searchlight on these materials and train students to search them as
important revealers of historical evidence.

You can apply "life-saving scissors," snipping away parts of a passage that
are irrelevant or tedious. Finally, when a document confronts a student with
insurmountable barriers, you can make individual provisions for that student.

The guidelines on the following pages, intended for students, originated
when Philip Montag and Julius Yashon, University of Chicago Laboratory
School social studies teachers, realized their students were struggling—and
sometimes losing the struggle—with extremely demanding documents from
the 1600s in colonial America. Some procedures, prepared at the request of
these teachers, helped students read with greater success. The "Ten Tips for
Reading Primary Sources" that follow are based on these guidelines.

It cannot be stressed too strongly that printed guidelines in themselves are
not likely to effect much of a change in habits. Those that follow are intended
as reinforcement for in-class instruction and as a reminder to students to
practice the new techniques from day to day. The most effective guidance is,
of course, tailored to the document at hand.

You will find further helps that can be applied to the reading of documents
in "When Their Reading's a Struggle" and in "Study Guides to Turn on
Reading Power" in Chapter 7. For a sample lift-off for a document, turn to the
section "Give a Mini-Preview" under "Helping Students *Want* to Read" in
this chapter.

TEN TIPS FOR READING PRIMARY SOURCES

As you read primary sources, you will not be accepting someone else's version of what happened in the past. You will be reading firsthand accounts by people who contributed to the making of history. Then—like a well-trained detective—you will be given the opportunity to reason out conclusions and make judgments based on the evidence you find in your reading.* *The tips that follow will help you in this rewarding search.*

Of course, you will not need to use every technique suggested with every document. Use as many of the techniques as necessary—or all of them—to grapple with the document and grasp its meaning.

1. MAKE THE MOST OF INTRODUCTIONS

As you approach a historic document, you will probably be supplied with a paragraph or two of background information. This introduction will place the document in its proper time and place in history, it may prevent your losing the meaning, and it should provoke your thoughtful reading. *Focus on this introduction.* Without it, a difficult document may seem like a large, meaningless piece that has fallen out of a jigsaw puzzle.

Suppose there were no introduction for, let's say, the Mayflower Compact. This historic document, with its extremely involved sentence structure and its archaic language, would lose much of its meaning. With an appropriate introduction, we can picture the storm-battered *Mayflower* rolling on a leaden sea while the Pilgrims gathered in the tiny ship's cabin and by the light of a flickering lamp signed their now historic Compact. And we realize why the Mayflower Compact was an important landmark along the road leading to democracy.†

2. KEY QUESTIONS WILL HELP YOU CRACK DIFFICULT READING

Is there a success secret for grasping the content of rigorous reading? One, among others, is to *approach your reading with questions.*

You may find that one or two key questions are presented to you in the document's introduction. These point the way *straight* to content that is crucial. Your class and your teacher may have raised questions. Then, too, you may find key questions at the close of the document.

---

* We are indebted to Martin W. Sandler, Edwin C. Rozwenc, and Edward C. Martin, authors of *The People Make a Nation* (Boston: Allyn and Bacon, 1975), for ideas and phrasings in this headnote.

† Adapted from Isidore Starr, Lewis Paul Todd, and Merle Curti, eds., *Living American Documents* (New York: Harcourt Brace Jovanovich, 1971), pp. v, 5.

In one group of readings, immigrants from Europe—the poor, the oppressed, the hopeful—express how they felt, what they thought, and what they dreamed about when coming to American. The following key question is provided to guide students to the very heart of the readings: From these readings, what hypotheses can you make about the dreams, hopes, and fears these immigrants had about coming to America?*

To grasp difficult original sources, *hold key questions in the forefront of your mind.*

3. YOU MAY WANT TO READ ONCE OVER LIGHTLY FIRST

Even your instructor, who has broad background and long experience in social studies, does not expect to grasp the content of difficult original sources in a single reading.

As you approach a difficult document, you may wish to "preview" it just to get the general drift. If you've already learned how to preview, you may need to revise your techniques. When you preview most informational writing, you read the introduction, "hit"" the first and last sentences of paragraphs, examine the concluding paragraphs. *Not so in many documents.* Often these have no neat introductions, no paragraphs with topic sentences, no neat wrap-ups. The documents you'll read are often excerpts from longer documents—and the opening and closing paragraphs are not the introduction and conclusion at all.

As you approach a difficult original source, it will often help to run through it lightly just to get a feel for the content. Now you've taken the chill off the reading. When you've finished prereading, try to express in your own words the gist of the selection.

4. NOW CLOSELY, THOUGHTFULLY, READ THE SELECTION

Is concentration sometimes a problem? Those key questions you're holding in mind should help you read searching intently for crucial content instead of dreaming your way through the selection.

Some passages, intended as they were for adult readers, are likely to be rigorous—a challenge to the most capable student. The meaning of difficult parts will sometimes escape you. Expect this! Successful social studies students say, "I didn't get that. I'll go over it again." A passage that blocked you at first may come clear with a third or fourth reading.

If you still can't grasp the meaning of a difficult part after repeated reading, just place a question-mark out in the margin and ask about that part in class next day.

---

* Sandler et al., *The People Make a Nation*, p. 47–48.

5. BREAK THE WORD BARRIER

Firsthand accounts from the pages of history were intended for adult readers; thus, the vocabulary in documents is likely to be adult. Make the most of any vocabulary aids that are supplied you. Definitions of difficult terms may be provided in the margin of the selection, in footnotes, or in a handy glossary supplied you by your teacher.

Documents of long ago may include words of long ago, or usages no longer in frequent use. When you turn to the dictionary for the meaning of a word you do not know in a document, you'll need to search the various meanings given to locate one that is the *perfect fit* for the context.

When in the Mayflower Compact, for example, the Pilgrim Fathers addressed King James as "our *dread* sovereign," they were intending to pay His Majesty a compliment. They intended the word *dread* to convey a meaning closer to "revered" than to "dreaded." When these Pilgrim leaders, founding a colony on a lonely shore, promised to enact laws "*meet* for the general good," they intended the word *meet* to mean "highly suitable" or "appropriate."

When documents abound with usages of a bygone day, you will have an advantage if you're aware that in some dictionaries the older meanings for a word are placed *first* among the meanings given. In other dictionaries, the most common *present* meaning is placed first. It is therefore essential to know the arrangement in the particular dictionary you're using. Of course, *all* dictionaries use "signal flags" to mark word meanings of long ago no longer in standard use. Students who probe the past should be alert to these signals placed just after a meaning. They are the labels *obsolete* and *archaic*.

6. "READ" PAINTINGS, PHOTOGRAPHS, AND DRAWINGS AS CAREFULLY AS YOU READ WORDS

Readers unsophisticated at inquiry in social studies may regard drawings, paintings, and photographs as if they were blank spaces in the page where they can "rest their eyes." Sophisticated readers, on the other hand, examine these sources carefully to search out important historical evidence. "We can tell much about a period of history by looking at the way artists of the time viewed it."*

These scholars also observe: "A picture, we often think, gives only facts. 'The camera can't lie' is a common expression. But pictures often express biased opinions."† We may need to ask ourselves: Is there a hidden purpose here? What is the artist attempting to do? Is this picture used in an attempt to persuade? Have details been deliberately selected to convey a certain viewpoint?

---

* Sandler et al., *The People Make a Nation*, p. xiii.
† Sandler et al., *The People Make a Nation*, p. 12.

During the period when America was being settled, some of the artists who portrayed the Indians who inhabited the New World did so with a hidden motive. One artist, for example, played up details intended to create *fear* of savages. Another advertised the *glory* of going to the New World and fighting the Indians (Sandler et al., 1971). Obviously, neither portrayed the whole truth about the Indians of the New World.

7. MAKE KEY IDEAS STAND OUT

Mark important ideas or jot down brief notes. Now you won't have to reread the whole selection when you return to review it later. You may want to jot down the answers to your preliminary questions.

8. USE THE MOST POWERFUL STUDY TECHNIQUE

What is the most powerful technique? It is the technique of self-recitation.* At a good stopping-point, ask yourself, "Just what have I read here?" Looking away from the page, try to recall—and recite to yourself—important content.

9. HOW FAST SHOULD YOU READ?

With original source material, your reading speed may be far below your rate of reading less demanding material. Speedreading has little status with original sources. Even your teacher must read difficult new documentary material slowly. *Really reading* a document of two or three pages may be the equivalent of reading forty pages of a novel for English class.

10. SHARPEN YOUR CRITICAL THINKING

As you read primary sources, you'll find yourself in the role of a source analyst and evaluator engaged in the search for the truth about the complex events of the past. From day to day you'll have the opportunity to practice skills of critical thinking—to separate the false from the true, to distinguish fact from opinion, to weigh evidence and make up your own mind.

You will need these skills every day of your life, in matters both large and small. Their importance cannot be overemphasized in a world that is so desperately in need of the guiding hand of clear thinkers (Starr et al., 1971).

---

* Walter Pauk, *How to Study in College* (Boston: Houghton Mifflin Company, 1962), p. 25.

Historians investigate the past so they can make wise decisions about the future (Starr et al., 1971). The more you sharpen your powers of critical thinking, the better you can cope with the problems of your world and the more you can influence the future.

To sum it up:

1. Make the most of introductions.
2. Hold key questions in mind.
3. Preread once over lightly.
4. Read the selection closely.
5. Break the word barrier.
6. "Read" paintings, photographs, and drawings.
7. Make key ideas stand out.
8. Use the most powerful study technique.
9. Put a brake on speed.
10. Sharpen your critical thinking.

Bibliography

Aukerman, Robert C. *Reading in the Secondary School Classroom.* New York: McGraw-Hill Book Company, 1972, chapter 7.

Banks, James A., with Ambrose A. Clegg, Jr. *Teaching Strategies for the Social Studies.* Reading, Mass.: Addison-Wesley Publishing Company, 1973.

Casner, Mabel B., and Ralph H. Gabriel. *Story of the American Nation,* teacher's manual. New York: Harcourt, Brace and World, 1967.

Duggins, James. *Teaching Reading for Human Values in High School.* Columbus: Charles E. Merrill Publishing Company, 1972.

Engle, Shirley H., and Wilma S. Longstreet. *A Design for Social Education in the Open Curriculum.* New York: Harper and Row, 1972.

Fraenkel, Jack R. *Helping Students Think and Value.* Englewood Cliffs, N.J.: Prentice-Hall, 1973.

Gross, Richard E., Walter E. McPhie, and Jack R. Fraenkel. *Teaching the Social Studies: What, Why, and How.* Scranton, Penn.: International Textbook Company, 1969.

Joyce, Bruce R. *New Strategies for Social Education.* Chicago: Science Research Associates, 1972.

Kellum, David F. *The Social Studies, Myths and Realities.* New York: Sheed and Ward, 1969.

Kenworthy, Leonard S. *Social Studies for the Seventies.* Waltham, Mass.: Blaisdell Publishing Company, 1969.

Krug, Mark M. "Primary Sources: Their Nature and Use in the Teaching of History." In *A New Look at Reading in the Social Studies,* edited by Ralph C. Preston. Perspectives in Reading Series, No. 12. Newark, Del.: International Reading Association, 1969.

Lee, John R., Stephan E. Ellenwood, and Timothy H. Little. *Teaching Social Studies in the Secondary School.* New York: Free Press, 1973.

Miller, Wilma H. *Diagnosis and Correction of Reading Difficulties in Secondary School Students.* New York: Center for Applied Research in Education, 1973.

Palmer, William S. "CONPASS: Social Studies—Suggestions for Improvement." *Journal of Reading,* 16, no. 7 (1973), pp. 529–538.

Panes, Paul. *Reading the Textbook: A Reading Improvement Manual for the Subject Matter Areas.* New York: Thomas Y. Crowell Company, 1972.

Preston, Ralph C. "Newer Approaches to Handling the Vocabulary Problem." In *A New Look at Reading in the Social Studies,* edited by Ralph C. Preston. Perspectives in Reading Series, No. 12. Newark, Del.: International Reading Association, 1969.

Preston, Ralph C., ed. *A New Look at Reading in the Social Studies.* Perspectives in Reading Series, No. 12. Newark, Del.: International Reading Association, 1969.

Preston, Ralph C., and Wayne L. Herman, Jr. *Teaching Social Studies in the Elementary School.* New York: Holt, Rinehart and Winston, 1974.

Preston, Ralph C., J. Wesley Schneyer, and Franc J. Thyng. *Guiding the Social Studies Reading of High School Students.* Washington, D.C.: National Council for the Social Studies, 1963.

Robinson, H. Alan. *Teaching Reading and Study Strategies: The Content Areas.* Boston: Allyn and Bacon, 1975.

Sartain, Harry W. "Content Reading—They'll Like It." *Journal of Reading,* 17, no. 1 (1973), pp. 47–51.

Shaftel, George. *Decisions in United States History,* teacher's guide. Lexington, Mass.: Ginn and Company, 1972.

Staff of the Social Studies Curriculum Center, Carnegie-Mellon University, Edwin Fenton, general ed. *The New Social Studies for the Slow Learner.* New York: Holt, Rinehart and Winston, 1969.

Thomas, R. Murray, and Dale L. Brubaker. *Decisions in Teaching Elementary Social Studies.* Belmont, Cal.: Wadsworth Publishing Company, 1971.

References

Association of Teachers of Social Studies of the City of New York. *Handbook for Social Studies Teaching.* New York: Holt, Rinehart and Winston, 1967.

Bailey, Thomas A. *The American Pageant Quiz Book.* Boston: D. C. Heath and Company, 1961.

Banks, James A., with Ambrose A. Clegg, Jr. *Teaching Strategies for the Social Studies.* Reading, Mass.: Addison-Wesley Publishing Company, 1973.

Bell, Earl, University of Chicago Laboratory School social studies teacher, in remarks to Ellen Thomas, June 1975.

Bormuth, John. "The Cloze Readability Procedure." *Elementary English,* 45 (April 1968): 429–436.

Brinton, Crane, et al. *Civilization in the West,* 3rd ed. Englewood Cliffs, N.J.: Prentice-Hall, 1973.

Carlson, Charles, social studies teacher at La Follette Senior High School (Madison, Wis.), in remarks to Ellen Thomas, June 1975.

Casner, Mabel B., and Ralph H. Gabriel. *Story of the American Nation,* teacher's manual. New York: Harcourt, Brace and World, 1967.

Engle, Shirley H., and Wilma S. Longstreet. *A Design for Social Education in the Open Curriculum.* New York: Harper and Row, 1972.

Flickinger, Alice, former University of Chicago Laboratory School social studies teacher, in remarks to Ellen Thomas, October 1969; September 1970.

Fraenkel, Jack R. *Helping Students Think and Value: Strategies for Teaching Social Studies.* Englewood Cliffs, N.J.: Prentice-Hall, 1973.

Hofstadter, R., et al. *The American Republic*, 2nd ed. (2 vols.) Englewood Cliffs, N.J.: Prentice-Hall, 1970.

Hozinsky, Murray, University of Chicago Laboratory School teacher, in remarks to Ellen Thomas, May 1970.

Kenworthy, Leonard S. *Social Studies for the Seventies*. Waltham, Mass.: Blaisdell Publishing Company, 1969.

Krug, Mark M. "Primary Sources: Their Nature and Use in the Teaching of History." In *A New Look at Reading in the Social Studies*, edited by Ralph C. Preston. Perspectives in Reading Series, No. 12. Newark, Del.: International Reading Association, 1969.

MacKinnon, Jeff., Bernard Bazan, and Charles Carlson, social studies teachers at La Follette Senior High School (Madison, Wis.).

Patrick, John, former University of Chicago Laboratory School social studies teacher, in remarks to Ellen Thomas, October 1964.

Preston, Ralph C. "New Approaches to Handling the Vocabulary Problem." In *A New Look at Reading in the Social Studies*, edited by Ralph C. Preston. Perspectives in Reading Series, No. 12. Newark, Del.: International Reading Association, 1969.

Reich, Krug, and Biller. *Building the Modern World*. New York: Harcourt Brace Jovanovich, 1969.

Reich, Strickland, and Biller. *Building the United States*. New York: Harcourt Brace Jovanovich, 1971.

Robinson, H. Alan. *Teaching Reading and Study Strategies: The Content Areas*. Boston, Allyn and Bacon, 1975.

Robinson, Helen M., in remarks in University of Chicago Reading Workshop, summer 1958.

Sartain, Harry W. "Content Reading—They'll Like It." *Journal of Reading*, 17 (October 1973): 47–51.

Schwartz, and O'Connor. *The New Exploring American History*. New York: Globe Publishing Company, 1974.

Shaftel, George. *Decisions in United States History*, teacher's guide. Lexington, Mass.: Ginn and Company, 1972.

Strang, Ruth, Constance M. McCullough, and Arthur E. Traxler. *The Improvement of Reading*. New York: McGraw-Hill Book Company, 1961.

Surgal, Joel, University of Chicago Laboratory School Social Studies Department teacher, in remarks to Ellen Thomas, July 1975.

Todd, and Curti. *The Rise of the American Nation*. New York: Harcourt Brace Jovanovich, 1969.

U.S. News and World Report. "The Shrinking Dollar." March 3, 1975.

Wallbank, and Schrier. *Living World History*. Chicago: Scott, Foresman and Company, 1974.

Wood, Leonard C., et al. *America: Its People and Values*, 2nd ed. New York: Harcourt Brace Jovanovich, 1975.

7

ENGLISH

As teachers plan a reading assignment, they often think, "This will confront some of my students with difficulties. How can I help them stretch and handle this difficult selection?" In the first section of this chapter we offer a grab bag of possible ways to help those students. These helps are intended for both troubled readers and top readers—for any student when the reading ahead may be a struggle. The contents of the grab bag are varied: providing a set to read better through a mini-preview, giving *preventive* instruction, building bridges to young people's concerns, walking students through the opening of a passage, reading aloud to *build reading power,* using advance organizers, using fasten-your-seat-belt tape recordings, using "life-saving scissors," and so on. In this chapter you will also find a section, "Study Guides to Turn on Reading Power." Here we offer tips for building solid reading help for students *right into the study guide.*

We do not intend this collection of helps "when their reading's a struggle" to be complete. Other parts of the book supplement it. As English teachers look out over their classrooms, they are likely to see Ted, who can barely handle material on sixth-grade level, sitting next to Dick, who can easily do college reading. Instructors will want to place materials of the right difficulty in the hands of each student. How this has been accomplished in actual classrooms is reported in "You Can Have a Silent Reading Teacher in Your Classroom" in Chapter 6. We hope the reader will consider this item a vital part of this chapter.

How can teachers learn, fairly easily, something about each student's strengths in reading—and the blocks in the way—in order to plan a year of more successful learning? In the section "Finding Out about Your Students' Reading" in Chapter 6 we suggest procedures for doing this, procedures that in a teacher's busy schedule require little time.

"Fun Fare for Vocabulary Growth" concludes this chapter. Here you will find an assortment of word play activities, activities to intrigue young people and turn them into dedicated word collectors. This fun fare will supplement the solid fare in Chapter 2, "Building Vocabulary."

Of course, you will want to individualize the approaches in this chapter; the procedures used should be appropriate to the interests and needs of your group. The contents are intended to supplement the more general reading improvement procedures in chapters 2 through 5. Although the examples in this chapter are from teaching English, most of the procedures are appropriate in other classes and will increase reading power in almost any subject.

WHEN THEIR READING'S
A STRUGGLE

> *Here is a "grab bag" of possible helps. They should help your troubled readers handle readings that might have overwhelmed them and should help your top readers stretch their abilities. It doesn't take a day of training in teaching reading to use these procedures.*

As you sit at your desk planning a reading assignment, you may be thinking, "This will be very difficult for some of my students. What can I do to help them read it?" You will find, on the pages that follow, a variety of possible ways to help those students.

What happens when students try to read their assignments, then put the book down day after day with "Too hard for me"? As time goes on, there may be a chain reaction: anxiety that makes it difficult for them to concentrate—fear that they will be exposed as poor readers—fear of even trying—losing out on practice, then dropping still farther behind—feeling the disapproval of parents—feeling themselves failures in their own eyes and those of their teachers and classmates—developing a negative self-concept—and, along with all this, feeling an aversion to anything between the covers of a book and to school as a place of failure.

What may happen when their teachers help them experience reading success? With time, anxiety may drop away, discouragement give way to hope.

Students may take hold, try again, and begin to grow in reading. Their parents may view them more favorably. As their sense of failure drops away, they are likely to develop more positive self-concepts. They may no longer regard reading as a disaster area. They may decide there is something to value between the covers of a book and that there is hope for them at school.

This section shares methods the authors and others have found helpful in enabling students to stretch and handle difficult selections. You will find much overlapping of procedures. Well aware of the diversity of teaching styles in English classrooms, the authors offer these procedures as a grab bag of helps. You are invited to reach into the bag and help yourself to whatever you find to your liking. Naturally, you will wish to select those helps that are in keeping with the needs of your students and the materials they are reading.

What Will the Trouble Spots Be?

You can help students read right past potential barriers if, as you plan an assignment, you search through the passage asking, "What will the trouble spots be?"

Give Preventive Instruction

As one instructor sits down to plan an assignment, she tries to imagine that she is one of her own students, with the reading power, the background of school courses, and the life experiences of that student. Her thoughts run like this:

> "What should students have gained after they have finished this reading? What blocks will stand in the way?" . . . "What background do they lack? What gaps should I fill in?" . . . "Here's an onrush of new characters. Shall I introduce some of them before students begin to read?" . . . "This part will be obscure. How can I help them get through it?" . . . "What words are likely to block them? Should I remove some of these blocks before they begin reading?" . . . "Will archaic expressions or dialect words seem like a foreign language? What about a glossary of these?" . . . "How can I give them something to look for as they read instead of turning them loose without a target?"

Now this teacher gives *preventive* instruction. Often the instruction most significant to students, the instructor concludes, is given *before* they start reading. Of course, when teachers anticipate too many trouble spots for too many students, they will undoubtedly want to assign a less difficult selection.

Students might be asked to mark possible trouble spots lightly in the margin (or the teacher might supply this reading guidance on a ditto): "Here's a crucial word—your comprehension will hinge on your finding out its meaning." . . . "This part will be difficult—slow down and read it several times." . . . "Here's a question to keep in mind as you read this part—it should clear it up." . . . "You may be lost here—just bring your questions to class."

Of course, when a work is difficult and lengthy as well, trouble spots will need to be anticipated and blocks removed at intervals during the reading; the students will need "booster-shots."

Give a Mini-Preview

What is our competition as we try to encourage today's students to find enjoyment and information in books? From early childhood, they have done much of their learning in front of the TV screen, which holds their eyes and minds through vivid color, flashing lights, arresting sound effects, and dramatic impact. All the devices of top photographers, skillful writers, talented actors, and compelling speakers are turned on, full force, to captivate and hold them. Small wonder little black-and-white marks "lying flat" on the printed page may seem a little lifeless in comparison.

When groups of poor readers were asked, "What makes reading easy?" they answered, "Interest" (Strang, 1965). Experienced teachers constantly observe how strong interest helps students dig out the meaning of difficult material, and, pulling them along, tends to speed up reading.

Television networks catch interest in coming attractions with intriguing previews. We might borrow this technique for coming readings.

Barriers Can Tumble

Julius Caesar may seem to be moldering in the dust of two thousand years, and the opening scene may be, for some readers, impassable. This is how, in one classroom, the instructor makes some of the barriers tumble:

> Before the students read the first line, I create a feeling of hail-fellow-well-met for Caesar. I create the holiday spirit—the excitement of Caesar's triumph after one of his most spectacular victories, the victory in Spain. I introduce Caesar as a leader idolized by his soldiers and by the commoners, the most

popular military hero in history. No wonder some Romans—Marullus and Flavius among them—fear that Caesar's immense popularity and his rising power will destroy Rome's jealously guarded freedom! The jealous, brooding Cassius; Marc Antony, once one of Caesar's soldiers, who idolizes him as do all his soldiers; Brutus, truly dedicated to the common good—these walk out onto the stage. Now after we read the opening scenes in class, *Julius Caesar* comes closer within reach.

One teacher realized that her not-so-able readers would have difficulty getting into even the fast-paced adventure story, "The Most Dangerous Game." This mini-preview—it took just sixty seconds to give it—sent them into this story with a "set" to read better and faster:

Did you ever hear of an "evil island"? In this story there *is* one in the Caribbean—an island that seems to broadcast vibrations of evil. It has an evil name among sea-faring men. Near this island the most fearless sailors sense they are in danger.

On a black tropical night a yacht is speeding past the evil island. Two sportsmen are on their way to hunt jaguars up the Amazon. One of the sportsmen, Rainsford, is alone on deck. Suddenly he is startled by a sound in the distance. Someone, off in the darkness, has fired a shot three times. Rainsford springs to the rail, straining to see through the darkness. Leaning precariously, he loses his balance—and the dark waters of the Caribbean close over his head. Struggling to the surface, he shouts with all his power, but his cries are not heard. The lights of the yacht become faint and finally vanish. There is only the evil island for Rainsford to swim to for safety.

Why is the island evil? *What* is the sinister secret? And what do you think is "the most dangerous game?"

"Leiningen versus the Ants," exciting though it is, can easily block students with its heavy load of difficult vocabulary on the opening pages. A quick sketch on the board of the layout of Leiningen's plantation, an introduction to some of the difficult key words, some intriguing plot-snatches about voracious ants "darkening the hills, ten miles long and two miles wide" and about a "dash against death," plus reading aloud the opening together—these should take down some of the barriers.

The two preceding mini-previews are clearly on the plot level. Until the less able readers know *what the selection says* on the surface, it is difficult for them to go on to depth questions calling for analysis and application.

Reading aloud until the student is "caught" is another form of mini-preview. Now teachers can capitalize on the fiction writer's narrative hook. With "The Diamond Necklace" it is good timing if, as the bell rings at the end of class, Madame Loisel is left in grief and despair, the fabulous diamond necklace borrowed from her wealthy friend mysteriously missing (Donham, 1975).

Mini-Previews Can Take Just Moments

Mini-previews can catch interest in moments. In assigning Thoreau, one instructor (Hillman, 1975) suggested to capable readers: "Tonight if you read carefully, Thoreau will tell you how to get rich." Many come next day with a new concept of riches—riches "in proportion to the number of things a man can do without."

The following mini-preview made the "Concord rebel" seem a little like one of today's student dissenters:

> At the end of his senior year at Harvard, Thoreau was asked to speak at his own graduation. He surprised some of his classmates, the parents who had come to attend graduation, and the august Harvard faculty assembled, by reversing one of the Ten Commandments: "Six days shalt thou devote to enjoyment and *one* to toil."

Sometimes the heading COMING SOON appeared in a special box on the chalkboard and under it an ad for a coming selection. This appeared just before Christmas:

COMING SOON:

How to make
your Christmas list

The selection coming soon was Emerson's essay, "On Gifts." Once under COMING SOON appeared the words, "How to Cure a Depression." The cure was revealed next day in Shakespeare's Sonnet 29.

Create a "You Are There" Effect

A mini-preview can throw students into roles, put them inside the shoes and skin of one of the characters in a story. Teachers might ask, "What would you do if *you* were in this situation?" and then present, for discussion, the painful dilemma of a character. In the example below, the instructor (McCampbell, 1975) used a role-play situation to involve students instantly with the hero's problem:

> In *Inherit the Wind,* the lawyer patterned after Clarence Darrow says of the young biology teacher: "It's the loneliest feeling in the world to stand when others are sitting." Before the classes start reading the play, they are given a sheet with this quotation printed at the top. They are then asked to make jottings of a time when they stood alone, or wanted to stand alone, or considered standing alone but did not. Now each student is already deep into the hero's problem.

Build Bridges to Young People's Concerns

Someone asked Edward J. Farrell, a supervisor of student teachers at the University of California, "What is the most serious shortcoming of the student teachers you observe?" Here is his answer (Farrell, 1966): "Their failure . . . to build bridges between students' concerns and experiences and the experiences recorded in literature. . . . Student teachers don't realize that assigning a selection and teaching it are not synonymous. . . . Bridges must be built for nearly every selection to be taught. When I am unsure about how to build, I inevitably fall back on the one constant we have, the emotional experiences of the youngsters. No matter how slow the class, the students will have had some experience with hate, with fear, with loneliness; some bent . . . toward honor, toward courage, toward love."

If we hope to really *teach* literature, Farrell suggested, we will plan lessons carefully, build bridges to student concerns, and set purposes through questions. He shared examples of his own bridges:

> There was the class of regular sophomores in which I disarmingly asked, "How many of you ever feel lonely?" After the diffident, numerous hands had been put down, I asked the students what they did when they were lonely. When many revealed that they sought the company of friends, I asked them to consider what it might be to be a king. Were kings more lonely than other people? If so, why? Eventually they were led into discussing the terrifying alienation of the regal Richard Cory.

> There was a class of college preparatory juniors in which I asked whether anyone had done homework for any class the night before. After the agonizing moans had ceased, I asked

how many of them would have preferred watching television or cruising around. When most of the hands arose, I asked the students why, then, they bothered to do the homework—why they didn't just go enjoy themselves. I was leading into the tension all of us feel between duty and pleasure, the tension at the heart of the poem I wished to teach, Frost's "Stopping by Woods on a Snowy Evening."

I have purposely enraged classes to get them into a story. At the beginning of one hour in a slow class, I passed out small pieces of paper and requested each student to write his name, fold the paper, and pass it forward. I took the pieces, placed them in a recipe box, asked for a volunteer to draw three names. When the students, dutifully docile till then, wanted to know what it was all about, I told them I had finished reading their last examinations, that almost all of them had done well, but that it was my policy in a class this size to fail at least a few students. Because I wanted to be fair, I thought the best procedure was that of drawing names. Within seconds all hell broke loose. I temporarily soothed ruffled tempers by saying I would reconsider my policy since it seemed so disturbing; now, though, I wanted to read them a story. I distributed the dittoed questions, and when it came, they were ready indeed for Shirley Jackson's "The Lottery."

Help Students Actually Start Their Reading

Students sometimes struggle with a page or two at the beginning of an assignment, then close the book with "I don't know what it's saying." Those first few pages, more than others, are often "stoppers."

Walk Students Through the Opening

When you walk students through the opening of a difficult play or novel, they are more likely to be able to walk alone through the rest of the reading. As they read the opening with you, they are introduced to the setting and characters, pick up the first plot threads, become aware of initial problems. They should then be given a problem or question, Finder suggested (1974), to bear in mind as they read on alone. This problem should lead them to attend to concerns central to the work—for instance, the sequence of incidents that make the final outcome probable or inevitable. Finder (1974, pp. 273–274) suggested how students might be helped to "step into" *The Glass Menagerie:*

First, students may be asked to read and discuss the initial description of the scene, here the Winfield apartment. A simple, straightforward explanation of vocabulary likely to cause trouble will suffice. . . . To help the students find their way into the action, read Tom's opening speech orally. Discuss briefly the family's situation—help them to see that the family is poor and in an ugly, demeaning environment, that the father has left them, and that Tom, his sister, and his mother constitute the family living in the apartment. Point out that Tom is "dressed as a merchant sailor." Ask what we are to infer from that.

To this point, the classwork has been aimed at helping the students begin to realize what the scene may look like, how the dialogue may sound, what kind of people Tom and Amanda are. This beginning sends them on their way to reading the play for themselves. Guide them by suggesting that, as they read, they bear in mind this problem: By the end of the play Tom leaves his mother and sister. Describe the sequence of events that lead to his leaving. Ask them to use the rest of the period to begin their reading.

Read Aloud—And Build Reading Power

Reading aloud to students can capture a class. And it can actually build reading power. The least successful reader in the class can enjoy these benefits.

A dramatic oral reading can give the class the experience of sharing the enjoyment of reading. It can prove to "tuned-out" readers that there is something to enjoy between book covers. It can intrigue students about what lies ahead. Reading aloud the opening may offer less confident readers hope of finishing an assignment; they have a tremendous psychological advantage in being already "into it." The oral reading creates *momentum* so that they may be able to carry on silent reading alone.

An oral reading by the teacher *need not be the only reading*. It can be followed by questions that require the students to return to the passage. Now that the chill has been taken off, insecure readers may take hold and make a real effort in a second reading.

Has any investigator done a research study on the correlation between eyes that light up with enjoyment and the achievement of students? The instructor's own appreciation for a selection has a chance to come through as he or she reads aloud to a class.

Along with benefits already mentioned, reading aloud can bring a host of other benefits:

1. Students are accustomed to the color, the arresting sound effects, and the dramatic acting on TV. Expressive oral reading can bring print "lying flat on the page" to life. Classes can become lost in a sensitive, dramatic oral reading.

2. Characters can spring to life through oral reading. If throngs of them crowd the pages at the beginning of a book or play (as in some of Shakespeare's plays), you have the opportunity to introduce and clarify these characters one by one.

3. Through dramatic reading plus commenting, you can make a remote, unreal setting—it might be Egdon Heath—as vivid as if it were before the class on a TV screen.

4. Openings sometimes move so slowly that they deaden interest. Teachers who read aloud can apply "life-saving scissors"; snip away certain passages, then quickly weave the parts together by telling the story.

5. Classes need not be passive while you are reading to them. Pausing, you can lead students to paraphrase difficult passages, thus strengthening their ability to interpret. Read silently, these passages might have been stoppers. You might draw students into the reading by reading difficult expository passages yourself, then having student-readers come in on the conversational passages.

6. While reading aloud, ask questions that elicit important skills of comprehension. These questions can lead students to focus on— and dig the meaning out of—the lines that yield the answers. You can paraphrase, and lead students to paraphrase, figurative expressions, thus helping them develop the power to handle figurative language alone. This procedure can lead students to focus on and interpret symbols and multiple levels of meaning.

7. Reading aloud can build word power. Oral readers can promote the growth of meaning vocabulary by quickly supplying the meanings for unknown words or leading students to figure out meanings. If students are deficient in word recognition, there is an opportunity to improve in this area. As you read the selection aloud, the students follow along, their eyes on their own books. As they *see* the printed word and *hear* it simultaneously, they recognize words that would otherwise seem unfamiliar. Some of these words become "sight words" of their own for future reading. The least proficient readers in the class can reap this benefit.

8. Oral reading can help to break the "period barrier." Some period pieces seem to today's students to be written in another language. The oral reader can translate *guerdon, forsooth, certe, wont, an,* and other strange or archaic expressions. Such expressions will

now be more familiar as the students continue their reading alone. Dialect barriers, too, sometimes fall through oral reading. As students listen to expressive reading of dialect, they recognize some words that would have blocked comprehension in silent reading, and they come to realize they can get the drift of other words from the context.

9. Poems cry out for oral reading. Like music, a poem *has* to be sounded. Reading a poem silently is like simply looking at a sheet of music without hearing the music and exclaiming, "Oh, isn't that beautiful!" (LaPorte, 1975). Poetic passages in prose selections, too, cry out for oral reading. An added benefit is that oral readers of poetry are constantly teaching, by example, that the vocal phrasing does not end at the end of a line unless the thought has been completed.

10. Some instructors encourage edge-of-the-chair listening by writing on the board two or three intriguing questions. The class is told, "Raise your hands when you *think* I have read the answer to the first question." Hands wave as students find the answers, which often call for between-the-lines reading.

11. Having understood and enjoyed your reading, underconfident readers may now make a genuine effort to read on alone. They have already picked up the first threads of the plot—now they have these threads to follow. You can suggest, "Though parts are difficult, see, you can get the drift." There will be an additional advantage if these students are given class time to begin their silent reading.

12. Reading aloud the opening of a selection acts as a speed device. It strengthens students' background for the selection and generates concentration—and along with these come speed. Even painfully slow readers are given hope. Part of their reading is already done, so there is less to do outside.

13. You have a special opportunity while reading aloud conversational passages. You can convey to students the extent to which, in silent reading, the reader's sensing the rise and fall of the speaker's voice, emphasis, and pause can help in grasping meaning. You can make the student aware that these characteristics of an utterance are revealed, to some extent, by punctuation.

14. You can constantly stir interest by leading students to anticipate —to try to predict—what lies ahead. You can close your reading with exciting questions—questions to *impel* students to read on.

15. Again, your oral reading *need not be the only reading.* Questions can require the students to return to the passage. Students can

be asked to verify points, to locate passages that support statements, to make interpretations. Now with a more positive mind-
set, discouraged readers may work their way through the selection. Thus the oral reading becomes an enabler. It has not taken
the place of silent reading—it has *made that silent reading
possible.*

Judy would have found the first scenes of *Othello* overwhelming had she
tried to read them alone. Her instructor read the opening scenes dramatically,
bringing regal Othello, gentle Desdemona, vengeful Iago vividly to life. This
introduction proved to be an enabler. Later Judy ran up to her teacher in the
hall, exclaiming, "Oh, I've just read the last act! It was so sad about Desdemona.
Othello was mad! And Desdemona tried to shield him!"

Teachers will want to consider *what* to read aloud and *when* during the delicate operation of planning the study of a selection. Passages beyond the opening of a selection often call for oral reading. As one instructor comments, "I
must read aloud scenes here and there through *Macbeth*, or I lose my students." Since many of the benefits here enumerated are of equal value to
superior readers, instructors will wish to include these students, too, in their
plans for sensitive, dramatic oral interpretations.

Of course, instructors will avoid making students overly dependent on oral
reading and will help gradually maturing readers advance along the road to
independence. Expressive oral reading, when planned to bring the benefits
mentioned and balanced with appropriate silent reading, can help students
reach that destination sooner.

Would You Like to Know What Happens?
Then Read Your Assignment!

Long before troubadours wandered through France and England singing and
reciting and captivating their hearers, listening to a good story came under the
heading of enjoyment. We can use the storyteller's art to lead right into any
work of fiction.

Excerpts from full-length books are often assigned to students in anthologies.
Why not tell the story leading up to the excerpt, catching the students up in the
excitement of the story?

A ninth-grade class was being assigned "The Bishop's Candlesticks," the
chapter or two from *Les Misérables* in which the saintly Bishop of Digne re-
generates Jean Valjean. The assignment might have been: "Read 'The Bishop's
Candlesticks' for tomorrow." Instead, the instructor decided to place the excerpt in its setting, telling the opening of the novel, bringing the characters to
life, promising a marvelous story. This "book bait" took four minutes:

Here is a chapter from one of the world's great books, *Les Misérables*. What does the title suggest? [The students respond, and the teacher touches on the degrading poverty of the "wretched ones" in France a hundred years ago.]

Jean Valjean is among those poor and unfortunate. The winter is severe, he can find no work, and his sister's children are starving. One night a baker, whose shop is nearby, hears a violent blow against a barred window. Jean Valjean has broken a pane of glass and has stolen a loaf of bread.

Now what seems today a very minor crime indeed was by the harsh laws of France then a serious crime. Jean is seized by the police and given a five-year sentence. Because of his tremendous strength, he is made a galley slave and chained down in the dark hold of a galley. There, conditions are unspeakable. At the slightest excuse he is flogged with agonizing cruelty. A man of great daring, Jean manages four times to escape. Once he escapes and hides in a convent, the home of Catholic nuns, where he lives in disguise as their gardner. He is pursued even there and recaptured. Once he pretends to be dead and is buried alive, along with the tools to dig his way out. But he is captured once more and returned to the terrible galleys. Each time he is returned, the sentence is lengthened as a penalty. When at last he is released, he has served nineteen years for stealing a loaf of bread. He is not, though, quite free. He has a brand for life: yellow identification papers that proclaim to the world that he is an ex-convict.

So Jean is cast adrift in a terrible condition of mind and soul—hard, disillusioned, cynical, hating mankind, no faith left in God, violent, savage, brutalized by the brutality he so long has suffered.

As our story opens, Jean has been traveling on foot all day. As night falls, he enters a little French town, seeking food and shelter. Everywhere—inn after inn—he is turned away, as the yellow passport reveals his past. Endlessly he walks. Finally, exhausted, he lies down on some stones in the town square. There a woman comes upon Jean, and pointing to a humble house in the shadow of a great cathedral, bids him, "Go there!" It is the cottage of an esteemed and aged bishop who lives like a humble priest—saintly, compassionate, deeply spiritual—and as deeply beloved.

Minutes later a violent knock is heard on the bishop's door.

What will happen when the saintly bishop meets the savage Jean Valjean—when gentleness meets violence? Is there a chance of redeeming so lost and desperate a person? If you want to know what happens, read "The Bishop's Candlesticks" tonight and we'll talk about it tomorrow.

Now the class—readiness high—stepped into the story. They were ready for the bishop's gentle welcome with supper and lodging, for Jean's stealing away in the night with the bishop's silver, for his capture and return by the gendarmes, for the bishop's saving him by assuring the gendarmes that the silver had been a gift to Jean, then his pressing on Jean the added gift of his treasured silver candlesticks: "Jean Valjean, my brother, I have bought your soul of you. I withdraw it from black thoughts and the spirit of perdition, and give it to God!"

Setting the stage transformed what might have been a listless reading into an involved and thoughtful one. The following night the teacher's own two-volume copy of *Les Misérables* went home in a student's book bag. Lead-ins like this might be preserved on cassettes and could become part of a growing collection.

Advance Organizers Upgrade Comprehension

Psychologist David Ausubel (1960) asked himself, "What happens when students read a 'prestructuring' statement *before* they read a long passage?" To answer the question he used a controlled study in which one group had the advantage of first reading a short introductory passage (500 words) that "ideationally organized" a longer passage (2500 words). The short statement mobilized relevant concepts already in the learner's mind, served as an anchoring focus for the reception of the new material and made the new material more familiar and meaningful. What happened as a result? The use of advance organizers definitely upgraded student comprehension of principles, facts, and applications—and aided retention, too. Few textbooks, Ausubel observed, come to the aid of students by providing prestructuring statements, and too few teachers provide advance organizers as they assign reading selections.

Advance Organizers Help Open the Door to Shakespeare

Students can sometimes grasp readings that are "beyond them" if you guide them to easier readings on the subject first. As you do so, you are providing them with one form of advance organizer. We are all aware of the value of advance organizers in our personal reading. We realize what a help it would be in trying to grasp a highly technical article on atomic fusion, for instance, to become oriented by reading a popular treatment first.

With Nancy, an average reader facing a difficult selection, an advance organizer opened the door to Shakespeare. Opening her book to *Richard III*,

Nancy was looking forward to enjoying the "world's greatest playwright." A throng of characters—thirty-eight of them—confronted her, their family relationships bewildering. The opening lines were not for the faint-hearted, as Richard soliloquized on and on through forty lines. Nancy's mind reeled under an interminable sentence, its subject *far* from its verb. She read, in Richard's words, that Clarence should be "mewed up," which meant nothing to Nancy. By now she had forgotten who Clarence was anyway. She put the book down, sighing, "Shakespeare is not for me."

Then Nancy sought out the reading teacher, who remembered the inspiring story of Richard III in Marchette Chute's *Stories from Shakespeare*. Perhaps this would help Nancy step into *Richard III*. "Shakespeare himself," explains Chute in the introduction (1956, pp. 14–15), "considered it of great importance that the stories of his plays should be clearly understood. It was the custom in his own day for an actor called the Prologue to come onstage before the action started and explain exactly what the play was going to be about. Moreover, Shakespeare chose stories whose plots were already familiar to his audiences. Most of his comedies and tragedies come from tales that had already been shown on the stage or were available in the bookstores. . . . Shakespeare never confused his own public, and he would not wish anyone to be confused today."

So Nancy was guided to *Stories from Shakespeare*. There she grasped the thread of the story and worked her way through the difficult opening. At the dramatic point where Richard woos Lady Anne as the corpse of her husband is borne through the streets of London, Nancy graduated to reading Shakespeare's version on her own. Then whenever she lost the thread, she found it again by turning to Chute's well-written story.

Many students need support as they read a drama from long ago. The opening lines of *Othello* abound with words dusty with centuries: *be-lee'd, 'sblood, off-capp'd, nonsuits, certes,* bookish *theoric, toged* consuls, *counter-caster, affined*. Of course, Shakespeare performed is an ideal way to open the door to Shakespeare. Teachers in a city high school report a "wonderful time" with Shakespeare through synchronizing the study of Shakespeare with theatrical presentations their classes can attend. "Pre-readings" in class through records or films are reading strengtheners for many students. They sometimes make possible a surprisingly successful silent reading at home, one in which the students return to the play and answer guiding questions.

Encourage an Easy-to-Difficult Sequence

How many times each school year do students say, "I'll go look it up!" The principle of the advance organizer can help them all through the year—whenever they are reading several references on a certain subject. They should be encouraged—until it becomes second nature—to read encyclopedias and other reference materials in an easy-to-difficult sequence. They should routinely turn first to the easiest reference for a quick orientation to the subject. For less capable high school readers the source could be *The World Book* or *Compton's Encyclopedia.* Then they may be ready to stretch their comprehension by undertaking more difficult readings—*Collier's* or *Encyclopedia International*—then perhaps on to the *Americana.* (The encyclopedias usually found in school libraries are listed and discussed in Chapter 5.) When, as standard procedure, students arrange their readings in an easy-to-difficult sequence, they have acquired a lifetime means of increasing their comprehension.

In one classroom the instructor (McCampbell, 1975) wrote her own advance organizers as her classes were reading the *Odyssey,* thus providing this easy-to-difficult sequence. As her students started each book, she included a organizer on their study guide. In a few lines she clarified the shifting settings, introduced the characters who were about to appear, and provided a plot-thread to hold on to. Incidentally, with long and difficult works, a single advance organizer as students begin the work will not provide enough support. Along the way they will need "booster shots."

*Commercial Study Guides Can Be
Advance Organizers*

With carefully selected students, commercial study guides to major works of literature, often displayed on racks in bookstores, can be extremely effective "advance organizers." Suppose a fairly capable reader, a conscientious student, has tried Faulkner's *The Sound and the Fury,* then closed the book, sighing, "*What* is it saying?" Used not as a substitute for the book itself but as an enabler, a good commercial guide can sometimes save such a book for this student and greatly enhance the student's enjoyment. The guide offers a chapter-by-chapter synopsis with critical commentary. Students who despaired over Faulkner may take hold again when oriented to the novel. And if they lose their way later on, they can find it again by returning to the guide. The authors have found the Monarch guides invaluable for conscientious students who need support in reading "difficult" books, for slow readers who need the boost the added background gives their speed of reading, and for foreign students who are reading English classics in a second language. You can suggest a guide to certain students, guide them in using it, sometimes supply the guide. Since you are aware that the student is using a guide, you can guard against overdependence.

In some classrooms well-written simplified classics are used as advance organizers. The simplified version is used not instead of the classic but *to make reading it possible.* Tom, our student, was losing a hard-fought battle over the *Iliad.* Then he read Alfred J. Church's simplified *Iliad,* and the door was opened to Homer's magnificent epic.

Masterpieces of World Literature (originally titled *Masterplots:* Magill, 1952–1969) contains short plots of the world's great fiction and is another source of advance organizers. The thread of plot this work offers has marked the way out of the labyrinth for students struggling with Joyce's *Ulysses* and *Portrait of the Artist as a Young Man.*

Try "Fasten-Your-Seat-Belt"
Tape Recordings

Readers may be familiar with the work of Laura Johnson (1973, p. 129), reading specialist at Evanston Township High School, in preparing read-along cassettes. She lures her reading holdouts by recording on tape the opening pages of "fasten-your-seat-belt" fiction. The student is offered a cassette player, earphones, a tape, and a paperback so shiny and colorful a student can't resist reaching for it. Carl, long a holdout, is caught by the picture of motorcycle and boy on the cover of *The Wild One.* "In nothing flat," Johnson writes, "motorcycles win out . . . , and he marches off to an empty carrel where he can listen to *The Wild One* in peace and quiet."

Turned on by an exciting opening, the students often read on to the last page by themselves. For those who cannot or do not, Johnson records entire paperbacks—fast-paced ones—as read-along books. Now the "non-print" students are held captive for hours in a world of printed words. As they follow along, their eyes on the book they *hear* a word at the same time as they *see* it, and they come to associated the *heard word* with the *printed symbol.* Thus they assimilate new words for future use in reading. Most importantly, reading is suddenly in the Fun Department. Psychological barriers may begin to fall as they have a reading experience without failure.

School Libraries Can Offer
Read-Along Tapes

English teachers in Johnson's high school have asked her to tape full-length novels, among them *Native Son* and *The Incredible Journey.* Tapes of these books and others are made available in the school library. Students go up to the librarian and ask, "Is there a tape of Sammy Davis's *Yes, I Can?*" No stigma is attached to checking out a read-along tape—the motive might well be the heightened interest of hearing a dramatic reading. Once under way, some students finish the books alone (Johnson, 1974).

Literature from anthologies can be recorded on read-along cassettes—perhaps just the opening pages, perhaps the entire selection. Parents and students (perhaps Future Teachers groups) who wish to serve a school might assist classroom teachers by tape-recording read-along collections.

For Poetry Holdouts, Try Choral Reading

In one Florida classroom (Hillman, 1974) the poetry studied had been too difficult for some of the students. Later they were caught up with choral reading, outdid themselves in interpreting poetry, and enjoyed it, too. Their teacher tells the story:

> We did choral reading of "The Bells," "The Song of the Chattahoochee," "The Creation," and other poems. Poor readers followed along in their books, becoming familiar with unfamiliar words as strong readers read the solo parts. Then they came in with enthusiasm on the refrains. Or the poor readers practiced the solo parts until they read them flawlessly!
>
> The real learning, I find, takes place as the students prepare the selection for presentation. When they read and reread the selection, argue about who should say what and how it should be said, they get the full meaning behind each word.
>
> Usually I divided the class into two groups (there were two readings of the poem), so that all could participate, yet each group would have an audience for its performance. Each group selected a director who would conduct the reading just as a director conducts a choir. But the entire group worked out the directions, and their interpretation dictated what these would be.
>
> I purchased some books of choral readings which supplied us all the directions. These started us off, but soon the students wanted to work out their own directions.
>
> The students read the poems with great depth of feeling. One of the advantages of choral reading is that one dares to be truly dramatic—something most of us can't do or won't do when we are reading alone. My students, including my least able readers, never interpreted poetry so well—or enjoyed it so much.

Break the Character Barrier

As students begin a long work of fiction, especially a play, there may be an onrush of characters on the opening pages. Students may become "lost in the crowd." To prevent this, the characters might be listed, with a sketch of each that brings each character vividly to life. In one classroom, younger students review this introduction to the characters by playing the game, "Who Am I?" A student gives an identifying statement, then calls on a classmate to name the character identified (Ravin, 1975). When family relationships are complicated, their instructor supplies a family tree.

In another classroom the instructor asks classes to cast the play with their classmates, at the same time catching up interest with intriguing snatches of the plot. With *She Stoops to Conquer or the Mistakes of a Night*, the teacher asks:

> Who in the class should play Charles Marlowe, an eligible but tongue-tied young bachelor who trembles and stammers with young ladies of high station but is *the* ladies' man with girls below his station—a tempting barmaid, for example? . . . Who in the class should play pretty Kate Hardcastle, a girl of wealth and culture, who sets her cap to catch this handsome bachelor? Knowing she hasn't a chance as a young lady of fashion, what do you think she does? [The class is quick to see that she will "stoop to conquer."] . . . "Who in the class should play Tony Lumpkin, a young rapscallion, a mischief-maker, the practical joker who causes the hilarious "mistakes of a night?" [The class clown is invariably selected to play Tony.] And so on.

Now the students have a feeling of "Hello, I know you" for Kate, Tony, old Mrs. Hardcastle, and the others, as the players they have chosen enact the opening scenes.

Incidentally, some plays offer highly appropriate reading for less able readers, since most passages are conversational, the sentences are usually short, and the vocabulary is fairly easy. If well selected, the plays can be high in interest for teen-agers.

Try "Nonreading" When Their Reading's a Struggle

Enriching the background for a selection is a tremendous plus. The more students bring *to* the reading, the more they take *from* it. Psycholinguists remind us how heavily readers depend on experience—real or vicarious—to bring meaning to and to draw meaning from the pages before them. Indeed, if the people, the places, the times, the happenings are remote from any experiences readers have had, they will find it difficult to read about those experiences even though the language elements are well known.

Classroom Visitors Can Be Enablers

We do not always think of classroom visitors as reading enablers. A senior boy who had spent his vacation at mountain-climbing school and was lost in a blizzard while assaulting a peak in the Tetons shared the dangers and lure of mountain climbing and gave his class momentum to read *Annapurna*. A history professor, a native of Germany who as a boy had lived through the days of Hitler, visited a high school class, brought those tragic times to life, and helped less able readers read *The Diary of Ann Frank*. A student who explored caves as a hobby took classes along, through a talk, down the dark depths and over the crevasses and served as an enabler for C. W. Beebe's "I Plunged into Darkness." An airplane pilot led students into *Night Flight*. With *every* increment in background, the reading process is eased. One teacher keeps a file of human resources; she often finds valuable resources no farther away than her school's student body.

A-V Aids Can Be Enablers

Far from replacing the reading, records and cassettes help make reading possible. Suppose some less-than-eager readers in a class in black literature are assigned a group of readings about slavery in the South. Among them is *To Be a Slave* by Julius Lester. Here black men and women who had actually been slaves reveal, through interviews and original narrative, how it felt to be a slave. Before trying the printed page, the students hear Ruby Dee and Ossie Davis (on Caedmon records) reading some of these moving slave narratives. The emotional impact is tremendous. The slaves seem to be speaking across the years— the students "live" the dehumanizing experiences. Fully involved now, they turn to *To Be a Slave* and dig in. The slave ship, the auction block, the plantation, slave quarters, emancipation—all are vivid experiences. Now many students will read this book more ably.

Excursions, television, films, filmstrips, slides, projected pictures, and models can be enablers. Now insecure readers, especially if supplied with guiding questions, may have a more successful reading experience.

Apply "Life-Saving Scissors"

How many of *us* would want to go on working if day after day we faced impossible tasks, constantly fell short, and looked forward to an official rating of "failure"? Young readers aren't very likely to take hold if their assignments are so long and so difficult they know they cannot cover the assignments even with their best efforts. Adjusting learning experiences so that young people come to believe in their own competence and, instead of rejecting learning, approach future tasks with confidence is at the heart of the mastery learning Dr. Benjamin Bloom (1971) so earnestly advocates.

Students Differ Astonishingly in Their Reading Rates

An astonishing range in reading rates exists, Grob pointed out (1970, pp. 285–288, 316), among students whose standardized test scores are *on* or *above* their grade levels. Then he asked us to consider: Is it always realistic to give across-the-board assignments?

> How long would it take you to read *Great Expectations* at 150 words per minute? . . . While the average reader in the class will finish *Great Expectations* after five days of two-hour readings, the students falling below a rate of 100 words per minute will need to spend two hours a day for 21 days. . . . Assuming that these students would have other academic responsibilities, it seems fair to conjecture that their likely work pattern would have to be 42 days of one-hour readings, or 84 days of half-hour readings.

Grob called attention to the academic crippling that may result from a low reading rate. And he urged us to make adjustments for the wide variations in study time required by students—so that we can help prevent this crippling.

Scissors Can Save an Assignment

We can sometimes make the reading ahead manageable for slow readers by assigning them just parts of an assignment. Reading a few chapters from a novel, a few scenes from a play, a few excerpts from a biography, even a single crucial page, seems preferable to the alternatives—being overwhelmed or giving up and losing out on practice. How can you fill in the parts that have been scissored? They can be sketched in orally or quickly summed up on a guide to study.

Since young people are painfully sensitive to being different, of course teachers will want to make adjustments for individuals inconspicuously. The teachers in the examples below do not make the slow readers in their classes feel like losers:

One teacher quietly suggests to certain students: "Be sure to read these parts—they're crucial to your understanding. Some of these others enrich, but they're not really crucial. Use your own judgment as to how much time you have."

Or: "These are the parts we're going to discuss in class. The other parts will add dimensions, but we won't have time for it all."

On a study guide, students find this suggestion: "Skip these pages if you're rushed. In case you omit them, here's a quick summing-up of the content." Of course, with this freedom of choice, students well able to read the entire assignment may elect not to do so. Then the teacher quietly suggests to these students: "You shouldn't be satisfied with doing just part—you're too good a reader." Or this incentive might be added: "If you complete *all* the reading, you'll have a chance to answer bonus questions."

With Dan and Debbie, *less* assigned reading worked out to be *more*, when their reading load was matched to their reading speed. Reading four hundred pages of *The Yearling* would have been impossible for Dan, a painfully slow reader. But it was a poignant experience for him to read the last two or three chapters—the shooting of Jody's fawn, Jody's running away through the sawgrass, his coming to understand that when life goes back on you, you "take it for your share and go on." Debbie had given up over the *Odyssey*. Her teacher suggested trying just the chapter about the enchantress Circe and sketched some exciting highlights: the mysterious wisp of smoke that led Odysseus' shipmates to the palace, the drug that transformed his comrades into swine, Odysseus' arming to go to the rescue, Hermes' giving the hero the white *moly*. Debbie was able to succeed with this one chapter. Then under this momentum, she completed some other highlight chapters.

Adjust the Deadline

In advocating mastery learning, Bloom (1971, pp. 51, 55) suggested that most of our students, indeed 95 percent of them, can master what we have to teach them. As one possible way to achieve this mastery, he urged that the *time available* for the learning task be made appropriate to each student's needs and characteristics.

Extending the deadline for a long assignment may make "mastery learning" possible for an extremely slow reader. And why should the deadline be rigid if relaxing it will contribute to the growth of a student? Earle and Sanders suggested (1973, p. 555):

> Sometimes a straightforward question, for example, "Would it be helpful if you had till tomorrow, or next Monday?" can guide the teacher in his decision. Surely it would do wonders for the student-teacher relationship by communicating the concern and flexibility that is the hallmark of the sensitive teacher.

How can you find out *which* students are in danger of academic crippling because they read slowly? Having the students read a typical selection in class and recording the elapsed time will help you identify the slowest readers. You will find other suggestions in "Finding Out About Your Students Reading" in Chapter 6 and under "Teacher-Made Tests" in Chapter 4. English teachers will be concerned to actively *improve* their students' rates. You will find ways to accomplish this in the section, "Rapid and Moderately Rapid Reading," in Chapter 4.

Of course, some selections will confront students with insurmountable difficulties. Then you will want to place in their hands easier-to-read materials. How to have on call reading resources matched to each student is suggested in "You Can Have a Silent Reading Teacher in Your Classroom" in Chapter 6.

We have offered in this section a "grab bag" of possible helps. Of course, hand in hand with these, there will be one additional help for students: gradually moving them from more reading guidance to less, then on toward independence in reading difficult selections. In the meantime, reading guidance appropriate to the learner, the learning situation, and the difficulty of the materials will be a *shortcut* to that destination.

STUDY GUIDES CAN TURN ON
READING POWER

*A study guide can help your students manage
unmanageable reading. Here are a dozen tips
for building solid assistance right into the guide.*

Study guides can help to turn on reading power. Students who would have found an assignment impassable can sometimes work their way through it when supplied with such a guide. The study guide itself can excite their interest, tailor the assignment to their individual needs and abilities, upgrade their comprehension, keep them on the job when the reading is rough going. Solid reading assistance can be built right into the guide.

When we tell students only "Read pages 78 to 95 for tomorrow," we are turning them loose without a destination. We are really saying, "Some important questions about our subject matter are answered in this reading assignment, but I'm not going to tell you what questions they are. You find the answers, come in tomorrow, and in our discussion I'll let you know what the questions were. If your answers fit my questions, you will be a winner; if not, you lose" (Earle and Sanders, 1973, p. 55).

We are on solid ground when, through study guides, we help students read with a questioning mind set. In an experiment with one thousand college students, those who approached their reading with questions showed decided gains in comprehension (Washburne, 1929). Questions asked *before* students do the reading help develop comprehension. If the same questions are not asked until *after* the students have completed the reading (unless they return to the passage and analyze it), comprehension is tested but is not likely to be developed (Niles, 1963, p. 2).

Not only can study guides help poor readers manage the unmanageable; they can also help good readers extend their abilities and manage more rigorous reading. On the following pages you will find a dozen tips for creating guides designed for these purposes. We hope you will find some of them suggestive, adjusting them according to the difficulty of the readings, the learning situation, and the capabilities of the students. Of course, even the most successful study guide should be supplemented with other types of reading guidance.

1. Take advantage of two wonder workers. What elements above almost all others help to turn on reading power? Two that may work magic are driving interest and clear-cut purposes. First, *let the task before the students be one they want to perform,* then *see that they understand clearly what they are to know and what they should be able to do when they complete the reading.* Now they may be able to digest reading matter that ordinarily would be well beyond them.

Questions for which students really want to find answers motivate their comprehension. Classes can develop their own study guides by raising questions about an exciting subject, or the instructor can contribute questions that invite reading. Possible ways to motivate reading are suggested in the section "Helping Students *Want* to Read" in Chapter 6.

2. Add a touch of novelty. Year after year students have been handed dittoed sheets of questions. They may react to another study guide as "just some more old questions." As you sit at your desk starting to prepare a guide, ask yourself:

"Is there a way to add a dash of novelty, originality, spice, variety? Can I possibly serve up the questions in some novel format?"

One instructor dittoed Shakespeare's Sonnet 116—the one with the line "Love is not love which alters when it alteration finds." The page was headed: How Can You Know When Love Is the "Real Thing?" The students were to explain the six tests for true love that Shakespeare suggested in the sonnet. The teacher used a numeral to mark off each of the six tests, then drew an inviting "balloon" from each test into the margin. The students were asked: "Inside each balloon explain in your own words the corresponding test for the 'real thing.'" Julie, a sophomore, interpreted "or bends with the remover to remove" in this way: "Real love lasts even though someone else comes along and tries to break it up." She explained "O, no! it is an ever-fixèd mark that looks on tempests and is never shaken" like this: "Lovers' quarrels can't shake a love that's true."

The circles ballooning from a poem invite students to fill them in. Students might be asked to explain in the balloons what pictures they see in the lines. Or the question might be free-response: "Draw your own balloons and write in whatever effect the poem, as you read it, is having on you."

A study guide for Emerson's essay "On Gifts" might look like a Christmas list. The student would fill in the names of relatives and friends, then name a gift for each person, one that Emerson would have approved.

To use a lively format, a social studies instructor has sometimes typed questions against the background of a dittoed map (Carlson, 1975). A map of Odysseus' wanderings might be dittoed and an intriguing question about each adventure typed at the scene of that adventure: Calypso's island, the coast of the Cyclops, Scylla and Charybdis. The students would make the journey with Odysseus via the map as they read and answered the questions. Study questions on the voyage of the *Kon-Tiki* or on stories of local color might also lend themselves to the map format.

The questions themselves can have a dash of spice. Questions in lively wording, questions with a believe-it-or-not flavor, striking statements that provoke analysis, questions close to the lives of students—these are not so likely to be "just the same old questions." We might even use pastel colored ditto paper instead of the "same old" white.

3. Use a mini-preview. TV networks catch interest in coming attractions with previews. We might borrow this idea to catch interest in the coming reading. A mini-preview like this one might head a study guide to "The World at My Finger Tips" (Lodge and Braymer, 1963, p. 280):

> What might life be like for a young person whose world is
> suddenly blacked out by blindness? How would he feel about
> it? What would he need to do to bring "light" back into his

world? This is one person's story of how he faced just such a situation. Because the story is autobiographical, the reader is able to share the experience at first hand exactly as it seemed to the author.

A mini-preview like this might invite reading of "The Telltale Heart" (Lodge and Braymer, 1963, p. 90):

In this tale of shock and suspense, Poe takes you inside the mind of a ——. But the opening sentence tells you the narrator is *not* insane. What are you to believe?

4. *Keep questions as few as possible.* The dittoed questions students are asked in the course of their high school years might, laid end to end, cross their football field several times! Again, they may react, "Oh, some more boring questions!" If questions are few but important, they are less likely to seem like chores.

5. *The order of the questions itself can give students support.* In what order do you arrange questions? Arranging them from easy to difficult, when this is possible, will encourage insecure readers. When students have to give up on an early item, they may lose confidence and make no attempt to answer the questions that follow. Simply placing the easier questions first provides some support.

6. *They can't build a second story first!* Which of the questions will prove easier for students? Generally, those that call for information directly stated in the black-and-white print will be easier than those that require reasoning *beyond* the print. Students cannot build a second story without a first story. They must first grasp specific statements made in the reading. They will then be better prepared to perform higher-level thought processes and answer higher-level questions based on that information—to grasp implications, infer relationships, draw conclusions, grasp the author's generalizations and make their own, evaluate, and make exciting applications to their own lives and the lives around them. Accordingly, instructors may wish to place first on a study guide the questions that help students pull out stated information. and only after that ask questions that call for inferential reading.

7. *Design study guides for mastery learning.* Matching our strategies to individual students so that these strategies provide clear evidence of learning success is one way to achieve the mastery learning Dr. Benjamin Bloom has so earnestly advocated. Study guides can include Part I, easier questions probing for the most essential content, and Part II, more difficult questions. Students for whom both parts would be overwhelming can be held responsible only for

Part I. The assignment can be modified for those students with a quiet word, the final decision being left up to the student: "If you complete Part I, you'll have the basic information. Try as much of Part II as you like, but this is optional for you." Through listening to class discussions, students who do not complete Part II can get some of the learnings they missed. One instructor routinely assigns to specific students the responsibility of answering certain questions on the study guide. Thus this teacher has an opportunity to match students and questions carefully.

A range in reading achievement that was dismaying confronted one teacher in her classroom as her students were starting the *Odyssey*. Could she prepare two different study guides so that her least successful readers could achieve mastery learning? Here, in her words, is how it worked out (Ravin, 1974):

> Most of my class read Robert Fitzgerald's superb but sophisti-
> cated translation. A few students for whom the adult *Odyssey*
> was out of the question read a well-written simplified edition.
> Students of widely differing ability did readings of widely dif-
> fering difficulty, covered widely differing amounts, and worked
> with widely differing questions. The students who used the
> simplified classic accepted it as a way to make progress in read-
> ing. Now all the students were *in* the assignment rather than
> out of it. Now all experienced at least some success with read-
> ing. Preparing two guides was not overwhelming. The ques-
> tions on the simpler guide were few but important.

We can build varying degrees of reading guidance, Earle and Sanders suggested, *into the questions themselves*. Students who have been labeled non-readers, they report (1973, pp. 551–552), have followed such study guides successfully. For students who cannot read well enough to comprehend material in paragraphs or sentences, they suggest writing short, simply worded questions and providing several alternative answers. For disabled readers these might be single words. The student's task is simply to turn to the reading selection and verify one of the answers. Or important details from the reading might be included in the question. The student turns to the selection and verifies the presence of these details.

Of course handicapped readers may now rest content with skimming for bits and pieces. But the questions in themselves require reading and provide some practice. Now they are *in* the assignment rather than on the outside looking in. Now they experience at least some success with printed matter.

When vocabulary difficulties might block students, a glossary of key terms supplied right on the guide can quickly remove these blocks. With archaic or dialect terms, such a glossary may be as necessary as the vocabulary section of a French or Spanish textbook.

8. *Study guides can supply "direction finders."* Teachers can provide strong support, when they wish to, by arranging the questions in the order in which the answers are found in the passage. They can provide even stronger support, when this is appropriate, by citing the page, column, paragraph, even the line where the answer can be located. Such support can often save an assignment for handicapped readers. Even though these readers may skim to find the answers, this much practice seems preferable to no reading practice at all. "Direction finders" may be needed for only the most difficult questions.

9. *Discourage skimming.* Won't even capable readers tend to skim rather than read a selection if supplied in advance with questions? Teachers can discourage skimming for bits and pieces of information by asking broad questions, questions inclusive enough to require thorough reading. Suppose the question is "Read this selection to compare life in a medieval castle with life in a modern apartment" (Niles, 1963, p. 2). Now the student must read closely in order to explore the different aspects of life in a castle. Of course, class discussions of the material covered and quiz questions covering it can also discourage skimming.

10. *Adjusting assignments can be routine.* If assignments are modified for under-par readers, won't these readers see themselves as second-class citizens? Perhaps they will not if assignments are adjusted routinely from the day school starts in the fall. Assignments can vary from one student to another according to specific interests and choices, some special contribution he or she can make to the class, individual reading power, and needs. One instructor tells classes from the first day of school in September: "I'm not teaching the class—I'm teaching *you!*"

11. *What about writing out answers?* Writing out answers may be necessary to pin down students to cover essential content. On the other hand, many students shy away from writing, and if it invariably accompanies reading, then reading becomes associated with a difficult chore. If the discussions in class are showing adequate mastery, instructors may not wish to require written answers.

12. *Guide students with a Guide-O-Rama.* What is the subject teacher's best friend? "The Selective Reading Guide-O-Rama," answer its creators, Cunningham and Shablak (1975). They explain the *why do's* and the *how to's* of it below.*

> Many students read every passage, every chapter, in mono-
> tone. All words, all phrases, all paragraphs are of equal im-

---

* Dick Cunningham and Scott L. Shablak, "Selective Reading Guide-O-Rama: The Content Teacher's Best Friend," *Journal of Reading*, 18 (February 1975): 380–382, summarized here with permission of the International Reading Association.

portance—or of none at all. In their struggle to read without a definite purpose . . . their minds wander, concentration wanes, and frustration sets in from lack of comprehension. Only the most masochistic of students will continue such an activity very long.

To prepare a Selective Reading Guide-O-Rama, we should first ask ourselves: "What is the purpose of this reading assignment?" Then: "What sections of the reading are necessary to achieve this purpose?" Then we should scissor any and all irrelevant parts. Last, we should ask: "What must the student do, operationally, to achieve the purpose—step by step, section by section?"

As the student works through the assigned reading, the Guide-O-Rama is on the desk before him or her. Here are some samples of the guidance it offers:

Page 61, par. 3 and 4. These two paragraphs describe (a) what the people of this area were up to, and (b) why they chose this particular spot. Do not read further until you are sure of these two points.

Page 42, par. 1. The question that is raised at the end of paragraph 1 will be answered in the remainder of this reading. State this question in your own words before reading further.

Page 61, par. 1. Read this paragraph quickly in order to get a sense of what is going on.

Page 44, par. 3 and 4. This material is interesting but not essential for understanding. You may read quickly or skip entirely if you wish.

Page 66. Slow down and read this entire page *very* carefully. It describes the living area in detail. When you have finished the reading, draw the living space as you imagine it in the space provided below.

Page 75, par. 3. This paragraph summarizes the entire reading selection. Read it slowly. If there is anything you do not understand in this paragraph, go back to the reading and check it over carefully. Ask me if anything still bothers you.

The designers of the Guide-O-Rama rightly call it a reading road map:

> Its purpose is to get a student safely to his destination. . . . The "map" includes helpful road signs such as . . . "Watch for the main idea here," "Read to find the six examples"; points of interest such as "Notice the analogy that the author uses here," "How does this compare with what you read on page 35?" and even detours, such as, "Skim these pages quickly," "Avoid this section entirely."

Classes that follow Guide-O-Ramas, their creators reported, comprehend better with this guidance, then later continue to comprehend *without* such guidance. As one teacher remarked, "This idea comes as close as I can to standing by my student with my hand on his shoulder while he reads the assignment."

13. *Won't preparing study guides be overwhelming?* Will conscientious teachers, in preparing study guides to keep students from being overwhelmed, overwhelm *themselves* in doing so? A simple guide with just one or two questions may provide all the guidance needed. Some sophomores were assigned the passage from the Bible in which King Solomon described the ideal wife. They might have been told, "Read *Proverbs* 31:10–31." Instead they approached the passage with these questions: "What in your opinion are the qualities of the ideal wife? List them. Now read *Proverbs* 31:10–31 and list the qualities King Solomon considered desirable. How do yours compare?" This brief guide gave the students purpose and definitely brought a lift to comprehension.

The reader in search of patterns to follow in preparing study guides and guidelines for using them will find these in abundance in Herber's *Teaching Reading in the Content Areas* (1970).

A creative teacher expresses this caution (Bell, 1975): "Students may regard study guides as setting limits. As they complete the guide, they may be thinking, 'Good! Now I'm through! I won't do one thing more.' In that case, study guides work against initiative—they may destroy more learning than they generate. My students do not always regard the questions on my study guides as handed down to Moses on Mount Sinai. They are also encouraged to go down fascinating, personal—perhaps more important—pathways."

JIM COULD HANDLE AWESOME ARISTOTLE

> *Here we share a study guide one of the authors prepared. We use the example of red-blooded teen-ager Jim and awesome, "antiquated" Aristotle because seldom have two seemed so far apart. The study guide brought Jim and Aristotle together.*

One of the writers faced a problem: how to help some less successful Laboratory School readers handle some rigorous reading—it happened to be a treatise by Aristotle, "On the Optimum Number of Friends." Overawed by the antiquity of Aristotle and his awesome name to begin with, these students were not likely to make it beyond the first two or three lines.

Making a study guide occurred to her—one that might walk the students past the difficulties. As she prepared it, she tried to imagine herself as Jim, one of the students. Her thoughts ran like this.

1. Could she build a bridge between Aristotle and teen-age Jim, who had close friends of his own and valued them?

2. Aristotle posed the question, "How many friends should we have?" Jim and the others should discuss this before they begin their reading.

3. Should she search the essay for words likely to block Jim, then re-move these blocks first?

4. Jim had already learned techniques for previewing. He should now be reminded to practice these techniques by previewing this essay.

5. Jim's own writing was sometimes chaotic. Like many students, he needed to learn to organize it—to brief his reader in his introduc-tion on what is to follow, to devote paragraphs in the body to dif-ferent aspects of the general subject, to "wrap things up" in a conclusion. The study guide should focus Jim's attention on how Aristotle does all this superbly.

6. The treatise on friendship is, among Aristotle's essays, relatively easy. At first the teacher hesitated to assist Jim to the extent of giving him "direction-finders," the numbers of the paragraphs where the answers to the questions could be located. She con-cluded that *this time* Jim would need this support. Hopefully, in the future she could withdraw this support and move Jim closer to independence.

7. Of course, Jim would not be able to think reflectively about Aris-totle's views on friendship unless he would first *comprehend* what those views were. So the questions on the guide should be se-quenced from literal questions, the answers to which are printed "in the lines," to the kinds of questions that require reading "be-tween and beyond the lines." With Aristotle's stated views pulled out and at his command, Jim would then be ready to go on to depth questions, those asking him to reflect on the soundness of those views and to make life applications.

How did it turn out? Teen-ager Jim read Aristotle successfully, was stimu-lated, did a little questioning of one or two of Aristotle's views, and philoso-phized quite a bit on his own on the subject of friendship.

Aristotle's "On the Optimum Number of Friends"

Are many friends really to be desired?

Introduction.*   In this essay, the Greek philosopher Aristotle talks to us— across nearly twenty-five centuries—about something as close to us as our own friendships.

The great philosophers agree with the common man on at least one point: that a true friendship is one of the rarest and most valuable experiences in life. In his own life Aristotle found friends to be a supreme source of happiness. A famous statue of Aristotle depicts him in an attitude of intent listening—we might imagine him to be deep in a searching conversation with a friend. The moving words he wrote as an inscription for an altar of friendship dedicated to Plato reveal the depth of his feeling for one of his closest friends.

In this essay Aristotle is asking a serious and important question: How many friends should we have? If we try to predict his answer, we may easily assume that he will encourage us to cultivate a wide circle of friends. Instead, Aristotle raises these questions: *Are many friends really to be desired?* How many friends should we try to have? If we cultivate a great number of friends, what kind of friends will they be?

If we were walking with Aristotle in an olive grove in Athens, he might offer this counsel: "Friends are essential for the good life. It is terribly important for you to have friends and to keep on having friends as long as you live." But then he would add a note of *caution*—and that is the heart of this essay.

Can you handle Aristotle's vocabulary?

You'll hurt your chances of grasping Aristotle's thinking if you have to fight for word meaning.

This section pinpoints words that may be unfamiliar. If you already know the meaning of the word *as it is used* below, don't bother to write in the meaning. However, if you aren't sure of the meaning, look up the word. Search out the meaning *that best fits the context* and write it in the blank [The guide included four more questions on words]:

---

* The authors borrowed an idea or two in this introduction from Paul B. Diederich and O. E. Palmer, *Critical Thinking in Reading and Writing* (New York: Holt, Rinehart and Winston, 1960), pp. 150–153. Ideas in the vocabulary preview are from Maxwell H. Norman and Enid S. Norman, *How to Read and Study for Success in College* (New York: Holt, Rinehart and Winston, 1971).

1. In the title "On the Optimum Number of Friends," *optimum* means _____.

2. In paragraph 3 (around line 2) Aristotle discusses friendships that are cultivated "with a view to *utility*." Here *utility* means _____.

As your first step, preview the essay

You've already learned how to preview an informational selection. As you know, you'll handle factual reading *better and faster* if, instead of just plunging in, you preview the selection before you read it thoroughly.

   Use your newly acquired preview technique to hit the high spots of the essay:

Examine the title.

Read the introduction.

Examine the first and perhaps the last sentence of each paragraph.
   Skim the paragraph.

Examine the conclusion.

Now can you answer these questions?

1. Do you now have a general idea of what the essay is all about and where it's going? What have you learned?

2. Did you spot some of the aspects under the general topic—*subtopics* that Aristotle will discuss? If so, what are they?

Then follow this study guide during your careful reading

1. When preparing a paper of your own, you write an introduction announcing to your reader what your paper will contain. Perhaps you raise broad problems which you will explore in the paper.
    Did Aristotle organize his essay with such an opener? If so, what does he announce as the content?

2. In the *body* of a paper that you are writing, you devote paragraphs to different aspects of your general topic. And so in this essay does Aristotle. Starting in paragraph 3, he turns his attention to three different types of friendship: two "lower" levels, then a third or "higher" level.
    a. Explain in your own words the two "lower" levels of friendship. (Aristotle devotes paragraphs 3 and 4 to these.) Why does he

counsel us against having too many friends of each of these
types?

   b. What characteristic, according to Aristotle, distinguishes the
third, or noble, level of friendship?

3. Even though friendships of type-three are noble and essential for
the good life, Aristotle now comes up with reasons—three of them
—for limiting the number of our type-three friends. What argument does he advance in paragraph 6? Paragraph 7? Paragraph 8?

4. In paragraph 9 Aristotle advances still another argument for limiting our type-three friends. This reason, he contends, lies in the very
nature of all of us. Can you state the reason?

5. In paragraph 11 Aristotle asks a probing question, "What is the
truth about those who *appear* to possess large numbers of friends?"
How does he answer this?

6. Well-organized informational writing usually does not break off
abruptly. When preparing a paper of your own, you often work out
a conclusion that adds a note of finality. Like your introduction,
this is likely to be general. It may offer a "recap" of what your paper
contains. It may drive home what you want, most of all, to leave
with your reader.

    Did Aristotle wrap up the content of his essay in a concluding
paragraph? If so, what is the gist of his conclusion?

Think these through

[The guide concluded with five more think-it-through questions.]

1. A senior boy has been elected to one school office after another all
through his four years of high school. Would Aristotle necessarily
conclude that he has been blessed with friends? Do you conclude
this?

2. What quality that Aristotle ascribes to a true friend would you
value most in a friend of your own? Do you consider it important
to relate in this way to your own closest friends?

3. Aristotle is deeply convinced that it is not possible to be a true
friend to many people. You have heard all his arguments. Do you
agree?

Again, a study guide with only a question or two may provide capable
readers with all the guidance needed. A teacher of capable seniors led her
students to the heart of Aristotle's essay with this single question (McGuire,
1974): "How does Aristotle answer the question: What is the optimum num-

ber of friends? And how does he arrive at this conclusion? Does his reasoning convince you?"

FUN FARE FOR VOCABULARY GROWTH

> *Word play activities can create excitement over words and turn students into dedicated word-collectors.*

Vocabulary work offers an opportunity for a variety of word play activities. Young people—troubled readers or top readers—seem to respond to this lighter approach. The teacher's own enthusiasm has a chance to come through during all this fun fare.

Many of the activities that follow reinforce vocabulary learnings. Often this reinforcement is multisensory—students *see* the new word, *hear* others pronounce it, *practice pronouncing* it themselves. It is often advisable for students to meet a new word in context a number of times after it has been introduced.

The activities are fast-paced, hands wave all over the room, and many take part. They offer a welcome change of pace within the classroom.

Activities to Enrich and Motivate Work with Context Clues

The activities that follow are offered for use along with the introductory principles and practices under "Vocabulary Development Through Context Clues" in Chapter 2. These activities are the fun fare—they are intended to follow the solid fare in that chapter.

Are you a good word detective?

Each student brings to class a useful new word in clue-rich context and reads the sentence aloud to the group. The others try to deduce the meaning. The student who answers correctly presents the next sentence. (This idea is adapted from McCullough, 1945, p. 3.) *Example:*

> I received the strangest note this morning. I've been puzzling all day long over its *cryptic* message.

The student who challenges the group with a word should be in command of the pronunciation and well prepared with the dictionary meaning that fits the context. Students rise to being the authority of the moment on their word! Students might rotate the responsibility for bringing a new word each day.

Sudents will need *much* help in formulating their own sentences for difficult words. It will be extremely helpful to guide them to those clear model sentences in a school dictionary of a difficulty appropriate for them to handle.

Winning streak

This game is played after a class has had introductory work on context clues. New words or words to be reviewed are printed at the top of index cards. Just below (or on the back of the card), the word appears in a sentence, one rich in context clues and close to the interests of the students. The sentence may be about happenings at school or about people they know.

The sentence below was used just after the big homecoming game (from Evans):

STENTORIAN

Suddenly the *stentorian* voice of the head cheerleader boomed over the loudspeaker. "Everyone up for the kickoff!"

The teacher reads the word aloud from the card and perhaps writes it on the board. Then he or she reads aloud the context clue. Students earn points for themselves by giving the correct meaning. Hands wave, and many take part.

In a variation of this game, the class divides into two teams. If individual students can give the meaning of the word without hearing the context clue, they earn two points for their team. If they must ask for the clue and can then give the meaning, they earn one point.

A vocabulary test with puzzle appeal

Books are open to a selection the students have not read. A number of puzzlers to be defined are listed on the board with the page and line where each is to be found. Students may make full use of all clues present, but they are not to turn to the dictionary.

The values and limitations of context revelation are driven home dramatically as students try—under the pressure of a test situation—to wrest the meaning from the clues.

What's missing?

Somewhere along the line as you teach the use of context clues, you might delete a new word in the midst of very revealing context, then prove to the students that they can reason out its meaning. In one classroom the teacher writes on the board a new word in revealing context, then covers the new word with a rectangle of cardboard hung on cellophane tape hinges. Then the teacher asks the class, "What meaning is called for here?" and then, "Just how did you know?"

> Presenting a prom involves an infinite number of little tasks. In printing the invitation, decorating the hall, and arranging and costuming the floor show, there are countless things to be done. The members of prom committees must attend to all these ⬚.

Students are quick to suggest "small details." The card is then lifted, and the word *minutiae* is revealed. The students are impressed that they have arrived at the meaning of the word without opening the dictionary and with no clues except those the context offered.

Activities to Enrich and Motivate Work
with Word Parts

These activities are offered for use along with the principles in Chapter 2 under "Greek and Latin Word Parts."

Whose family tree grows largest?

Younger students draw a tree, print a word ancestor (*poly-*, for example) on the trunk, then write in members of the *poly-* family on the branches. Whose "family tree" will grow largest within the time limit? It's fair to consult a student dictionary. (Idea from Kalk, 1975.)

Or each student selects a different prefix or root, goes to the board, and creates a tree. Soon trees are branching, spreading, and growing all over the chalkboard.

Word coinages

After students have studied certain Greek and Latin word elements, the teacher coins words by combining familiar parts, then tests students with coinages like those below. Students, too, may come up with some very original coinages:

magnomarshmallowphile   a lover of big marshmallows.

teacheritis   irritation, affliction caused by a teacher (idea from Feiman, 1970).

neologophile   a lover of new words.

ultrahyperpolysyllabic words   words that have an inordinate number of syllables.

Teasers

The study of word parts offers an opportunity to use the light touch—and provide practice—with teasers like these. The examples (from Greene, 1962) are intended for upperclass honors groups:

Which would you rather meet—a *philanthropist* or an *anthropophobiac?*

How would a *misogynist* feel in a *gynarchy?*

Would a walk to his office be harder for a man with *cephalalgia, podagra,* or *dermatitis?*

A *quaver,* in music, is an eighth note. Then what is a *demihemisemiquaver?* You already know the meanings of *demi-, hemi-,* and *semi-.* [Answer: a sixty-fourth note.]

If you were in an uncivilized land, which would you try most to avoid —the *entomologists,* the *anthropophagi,* or the *ichthyophobiacs?*

Chain reaction

As classes work with word parts, a teacher can easily make them aware of "chain reactions." Students who have learned *micro-* in the word *microscope* and *chrom-* (color) in *polychromatic* might—to their delight—find that they can use these parts to figure out the impressive-looking *microchromaphotograph* (a color photograph taken through a microscope). Then they might use *chrom-* to figure out that *dyschromatopsia* (*dys-,* bad; *chrom-,* color; *op,* sight) is simply a forbidding word for a form of color-blindness. As they work with *dyschromatopsia,* they pick up the new part *dys-.* They use this part, in turn, to unlock *dysfunction, dyspepsia,* and *dysrhythmic.*

Race track

A race track is labeled with a conspicuous START and FINISH LINE and is marked off into small spaces (Gainsburg, 1967, p. 117). A prefix or root that has been studied is printed on each space. Players throw the dice, then advance their token along the track the corresponding number of spaces. They may remain on that space *if* they can give the meaning of the word part printed there plus one English derivative. The first player to cross the finish line wins. A race track can be quickly drawn on the board or on poster paper.

Learn to count and learn new words

An English teacher reports (Kaplan, 1970), "The study of meter in poetry affords an ideal time to learn the number prefixes. Terms like *dimeter, tetram-*

eter, *pentameter, hexameter,* appear forbidding to students—at first. I suggest that all you have to do is learn to count in Greek! As we work with *mono-, di-, tri-, tetra-, pent-, hex-,* etc., derivatives like *monotonous* and *Pentagon* come up for discussion and reinforce the meanings of the Greek parts."

Activities to Enrich Work with Word Origins

The activities that follow are offered for use along with the introductory material in Chapter 2 under "Word Origins Fix Meanings and Stir Interest."

What's the good word?

Students are given a clue in the story of a word's origin. They are to try to find the "good word" and bring it to class next day.

Word clue.   Once in history a word caused the death of 42,000 people. Forty-two thousand people were killed because they could not pronounce one word. Look for it in your Bible—in the twelfth chapter of the book of Judges.

Answer: shibboleth.   Two tribes of ancient Israel were at war. The men of Gilead were victors over the men of Ephraim. Certain fugitives pleaded with the victors, "We're not enemies—we're not Ephraimites. Let us go free!" The Gileadites named a condition: "If you're not our enemies, then prove it by pronouncing *shibboleth."* The Ephraimites could not say *sh*—the sound was not in their language. Their pronunciation soon betrayed them. The Bible concludes the story: "If he said 'sibboleth,' . . . they would seize him, and slay him at the fords of the Jordan. Thus there fell at that time forty-two thousand of the Ephraimites."

The students now retain more readily a current meaning of *shibboleth:* a criterion to distinguish the "ins" from the "outs," or a custom, habit, mode of dress, or pet phrase which distinguishes a certain group.

Word clue.   What word meaning "wise and faithful counselor" spans more than thirty centuries back to the Trojan War? Look for it among the Greeks, not among the Trojans.

Answer: mentor.   When Ulysses left Ithaca for the Trojan War, he entrusted the education of his son Telemachus to his trusted friend, Mentor. During Ulysses' long absence, Mentor served the boy faithfully as wise counselor, guardian, and teacher. Today, across a span of three thousand years, the word still means a wise and faithful counselor.

Word clue.   What word for loud or powerful also reaches across three thousand years to a character in Homer who had a voice as powerful as those of fifty men?

Answer: stentorian. This word comes from Stentor, who was the Greek army's herald during the Trojan War. Heralds needed loud voices so they could make themselves heard in the days before public address systems (from Evans).

Word clue. What word for "fat" comes from Latin and suggests too much body?

Answer: corpulent. The Latin *corpus* means body.

Word autobiographies

One teacher (Wiersma, 1963) asks classes, "Why not shake hands with a word and get to know it better?" From words encountered in reading or discussion, she compiles a list of those with exciting stories. Each student selects an interesting word, researches it, and presents its life story. A format is agreed on: origin, meaning, changes, sentences illustrating the use of the word, and the like. The classroom is well stocked with books on derivations.

Collector's items from mythology

During the study of mythology, students are on the lookout for words whose origins span more than thirty centuries to the world of the Greek and Roman gods and heroes. They collect and discuss words like *siren, atlas, cereal, lunatic, oracle, hector, tantalize, mercurial, iridescent, jovial, Stygian, chaotic, Herculean, labyrinth, lethal, mentor, halcyon, martial, titan, odyssey, stentorian, psyche, demigod, narcissistic, chimerical, cupidity, nemesis, saturnine, procrustean,* and *protean.*

What's in a name?

Words originating in people's names often have fascinating stories. The guillotine, for instance, bears the name of Joseph Ignace Guillotin, a humane French physician who in 1789 proposed its use as more merciful than hanging. Each student might select from a list supplied by the teacher a word that interests her or him and report its story. "People words" include *atlas, boycott, maverick, martinet, echo, cereal, mesmerize, salon, fuchsia, vandal, philippics, quixotic, chauvinism, diesel, pasteurize, malapropism.* Appropriate words are suggested in *People Words* (Severn, 1966) and *Name into Word* (Partridge, 1949).

Words from faraway places

Words now common property originated from the names of faraway places where memorable events occurred. Each student might select a word from a list supplied by the teacher and tell its lively story. The list might include *bedlam, mecca, shanghai, marathon, colossal, meander, academy, maelstorm, laconic, waterloo,* and *babble.* Words of varying difficulty levels are suggested in *Name into Word* (Partridge, 1949).

Activity for Dictionary Study

Secondary school students often need far more introductory explanation and follow-up practice with dictionary skills than might be realized. The activity on the next page reinforces important work with pronunciation aids.

Word champ

This activity challenges students who have just learned to sound out difficult words by using the diacritical marks and accent marks in the phonetic entry in the dictionary, together with the pronunciation key. Sounding out the "word champ" is the pay-off! (Incidentally, the champ can be found in *Webster's Third New International Dictionary*. It means about the same as *silicosis*.)

Miscellaneous Fun Fare

Word charades

After certain words have been studied, selected ones that lend themselves to charades are printed on slips and dropped into a box. Each student pulls out a slip, then presents a pantomime that suggests the meaning of the word. Class members are to guess the word that is being dramatized. A popular football player pantomimed primping in a beauty salon to depict *pulchritude*. For *serendipity*, a student pantomimed looking through a book, then finding an unexpected dollar bill (Rhinestine, 1970).

What would you do with . . . ?

A particular teacher piques interest by writing on the board a question like this: "What would you do with a cortege?" Her students suggested, "Lock it in a cage," "Keep it in my locker," "Send it to a girl before a dance," and "March in it slowly." Curiosity prevailed; many looked up the word and knew its meaning the next day. They found the question still on the board, and some were amused by their guesses of the day before (Robinson, 1957).

Classroom conversation

After certain words had been studied, the teacher announced the topic for a classroom conversation. Each student was to take part in the conversation by contributing a sentence using one of the new words. Since Queen Elizabeth and Prince Philip were making an official visit, the teacher announced as the topic the visit of the Queen. On the list was the word *fetid*. How could the class converse about the lovely queen using the unlovely word *fetid*? A student came up with "The garbage in the Queen's kitchen was fetid."

text cont. pg. 367

Below is one of the longest words in the English language. Try out your ability to work out pronunciation and accent by using principles you've learned in class and by referring to your dictionary's pronunciation key when necessary.

Take care to accent the word correctly. Stress *most strongly* syllables with a heavy accent mark. Stress *less strongly* (but still stress) syllables with a lighter mark.

Can you pronounce the "champ" in class?

PNEUMONOULTRAMICROSCOPICSILICOVOLCANOCONIOSIS

(nū′ mə nō əl trə mī krə skäp′ ic sil′ə kō val kā′ nō kō nē ō′ səs)

Do you see any familiar parts? Can you make a guess at the meaning?

I'm thinking of a word

This drill is fast paced, many participate, and students practice and hear the pronunciations of their new words. Using words already studied, the teacher or a student leader supplies a double hint—the meaning of the word and its first and last letters. Students guess the word. Examples:

> I'm thinking of a word which means *predicament* or *plight*. It starts with *d* and ends with *a*. What is it? (Answer: *dilemma*)
>
> I'm thinking of a word which means *destroy completely*. It starts with *a* and ends with *e*. What is it? (Answer: *annihilate*)

Match-ups

The teacher or a group of students compiles a list of useful new adjectives (in good taste) that can be used to describe the personality traits of classmates, of other students, or of staff members of the school. Using their dictionaries, students match adjectives and people they know, then compare the match-ups.

Adjectives such as these lend themselves to this kind of practice: *loquacious, irrepressible, versatile, sophisticated, petite, argumentative, bland, imperturbable, vivacious, dynamic, benign, jocular, gregarious, affable, effervescent, vociferous, diminutive, altruistic, amiable, benevolent, stalwart, sage, animated, beneficent, scintillating, chic, sapient, sedulous, erudite, articulate, sanguine, pedagogical.* One teacher asked the class: "Which one of us is vociferous? Petite? Articulate? A pedagogue?"

Name calling

Teachers sometimes use arresting and descriptive new words to characterize students or their activities. On a day when one teacher (Kaplan, 1970) seemed to run into the same three girls everywhere—in the halls, the library, the cafeteria—she exclaimed, "You three surely are ubiquitous!" The dictionary was quickly consulted. The morning after her students had taken part in a play, she greeted them with "Good morning, my little thespians!" Parents reported the word came up for discussion that night at dinner. One teacher concluded a class period spent on vocabulary work with the comment, "You're turning into ultrahyperpolysyllabic sesquipedalianists—and logophiles, too!"

Teachers' original word uses

The teacher's own vocabulary, we have noted, can be a major motivating factor. Dedicated word lovers themselves, teachers can inject interest and humor into word study with their own original word uses.

One day a teacher walked into class and announced, "Today is Serendipity Day!" The class was to have an unexpected treat—the playing of a recording by the Smothers Brothers of *Aesop's Fables*. The regular lesson time had been preempted, and each student had become a serendipidist! (Rhinestine, 1970).

Another teacher gave his class a mild lecture, then added, "I just felt like pontificating," and in doing so, created just the right moment to teach the new word and its derivation.

Words so used often become "in" words, which students enjoy using in class and in their own speech and writing.

Notes on students' papers

One teacher (Kaplan, 1970) piques interest in words by writing notes on her students' papers: "Shame on you! You've committed a tautology!" or "You've used a flagrant pleonasm!" or "You have here a superb example of zeugma!"

Loaded paragraphs

After certain words have been introduced and need reinforcement, teachers sometimes create original materials loaded with the new words. In the exercise below, students are asked to explain the different maniacs who attend the "mania party":

> Have you ever been to a *mania* party? You must act the role of your favorite mania, within reason. The *megalomaniac* might appear as Napoleon with hand in coat. The person with the lighted candle and that glitter in his or her eye might portray the *pyromaniac*. It is fairly easy to pretend to be a *dipsomaniac* by staggering and carrying a bottle. The *kleptomaniac* might spend the evening attempting to steal pocket handkerchiefs, jackets left on chairs, et cetera. You'll have to figure out how to *act* like the following maniacs without destroying your image: *nymphomaniac, monomaniac, theomaniac.*

Fill the blank

This activity is fast-paced, all participate, and students practice new words and hear their pronunciations. Using words from a group already studied, each student composes a sentence leaving a blank where one of the new words is to be inserted. A student might write: "The Junior-Senior Prom is a _____ affair." (The word in mind is *convivial*.) The student reads his or her sentence, then calls on someone. If the classmate fills the blank correctly, it becomes his or her turn to offer a sentence.

Students' original sentences are usually close to teen-age interests; they invest the word with meaningful associations and help the meaning stick.

Laziness is not _____ to a record of all A's. (*conducive*)

Sophomores often _____ a prominent senior. (*emulate*)

After receiving my paycheck, I felt _____. (*affluent*)

A wall of words

A section of the chalkboard is set aside as a "word wall." The students are invited to write here in colored chalk new words they have collected, with their meanings. They initial each word they contribute. The wall is soon splashed with colorful words—an eye-catching reminder to keep vocabulary growing. Students who contribute a word that will be especially useful to their classmates teach that word to the class (Matthai, 1973).

What's the password?

The teacher asks a group to find a useful new word during their silent reading in class that day. They are to give it as the password as they walk out of class. At the door the teacher stops each student with "What's the password?" Each student then pronounces a new word, presents it in context, and "teaches" it to the teacher. From then on, passwords often become "in" words that teacher and students use in class in lighthearted, original ways.

Great words

The teacher prefaces a study of "great words":

> During the course of human history, people have come to clothe their highest ideals and aspirations in words. The very existence of these words has uplifted the race. If these concepts did not exist, human beings could not aspire toward them. These words can make us "better than ourselves."

The class discusses some "words to live by" suggested by the teacher, perhaps *compassion, integrity, magnanimity, empathy*. The students, too, suggest "great words." Words studied might include *fortitude, altruism, fidelity, maturity, steadfastness, serenity, wisdom, fraternity, indomitable, invincible, ethical*.

Word of the day

In one class the students are always on the lookout for words "headlined" in the news of the day. Then the teacher headlines one of the words in a prominent corner of the board as the Word of the Day. The word is introduced in lively, timely context. One day when tensions between two nations had just been relaxed, the Word of the Day was *détente*. One day when the Academy Awards were in the spotlight, the Word of the Day was *accolade*.

Give me a clue!

From a group of words already studied, the class selects one—let's say, *incongruous*—while a student is out in the hall or just closes his ears. Then that student tries to guess the word the class selected. The others provide clues, either direct or oblique, to aid the guessing. Hints for the word *incongruous* might be "wearing a bikini in the snow," "diving into the swimming pool with track shoes on."

From aardvark to zygote

Here are some teasers that add a lighthearted touch. They send students hurrying to the dictionary or stimulate them to work out the meanings through carefully considering the context:

Which would you rather have—a flattering *epithet* or a flattering *epitaph?* (Rosenberger, 1947, p. 14).

Is coming to our class an *onus* or a *bonus?*

Are you your parents' *prodigy* or your parents' *progeny?*

Can you figure out the meaning of *propensity* in Ogden Nash's couplet?
"Boys seldom have a *propensity*
Toward girls of such immensity."

Should a ninth-grader be flattered to be called *sophomoric?*

If you are *fatuous*, should you decide to go on a diet?

Do you think you should be glad to have someone's *fulsome* praise?

Would you like to have a *cache* of cash?

If you were *eschewing* a chocolate marshmallow sundae heaped up with nuts, would you be preparing it in your mouth for swallowing?

Why can you "bask in the sun" but never "bask in the shade"?

Would you choose this age in life—*dotAGE?*

Would you use the word *stentorian* to describe a lullaby or a foghorn?

If someone said you are *anathema* to him, would you be flattered or never speak to him again?

Are you likely to be *confident* of your *confidant?*

If you were *pseudosophisticated,* would you really know your way around socially?

Is a *mountebank* a quack doctor or part of a mountain? (Rosenberger, 1947, p. 107).

Would you wish to be noted or *notorious?* (Rosenberger, 1947, p. 14).

Where are you most likely to find a *thespian*—behind a counter, behind bars, or behind footlights? (Rosenberger, 1947, p. 33).

If you were *bibulous*, would you read the Bible, prepare bibliographies, or visit bars? (Rosenberger, 1947, p. 100).

Would you rather be a *cad* or a *cadaver?*

What kind of person are you if you're the *quintessence* of *effervescence?*

Would a teacher be likely to prefer a class to be *vociferous, tractable,* or *erudite?*

The Great Pumpkin arrives

Special days—Halloween, Thanksgiving, Christmas—bring opportunities for "fun fare." Around Halloween the Great Pumpkin rises out of the pumpkin patch—at least in one classroom. A large, inflatable jack-o-lantern appears. This jack-o-lantern has two faces: one beaming, one gloomy. Turning the unhappy face toward the class, the teacher asks: "Does Jack look *disconsolate* [*morose, despondent*]?" "What do you think that means?" Then showing the happy face, she asks: "Now does Jack look *ecstatic* [*sanguine, beamish*]?" "What do you think that means?" "Is Jack *rotund?*" and so on. The words become "in" words, like the passwords described earlier.

Christmas offers other opportunities: "Suppose your wide-eyed three-year-old brother starts to climb the Christmas tree, will you *remonstrate?*" "Would you like to have your birthday *coincide* with Christmas?" "On the community tree in the Civic Center are *myriads* of colored lights."

Turn your old words in for new

Working with words from a group already introduced and studied, students have the satisfaction of turning their everyday, familiar words in on new words (Rosenberger, 1947, p. 78). The teacher or a student asks, "Can you trade in the old, familiar words *painfully moving* or *touching* on a new word?" Students respond with *poignant.* "Can you turn the old, familiar words *spirit of good fellowship* in on a new word?" Students answer with *camaraderie.*

Vocabulary Parcheesi

Vocabulary Parcheesi is an original way to review words students have already studied. New words, perhaps in a snatch of context, are pasted on the spaces on a Parcheesi board, except for the "safety" spaces. A player throws the dice and is entitled to move forward as indicated by the dice *if* the player can give the meaning of the word on the space where he or she lands. Rules for Vocabulary Parcheesi:

1. So that the game will have maximum learning value, the students are given time before they begin to play to look over the board and study any words they are not sure of.

2. Each player has only one marker.

3. A player must throw a 5 to enter the game.

4. A player may move the number of spaces indicated by the dice *if* he or she can give the meaning of the word on the space where the marker will land.

5. A player who lands on the space with another player "sends the other player home."

6. The teacher judges the accuracy of the answers.

7. If a player fails to give the meaning of a word, the opportunity is thrown open to someone else, and 5 free spaces are awarded for the correct answer. In case no player knows the answer, the teacher supplies it.

8. Players are expected to pronounce the word, then to give its meaning.

9. In order to go "home," a player must throw the exact count required to arrive there. The player may throw this count on one of the dice or as the total of both dice.

10. The first player who arrives "home" is the winner.

You can use the same Parcheesi board with other vocabulary words and for a variety of other activities if, instead of pasting words on the spaces, you number the spaces, then type a list of words (or other tasks) on a ditto, numbering these correspondingly. You then supply a dittoed list to each player. Of course, students can prepare the board.

Browsing box

One teacher (Kaplan, 1970) suggests a large browsing box. Students with an extra five or ten minutes at the end of the period can select a word activity from it. Compartments with standup flags and colorful folders catch the eye. Activities include clippings of the "Wit-Twister" column in *Saturday Review*,

"You Can Enrich Your Word Power" from *Readers Digest*, games like Perquacky, Jotto, Probe, and Scrabble; and word puzzles, including crosswords.

Bibliography

Adams, W. Royce. *How to Read the Humanities*. Glenview, Ill.: Scott, Foresman and Company, 1969.

Aukerman, Robert C. *Reading in the Secondary School Classroom*. New York: McGraw-Hill Book Company, 1972, chapter 8.

Berg, David W. "Independent Study: Transfusion for Anemic English Programs." *English Journal*, 59, no. 2 (1970): 254.

Developmental Reading, OSSTF Resource Booklet. Toronto: Ontario Secondary School Teachers' Federation, 1972.

Doemel, Nancy J. "Vocabulary for Slow Learners." *English Journal*, 59, no. 1 (1970): 78.

Finder, Morris. "Teaching to Comprehend Literary Texts—Drama and Fiction." *Journal of Reading*, 17, no. 4 (1974): 272–278.

Grob, James A. "Reading Rate and Study-Time Demands on Secondary Students." *Journal of Reading*, 13, no. 4 (1970): 285–288 ff.

Hillocks, George, Bernard J. McCabe, and James F. McCampbell. *The Dynamics of English Instruction, Grades 7–12*. New York: Random House, 1971.

Johnson, Laura S. "Cool It, Teach! and Tape All of It!" *Journal of Reading*, 17, no. 2 (1973): 129–131.

Manzo, Anthony V. "CONPASS: English—A Demonstration Project." *Journal of Reading*, 16, no. 7 (1973): 539–545.

Meade, Richard A., and W. Geiger Ellis. "Paragraph Development in the Modern Age of Rhetoric." *English Journal*, 59, no. 2 (1970): 219.

Robinson, H. Alan. *Teaching Reading and Study Strategies: The Content Areas*. Boston: Allyn and Bacon, 1975, Chapter 9.

Smith, Frank. *Understanding Reading*. New York: Holt, Rinehart, and Winston, 1971.

Smith, Richard J. "English Teacher as Reading Teacher." *Journal of Reading*, 16, no. 3 (1972): 245–250.

Smith, Richard J., and Karl Hesse. "The Effects of Prereading Assistance on the Comprehension and Attitudes of Good and Poor Readers." *Research in the Teaching of English*, 3, no. 2 (1969): 166–177.

Tooze, Ruth. *Storytelling*. Englewood Cliffs, N.J.: Prentice-Hall, 1959.

Willson, Norma. "The Recalcitrants." *English Journal*, 59, no. 1 (1970): 105.

Wright, Dorothy. "Try a Quest." *English Journal*, 59, no. 1 (1970): 131.

References

Ausubel, David P. "The Use of Advance Organizers in the Learning and Retention of Meaningful Verbal Material." *Journal of Educational Psychology*, 51, no. 5 (1960): 267–272.

Bell, Earl, University of Chicago Laboratory School teacher, in remarks to Ellen Thomas, July 1975.

Bloom, Benjamin S. "Affective Consequences of School Achievement." In *Mastery Learning: Theory and Practice*, edited by James H. Block. New York: Holt, Rinehart and Winston, 1971, pp. 16–19.

Bloom, Benjamin S. "Mastery Learning." In *Mastery Learning: Theory and Practice*, edited by James H. Block. New York: Holt, Rinehart and Winston, 1971.

Carlson, Charles, social studies teacher at La Follette Senior High School (Madison, Wis.), in remarks to Ellen Thomas, June 1975.

Chute, Marchette. *Stories from Shakespeare*. Cleveland: World Publishing Company, 1956.

Cunningham, Dick, and Scott L. Shablak. "Selective Reading Guide-O-Rama: The Content Teacher's Best Friend." *Journal of Reading*, 18 (February 1975): 380–382.

Donham, Virginia, former teacher at New Trier High School (Winnetka, Ill.), in remarks to Ellen Thomas, July 1975.

Earle, Richard A., and Peter L. Sanders. "Individualizing Reading Assignments." *Journal of Reading*, 16, no. 7 (1973).

Evans, Edna Hoffman, English teacher at Phoenix College (Ariz.), 1968.

Farrell, Edmund J. "Listen My Children, and You Shall Read." *English Journal*, 55, no. 1 (1966): 43–45.

Feiman, Sharon, former University of Chicago Laboratory School English teacher, in remarks to Ellen Thomas, May 1970.

Finder, Morris. "Teaching to Comprehend Literary Texts—Drama and Fiction." *Journal of Reading*, 17, no. 4 (1974).

Gainsburg, Joseph C. *Advanced Skills in Reading*, Book 3. New York: Macmillan Company, 1967.

Greene, Amsel. *Word Clues*. New York: Harper and Row, 1962.

Grob, James A. "Reading Rate and Study-Time Demands on Secondary Students." *Journal of Reading*, 13, no. 4 (1970).

Herber, Harold. *Teaching Reading in the Content Areas*. Englewood Cliffs, N.J.: Prentice-Hall, 1970.

Hillman, Peggy, former English teacher at St. Petersburg High School (Fla.), in remarks to Ellen Thomas, October 1974.

Hillman, Peggy, former English teacher at St. Petersburg High School (Fla.), in remarks to Ellen Thomas, September 1975.

Johnson, Laura S. "Cool It, Teach! and Tape All of It!" *Journal of Reading*, 17, no. 2 (1973).

Johnson, Laura S., reading specialist at Evanston Township High School (Ill.), in remarks to Ellen Thomas, November 1974.

Kalk, Sharon, University of Chicago Laboratory School teacher, in remarks to Ellen Thomas, July 1975.

Kaplan, Ruth, former University of Chicago Laboratory School English teacher, in remarks to Ellen Thomas, May 1970.

LaPorte, Emma, former teacher at New Trier High School (Winnetka, Ill.), in remarks to Ellen Thomas, March 1975.

Lodge, Evan, and Marjorie Braymer. *Adventures in Reading*, Book 9. New York: Harcourt, Brace and World, 1963.

Magill, Frank N., ed. *Masterpieces of World Literature*. New York: Harper and Row, 1952–1969.

Matthai, Ann, University of Chicago Laboratory School English teacher, in remarks to Ellen Thomas, December 1973.

McCampbell, Darlene, University of Chicago Laboratory School English Department chairperson in remarks to Ellen Thomas, July 1975.

McCullough, Constance M. *Elementary English Review*, 22 (January 1945).

McGuire, Eunice, University of Chicago Laboratory School English teacher, in remarks to the English Department, May 1974.

Niles, Olive S. "Help Students Set a Purpose for Reading." *English High Lights*, 20 (April–May 1963).

Partridge, Eric. *Name into Word*. London: Secker and Warburg, 1949.

Ravin, Sophie, University of Chicago Laboratory School English teacher, in remarks to Ellen Thomas, November 1974.

Ravin, Sophie, University of Chicago Laboratory School English teacher, in remarks to Ellen Thomas, July 1975.

Rhinestine, Hope, University of Chicago Laboratory School English teacher, in remarks to Ellen Thomas, May 1970.

Robinson, Helen M., in lecture to a class at the University of Chicago, summer 1957.

Rosenberger, Marjorie. *Mark My Words*. Yonkers-on-Hudson: World Book Company, 1947.

Severn, Bill. *People Words*. New York: Washburn, Ives, 1966.

Strang, Ruth, in lecture to class in the teaching of secondary school reading, University of Chicago, summer 1965.

Washburne, John N. "The Use of Questions in Social Science Material." *Journal of Educational Psychology*, 20 (May 1929): 321–359.

Wiersma, Mildred Z. "Ceiling Unlimited." In *Readings on Reading Instruction*, edited by Albert J. Harris. New York: David McKay Company, 1963, pp. 253–257.

SCIENCE

A new physics teacher in the Laboratory School appeared in the doorway of the reading consultant's office: "My classes need rescuing. They have no idea what reading in physics demands! I'd like to work on this with them next week." A good many long-hours-after-school-later, the teacher and consultant had planned a rescue operation. It appears here as "First Aid for Physics Students," the opening section of this chapter.

One day the biology teacher commented to the consultant, "My students read the lab procedures carelessly. Though they're assigned for reading the night before, many come to the lab unprepared. Maybe we could work out some guidelines." The approach to reading laboratory procedures that they developed—and the results in the laboratory—are shared in the second section of this chapter.

One day the reading consultant asked some biology classes, "What helps do you need in order to study better?" Many students gave this suggestion among others, "Help us pronounce difficult terms!" Some simple aids that solved this problem for them appear in the closing section of the chapter.

Of course, other needs confront students as they learn from the printed page in science. The section in Chapter 5 on reading skills for problem solving was prepared with the needs of science students in mind. Because of the close similarity between reading in science and reading in mathematics, almost all the approaches and devices suggested in "Helps for Improving Mathematics Reading" in Chapter 9 will prove equally helpful in science.

The comprehensive section on upgrading students' textbook reading in Chapter 3 was originally developed for use in Jerry Ferguson's biology classes because of his concern for helping his students learn how to approach their new textbooks early in the course. "Giving students reading techniques," he comments, "is a necessary and rewarding introduction to the course—it pays off all year in increased efficiency for students."

FIRST AID FOR PHYSICS STUDENTS

It was easy to see that his students were not grasping important content in their physics textbook. Here's how Richard Kimmel conducted a rescue operation.

Early in the school year the physics teacher appeared in the reading consultant's doorway. He announced: "My classes need rescuing. There's a *very* low level of independent reading." Toward the end of the year he reported: "My students are *much* better equipped to read. Now I can make an assignment with more confidence that they will come next day prepared for classwork based on their outside reading."

What happened in between? First, the classroom teacher and the reading specialist prepared guidesheets, which appear in this chapter, to be placed in the hands of students. But these were intended to supplement something of far greater importance—instruction in the new approaches by the classroom teacher.

How did the teacher give that instruction? Here, in response to interview questions, he explains his procedures:

Question. Students do not always recognize their need for reading helps. How did you create a sense of need?

Answer. I assigned a simple chapter to read at home, then in class let the students flip through it to refresh their memories. Then they put their books away and answered some quiz questions. I gave the impression that it was more like a game, "to learn about their reading." When they went over their own answers in class, they learned they had not done at all well.

Question. What help did you give?

Answer. I introduced the "OK4R" approach as a package. We previewed a chapter, and the class saw how this gave them the organization of forget much that they learned in physics. But the reading approaches and techniques will be theirs the rest of their lives.

Question.   How did the students respond?

Answer.   The first reaction of some was "I've seen that before." But I think I had almost universal endorsement from the beginning. They picked out their favorite tips. Some would come into class excited: "You know I had trouble with a passage last night and tried the helps, and they really worked," or, "I was prepared for that test. The reading tips really helped me pin down that chapter."

the chapter quickly. Then we took sample sections and analyzed the difficulties involved in reading those sections. I drew attention to an appropriate reading tip offered in "OK4R," and we applied "first aid" to the sections. They saw for themselves that, indeed, the reading helps *helped*.

With some of the "Special Strategies for Reading Physics" [see the student guidesheets] I waited until the point in the course where that particular strategy was called for. For instance, I postponed the "back-and-forth strategy" for reading illustrations, charts, and figures until the class was confronted, in the chapter on acceleration, with quite difficult figures—with difficult graphs to read back and forth.

I often told anecdotes about how I constantly use the pointers myself—how they help me in my own doctoral work in physics. For instance, I told them how I often stare at the ceiling while I self-recite on what I have just read.

All year long we reinforced the pointers. We would take out our textbooks, read a section or two in class, have a discussion, point out that a crucial idea was not pinned down well enough, then apply a helpful pointer from the reading guidelines. I discovered that many students need continuing help—this is not the casual approach to reading that they are used to.

Question. How did you avoid turning students off by what might seem to be a lock-step method of study?

Answer. From the first, I gave the pointers as suggestions, not as orders: "Use whatever works for you. Here's a pointer that perhaps will be a help. Discard it if you don't need it."

Question. Why did you call this approach OK4R? Hadn't some of your students already met the same approach in their biology class where it was called PQ4R?

Answer. The reading specialist and I wanted to give the method status with upper-class students. We wanted to refer to Dr. Walter Pauk's Reading-Study Center at Cornell, where he originated the name OK4R. We wanted to impress the students that this is "college stuff."

Question. What were the results?

Answer. I feel that my students were much better equipped after they had had the reading helps. I could assign reading with more confidence that they would come to class prepared for classwork based on that reading. But I feel that I could get even better results if I devoted more energy to it during the year—some of the students fell behind. I feel that the approach to reading is as valuable as anything they can learn about physics. Unless they go on in science, they will

FIRST AID FOR PHYSICS STUDENTS
The OK4R Approach to College Reading

*Dr. Walter Pauk of the Cornell University
Reading-Study Center helps college students
streamline their study. Their grade point
averages go up when they use OK4R.**

Psychologists at top universities have experimented for years to find out how students learn most easily. The OK4R procedure offers a package of the most powerful study techniques known for mastering a textbook chapter.

Here is OK4R tailored to your physics textbook. It should prove extremely effective to the student seriously bent on learning physics. The steps are:

> 1. Overview
>
> 2. Pick out Key Ideas
>
> 3. Read
>
> 4. Recite
>
> 5. Reflect
>
> 6. Review

Of course, you will not need each strategy in every assignment. Use as many as necessary, in the order you find best, to grapple with and grasp the content of the chapter.

1. Overview the chapter

Ask yourself, "What is my purpose in reading this chapter?"

Examine the title.

Read the chapter introduction (first paragraph or two or three).

---

* Dr. Pauk's solid results with students as Director of the Cornell University Reading-Study Center are well known. We have used the name "OK4R" and have adapted this approach to physics with his generous permission. Walter Pauk, *How to Study in College*, 2nd ed. (Boston: Houghton Mifflin Company, 1974) is an excellent source of practical helps.

"Hit the headings" (in large or boldface print).

Glance at the pictures, charts, and diagrams.

Read the chapter summary.

And then:

Mark the purpose in those first paragraphs, or *note* it quickly in the margin.

How does this chapter fit into the orderly progression of chapters in the book?

2. *Now read section by section to pick out the key ideas*

Note the numbered sections of the chapter. Each is a small, manageable bite for you to digest.

You'll find that some of these sections are quite easy. Then just pick out the key ideas from the supporting material.

> Converting main headings into questions will sometimes guide you to the key ideas. You may find the boldface heading, **The Sources of Energy.** Quickly shift it into the question, "Just what are the sources of energy?" You may find a heading like this, **Uniform Velocities Can Be Calculated.** Rephrase it quickly: "How can uniform velocities be calculated?"

Mark the key ideas and any important details, or, if you own the book, note them down in the extra-wide margins that your book provides just for that purpose.

3. *Closely, thoughtfully, read the difficult passages*

Some passages in physics are rigorous, a challenge to the most capable student. The authors proceed, through a highly complex argument, step by step to a logical conclusion. Each step is built on full understanding of preceding steps. Try not to go on to the next step until you fully understand the one before.

The meaning of difficult parts will often escape you. Expect this! Successful physics students say, "I didn't get that. I'll go over it again." A passage that blocked you at first may come clear with a third or fourth reading.

> If you still can't get it after repeated reading, it may be time to stop and take a rest. In your notebook, carefully write out a question that pinpoints what confuses you, so that you can ask

your question next day in class. (Your teacher will be delighted to answer it and to see that you are so thorough in doing your assignments.) Now you can skip the confusing part with a clear conscience and continue reading.

Mark important ideas or note them down. *Make the key ideas stand out.* If you own the textbook:

Jot notes in the margins.

Sketch quick vertical lines at the left of crucial passages.

Bracket key ideas.

Underline.

Now you won't have to reread the whole chapter when you return to review it later on.

4. Recite to yourself

Look away from your physics book while you recite to yourself the important ideas. "Firm up" your learning.

> You recall that Dr. Walter Pauk, one of the nation's top study experts, helps college students study better and faster. As they follow his directions, their grade-point averages go up.
> Dr. Pauk advises students, *"Use the most powerful study technique known to psychologists:* keep the print out of sight perhaps 50 percent of the time you're studying."

Cover a passage with your hand or with a card, or just look away from the book. Can you recite or write the important points to yourself? Now look back at the print to check yourself.

Cover a crucial diagram or graph. Can you still *see* it before you in your mind? Can you draw it yourself? Could you explain it in detail to a puzzled friend?

If you merely reread a difficult passage, you can dream all the way through. The cover-up technique *forces* you to concentrate while you struggle to recall what's underneath.

> When Dr. Pauk's students at Cornell, in repeated experiments, spent *one* minute self-reciting on a passage they had just read, they nearly *doubled* their retention of the content.

5. Reflect

Is reflective thinking built right into the way you operate in reading physics? Do you probe for *whys*, challenge the authors' reasoning, predict outcomes, relate what you are reading to experiments in class, to the world outside your classroom, and to what you have read before? Do you make some intuitive leaps for yourself, speculate and wonder, ponder what mysteries Nature may be hiding in the subtle physics of our dynamic, wondrous, ever-changing universe?

6. Review

Recapture the broad chapter plan. You've been concentrating on the numbered sections of the chapter, even on bits and pieces within those sections, perhaps like the meaning of some difficult concept, such as *field*. You may have lost the broad chapter plan.

Now give the chapter one more run-through. Repeat the overview step. Call the broad chapter plan back to mind. You've attended to the small pieces of the jigsaw. Now look once more at the total picture.

Check yourself on the crucial content. Leaf through while you self-recite on the essential content. If you've marked your book, the important points will now flag you. Reread if some of these points have slipped away. Then space out future reviews to freshen up your memory.

Now everything you want from the chapter should be *yours—to stay*.

SPECIAL STRATEGIES FOR READING PHYSICS

1. *Always have your standard equipment ready:*

• Scratch sheet

• Sharp pencil

• Graph paper

• Ruler

It's impossible to study physics without some graph paper and a ruler and a scratch sheet in front of you *and a pencil in your hand*. They help you to pin down elusive ideas.

Your mind will sometimes reel under a weighty passage. Then it may be extremely difficult to keep on concentrating. If you can't grasp a difficult concept like *vector acceleration*, there's a rescue technique for you:

> Attack the passage again with a view to jotting down the meaning in your own words. This rivets your attention and may give you a breakthrough.

Students often say, "I read that, but I can't remember it." If you're struggling to remember the concept of *continuous variable*, you might write down the meaning in words—your own words—several times.

Sketch constantly as you study. Good physics students aren't spectators who passively view the authors' drawings or examples. Make up your *own* examples. Sketch your *own* figures. Translate the printed explanations into your *own* pictures on your *own* graph.

Sketching your own figures and making up your own examples helps you really to *see*, to bring hazy relationships into sharp focus.

Now you're involved in kinesthetic (muscular) learning.

> In many students motor memory is one of the strongest learning channels of all. Just the act of making these jottings—even if you lose them forever—will put you ahead. The muscular act of writing, in and of itself, will have strengthened your learning.

Answer the authors' questions. Right in the middle of explanations in your textbook, the authors may suddenly direct questions to you—point-blank. Or they may suddenly confront you with an important mathematics problem. Your scratch sheet is handy for working out the answers.

Zero in on the check-yourself sections. The authors have placed self-check sections and questions to test your understanding at the end of, and perhaps throughout, each chapter. Work through them as you come to them, with your ruler, paper, and pencil, and you'il be changing half-learned material into fully learned material.

2. *Use the physicist's "back-and-forth"*
   strategy when you're referred
   to a figure.

Shift your eyes from the verbal explanation to the figure as needed. Words like these flash a special signal: "in Figure 2–3," "as shown in Figure 2–6," "notice in Figure 3–5." They're signaling that you should shift to a back-and-forth reading strategy.

When a chart or diagram is present, read the words of explanation with special care. When the authors refer you to the figure, *shift your eyes and thoughts to that figure.*

Zero in on the caption. When it refers to specific features of the diagram, or to lines and points of the graph, locate these precisely. Continue this precision back-and-forth reading as needed.

You'll discover, for example, that the graph of position versus time for any object—an airplane or a car—calls for perhaps as many as six of these back-and-forth movements.

Next, can you draw the figure for yourself and explain it to a friend? Don't leave it until you can.

3. *Make the "official" language*
   of physics your own

When key terms or concepts are first introduced to you in any textbook, the authors usually flag you with a conspicuous signal. The signal used in your textbook is probably boldface or colored or italic type. Words so designated are likely to be important "official" terms.

"Official" terms ought to be collector's items. A single unknown term (like *instantaneous speed*) may devastate your understanding of a crucial passage. And every new "official" term is basic for future learning—to the last day of the course and beyond.

> To clear up unfamiliar, general terms, turn to a general dictionary when you need to. Do you really know words like *enigma* and *ambiguity*? Of course, you have a vague understanding. But can you express their meanings precisely?

4. A specialized requirement for physics reading: a high degree of skill in visualizing

> *A reading manual written by two Harvard experts and designed to strengthen the reading skills of students at Harvard strongly stresses the skill of visualizing.**

This skill is crucial in physics, where much reading time isn't reading time at all; it's visualizing time. Physics reading constantly demands complete stops for mental pictures.

Actually, almost every page of certain chapters demands that you form mental pictures. When you come to the section on adding vector velocities, *see* your canoe in the river. Feel what it's like to paddle toward shore yet at the same time be carried a little bit sideways by the current.

The canoe scene is an easy starter example. But as you advance through the course, you'll need to develop skill in visualizing highly complicated situations.

Making your own sketch of what you've read helps you really to *see*, to bring hazy impressions into sharp focus as if on a screen in your mind.

5. How fast should you read rigorous passages in physics? Maybe one-tenth your average rate!

In the world of physics, speedreading has little status. This is because the slowest readers in physics often prove to be the most efficient. It's the high-speed readers who often have the greatest difficulty with their assignments. They're so used to whipping through their ordinary reading that they're unable to shift gears and read their physics slowly unless they make unusual effort.

---

* S. Vincent Wilking and Robert G. Webster, *A College Developmental Reading Manual* (Boston: Houghton Mifflin Company, 1943).

Even physics instructors, with broad backgrounds in physics and long experience in reading about it, find that they must read difficult new material slowly. Very slowly. *Really reading* three pages in physics may be the equivalent of reading fifty pages of a novel for English class.

In reading the opening chapters of your textbook, you *spend* time to *save* time. Get the basics firmly through precision reading, then build on these for a successful year.

UPGRADE STUDENTS' READING OF
LABORATORY PROCEDURES

*"My students used to read their laboratory pro-
cedures carelessly—then muddle through their
investigations," Jerry Ferguson, University of
Chicago Laboratory School science teacher,
reports. "Then I upgraded their reading and
changed lab day into a smooth operation."*

Picture a laboratory where students walk in on lab day having read the assigned
procedures only superficially—indifferently informed about the activity ahead
—uncertain about their objectives. Their experimenting time slips away as
they try, at the last minute, to find out what they are to do, leaning on their
teacher or on each other, and asking unnecessary questions. They lose time correcting errors and perhaps doing the investigation over. As the bell rings, some
have failed to finish the experiment.

Picture another lab where students arrive oriented to the investigation ahead
and informed about how to proceed. They quickly secure the materials they
need, operate without pressure, correct fewer mistakes, work with appropriate
independence, and finish the investigation on schedule. What makes the difference? Several factors. Probably among the foremost is the degree of expertise
the students have developed in reading the procedures.

Because activities in the laboratory are the heart of many science courses, and
the laboratory is the place where students *practice* the scientific method rather
than merely read about it, proficiency in reading investigative procedures is
likely to be an important plus for the student.

Reading May Require a New Look

Why is reading likely to call for a new look as students in a new science course
try to read the procedures they must carry out in the laboratory? A pattern of
writing never before encountered may confront them. They must grapple
with directions for carrying out a process—often a long and complicated
process involving many steps. The sequence of steps may be crucial. A single
unknown word may throw off the entire experiment. Drawings, diagrams, and
photos take on special importance because they convey a vital message.

Perhaps for the first time, students must translate reading into action within
a rigid time limit. Their reading time must not encroach upon doing-the-job
time. Students must read the direction pattern with in-depth comprehension.
Perhaps nowhere in all their years at school have they had a chance to *learn*

to cope with this type of reading. If they read lab instructions as they have done other reading in the past, they may lose out before they have read two or three steps.

Teacher and Consultant Develop Guidelines

Intent on improving efficiency in the laboratory, Jerry Ferguson, University of Chicago High School science teacher, enlisted the help of the reading consultant. In the laboratory instructions that confront his students all through the year, an identical pattern of writing occurs scores of times. Perhaps proficiency in handling this pattern might be developed relatively quickly during the opening weeks of the course in the fall. Perhaps teacher and consultant might work out together some this-is-how-to-read-it suggestions.

The guidelines that evolved were entitled "A Scientist's Approach to Reading Laboratory Procedures" and were printed as a four-panel foldout, which students would keep for reference in their looseleaf notebooks and to which they could refer while doing advance reading of the procedures at home. A complete set of instructions for a laboratory investigation—an experiment the teacher had selected as representative—was reproduced, with permission of the publisher, in the two center panels of the foldout. The pointers for efficient reading appeared on either side. Highway signs—SLOW, STOP, and WARNING—in attention-catching red or yellow, were positioned appropriately, adding page trim and color.

To bombard the class with the guidelines, a striking "billboard" was hung on the rear wall, where it dominated the laboratory. To enlarge the guidelines to this billboard size, they were abridged, typed on an IBM Executive typewriter, and reproduced by a photo blowup process.

The content of the students' foldouts is offered here under "A Scientist's Approach to Reading Laboratory Procedures."

Classes Profit From How-to-Read-It Sessions

In September, before his students had an opportunity to fall into inefficient habits, the teacher (Ferguson) acted to develop *efficient* habits.

On the day before the first laboratory session, he stressed expertise in reading laboratory procedures as a must for the course ahead: "You'll need to come in tomorrow with what you are to do *already fixed in mind*. Your experimental work will fill the entire period. Time used in class for *reading* the procedures is time lost in the *doing* of them. As the course progresses, the investigative

text cont. pg. 394

A SCIENTIST'S APPROACH TO READING
LABORATORY PROCEDURES

Study the **title.** ⟶
It quickly clues you in to the type of activity ahead.

Read the **introduction.** --->
This orients you—may supply critical information—charts your direction. It helps you to set your overall purpose, lets you know the why of the whole procedure.

Ask yourself: "How does this relate to what I've studied?"
"Where am I going in this investigation?"

Note mentally **materials** you'll need.

Try this approach for a detailed procedure:

1. **"Pre-read" the entire procedure** and also the **discussion questions.**
   Read these through "once over lightly."

   Ask yourself, "What, in general, am I to do?" Now each step in the process takes on meaning. It falls into place in relation to the whole.

2. **Read the procedure a second time,** step by step, with great care!

   Make a complete stop after reading each sentence or each step, whenever necessary, to make sure you understand just what you are to do. "Thought time" is needed in addition to reading time.

   Are you having difficulty concentrating on a complicated step? It may help to **form a mental picture** of yourself performing the step.

   Seeing yourself perform the step may help you to *rivet* your attention on the meaning—it forces you to take in what's being said.

   If you read without this visual image, your reading may be passive, with your thoughts worlds away.

   Read the diagrams as well as the text.
   As you read, you'll find frequent references to diagrams. These are often quick, vivid, easy-to-grasp—they give you instant "how-to-do-it" insights—save you working time.

   When you are first referred to the diagram, shift your attention to the diagram. Read the caption, then examine the diagram carefully, noting each label and its corresponding part. Whenever a subsequent sentence mentions something pictured in the diagram, look back at the diagram, if you need to, after you've read the sentence.

   Diagrams often clarify methods and processes for you every step of the way—show you what to do and what not to do.

5–4 Investigating the composition of water. *

In this investigation you will see a compound broken down into the separate elements that form it. You will split water into two gases by passing an electric current through it. This process is known as electrolysis (e-lek-TROL-uh-sis). The gases will be collected and tests will be made to identify them. Your observations should help you to understand the relationship between atoms and molecules and between elements and compounds. These observations will also help you to understand the nature of chemical changes.

Materials

Electrolysis apparatus (See Figure 5–5.)
   Water-acid solution (100 parts water mixed with two parts concentrated sulfuric acid)
DC power supply (or two 6-volt dry cells connected in series)

Figure 5–5 *How to set up the electrolysis apparatus.*

Procedure

1. With the stopcocks open, pour the water-acid mixture into the reservoir until the liquid level reaches the bottom of the stopcocks. (See Figure 5–5.) Pour the acid mixture carefully. Close the stopcocks.

2. Connect the wires from the electrodes to the terminals of the DC source. If you use a DC power supply, start with a low voltage and increase to a higher voltage. If you use dry cells, connect each pole to one of the electrodes. Do you observe any reaction? Next, connect another battery in series with the first. Use only one wire to connect the two batteries, the positive pole of one to the negative pole of the other. Connect the remaining poles directly to the electrodes as in Figure 5–5.

3. Observe the process closely for 15 minutes. List at least ten observations. Be sure that they are really observations and not assumptions.

4. Your teacher will perform tests for two common gases to help you identify some of the substances that were produced in the process.

* Reproduced with permission from *Biological Science, Molecules to Man*, Blue Version, by Biological Sciences Curriculum Study. Boston: Houghton Mifflin Company, 1968.

Discussion

1. Did you notice bubbles rising from the electrodes? How do they differ in each tube? Do they rise to the surface at the same rate?
2. What happened to the water in each tube? Form a hypothesis to explain your observations.
3. What is the ratio of the volumes of gas in the two tubes? Did this ratio remain constant during the observation time?
4. What is the probable ratio of hydrogen particles to oxygen particles in a molecule of water?
5. What is the relationship between the volume of gas produced at a terminal and the electrical charge on that terminal?
6. What is the effect of the increase of voltage? What would you expect with further increase in voltage?
7. What is the function of the electric current in the electrolysis of water?
8. As the teacher opened the stopcock to collect the gases, which test tube was held upside down? What can you tell about the gases from this technique?
9. Write a short paragraph summarizing the results of the tests.
10. Complete the equation to show how many atoms of each gas would be produced by splitting two molecules of water.

$$2H_2O \longrightarrow ? + ?$$

Terms in *boldface italics* say, "Stop! Look! Learn!" These are highly important "official" scientific terms.

The authors "signal" other important terms with italic type without the boldface.

Reach for your dictionary, when necessary, for unfamiliar general terms. Make sure you know the meaning of abbreviations and symbols. A single word left unknown—or left with an imprecise meaning—may ruin your entire experiment.

You can have instant access to forgotten technical terms through the glossary or index of your textbook.

> LEARN TO HANDLE EXPERIMENTAL PROCEDURES LARGELY ON YOUR OWN. COME TO LAB PERIOD ALREADY INFORMED ON WHAT TO DO. YOU'LL NEED THE ENTIRE PERIOD FOR EXPERIMENTAL WORK.

◄ ○○○○○ **Note warnings!**

Italic type—with or without the word CAUTION—is sometimes a "danger flag" alerting you to possible "traps." (See Step 1 under "Procedure" for the experiment.)

Overlooking a warning may:

Cause injury to yourself or a classmate.
Ruin your experiment.
Damage expensive equipment.

Anything **quantitative** is a possible **danger-spot.** "Zero in" on <u>amounts</u>, <u>distances</u>, <u>timing</u>, and <u>temperatures</u>—and later make your measurements with precision.

Reread as often as necessary:

Note that each step is built on full understanding of preceding steps.

A single error in any step may throw off the rest of the process.

3. **Add a last quick "run-through"** to fix in mind the procedure as a whole.

4. During laboratory period, **carry out the steps to the letter in the order given.**

Timing for fifteen minutes means precisely fifteen minutes by the second hand. (See Step 3 under "Procedure" for the experiment.)

The sequence of steps is critical.

If something goes wrong:

Rethink the purpose, reread the procedure, and recheck your actions.

No question should remain unanswered.

Jot down questions to ask in class.

> Precision reading of the directions for an experiment is an essential tool of learning in science. It should enable you to work through experiments far more accurately and quickly. Clumsy reading does not pay as you strike out blindly, blunder, then lose time correcting errors and perhaps redoing the experiment.

procedures will become more complicated. Reading in class will be out of the question—you'll hardly have time to say 'Good morning'! If you try to crowd your reading into the lab period as your fifty minutes are ticking away, you may have chaos. If you read the procedures *before* you come, you'll be more confident and efficient."

Having distributed the foldouts, the instructor then guided the class through the suggested reading approach, using the investigation assigned for the next day. He concluded, "Does anyone have the procedure perfectly in mind—just what you are to do tomorrow? No? That's understandable—this is rigorous reading. So you'll want to reread it tonight.

"Of course, your memory for the details will not be perfect. You should *expect* to look at the printed procedure during the experiment tomorrow. But you'll look and say, 'Oh, I remember—I cut the corks now.' This will take *minimal* time compared with the time it would take you to do an initial reading. Perhaps you'll want to give the procedure a quick run-through just before class tomorrow."

As the instructor observed the students' performance during the next day's lab session and later examined their written lab reports, he noted continuing reading needs. These he discussed with the class a day or two later. There was guidance as needed during the first two or three months of school.

Classes Help Develop Guidelines

There is no intention of straitjacketing students into a rigid procedure. The guidelines are offered as tips that are likely to prove helpful. Teachers may prefer to involve students in developing the guidelines. Teachers might project on a screen before the class a set of laboratory instructions, then pose the question, "Suppose you wished to read these directions, then carry out the investigation without a word of help or explanation from your teacher. How would you read the directions *ideally?*" When students focus their attention on how to read procedures *ideally,* they often come up with highly practical suggestions. These teachers can combine with their own expertise to evolve the final guidelines.

Students Assess Their Own Skill in
Reading Procedures

A Self-Rating Checklist for Reading Laboratory Procedures centered each student's attention on "need areas" and pointed the way to improvement. Students evaluated themselves at intervals, keeping their checklists for before-and-after-comparison in their looseleaf notebooks. The instructor evaluated the students' reading competencies on an accompanying scale and discussed with individuals any marked disparity between their own evaluation and the instructor's evaluation of them. Each student set as a personal goal the rating he or she hoped to attain on the next evaluation.

Have Students Improved Their Reading of Procedures?

How has "Operation Reading" worked out? The instructor comments (Ferguson, 1969, pp. 118–119): "In the years before we had the 'directions drive,' many students had no approach other than a hit-or-miss reading. Now most of them come to the lab prepared. The many students who follow the guidelines on the foldout are confident, efficient, and pleased with the results. They find that they can work steadily, yet not hurriedly, and do not get lost in the process of working. They do not have to correct as many mistakes but can proceed smoothly and without much pressure. The few who start out by ignoring the outlined reading procedure become confused and pressured enough to have to start over, or find themselves wasting too much time, or frequently find that they cannot complete the work at all. The truth becomes evident to them, and the vast majority of these doubters reform their reading procedures before many sessions have passed.

"Periodic reminders to follow the successful procedure must be given— though with decreasing frequency—as the first semester progresses. Once a student has panicked under the stress of not being prepared, he serves as his *own* moving spirit. The long-range result of our project has been more efficient laboratory sessions and a saving of countless hours of working time."

When Students Design Their Own Procedures

Students who have learned to read experimental procedures precisely have an advantage later in the course *when they design their own procedures*. They are likely to make sounder decisions because they have observed with what precision, with what rigorous preparation, with what logic a scientific investigation must be devised.

Isn't a Compelling Interest in Laboratory Work Enough?

Isn't a student's compelling interest in science enough to bring about efficient reading? Surely, genuine drives for reading are of immense importance in the

text cont. pg. 398

SELF-RATING CHECKLIST FOR READING LABORATORY PROCEDURES BEFORE COMING TO LABORATORY PERIOD

NAME   PERIOD   DATE

This checklist is intended to focus your attention on any "need areas" and point the way to improvement. Your teacher will also evaluate you.

Consider how you stand on each of the points below, using the scale from "poor" to "excellent" on the next page. Then rate yourself from 1 to 10 in the space before the numeral.

Points to consider

_____ 1. Do you orient yourself to the investigation ahead—learn the *why* of the whole procedure—by studying the title and getting a thorough grasp of the introductory statement of purpose?

_____ 2. Do you come to laboratory period already familiar with the materials you'll need?

_____ 3. Before doing your intensive reading of the procedure, do you pre-read all of it (and also the discussion questions) to learn what, in general, you will be doing?

_____ 4. When, as you do your intensive reading, a difficult step needs clarifying, do you stop, reread, and reflect to make certain you understand just what you are to do?

_____ 5. A single word, symbol, or abbreviation that you do not know may ruin your entire investigation. Do you stop and learn the meaning whenever one of these is unfamiliar?

_____ 6. Anything quantitative is a possible danger spot. Do you zero in on amounts, distances, timings, and temperatures—and later make your measurements with precision?

_____ 7. Are you alert to, and alerted by, CAUTIONS and WARNINGS?

_____ 8. Do you read the diagrams and drawings for the quick how-to-do-it insights they offer?

_____ 9. Are you aware that the sequence of steps is critical, and are you alert to this sequence as you read?

_____ 10. Have you eliminated asking questions of your instructor when the answers are clearly stated in the procedures themselves?

_____ 11. Do you come to laboratory periods having made all possible preparations outside of class and having freed the period for experimental work?

_____ 12. Are you gradually eliminating the errors, the lost time, and the redoing of investigations that result from reading the procedures superficially?

_____ 13. Are you moving toward handling procedures for laboratory work largely on your own?

_____ 14. Is reflective thinking built right into the way you read and the way you operate in the laboratory? Do you speculate, anticipate outcomes, make predictions, seek the basic *why* a thing does so and so, draw conclusions, and make applications to the world outside the laboratory and to your own experiences?

Your own general evaluation

Now that you have considered your specific strengths and weaknesses, give yourself a general rating on the scale below. Place a single check mark at the appropriate point on the scale.

Your teacher's evaluation

Set your own goals

At intervals you will be asked to assess your reading competence. What general rating do you hope to reach by the next evaluation?

Place numeral here: _____

An Added Plus-Factor

As you improve with each of these evaluations, you are learning to do rigorous reading of lab procedures. And there will be an added plus-factor. When you devise your *own experimental procedures*, you will make sounder decisions, for you will already have observed with what *precise planning*, with what *rigorous preparation* investigative procedures must be devised.

---

reading development of students. But do these automatically ensure that the students will develop the most rapid, labor-saving, and effective techniques? When students caught up with interest in an exciting problem have the added advantage of their teacher's guidance in the most effective techniques, an ideal situation is created. The immediate need motivates students to learn the facilitating skills. They are likely to react, "That really works!" Satisfaction leads to continued use of the skill and to its reinforcement.

Neither powerful incentive for reading nor the teacher's guidance in reading approaches is fully effective without the other; together, they can be a potent force for giving the student a complete collection of reading skills for science.

WHEN SCIENCE WORDS COME BY THE YARD

Students can quickly learn to zero in on the pronunciation aids in their textbook.

A reading consultant asked science classes, "What helps do you need in order to study better?" Many students responded, "Help us pronounce difficult terms." Aids to pronunciation were already clearly present for every difficult technical term in their textbook, but somehow they did not appear to be aware of them.

A simple explanation like the one below, followed by practice in natural situations, solved the problem for these students.

> Some official terms in biology come by the yard. They look as if they would be staggering to pronounce: *platyhelminthes, schizomycetes,* or *echinodermata.*
>
> But just after the term in your textbook—"fenced in" by parentheses—you'll find it divided into short, easy-to-manage, pronounceable parts. You can count on the authors to give you this help *every time a difficult "official" term is introduced.*
>
> *flatly bilateral**
>
> Some seven thousand species of worms that are "flat as a pancake" make up the phylum *Platyhelminthes* (*plat* ih hel MIN theez), a Greek word meaning, literally, flat worms. Just about all the. . . .

---

* Excerpt from Harold A. Moore and John R. Carlock, *The Spectrum of Life* (New York: Harper and Row, 1970), p. 68.

And there's a handy pronunciation key on page _____ to help you sound out troublesome letters or combinations.

You'll notice that one syllable stands out because it's printed in *capital letters*. This syllable carries the major or *primary accent*. When you come to this syllable, you'll say it with special force. Sometimes a word is so long that it needs an extra accent. This second accent, a weaker one, is called the *secondary accent*. In this particular case, this syllable is printed in *italic type*. You'll stress this syllable not quite so strongly as the one with the primary accent but more strongly than the unaccented syllables.

Attack the word now, part by part, working out both pronunciation and accent carefully. [The instructor "walks" the students through this process.] Now say it again and again until you're comfortable forming the sounds.

Some students are "half-glancers"—they slide over the pronunciation of difficult new biological terms. Then what happens? They learn the term only vaguely, and it easily slips from their memories.

TAKE TIME to work out the pronunciation of important new terms. SAVE TIME when the term slides more easily— and lastingly—into your science vocabulary.

Of course, helping students zero in on pronunciation aids is just one way to help them master the vocabulary of science. Since proficiency in learning the meanings of scientific terms is so vital to reading in science, instructors will want to refer to the approaches and procedures suggested in Chapter 2, "Building Vocabulary." Many of the procedures suggested in "How To Master the Vocabulary of Mathematics" in Chapter 9 will also prove helpful in science.

Bibliography

Adams, W. Royce, *How to Read the Sciences*. Chicago: Scott, Foresman and Co., 1970.

Aukerman, Robert C., *Reading in the Secondary School Classroom*. Chapter 9. New York: McGraw-Hill Book Co., 1972.

Herber, Harold L. "Teaching Reading and Physics Simultaneously" in *Improvement of Reading Through Classroom Practice*, ed. J. Allen Figurel, International Reading Association Conference Proceedings, No. 9 (Newark, Delaware: International Reading Association, 1964), pp. 79–80.

Pauk, Walter, *How to Study in College*, 2nd ed. Boston: Houghton Mifflin, 1974.

Robinson, H. Alan, *Teaching Reading and Study Strategies: The Content Areas.* Boston: Allyn and Bacon, 1975, pp. 99–126.

Shepherd, David L., *Comprehensive High School Reading Methods.* Columbus, Ohio: Charles E. Merrill Publishing Co., 1973, pp. 213–50.

Thelen, Judith N., "CONPASS: Science—Learning in Several Directions," *Journal of Reading,* XVI (1973), pp. 525–28.

Reference

Ferguson, Jerry. "Teaching the Reading of Biology." In *Fusing Reading Skills and Content,* edited by H. Alan Robinson and Ellen Lamar Thomas. Newark, Del.: International Reading Association, 1969.

MATHEMATICS

This chapter was prepared with the help of two consultants: Richard H. Muelder, mathematics teacher at the University of Chicago Laboratory School and former chairman of the Mathematics Department; and Max S. Bell, Associate Professor of Mathematics Education, University of Chicago.

Many of today's textbooks in mathematics confront students with page after page of specialized, often rigorous reading. With a frequently recurring pattern of a passage of analytical exposition followed by a set of problems, these textbooks make new demands on reading power.

What a sudden adjustment students must face if they have acquired only a once-straight-through approach to reading! They must now draw out the meaning from dense analytical passages. They may find telegraphic explanations that require filling in the inner steps, passages that call for visualizing or sketching, reading that requires shifting back-and-forth between a text explanation and a diagram. If they continue reading in the old familiar way, parts of their textbooks may lose them before they have read two or three sentences.

Clearly, the classroom instructor who provides students with appropriate reading guidance is helping ensure success in the immediate course and in all advanced mathematics work. And, in an age of exploding mathematical knowledge, the instructor is helping to prepare them for self-education in any occupation involving mathematics. Some specifics in a course in mathematics may become obsolete tomorrow. *The reading competencies that enable students to update those specifics are not likely to become obsolete.*

We offer in this chapter three items for your consideration. First, you will find some comprehensive guidesheets written directly to the student. These discuss why the reading in modern mathematics courses requires a new look; then, specific approaches and techniques are suggested for the student to try on an assignment *tonight*. Next, we offer the instructor a miscellany of possible procedures for upgrading reading. Here a successful mathematics teacher discusses how, early in the course, he starts his students on the road to better reading. The last item deals with what many students consider their "disaster area" in mathematics: word problems. You will find suggested here an assortment of possible techniques for trouble-shooting word problems.

STUDENT GUIDESHEETS TO UPGRADE MATHEMATICS READING

> *Here are instructional materials that talk right to students about how to read their mathematics textbooks. They are intended to help students accept their share of the responsibility for their own learning through reading in mathematics.**

A reading consultant asked a group of mathematics teachers, "What bothers you most about your students' reading?"

Here is what they answered:

"They read the explanations like a novel."

"They bypass the reading completely—they skip on over to the problems."

"They lean on me too much—count on me for all the explaining."

"They slide over important new terms."

"They give up too easily. They don't know what it means to read and reread a difficult passage until it comes clear."

---

* Preparing the guidesheets was a Laboratory School project in which five mathematics teachers and the reading consultant worked together. The teachers were Richard Muelder of the Laboratory School, and Sylvia Auton, Max Bell, Paul Moulton, and George Richardson, formerly of the Laboratory School.

The consultant suggested that perhaps together they might work out some ways to improve the reading of the mathematics textbook the following fall. In informal interviews with each teacher, she asked questions like these, drawing out each teacher's insights:

"How do you help students master difficult terms?"

"How should they approach the reading of pages and pages of expository reading?"

"How do you help them read diagrams?"

"How do you encourage an appropriate speed?"

"How do you help them read theorems?"

She then compiled the best suggestions of the teachers, with added ideas of her own, into some comprehensive guidesheets to be placed in the hands of students. Designed as a section for students' looseleaf notebooks, they are intended to supplement something of far greater importance: instruction in the new approaches by the classroom teacher.

What was the rationale of these teachers as they planned an intensive effort to upgrade their students' reading of the textbook? Today's textbooks, they reflected, are written *directly to the student*. In quality textbooks, new principles, new concepts, and new technical terms are carefully explained—often with a generous supply of clarifying examples. With adequate guidance, many students can accept a share of the responsibility for their own learning. If, as the course develops, students grow in their ability to draw meaning independently from a page of mathematical content, they are moving toward mathematical maturity. Contrast their development with that of the students who turn to their teacher to *give* them the course by explaining every reading assignment in class. Indeed, *over*-explaining makes it unnecessary for students to read any of the explanatory passages. Lacking experience and practice from day to day and having no opportunity to gain confidence and self-reliance, some students may become virtual nonreaders of mathematics.

It is apparent that some analytical passages will require extensive preliminary explanation by the teacher. Other passages students can be expected to read and master—to a degree—on their own. Students often rise to expectations. When it is clearly the teacher's expectation that they read an assigned passage carefully before it is all explained in class—that, having had adequate guidance, they will do a share of their own learning through reading—many students can advance along the road to independence.

Perhaps negative attitudes, difficult to change once formed, would be less likely to develop if students were introduced *early in the course* to effective study-reading techniques. Perhaps they would feel more at home and at ease with their new course and their new textbook.

Surely, giving students the specialized approaches and techniques which they *must* have for reading mathematical materials should be among the objectives of mathematics education. Classroom teachers who develop these competencies are helping students achieve better not only in their courses but in every future mathematics course. And they are equipping them for self-education in trades and professions that involve mathematics. Some of the specifics in the immediate course may become obsolete tomorrow. The reading competencies that equip students to update those specifics are not likely to become obsolete.

The student guidesheets that follow were prepared in sections so a teacher can cover the content in manageable installments. First is an introductory section, "Reading in Mathematics Calls for a New Look." The next section, "A Higher-Level Reading Approach for Mathematics," suggests a specific approach for grasping passages of explanation. The last section, "How to Master the Vocabulary of Mathematics," offers the student some effective techniques for learning new technical terms.

It cannot be emphasized too strongly that printed guidelines in themselves are not likely to bring about much of a change in habits. Our guidesheets are intended as reinforcement for in-class instruction, as a convenient reference for students, and as a reminder to students to *practice* the new techniques from day to day.

STUDY BETTER AND FASTER WITH HIGHER-LEVEL STUDY SKILLS*

From time to time in mathematics class you'll be given tips on highly effective study techniques. You can take advantage of these to learn the *maximum amount possible from every moment you spend studying.*

Capitalize on scientific learning procedures

Psychologists at top universities have been experimenting for years to find out how students learn most easily and well. Methods that have proved effective with thousands of college students are called higher-level study skills. Through these you can learn more easily, remember longer, and conserve your study time. You'll need to cultivate these techniques as you enter a higher-level mathematics course.

You can develop higher-level skills

Of course, effective study methods aren't inherent—they're acquired. *You can develop these skills.* In many classes, some students with extraordinary ability achieve little. Others with less ability achieve highly. What makes the difference? Often it's knowing how to study.

After all, instructors don't grade students' intellects but the quality of work they do. It's important to make the most of your capabilities. Higher-level study skills can help you do this.†

A package of powerful techniques

You'll soon be introduced to higher-level approaches in class and through a series of guidesheets. First we'll talk about why mathematics calls for a new look at reading. Then we'll discuss an approach that should help you comprehend difficult material, concentrate better, and remember what you read. We'll show you some ways to master the technical vocabulary of a new math course. We'll go over "the most powerful study technique known to psychologists." We'll give you some tips on what to do when you just can't seem to get it.

There are three things for you to do:

1. Make the most of tips in class from your instructor.

2. Read the guidesheets that follow, then file them in your notebook for reference.

---

* The term "higher-level study skills" belongs to Francis P. Robinson, who uses it in his *Effective Study*, 4th ed. (New York: Harcourt, Brace, and World, 1970).

† Ralph C. Preston and Morton Botel, *How to Study* (Chicago: Science Research Associates, 1974), pp. 2, 3.

3. And last—without which there will be no value for you, now or ever—
practice your higher-level study skills, from here on.

A fair exchange?

An expert who counsels college students commented, "You will probably put forth more effort every hour you spend studying than you've put forth in the past. Are you willing to do this—and then finish the job with *more learned and more remembered in the process?* Scientific study procedures have enabled thousands of students to do that very thing: swap extra effort for better performance—and perhaps more free time. Fair exchange?"*

READING IN MATHEMATICS CALLS FOR A NEW LOOK

Rewarding reading, page after page of it, is ahead for you in the "new math." You'll probably find the demands to be a challenge. You'll need some new strategies to keep on top of your assignments.

Once many students manipulated mathematical processes with slight understanding. They didn't *do* mathematics, they merely made mathematical marks! Now the demands are far more exciting and exacting: React! Interpret! Question! *Think your way to understanding!*

Chances are you'll find this thinking-through process more to your liking than superficial reading.

Read your mathematics textbooks as you've done your reading in the past, and parts may lose you before you've read two or three sentences. Read them with an approach tailored to the new demands, and you should:

1. Get a breakthrough with passages that might otherwise block you.

2. Work through problems far more accurately and quickly.

3. Build a solid foundation for the rest of the course and save many hours in future study.

These pages, and future ones like them, will start you on your way to handling such rigorous reading.

Why a new look at reading?

Why will mathematics require new approaches to reading?

Your textbook probably has a do-it-yourself format—a recurring pattern of several pages of explanation followed by a set of problems. Sometimes your instructor will preview this explanation in class. Other times you'll be expected to read and master it completely on your own.

---

* Thomas F. Staton, *How to Study* (Montgomery, Alabama, P.O. Box 6133, 1968).

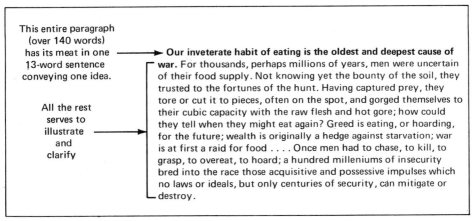

This entire paragraph (over 140 words) has its meat in one 13-word sentence conveying one idea. ⟶ **Our inveterate habit of eating is the oldest and deepest cause of war.** For thousands, perhaps millions of years, men were uncertain of their food supply. Not knowing yet the bounty of the soil, they trusted to the fortunes of the hunt. Having captured prey, they tore or cut it to pieces, often on the spot, and gorged themselves to their cubic capacity with the raw flesh and hot gore; how could they tell when they might eat again? Greed is eating, or hoarding, for the future; wealth is originally a hedge against starvation; war is at first a raid for food . . . . Once men had to chase, to kill, to grasp, to overeat, to hoard; a hundred milleniums of insecurity bred into the race those acquisitive and possessive impulses which no laws or ideals, but only centuries of security, can mitigate or destroy.

All the rest serves to illustrate and clarify ⟶

Figure 9–1. *Paragraph with only a single concept. (Text excerpt from Will Durant, "Why Men Fight," Saturday Evening Post, 210 [July 10, 1937], p. 23. Used with permission).*

You'll probably find *more information delivered to you per square inch, per sentence, per page, than in any textbook you've ever met.* You may en-counter written material with crucial information more concentrated than you have ever encountered before.

Accustomed as you are to the spread-out meanings that characterize much of your reading matter in social studies and English, you might be at a loss when you first encounter extremely dense writing—if you were not alerted.*

Here are examples of writing that contrast markedly in density. In social studies, for example, you're often expected to grasp from a single paragraph *only a single concept* (see Figure 9–1).

In mathematics, paragraphs, or even single sentences, are packed with concepts. The brief textbook paragraph in Figure 9–2, for example, carries a load of *four concepts.* All demand your thorough understanding. Every word serves a function *served by no other.* What is said is said once and for all.

Difficult new technical terms crowd the textbook pages—you're virtually learning a new language, the "official" language of mathematics. Easy, fa-miliar words appear with unexpected new meanings. The everyday word *exactly* suddenly becomes technical—with a precise meaning! *Between* takes on a special meaning—so do *any, if,* and *or!*

Rote memory is no longer enough. You'll acquire a working understand-ing, but learn to use these terms rigorously and intelligently.

---

* Joseph J. Schwab, *Biology Teacher's Handbook* (New York: John Wiley & Sons, 1964), p. 449.

QUADRILATERALS IN A PLANE

We recall, from Section 5–8, the definition of a quadrilateral.

This brief passage is *loaded* with important concepts.

Every one is *crucial.*

Hardly a word can be slighted!

Definition

Let *A, B, C,* and *D* be four points of the same plane. If no three of these points are collinear, and the segments $\overline{AB}$, $\overline{BC}$, $\overline{CD}$, and $\overline{DA}$ intersect only at their end points, then the union of these four segments is called a *quadrilateral.* The four segments are called its *sides,* and the points *A, B, C,* and *D* are called its *vertices.* The angles ∠*DAB,* ∠*ABC,* ∠*BCD,* and ∠*CDA* are called its *angles.*

Figure 9–2. *Paragraph loaded with concepts. (Text material reprinted from* Geometry, *2nd ed., by Moise/Downs, copyright ©️ 1975 by Addison-Wesley Publishing Company, Inc., p. 281. Reprinted by permission of the publisher. All rights reserved.)*

*New expectations need a
new time allotment*

Clearly, more of your study time in mathematics will now be spent in reading. What part of it? Though assignments from day to day vary, and the needs of individual students do, too, on the average, about one-third of your study time should be allotted to reading.

If you slight the preliminary reading, you'll make hard work for yourself as you strike out blindly, make errors, reinforce your errors, and have much to relearn. You'll be building your future leaning on quicksand, for each explanatory passage rests squarely on the ones before.

*How fast should you read
in mathematics?*

Did you turn through the pages of your textbook when you first received it? How much time do you think reading just three or four pages of explanation might take you?

Recently speedreading techniques have been spotlighted on TV. We've all heard claims for a breakthrough toward fantastic speeds: "See a paragraph at a glance with total recall. The greater the speed, the better the comprehension."

A highly competent scholar with special aptitude in mathematics was asked how rapidly he read difficult new mathematical material. He answered, "About one-tenth the usual rate! 'Reading once straight through' patterns are not appropriate. Eyes do and *should* regress, or make backward movements, often. Complete stops are called for frequently. Thought time is essential in addition to reading time."

Preparing for the higher-level reading approach

Suppose it's 7:30 tonight. You've watched the news, had dinner, and now you're starting your math assignment. How do you handle the job and *learn and remember the maximum amount possible in the process?*

As we pointed out previously, your textbook has a do-it-yourself format— a recurring pattern of passages of explanation followed by a set of problems. Sometimes your instructor will preview the explanation in class. Other times you'll be expected to read and master it completely on your own.

No one should expect to comprehend such an assignment in a single reading—not the most gifted reader, not a skilled mathematics scholar. So, first of all, you should plan to do more than one reading.

You may need to put the brakes on runaway speed.

In actual experiments the slowest readers in mathematics have often proved to be the best. In fact, the students who have the greatest difficulty reading their math assignments are often rapid readers. They've become so accustomed to speeding through other reading that they're unable to shift gears and read slowly unless they make unusual effort.

Three pages of difficult new reading assigned to you in mathematics may be equivalent to forty or fifty pages of a novel for English class and to twenty or thirty pages of a chapter for social studies.

On the other hand, you may be able to cover *familiar* material in mathematics quite rapidly. The efficient student learns to vary the tempo of his reading to the task at hand.

Your in-depth reading should result in *time saved.* Later your thorough understanding will *give you insights faster.*

A HIGHER-LEVEL READING APPROACH FOR MATHEMATICS

FIRST READING

PRE-READ TO LOOK OVER THE TERRAIN

> ONCE
> OVER
> LIGHTLY

Read the passage through—once over fairly lightly—to get a feeling for the content.

1. *Use a moderate speed in general, but vary it as you need to.*

You may need to read some parts slowly to help you get the drift. If you pre-read dense passages too rapidly, you may get nothing.

On the other hand, this is *not* your intensive reading. This is a PRE-VIEW—where you determine what the whole thing is all about. If somewhere on the page there are parts you don't understand, don't feel compelled to dig for every meaning. You're going to return later anyway.

2. *Read with a questioning mind set.* Ask yourself:

"How does this relate to what I've been studying?"
"What's the author driving at? Where is all this leading?"
"What should I look for when I go back and really study this
     section?"

You might jot down questions you'll want to answer during your second reading. Use sheets from a 4 × 6 memo pad and keep them between related pages of your book. Or, if you own the book, make your jottings in the margin.

Why pre-read?

1. *You've taken the chill off the reading.* You have a general view of what it's all about and where it's going.

2. *Now you should not be lost among meaningless details.* These should fall into place in relation to the whole. You should retain them with less effort.

3. *You should comprehend difficult passages more readily.* A sentence or a paragraph that might have been a "stopper" for you on an early page of the assignment may be quite clear in the light of your survey of the entire section.

Don't conclude that pre-reading is difficult and time consuming. It's the first step in an approach which, when practiced and perfected, should enable you to do *more good studying in the same time*—hopefully in less.

Skillful pre-reading will not be instant. As with any skill development, your techniques improve with practice.

SECOND READING

**IN-DEPTH READING IS
THE NEXT STEP**

After you've pre-read, you're ready for your close, intensive reading of the passage. You may be reading for a depth of comprehension never before demanded.

Go in with a question!

 As you probe more deeply in your second reading, questions should come constantly to mind. In an actual experiment, college students who approached a reading selection with questions in mind showed decided gains in comprehension. In another investigation they showed better immediate retention on tests just after the reading—and better *long-term* retention, on tests two weeks later.

A questioning mind set is a powerful aid to concentration. Holding questions in the forefront of your mind, you now read searching intently instead of dreaming through the assignment.

Read to pull out the meaning of each word and phrase and sentence

Each step is built on *full understanding* of preceding steps!

When a passage is difficult, stop during this second reading and think over each sentence to be positive the meaning is clear to you. Try not to go on to the next sentence until you fully understand the one before.

The meaning of difficult parts will constantly escape you. Expect this! Read and reread as often as necessary.

Not a single line—hardly a word—may be slighted. Noticing that the authors have used *the* instead of *an* or that they have used *or* instead of *and* may be crucial. Observing that the wording is *at least one*, not *exactly one*, is often critical.

Your index offers instant access to forgotten meanings

Suppose you can't remember the meaning of a technical term you've already met. The word "between," you recall, has a precise mathematical meaning. Suppose you're reading a passage, see the word *between*, and find that its mathematical meaning has slipped your mind. If you slide over this, two or three sentences later you may have lost the meaning of the passage.

You need not leaf through countless pages searching for the meaning of "between." You have the meaning right at your fingertips through the alphabetical index of your textbook. In just seconds, it will guide you to the original textbook explanation of the term.

Complete stops are often needed

In social studies and English you often follow a reading-straight-on pattern. Not so in mathematics! Perhaps 50 percent of your reading time you will "read" standing still!

Read, then stop at the end of a sentence to ask, "Do I understand?" or, "Can I give an example?"

If the authors ask, "Why is something true?" don't just *read* the "Why?" Stop to reflect, "Indeed, why?" If the authors state, "It is obvious that . . . ," ask yourself, "Is it obvious to me?" Then stop and think things over until you're certain that it is. Often it is far from obvious until you've thought it through.

Stop often and ask, "How do the authors have a right to say that?" "How can they justify saying that?" If you read on, thinking, "I'll accept that without question," you may soon forget what the authors have said. But if you've questioned it and convinced yourself it's right, you're much more likely to remember.

There's another reason for asking, "Do the authors have a right to say that?" Perhaps they have no right! All of us make mistakes, and authors are no exception. You'll catch occasional mistakes in textbooks: statements that are inconsistent and untrue—misprints, too. You might lose out on understanding an entire assignment because the author or printer made a mistake you failed to detect. So stop frequently to ask not just, "Why is this true?" but "*Is* it indeed true?"

Attend to diagrams and figures

This crucial part of your intensive reading is discussed next and given special attention because of its importance.

> TAKE TIME for precision reading!
>
> SAVE TIME when things go right!

Your eye movements as you read mathematics may differ markedly from those in other kinds of reading. Your eyes may go backward and forward many times—suddenly drop down below the line—make vertical sweeps— even describe arcs and diagonals! A highly skilled reader might make such movements as these while *expertly* reading a diagram in the textbook!

As you read your textbook, you'll find many references to figures: "in the figure you see," "as shown on the right below," "in the above figure."

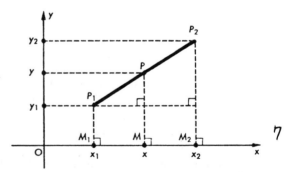

7

Figure 9–3. *Examine it carefully! (Reprinted from Geometry, 2nd ed., by Moise/Downs, copyright © 1975 by Addison-Wesley Publishing Company, Inc., p. 397. Reprinted with permission. All rights reserved.)*

*Shift your eyes from text to
diagram as needed*

When a figure is present, read the textual explanation with special care. When referred to the diagram, *shift your eyes and thoughts* to the diagram. When lines, angles, and points are mentioned in the explanation, locate on the diagram the letters and numbers that designate these. Continue this back-and-forth reading as needed.

If the book is your own, you may wish to make certain features of the diagram stand out by tracing them with colored pencils. For example, you might use different colors to trace overlapping triangles so that each separate triangle stands out distinctly. If in geometry you've studied congruences, you'll want to mark or code figures in such a way that they convey information about sides and angles that are congruent.

*Conceal the explanation and
see if you can supply it*

Did you really understand the diagram? Check yourself by covering the explanation. Look at the diagram alone and see if you can give the explanation.

Reread the explanation, referring back and forth once more until you're sure you understand the figure.

*Conceal words and diagram and
try to visualize the figure*

Try to see the figure in your imagination, or draw essential parts on a scratch sheet. Then check the accuracy of your mental picture.

Much reading time in mathematics isn't actual reading time at all, it's visualizing time. *Complete stops* for mental pictures are constantly called for.

**SUCCESSFUL STUDENTS USE
A SCRATCH SHEET**

If you merely look at your book as you study, your reading may be passive, with your thoughts worlds away. *Think on paper* as you go, and you'll have a powerful device for comprehension, concentration, and retention. It's impossible to study mathematics without pencil work.

Capsulize important ideas

You may want to jot down the gist of difficult passages. Forcing yourself to restate a difficult idea rivets your attention on its meaning and helps you grasp elusive concepts. Ask yourself, "What did it say? How would I say it?"

Fill in steps of each process

As you advance to a higher mathematics course this year, the authors will count on you to fill in parts of processes. They will often give just telegraphic explanations, leaving out inner steps. These you must fill in. You can often work out inner steps on your scratch sheet in just seconds.

If the book is yours, you may prefer to work out inner steps right in your textbook—then they'll be right there for you when you need them.

Answer the authors' questions

Right in the middle of explanations the authors of your textbook may suddenly direct questions—point-blank—at you, the student reader. Your scratch sheet is conveniently at hand for working out the answer.

Sketch constantly as you study

Good mathematics students aren't spectators who passively view the drawing or example in the book. Make up your *own* examples. Compare yours with the authors' and with the definition given.

Draw a sketch, for example, of the graph of a solution set. First, draw a figure of what you think it *is*. Then draw what you think it is *not*. Ask yourself, "Why *isn't* this the graph of a solution set?"

If you own the book, you may wish to make additions to figures in your textbook. For geometry, we've mentioned coding figures in such a way that they convey information about congruent sides and angles.

You'll run across assignments in which the authors give a definition without an accompanying diagram or example. If these are lacking, it's often wise to make one of your own.

If the authors have given a good account, their specifications should be clear enough for you to draw a figure or create your own example. When the book describes a parallelogram, for example, you should be able to translate the words into a geometric picture. When the authors say an operation is *commutative*, you should be able to give an arithmetical example.

If you read the definition and illustrate it, watch it develop, see it build up, then the new concept should take on fuller meaning. Sketching your own figures and making your own examples helps you really see—hazy relationships become sharply focused.

You may be thinking, "That's a lot of work and time and bother." Actually you'll make many of your jottings very quickly.

> YOUR SCRATCH SHEET SHOULD INTENSIFY YOUR CONCENTRATION. BEING ACTIVE WITH A PENCIL HAS A "NO-DOZE" EFFECT!

ADD A LAST QUICK RUN-THROUGH

Your second reading has been a close, intensive reading; you've attended to every word and tiny subscript. You may have lost the whole in the parts!

To be sure you have the broad view again, you may wish to add a final rapid reading. This should wrap things up—put them once more in perspective.

In summing up:

1. Pre-read to orient yourself to the passage.

2. In a second, in-depth reading, study for full comprehension. Attend to diagrams and figures and examples—and sketch or make your own.

3. Think on paper as you go, with a scratch sheet.

4. Add a final run-through to regain the broad view.

> YOU HAVE BEEN GIVEN SOME POWERFUL TOOLS FOR COMPREHENDING EXPLANATORY PASSAGES IN MATHEMATICS AS WITH ALL TOOLS, THERE WILL BE NO VALUE FOR YOU NOW OR EVER UNLESS YOU PRACTICE USING THEM.
>
> YOU'LL PROBABLY PUT FORTH MORE EFFORT PER HOUR THAN IN LESS EFFICIENT STUDY. THE RESULTS? THE MAXIMUM LEARNING FROM EVERY MOMENT.

WHEN YOU JUST CAN'T GET IT

Here are some secrets good students have for getting a breakthrough:

1. *Reread.* Successful math students read explanations again and again. A passage that blocked you at first encounter may come clear with a fourth or fifth reading.

2. *Restate.* Trying to re-express an idea forces you to concentrate on what is being said—it may clinch your understanding.

3. *Read on.* If after repeated efforts the meaning still escapes you, read on in the assignment, then return later. The difficulty may clear up in the light of the rest of the passage.

4. *Try again after time has passed.* Try a change of pace. Turn to other activities. Sleep on it. A difficult passage often hits you differently later. We've all experienced struggling—only to see something clearly the next morning.

5. *Search out other books.* The explanation in another mathematics textbook is often helpful. Your instructor can suggest books that parallel yours. You would naturally expect several explanations to be clearer than a single explanation.

    The kinds of questions you should ask yourself when you just can't get it are suggested in a classic little paperback by Gyorgy Polya, *How to Solve It* (Anchor Books).

6. *Consult a friend.* But let him or her *help* you. It honestly takes the fun out of it if you're *told.* Furthermore, it is doubtful that you have learned something you can use independently another time.

7. *Not a single question should remain unanswered.* Other concepts will be built on that concept not mastered! Unanswered questions pile up! Jot down questions to bring to class or conference, or put a question mark in the margin where things went awry.

> MATHEMATICS IS CUMULATIVE. TO THE LAST PAGE, YOU'LL BE CALLED ON TO USE ANYTHING AND EVERYTHING YOU'VE LEARNED BEFORE! YOUR THOROUGH UNDERSTANDING SHOULD PAY DIVIDENDS IN FUTURE STUDY.

HOW TO READ A THEOREM WHEN THE PROOF IS SUPPLIED TO YOU*

In addition to the general suggestions for reading *all* mathematics in the guidesheets you've just read, working with the proofs of theorems requires some additional techniques. If these next few pages concerned with geometry are not now useful to you, skip over to the section on "How to Master the Vocabulary of Mathematics."

When the proof of a theorem is on the page before you, supplied you by the authors complete with every step, try to resist the temptation to be a mere spectator! Rather than passively accepting what others have thought out for you, involve yourself *actively* in the proving process. Here are some tips:

1. *Have a scratch sheet at hand.*

2. *Use a cover card* (an index card) to conceal the proof written out in the book for you. Expose the statement of the theorem, any restatement, and the diagram, if one is provided. Cover the rest.

3. *Give the statement of the theorem a careful first reading* in order to orient yourself.

4. *Read it a second time to search out (a) what you're to prove and (b) what is already given.* Make sure you understand perfectly what you already have and what you're aiming at. Jot these essentials on your scratch sheet or in your textbook, if it's your own.

5. *Look up forgotten meanings.* No term should remain unknown. Your

---

*Several of the suggestions that follow have been adapted from Henry Swain, *How to Study Mathematics: A Handbook for High School Students,* rev. ed., 1970. It is published by the National Council of Teachers of Mathematics, 1201 Sixteenth Street, N.W., Washington, D.C. 20036.

index will guide you to the full explanation of technical terms in just seconds.

6. *"Read" the geometric picture, or supply one yourself.* As you read the statement and restatement, refer constantly to the figure, if one is present. Make your own drawing on your scratch sheet. Work in pencil, not pen, drawing as accurately as possible. Keep your sketch small.

   Sketch your own figure when none is provided. If you read the theorem, then illustrate it yourself—see it develop—the chances of your fully understanding are multiplied. Your diagram will often bring into clear focus facts, principles, and relationships that seem hazy when expressed in words alone.

   A prime help in mastering theorems is to form a "picture-theorem" association. Eventually you should have instant recall of picture, idea, and statement of theorem—in that order.

7. *Now try proving the theorem yourself,* as if no proof were supplied to you. If you succeed in working out a proof, check it out against the proof in the book. Of course it is possible that two different proofs may be equally correct. If you think you have discovered a new proof, discuss it with your teacher.

8. *If you don't succeed in working out a proof,* lift your cover card and take a quick look at the proof you've concealed. Then try once more to construct the proof on your own.

9. *If you still can't work out the proof,* work carefully through the explanation given by the authors, carrying out details on your scratch sheet as you go along. Find out how the theorem *is* proved.

10. *Last, fix the "key ideas" of the proof in mind.* Before you leave your study of the theorem, whether you proved it yourself or took the authors' help, analyze the proof so that you can state the key ideas, the key steps of the proof.

Can you predict the next move?

In the game of chess, it's a challenge to try to predict the next move of an expert opponent. In geometry, it's a challenge to try to anticipate the authors' reasoning and predict the "next move" in a proof. Here's a way to actively involve yourself in the "proving-process."*

1. Supply yourself with two 3 × 5 index cards.

2. Use the index cards to *conceal the proof* supplied you by the authors. Cover the STATEMENTS with one card and the REASONS with the other.

---

* Paul Moulton, former University of Chicago Laboratory School mathematics teacher, in conversation with Ellen Thomas, May 1967.

3. *Read* the *statement* and restatement of the *theorem*, examine the diagram, and search out what you're to prove and what's already given.

4. With the first STATEMENT concealed, ask yourself, *"What will the authors' first statement be?"* Formulate your "considered guess." Then lift your card and see if you predicted correctly.

5. Next ask yourself, *"What will the authors give as a reason?"* Formulate your answer. Lift your card and check.

6. Continue to *match wits* with the authors through the sequence of STATEMENTS and REASONS, lowering your card step by step.

> SOMETIMES THE ORDER OF STEPS IN A PROOF IS NOT RIGID. YOU ARE NOT NECESSARILY IN ERROR IF YOU PREDICTED THE STEPS IN A DIFFERENT SEQUENCE.

As in a chess game, you will not chalk up all successes as you try to foresee the next move. The fact that you made a prediction means that you're no longer a spectator.

Should you memorize theorems?

Some students get the impression that memory is beneath them—that it's not an acceptable avenue for learning. This impression should not become an excuse for vague half-learning of basic material.

Theorems are essential tools you'll work with constantly and should be remembered. Much of your mastery will occur naturally as you go over them constantly, reread them, and apply them to problems. Regardless of whether mastery comes about through your day-to-day involvement with the material, you must have your stock of remembered theorems—remembered not by rote but with full appreciation of their meanings.

HOW TO MASTER THE VOCABULARY
OF MATHEMATICS
(Put these tips to work, and your dividends may be dramatic)

As you begin a new course in mathematics, it may seem as if you're learning a foreign language. Difficult new technical terms crowd the pages. Easy, familiar words appear with unexpected new meanings. The everyday word *between* suddenly becomes technical—with a precise meaning! The word *exactly* takes on a special meaning—so do *any*, *if*, and *or*!

Rote memory is no longer enough. You must acquire a working understanding, learn to use the new "word tools" rigorously and intelligently. Once an unfamiliar term is defined, or a familiar term is defined with a new meaning, the authors will use it again and again, assuming ever after that you understand it.

Pass over these new terms lightly and word blocks will soon obstruct your learning—your reading will become an obstacle course.

Learn the new terms thoroughly at the time they're introduced and you'll have precision tools for grasping essential new knowledge to the last day of the course.

Clearly, your vocabulary now becomes a tremendous asset. Fortunately, learning experts—in actual experiments with students—have researched learning and retention techniques. Some of the procedures suggested here are based on years of experiments in the psychology of learning.

How will the authors alert you to
important terms?

When key terms or concepts are first introduced in textbooks, the authors usually flag you with a conspicuous signal. The signal used may be **heavy**

Figure 9–4.   *An obstacle course?*

black (boldface) type, *italics*, or color. Words so designated are crucially important "official" mathematical terms.

In the passage shown in Figure 9–5, an important term stands out on the page because it is in **boldface italic type.**

You might make it a thirty-second assignment to scan your own textbook and see how the authors signal important new terms.

Sometimes there is an "explosion" of new words, like the one in Figure 9–6, in a brief space. Yet every new term is basic for your future learning and calls for thorough learning and retention.

Tips for learning difficult technical terms

1. *Attend to each term* when first it appears. Read reflectively to grasp what the definition is saying—not to memorize by rote but to gain a real appreciation of the meaning.

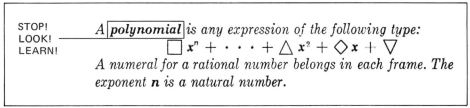

STOP!
LOOK!
LEARN!

A $\boxed{polynomial}$ *is any expression of the following type:*
$$\Box\, x^n + \cdots + \triangle\, x^2 + \Diamond\, x + \nabla$$
*A numeral for a rational number belongs in each frame. The exponent **n** is a natural number.*

Figure 9–5.   *Boldface italic type. (Text excerpts from Mervin L. Keedy, Richard E. Jameson, Patricia L. Johnson, and Joseph Ciechon, Exploring Geometry. New York: Holt, Rinehart and Winston, Inc., 1967, p. 168.)*

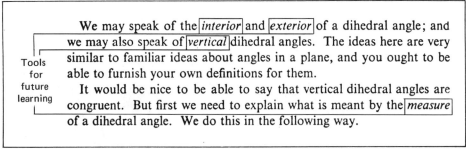

Tools for future learning

We may speak of the $\boxed{interior}$ and $\boxed{exterior}$ of a dihedral angle; and we may also speak of $\boxed{vertical}$ dihedral angles. The ideas here are very similar to familiar ideas about angles in a plane, and you ought to be able to furnish your own definitions for them.

It would be nice to be able to say that vertical dihedral angles are congruent. But first we need to explain what is meant by the $\boxed{measure}$ of a dihedral angle. We do this in the following way.

Figure 9–6.   *"Explosion" of new words. (Reprinted from Geometry, 2nd ed., by Moise/ Downs, copyright © 1975 by Addison-Wesley Publishing Company, Inc., p. 281. Reprinted with permission. All rights reserved.)*

2. *Take the new word apart if you can.* Do you recognize a familiar part? If, for example, you recognize the prefix *poly-*, meaning *many*, you already have a hold on *polynomial, polygon,* and *polyhedron.* If you recognize the word part *equi-*, meaning *equal*, it helps you unlock *equidistant, equiangular, equivalent,* and *equation.* The familiar prefix *co-*, meaning *with* or *together with,* can help you master *coordinate, collinear, cosine,* and *cotangent.*

3. *Read and reread as often as necessary.* Reading-once-straight-through patterns are not appropriate. Complete stops are called for frequently. Thought time is essential in addition to reading time.

4. The authors' definition of a new term is almost always followed by examples. *Examine these examples critically* and figure out whether in fact they do follow the definition. If examples are not given, try to create some of your own.

5. *Try to think of counter examples,* examples that do not come under the definition. In arriving at these, you may find it helpful to change a word or two in the definition.

6. *Read the definition,* as you read all mathematics, *pencil in hand.* Make jottings and create your own examples.

7. Suppose, as you're reading the definition of the new term, you encounter a technical term you've already met in the course whose meaning now escapes you. We all forget! You have the meaning right at your fingertips through the index of your book. *Use the index for instant access to the original explanation of the forgotten term.*

8. As you're working with the new term, try to *express its meaning in actual words—your own words.*

9. You may find a "List of Some Important Terms to Learn" toward the end of each chapter. You'll want to *check your understanding of this list.* The terms the authors have selected for this list are crucial. You may also want to *make your own list of key terms and their meanings.*

10. Make an effort to *use your new mathematical terms.*

In summing up:
1. Read reflectively.
2. Look for familiar word parts.
3. Reread.
4. Scrutinize the examples.
5. Make up counterexamples.
6. Be active with a pencil.
7. Use the index.
8. Self-recite.
9. Review.
10. APPLY YOUR NEW LEARNINGS.

Mastery of new terms

Should you memorize the meanings of new terms? Chances are you won't need to. Mastery will often come about naturally as you go over the material, reread, do problems. This is not to endorse imprecise half-learning of essential terms. Terms in mathematics are rigorously defined. It's essential to get strict meanings in mind. Retaining a very close approximation of what has been said will be a tool in future learning.

A study expert at Cornell University counseled students, "Learn the language of mathematics, and learn to use the words precisely. Only then can you fully and accurately communicate with others, orally or in writing, in the realm of mathematics."* And only then can your instructor and your textbook authors communicate with you.

The dividends will be high: your quick command of terms all through the course and clearer insight into related theorems and problems. In actual experiments with students, those who gave special attention to mastering the technical terms in mathematics made impressive gains in vocabulary and in problem solving too.

Key terms should be "collector's items"

You may want to set aside a section of your notebook as a Mathematics Glossary. As you run across each new key term, collect it for your glossary. Keep this record up to date. Take about two minutes—that's all you'll need—to make each entry.

You may find the "divided page" handy (see Figure 9–7). Make a line down the middle of a page in your notebook. In the *Key Term* column to the left, record the new word. In the *Meaning* column to the right, enter the meaning with precision.

The divided page is handy when review time comes. The dividing line makes it possible to conceal the meaning completely as you check your understanding of a term later.

Mark the end of each unit, perhaps with a double line. Now when you want to go back and check on the new words you've studied in a certain unit, you'll know where to find them.

If you were to do nothing more than record the new words you'd met in a unit and then lose your glossary, you would still have an advantage. The muscular act of writing, in and of itself, would already have strengthened your learning.

Use the most powerful study technique

Students often ask, "How can I retain what I study?" You can *learn for the future* with what the Cornell expert calls the "most powerful study technique known to psychologists."† This is the technique of *self-recitation*.

---

* Walter Pauk, *How to Study in College* (New York: Houghton Mifflin Company, 1962), p. 119.

† Pauk, *How to Study in College*, p. 25.

THE "DIVIDED PAGE"

Key Term	Meaning

Test Your Understanding by Covering This Side.

Figure 9–7. *The divided page.*

Conceal the right-hand side of your divided page with your hand or with a cover card (an index card) and try to express the meaning—not by rote, but with full appreciation of the content. Then lift the card and check. Continue checking until you have full understanding. Mark terms that are especially difficult, and doublecheck these next time.

You'll find a cover card handy in other ways. Using a card to work through chapters as you review is often more effective than rereading. You can reread material and dream all the way through. The cover card forces you to concentrate as you struggle to recall what's underneath.

Use your senses

Multisensory study can speed and strengthen your learning. Eyes are just one of your learning channels. Use your eyes only, and you turn on just one-third of your sensory channels for mastering a new term. What other learning channels can you use? Your auditory and motor channels.

> "See it!
> Say it!
> Hear it!
> Draw it or write it!"*

As you study, *see* the material as you read the word and reflect about its meaning.

Then *say* the new term and formulate its meaning, aloud or in a whisper. Now you're adding kinesthetic learning. As you form the sounds, the muscles of your throat, tongue, and lips are reinforcing your retention.

And as you say it, *hear* it. Now you call in hearing, another learning channel.

Draw a figure to illustrate the term or *write* down its meaning. Now you bring more learning power into play—your motor equipment. Jot down just a key word or two in the definition as you express the content to yourself. Pencil work helps concentration; it has a "no-doze" effect. You can be assured that any writing you have already done on a scratch sheet or on the divided page has already reinforced your learning.

"See it! Say it! Hear it! Draw it or write it!" is all-out study, a four-way reinforcement. The variety itself helps you recall. The change of pace— eyes, voice, ears, pencil—keeps you alert and increases absorption.

To retain longer, space out your reviews

You can remember longer simply by the way you place your reviews. You can place your first review to minimize forgetting. Suppose you read your math assignment today. When will forgetting take its greatest toll? If your forgetting is typical, the greatest loss will be within one day. Arrange your first review to check this drop. Place it from twelve to twenty-four hours after you study your math. Reinforce immediately, and you will remember much longer. It might be a good idea to review the previous assignment immediately before going on to the new assignment.

A study expert pointed out the "curve of forgetting" to military officers returning to academic study after being out of school for several years.†

---

* George J. Dudycha, *Learn More with Less Effort* (New York: Harper and Row, 1957), p. 96.

† Thomas F. Staton, *How to Study*, p. 59.

The first student studied one hour on September 30, and six weeks later retained very little, as illustrated in Figure 9–8.

The second student studied only thirty minutes on September 30, but spaced out the reviews—fifteen minutes on October 1 and ten minutes more on October 8. On November 8 it took this student just a five-minute review to bring back what was wanted—with 100 percent mastery! (See Figure 9–9.)

Both students studied just one hour, but the one who spaced out the review had far better retention.

Your glossary of terms lends itself to spaced reviews. You can have a quick run-through waiting for a friend, riding to school, waiting for a bus, between classes, just before a test.

Take care, though, that your run-throughs don't become unthinking, mechanical repetitions. Your instructors hope that as you review your terms and their meanings, you will focus on *what the definition is really saying*. They sound this warning: though precise understanding is absolutely essential, too much stress on rote memory of words may destroy your grasp of their real meanings.

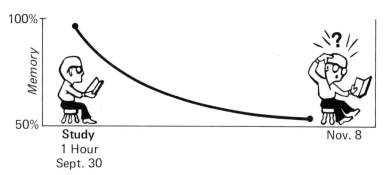

Figure 9–8.　*Curve of forgetting. (Drawing reproduced by permission of Dr. Thomas F. Staton.)*

Figure 9–9.　*Spaced reviews. (Drawing reproduced by permission of Dr. Thomas F. Staton.)*

You'll find that spaced-out reviews will pay you high dividends in aspects of geometry other than vocabulary and in school courses other than geometry, too.

> LEARN THE NEW TERMS FROM DAY TO DAY! THEY'LL BE YOURS TO THE LAST DAY OF THE COURSE—AND BEYOND—AS TOOLS FOR GRASPING ESSENTIAL NEW KNOWLEDGE.

HELPS FOR IMPROVING MATHEMATICS READING

Here are some tools for learning what students need as they read mathematics—then starting them along the road to better reading.

How can a mathematics instructor get insights into the reading competencies of students? How can he or she upgrade their mathematical vocabularies? Help them read the textbooks better? Encourage mathematical thinking in their lives outside the classroom? Help create lifetime readers in the field of mathematics? The resourceful teacher will use the suggestions here, improve them, and increase and multiply them.

Standardized Reading Scores Talk to the Mathematics Teacher

Even before they meet their classes on the first day, mathematics teachers can take steps to improve their students' reading. Through the standardized reading scores in their cumulative folders, they can have a preview of the diversity in reading levels they will face within their classes. Even in homogenous classes, a span of difference of six full years is not unlikely. One teacher of high school sophomores, whose students' reading scores were spread from sixth-grade level all the way to first-year college, commented: "I try to put myself in the position of the students at the different levels. I try to imagine how the sixth-grade-level reader will react to being faced each day with a high school sophomore's text and whether the college-level reader is likely to be challenged by that same high school sophomore's textbook" (Muelder, 1966, pp. 102–103).

Students' folders often include sub-scores in vocabulary, comprehension, and speed of reading. These scores tell teachers about possible trouble spots; by looking at these teachers can begin to get some rough insights into the problems of individuals. By noting low vocabulary scores they can identify the student whose deficiency in general vocabulary may possibly block comprehension in reading mathematics. Through noticing the combination of high speed scores with low comprehension scores, they can discover those who may need help in adjusting speed downward for densely packed passages in mathematics. Low comprehension scores suggest that there may be a difficulty in important comprehension skills. Such insights can be followed by appropriate steps to help students (Muelder, 1966, p. 103).

Standardized reading scores can help teachers match students' abilities with the materials they read. They are a factor to be considered as teachers select textbooks to be used by various homogeneous classes or for heterogeneous classes. They are a special aid to those who are selecting reading materials for enrichment. No matter how great the diversity of reading levels within a group, the teacher can often get the right book into the hands of the student through supplementary materials. With guidance, the poorest reader can experience some measure of success, and the most highly gifted can read books that stimulate and challenge (Muelder, 1966, pp. 103–104). Word problems that are beyond a disadvantaged reader's reach can sometimes be rewritten on a level easier with respect to reading. Here, too, knowing the general reading level, even as roughly as represented by a standardized test score, is an advantage.

In schools that do homogeneous grouping, standardized reading scores are one factor to be considered in assigning students to the appropriate group. Traditionally, achievement and aptitude in mathematics, grades in mathematics, and intelligence scores have been considered. Modern textbooks confront the student with many pages of reading on the analytical aspects of mathematics; thus, another factor predictive of success in mathematics is reading achievement.

How Well Can a Student Handle a Textbook Passage?

While offering useful general insights, standardized tests are silent on important questions: What are the students' special reading competencies for mathematics? How strong are their mathematics vocabularies? Ordinarily the vocabulary section of reading survey tests covers only general vocabulary. And the comprehension section does not test the student on passages with mathematical content.

Is there a way a teacher can assess students' competencies in handling the actual textbook explanations they will be assigned all year? Having selected a passage the students might be expected to handle alone, you might direct them: "Study this passage right here in class as if you were preparing for a test on what it says. A little later, you will have some questions. Use a scratch sheet, if you wish, to make notes and jottings."

Students who fail to complete the passage within the time given should note on their papers the point where they stopped. All should hand in their scratch sheets. The quality of students' jottings, their answers to the quiz questions, and your observations while they are working should provide important insights.

1. Can students handle the textbook, or does it appear to be beyond them?

2. Can they master clearly explained technical terms independently? Grasp key concepts? Get the message of diagrams and figures?

3. Do they use a scratch sheet to study actively—to jot down important ideas, make their own sketches, fill in the inner steps of explanations?

4. Do they appear to be extremely slow readers?

Pre-Teaching To Remove Vocabulary Blocks

Teachers can remove blocks *before* their students read an assignment by searching through the assigned reading beforehand, pulling out words that will cause difficulty, and teaching them in advance in the context in which they will be encountered. For example (from Moulton, 1969):

> In assigning pages on the properties of numbers, a possible block to understanding might be the word *commutative*. The word is placed on the chalkboard—its syllables marked off with vertical lines or short dashes:
>
> com | mu′ | ta | tive
>
> The students are guided in pronouncing the word part by part. At every opportunity teachers point out to students that long, formidable mathematical terms often have familiar parts.
>
> With *commutative*, a teacher might ask, "Can you see a word you know within this word?" Students quickly respond, "Oh, commute." Next the teacher asks, "What does *commute* mean?" Then the teacher guides the class in learning the technical meaning, the word's length no longer making it appear forbidding. As the teacher encourages students to examine word parts, he or she is helping to alter the habits of the many poor readers who are inclined to glance at the first few letters of a forbidding word, then dismiss it with "Too hard for me."

Numbers of words can be brought within the reach of readers through part by part analysis.

Greek and Latin Word Parts

Greek and Latin word parts enter into the formation of many technical terms in mathematics. Mastering the easy-to-learn number prefixes *mono-, pent-, oct-, dec-, cent-, mill-,* and the others is, of course, a stride ahead. Students are often fascinated with the way Greek and Latin parts set off a chain reaction. Teach them the Greek prefix *poly-* in *polynomial,* and they already have a hold on *polygon, polyhedron,* and others. Teach them the Greek root *-hedron* in *dihedron,* and they have a handle for grasping *tetrahedron, pentahedron, octahedron,* and others. Teach the Latin prefix *inter-,* meaning "between," and you help them unlock *interpolate, intersect,* and *intercept.* Teach the Latin prefix *co-* or *con-,* meaning "with" or "together with," and you give them a hold on *coefficient, coordinate, collinear, coplanar, cosine, cotangent, conjugate,* and *conjunction.* You can help them grasp the formidable looking term *trichotomy* through the Greek parts *tri-* and *-tom* meaning "cut."

Terms like the following are likely to repay this sort of analysis, especially with students who have rich language backgrounds: *subscript, transpose, circumference, rectangle, equilateral, equivalent, bisect, perimeter, symmetry, diameter, concurrent, tangent, cotangent, finite, infinite, geometry* and *permutation.*

Help-Yourself Vocabulary Methods

Pointers to help students develop on-their-own competency in mastering technical terms are offered in the preceding item, "How To Master the Vocabulary of Mathematics." There you will find tips for students on how to read the defnition of an "official" term—how to turn on multiple strength learning—how to make the new term theirs to stay.

Students Should Meet the Textbook

Today's publishers are providing students with textbooks that have superior aids for reading and study. Many of these aids, however, will be lost on students. There is evidence that even superior students do not make good use of such facilitative cues unless they are given special instruction (Robinson, 1961, p. 30). Time spent early in the course on a "meet your textbook" session will reward students by improving the caliber of their independent study.

Students should come to know and *use* these study helps in their new textbooks:

The table of contents with its concise, sequential listing of major topics covered

Lists of mathematical symbols for easy reference

Large-size or boldface headings that announce the content of a section

Italics, boldface or color used to signal "official" terms

Italics, boldface, or color used to call attention to concepts, rules, or principles that should be learned and to flag these for easy reference

Typographical danger signals of pitfalls to avoid

Aids for pronouncing and accenting difficult new terms (if these aids are present)

Chapter summaries that wrap up big ideas

Self-check tests at the close of chapters

Table of squares and square roots

Reference list of axioms

Glossary

Index

Once these study aids have been pointed out to students in connection with a single chapter, the students should have them at their command for all the chapters.

Help Students Step into a Unit

As students approach new work, it is well to help them step into their reading by previewing the coming unit. Too often, new work is simply taken up detail by detail with little thought of relating details to the structure of the whole. Through this preview the students should see the main concepts and principles in their relations to each other and to previous work. The preview can be a well organized talk by the instructor—in most cases, it need not be a long one (Butler and Wren, 1965, p. 134). In addition to helping the class view the total picture, the preview provides background understandings, and these, too, make for better reading.

Make Dramatic Assignments

"Do the problems on page 37," students are sometimes told. "And, by the way, read the two or three pages just before the problems." They may drudge through the two or three pages, their motivation only to get the reading over with—if indeed they read the pages at all.

Contrast their reading with that of students whose teacher pulls out a dramatic "believe it or not" problem from the coming assignment:

> "What is the probability that among you twenty-five people in the class two have the same birthday?" To the surprise of the class, the teacher then proves that there is an even chance that two have the same birthday. Next he adds another class and works with fifty students. He proves that it is statistically certain that two have the same birthday. Now the minds of many students are alive with questions: "How can we calculate the probability that a certain event will occur?" "What are the reasons behind this type of calculation?" "Just what is meant by statistical certainty?" As they leave class the teacher reminds them, "You'll find all the answers in your reading for tomorrow."

Even students who are not mathematics oriented sometimes dig into this assignment (Muelder, 1970).

Guiding Questions

Teachers can help students get through a difficult assignment by examining it ahead of time for probable points of difficulty, then supplying guiding questions that will help them work their way past these difficult spots. Niles (1963, p. 2) suggested another reason for formulating preliminary questions: "Asked *before* students read . . . , such a question should help *develop* comprehension. If the same question were not asked until *after* students had read a passage [unless the students return to the passage and analyze it], comprehension would be *tested* but not developed." One would naturally expect students to comprehend better if they approached their reading with purpose questions—if they knew what they should understand and know and what they should be able to do at the completion of the reading.

Hold "How to Read Your Textbook" Sessions

Today's textbooks *talk directly to the students*. Frequently there is a recurring pattern of explanation followed by a set of problems. Once students have been given adequate guidance, many can accept a share of the responsibility for their own learning through reading.

One teacher (Muelder, 1966, pp. 104–110) reports good results from sessions like this:

Early in the course—the first time the class is faced with some pages that introduce new material—I make an assignment that is 100 percent reading. The students are given no problems to work for next day. I have two definite purposes in assigning "pure" reading: (1) to emphasize for the class the importance of becoming successful readers of mathematics, and (2) to set the stage for giving some reading instruction. During part of the class hour we discuss why reading in mathematics differs from reading in other school subjects. Then I suggest some procedures to help the students become successful readers. [See "Reading in Mathematics Calls for a New Look" and "A Higher-Level Reading Approach for Mathematics" earlier in this chapter.]

Early the next class meeting, before the reading is explained or discussed, there is a short quiz. This serves three purposes: (1) to help me evaluate my instruction in reading mathematics, (2) to jolt overconfident students who weren't quite convinced of the need to read and reread mathematical content, and (3) to reemphasize my conviction that reading in mathematics is something to work on.

The results, by the way, have convinced me that a one-shot effort is not enough—that I must reinforce, remind, and review in classroom and in conference.

How You *Should* Have Read It Sessions

The same teacher (Muelder, 1966, p. 111) suggests that a classwide disaster brought on by careless reading of an assignment may be the right moment to walk the students through a model reading:

Begin by having the class read the assignment through once, at a moderate speed, to get the general drift. Then briefly discuss the major ideas. Discourage too much detail; the purpose of the pre-reading was simply to get the broad picture. Then have students, in turn, read parts of the assignment aloud—slowly. Interrupt at crucial points—when the student should stop and draw a picture, when he should do some figuring, when he should find another example, when he should shift his focus to a diagram. Interrupt the reader—and let students do so—to ask questions. When the students have finished this slow rereading, have them all reread the assignment a second time at a moderate pace.

Finally, have them close their books and take a quiz on the content covered in this "model" reading, and reveal the an-

swers immediately. Most of the students will be delighted at
the results. Compare their success this time with past "dis-
asters," and suggest that perhaps their improved scores are the
result of their more careful, more thoughtful, more intelligent
reading. All through the year, in emphasizing how students
are expected to read an assignment, their experiences doing
this model reading can serve as referents.

Guide Under-Par Readers
to Easier Textbooks

Textbooks in introductory mathematics courses vary considerably in the reading demands they make on students. Some are expressly designed to meet the
needs of below-average readers and carefully control the level of reading difficulty throughout the book. When sections of a textbook are clearly beyond
some readers, they may profit from reading the corresponding sections in a
textbook easier with respect to reading. Possibly, with their background understandings thus strengthened, they may be able to extend their reach and handle
their "too difficult" textbook.

Top readers, too, should not be overlooked. They can be sent to an advanced
textbook, one which presents them with a challenge to "stretch their reading
muscles."

Mathematical Thinking Outside the
Classroom

Clear, insightful thinking was never so vital as today. In an age of bewildering
and complex problems, tremendous forces are at work to confuse thinking.
Training in critical reading in mathematics could be a counterforce. Although
all instructors hope students will transfer habits of critical thinking and
reading developed in mathematics class to life outside the classroom, little is
found in most mathematics textbooks to encourage this transfer. Perhaps it
should be more than a byproduct to be hoped for—rather, a definite outcome
to be worked for (Butler and Wren, 1965, p. 165).

Classes should find it fascinating to practice applying techniques of deductive reasoning to the affairs of daily life. *What's wrong with this thinking?* can
become the watchword as they examine excerpts from magazines and newspapers, from TV broadcasts, from conversations heard around school. Are
there unstated premises here? Are they valid? Is this a case in point? Does the
conclusion necessarily follow? The class might cull examples from their read-

ing and listening and make notebooks or placard the classroom with displays of ads and clippings.

Certainly, few other teachers command the expertise of mathematics teachers in developing discerning readers of statistics. People are inclined to revere statistics. They are likely to be unaware that in popular media and elsewhere, statistics, with their aura of objectivity and authority, can be highly misleading, that reports bulwarked with figures as "evidence" can be used to distort political, economic, and social trends, opinion polls, business conditions—even the census! Darrell Huff (1950) opened the bag of statistical tricks in an article, "How to Lie with Statistics." He alerts the reader to such mischief-makers as the "sample with built-in bias," the "truncated or gee-whiz graph," the "well-chosen average," the "unwarranted assumption or *post hoc* rides again," and others. Advanced high school readers and college readers are likely to enjoy and profit from this article. A paperback *How to Lie with Statistics* (Huff and Geis, 1954) is also available.

An assignment like this can have appeal and value:

> As you come across statistics in your reading and listening this week, jot down some of the statistics or bring the clippings to class. Cull examples from your daily paper, your weekly news magazine, from speeches of legislators and political candidates, from TV newscasts, panel discussions and interviews, and from advertising. Do these statistics appear to be sound? Do any of the reports appear to misinform? How much attention should be paid to this evidence? Ask your classmates to weigh the possibility of distortion. Be prepared to comment yourself.

Such an assignment might be ongoing, with the clippings deposited in a growing critical reading file.

Current affairs materials offer a promising opportunity for team teaching between a mathematics teacher and a social studies teacher. In a joint assignment, students might be asked to analyze the speech or public statement of some prominent figure, a speech or statement citing statistical evidence.

Create Readers in Mathematics for Life

A library of attractive and inviting books on mathematics on instant call within the classroom can be a daily stimulus to enjoy reading, practice it, and make it a lifetime habit. Books that convey the fascination of mathematics span an exceptionally broad range of reading levels. The colorful, profusely illustrated *Wonderful World of Mathematics* by Lancelot Hogben is within the reach of many below-standard readers. A book to stretch the reading power of top readers is George Gamow's *One, Two, Three Infinity. Mathematics on Vacation*, edited by Joseph S. Madachy, opens a world of mathematical fun with its mathematical puzzles, pastimes, and curiosities, as does the advanced *Hungarian Problem Book*, translated by Elvira Rapaport. *Changing Careers in Science and Engineering* by Sanford C. Brown (MIT Press) invites readers who want to learn more about a life work in these fields. You might speak to the class intriguingly about books like these, giving a thumbnail sketch of the content or reading aloud an inviting passage. Students who would never voluntarily reach for a book in English class may reach for one here. They may find these books hard to put down and spend many hours reading outside class— with all the gains this added practice brings.

Through this "library," specialized reference materials in mathematics can be on call in the classroom. As students turn to these, the teacher has an opportunity to guide them in the techniques of searching out answers for themselves in the field of mathematics, thus strengthening their equipment for continuing their mathematics education long after school courses are over.

Books from the school library may sometimes be available, on long-term or short-term loan, for classroom collections. The lists below offer "book bait" for students reading on a wide diversity of levels. They are available from the National Council of Teachers of Mathematics:

Mathematics Library: Elementary and Junior High School. Clarence Ethel Hardgrove and Herbert F. Miller. This is an annotated bibliography of enrichment books from grades K–9, classified by grade level. 1973.

The High School Mathematics Library. William L. Schaaf. This annotated bibliography of enrichment books includes about 800 entries, classified by topics, which cover the principal areas of today's high school mathematics. A list of periodicals with a directory of publishers is included. 1973.

A *Bibliography of Recreational Mathematics.* William L. Schaaf. Works are classified under 113 headings, including mathematics in nature, art, club programs, cryptography, string figures, and others. 1973.

TROUBLESHOOTING WORD PROBLEMS

Word problems are one of the real trouble spots for students in mathematics. Reading guidance may be part of the solution.

Ask students the most difficult part of courses in general mathematics and introductory algebra, and they are likely to answer, "word problems." With many of these students their approach to the *reading* of the problem is a source of difficulty. Some have developed a deep-seated dread of these problems. After an inadequate reading, they are inclined to panic. Some are impatient. They dismiss a problem as "too hard for me" if they cannot see and organize the relationships almost instantly. Many are not aware of the close, concentrated reading that word problems demand. They do a helter-skelter reading, then strike out blindly.

Reaching all these problem readers taxes the resourcefulness of any teacher. Some possible ways of troubleshooting word problems through improving reading are offered here.

One Step at a Time

Encouraging a step-by-step procedure may persuade superficial readers to give word problems a more deliberate reading and may help tranquilize those who are fearful. Of course, students should not feel locked into a rigid progression of steps, nor should they conclude that there is only one acceptable way to solve a problem. What is of value is learning to analyze the problem systematically.

A step-by-step sequence like the one below should help students learn to attack word problems. (Modifications would have to be made before it could be applied in algebra.)

Let us suppose, for example, that it's during the World Series. You assign the following problem:*

> Johnny Bench has 13 hits for 37 official times at bat. If he has a great day and goes 5 for 5 in today's game, by how many points will his batting average increase?

Step 1: Read the problem thoroughly, asking, "What is this all about?" Size up the problem situation. Is there a word you don't know? Now is the time to check up on its meaning. A single word left unknown—a slip-up because of one *unc*lear meaning—may make the rest of your efforts ineffective.

The student's thinking should run something like this, "This problem is all about batting averages and comparing two of them." If the student does not know what "he goes 5 for 5" means, he or she must find the definition before proceeding further. Of course, students should have the background informa- that batting averages are decimal fractions between zero and one, rounded to three places.

---

* Richard Muelder, University of Chicago Laboratory School mathematics teacher and former chairman of the Mathematics Department, devised the baseball problem and helped apply the sequence of steps to it.

Step 2: Reread the problem, asking, "What am I to find here?"   Make sure you understand precisely what the problem asks for. The student should think, "I need to figure two batting averages—one for Bench's present record and a second after today's game. Then I'm to figure the increase."

Step 3: Ask yourself, "What facts are given?"   What information is already supplied you in the problem? Make jottings. The student might think, "I know the number of Bench's hits and times at bat right now, and I know that he adds 5 to each of them in today's game."

Step 4: Plan your attack.   Read the problem through once more, asking, "What processes will I use?" or "What formulas will I need?" Plan the steps you'll take in finding what's required. Continue to make jottings.

The student's thinking should run something like this: "I must divide the total times at bat into the number of hits to find the batting average. First, I'll divide 37 into 13 so that I can get Bench's first average. Then I must add five to each of these in order to learn his new record. Then I must divide 42 into 18 to determine Bench's new average. And last, I must find the difference between his first and his second average."

Step 5: Estimate the answer.   Ask yourself, "What would a reasonable answer be?" The student might estimate something like this: "Both 13/37 and 18/42 are batting averages over .333 but under .500. So their difference will be a decimal fraction less than ½."

Step 6: Carry out the operations.   Now carry out the planned operation. Hopefully, the student will obtain, as an answer, an increase of .077 in Bench's average.

Step 7: Check your work.   Compare the answer you arrived at with your estimated answer. Go back to the original problem and check your results against the conditions of the problem. See if your answer fulfills those conditions.

No one can bat over 1.000. Thus, if the student gets the spectacular increase of over 3.300, something is wrong! Check by asking, (1) Was my error caused by an error in arithmetic? or (2) Did I misunderstand the problem?

It should be noted that with the mature problem solver there is no dichotomy between reading time and figuring time. The student reads and figures—getting notions, discarding one, trying another—not one and then the other but "all mixed in" (Bell, 1970).

In summing up, students may reach the answer on a ladder of the steps shown in Figure 9–10.

Word problems in algebra can be attacked by using a modified version of the strategy described in the ladder. The flow chart in Fig. 9–11 illustrates how to set up a problem with one variable. In time, the student will go through these

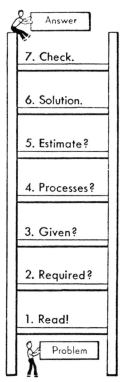

Figure 9–10. *Ladder of steps. (From William Betz, A. Brown Miller, F. Brooks Miller, Elizabeth Mitchell, and H. Carlisle Taylor,* Everyday General Mathematics, Book 1, *rev. ed. Boston: Ginn and Company, 1965, p. 71. Reprinted with permission.)*

steps automatically. Speed and accuracy are likely to be improved tremendously. A flow chart will be most effective if its use is illustrated with specific problems, if practice is provided, and if students *see the results* in arriving at solutions efficiently.

Try Data Diagrams

It may be helpful to draw a picture or a simple sketch of just what is going on in the problem. On a data diagram, like the one in Figure 9–12, the student sets down, as briefly as possible, all the given facts.

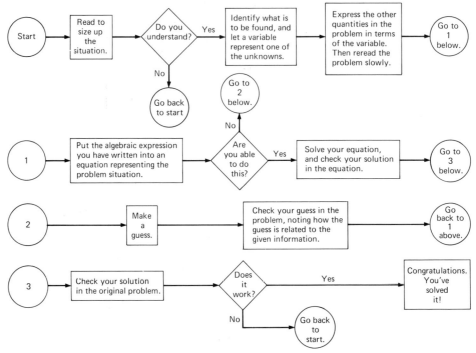

Figure 9–11. *Flow chart for solving a word problem in algebra. (Contributed by Richard H. Muelder, University of Chicago Laboratory School mathematics teacher.)*

Mr. Greene is to land at the airport at 9 p.m. Mrs. Greene, who lives 20 miles from the airport, is to meet him. If she leaves at 8:15 and averages 30 mph, will she be on time?

```
SHE                                                           HE
LEAVES   ——————  ←———— 20  MILES ————→  ———→  ARRIVES
8:15                        30  MPH ————→                      9:00
```

Figure 9–12. *Data diagram. (From Dunstan Hayden and E. J. Finan, Algebra One. Boston: Allyn and Bacon, Inc., 1961, pp. 275–276.)*

> Mr. Greene is to land at the airport at 9:00 p.m. Mrs. Greene, who lives 20 miles from the airport, is to meet him. If she leaves at 8:15 and averages 30 mph, will she be on time?

With the diagram, students see the problem situation *visually*, and as they do so, they can often detect relationships and formulate mathematical expressions of them.

Good Guesses Help Toward Solutions

The step-by-step procedures previously suggested include a helpful guessing step. Unless the problem situation is too involved, students often move closer to the solution when they ask themselves, "What is a reasonable answer in the light of the facts given?" Formulating an informed guess leads students to *think through* the problem situation and to detect elements and see relationships they can use in moving to a solution. Instructors should point out the difference between a *good guess* based on systematic consideration of the data and a *haphazard guess* based on little thought. They should make clear that they are not teaching students to get quick answers by guessing.

"It's not important," one teacher observes (Muelder, 1966, p. 112), "that the student's guess be accurate. What is important is that he test his guess with the data given, and in so doing see how the data are related to the answer wanted. After having done this, he can often set up a problem using a variable, replacing his previous guess with the variable. He can then proceed to solve the problem."

Students can be given extra "guessing practice" through problems with multiple-choice answers. Problems can be dittoed with several estimated answers printed below each problem. Students are asked to think through the problem data carefully, cross out answers that would be ridiculous, and choose their guess.

Verbal Check—Superior Reading Practice

Showing students how to make the verbal check—how to rethink the problem situation—can be excellent reading practice; in many cases, teachers find, fully as valuable as the original problem solving itself (Matchett, 1971). Students should appreciate the *why* of the verbal check:

> Don't be satisfied with substituting the answer you arrived at in an equation you made yourself. This, of course, is *not* a

check for verbal problems since you may have made an error in writing the equation in the first place. If you are satisfied merely to substitute in the equation, any errors in *thinking through the information* will, of course, escape you.

A complete check, therefore, should include (1) a *mathematical check* to catch any errors in your computations, and (2) a *verbal check* to verify your thinking through the information.

Now is the time to substitute your answer in the equation in order to catch any errors in the mechanics of your computations.

For your verbal check, return to the original problem. Check your results against the conditions of the problem. Substitute according to the original conditions and see if your answer fits into the picture. If it does fit, you are likely to have solved the problem correctly.

How-to-Read-It Sessions

Try holding sessions in which you concentrate on guiding students through the reading of verbal problems—through the stage of formulating the open sentence but no further. Guide them through a sequence: read for the drift of the problem ("What am I to find?"), note what is given, make a "data diagram," plan strategy, and so on. In these practice sessions, have them concentrate only on *reading and thinking through the information*. They need not spend time performing the computations.

It may help to encourage students to imagine themselves as participants in word problems: *You* are in the speeding car which must come to a stop when traveling a certain number of miles per hour. *You* are in racing boat A which may or may not overtake boat B.

Try Pre-Reading Sessions

One instructor (Junker, 1970) sets aside class time for students to pre-read word problems that have just been assigned for homework. While in class, students read the problems silently. This is *reading* practice—they stop short of carrying out the computations. They are encouraged to ask questions at points where they foresee difficulty and to work out their trouble spots in class. She also holds post-reading sessions in which the students discuss freely the difficulties they had reading last night's problems. She reminds her students, "If you slight the reading, you'll make hard work for yourself as you strike out blindly, make errors, and have much to do over."

Is a Once-Through Reading Enough?

To prove dramatically the necessity for rereading, students might be given an interesting problem and asked to read it through once *at their normal reading speed.* Only this single reading is permitted. Then, without looking at the problem again, they are to answer questions on the conditions described in the problem. When the students have tried *all* the questions, they are to check their answers with the original problem (Hayden and Finan, 1961, pp. 275–276). The message comes through loud and clear, that close reading and several readings are essential to "pull out" all the information in a problem.

"Translate" the Words into Symbols

Write out the statement in the problem across the chalkboard in one long line. Then show, just below, how the verbal statement can be written in a mathematical statement by substituting the right mathematical symbols for the words. This "translation device" is often effective (Welchons et al., 1970, p. 42).

Try Reading Problems Orally

Another teacher (Muelder, 1966, p. 112) finds oral reading to have special values. "When a student comes to me for help with a word problem, I often have him read the problem to me orally, assisting him when it seems appropriate. As he reads aloud, I learn something about the nature of his reading blocks. The student whose difficulty with a problem results from a reading disability is often able to solve the problem if he *hears* it. The emphasis in schools on silent reading leads students to think it's somehow wrong to read aloud to oneself. This not the case with word problems. I suggest to students that they bring all possible learning channels to bear, including hearing."

Try the "Easy Numbers" Technique

The "easy numbers" technique can be extremely helpful to students: "Have you ever read a problem, thought it too complicated, and just guessed what to do? We have already suggested rewriting a problem in your own words. Another way to rewrite a problem is to substitute 'easy' numbers for those in the problem. 'Easy' numbers give a quick solution and show how to solve the original problem" (Bernstein and Wells, 1969, pp. 301–302). For example:

> An airplane averaging 238 miles per hour flies from New York to Detroit in 2¾ hours. How far is it from New York to Detroit?

Solution:

> REWRITE An airplane averaging 200 miles per hour flies from New York to Detroit in 3 hours. How far is it from New York to Detroit?

> Do you see that the answer to this easy problem is 600 miles? It must have been found by 3 × 200. Therefore, we solve the original problem by 2¾ × 238.

Simplify Problems for Under-Par Readers

When word problems are beyond handicapped readers, they can sometimes be rewritten on an easier reading level, then dittoed for the students. The general vocabulary can be made easier, the sentence structure simplified, and the sentences shortened. Reading consultants can suggest methods of bringing verbal material within the grasp of below-average readers. Your folders of simplified problems will grow and will enrich your resources year after year.

Tap Student Interests

Through original problems, it is sometimes possible to tap the interests of students, to bring problems within the range of their everyday experience, and to make these problems seem real. Students whose world is cars might be asked, "How much can Al save on his new accessories: six-volt spotlight, turn signals, new rearview mirror, and so on—when these are on sale at a 20 percent reduction?" "What is the percent of increase in the cost of liability insurance for a male driver under 25?" "What was Bill's average annual depreciation per mile?" "What was the average asking price of the cars Janice considered while shopping for her car?"*

---

* The ideas related to problems of interest to students are from Nila Banton Smith, *Be a Better Reader*, Book 4 (Englewood Cliffs, N.J.: Prentice-Hall, 1963).

If students are sports minded, problems about sports can tie mathematics to their interest while capturing a bit of the excitement of the sports event itself: "Which yacht, *Seawind, Spray,* or *Green Wave,* won the race when the elapsed times were corrected?"

Problems about sports can take on interest through timeliness; they can ride the crest of seasonal enthusiasms: "Which of the two old rivals—Grant High or Williams—had the better final standing in the North Central Football Conference?" "How many hits must ace shortstop Bill Rawls get his next 25 times at bat to average .300?"

Problems that are real and practical, that are within the comprehension and experience of students, and that are solvable by elementary algebra appear to be very scarce. Teachers will wish to detect, select, and create such problems (Butler and Wren, 1965, p. 383).

Relate Problems to Job Ability

In communities where graduates are likely to be looking for work within the community, students or the teacher might ask prospective employers, "What problems would you like your employees to be able to solve?" (Willoughby, 1970, p. 276). A student hopeful of becoming an auto mechanic might feel genuine interest in solving a real problem supplied by a professional mechanic. File folders containing problems related to a variety of types of jobs can be built up over the years.

Have Students Bring in Live Problems

Students can be encouraged to bring in live problems—those that confront them in their personal lives. The problems they come up with are likely to be practical, to have teen appeal, and to testify to the fact that mathematics does meet personal needs.

Bibliography

Aukerman, Robert C. *Reading in the Secondary School Classroom.* New York: McGraw-Hill Book Company, 1972, chapter 10.

Brown, Sanborn C. *Changing Careers in Science and Engineering.* Cambridge, Mass.: MIT Press, 1972.

Butler, Charles H., and F. Lynwood Wren. *The Teaching of Secondary School Mathematics.* New York: McGraw-Hill Book Company, 1965.

Dudycha, George J. *Learn More with Less Effort*. New York: Harper and Row, 1957.

Gamow, George. *One, Two, Three Infinity*. New York: Bantam Books, 1971.

Herber, Harold L. *Teaching Reading in Content Areas*. Englewood Cliffs, N.J.: Prentice-Hall, 1970.

Herber, Harold L., and P. L. Sanders, eds. *Research in Reading in the Content Areas: First Year Report*. Syracuse: Reading and Language Arts Center, 1969.

Hogben, Lancelot. *Wonderful World of Mathematics*. New York: Doubleday and Company, 1968.

Madachy, Joseph S. *Mathematics on Vacation*. New York: Charles Scribner's Sons, 1975.

Pauk, Walter. *How to Study in College*. Boston: Houghton Mifflin Company, 1962.

Rapaport, Elvira, trans. *Hungarian Problem Books 1 and 2*. (2 vols.) New York: Random House, 1963.

Robinson, Francis P. *Effective Study*. New York: Harper and Row, 1961.

Robinson, H. Alan. *Teaching Reading and Study Strategies: The Content Areas*. Boston: Allyn and Bacon, 1975, chapter 8.

Shepherd, David L. *Comprehensive High School Reading Methods*. Columbus: Charles E. Merrill Company, 1973, chapter 11.

Staton, Thomas F. *How to Study*. Montgomery, Ala.: P.O. Box 6133, 1968.

References

Bell, Max S., former University of Chicago Laboratory School Mathematics Department chairman, in remarks to Ellen Thomas, August 1970.

Bernstein, Allen L., and David W. Wells. *Trouble-Shooting Mathematics Skills*. New York: Holt, Rinehart and Winston, 1969.

Butler, Charles H., and F. Lynwood Wren. *The Teaching of Secondary School Mathematics*. New York: McGraw-Hill Book Company, 1965.

Hayden, Dunstan, and E. J. Finan. *Algebra One*. Boston: Allyn and Bacon, 1961.

Huff, Darrell. "How to Lie with Statistics." *Harper's*, 101 (August 1950).

Huff, Darrell, and Irving Geis. *How to Lie with Statistics*. New York: W. W. Norton and Company, 1954.

Junker, Gladys, former University of Chicago Laboratory School Mathematics Department member, in remarks to Ellen Thomas, June 1970.

Matchett, Margaret, University of Chicago Laboratory School mathematics teacher, in remarks to Ellen Thomas, November 1971.

Moulton, Paul, former University of Chicago Laboratory School mathematics teacher, in remarks to Ellen Thomas, May 1969.

Muelder, Richard H. "Helping Students Read Mathematics." In *Corrective Reading in the High School Classroom,* edited by H. Alan Robinson and Sidney J. Rauch. Perspectives in Reading Series, No. 6. Newark, Del.: International Reading Association, 1966.

Muelder, Richard H., University of Chicago Laboratory School mathematics teacher and former chairman of the Mathematics Department, in remarks to Ellen Thomas, June 1970.

Niles, Olive S. "Help Students Set a Purpose for Reading." *English High Lights,* 20 (April-May 1963). Chicago: Scott, Foresman and Company.

Robinson, Francis P. "Study Skills for Superior Students in Secondary School." *The Reading Teacher,* 15 (September 1961).

Welchons, A. M., W. R. Krickenberger, and Helen R. Pearson. *Algebra, Book One,* annotated ed. Lexington, Mass.: Ginn and Company 1970.

Willoughby, Stephen S. "Issues in the Teaching of Mathematics." In *Mathematics Education,* edited by Herman Richey. 69th Yearbook of the National Society for the Study of Education, Part 1, 1970.

INDUSTRIAL ARTS AND VOCATIONAL EDUCATION

Herbert Pearson, University of Chicago Lab-oratory School industrial arts teacher, served as a consultant for this chapter.

Students with reading difficulties often gravitate to technical courses, hoping for a haven at school where reading is not demanded. Instructors express concern over the gap between the reading competencies these students bring to their courses and the demands that will confront them from day to day. Teachers without formal training or experience in teaching reading can take action to narrow this gap—in the daily work of the course with no undue investment of class time. There should be these dividends for students: better mastery of the immediate course, and better reading for advanced technical courses and apprenticeships and for self-education after school courses are over.

The problem of upgrading reading in technical courses is a special one—but *so is the opportunity*. Where, if students are interested in technical subjects, is reading closer to doing their "own thing"? In wood shop, the printed words on the page may be related to making a pair of water skis; in electronics, to checking out what's wrong with a transistor radio or stereo; in metal shop, to improving scuba diving equipment; in auto mechanics, to getting more "go" out of a motor bike or car. Here reading ability can be turned into *job* ability. Students realize they *must* be able to handle technical reading or be shut out of the job market for all but the simplest manual labor.

In this chapter we offer for your consideration first a section suggesting approaches and devices which should help readers (particularly those less capable) handle the heavy vocabulary load in technical courses. Next we offer guidelines for helping students read—with the precision demanded—the often complicated directions that crowd the pages of their textbooks and job sheets. The last item presents a strong case for a technical library right in the shop or classroom. Here students can acquire find-it-yourself procedures to keep their technical knowledge up to date and growing—for life. And here, in fascinating how-to-do-it books and colorful popular magazines, there will be a silent reading teacher daily inviting them to *practice* reading.

HELPING STUDENTS LEARN TECHNICAL VOCABULARY

The vocabulary load in technical courses is crushing for many students. There's an urgent need for effective vocabulary learning.

In technical courses, difficult vocabulary terms—sometimes hundreds of them —come crowding upon the student. A precise working understanding is often crucial. Not knowing the difference between *drilling* and *counterdrilling* can mean disaster for that study desk the student is making. New technical terms pile up and must be mastered from day to day. To the last day of the course, words will be precision tools for grasping essential new knowledge.

In some respects there is a unique opportunity in the technical classroom for effective vocabulary learning. Here, daily, there are live experiences with words. Students *see* the referent for many printed symbols right there before them in wood, metal, plastic. As they learn the new term *engine lathe*, they see, hear, touch, and manipulate the actual machine. As they learn the term *knurling*, they observe, then perform, the process. When they meet *micrometer caliper*, they pick up the instrument and hold it in their hands *to do a job*. Here "print-shy" readers may change their attitudes toward words. As they turn the pages of a popular magazine on mechanics, printed symbols on the page may stand for fascinating parts of a mini-bike—and printed words tell how to repair it.

It might be argued that the school shop or the technical classroom should provide a reading-free environment—a place at school where the discouraged reader can succeed *without* the printed word. But this is not realism. Let us rather examine the possibility of exposing individuals to powerful reading stimuli—indeed, of bombarding them with printed words. A miscellany of possibilities for increasing technical word power through many such exposures is now offered.

Take Down the Obstacle Course

You can remove roadblocks *before* your students read by searching through textbook or job sheet beforehand, pulling out significant difficult words, and teaching them in advance in the context in which they will be encountered. As you do so, you will be taking the chill off the reading, and discouraged readers may take hold.

Numbers of technical terms can be brought within the reach of student readers through part-by-part analysis. A word like *superconductivity* may appear overlong to some readers. They are frightened by seven syllables and give up. It is immensely helpful simply to show students that long, difficult-looking words often have familiar parts—here, the obvious *super* and *conduct*. This takes just minutes. Students are likely to "see into" words as you analyze them if, on the chalkboard, you mark off longer words into easy to manage parts:

super / conduct / ivity

With *carbonaceous*, students might be asked, "Can you see a word within the word?" as you print the word on the board. Some will discover *carbon* quickly. You might highlight the base word on the board in some way, perhaps by underlining:

carbonaceous

Then the class can move on to learning the technical meaning—the word's length no longer making it appear forbidding.

With *dynamometer* printed on the chalkboard, you might ask, "Is there a part you know?" Students are likely to respond, "Oh, dynamo!" They now perceive that the long word *dynamometer* is a not too difficult word with *meter* (which may already be familiar) tail-ending it.

If *commutator* should be a hurdle, you might suggest, "Can you strip this one down?" When the students discover *commute*, you might ask, "What does *commute* mean?" then guide them in mastering the specialized meaning.

Printing the term on the board accents its appearance and spelling and helps students to "take a mental picture." If in future reading they are to recognize the new term instantaneously, they must have this "mental picture."

The terms that follow, found in various technical textbooks, lead themselves to the question, "Can you take this word apart—break it into its building blocks?"

set-over	demagnetize
spotfacing	electromagnet
setscrew	variometer
casehardening	variocoupler
monotype	magnetometer
ultrasonic	equipotential
photosensitive	interelectrode
photoconductive	transconductance
micrometer	electrodynamometer
autotransformer	microminiaturization
accelerometer	radiometallography

Familiar parts discovered in these words are handles to take hold of in remembering their meanings. Terms that lend themselves to part by part analysis are numerous in technical courses.

Teach Jackpot Word Parts*

Students who master the easy-to-learn Greek and Latin word parts for numbers take a stride ahead in technical vocabulary. In a few moments of turning through the index of two or three technical textbooks, one can find all these derivatives: *unipolar, unishear, monoblock, monotype, monochrome, bimetal, bilateral, binary, trimetric, quadrant, quadrilateral, tetrahedron, pentagon, pentagrid, hexagon, hexahedron, hexode, heptagon, octagon, octahedron, octode, nonagon, decagon, dodecagon, dodecahedron, centimeter, millimeter,* and others. Here, again, the familiar part gives the student a peg on which to hang retention of the meaning. A complete list of useful number prefixes is under Level 2 of the list of Greek and Latin word parts in Chapter 2.

---

* Ward S. Miller uses the term "jackpot" vocabulary lessons in *Word Wealth* (New York: Holt, Rinehart and Winston, 1967).

Multimeaning Terms Call for
Special Handling

Many words take off their easy, familiar meanings and put on difficult technical meanings the minute the student walks through the door into the shop. Word like *lap, polish, rack, tolerance, quench, cast, dog,* and *boss* suddenly take on technical meanings that must be learned with precision. *Hard* and *tough* look like everyday words to students and are likely to be thought similar in meaning. Now they become important in describing certain properties of metal and must be carefully differentiated. Since students must relinquish their preconceived ideas of such terms as easy, some of these terms may call for special handling through emphasizing their technical meanings during explanations and demonstrations.

Meet Your New Shop

The more numerous the exposures to a printed word, the more likely students are to form the visual image necessary to incorporate it into their vocabularies. On the first day in a new shop class, when interest is high, a floor plan of the shop can be given to each student (Funk, 1961, p. 25). On it various pieces of equipment—engine lathe, shaper, milling machine, table saw, jointer, planer, and others—are located and numbered. The machines themselves have identification signs conspicuously attached. Eager to learn about the equipment they will be using, the students move around the shop with their floor plans. As they circulate, they complete a numbered sheet, writing the name of each machine after the number corresponding to that on the floor plan.

Safety Signs Send Out Verbal Stimuli

Shop safety signs, which students will live with from day to day, further expose students to the stimuli of printed words. As the teacher directs attention to a prominent sign and forcefully drives home its message, students may come to retain an image of the printed symbols. For still another exposure to words, bulletins on shop safety might be read aloud to under-par readers as they follow the printed words silently.

Label Everything in Sight!

Almost everything in the shop or classroom can be conspicuously labeled. The tools on the tool racks can be labeled. The materials in drawers or in storage cabinets can be prominently labeled (El Monte Union High School District, 1966, p. 9). Each time students remove or replace a tool from a rack or open the door of a cabinet, they are pelted with words. They may come to associate the symbol with the object, retain a mental picture, and make the word their own for future reading.

One teacher demonstrated the use of a machine—a squaring shear, for example—with eye catching name cards attached to important parts (Schramm, 1954, p. 278). Small magnets designed to hold cards were used to attach the labels. Interest was caught by this novel and effective way of presenting vocabulary. Later the name cards were removed, and the students were asked to re-attach them to the right parts. As they manipulated each label, they strengthened their visual image of each term—*extension arm, cutting blade, bed, foot treadle,* and others. The teacher coated the cards with clear lacquer and stored them in a card file.

Bulletin boards, too, can teach vocabulary. One teacher displayed a wood selection chart with forty-eight kinds of hardwoods and softwoods, each of these conspicuously labeled. Students could be seen lingering before and after the class hour, studying this chart. Colorful charts supplied by businesses and manufacturers expose the student to additional verbal stimuli.

Dittoed job sheets are often accompanied by diagrams and drawings. These provide still another opportunity for prominent labels.

Demonstrations Are an Opportunity Plus

The instructor's frequent demonstrations of equipment and processes in technical courses offer a superlative opportunity. Is there a better setting for synchronizing *hearing* the word and *seeing* it, a coordination conducive to acquiring vocabulary? Auditory memory is involved as students hear their teacher use the word during the demonstration. Most important if reading capability is to benefit, visual memory becomes involved, if, at the same time, students see the word displayed during the demonstration. Here again they have a chance to photograph the word in their mind's eye and add it to their sight vocabulary. If demonstrations are conducted without printed words, this special opportunity is lost.

How can teachers spotlight printed words while they have their hands full giving a demonstration? Classroom flip charts with pages that flip over easily can present the terms to view. A portable stand that can be moved anywhere in the shop makes displaying the charts quite easy. As you demonstrate knurling on an engine lathe, you can direct attention to the term *knurling* in large print on a chart nearby. As you demonstrate uses of the circle saw, each important new term—*ripping, crosscutting, mitering, dadoing, beveling,* and others—

takes the spotlight. Students can sometimes profit from helping prepare the charts. Charts supplied by industry can add to the classroom resources.

In reviewing terms just taught, a teacher working with younger children pointed to the printed terms on the chart. The students enjoyed getting the actual objects—nail, screw, dowel—and holding them up beside the printed symbol (Ferrerio, 1960, p. 19).

Sometimes the chalkboard is the convenient place to display charts that highlight words. How to put these up quickly while preparing a demonstration? As a simple solution, one teacher (Schramm, 1954, p. 277) inserted the pointed end of an unopened brass paper fastener under the molding at the top of the chalkboard. The round top of the fastener gripped the charts, posters, and drawings in place firmly.

Schramm also found it helpful to have tools in full view during a demonstration. He constructed a simple portable chalkboard with a handy magnetic toolholder held by a strip of plywood to the top of the chalkboard. The magnet held up small hand tools. On the background of the chalkboard he could label the tool and its parts with prominent printed labels. A "Magnagrip" tool holder can be secured from the Phelon Magnagrip Company, East Longmeadow, Massachusetts 01028.

One teacher had an ingenious way of spotlighting a term at just the right moment (Schramm, 1954, p. 279). Have you ever wished, he asked, that you could reveal the name of each part of a tool or machine just when you need to during a demonstration? To solve the problem he prepared large drawings of various tools and machines, omitting the names of the parts Then he covered the drawings with clear cellulose acetate. As he proceeded with his demonstration of the actual equipment before the class, he printed the name of the part he was explaining, using a china marker. For emphasis, he sometimes printed the labels in color, using different colored china markers. The markings could be easily removed from the acetate. The drawings were on hand for follow-up reinforcement and testing and for use year after year.

Contrast reading-oriented demonstrations, like the ones just described, with those in which the student simply hears the word and there *is* no printed symbol. Printed words thus spotlighted should add up to better reading.

Turn Job Sheets into Better-Reading Devices

As their teachers can substantiate, many students lack the reading power to handle the job sheets intended to guide their work in the shop from day to day. It may be possible to transform these guidesheets into better-reading devices.

Handicapped readers often shy away from the printed word. They prefer to depend on the spoken word, to get by without reading by turning to their teacher for information. But since drawing out meaning from printed material is vital to their success as technical workers, they should be led back to the printed page as a source of information whenever possible.

One teacher developed a type of lesson intended to help students handle their immediate job sheets and improve in reading, too (Levine, 1960, pp. 22–24). Picture the groups confronted with a job sheet that started like this:

Unit: How to turn tapers by the offset
tailstock method
Topic: Checking offset with dividers

> 1. Set the legs of the dividers to the required offset. Adjust set-over screws until the distance between the index line on the base and the index line on the tailstock body corresponds to the setting of the dividers.

And this was just the first step!

First, the teacher demonstrated the required processes orally, introducing the class to the equipment with which they would be working. Attention was directed to the chalkboard where the teacher had printed the key words of the job. Among these were the following:

1. required offset

2. set-over screws

3. corresponds to the setting

4. tailstock body

5. index line

As a check on understanding, the teacher pointed to the phrase on the board and asked a student to indicate the equipment (set-over screws, for example) and to give the function, or to demonstrate or explain the process. Again, headlining the phrases on the board concentrated attention on their appearance and spelling. Sometimes the teacher erased the words and called on certain students to write them in again, asking the others to watch the board and be ready to help their classmates. After this thorough pre-teaching of key vocabulary, the teacher or a student read the job sheet aloud while the students followed along silently. As they did this, their understanding of words they could not recognize on the page was made possible by the *heard* word. Many proceeded with their work, now capable of reading the job sheets for themselves. Of course, all this support for students—this oral-silent reading procedure—is appropriate only for those who have problems reading the job sheets.

Elicit the Use of New Terms

Students can be led to *use* the new terms immediately. A shop teacher who has just demonstrated mitering a board asks his class, "What did I just do to this board?" The students reinforce their new learning as they answer individually or in chorus. Holding up the miter-gage or the push stick, or pointing to the rip-fence, the teacher asks, "What did I just call this?" Again, there is the opportunity to say and to hear the new words.

Bring Job Sheets into Closer Reach

When job sheets, textbook directions, and the like are beyond the reach of certain readers, they can be rewritten on an easier level. The general vocabulary can be made easier and the sentences can be shortened to include only a single direction in each. A reading consultant can suggest ways of bringing directions within the grasp of under-par readers. Resources of simplified materials can be enlarged year after year.

Non-Print Materials Can Reinforce Reading

For individuals who need further reinforcement in recognizing important terms and following directions, the teacher might record a series of directions on a tape. Using earphones, the students read the words on the page silently while reinforcing their reading through listening. They play and replay the tape as often as necessary. Through this reading-hearing procedure, they come to associate the word they see printed on the page with the word they hear. After this reinforced reading, some students can work away from the tape recorder using only the printed directions. Thus they are grasping the directions for their current project and learning to read better besides.

Films and filmstrips can be used to introduce new terms. During a film the students both hear and see the key terms and see the tools and materials pictured.

Can You Answer the Boss's Note?

The teacher clips an advertisement for a carpenter's assistant from a newspaper (El Monte Union High School District, 1966, pp. 10–11). The teacher asks, "If you were to get this job, what do you think you would have to do?" The students talk this over.

The teacher goes on, "Here is a copy of a note you might get on the first day of your new job," and projects on a screen a blow-up copy. The note is read aloud, and here is the boss's message:

I am up on the tenth floor. Bring me the following tools:

mallet	gouge	pliers
chisel	hammer	coping saw
brace	hand drill	hacksaw
bit	plane	clamp
Hurry!		

The teacher then asks, "What will you need to know to be able to answer the note?" The students respond, "The tools the carpenter mentioned."

The tools the carpenter needs are laid out on a workbench. Their names have been printed on large word cards. The students are asked to match each name card with the corresponding tool.

After tools and cards have been matched, the teacher removes the tools, but leaves the word cards. The students now work only with the printed symbols. Asking the class to keep in mind the *use* of each tool, the teacher suggests that certain words can be grouped together because their uses are similar. Questioning is continued until the name cards have been arranged into five groups:

> mallet, hammer
>
> chisel, gouge
>
> pliers, clamp
>
> coping saw, hacksaw
>
> brace, bit, drill

In summing up, the class discusses the question, "How can this help you to be a good carpenter's assistant?"

When follow-up is needed, the tools are again laid out and matched with their labels, then removed as the students work again with only the symbols. This concentrated effort, the teacher finds, will fix basic terms.

Name That Tool!

The teacher introduces the class to tools, parts of tools, types of lumber, varnishes, stains—whatever is needed to complete a project. As this is done, the printed names are displayed and stressed. Later the teacher hangs a number on each item and gives each student a numbered sheet. The student is asked to write down the name of each piece of equipment or material. The teacher is enlisting kinesthetic (muscular) learning, which in many individuals is one of the strongest of all learning channels. The motor act of writing the new term, in and of itself, is likely to strengthen the learning.

A similar purpose can be served by sheets dittoed with drawings of machines or tools, a wood plane, for example. There are blanks to fill in instead of labels for the various parts, and the student is asked to fill in the name of the part.

Record New Terms

Supply houses are often generous with large advertising calendars. As one more way of enlisting motor memory the student might write on today's date the new technical words learned today. If spelling is a problem the word's trouble spots might be printed in extra-large letters or in color (Ferrerio, 1960, p. 20). Students might also prepare their own calendars to help develop a key word list.

Some teachers suggest that students record words for special study in a vocabulary notebook. They might group them under various classifications: cutting tools, hammering tools, electric tools, and so on.

Flash cards offer another possibility for enlisting "muscular memory." The student prints the term by itself on one side of a 3 × 5 card and writes the meaning on the reverse side. In checking, the student looks at the new term and thinks, "Do I know its meaning?" or, operating the other way, reads the meaning and asks, "Can I supply the new term?"

Play Up "Words of the Week"

A sign with movable letters is displayed before the class (Ruskin, 1966, p. 45). Each week crucially important words are highlighted by spelling them on the sign. The teacher plays up these words in demonstrations and discussions, and they turn up on quizzes. The sign is just one more way to underline for students the importance of building their technical vocabularies.

Point Out the Index for Easy Finding

As already mentioned, some students are allergic to print. They want *spoken* answers and like to get these by leaning on their teacher, asking often, "What does this word mean?" Such questions are an opportunity for the teacher to ask, "Have you tried to find out?" If students start leafing absently through the pages of a book, guide them to the index. Demonstrate its value as an aid to instant finding. If necessary, assist them appropriately as they read the explanation of the term. If the book has a glossary, alert them to its value.

The Dictionary Is a Vital Tool

Classroom dictionaries to which students can turn for unknown general terms should be part of a vocabulary "tool kit." Helping the student *use* this tool is strengthening the power to read and learn independently *for life*.

Some students may be lost when they open the dictionary and find their choice of a number of definitions. Of course they should not select the first one, as many are inclined to do—or the easiest—or the shortest—but they should search out the "best fit" in view of the context. Guided practice tied in with live reading situations is ideal.

Simplified dictionaries should be standard equipment in classrooms where there are deficient readers. What is to be gained if a student deficient in vocabulary looks up *automatic* and finds the meaning *done without volition?* Too often a shabby college-level dictionary which has been knocking around the classroom for years is the only one to which poor readers can turn. For younger and less able readers, elementary and junior high school dictionaries should be within reach. The reader will find student dictionaries discussed and listed in Chapter 2.

ROAD SIGNS FOR READING DIRECTIONS IN TECHNICAL COURSES

Here's how Herbert Pearson, University of Chicago Laboratory School industrial arts teacher, equips his students to read directions—and in the process guides them toward independence.

Examine most textbooks in technical courses, and you will find a "directions explosion." Students are faced with the task of reading directions almost every class period from the first to the last day of the course. Teachers of technical courses everywhere are concerned about upgrading the reading of directions. Surely, improved proficiency should bring immensely important gains for students in more efficient, more productive work sessions.

Reading approaches call for a new look as students begin to study a technical textbook. Perhaps they have never before encountered the rigorous direction pattern now confronting them. Suddenly they must work their way through complicated processes involving many steps. Each step is built on full understanding of preceding steps and must be read with concentrated attention. Attending to the *sequence* of steps may be crucial. Drawings and photos take on critical importance, for each conveys a vital message. As in much scientific writing, readers must often shift their focus from the printed matter to the graphic aids, then back again. Difficult new technical terms come crowding in. Mistaking the term *drilling* for *boring* is costly; it may mean disaster for a student's project.

Perhaps nowhere in all the students' years at school, unless in the science laboratory, has there been occasion to cope with directions so demanding. If they use approaches that have served them in the past—approaches suitable for the broad meanings that characterize much reading matter in English and social studies—the directions may lose them before they have read two or three steps.

In the University of Chicago Laboratory School, the instructor and the reading consultant noted that the direction pattern recurred hundreds of times in the textbook used in the drafting course. They concluded that proficiency in handling this pattern might be developed relatively quickly during the opening weeks of the course. Perhaps together they could work out some practical helps for students.

The guidelines that evolved were printed as "Road Signs for Reading Directions," a three-panel foldout (following this section) that students kept for handy reference in their loose-leaf notebooks.* A sample set of directions from the textbook was reproduced in the center panel; the guidelines appeared on either side. Highway signs SLOW, STOP, and WARNING, in red or yellow, were positioned appropriately, adding page trim and color. As an extra, constant, and powerful stimulus, the Road Signs were abridged, typed on an IBM Executive typewriter, enlarged by a photo blow-up process, then displayed on the wall on a striking 4′ × 10′ "billboard."

Aware that printed materials would not bring results without instruction, reinforcement, and supervised practice, the classroom teacher planned a how-to-read-directions session. On a day when the need for reading directions was *right there and right now*, the instructor gave out the guidelines and talked about them with each class. The students discussed the suggested procedures and took notes right on their foldouts. During the weeks and months that followed, there was reinforcement as needed.

---

* James Bigaj helped Herbert Pearson develop his original guidelines when he was interning as a reading consultant in the University of Chicago Laboratory School. Mr. Bigaj is now Reading Consultant for grades kindergarten through twelve in the Milwaukee Public Schools, Wisconsin.

ROAD SIGNS FOR READING DIRECTIONS
IN DRAFTING

1. **Study** the **title.**
   It clues you in to the type of activity ahead for you.

2. **Pre-read** the **entire procedure** to get the general drift.
   Ask yourself, "What, in general, am I to do?" Now you've set your direction. Now each step in the process takes on meaning. It falls into place in relation to the whole.

3. **Read** the **directions a second time**—step by step—with great care!

   Make a complete stop after reading each step, if necessary, to be sure you understand just what you are to do.
   Thought time is needed in addition to reading time.

   Form a **mental picture** of yourself performing each step.
   Seeing yourself perform the step rivets your attention on the meaning.
   If you read without this visual image, your reading may be passive—with your thoughts worlds away.

   Look up any **technical information** you lack.
   Use the appendix or tables of your textbook.

   "Read" the **photographs** and **drawings.**

   As you read your textbook, you'll find countless references to illustrations.
   These give you instant how-to-do-it insights and save you working time.
   When you are referred to an illustration, shift your attention to the illustration. Read the title—then examine the illustration carefully, noting each label and its corresponding part. When lines, angles, and points are mentioned in the printed matter, locate in the illustration the designated letters and numbers.
   Illustrations often clarify methods and processes every step of the way, show you what to do and what not to do, and provide helpful examples to follow.

4. **Zero in** on amounts, distances, timings, and temperatures. And later make your measurements with precision.

   Quantitative measures flash a warning signal! They're danger spots!

   Reread as often as necessary.

   Note that each step is built on full understanding of preceding steps.

Instructions for (a) and (b):
1. Strike arcs R_1 = radius R (given radius).
2. Draw construction arc parallel to given arc, with center O.
3. Draw construction line parallel to given line.
4. From intersection C, draw CO to get tangent point T_1, and drop perpendicular to given line to get point of tangency T_2.
5. Draw tangent arc R from T_1 to T_2 with center C.

Figure 10–1.   *Reproduced with permission from*
Basic Technical Drawing *by Henry Cecil Spencer, Macmillan Company, New York, 1962.*

5.   Unknown terms say "Stop! Look! Learn!"

A single word left unknown may make it necessary to redo your entire project.

You can have instant access to full information on many technical terms through the index of your textbook. Turn to a trade dictionary to clear up the others.

Make sure you know the meaning of abbreviations and symbols.

LEARN TO HANDLE DIRECTIONS LARGELY ON YOUR OWN.

*463

6. **Add** a last quick **run-through** to **fix** in mind the **procedure** as a whole.

7. **Carry out** each **step** in the order given.

   The order of steps is critical.

   A single error in any step may throw off the rest of the process.

8. If **something** goes **wrong:**

   Reread the procedure and recheck your actions.

9. **No question** should **remain unanswered.**

   If you don't know, don't guess—ask!

PRECISION READING OF DIFFICULT DIRECTIONS IS AN ESSENTIAL TOOL IN TECHNICAL DRAFTING.

Clumsy reading does not pay as you strike out blindly—blunder—then lose time correcting errors and perhaps doing the entire project over. TAKE TIME for precision reading! SAVE TIME when things go right!

Has the "directions drive" proved effective? Following the first session, the instructor observed a tendency to approach directions more carefully, to eliminate unnecessary questions, and to require less supervision. He estimated fifty percent of the students' questions were eliminated before Christmas vacation. The class time invested, he concluded, was not lost—it was saved many times over through more productive class sessions. More of his own time was freed for instructing students in the practical techniques of drafting.

There was no intention to lock students into a rigid procedure. The guidelines were intended to suggest that rigorous directions should be approached with some degree of system, to discourage the impression that a whip-through reading is enough, and to convince students that rereadings are not only expected but desired. Students were encouraged to view the guidelines as tips that would very likely prove helpful.

During the class sessions that followed, students often spread out the foldouts on their drawing tables for reference. As students ran into a snag, the teacher would refer them to an appropriate guideline. The colorful billboard, which daily and hourly *shouted* its message to approach directions carefully, was used constantly with individuals and groups. If a student had read a step in the procedure carelessly, the teacher might point to the tip, "Try to form a mental picture of yourself performing each step." If students had failed to attend to a key term, the teacher would indicate the pointer, "Unknown terms say STOP! LOOK! LEARN! Turn to your index." He often needed to direct attention to "Reread the directions and recheck your actions."

While there is generous help when appropriate, the teacher discourages overdependence. "I don't want to teach mechanical drawing; I want to teach students *how to learn* mechanical drawing." If answers are readily available through reading, students are encouraged to discover these for themselves. "I'm the laziest guy in the class," the teacher tells his classes, smiling. "I *hate* to answer questions." Then by deft questioning, he will stimulate thinking, lead students to eliminate unpromising possibilities, then guide them back to the textbook to search out their own solution. Students take deeper pride, he observes, in on-their-own discoveries than they do in gift-wrapped solutions. (For under-par readers who have difficulty recognizing the words of the directions, special helps are suggested in the preceding section, "Helping Students Learn Technical Vocabulary.")

"I have broader goals," he comments thoughtfully, "than those immediately at hand in drafting. I'm trying to help students work out solutions in school, in working, in living—to help them learn to apply the experiences of others, like those distilled in their textbook, in solving their own problems maturely."

As opportunities arose, this instructor encouraged his students to apply their new techniques to the directions on job sheets, on instruments and tools, and on the labels of containers. He would often drive home their value as he helped a student with a personal project, such as assembling a new bicycle.

As the months passed the teacher observed that his students took out their foldouts less often, yet they continued to approach directions with care. Many who had demonstrated no approach other than helter-skelter reading, then blundering through, now had an effective approach built into their permanent habits.

As the instructor worked on upgrading reading, he did some reflecting about students' basic tools of learning. Technical teachers would not for a moment consider letting students use the *physical* tools of their courses without special training. Their classes are trained with precision to use shapers, milling machines, and lathes. Yet students are often given little guidance in using another tool of learning—their textbooks.

The technical worker will need various competencies for drawing information from the printed page. Highly important among them is skill in reading directions. Students who develop direction-reading expertise are better equipped to succeed in vocational courses, in an apprenticeship, or in technical courses in college; they are better able to meet the reading demands of creative hobbies in the home and to continue their self-education in jobs and careers in the technological world.

The guidelines suggested here are adaptable to directions in other technical courses—woodworking, metal working, machine tool, foundry, welding, printing, carpentry, heating and ventilating, electronics, and others.

A SHOP LIBRARY CAN TURN ON READERS

Herbert Pearson's technical library is often the busiest part of the shop.

You can get a good thing going in a shop or technical classroom library. Students who would not be caught reaching for a book in the school library may reach for one here. Here, each time they come to shop, attractive how-to-do-it books and colorful popular magazines can invite them to *practice* reading.

Picture a turned off reader—yet a student geared up with mechanical interests—walking into this library. Reading in English class was never like this! On a bookshelf is the brightly colored new *Honda Repair and Tune Up Guide*. On display, as in the corner magazine store, are *Popular Mechanics, Mechanix Illustrated, Science and Mechanics, Popular Science,* and others. The shiny cover of one offers a preview of the cars and drivers slated to appear at the Indianapolis speedway. The equally bright cover of another invites the student to build a sailplane from a kit. Inside are plans for building a combination desk and workbench, tips for choosing the right caulking for a boat, suggestions for sprucing up a car to make it worth more at trade-in time. The student sees a pamphlet, "Careers in Technical Occupations," and looks it over. It invites you to check out your abilities and limitations, size yourself up, and perhaps make some plans for *the* job someday. (Lists of free or low-cost pamphlets on vocational opportunities in technical fields are available from the United States Printing Office, Washington, D.C. A list will be mailed on request.)

With the teacher's guidance, the student soon comes to regard the library as a technical know-how center. The doors of the tall cabinet of how-to-do-it books are always open. Books with hundreds of simple diagrams and pictures ease the way to solving in-class (and sometimes out-of-class) problems. There is no period of waiting, no cooling of enthusiasm or drop in interest while running to find a book in the regular school library. The need is right there and right now, and so is the book. Students can reach for *Experiences with Electrons, General Shop for Everyone, Modern Metalworking*, the bright-colored *Chilton's Automobile Repair Manual*. The pamphlets supplied by industry are inviting. One of these, *The ABC's of Hand Tools* (General Motors), clarifies the use and care of small hand tools through Walt Disney drawings. The student may gain a new view of what is between the covers of a book. Answers are right there—in *printed words*.

Through this library, reference skills for reading technical material can be taught *right in shop*, at the time the student is caught up with a problem. In minutes an instructor can teach students to value and use a book's index as an aid to instant finding of what they are looking for. With guidance, students can learn to scan pages rapidly to find their target information. These find-it-yourself procedures will be a built-in part of their learning equipment when confronted with exploding technological advances after schooling is over.

Simple check-out procedures encourage students to practice out-of-class reading. They write their name on the card, then leave the card with the teacher or a student librarian. The loan period is flexible, in keeping with the current project and the demand for the book by others. Books that everyone needs at once do not circulate; they must be read in the library.

The books span a broad range of reading difficulty levels. They are processed in the school library, yet considered a permanent part of the classroom collection. Paperbacks on a variety of technical and practical subjects are available at low cost through the Popular Science Book Club, 44 Hillside Avenue, Manhasset, New York 11030.

Benefits of a Shop Library

Here are some of the benefits a shop library may bring to turned off readers:

1. Their strong interests in shop-related subjects can help remove psychological blocks to reading progress.

2. The world of words has never been their world. Now, for the first time, they may spend many hours in the world of printed words. They meet new words repeatedly in similar and different settings, often with a little increment of meaning with each encounter, and gradually incorporate the words into their vocabulary. Reading practice tends to strengthen comprehension.

3. An impelling interest in a subject may enable students to handle "far too difficult" books and to stretch reading power.

4. As they learn to search out answers for themselves in books, they are better able—through reading—to continue their technical education.

5. The inviting do-it-yourself projects in popular magazines and in books often lead to home hobbies.

6. Young people's self-concepts can be altered when they experience success. Success through and with reading in shop class sometimes helps them succeed better in the broader school situation.

Staggering sums are required to reclaim students who leave the doors of their schools without reading power and without earning power. The sum expended to finance a shop library is an investment in *prevention*.

Bibliography

Derby, Thomas L. "Informal Testing in Vo-Ed Reading." *Journal of Reading*, 18, no. 7 (1975): 541–543.

Frederick, E. Coston. "Reading and Vocational Education." In *Fusing Reading Skills and Content*, edited by H. Alan Robinson and Ellen Lamar Thomas, Newark, Del.: International Reading Association, 1969, pp. 145–150.

Johnston, Joyce D. "The Reading Teacher in the Vocational Classroom." *Journal of Reading*, 18, no. 1 (1974): 27–29.

Robinson, H. Alan. *Teaching Reading and Study Strategies: The Content Areas*. Boston: Allyn and Bacon, 1975, pp. 222–225.

References

El Monte Union High School District. "The Reading Program and Industrial Arts," *Workshop for Reading in the Content Areas*. El Monte, Calif.: El Monte Union High School District, 1966.

Ferrerio, Anthony J. "Try Industrial Arts for Retarded Readers." *Industrial Arts and Vocational Education,* 49, no. 2 (February 1960).

Funk, Gordon. "Reading and Industrial Arts: Interview." *Industrial Arts and Vocational Education,* 50 (October 1961).

Levine, Isidore N. "Solving Reading Problems in Vocational Subjects." *High Points,* 42 (April 1960).

Ruskin, Arnold P. "Teaching Vocabulary in Industrial Arts." *Industrial Arts and Vocational Education,* 55 (February 1966).

Schramm, Howard R. "Helpful Teaching Aids for Industrial Education." *Industrial Arts and Vocational Education,* 48 (October 1954).

TYPEWRITING AND BUSINESS EDUCATION

The reading helps in this section were prepared with Faynelle Haehn, University of Chicago Laboratory school typewriting teacher.

One day a reading consultant asked a typewriting teacher, "What bothers you most about the reading of your students?"

The teacher answered, "They read directions superficially—even my class of particularly bright seniors. It's the major block to their progress in typewriting."

Together the typewriting teacher and the reading consultant examined the frequently missed directions in the textbook, then decided to involve the classes in an intensive directions-reading drive. The methods and materials they developed, including detailed guidelines for students, appear in the first section of this chapter.

Next, they considered the problem of proofreading. Many students, the teacher reported, proofread carelessly or not at all. Techniques for *finding* errors would not be enough. The student must *want* to find them. The two of them researched proofreading techniques, planned some guided lessons, and prepared another set of pointers for students, which is the second section of this chapter.

Last, they turned to developing a reading competency unique to typewriting: the reading of straight copy while typing a passage. They happened upon some research that reported techniques used by world champion typists—then, as a motivator, they incorporated tips from the champions into a third set of pointers for students. You will find these in the last section of this chapter.

Here is the teacher's unsolicited comment: "I like teaching reading. So will you! You will find it one of the most rewarding areas of teaching typewriting."

Business Education Teacher Upgrades Reading Directions

There's a "directions explosion" in business education. The future secretary, typist, file clerk, office manager, operator of office machines, and data processor must grasp countless directions for carrying out a process—often a complicated process involving many steps. Frequently they have only hit-or-miss procedures for this critically important type of reading.

There's a "directions explosion" in the typewriting textbook. In one widely used text more than 1200 directions confront the students. Teachers observe that careless reading of directions is a frequent roadblock to progress in typewriting. Upgrading direction-reading techniques should mean time saved to the last day of the course as students eliminate nonessential questions, require less supervision, and work through practice after practice more accurately and quickly.

The Right Moment to Teach the Reading of Directions

At University High School in Chicago the typewriting teacher capitalizes on the right moment to give instructional guidance:

1. Students return to school those opening days in September with high resolves, "This year I'll do my very best." In a how-to-do-it session shortly after textbooks are distributed, the instructor accents competency in reading directions as a must for success in the course ahead.

2. A classwide catastrophe in practice work brought on by misreading directions may offer the opportune moment.

3. Instruction or reinforcement may be appropriate at a point in the textbook where directions become noticeably more difficult.

4. Reinforcement may be desirable at the stage where the work becomes individualized and students are expected to complete their practice work independently. Now, do-it-yourself techniques become critically important.

Classes Help Develop Guidelines

Concerned that many students used no approach to directions other than haphazard reading, the typewriting teacher and the reading consultant went into action. Together they decided to involve the classes in developing their own guidelines. They planned a lesson in which the students were confronted with rigorous directions for aligning and typing over words, a complicated procedure involving a series of numbered steps. These directions were projected onto a screen before the class with the opaque projector.

The instructor asked each class, "Suppose you wished to follow these directions without a single error and without a word of help or explanation from your teacher. How would you go about reading them?" With their attention focused on how they would read the directions ideally, the students came up with some highly practical pointers. These the teacher recorded in shorthand. The students' suggestions were then combined with the teacher's expertise and the insights of the reading consultant to evolve the final guidelines.

Students Observe Road Signs

The guidelines that follow were printed as a colorful three-panel foldout. Sample directions from the textbook (those for aligning and typing over words) were reproduced in the center panel of the foldout. The guidelines were printed on either side. Highway signs SLOW, STOP, and WARNING, in red and yellow, were positioned appropriately, adding page trim and color. As an added, constant, and powerful stimulus, the guidelines were abridged, typed on an IBM Executive typewriter, enlarged by a photo blow-up process, then displayed on the classroom wall on a striking 4′ × 8′ "billboard." The foldout was kept for reference in the students' own typewriting folders.

How-to-Read-Directions Sessions

Aware that the printed foldout was not likely to mean much to students unless accompanied by instruction, the teacher planned how-to-read-directions ses-

text cont. pg. 477

CAN YOU DO PRECISION READING OF
DIRECTIONS IN YOUR TYPING TEXTBOOK?

1. **Study the title.** ⟶　⟶　⟶　⟶　⟶　⟶

   It quickly orients you. In just a word or two, it clues you in to the type of activity ahead.

2. **Preread the entire procedure.** -- ➤ -- -- ➤ -- -- ➤ -- ➤

   Read it through once over lightly. Ask yourself, "What, in general, am I to do?"

   SLOW

   Now you've set your direction. Now each step in the process takes on meaning. It falls into place in relation to the whole.

3. **Read,** then **carry out each step**—with great care!

   Adjust your speed of reading to the difficulty of the step.

   STOP

   Make a complete **stop,** if necessary, after reading each difficult step, to be sure you understand just what you are to do in carrying out that step.

   Thought time is needed in addition to reading time.

   Are you having difficulty concentrating on a difficult step? It may help to try to form a mental picture of yourself performing the step.

   Seeing yourself perform the step rivets your attention on its meaning —forces you to take in what's being said.

   If you read without trying to form this visual image, your reading may be passive, with your thoughts worlds away.

   Reread as often as necessary. Each step is built on full understanding of preceding steps.

   A single error in any step may throw off the rest of the process.

> Precision reading of difficult directions is an essential tool of learning in typing. It should enable you to work through practices *far more accurately and quickly*. Clumsy reading does not pay as you strike out blindly—blunder—then lose time correcting errors and perhaps doing entire practices over.

Unknown terms say "Stop! Look! Learn!" ═══ ➤ ── ➤ ── ➤ ──

A single word left unknown—an imprecise meaning—may necessitate redoing the entire practice.

You can have instant access to forgotten meanings through the index of your textbook or the diagram of typewriter parts.

Consult your **dictionary,** when necessary, for unfamiliar general terms.

45E: Aligning and Typing Over Words*

LOCATE: Aligning Scale **33**; Variable Line Spacer **3**.

1. **Type** the following sentence but do not make the return:

    I think I can align this copy.

2. **Move** the carriage so the word *think, align,* or *this* is above the scale. Note that a white line points to the center of the letter *i* in the word.

3. **Study** the relation of the top of the scale to the bottom of the letters with down stems.

    It is important for you to· get an eye picture of the exact relation of the typed line to the top of the scale so you will be able to adjust the paper correctly to type over a word with exactness.

4. **Remove** the paper; reinsert it. Gauge the line so the bottoms of the letters are in correct relation to the top of the aligning scale. Operate the variable line spacer **3** if necessary to move the paper forward or backward. Operate the paper release **16** to move the paper to the left or right if necessary when centering the letter *i* over one of the white lines on the scale.

5. **Check** the accuracy of your alignment by setting the ribbon control **22** for stencil position and typing over one of the letters. If necessary, make further alignment adjustments. *Return the ribbon control to typing position.*

6. **Type** over the words *think, align,* and *this* in the sentence, moving the paper forward or backward, to the left or right, as necessary for correct alignment.

7. **Repeat** Steps 1, 3, 4, 5, and 6.

---

* Reprinted with special permission from *20th Century Typewriting* by D. D. Lessenberry, T. James Crawford, and Lawrence W. Erickson. Cincinnati: South-Western Publishing Company, 1967.

◄••••••• **Note warnings.**

In your textbook, italic type is often a "danger flag," a caution against possible errors.

Focus full attention on **drawings** and **diagrams.**

These are quick, vivid, easy-to-grasp—give you instant how-to-do-it insights —save you working time.

They may clarify procedures every step of the way, show you what to do and what not to do.

Far from repeating what the words have already said, they sometimes convey a message words could not possibly express.

Carry out each **step** to the letter—in the order given.

The sequence of steps is critical.

If **something** goes **wrong:**

Reread the procedure and recheck your actions.

LEARN TO HANDLE DIRECTIONS LARGELY ON YOUR OWN. EMPLOYERS LIST "FOLLOW-THROUGH" WITH DIRECTIONS AS ONE OF THE TOP ASSETS OF EMPLOYEES.

sions. There was follow-up then and later as she guided the class through the suggested procedures under supervision.

There was no intention to lock students into a rigid procedure. The guidelines were intended to convey the idea that difficult directions should be approached with system, to discourage the impression that a once-over-lightly reading is enough, to inform students that rereadings are not only expected but desired. Students were encouraged to view the guidelines as tips that were likely to prove helpful, and to use these flexibly, adapting them to the demands of the task before them at the moment.

Has the reading effort proved effective? From the first how-to-read-it session, the instructor observed a tendency to approach directions more carefully, to eliminate careless errors, and to work more independently.

Students Assess Their Own Skill

The Self-Evaluation Checklist for Reading Directions, reproduced below, centered each student's attention on need areas and pointed the way to improvement. The classes had a part in developing this checklist. One day they were asked to think about their own areas of need and each student was to write these down on an index card. From these cards and the discussion that followed, the teacher and the consultant evolved the checklist.

The students evaluated themselves at intervals and filed their checklists in their folders. The instructor evaluated the student's competency on an accompanying scale and discussed with individuals any marked disparity between a student's evaluation and that of the teacher. Each student set as a personal goal the rating she or he hoped to attain on the next evaluation. The teacher was alert for the first signs of progress and accorded these recognition and praise. Improvement was reflected in grading.

Students Zero in on Directions

The directions in the textbook, the teacher noted, appear in a variety of types, sizes, and colors. Some of these directions are simple and present no reading problems. Nonetheless, they are frequently missed, often through carelessness and oversight.

Students were asked to search selected pages of their textbook with these questions in mind: "How do the authors focus your attention on exactly what you are to do? Do they catch your eye through the type and the size of the print? Through the use of color? By other means?" Students were quick to spot in their particular textbook the following types of attention catchers: marginal

text cont. pg. 480

SELF-EVALUATION CHECKLIST FOR
READING DIRECTIONS

NAME   PERIOD   DATE

This checklist is intended to focus your attention on any need areas and point the way to improvement. Your teacher, too, will evaluate you.

Consider how you stand on each of the points below, then rate yourself from 0 to 10 in the space before the numeral. A score of 0 means you never do this; a score of 10 means you have mastered the point and do it consistently.

Points to consider

_____ 1. Do you focus full attention on directions in whatever format you find them—numbered lists, brief directions in the margin, directions inserted right into the copy, and so on?

_____ 2. At the end of an especially difficult step, do you stop, reflect, and reread, if necessary, to make sure you understand just what you are to do?

_____ 3. Do you make sure you understand the meaning of unfamiliar key terms?

_____ 4. Do you examine photographs and drawings?

_____ 5. Are you moving in the direction of independence in handling directions largely on your own?

_____ 6. Are you gradually eliminating errors due to superficial reading of directions?

_____ 7. Are you less and less often having to redo practices because of superficial reading?

Now that you have considered your specific strengths and weaknesses, give yourself a general rating by placing a single check at the appropriate point on the scale below.

Your own general evaluation

Your teacher's evaluation

Set your own goals

What general rating do you hope to attain before the next evaluation? Place numeral here: _____.

directions in eye-catching red, red italics inserted right into the copy, headings in boldface type, black italics specifying line length and spacing, boldface terms that signal warnings, instructions boxed off in black lines.

The different formats for directions were then illustrated on a wall poster with the heading "Zero In on Directions—Wherever You Find Them." Full textbook pages illustrating various ways the author calls attention to directions were displayed on the poster. Each type of attention-catcher was conspicuously labelled in the margin of the poster. A vivid red cord led from the label to the sample direction. Daily this placard sounded an alert.

Teacher Projects an "Aid-less" Page

To dramatize the value of aids for grasping directions provided them in their textbooks, the teacher projected on a screen before the class a page with all these aids opaqued with white correction fluid. *Missing* from the page were the marginal directions in color, boldface type, numerals indicating a series of steps, boldface headings that give directions, directions inserted into the copy to be typed, and drawings clarifying exactly what to do.

The class was encouraged to react to this "aid-less" page. One student commented: "It isn't friendly. It doesn't talk to you. It doesn't come to help you. You have to fight with it to pull out what it wants you to do. You have to tussle with it."

When, in contrast, a page complete with all of these aids was later flashed upon the screen, the students had a new appreciation for the help these aids had to offer. They realized that typographical and other helps they had sometimes overlooked were clearly important and would merit their close attention.

How-to-Do-It Insights from Drawings

The teacher also projected on the screen directions from the textbook *with* a drawing showing how to reach for the letter *t* (see Figure 11–1), followed by the same directions from which the drawing had been removed with white correction fluid. She commented, "It may cost publishers several times as much to reproduce a drawing as it does to use regular type. If you don't notice the drawing, this money's lost. Why do they go to all this expense?"

One student reacted: "You quickly see *exactly* how to reach for the *t*. It would take a good many words to tell you just how to hold your wrist and fingers, and even then the words couldn't possibly tell you as well as the picture."

REACH TECHNIQUE FOR T

Reach the *left first finger* to **t** without arching the wrist or moving the hand forward.

```
tt tf tf tt ftf tf tt ftf

tf the flat the left that
```

Figure 11–1.　*An important drawing. (Reproduced with special permission from* 20th Century Typewriting *by D. D. Lessenberry, T. James Crawford, and Lawrence W. Erickson. Cincinnati: South-Western Publishing Company, 1967, p. 8.)*

Students Build "Bank Accounts"

Progress was dramatized through "bank accounts" of points. Students started with a "deposit" of one hundred "direction points." They might increase this deposit by following accurately an exceptionally challenging set of directions. If they succeeded in following these without an error, they "deposited" ten points to their account. For each error in following directions, one point was deducted from the "deposit." An impressive "bank balance" at the end of a marking period was reflected in the student's grade.

It should be added that the points penalty is not invoked until the student is oriented to difficult new practice work. With business letters, for example, there are no deductions before the students' third experience.

Dividends from the Directions Drive

Students were quick to note certain plus values as they sharpened their directions-reading skills:

1. More of their practice exercises were going right the first time, not the second, third, or fourth.

2. They were saving many hours of working time as they eliminated errors and typed fewer practices over.

3. On occasions when the work was individualized, they were more productive.

4. Their stepped-up proficiency was bringing an improvement in their grades in typewriting.

5. They were acquiring an asset vital in many careers: the ability to read and grasp directions and to follow through.

The dividends are high. As the year progresses, there is less page trim in red pencil. Students less often lean on the teacher and ask nonessential questions. The time spent in the directions drive has been saved many times over through more efficient, more productive class sessions.

Pointers on Proofreading

Not just the business education student but the writer of papers for any course is constantly called upon to proofread. Yet seldom do students have on call highly skilled proofreading techniques. The following pointers, addressed directly to students, are intended to supplement classroom instruction.

WHAT IS YOUR P.Q.?
Detect Your Errors with Near-Perfect Accuracy

"When I got that paper back, four errors were marked," the student bewails, "and I should have found every one of them myself!"

What is *your* Proofreading Quotient? Do your papers come back with page trim in red pencil indicating errors you yourself could easily have eliminated? Here are twelve tips to send your P.Q. soaring.* You can put these to work for instant error reduction. With effort and persistence you can advance toward perfect accuracy in error-detection—the standard of business. When only an occasional error remains undetected, you've attained a near-genius P.Q.

At present you're concerned with turning out perfect assignments for your class in typewriting, for themes and research papers for courses at school, or for your own personal typewriting. Later on, you'll find your sharpened proofreading techniques are a definite plus whatever your role in the business or professional world.

DO *regard proofreading as productive*

Some students regard proofreading as a nonproductive aspect of typewriting —they feel a compulsion to hurry through it to get on with more result-producing work.† But what phase of your work is more result-producing than proofreading? It can transform a "not-so-perfect" product into one that's letter-perfect—turn a product that would have produced a negative reaction into one you can be proud of. Certainly proofreading should be regarded as a highly important, time- and effort-consuming aspect of your course in typewriting—one which will be richly rewarded.

DO *assume your paper is* "guilty" *of errors*

Overconfidence can undermine a potentially high P.Q. One expert offers this suggestion: "A transcript should be assumed guilty of errors until it is proved innocent. Errors creep into one's work unknowingly and must be ferreted out."‡

---

* Prepared by Ellen Lamar Thomas and Faynelle Haehn, University of Chicago Laboratory School typewriting teacher. Before Miss Haehn revealed the twelve tips, she involved her classes by having them try to predict what these tips would be. The twelve tips were later taped under transparent plastic on each student's desk, reminding him each day to "watch your P.Q."

† Alan C. Lloyd, "Let's Make Proofreading Affirmative," *Business Education World*, 30 (March 1950): 335.

‡ Leroy A. Brendel, "Yes, They Proofread IF—" *Journal of Business Education*, 29 (March 1954): 242.

DO *give proofreading "prime time"*

How often students proofread in haste the last few seconds of the class period, then tear the page from the typewriter with a relieved "That's done!" Or postpone proofreading a major paper until late the night before the deadline or even the last brief moments before they rush to class.

Clearly, proofreading merits "prime time" and unhurried time. Your P.Q. is upward-bound when you deliberately allot time for proofreading as you schedule your activities in a class period in typewriting or budget your study time for writing an important paper at home.

Ideally, important projects should have an additional check some time later. If a time interval elapses between your typing and the final checking, you'll return to your manuscript with mind and eye refreshed. This will help you ferret out those last, elusive errors. Allowing an important paper to lie untouched overnight should help freshen your eye for errors.

DO *proofread with close attention*

One writer refers to a "sixth sense" that may attract the eye to that "something is wrong spot" on the copy.[*] Experienced proofreaders, however, do not trust this mystical sixth sense. On the contrary, they observe in themselves and in others a dangerous wishful-thinking tendency, a seeing-what-you-want-to-see inclination. The eye, they note, has a way of passing over the lines of typescript and seeing what the *mind wishes were there* instead of what the fingers have actually put there.[†] This tendency is particularly strong with words that are "look alikes," such as *that* and *than, now* and *not, it* and *in, ever* and *even, yet* and *yes.*

DO *proofread once for thought conveyance*

At minimum, proofreading to detect errors requires two readings: first for the meaning of the passage, second for the mechanics. And, in copy of special importance, proofreading may extend to several readings, each performed with a particular purpose in mind.[‡]

Proofread one time through with your attention focused on catching errors *in conveying the meaning precisely as was intended.* Do you have a superior P.Q. for catching meaning errors? Some of these are highly elusive. The following checklist should alert you to possible errors.

1. Have you repeated words? Substituted words? Transposed words? Transposed lines?

2. Have you omitted a word or a phrase? Used a sentence fragment?

---

[*] Brendel, 1954, p. 242.

[†] Lloyd, 1950, p. 335.

[‡] Leroy A. Brendel, "Pinpointing Critical Areas of Proofreading," *Business Education World,* 47 (November-December 1966): 18.

3. Have you omitted a letter and, in so doing, altered a word's meaning?

4. Have you omitted a paragraph or an entire section?

5. Have you been misled by a sound-alike—a word that sounds like the correct one but means something different (e.g., *effect* for *affect*)?

6. Have you altered the intended meaning through an error in punctuation?

7. In the light of the meaning, are there errors in the use of capital letters?

8. Are there errors in the agreement of verbs with their subjects? Pronouns with their antecedents?

9. Is there any break in the continuity of thought content from one page to the next? As you removed one page from the typewriter and started the next, have you repeated the last word on the page or omitted a word?

This is the time to *tune out* your attention to mechanical errors and *tune in* your attention to errors in the meaning. Conversely, during the next step, when you want to concentrate on the details of mechanics, do not let yourself become caught up and diverted by the "story."

DO detect errors before your paper is removed from the typewriter

It should be your standard operating procedure to try to catch *every error* before your paper is removed from the machine. This saves you all the time and bother of having to reinsert and realign your paper.

To proofread for errors in thought conveyance (and placement), keep the full page exposed to your view. To detect errors in the content, you may require considerable sweep of meaning.

To proofread for mechanical errors, roll the copy back to the top line. A trade secret of some expert proofreaders is to follow each typewritten line with a pencil along the paper bail, moving the copy up one line at a time. Make a very light check in the margin of the line that contains the error, and correct all your errors as soon as you have finished checking.*

DO zero in on individual letters

When you do your ordinary reading for information and enjoyment, you sweep up many of the words as wholes. All you need do to recognize many familiar words is to glance at just part of the word. While highly desirable in ordinary reading, this whole-word response makes you error-prone in proofreading. Habituated for years to pick up words as units, you are likely to overlook such errors as *gound* (for *ground*), *dont* (for *don't*), *explian* (for *explain*), and *aud* (for *and*).†

---

* Brendel, 1966, p. 18.

† Joseph Lasky, *Proofreading and Copy-Preparation: A Textbook for the Graphic Arts Industry* (New York: Mentor Press, 1941), p. 75.

Joseph Lasky, author of a classic how-to-do-it book for proofreaders in the graphic arts industry,* underscored this suggestion: "The average reader reads the word *furnshing*, sees it as a complete word picture, and is unlikely to notice the absence of the letter *i* between the *n* and *s*. As you proofread the word *furnshing*, read each separate letter. When you read the word mentally, letter by letter, *f-u-r-n-s-h-i-n-g*, you thereby instantly note the omission of the letter *i*.

"The average reader reads the word *asssistant*, responds to the word as a unit, and may be completely oblivious to the extra *s*. Read the word mentally, letter by letter, *a-s-s-s-i-s-t-a-n-t*. When you read each separate letter, the extra *s* between the *a* and the *i* becomes glaringly conspicuous." Lasky calls the error in which a letter is unintentionally doubled a "doublet." He notes that this is one of the most treacherous of errors and that even professional proofreaders overlook this type of error constantly.

He goes on, "The person reading normally may not notice anything amiss with *superoirity*. Attack it letter by letter to read it *s-u-p-e-r-o-i-r-i-t-y*. The transposed *i* and *o* are now observed with ease."

So crucially important is this letter focus, Lasky asserted, that professional proofreaders have a technical term for it. They refer to it as *focus of attention* and define it as *focusing the mental attention on the separate letters of a word simultaneously with visual concentration.*

He observed, "Focus of attention is vitally necessary. It is impossible to attain accuracy in proofreading unless one learns to synchronize the focusing of the eyes with the focusing of the attention."

Obviously, letter focus involves a drastic departure from lifelong reading habits; it calls for a constant struggle to resist the habitual whole-word response. To retard the rapid sweeping up of whole words, some students find it helpful to move the blunt end of a pencil or pen along slowly under each word.†

Won't focusing on each letter be unduly time consuming? With practice, you'll learn to read letter by letter very quickly.

Summing it all up: Zero in on letters. Don't be a half-glancer. There may be an error lurking in the part of the word you barely glanced at.

DO reduce your reading speed if necessary

As you do your ordinary reading in books at home or at school you often race along, lost in the meaning of what you are reading, hardly conscious of the words or sentences. Your purpose is information or enjoyment. As you do proofreading, you direct your attention to every letter, every punctuation mark, every capital, every space. Your purpose is no longer getting meaning —it's *detecting errors.*

---

* The suggestions for students on *focus of attention* have been adapted from Lasky, *Proofreading and Copy-Preparation*, pp. 75–76.

† Robert L. Coard, "Proofread, Proofread, Proofread!" *Journal of Business Education*, 33 (October 1957), p. 21.

For years you may have done your ordinary reading from 250 to 400 words per minute. Long habituated to this more rapid reading, you may now feel the pull of a "runaway" reading rate in proofreading.

The ideal toward which every proofreader should strive, Lasky observed, is *absolute accuracy* in reading performed in the *shortest amount of time*. The paramount consideration, he underscored, is *accuracy*.*

Too many slip-ups? Perhaps you need to put a brake on speed. This will call for conscious effort.

DO *proceed with caution when checking numbers*

Errors in a sequence of numbers may easily escape your glance. It is imperative to check each numeral with the corresponding number in the original copy.

DO *turn concentration into speed*

Vigorous concentration helps you spot errors instantly. Lasky offers this suggestion: "If you are not positive that you have actually taken in every word—every letter—every punctuation mark on which your eyes have focused, stop at once and read them over again. You may fail to see conspicuous errors if while looking directly at them, you are subconsciously thinking of possible errors you may have overlooked in the preceding line. Reread to remove this subconscious worry. Now you can concentrate all your attention on the 'current' copy."†

Better still, avoid the necessity for frequent rereading. Try to develop "miss-proof" concentration.

DO *have the mechanics of English at your command*

A dictionary and a handbook of English usage should be conveniently at hand whenever you proofread. *But the less often you must consult these, the better.*

You can turn a command of English into high-speed proofreading. When you have, on instant call, the rules of spelling, punctuation, capitalization, word division, you will not have to stop and verify a doubtful point. The more you know and the surer you are that you know, the speedier you will become. ‡

DO *turn your errors into improvement*

Making occasional errors is natural. Excessive worry over these is unproductive. One expert gave this counsel: "Accuracy in typewriting is primarily

---

* Lasky, 1941, p. 78.

† Lasky, 1941, p. 78.

‡ Lasky, 1941, p. 79.

knowing what words to be careful of. When you proofread painstakingly, you discover many of the tricky words and pitfalls; and, having discovered them, you can work to dispose of them. Practice in extremely careful proofreading is just about the best practice possible in improving typewriting accuracy, and it is not uncommon to find that the best proofreaders are also the most accurate typists."*

You can eliminate errors, then, when you analyze them with questions like these in mind: "What error-demons should I look out for? What are my need areas? What kind of practice will benefit me most?"

You can turn your errors into assets if you regard each error as a clue pointing the way to improvement.

In Summing Up
1. DO regard proofreading as productive.
2. DO assume that your paper is "guilty" of errors.
3. DO give proofreading "prime time."
4. DO proofread with close attention.
5. DO proofread once for thought conveyance.
6. DO detect errors before your paper is removed from the typewriter.
7. DO zero in on individual letters.
8. DO reduce your reading speed if necessary.
9. DO proceed with caution when checking numbers.
10. DO turn concentration into speed.
11. DO have the mechanics of English on instant call.
12. DO turn your errors into improvement.

---

* Brendel, 47, p. 18.

Suggestions for Reading Copy

Reading straight copy while typing a passage from the textbook is drastically different from ordinary reading. The following suggestions, written for students, help them acquire this specialized skill.

DEVELOP PROFICIENCY PLUS IN READING COPY
Eliminate Errors in Reading Straight Copy for Typewriting

Why not develop proficiency *plus* in reading copy? Sharpen your copyreading techniques, and you've taken a long step in the direction of error-free typewriting. Clumsy copyreading does not pay, as you may bungle practice work, then lose valuable time correcting errors and perhaps typing entire practices over. Five- and ten-minute straight copy typing tests are required of many job applicants. You may want highly skilled copyreading techniques for getting THE job someday.

You may be thinking, "I'm already a good reader." But reading straight copy from your typewriting textbook calls for some *new, drastically different, and highly specialized procedures.* As you do your ordinary reading, you're often completely lost in the meaning—swept across the lines and pages by interest—scarcely conscious of words or sentences. Your objective here is information or enjoyment. But as you read straight copy in typewriting, your purpose is different. You're transferring what you read letter by letter, punctuation mark by punctuation mark, and space by space from the copy in your textbook to the sheet of paper you've inserted in your typewriter. Your eyes grasp the words and letters—your nerve impulses flash the signals—your finger movements make the transfer. Your purpose is no longer getting meaning; it's reproducing symbols.

What habits and techniques of reading are important in reading straight copy for typewriting?

A doctoral student at Harvard University researched copyreading techniques.* Among his subjects were winners of the coveted title of World's Champion Typist. How did world champions read copy while attaining their fantastic speeds? Did they read it rapidly or slowly? eyes on the immediate copy or far ahead? taking in words by parts or wholes? with or without attention to what the page was saying?

The eleven *do's* for you that follow are based primarily on the conclusions of this Harvard researcher. Why not get the techniques of world champions going for you in your own day-to-day reading of copy?†

---

* The writers have based many of the suggestions in this section of the chapter on the findings reported by Robert C. Fuller in his doctoral dissertation, "Reading Factors in Typewriting," completed at Harvard University and published by Oklahoma A. and M. College, Stillwater, in 1945.

† Faynelle Haehn is a University of Chicago Laboratory typewriting teacher. Before Miss Haehn revealed the eleven tips based on the techniques of world champions, she involved the classes by asking them to see if they could predict what these tips would be. The eleven tips were later taped on each student's desk under transparent plastic.

DO extremely close, attentive reading

Close, attentive reading is a number-one aid. You're on your way to skilled copyreading when you zero in on details: letter sequences, number sequences, punctuation, capitalization, spacing, paragraphing.

DO move your eyes across the line without backward eye jumps

Keep your eyes advancing as consistently as possible in a left-to-right direction. This should help you develop continuity and a flowing performance. Full concentration should help you do this. When your thoughts don't stray from the copy, you'll need few backward eye jumps to see if you overlooked a word or made some other error. A backward glance occasionally, however, may be unavoidable to check on some detail.

DO cling with your eyes to the immediate copy

Shifting your eyes away from the copy results in wasteful pauses. You may become disoriented because you've lost your place. And when you find your place again by holding a certain word in mind, you may pick up the same word but in a later line, omitting everything in between.

You'll need to make exceptions to the practice of keeping your eyes on the copy during the initial stages of learning to type. At that stage, you're expected to use your eyes to guide your hands and fingers. Later on, when your kinesthetic sense takes over, only an occasional glance away from the copy will be called for.

DO NOT read ahead of the point necessary to supply copy to your fingers

Students are sometimes urged to expand their "eye stretch" in typewriting to take in four or five words at a single glance. This advice, however, doesn't seem to stand up. High-speed typists do not appear to take large eyefuls. A contestant who walked away not once but many times with the title of World's Champion Typist submitted to tests that filmed eye movement. The film revealed that he was attaining his lightning speeds while taking in only a fraction (*just seven-tenths*) of a word at a glance.

Do not read in advance of the place necessary to supply copy to your fingers as it is needed. When your eyes sweep too far ahead and overreach the task at hand, new material may capture your attention. You may pick up words and punctuation glimpsed a sentence or two later on and find that these have intruded, unwanted, into your present copy.

How far should your eye outpace your fingers? One researcher reported a probable tendency for the eye to outdistance the hand by one second. In terms of spaces, the distance ahead varies, of course, with speed. In typing 40 words a minute, the eye probably travels about 3½ strokes ahead of the hand; in typing 20 words per minute, 1⅔ strokes; 30 wpm, 2½ strokes; 50 wpm, 4⅙ strokes; 60 wpm, 5 strokes; 100 wpm, 8⅓ strokes.*

Summing up: Let your eyes take in no more than a word or two (about a second's typing speed) in advance of the word you're typing.†

DO zero in on parts of longer, less familiar words

You'll read, spell, and typewrite *boy* without much conscious effort. On the other hand, you'll need to attack longer, less familiar words by giving full attention to letters and letter groups. You'll find this to be good practice even when you're an advanced typist. According to the Harvard study, the eyes of the world's champion followed word detail.

Do you sometimes add an extra letter? An extra syllable? Omit a letter? Use the wrong word ending? Errors like these may result from imprecise reading. To eliminate them, form a mental image of the sequence of letters. Break the word down into its natural divisions. You can attack compound words like *nonetheless* and *bookkeeping* by breaking them into their component parts. Other words you can attack part by part: *un-dip-lo-mat-i-cal-ly.*

Three stages of learning

You may have observed that the way you read copy and the way you type it are closely related.‡ In the early stages of learning to type, you see, think, and type letter by letter. This is called the "stroke response." On this, the lowest level, you attend to the letters of even the simplest words in the copy, and you type these a stroke at a time.

As you advance, you come to see, think, and type the word as a unit rather than letter by letter. This is the word recognition level, appropriate for short, easy words.

You'll find yourself shifting from one of these responses to another within a word, within a line, or within a sentence. This is the "combination response," in which you see, think and type some sequences letter by letter, others part by part or word by word, and still others word group by word group.

In the "combination response," you're recognizing and responding appropriately to word parts or words of varying difficulty. For short, easy parts or words you're making automatic responses. For unfamiliar or difficult parts or words, you're giving full attention to letters or groups of letters, and stroking

---

* Fuller, *Reading Factors in Typewriting,* 1945, p. 97.

† D. D. Lessenberry, T. James Crawford, and Lawrence W. Erickson, *Teacher's Manual for 20th-Century Typewriting* (Cincinnati: South-Western Publishing Company, 1967), p. 22.

‡ The entire explanation of the interrelationship between the way copy is read and the way it is typed is drawn, with special permission, from page 25 of *Teacher's Manual for 20th-Century Typewriting* by Lessenberry, Crawford, and Erickson.

accordingly. You're typing long words by the stroke response or by a combination of stroke and syllable response. Listen to the performance of any expert typist and you'll hear these patterns in operation. Ultimately, shifting from one response to another becomes automatic.

DO proceed with caution with word centers—they're danger spots!

Word centers flash a bright red warning signal. Many of the so-called mechanical errors in typewriting appear to involve letters at or near the *centers* of words. There's a tendency in reading to sweep up a word as a unit and to overlook the sequence of letters near the center. Signals for beginnings and endings often come through loud and clear to the typist. Not so with centers. The syllable most frequently missed in typing the word *pronunciation* or *repetition,* for example, is an inner syllable (pro*nun*ciation, rep*e*tition).

Don't be a "half-glancer" at long or difficult words. Zero in on letters or letter-groups in their centers.

DO resist getting lost in the meaning

Reproducing symbols is your purpose as you read copy, not reading for meaning. Nonetheless, until you develop automatic typing habits, it seems good to grasp sufficient meaning so that the sense helps carry the line forward. Give enough attention to the content so that the right words seem to chain together and the sense helps you reproduce them in the correct order. Skipping words or word-groups, even whole sentences, may result from reading along while completely oblivious to the meaning.

Once you develop automatic typing habits, however, you'll probably give slight attention to the content of straight copy. You are concerned primarily with word detail instead of meaning. Fast, accurate typists are often unable to tell you the theme of a timed practice they have just finished typing. They copy foreign words with impressive speed and accuracy without the slightest conception of what they mean.

DO resist becoming absorbed in what the page is saying

When the copy becomes *too* interesting and your thoughts are deflected away from word detail, an error-making tendency results. Caught up in the content, you may lose conscious control. When this happens, refocus your attention and continue under conscious control.

DO expect to reduce your speed for numbers

Even professional typists, unless they are statistical typists, do not attain the high speed with numbers that they do with the alphabet. *Expect* to slow down for numbers. Making those longer reaches to the top row takes time!

A "reachable" goal for a student is being able to type number and symbol copy at least half as fast as your straight copy speed.

Here's a tip for a long sequence of numbers. Read the numbers within the series as you do syllables within a word. Take eyefuls of groups of two or three numbers at a time. If commas are present (as in the sequence 97,281,645), the comma breaks should serve as the dividers.

One observer commented, "Whether we like it or not, we have become a generation of numbers. We eat, sleep, and live using all forms of numbers and symbols. As our society progresses toward an even higher level of technical achievement, we can assume that our lives will become even more influenced by the use of numbers and special characters."*

DO *bring your reading rate down to your typing rate*

Someone may be thinking, "Perhaps if I just read faster, I'll increase my speed in typing." Actually, far more frequently it is advisable to *put a brake on speed* of reading.

Perhaps you can *type* approximately 50 words a minute, while for years you have *read* from 250 to 400 words a minute. Your eyes may tend to race ahead of your fingers. Top-speed readers may have a special problem. While their fingers are copying from one line, their eyes may be a line or more ahead. Transposition errors may result. The tendency to speed along more rapidly than one can type also leads to errors as you lose your place in the copy.

In the case of extremely slow readers, errors may occur as a result of reading too slowly. The average student, however, will need to read straight copy far more slowly than ordinary reading. *Adjusting your reading rate downward may call for conscious effort.*†

DO *develop concentration*

Never allow your mind to wander from the copy you are typing. Wavering even for an instant may make you make errors.‡

Copyreaders who are not "with it," type words out of place, omit important words, reverse the order of words and letters—even insert words that are in their minds instead of in the copy! When you turn off helter-skelter thoughts and turn on vigorous concentration, you should work through practice after practice more accurately and quickly.

---

* Glen L. Boyer, "Develop a Positive Attitude to Number and Symbol Typing," *Business Education World*, 49 (December 1968): 19.

† Fred C. Cook, "Perfect Typing Every Time," *Business Education World*, 49 (October 1968): 20.

‡ Richard D. Featheringham, "Principles for Producing Master Typists," *The Balance Sheet*, 47, no. 7 (March 1966): 299–300.

In Summing Up

1. DO extremely close, attentive reading.
2. DO move your eyes across the line without backward eye jumps.
3. DO cling with your eyes to the immediate copy.
4. DO NOT read ahead of the point necessary to supply copy to your fingers.
5. DO zero in on parts of longer, less familiar words.
6. DO proceed with caution with word centers. They're danger spots!
7. DO resist getting lost in the meaning.
8. DO expect to reduce your speed for numbers.
9. DO bring your reading rate down to your typing rate.
10. DO develop concentration.

FOREIGN LANGUAGES

This chapter was developed with the help of
Milton Finstein, former University of Chicago
Laboratory School French teacher, and Emma
LaPorte, former Spanish teacher, New Trier
High School, Winnetka, Illinois.

One day a French teacher had a rather frustrating experience with his class. As an assignment, the students had been asked to read a passage in French about the province, La Bretagne. Most of them had dutifully decoded the words, but they had not *read* the selection. In the discussion that morning they showed little grasp of the meaning.

Are there effective ways, the teacher asked himself, to divert attention from merely decoding words and center it on meaning? What about well established techniques for improving comprehension in reading English? Why not apply these to comprehension in a foreign language? Perhaps the school's reading consultant might have some suggestions. A team effort of classroom teacher and consultant resulted. The methods they found effective are shared in this chapter.

First, they turned their attention to reading readiness. The procedures they worked out to make students *ready* to grasp meanings are offered in the first section of this chapter.

Then they considered the question, "Are there techniques for learning

English vocabulary which should promote vocabulary accretion in a foreign language?" The methods they found effective are incorporated in the second section, which contains some comprehensive vocabulary guidesheets directed to students.

Next, they examined the question, "Just how can a student derive a word's meaning from the context?" A miscellany of specific helps resulted—the third section in this chapter.

Turning once more to helping students grasp the meaning of a passage, they adapted the widely known PQRST approach, a cluster of techniques for upgrading comprehension in English. This approach is detailed in some student guidesheets in the fourth section of this chapter.

The writers are indebted to Emma LaPorte, versatile linguist and teacher, for her help in broadening the application of this chapter to languages other than French, and for the many lively examples from her classes.

What about "Reading Readiness" to Upgrade Comprehension?

Students can be made ready to focus on the meaning of a passage.

A student studying a foreign language looks up from the text and exclaims, "I've read it, but I don't know what I've read!" He or she has worked meticulously through the selection, pored over the vocabulary section, studied each verb ending dutifully—attended to everything *except the meaning*.

What about reading readiness to help the student concentrate on the thought of the passage? Highly effective in motivating English reading, creating readiness may be even more vital with students facing the obstacle course of foreign language reading. Among other components,* reading readiness involves interest caught up beforehand—anticipation—zest for the reading.

When readiness is created through interest, foreign language students will be more intent on grasping the meaning behind the words. As extra dividends, the interest pull may tend to increase their speed, and a rigorous passage should seem less forbidding to students.

In this section you will find a dozen possibilities for creating interest readi-

---

* According to the literature on teaching reading in the English language, creating reading readiness for each assignment involves, in addition to creating interest, the following: providing background experience or relating the assignment to the student's experience, preparing the student to cope with the vocabulary of the selection, helping the student read with purpose, and helping the student know how to read to accomplish this purpose.

ness. They are offered with the thought that the creative teacher will find them suggestive, improve on them, and increase and multiply them. In classes where English is not spoken, it is possible to create this readiness using the second language.

Give Assignment-Making Prime Time

How many assignments will a teacher make in a lifetime? Perhaps two or three a week to each of five classes, for thirty-six weeks of the year, for thirty years or so of teaching. This adds up to 25,000 assignments! And how many hours will students spend at work on these assignments? The total is now astronomical!

"I want these hours well spent," comments a Spanish teacher, "so I give making the assignment unhurried prime time during class period. I find that a good send-off on each assignment upgrades the quality of study during the many hours students spend over their Spanish alone."

Search the Assignment for Interest-Catching Content

Pull out in advance an arresting bit of information, a believe-it-or-not statement, a dramatic situation.

During your own school days you may have read about the Visigoths in Caesar's *Commentaries on the Gallic Wars* with something less than compelling enthusiasm. Catherine Hughes, a Latin teacher, told how she turned on her classes:

> It takes four days to create a feeling of "hail fellow well met" for Caesar. I raise exciting questions: "Why did Caesar *have* to win spectacular glory—*desperately* want and need to become the idol of the people?"
>
> "When winter came and the army went into winter quarters, why did this great soldier turn to writing? How did his destiny, indeed *Rome's* destiny, hinge on these writings?"
>
> "If it had not been for Julius Caesar, how might your life today be different?"

It took just moments for this French teacher to stir interest in reading a passage in French about the Louvre:

> When you go to Paris, you won't want to miss the Louvre. You'll find eight full miles of galleries—more than a quarter

of a million prized works of art! When you come to class to-morrow, can you tell us some of the fabulous art works you'll see there?

Ask Preliminary Purpose-Questions

"Read the next chapter in *José*" is one possible way of making a Spanish assignment for tomorrow. Students may drudge through the passage, their highest motivation being to get the reading over with. Contrast this reading with that of the student who approaches the chapter with interest catching purpose-questions:

> In your reading in *José* for tomorrow, Elisa will face a problem of parental control. She's unwilling to marry the man her mother has chosen and strictly forbidden to marry the one she loves. Disinhcritance is the custom when a daughter defies her parents. Is there hope for Elisa's marriage to her favorite? A legal loophole? Compare her circumstances with the freedom of young people today. Would Elisa face this problem if she were living here today?

One teacher whose students were reading the epic *Araucana* took on the class in a debate:

> For tomorrow you'll be reading how the conquistadores enslaved the Incas and put to death their great chief Atahualpa. Which side was in the right? Tomorrow I'll take the side of the conquistadores. *You* come prepared to plead the case of the Incas. Look for evidence in your reading that the Incas were grievously wronged.

Reading becomes an active search for debate points rather than a passive translating of words.

A Latin teacher assigning Aeneas' visit to Dido's palace asks this question:

> Now Aeneas is a dashing widower and Queen Dido, a charming widow. In your reading, you'll find Dido inviting Aeneas to a banquet at her palace. How does it come about that after this meeting—this *one* meeting—Dido is deeply, hopelessly in love? Was it just love at first sight? Or was there something more?

Interest caught up, the students now read *anticipating meaning*. They discover that Aeneas fancied that the young lad holding his hand as he strolled to the palace was his son Ascanius. Actually it was Cupid, tagging along in disguise. At the banquet Cupid ensconced himself in Queen Dido's lap and from this vantage point left love arrows deep in her heart (Hughes).

Foreign language teachers will be interested in the effect of preliminary questions on comprehension when students are reading in English. In a study with 1,456 students, the effectiveness of accompanying reading with questions versus assigning it without questions was explored (Washburne, 1929). Providing questions brought decided gains in comprehension. Where should the questions be placed? This, too, was explored. Two placements proved effective: before the entire selection or before the part of the selection in which the question was answered.

Niles (1963) had this to say of purpose-questions: "Asked *before* students read . . . , such a question should help *develop* comprehension. If the same question were not asked until *after* students had read the passage [unless the students return to the passage and analyze it], comprehension would be *tested* but not developed.

Unless practice on skimming is the intention, preliminary questions should be sufficiently broad to require a grasp of the essential content. If the questions demand only directly stated details, students may skim for bits and pieces and bypass important content.

Make a Striking Statement

Instead of, "For tomorrow read the selection on Napoleon," a teacher might distribute two dittoed statements: one lauding Napoleon extravagantly, the other condemning him as one of the arch-villains of history. Students are to find data supporting each of these views: "He was one of the most worshipped and one of the most despised men in history. Read to find out why and what *you* think of him."

Instead of, "For your assignment, read about Niobe," a Latin teacher might suggest, "A waterfall on Mt. Sipylus in Greece is said to be made of tears. Whose tears? Why is she weeping? Why is her grief so deep she can never stop?"

If You'd Like to Know What Happens, Read Your Assignment

When the reading lends itself, a teacher might preview the content up to a climax of interest, then break off, saying, "If you want to know what happens, read your assignment."

A Spanish class was assigned a passage on the Christ of the Andes. The teacher previewed it: "Because of a bitter quarrel, this magnificent statue came close to never being built." She recounted the conflict that arose between Argentina and Chile. Which country should the statue face? One insisted, "It must face our nation." The other countered, "But Christ has never turned his back on us before." So bitter was the quarrel that it seemed unlikely the statue would ever be constructed. Then suddenly Chile changed its mind. It preferred that the statue face the other country! "But why?" the teacher queried. "Can you find out why this devoutly Catholic nation should suddenly prefer for Christ to face the other way? Read your assignment and find out why."

The students discovered that Chile had decided that Argentina could not be trusted. Christ should face the other nation and keep an eye on it forever! And as they read, they absorbed additional information about the statue—who the sculptor was, what it cost, how the money was raised among desperately poor people, what the statue symbolizes.

Place Questions Strategically as Students Sightread

As students are sight-reading in class, anticipatory questions can help divert their attention from individual words and center it on the thought just ahead: "You know this character—his feelings, his motives, his temperament. What do you think he will do next?" Or "What will Marie now reply to the young man?"

How Would You Conclude This Story?

A question like the following directs attention to the thought content of fiction: "Your assignment for tomorrow will take you to the end of the chapter. By then, the characters will be familiar, the struggle developed, the situation clear. How do you think the author will conclude the story?" Or, with creative students: "If you were the author, how would you end the story?" Students who have just struggled mightily to foresee the outcome are likely to read on, eager to find out how the story actually turns out.

Start Reading the Selection in Class

Read the opening—if only a few lines—with the students in class, and break off at a point where there is something to anticipate. Then ask, "Can you foresee what's coming?"

A Spanish class read this single opening sentence: "The nights in Cordoba are just too long." Then the students came up with guesses about the content: "The setting is southern Spain—the nights are literally long." "It's about a character who lies awake, troubled. The nights seem endless." As they read the assignment, they discover that a man has journeyed to a friend's home to collect a debt. There he will lodge overnight. His host receives him courteously, wines and dines him, then ushers him to his bedroom. To postpone being pressed for the debt, the host *indeed* prolongs the night. The bedroom has no windows, the clock has been hidden, the servants—if summoned—have been instructed to insist that daybreak has not yet arrived. The guest was immured three nights. That night in Cordoba was indeed "too long."

Teachers can capitalize on the fiction writer's narrative hook—reading a selection at sight until the student is caught. With "The Diamond Necklace" it is good timing if, as the bell rings at the end of the class hour, Madame Loisel is left in grief and despair, the fabulous diamond necklace borrowed from her wealthy friend mysteriously missing.

Help Students Step Right into Their Reading

To students reading in their native language, the opening of a work of fiction may be confusing—a large cast of strange characters, an unfamiliar setting, an undelineated situation, the first threads of two or three plots. To students reading in a language *not* their own, these plots and characters may seem as confusing as Tolstoy's.

A teacher can help students step right into fiction by providing an easy preview—introducing the characters, defining the plots, intriguing the class with promise of dramatic situations. Such a preview, dittoed or presented orally, *pre*-focuses attention on the thought content.

In novels like those of Balzac, page after page of description may precede any narrative hook. An exciting preview will help students work through these pages.

Have Students Share Background Experiences before Reading

How much more readily we comprehend when reading in our mother tongue *if* the terrain is familiar. In reading a language not our own, how clearly important is background experience.

A class-wide "experience exchange" can enrich the background that students bring to a selection. Before reading about Jeanne d'Arc, a French teacher might ask, "What do you already know?" Now students share snatches of Jeanne's story: the visions she felt came from Heaven, her military genius and her liberation of Orleans, her trial as a witch and a heretic, facing death with high courage.

Assign Reading That Forms a Unit

Ordinarily the end of an assignment should coincide with the end of an episode in fiction and with the end of a thought unit in nonfiction. "Translate down to line thirty" may do violence to the natural divisions of the content, making it extremely difficult for the student to center his attention on the meaning.

Bring the Reading Close to the Students

Faraway times and happenings can come close when questions tap the interests of teenagers, especially personal problems—friendship, love, self-confidence, family relationships, personal values, social problems.

Friendship: Whom would you prefer as a friend—Cyrano or Christian?

Self-confidence: How much of Cyrano's suffering over his nose was self-inflicted? Is there evidence that people forgot his nose and loved him anyway? Are many such sufferings self-inflicted?

Family relationships: Has something like this ever happened in your family? Did you react like this character?

Values: Which character do you admire most? Why?

Social problems: The conquistadores displaced the Peruvian Indians "to make way for progress." Near you, in your own city, families from a ghetto are being displaced to make way for the new campus of a great university. Can you find, as you read your assignment for tomorrow, similarities between the displaced Indians and the displaced ghetto families?

Again, questions asked *before* the reading can help develop comprehension. Questions asked *after* the reading often merely test it.

The Question of Dependence

Will students become overdependent as a result of undue advance preparation for each reading assignment? Clearly, sending students into an assignment with

"Read the next five pages" is one extreme. Crippling them with *over*preparation is another. Factors a teacher may wish to consider during the delicate operation of planning the assignment will be the pull of the selection itself, enthusiasm of students for the language, and, of course, the level of achievement of the students.

Certainly, students should gradually advance in the direction of on-their-own readiness. They should develop the ability to preview an informational selection, get a general view of what it's all about, then decide for themselves, "What should I look for when I go back and read this more carefully?" (Tips on how to preview are offered in the PQRST Approach later in this section.) On occasions when students are assigned broad collateral reading, the instructor has an opportunity to check on how well they can perform with less direction.

Niles (1963), a long-time advocate of a thinking approach to reading, has this to contribute: "Secondary teachers may feel there is too much 'hand-holding' in this directed-reading-lesson approach. In a sense good teaching *is* hand-holding; it is leading the students through a process until they can 'walk alone.' And rarely does this time come abruptly."

Indeed, the right degree of hand-holding may help them walk alone sooner.

Student Materials for Mastering Vocabulary

"I've looked that word up four times," students sometimes say, "but I still can't remember it." Here are some techniques to help them put new words on instant call. The guidesheets that follow, addressed directly to students, were developed as a section for their looseleaf notebooks. They are intended to supplement and reinforce in-class instruction.

Ways to Improve Context Clue Power

Here are helps to sharpen techniques for making full use of context revelation.

Teachers often observe that foreign language students need to strengthen their context clue power. Students are so worried about missing little words, they miss the larger thought. They exhaust themselves looking up each word they don't know. Then they slight the job of comprehending because their time and energy are gone.

Just how can students make the context reveal more about a new word's meaning? What specific types of context clues will they find? What kind of practice work is likely to be to their advantage?

text cont. pg. 515

You may feel as if you're confronted with a "new word explosion" as you first leaf through the pages of a foreign language textbook. Clearly you'll be spending a good many hours with vocabulary in the course of a year's work in a foreign language.

How can you learn the maximum amount possible from every moment you spend in vocabulary study? With what procedures should you react when you encounter an unfamiliar word? Under what circumstances? In what order? What techniques have proved effective with language students in helping them cope with heavy loads of vocabulary? How can these techniques get going for you in foreign language study?

Here are a few vocabulary tips at your fingertips. You can take advantage of them to pack sixty seconds of faster, firmer learning into every minute of study.

TIP 1

Does the context clue you in on the new word's meaning? A university expert on reading in a foreign language had this advice for students: "The following method is guaranteed to waste a maximum amount of time and to produce minimum results. Start off with the first word of the assignment, read along until you come to a word you don't know, and look it up in the vocabulary. Then read along to the next word you don't know, look that up in the vocabulary, etc., *ad nauseam*."

"A cardinal rule to follow is this: *Never look up a word in the vocabulary until you have read the immediate context in which it occurs. . . .*"[*]

A vital skill for you

Indeed, context suggests the meaning so often that one of the most vital skills for you to acquire is the use of context revelation. Whenever a new word confronts you, search the context to detect clues to its meaning. As you do so, you may develop a psychological set toward the word—you may "lay the first layer of cement for fixing the term in your vocabulary."[†]

How far beyond the word should you read? The university expert continued: "It would be idiotic to look up a word before reading through the whole sentence in which it occurs." In some cases you may want to read through the whole paragraph or beyond.

---

[*] William G. Moulton, "Study Hints for Language Students," in *How to Study in College*, 2nd ed., by Walter Pauk (Boston: Houghton Mifflin Company, 1974), pp. 266–268.

[†] Philip B. Shaw, *Effective Reading and Learning* (New York: Thomas Crowell Company, 1950), p. 290.

A flash revelation?

As you read on, you may suddenly have a flash revelation of the meaning. You may encounter the puzzling word in another setting—this one rich in added clues. You may come across a photograph or drawing with details that illuminate the meaning. Of course, illustrations are part of a word's environment and often reward you with clues.

Perhaps, at your first encounter with the word, you found yourself deliberating over two or three possible meanings. As you discover further clues, you may find you can now commit yourself to one particular meaning.

Among your vocabulary competencies should be *sharp powers of clue detection.* You'll make a conscious, deliberate attack on the context to wrest from it all it will reveal of the new word's meaning. In class your teacher will probably alert you to some of the context clues that abound to help you in your reading.

When you first *practice* exploring context, you will want to check your tentative meanings immediately by consulting the vocabulary section of your foreign language dictionary.* Later, the decision when *to* and when *not* to look up a word will be guided by the *do's and don'ts of using context,* to be suggested later.

TIP 2

Does the word (or group of words) look like some word or expression you already know? New words that are related to well-known English words should yield their meaning quickly. They do so because they have an ancestor in common with the English word, resemble it, and have the same or a similar meaning. Such words are called "cognates."

A family resemblance

Like members of a family, all the "relatives" below look alike. They all mean *captain:*

> *capitaine* in French
>
> *capitán* in Spanish
>
> *Kapitän* in German
>
> *capitáno* in Italian
>
> *capitaneus in Latin*

Luckily, you'll find cognates at every turn in languages that have become interrelated in their historical development. You'll want to make the most of these look-alikes.

---

* Louise C. Seibert and Lester G. Crocker, *Techniques for Reading French* (Baltimore: Johns Hopkins University Press, 1958), p. 54.

Deceivers

Will the use of cognates ever lead you astray? Some cognates, indeed, are deceivers. In French and Spanish, the words *actuel* and *actual* look easy. But, surprisingly, they mean "existing right now," "immediate," not the so-obvious "actual" or "real" or "genuine." *Pain* in French means bread, and *dispenséme* in Spanish means "excuse me," not "dispense with me!"*

Yes, there are notorious *false cognates*. Some of these you'll recognize because their meanings fail to click with the context. Others your teacher will call to your attention. Fortunately, there are relatively few false cognates. The large numbers of true cognates contribute greatly to the effectiveness of intelligent guessing.

TIP 3

Can you discover a clue in a familiar part? Take the word apart if you can. Do you recognize any part—a prefix, a root, a suffix? Guess all you can from any part you recognize. When you *do* discover a part you know, your gain is usually great.†

In French, Spanish, German, and Italian, the following prefixes help you "unlock" numbers of words:

con-	together, with
inter-	between
pan-	all
re-	again
trans-	across

In all four of these languages, the following roots help you reason out the meaning of a far-flung family of related words:

dic-	say
audi-	hear
graph-	writing, record
scrib-	write
voc-	call

Though it is not often possible to get at the precise meaning of a word through its component parts, a part you recognize helps you remember the

---

* Richard A. Kalish, *Making the Most of College* (Belmont, Calif.: Wadsworth Publishing Company, 1959), p. 223.

† Shaw, *Effective Reading and Learning*, p. 290.

meaning once you've ascertained it. It's a handle to take hold of in retention.

Is there a preferred sequence for exploring the new word's context, giving thought to cognates, analyzing word parts? Not really! Actually, you may get a notion from any one of these—test it—then discard, modify, or confirm it.

TIP 4

If tips 1, 2, and 3 haven't yielded all the meaning you want, turn to the vocabulary section or reach for your foreign language dictionary. If you require a more precise meaning or if your tentative meaning needs verifying, now is the time to look the new word up. This timing gives you full benefit of the mental set you developed by trying to deduce the meaning.*

You may be wondering, "Just *when* should I rely on context, and when should I look the word up?" Here in a capsule are a few do's and don'ts:

DO'S AND DON'TS OF USING CONTEXT

Do rely on clues—from context, cognates, and word parts:
1. When you have highly revealing clues and when the meaning you arrive at definitely clicks with the rest of the passage.
2. When, in view of your purpose in reading the selection, you need only the approximate meaning.

Don't rely on clues—look the word up:
1. When the word is a key word, crucial to your understanding, and full comprehension is important to you.
2. When you require a precise meaning. It usually takes the dictionary to pin the meaning down.
3. When the clues suggest several possibilities, the meaning might be any one of several—and you don't know which.
4. When you don't know the nearby words.
5. When you have encountered a word a number of times, you realize that it is one you will meet again, and you want to master it thoroughly for future reading.

TIP 5

If the word is an important one for you to retain, you may wish to record it (on a divided page in a notebook or on flash cards) for future study. Students say, "I've looked that word up four times, and I still can't remember it!" You can put words on instant call through powerful techniques for retention. Which words are you likely to want to record to work on further?

---

*Shaw, *Effective Reading and Learning*, p. 290.

WORD OR IDIOM	MEANING	ILLUSTRATIVE SENTENCES (Optional)
		Test your understanding by covering answers.

Figure 12–1. *The divided page.*

1. By the time a word has blocked you three times, chances are it will block you many times more. If you own your book, you might make a dot in the vocabulary section beside a word each time you look it up —then record for special study words that have three dots.
2. You may want to record deceptive cognates, but you probably won't need to record words with exact or almost exact correspondents in English.
3. You will very likely wish to record your "error demons"—words whose meanings persistently elude you.
4. Troublesome idioms should be recorded.
5. Your teacher will stress words you'll run across often.
6. Authors of textbooks often spotlight words they consider essential through the vocabulary lists that accompany each lesson.

How to make and use a divided page

Rule off a sheet of notebook paper vertically into three columns. Enter the word or idiom in the first column; the particular meaning in the center column; and original illustrative sentences (if you wish to include these) in the third column.

Now turn on the "most powerful study technique known to psychologists": self-recitation.* Conceal the meaning column with your hand or with an index card used as a cover card, and try to express the meaning. Then lift the card and check. Keep checking until you have full mastery.

---

* Pauk, Walter, *How To Study in College* (Boston: Houghton Mifflin Company, 1962), p. 25.

```
┌─────────────────────────────────────────────────────┐
│                  VOCABULARY TERM                      │
│                     OR IDIOM                          │
│                                                       │
│                                            ╲          │
│   Print here: _____ SE METTRE A _____          │
│                                                       │
│                                                       │
│                                                       │
│                                                       │
│                                                       │
└─────────────────────────────────────────────────────┘
```

```
┌─────────────────────────────────────────────────────┐
│                                                       │
│                                                       │
│   Write meaning here: ____ to begin to _____        │
│                                                       │
│   ─────────────────────────────────────────────      │
│                                                       │
│   Write brief illustrative sentences (optional) below:│
│                                                       │
│            Il se mit à pleurer.                       │
│                                                       │
│                                                       │
└─────────────────────────────────────────────────────┘
```

Figure 12–2.   *Flash cards.*

Or operate the other way. Expose the meaning column, conceal the new word column, and see if you can supply the new word. Mark items that are still "error demons" and double-check these next time.

How *not* to learn vocabulary is to read and reread dutifully (and all too often dreamingly) a list of new words and their definitions. How to *learn* vocabulary is to spend much of your study time (perhaps as much as four-fifths) in self-recitation. The cover card *forces* concentration as you struggle to recall what's underneath. You can fold your "current" page, carry it around with you, and work on it during odd moments.

How to use flash cards

You may prefer standard 3 × 5 index cards for your word collection. Record the word or idiom by itself on one side of the card and the meaning on the reverse side. Look at the word, then ask yourself the meaning. Or check yourself the other way—work from the meaning to the new word.

Flash cards offer several advantages over the divided page: (1) As you study, you can separate your cards, with rubber bands, into an "I do know" pile and an "I don't know" pile. (2) You can shuffle the cards and shift their order frequently. (3) You can "retire" words that you feel have become permanently yours, replace these with new ones, and free yourself to concentrate on current problem words.

You may be thinking, "That's a lot of work and time and bother!" Of course, recording a word takes time—probably, for each entry, three or four minutes of your too-crowded day. But you'll actually be making entries for relatively few words. Mastery of many words will come about naturally as you go over a lesson—meet them in reading—hear them in class. Thus, there is no necessity for recording most of the new words you'll meet.

Then, too, the *very act* of entering a word will help you remember the word. If you were to do no more than make the entry, then lose your word collection never to find it again, you would still be ahead. The mere motor act of writing, in and of itself, would have strengthened your learning.

How to make a word entry

You can pack three or four minutes of concentrated learning into the very act of recording the word.

Enter the word and its meaning on the divided page or flash card so that they are letter perfect. *Printing* the word will eliminate any confusion later about its spelling. You will soon be learning some powerful techniques for retention. Remember: if your entry itself is inaccurate, you will have learned for the future—*wrong*.

Nouns should be recorded with the singular article as an aid in learning the gender: in French, *le gateau, la mer, un arbre*; in Spanish, *el cometa, la carne, un arbol*; in German, *das Autofahren, die Decke*.

As you're recording the word, pronounce it—aloud or in a whisper—until you're comfortable forming the sounds.

WOULD YOU LIKE A CLINCHER?

Would you like a clincher for retention? If so, you might add to your divided page (third column) or to your flash card (meaning side) three short sentences of your own in which you use the word. Takes too much time? Chances are you'll *regain* the time through firmer learning. And you should collect an important fringe benefit in the ease with which the new word now slides into your own speaking and writing.

"See it! Say It! Hear it! Write it"

As you go over the words in self-recitation, you can turn on multiple-strength learning. If you learn a word with your eyes alone, you'll be using just one-third of your sensory learning channels for mastering new words. The word may remain with you only briefly. Why not use all-out VAK learning—Visual, Auditory, and Kinesthetic?

College students are advised, "Use your eyes in learning—then add your ears and muscles."

See it!

Say it!

Hear it!

*Write it!**

1. Use your eyes as you *see* and reread the word and its meaning. "Photograph" the word with your mind. Close your eyes and see it! Then check your mental image with the card.

2. *Say* the word—aloud or in a whisper. Now you've added kinesthetic (muscular) learning as you involve the muscles of your throat, lips, and tongue.

3. Strengthen learning with your ears as you *hear* yourself say it. Now you've brought to bear your auditory memory.

4. Add kinesthetic learning again as you write down the word and its meaning. You've now involved motor memory, which in many students is the strongest of the learning channels. If spelling is a problem, you might print the trouble spots in large letters or colored ink.

This is four-way reinforcement. The variety itself helps you recall. The change of pace—eyes, voice, ears, pencil—keeps you alert and increases absorption.

Keep your current working group of words manageable. An unwieldy pack of flash cards or a long, forbidding list may seem overwhelming. You might prefer to work on words in groups of five. Short-term goals, readily reachable, will bring you a sense of accomplishment and satisfaction.

*How to retain longer through
spaced reviews*

You can remember longer simply by the timing of your reviews. You can plan your first review to minimize forgetting. Suppose you read an assignment today. When will forgetting take its greatest toll? If you are typical, the greatest loss will be within one day. Arrange your first review to check this drop. Place it from 12 to 24 hours after you study. Reinforce immediately what you learned, and you will remember it much longer.

---

* George J. Dudycha, *Learn More with Less Effort* (New York: Harper and Row, Publishers, 1957), p. 96.

*How to use the memory aid
of "overlearning"*

Learning for the future requires *overlearning*. A football player learns to take his man out in a run around left end. Then he goes over and over the play until he overlearns it. He does this so there will be no forgetting and confusion. An actor memorizes his lines well enough to deliver them without error. Then he continues to go over them until they are automatic.*

Learning experts say that *minimal* learning is not enough. When you can say, "I have learned this material," you should then spend perhaps one-fourth the original time overlearning it.

Dividends will be high. In one study, students who overlearned a vocabulary lesson remembered *four times as much* after 28 days had passed. Now, before important tests, a quick run-through may be all you need.

Put these techniques to work each day

You've just had some tips on study techniques, some of the most powerful known to learning experts. Use them only late on nights before a test and the dividends will be doubtful. New words accumulate so rapidly that you would be not unlike a piano player who, instead of practicing faithfully an hour a day for a year, tries to practice 365 hours without stopping! But put these tips to work for you each day, and your dividends can be dramatic.†

Have you really overwhelmed those words?

A written test to check your mastery of new words is an important final step. Oral run-throughs may deceive you. You may think you can write and spell the words correctly when, if you should actually try, you would fall short.

As a final step, pull ten or twenty cards at random from your flash cards or select works at random from your divided page, and see if you can indeed write out the words and their meanings. If you pass your written self-test with colors flying, chances are the words are yours to stay.

---

* Kalish, *Making the Most of College*, p. 119.

† Charles Hundley, former University of Chicago Laboratory School Latin teacher, in remarks to the writers, March 1970.

The context clues discussed below will be identical with those that abound to help students as they read English. Brief, easy-to-grasp descriptions of ten specific types of context clues are offered in Chapter 2.

Make the Most of Context

Some teachers prefer to work with context entirely in natural, incidental situations as their students meet new words in passages they are reading in the second language. Others prefer to work initially with English sentences carefully contrived to sell the students the value of context exploration and to exemplify each type of clue. Such sentences are offered in the exercise "What Is Your Context Clue Power?" in Chapter 2. Since the entire section on developing context clue power in reading English is applicable in foreign language reading, the reader is also referred to that section in Chapter 2.

The reader may also wish to examine the superlative explanations and stimulating practice work—applicable in any foreign language—offered in *Techniques for Reading French* by Louise C. Seibert and Lester G. Crocker (Baltimore: Johns Hopkins University Press, 1958), pages 44–87.

Don't Use the Dictionary

A French instructor whose students are overly dictionary-prone tells them, "You can probably deal with *more than half* of the new words you meet in French without looking them up. Suppose you decide to abandon your dictionary or the vocabulary section for all those words. Just how *will you* get at the meaning?" After the students have been introduced to various types of clues, this is their assignment:

> Read this short passage and list the words that were unknown to you. Place a check mark before those whose meaning you could approximate either through context clues or through cognates.

Next day in class the instructor asks, "What led you to the meaning?" The students discuss clues that proved revealing. As they run into misleading clues and false cognates, they realize the importance of checking to be sure their intelligent guesses conform to the thought of the rest of the passage. They also discuss when it is essential to check or verify the meaning. Much day-to-day practice in natural reading situations follows.

Are You a Good Word Detective?

After an introduction to various types of context clues, students test their powers of clue detection. Using a short dittoed selection, a Latin teacher (Schroth, 1968) has students search the context for clues to the meaning of ten selected words that have been enclosed in boxes (as they appear in the dittoed selection) and numbered from 1 to 10. They are also asked to analyze and write down just how they arrived at each guess.

The boxed-in words should be important to the meaning of the passage, should be unknown to the students, should have fairly revealing context, and should exemplify the various types of clues. Obviously they should not be cognates or words with Greek or Latin prefixes and roots that give away the meaning. Students who arrive at the correct meaning can share their success secrets.

An Open-Book Test with Puzzle Appeal

Here is a test with puzzle appeal. Books are open to a selection the students have not read. A number of words to be defined are listed on the board with the page and line where each is to be located in context. The students may make full use of all clues present but are not to consult the vocabulary section. The values and limitations of context revelation are driven home dramatically as the students try—under pressure of a test—to wrest the meaning of the puzzlers from context clues.

What Can You Learn in One Minute?

Using short passages, such as the vignettes in the French or Spanish *Reader's Digest*, students are asked, "What can you learn in one minute?" With the watch ticking away the minutes, they are forced to make the most of context. Students report the information they could glean from the passage when time did not permit their reaching for the dictionary. They often surprise themselves.

Can You Skim a News Story in One Minute?

While reading foreign language newspapers, students are led to observe that owing to their structure, news stories can be skimmed very rapidly. The headlines and the opening sentence or two of a straight news story yield the gist. From then on in the story, the content tapers off in importance. Against a one-minute time limit, students skim the headlines and the leads to get the gist of front-page stories. Under time pressure, they are forced to make the most of context.

THE PQRST APPROACH TO READING FOR MEANING IN A SECOND LANGUAGE

Here is a package of meaning-getting techniques. It incorporates more than thirty years of research on reading comprehension.

Ask teachers of a foreign language what bothers them most about their students' reading and they are likely to respond, "When they turn to the selection, they have no response other than plunging in and plodding through. They 'read' until they encounter an unknown word, then pore over the vocabulary. And on they plod—from the first word on the first page to the last word on the last. When they close their books with the assignment 'completed,' they have little grasp of the meaning behind the words."

What about using well established procedures for reading English to improve foreign language reading? The "PQRST" approach, when adapted to the reading of a second language, should serve the same purpose it serves in English: to provide students with sound *meaning-getting techniques.*

PQRST stands for the five steps in the procedure—Preview, Question, Read, State (self-recite), and Test. It is based on Francis P. Robinson's widely known SQ3R approach, which proved itself in World War II, when young recruits were rushed through training courses. In a national crisis, Robinson, an expert on the psychology of learning at Ohio State, was called in as a consultant on fast, effective study-reading. Incorporating the results of some thirty years of investigation, he designed a package of effective procedures.

An adaptation of PQRST for foreign language reading follows. The procedure is appropriate when the student's task is grasping the meaning of informational writing. Obviously, many of the guidelines can be used to special advantage by intermediate and advanced foreign language students because of their greater vocabulary resources. Students who use the language to do close reading of scientific or other technical materials should find it extremely helpful. While parts of the approach are applicable to the reading of fiction, obviously the Preview step does not lend itself to reading when suspense about the outcome is important.

Since foreign language teachers differ in their methods and since different types of reading matter confront the student with special problems, the teacher may wish to adapt the procedure freely.

Foreign language students seriously bent on improving their reading are likely to find this approach to be a long step toward reading for meaning and ultimately to be a shortcut toward more rapid reading.

THE PQRST APPROACH TO READING FOR
MEANING IN A SECOND LANGUAGE

Just survey, the first time through

PREVIEW

ONCE
OVER
LIGHTLY

Before starting your thorough reading of the passage, spend a few minutes in an advance survey.

1. *Examine the title.* This is often the writer's "label" for the content. It may clue you in on the general content in a moment or two.

2. *Skim the entire passage to get a general view of what it's all about.* College experts on reading in a foreign language offered these suggestions: "The first thing to do . . . is to understand what the author is writing about. . . . The second step is to grasp rapidly the significance of some of the key words which will narrow the scope, and focus the mind on one particular aspect [or on particular aspects] of that subject."

Suppose, for example, the subject in general is a tropical forest. You may be able to grasp this fairly easily. Then try to narrow the scope. Ask yourself, "What special aspects? Its beauty? Its vegetation? Its ferocious beasts? Hunting? Its dangers?"* Looking for key words may help you to zero in on particular aspects.

Are photographs or drawings present? If so, examine these. They may offer instant insights into the content.

During your preliminary survey, it may help you to hit the strategic spots of well-organized informational writing:

a. Examine the opening paragraphs of the selection. Here authors often announce the general content—tell you what they're going to tell you—conveniently brief you on what's ahead.

b. Next, skim through the body of the selection. Try now to narrow the scope. It may help to examine the first and perhaps the last sentences of paragraphs. In expository writing, beginnings and endings are often heavily freighted with meaning. Topic sentences are frequently located here. These may announce aspects under the general topic.

c. Examine the conclusion. Here the authors often wrap up important content—drive home what they want most of all to leave with the reader.

You'll find exceptions to all that's been said. The organization of prose is not always neat. Introductions may fail to announce and conclusions may fail to wrap up. Topic sentences are not always first or last—or even present

---
* Adapted from Louise C. Seibert and Lester G. Crocker, *Techniques for Reading French* (Baltimore: Johns Hopkins University Press), pp. 147–148.

at all—in paragraphs. Your skimming techniques cannot be rigid. A flexible "floating" down the page or through a paragraph looking for key words and following one promising lead after another is often desirable.

3. ***Rest content with the general import.*** Much of the content will elude you as you preview. Expect this! Your purpose, this first time through, is not to grasp details. You're going to return later anyway.

4. ***Do not stop during the preview step to look up unknown words, even though words clearly important may not all be familiar.*** You might make an exception only if a strange word completely blocks your getting the gist of a section of some length or import.

5. ***Call upon your own background information.*** Summon up your own ideas and experiences on the topic. Ask yourself, "What do I already know about this?" You may have learned related ideas while studying other subjects. You'll grasp the meaning better if new learning clicks with something you already know.

6. ***Go in with questions.*** Your interest or suspense may be aroused as you're making this survey. Ask yourself, "What should I expect to know about this subject after I've read intensively? What should I look for when I go back and read the selection more carefully?" It may be extremely helpful to jot down questions you'll want to answer during your second, your more thorough reading.

Why Preview

1. Without the preview step, your translating may be "a kind of extended puzzle involving a painful putting together of meaningless pieces." Like a jigsaw, the little pieces will fall into place more easily after you've glimpsed the total picture.*

2. Knowing the general drift of the selection should aid you greatly during your second reading. It should help you guess at meanings of strange words and recognize those already familiar.

Go in with questions

QUESTION

Chances are your preview has left you with gaps in the picture that you wish to fill. You may have jotted down some questions. Then, too, your instructor, your classmates, or the authors of your textbook may have raised important questions.

---

* Milton Finstein, Etiennette Pillet, and Roger Pillet, *Pas à Pas: A Sequential Introduction to French* (Chicago: The Laboratory Schools, University of Chicago, 1965), p. 170.

1. *Now focus on what you're looking for.* Hold what you're after in the forefront of your mind.

2. *Through questions, your reading should become an active search for meaning.* Students often "read" a foreign language selection with their minds worlds away, aimlessly looking up one word after another. In grasping the meaning *behind* the words, they're "dropouts." When you approach your reading with questions, you'll have a powerful study technique to concentrate your attention on the *thought* of the passage.

In-depth reading is the next step

READ

You've previewed to get a view of what lies ahead in the passage, and you are holding in mind some questions. You are now ready to do your in-depth reading.

1. *Now read to find the answers to your questions and other important content.* New questions may need to be added while you are reading.

2. Now is the time to "turn detective" and *try to deduce the meaning of each strange word.** Read *past* the unknown word—to the end of the sentence, perhaps to the end of the paragraph. Ask yourself:

a. What light do clues in the context throw on the word's meaning?

b. Does its similarity to an English word give you a clue? Is there a well-known root, prefix, or suffix? Guess all you can from any of these clues you find.

c. If no knowledge you possess gives the unknown word meaning, if your guess makes the rest of the sentence ridiculous, or if several uses have marked the word as a common, useful one which you will very likely meet again, look it up in the vocabulary section or in your foreign language dictionary.†

Looking up one word right after another is "guaranteed to waste a maximum of time and produce minimum results."‡ Turning mindlessly to the dictionary, someone observed, exercises only your *thumb.* Trying first to wrest the meaning from context and word parts vigorously exercises your mind. Your dictionary should not be your first resort but your last.

---

* Willis Jones, "Cultivating Reading Speed in Spanish," *Modern Language Journal*, 41 (March 1957): 128.

† Jones, "Cultivating Reading Speed in Spanish," p. 130.

‡ William G. Moulton, "Study Hints for Language Students," in *How to Study in College*, 2nd ed., by Walter Pauk (Boston: Houghton Mifflin Company, 1974), p. 266.

Tell yourself what you've read

STATE

Your second reading has been a close, intensive reading. You've been puzzling out individual words, attending to the bits and pieces. During this step, concentrating on the broader meaning has been difficult.

To return to the jigsaw, you've been painfully putting together the little pieces of the puzzle and may for the moment have lost the total picture. Now that the pieces are together, you need to look at the total picture.*

Just what have you read? You may wish to pause now, look away from your book, and see if you can recite to yourself what you've read (if you're an advanced student, preferably in the foreign language). If it's difficult, that's your cue to reread appropriate parts.

Add a final run-through

TEST

Now add a final rapid reading to test whether you can read the passage fluently. Now is your chance to get in some *extremely effective practice* on reading for meaning. You've already removed many of the blocks that stood in your way. Try to read now with full appreciation of the meaning.

Advanced students may expect to move gradually toward this ideal: Try, as much as possible, to obliterate any thinking in English. The ideal is not to replace the passage with its English equivalent, but to get the writers' thoughts *in their own words*, with whatever overtones the style and language provide.†

Would you like an extra bonus in speed of reading? Read the passage over and over until it seems almost as easy to you as English. These added run-throughs yield surprising dividends in speed. You can increase your speed considerably simply by knowing what's coming. The more times you practice a selection, the faster and smoother your reading becomes. You may be well on your way to reading at speeds you never imagined possible.‡

Is this approach time consuming?

The expert use of new procedures will not be instant. You'll improve your techniques with practice. Ultimately this new approach should *conserve your study time*. When practiced and perfected, it should enable you to do more effective studying in the same time—probably in less. It should help you gain the *maximum results from every moment* you spend in foreign language reading.

---

* Finstein, Pillet, and Pllet, *Pas à Pas*, p. 177.

† Jones, "Cultivating Reading Speed in Spanish," p. 130.

‡ Jones, "Cultivating Reading Speed in Spanish," p. 128.

References

Hughes, Catherine, former Foreign Language Supervisor, schools of Gary, Indiana.

Niles, Olive S. "Help Students Set a Purpose for Reading." *English High Lights*, 20 (April-May 1963): 2.

Schroth, Ruth, former University of Chicago Laboratory School Latin teacher, in remarks to the writers, May 1968.

Washburne, John N. "The Use of Questions in Social Science Material." *Journal of Educational Psychology*, 20 (1929): 321–359.

13

HOME ECONOMICS

The reading helps in this section were pre-pared with Dorothy Szymkowicz, University of Chicago Laboratory School home economics teacher.

One day a reading consultant was invited to visit a foods class. She found the teacher carefully pre-teaching vocabulary. The class was preparing to make spaghetti, and the teacher was painstakingly teaching *colander*, surrounded by chopped onions, tomato sauce, and Parmesan cheese! When, after the closing bell, the consultant expressed her delight at finding a part-time "reading teacher" in a home economics classroom, a cooperative venture to try to up-grade reading—a sharing of insights of classroom teacher and consultant over the years—was born.

The teacher posed their first problem: "Students tend to be over-confident with directions. How can we equip them to handle the directions on packaged products? Almost everything will be prepackaged for the homemaker of tomor-row!" The methods and materials they worked out together, including a set of guidelines for students, are shared with you in the first section of this chapter.

Next, they turned to the reading of recipes. "Here," the teacher commented, "deficiency in reading is disastrous to a successful food product." Could they work out ways to develop expertise in reading recipes? The procedures they developed, including another set of guidelines for students, are detailed in the second section of this chapter.

Next, the teacher suggested, "Can we help students handle the complicated, often bewildering, directions on a sewing pattern?" The reading guidance that resulted, along with a third set of guidelines, is shared in the concluding section of the chapter.

How has the reading venture worked out? Has there been a change in the students' reading behavior? On the pages that follow, the teacher makes some interesting observations.

In these projects, the teacher had the enthusiastic help of intern reading consultants: Phyllis Brannan, Terri Heimann, and Joan Gilpatrick.*

Of course, reading in home economics calls for a wide variety of skills. The procedures discussed here happened to meet some special needs in one teacher's classes. For other ways to improve reading in home economics, turn to the Subject Area Index in Chapter 1.

How to Read Directions on Package Mixes

A home economics teacher talks about her students' reading before and after her guidance.

Ours is an age of directions. In the future, nearly every food product for the home will be prepackaged with directions. Even today there are few commodities offered to the consumer without some kind of directions attached. The homemaker must read the directions on a package mix for party cupcakes, follow the directions for washing a delicate sweater, carry out the instructions for attaching a new accessory to the vacuum cleaner.

Directions on packages are often short and concise *and highly deceptive*. These "simple" directions are densely packed with detail and require slow, precise, and thoughtful reading. Advertisers who give the impression that the result will work out perfectly often fail to stress that the directions must be followed precisely—*step by step*—if the perfect result is to follow. Students—and even experienced homemakers—tend to be overconfident when they see "simple" directions. They have simply never been briefed on the appropriate reading techniques.

To equip students to deal successfully with the directions on package mixes (and, more broadly, the directions on products for the home of any type), a

---

* Phyllis Brannan is now Reading Consultant, Washtenaw Intermediate School District, Ann Arbor, Michigan. Terri Heimann was formerly Language Arts Consultant for the Interrelated Language Skills Center, Milwaukee Public Schools. Joan Gilpatrick is Reading Specialist, Glenbrook North High School, Northbrook, Illinois.

home economics teacher and a reading consultant prepared a set of guidelines, "Direct Success with the Directions on Package Mixes." The teacher reports the results of a "before and after" experiment (Szymkowicz, 1969):

> In the students' first experience with package mix, no special guidance in reading was given. The students were told only to follow the directions on the package. Their remarks were "That's easy!" and "No challenge in that!" As they worked, they paid slight attention to the directions. They merely glanced at a word or two now and then and guessed the rest, or asked one another what to do next. Some students never once looked at the printed directions. As the work progressed, students were beginning to look completely lost. With many, the final step was guessed, and the concoction was thrown into the baking pan in utter despair. Some ovens were not checked for the correct temperature. One oven was quite cold! Most students, having expected the mix to work perfectly, were very disappointed in the results. The conclusion of the group, to their own surprise, was that they had misjudged package mixes and that it was easier to make a product from scratch.
>
> A day or two later, the guidelines were used with the same group of students. This time I guided the class through a thoughtful reading of the guidelines, applying them to another set of directions on another, different package mix. After this "reading lesson," the students, on the whole, carried out the step-by-step procedures with much better results. Although there were still some difficulties, this time they involved practical skills, not reading skills.

The guidelines were kept for future reference in the students' looseleaf notebooks. There they were available to consult and review as needed. The teacher constantly broadened the application of the direction-reading techniques, encouraging the same precision with the directions on home appliances, on the labels of all household containers, and on the tags attached to ready-made garments.

How did the "directions drive" work out? As the weeks passed, many students read directions with never-before precision, asked fewer nonessential questions, and required less supervision. They became aware that the fine print on an inconspicuous label can mean the difference between delight in their purchase and disappointment. When the course ended, these consumers of tomorrow were better equipped to cope with the "directions explosion" that will confront them when they buy packaged products.

"Self-Evaluation Checklists" can be used to focus students' attention on their need areas in reading directions and point the way to improvement. The reader will find an example, adaptable to home economics, in Chapter 11.

DIRECT SUCCESS WITH DIRECTIONS ON
PACKAGE MIXES

PART I. READING THE DIRECTIONS

1. **Pre-read** the entire **directions.** Read them once over lightly to get a general idea of the materials and procedures.

   Check to see if you have all the necessary equipment and ingredients.

2. **Reread** the **directions** precisely.

   Notice that they're written in simple, concise, easy-to-grasp steps.
   Make a complete stop after each step, if necessary, to be sure you understand just what you are to do. Try to form a mental picture of yourself carrying out each step.

   Study the "here's how" illustrations. These will save you working time. Though many processes are difficult to explain in words, you can get instant insights from an illustration.

   It takes just a glance to see that the topping mix goes in the center as well as on top. ——————▶——————▶——————▶——————▶

   Be alert for action words. Turn to the glossary of your cookbook to clear up terms you do not know. *Blend* and *beat* may seem to differ only slightly, but there's a decided difference in the action called for—and a world of difference in the way your coffee cake may turn out.

   Focus sharply on descriptive words—such as *glass*, *round*, or *square* pan. These can be critically important. The oven temperature often changes with the type of pan used.

   Reread as often as necessary for a thorough understanding of the procedures. A single error in any step may make the kitchen where you're working a disaster area.

> TAKE TIME FOR PRECISION READING!
> SAVE TIME WHEN THINGS GO RIGHT!

PART II. CARRYING OUT THE DIRECTIONS

1. **Assemble** all the equipment and ingredients you'll need. Double check the directions to be sure you have everything ready.

2. **Attend** to preliminary steps like these:

   Preheat the oven.

   Grease and flour the baking pan.

Cinnamon Streusel Coffee Cake *

PREHEAT OVEN TO 375°. (350° for glass pans.)
Generously grease and lightly flour bottom of 8 or 9-inch round or square pan.

BLEND in small (about 1½ quart) mixer bowl
Coffee Cake Mix
1 egg
½ cup milk
at low speed until all ingredients are moistened.

BEAT 2 minutes at medium speed or 300 strokes with a spoon.

SPREAD half of batter in pan; sprinkle with half of **Topping Mix.** Spread with remaining batter and sprinkle with remaining Topping Mix.

BAKE 375° 8-inch pan............35 to 40 minutes
9-inch pan............30 to 35 minutes
Serve warm.

Reproduced from Pillsbury Cinnamon Streusel Coffee Cake Mix.

3. Now **carry out** each step in the process.

   The order of steps is critical.

   <u>Measure acurately</u> with standard measuring equipment.

   > Be precise with amounts, timings, and temperatures. Quantitative measures flash a bright red warning signal. They're danger spots!

   <u>Time carefully.</u> Notice the time specified for beating.

   > Beating for "two minutes" means precisely two minutes. It's difficult to guess two minutes accurately.

4. **Time** the cooking process precisely.

   > When the time for a process is specified, it's essential to use a clock or timer.

   > Note that the timing may change with the type of pan you use.

5. In case of failure, **reread** the directions. Search out the cause and **vow to succeed** next time. Failures are usually due to your interpretation of the directions, not to the contents of the package. Package mixes are perfectly tested for a perfect product.

How to Read a Recipe

Students can improve their competencies in
reading recipes relatively quickly. Better use of
class time is one result.

How many times will students follow a recipe in the course of a class in foods preparation! Here, day after day, they must read an almost identical pattern of directions. Without reading guidance, students tend to be "direction dropouts." They often glance at two or three words, then turn to their teacher with questions. *With* guidance, many can acquire recipe reading techniques relatively quickly. The results? Better food products, better use of both student and teacher time, and better foods preparation in the home after school days are over.

Using the guidelines, "How to Read a Recipe Successfully," a home economics teacher guides students through a model reading of a recipe. The students discuss the how-to's and the why-do's of the suggested procedures; they talk over the critical importance of understanding each term; they become aware that a single punctuation mark can mean the difference between failure and success. The guidelines, printed on a colorful foldout, are kept for future reference in their notebooks. A striking wall-size billboard on which the guidelines have been enlarged by a photo blow-up process dominates the kitchen area of the classroom. Throughout the course the teacher refers to the billboard frequently. A single reading lesson with no follow-through, the teacher observes, has little permanent effect on student behavior.

After their directed reading of the recipe, most of the students read recipes more precisely and are more successful with their products. Some who have viewed themselves as scholastic misfits experience their first sense of accomplishment and confidence in foods class. The lift to their self-concepts through these experiences of success and approval could well lead to better achievement in the broader school situation.

Tape Recorded Directions to the Rescue

Below-average readers often congregate in homemaking classes. For individuals who need reinforcement in recognizing the words of the directions, the teacher might record a series of directions on tape. Using earphones, the students read the words of the directions silently while reinforcing their reading through listening. They play and replay the tape as often as necessary. Through this reading-hearing procedure, they come to associate the word they see printed on the page with the word they hear. After this reinforced reading, some students can proceed with their work away from the tape recorder, using only the printed directions. Thus they are grasping the directions for their current project, and learning to read better, besides.

How to Read a Sewing Pattern

Through guiding students in reading, a home economics teacher frees time for better service to students.

Anyone who opens a sewing pattern for the first time is likely to be bewildered by the many pieces, the different "views," marking symbols, cutting layout, the special language of the sewing guide, the detailed steps. How confusing all these must be to the beginning student!

Aware of the special need for instruction in reading such complicated directions, a home economics teacher and a reading consultant developed "Guidelines on How to Read a Sewing Pattern." Intended as an insert for students' looseleaf notebooks, they supplement and reinforce in-class instruction.

Excitement is in the air on the day the students bring to class their newly purchased fabric, zippers, buttons, and their intriguing new patterns—all to go into the making of THE dress or shirt. As the period starts, the teacher passes out the guidelines and sets the stage for the reading instruction:

> You've bought your materials and your pattern, and you're eager to go ahead. That one dollar pattern is a gold mine of information—but it's no use to you if you can't understand it. Knowing how to read it will help you become a make-it-yourself expert. You'll go home and sew just as well *there*, where you no longer have me to help you. How easy it will be for you to make a becoming dress for yourself—*when* you've learned how to read your pattern! You'll work ahead faster here in class, too. You won't have to ask unnecessary questions or lose time waiting in line for me to answer. How much time can I give each one of you if all of you, instead of consulting your patterns, come to me at once with questions!

The teacher now leads the class through their study of the reading guidelines, applying them to the parts of the pattern: the envelope, general directions, marking symbols, diagram of pieces, cutting layout, sewing directions, symbols on the pieces themselves. As a step along the road to independence, the teacher introduces the students to a colorful sewing resource book, *The Simplicity Sewing Book* (New York: Simplicity Pattern Co., Inc., 1970) in which they

text cont. pg. 536

If the oven is to be used, **locate temperature** required.

Think ahead! And at the appropriate time preheat your oven. Light your oven *before* assembling your ingredients. It will take about ten minutes for it to reach the temperature desired.

PART 1. MATERIALS

Read through the **entire recipe** with special care.

Descriptive words sound an alert. These are "key terms" to cooking success. ⟶ ⟶ ⟶ ⟶

Focus sharply on abbreviations. -----➤ -----➤ -----➤ -----➤

Remember: tsp. means teaspoon;
tbsp. means tablespoon.

Note carefully quantities you'll need. •••••➤ •••••➤ •••••➤ •••••➤

Unknown terms say **Stop! Look! Learn!**

A single word left unknown may ruin your batch of cookies.

The index of your cookbook or its "List of Terms Used in Recipes" should give you instant access to the meanings.

Assemble your **ingredients** and **utensils.**

Then doublecheck. Reread Part I of the recipe to be certain you have everything you'll need.

RECIPE FOR EASY SUGAR COOKIES

Part 1

1½ cup sifted flour

1 tsp. cream of tartar

½ tsp. soda

¼ tsp. salt

½ cup shortening

1 egg

½ cup sugar

½ tsp. vanilla

OVEN TEMPERATURE 375°

PART 2. METHOD

Carry out all the **steps** one by one in the **order given.**

Notice that the ingredients are conveniently listed in the order in which you'll use them.

Watch for special action words—for example, *sift, beat, cut in, mix*—and perform the technique called for. Remember that specific words are used for a purpose. Though some words may seem to differ only slightly, there's a *decided* difference in the action called for and a world of difference in the way your cookies may turn out!

CAUTION

Focus on descriptive words.

Zero in on amounts, timings, temperatures.

Quantitative directions are danger spots.

Carry out each step—with great care!

For example, add the egg mixture to the flour, not the flour to the egg mixture.

Reread as often as necessary.

A single error in any step may make your cookies not a delight but a disaster.

Then *time* precisely.

Note the description of the finished product.

> TAKE TIME for precision reading!
> SAVE TIME when things go right!

Part 2

1. Sift together flour, cream of tartar, soda, and salt.
2. Cut in shortening until like fine crumbs.
3. Beat egg with sugar and vanilla.
4. Add egg mixture to flour mixture and mix well. Dampen the hands with water, and roll into balls the size of a walnut.

5. Place balls one and a half inches apart on an ungreased cookie sheet.
6. Flatten first cookie with bottom of dampened glass tumbler.
7. Dip tumbler into the sugar and then press all the cookies.

8. Bake in a moderate oven 375° until *pale brown*—about *six to ten minutes.*

can find the answers to many of their questions. This, it is explained, will always be close at hand—theirs to reach for at the moment of need. The teacher points out the clear "this-is-how-to-do-it" illustrations and the simple explanations of sewing terms they may not know. Reinforcement of the newly acquired techniques is ongoing during the weeks and months that follow.

Does behavior change as a result of special instruction in pattern-reading techniques? The teacher comments:

> *Without* instruction, many students are question-prone. They look for the easiest and quickest way to learn a new technique, and that is to try to get all the answers they can by asking their teacher. Searching out information for themselves on their pattern or in a sewing resource book may not have occurred to them. *With* guidance in reading a pattern, they are likely to require much less supervision and to work with an appropriate degree of independence. My time is freed to give essential instruction in construction techniques. The students usually find their first encounter with a pattern rewarding rather than frustrating, avoid mishaps with their garments, and experience the satisfaction of successful on-their-own accomplishment. Many, in future years, will be able to make quality garments without professional help. Their pattern reading expertise will enable them to continue their sewing education after school days are over.

GUIDELINES ON HOW TO READ
A SEWING PATTERN

STUDY THE ENVELOPE

Front: Visualize your completed garment. You will usually find several styles pictured. Fix firmly in mind the letter or number of the view you have selected.

Back: Read the description of the garment so that you understand how the pictured garment fits the description.

Check the list of necessary materials, both fabric and notions, to make sure you have all items ready before you begin.

> Locate a sewing resource book for quick reference.

PREVIEW THE ENTIRE PATTERN GUIDE

All pattern guides include the following important sections, but their placement varies from one brand of pattern to another. Locate each section on your particular guide. Know the general purpose of each section.

Identify each section:

1. General directions for preparing the pattern and fabric and explanation of pattern marking symbols. In addition, there are generally some helpful cutting and sewing pointers. (These may be in one place or scattered in several places on the pattern guide.)

2. Selection of pattern pieces (labels and diagram).

3. Views for laying out the pattern and cutting.

4. Detailed steps for assembling and sewing.

MAKE A PREPARATORY STUDY

Understand the pattern marking symbols. Study these thoroughly. You cannot follow the rest of the directions unless you clearly understand these symbols.

Identify each pattern piece. To guide you in this identification, the following are provided:

1. A list of piece requirements for your particular view.

2. A diagram of all the pieces in the envelope.

3. Labels corresponding to these pieces.

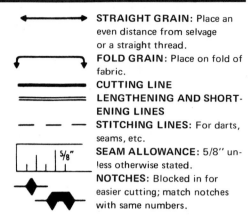

STRAIGHT GRAIN: Place an even distance from selvage or a straight thread.

FOLD GRAIN: Place on fold of fabric.

CUTTING LINE

LENGTHENING AND SHORTENING LINES

STITCHING LINES: For darts, seams, etc.

SEAM ALLOWANCE: 5/8" unless otherwise stated.

NOTCHES: Blocked in for easier cutting; match notches with same numbers.

Figure 13–1. *Pattern marking symbols (reproduced with permission of* Simplicity Pattern Company, Inc., *New York, New York).*

Identify those pieces which you need for your view. Replace unneeded pieces in your envelope.

PREPARE YOUR FABRIC

Does your fabric need special preparation? Read carefully the section on fabric preparation in the general directions, and proceed as required.

Unknown Terms Say "Stop! Look Up! Understand!"

A single term left unknown may make it necessary to redo an entire operation and may even result in permanent damage to your fabric. Terms like *bias, selvage,* and so on, should be clearly understood. You can have instant access to the meaning of an unknown term if you consult the glossary or index of a sewing resource book. Here you will find a helpful definition or description and often an illustration or diagram.

Diagrams are timesavers. They often make the meanings of terms instantly clear. Note how the diagram at the left clarifies the meaning of the term *bias.*

Figure 13–2. *On the bias.*

PREPARE YOUR PATTERN

Does your pattern need adjusting? Check your body measurements with the measurements on the envelope. If adjustments are required, proceed as follows:

1. Consult the printed directions and diagram for lengthening or shortening.

2. Locate on the pattern itself where the adjustments in length are to be made.

3. Carry out each direction.

4. Of course you will want to try on your garment and perhaps adjust it further while you are sewing.

> A GARMENT THAT IS FLATTERING TO YOU SHOULD BE A PERFECT FIT. IT IS EASIER TO MAKE SUCH A GARMENT FROM A CAREFULLY ADJUSTED PATTERN.

PREPARE FOR CUTTING

1. Locate the cutting layout that combines the following:

Your view.

Your fabric width.

Your size.

With or without nap.

2. Circle your cutting layout so that it stands out from others.

3. Study your layout carefully before you do any placing or pinning.

Note the markings and symbols that are used, and make sure of their meanings:

Dark or shaded sections.

Arrows.

VIEW 1 blouse

35″ 36″ fabric without nap
sizes 5/6, 7/8, 9/10
sizes 8, 10
NOTE: Cut one D.

Figure 13–3. *Label for cutting layout (reproduced with permission of* Simplicity Pattern Company, Inc., *New York, New York).*

Figure 13–4. *Cutting layout (reproduced with permission of* Simplicity Pattern Company, Inc., *New York, New York).*

Labels.

Letters or numbers.

Notches.

a. Identify each pattern piece by shape and letter.

b. Note on the layout the position of the fold and selvage.

c. Study carefully the arrangement of the pieces on the fabric.

d. Be alert for these: right and left side of pattern, symbol for grain of fabric, symbol for fold of fabric.

4. Place your pattern on the fabric so that it corresponds exactly to the diagram. Make sure that no piece has been forgotten and that every piece is correctly arranged before you do any cutting. If you cut with a single piece misplaced, you are likely to run short of fabric.

5. Before you cut, be sure you have identified the cutting line on the pattern. *A garment that hangs correctly is a garment that is cut correctly.*

MARK YOUR FABRIC

Several possible ways of marking your cut fabric may be suggested on the pattern guide. After selecting your method, follow each direction carefully. Refer to a sewing resource book if the marking operation is not clear. Be certain which symbols must be clearly marked on the fabric, for instance, darts, button placements, pleats, pockets. Recheck to be positive that you have made all the required markings.

SEW YOUR GARMENT

Locate the step-by-step sewing directions for the view you have selected, and proceed to follow them.

Figure 13–5. *Marking methods (reproduced with permission of Simplicity Pattern Company, Inc., New York, New York).*

1. The sequence of steps is critical. Carry out each step in the order given.

2. Make a complete stop after reading each step, if necessary, to be sure you understand what you are to do. Thought time is needed in addition to reading time.

3. Each word requires precise understanding.

4. A concisely stated step does not necessarily indicate a quick, easy operation. The operation called for may be quite lengthy.

5. Shift attention to diagrams as needed. Diagrams often give you instant how-to-do-it insights—save you working time. They often clarify processes each step of the way. They show you what to do and what *not* to do.

6. Note warnings. Words in large print or boldface type may be danger flags alerting you to possible pitfalls.

7. Take careful note of seam allowance and other measurements and be accurate with your measurements.

8. Reread as often as necessary. The moments you spend in rereading may save you hours of ripping and re-sewing.

9. Refer to a sewing resource book to clear up any operation you are doubtful about.

10. If something goes wrong, reread the procedure and recheck your actions.

UNIT 2
back and yoke back

STAY-STITCHING

a—Make darts in back;
clip and press toward center

Stitch center back seam
to notch.

STAY-STITCHING

b.

b—Make dart in yoke;
press toward center.

c—Machine-baste interfac-
ing to WRONG side of
yoke 1/2" from outer
edges. Trim interfacing
close to stitching.
With RIGHT sides to-
gether, pin back to
yoke, matching centers and small dots
Stitch seam; press up.
On OUTSIDE, top-stitch 3/8" above seam.

Figure 13–6. *Sewing directions (reproduced with permission of* Simplicity Pattern Company, Inc., *New York, New York).*

FOLLOWING THESE GUIDELINES ON HOW TO READ A SEWING PATTERN SHOULD HELP YOU SEW IN-DEPENDENTLY and SKILLFULLY.

PRECISION READING OF DIRECTIONS + CAREFUL WORKMANSHIP = A BEAUTIFUL, CUSTOM-MADE GARMENT.

Reference

Szymkowicz, Dorothy. "Home Economics and Reading." In *Fusing Reading Skills and Content*, edited by H. Alan Robinson and Ellen Lamar Thomas. Newark, Del.: International Reading Association, 1969, pp. 62–66. Paper first presented at the 1969 International Reading Association Convention, Kansas City.

14

MUSIC

This section was prepared in consultation with Frank Tirro, former University of Chicago Laboratory School music teacher and chairman of the Music Department. Mr. Tirro is now chairman of the Music Department of Duke Univerity.

Music courses often demand an extraordinarily high level of reading competence, and it is frequently the students' ability to read—not their musicality or intelligence—that determines success or failure in music. This is the observation of Frank Tirro, teacher of music theory and music history.

He emphasizes the rigorous reading that confronts students in certain textbooks: "A music theory textbook is almost in a class unto itself. Each word of explanation, each note or other symbol on the musical staff, must be carefully considered, tasted, swallowed, and rechewed like a cow's cud. One does not really *read* a theory book. One grapples with it in a life-and-death struggle. Perhaps in all reading situations the teacher is well advised to introduce students to the particular reading techniques of the discipline in question. In music it would be sadistic not to do so" (Tirro, 1969).

He urges other music teachers to become part-time reading teachers and reports his own activities in helping students digest their music textbooks: "It becomes obvious that early in the year, time must be taken to study and prepare an assignment in these courses. Instead of dictating the assignment traditionally, then sending the student home or to the library with no further instruction, it becomes clearly preferable to make the assignment and then dedicate the next few class periods to its actual preparation, the teacher demonstrating how to attack the chapter—previewing, questioning, reading, self-reciting, and so on—and then supervising students in the same processes. The teaching of method and technique is infinitely more important at this stage of the course than attempting to move directly to content. When method is faulty, the acquisition of knowledge in any form is likely to be faulty."

Two of the areas Mr. Tirro focuses on are discussed specifically in this chapter. In planning this instruction, Mr. Tirro and the reading consultant combined their insights. First, we consider the reading of musical examples and then study-techniques for the vocabulary of music. The reading-study approach to which Mr. Tirro introduces his students early in the school year is explained in Chapter 3, in the section on PQ4R. Instructors of music appreciation courses, too, can take advantage of this approach to make their students more efficient readers of their textbooks.

READING TECHNIQUES IN TEACHING MUSIC

In certain areas of music education, it is the student's reading competence that determines success or failure.

The opening weeks of a course in music theory, music history, or music appreation are the right time to help students learn to handle the heavy load of musical terminology in their textbooks. A special need—indeed, a crucial need —is a strategy for reading a *musical example*. A musical example is an explanation of a term or concept, not in words, but in notes and symbols on the musical staff (see Figure 14–1). Students often barely glance at these examples or bypass them completely. A reading technique that is unique to music is called for. Only the music teacher has the expertise to develop highly skilled readers of musical examples. And, of course, students need guidance in music, as well as in other disciplines, in learning to cope with a multitude of new terms and concepts. The rest of this chapter, therefore, consists of pragmatic tips for reading musical examples and for mastering the vocabulary of music.

TEN TIPS FOR READING A MUSICAL EXAMPLE

As you read your textbooks in music courses, you will meet explanations of new terms or concepts followed by clarifying examples. These examples—unlike those in your textbooks in other subjects—are not written in words. Instead, they are *printed in notes and symbols on the musical staff*. Bypassing these examples can be disastrous to your understanding of the term or concept.

You're likely to need a special strategy for attacking musical examples. The tips that follow should prove effective for the student who is seriously bent on mastering the vocabulary of music.

Of course, you will not need to use every technique suggested with *every* new term. Use as many of the techniques as necessary—or all of them—to grapple with the new term and grasp its meaning.

1. Most musical examples are meant to flash a warning signal: REDUCE SPEED!

2. Read the author's words of explanation with special care.

3. When the author refers you to the musical example, *shift* your eyes and thoughts *to the musical staff*. Note whether the passage is a musical excerpt or a devised textbook example.

4. When key signatures, notes, intervals, and the like are mentioned in the verbal explanation, locate these on the musical staff. *Continue* this *back-and-forth reading* as needed.

5. *Hum* or *whistle* the *passage* (or part of it) or *play it* on a musical instrument.

   a. Note the clef, the key, the meter, and the tempo.

   b. If the passage consists of a sequence of single notes instead of chords, hum or whistle the melody to yourself.

   c. If the rhythm is important to your understanding of a term or concept, you will find it helpful to tap the rhythm. Use your finger, not your foot. Finger tapping is more likely to be a conscious gesture. Foot tapping usually degenerates into unconscious motion.

   d. Chordal passages should be played on the piano.

6. *Read and reread* as often as necessary. Complete stops are called for. Thought time is needed in addition to reading time.

7. Read with pencil in hand and staff paper before you. Try to *make up* on staff paper an example of your own that fits the author's specifications. Now compare your own example with the author's and with the verbal explanation. Have you indeed "translated" the words into a musical example?

We have already mentioned the fact that notes which have the same letter name are regarded as equivalent. This is evident in the following theme.

Example 26. MOZART: *Symphony in D major, K.385* ("Haffner")

Do back-and-forth reading between printed words and musical staff.

The half note D in the second measure is not different from the first note of the theme, but merely another occurrence of the same note in a different octave. Both notes are called D. Similarly, all the notes in the third measure are C♯'s and all the notes in the final measure are A's. This reflects the operation of the principle of 8ve equivalence previously described (page 8). *Inversion*, a primary technique of chord generation, is dependent upon the principle of 8ve equivalence. We shall consider chord inversion in subsequent chapters; here we limit discussion to interval inversion. This is shown below.

Example 27.

Unison = 8ve

Figure 14–1. *Inversion of intervals (from Allen Forte, Tonal Harmony in Concept and Practice. New York: Holt, Rinehart and Winston, Inc., copyright © 1962, p. 15. Reprinted by permission).*

Creating your own example is a powerful technique. It helps bring hazy understandings into sharp focus. If you study the verbal explanation, then "illustrate" it—watch it develop, see it build up—the new term or concept should take on full, clear meaning.

You might also make up an example that does *not* fit the author's specifications and think through the reasons why it does not fit. Bring your example to class and discuss it with your teacher and classmates.

8. Turn on the "most powerful study technique known to psychologists" —*self-recite* on the new term.* Cover the words of explanation. Look at the musical example and see if you can supply the explanation in your own words. If you can't, recheck the explanation.

Now operate the other way. Expose the words, cover the musical example, and see if you can "see" the musical example.

9. All through this process, *turn on triple-strength learning*: visual, auditory, kinesthetic. If you try to learn a musical term with your eyes

---

* Walter Pauk, *How to Study in College* (Boston: Houghton Mifflin Company, 1962), p. 25.

alone, you'll be using just one-third of your sensory channels for mastering the printed page. Use your eyes—then add your ears and muscles.

Learn with your *eyes* as you *read* the words of explanation and the musical example. Strengthen learning with your *ears* as you hear yourself *hum* or *play* the example. Now you've brought to bear your auditory memory. Add *muscular learning* as you *write* your own example on staff paper. Now you've involved motor memory—one of the strongest learning channels for many students.

10. Make an effort to *use* the musical term or concept. Whenever you hear a music selection on TV or radio, on a record, or at a concert, apply and reinforce your new learnings. Now the term is likely to be *yours to stay.*

In Summing Up—
1. Reduce speed.
2. Read the words of explanation.
3. Focus on the musical example.
4. Do back-and-forth reading.
5. Hum, whistle, or play the passage.
6. Reread.
7. Make up your own example.
8. Self-recite.
9. Turn on triple-strength learning.
10. USE your new term or concept.

SOME STUDY TECHNIQUES FOR THE
VOCABULARY OF MUSIC

As you begin to study music seriously, it may seem as if you're learning a foreign language. Difficult and unfamiliar technical terms come crowding. Once an unfamiliar term is defined, the author will use it again and again—assuming ever after that you understand it.

Rote memory is not enough. You must acquire a "working understanding"—learn to use the new word tools rigorously and intelligently. Pass over these new terms lightly, and word blocks will obstruct your learning; your reading will become an obstacle course. Learn the new terms thoroughly at the time they're introduced, and you'll have precision tools for grasping essential new knowledge to the last day of the course—and beyond it.

Clearly, your vocabulary competencies now become a tremendous asset. Fortunately, learning experts at a number of universities, in actual experiments with students, have researched learning and retention techniques. Some of the procedures suggested here are based on years of experimentation in the psychology of learning.

*How will the author alert you
to important terms?*

When key terms and concepts are first introduced to you in your textbook, the author flags you with a conspicuous signal. The signal used is likely to be *italic* or **boldface** type. Words so designated are highly important "official" terms or concepts.

Figure 14–2.   *Hurdles!*

In the passage on the next page, the author makes important terms stand out on the page by using italic type:

TIPS FOR LEARNING KEY TECHNICAL TERMS IN MUSIC

1. *Attend to each new term* when first it appears. Read reflectively to grasp what the explanation is saying—not to memorize by rote, but to gain a real appreciation of the meaning.

2. *Read and reread* as often as necessary. Reading-once-straight-through patterns are no longer appropriate. Complete stops are called for frequently. Thought time is essential in addition to reading time. Even your instructor, with broad background and long experience, must read difficult new material extremely slowly.

3. Suppose, as you're reading the explanation of a new term, you encounter a musical term you've already met whose meaning now escapes you. We all forget! You have the meaning of many such terms at your fingertips—through the *index* of your textbook. It offers you instant access to the original, full textbook explanation of many terms.

4. You may wish to *consult a dictionary of musical terms* for those not included in your index. A reference that offers you clear, readable explanations is Willi Apel, *Harvard Dictionary of Music*. Music textbooks of high quality are often difficult. General vocabulary terms that you do not know may be frequent. To remove these roadblocks to your understanding, consult your general dictionary.

5. The authors' definitions of new terms are almost always followed by musical examples. *Examine* these *examples* critically and figure out how they follow the definition. You'll find a special strategy for reading musical examples earlier in this chapter.

6. *Challenge the authors*. Try to think of exceptions. Stop often and ask, "How do they have a right to say that?" "How do they justify saying that?" If you read on thinking, "I'll accept that without question," you may soon forget what the authors have said. But if you've *questioned* it and convinced yourself it's right, you're far more likely to remember. Does your own musical experience support the authors' contention? Bring your exceptions to class and challenge your teacher.

7. *Read* the explanation of the new term *with pencil in hand*. Make up your own examples on staff paper.
   Students often say, "I learn new terms, but I can't retain them." You may find it helpful to record the meaning, and perhaps an example, of difficult new terms on a flash card or in a notebook, not by rote but with full appreciation of the content. Take two or three minutes— that's all you'll need—to make each entry. If you were to do nothing

The Auxiliary Note and the Passing Note

**STOP!
LOOK!
LEARN!**

**TOOLS
FOR
FUTURE
LEARNING**

The Beethoven themes above also illustrate two melodic events of fundamental significance to the study of harmony. First, in Example 15 attention is drawn to the note marked *aux.*

This abbreviation stands for auxiliary note, a note that stands at the interval of a 2nd above or below two occurrences of a more important harmonic note. In this instance the auxiliary note D stands between two C's, C being the more important note since it belongs to the C major triad, which is the keynote or tonic triad. The second melodic event of fundamental significance is marked *pn* in Example 16. This abbreviation stands for passing note, a note that passes between or connects two more important harmonic notes. Here D, the passing note, stands between E♭ and C, which belong to the C minor triad, the tonic triad in the key of C minor. The passing note differs radically from the auxiliary note. The auxiliary note departs from and returns to the same note. The passing note connects two different notes.

Auxiliary notes and passing notes are often chromatic. In such cases spelling depends upon the function of the note. For instance, in the Haydn theme below we find a chromatic passing note which connects scale degrees 1 and 2. Since the passing note ascends, it is spelled G♯, not A♭. The latter would be the correct spelling for a descending passing note.

Example 17. HAYDN: *Symphony in G major, No. 94*

In the passage quoted below the chromatic auxiliary note is spelled F♯, not G♭, since it ascends to the main note.

Example 18. HAYDN: *Symphony in C minor, No. 95*

Figure 14–3.   *Auxiliary note and passing note (from* **Allen Forte,** Tonal Harmony in Concept and Practice. *New York: Holt, Rinehart and Winston, Inc., Copyright © 1962, p. 10. Reprinted by permission).*

more than *record* the new terms and definitions and then lost your flash cards, you would still have an advantage. The muscular act of writing, in and of itself, would have strengthened your learning.

8. *Self-recite.* Cover the words of explanation, and see if you can supply the explanation in actual words—your own words.

   You may find a "list of some important terms to define and memorize" toward the end of each chapter. You'll wish to check your understanding of these terms. The terms the authors have selected for this list are crucial.

9. Some of your new technical terms will involve difficult musical concepts. Even with the systematic, effective procedures suggested here, the meaning of some of these terms will probably elude you. Your teacher will preview some of the most difficult terms in class *before* you read your assignment. Mastery of some will come about later as you work through the exercises or as your teacher explains the material or discusses it with you.

   No question should remain unanswered. *Jot down questions* to bring to class.

10. Make an effort to *use* your *new* musical *terms.* Whenever you hear a music selection on TV or the radio, on a record, or at a concert, apply and reinforce your new learnings.

In Summing Up—
  1. Attend to each term.
  2. Reread.
  3. Use your index.
  4. Consult your dictionary.
  5. Scrutinize the examples.
  6. Challenge the authors.
  7. Be active with a pencil.
  8. Self-recite.
  9. Bring questions to class.
  10. APPLY YOUR NEW LEARNINGS.

Reference

Tirro, Frank. "Reading Techniques in the Teaching of Music." In *Fusing Reading Skills and Content*, edited by H. Alan Robinson and Ellen Lamar Thomas. Newark, Del.: International Reading Association, 1969, pp. 103–107. Paper first presented at the 1969 International Reading Association Convention, Kansas City.

LIBRARY SERVICES

The library should be a vital communication center in every junior high school, senior high school, and college. Here students should be able to find materials, print and nonprint, to help them complete their assignments and to suit their host of leisure time purposes. Here they should be conscious of a partnership between their classroom instructors and the library staff.

Librarians at the University of Chicago Laboratory School, and certainly in many other places, attempt to come to know their patrons, their reading levels, and their interests. They also often work with teachers in helping students learn the variety of reference techniques needed for units of work. The closer the liaison between the instructors and the librarians, the more the students will benefit. Librarians who are aware of assignments in advance can prepare the library environment so that students will make maximum use of its offerings.

Just as the classroom teacher's role in the reading program is usually twofold, so is the librarian's. Each should play a unique part in helping students improve their reading ability and in motivating students to turn to reading to satisfy individual needs (recreational, informational, spiritual) and to fulfill assignments.

Librarians everywhere face the persistent problem of coping with the individual needs of students in large school populations. Hour after hour, all through the school day, they attempt to get the right books into the hands of students. They will have an invaluable tool to assist them if they can have—on instant call—information about the general reading achievement of each student.

At the University of Chicago Laboratory School the reading consultant provides librarians with a simple, handy device: an "instant reading level file," with a card of useful information about the reading of each student. On the pages that follow we share with you how to make and use such a file.

Librarians Can Lead the School in "Operation Match-Up"

> *With a handy "instant reading level file"** *librarians can translate impersonal standardized test scores into the personal needs of students. How often these scores gather dust in some remote file case! With quick access to these, librarians can often match the reading reach of students and the materials they read. And they can be a force for a far-reaching "Operation Match-Up"—all through the school.†*

Librarians are confronted hourly with a broad span in reading achievement. Among students crowding around the charging desk for books to do the same assignment—on, say, Shakespeare's theater—there may be one who should be guided to a book of sixth-grade difficulty and another who can handle college reading. Without guidance, poor readers may select books years beyond their reach and, deprived of practice, fall even farther behind. Gifted readers may mark time all year instead of moving closer to their full potential.

Through daily contacts, librarians can influence the choice of reading materials throughout the school. They can sometimes make successful reading experiences possible for students who might otherwise drop out. And they can share with instructors in every classroom the conception of the school's reading range as an exciting challenge.

Put Scores on Instant Call

Librarians can have insights at their fingertips through an "instant reading level file." It is a file of cards arranged alphabetically for every student in the school.

---

* The "instant reading level file" was the subject of an article, "Instant Access to Students' Reading Levels" by Ellen Lamar Thomas in *School Library Journal*, 12, copyright © R. R. Bowker, 1966, pp. 49–52. Parts are reprinted here with special permission.

† Librarians guide students to successful reading experiences daily at the University of Chicago Laboratory School. They include Head Librarian Blanche Janecek, librarians Mary Biblo, Frances Serpe, and Winfred Poole; also Floyd Fryden, Judy Geneson, Stephanie Goldsmith, Sylvia Marantz, and Susan Peters, former librarians in the Laboratory School.

Student *Davis, Tom*   Class   *9*

Confidential

Gates-MacGinitie Reading Test, Form 1[3]

	Grade Level	I.Q. *106*
Comprehension	*7.2*	
Vocabulary	*6.9*	
Speed and Accuracy		
Number Attempted	*9.2*	Interests:
Number Correct	*6.8*	*space*
		stock cars
	Percentile Band	
STEP Social Studies	*17-37*	*wants to be*
STEP Science	*42-71*	*auto mechanic*

Figure 15–1. *Instant reading level card. A card like this places at the librarian's fingertips insights into each student's reading power and possible interests. (Gates-MacGinitie Reading Test, New York: Teachers College Press, Columbia University, 1965.)*

On each card is test information that throws light on reading. At the University of Chicago Laboratory School, librarians consult such cards from day to day. Of course they recognize the file as only one tool in reading guidance—one that must be supplemented with all the resources of a trained librarian: thorough knowledge of materials and their difficulty and, most important, knowledge of individual students. The limitations of standardized test scores are recognized, and the scores are regarded as just a suggestion of the student's reading level. It is also fully recognized that reading strength is not identical in all subject areas.

Since publishers' appraisals of the difficulty of books are often expressed in grade levels, it is convenient if the scores are stated in grade levels rather than, or in addition to, percentiles or stanines. Many tests yield scores in grade levels. Of course, percentiles and stanines are suggestive of a student's relative standing. The breakdown into vocabulary, comprehension, and speed is useful in suggesting to the librarian the student's strengths and needs in these particular areas. "STEP" scores* in social studies and science are recorded because they

---

* *Sequential Tests of Educational Progress*, Series II (Princeton, N.J.: Cooperative Test Division, Educational Testing Service, 1969–1971).

have something to suggest about the student's "reach" when reading books in these particular fields. Favorite pastimes, interests, and possible vocational choices are a useful addition.

Other Resources Must Supplement the File

Gleanings from students' cards are adjusted in the light of all the librarian knows about students, their motivations, drives, interests, backgrounds, and other factors. No student is locked into books on a certain level. A student possessed with interest in a subject (cars, for example) may, by virtue of background information and technical vocabulary, command far more reading power on this topic than reading scores suggest.

Help Rescue Retarded Readers

A stand-up tab on the card of each student enrolled with the reading teacher can be a signal to librarians for "special handling." If certain sophomores, for example, are unable to read much beyond the level of sixth graders, the special reading teacher will give materials and assignments with which they can succeed and progress, but the special teacher can work with each student only two or three hours a week. During the rest of the week—in English, science, social studies, and mathematics—readings may be years beyond such students unless the total curriculum is adjusted to their needs. Most often the curriculum is not altered, so they simply cannot cope with the rest of the school program. They lose hope and purpose. Librarians can help get the right books into the hands of these students, making a measure of success possible. Librarians can help overcome a failure mind set and help alter the damaging self-concept that has determined much poor reading behavior.

There is a special need when conscientious students overachieve, pushing beyond their powers at the sacrifice of school activities, recreation, and friendship. A senior reading around ninth-grade level may face the same assignment as others in the class who can read on college level. By providing an easier-to-read book that supplies the materials this senior needs, a librarian can help to ease the pressure.

Of course poor readers are sensitive about their handicap and are reluctant to accept materials that make them appear different. A book should not offend these students through its format, and there should be no notation of its difficulty. Librarians can guide these students inconspicuously, with casual comments: "All these books are excellent. This one has some material that may be useful. Why not look it over and see if you like it?" "You may want to read this as background before you read this." "You can take this now, if you wish, but you'll probably enjoy it much more in a year or two."

Of course, multilevel print materials alone will not solve the problems of retarded readers. Multimedia materials should also be used. Scores on the cards can alert librarians to the less verbally oriented students. Having identified the students, they will sometimes find it appropriate to provide filmstrips, slides, or other nonprint materials. Suitable print materials should be complemented with instruction on essential reading skills in subject classrooms and through the school's special remedial services. Little is gained by supplying poor readers with easy materials and leaving them there, so that they never stretch their reading power. *The goal is a sequence of increasingly difficult readings with students held to all they can do.*

A librarian often finds it possible to advance students to a more difficult book when they are caught up with interest in a topic. One librarian comments: "I find the days just before a vacation a good time to suggest something more difficult. During the vacation the student will not have to hurry in reading. Other times I suggest a more difficult book on a try-it-out basis. 'Here's a book like the one you liked—only slightly harder. You might try a few pages and see how it goes.'"

The File Can Spotlight Top Readers

The abilities of gifted readers often go unobserved. The reading levels in the file can help librarians identify these students. Top readers who habitually reach for an easy book can then be guided to works that broaden, stimulate, and challenge.

Reading Scores Have Top Security

Of course the file should have a Top Secret security rating and must be out of the reach of student assistants. It would be shattering for a junior to come across his or her card and find a score on seventh-grade level—or to learn this from a student assistant who had seen the file.

Distribution Charts Can Alert a School to Its Broad Reading Range

Reading level distribution charts (see Figure 15–2) for each grade in the school can show at a glance the spread in reading comprehension within each grade

```
┌─────────────────────────────────────────────────────────────┐
│                       NINTH GRADE                           │
│                                                             │
│  Reading Comprehension Levels        Number of Students      │
│                                                             │
│     11th-grade or above          (14)  / / / / / / / / / / / / / /    │
│     10th-grade                   (11)  / / / / / / / / / / /          │
│     9th-grade                    (20)  / / / / / / / / / / / / / / / / / / / /  │
│     8th-grade                    (13)  / / / / / / / / / / / / /      │
│     7th-grade                    (13)  / / / / / / / / / / / / /      │
│     6th-grade                    (13)  / / / / / / / / / / / / /      │
│     5th-grade                     (9)  / / / / / / / / /              │
│     4th-grade                     (7)  / / / / / / /                  │
└─────────────────────────────────────────────────────────────┘
```

Figure 15–2. *Reading level distribution chart. Reading level distribution charts reveal at a glance the spread of reading scores within a class and the number of students who scored on each level. (The reading levels illustrated are not those of the University of Chicago Laboratory School but are representative of the distribution for a number of high school populations in public schools.)*

together with the number of students who scored on each grade level. When circulated far and wide throughout a school, these dittoed sheets can have an impact on teachers who are selecting books for reading lists or considering new textbooks. The charts can be prepared in just an hour or two simply by turning through the cards in the file box and recording on the appropriate grade level a tally for each student.

The message of the chart above comes through loud and clear. Instructors see their students spread out over more than eight grade levels. The chart nudges them to provide enough sources—and enough copies—at the often neglected lower and upper extremes.

Librarians find the distribution sheets immensely helpful. After examining them, they can enter classes to advertise books armed with some knowledge of what the students in those classes can read. If librarians are searching out sources to list on a bibliography for groups working on a special assignment, they can gain from the charts insights into what those students can profitably use.*

A librarian cautions: "No one should give the impression that matching reading materials to the reading power of students is easy. We often fail. It is a

---

* Ideas based on Sylvia Marantz, "Reading: A Hot Issue for a Cool Librarian," *Fusing Reading Skills and Content,* edited by H. Alan Robinson and Ellen Lamar Thomas (Newark, Del.: International Reading Association, 1969), pp. 122, 124.

goal to work toward a little at a time, as we seek to expand our knowledge of materials and deepen our knowledge of the students as individuals."

The reading level file becomes well worn during the school year through frequent use. In free moments some librarians even sit down with the box and study the cards. One reports: "Now when students come crowding in and it is difficult to leave even for a moment, their reading levels click into mind."

FINE ARTS

A dedicated "reading teacher" is where you find one. In the University of Chicago Laboratory School there's a great one in art class. There Operation Reading is a full-scale, year-long project, built right into the art curriculum. There, in the art history, design, and photography courses—courses where reading often plays a minor role—Robert Erickson, department chairperson, sells his students reading, improves their reading, helps them find themselves through reading (Erickson, 1968, 1969).

What will you find if you look in on one of his reading oriented art classes? Shelves and shelves of books with colorful covers and intriguing content are standard equipment—as much so as paints, brushes, and palettes. Students reach for a book to find a stimulating new idea for a project, to study a technique, to search out information related to an assignment, to explore a philosophy, or just to browse. The demand for books is so great that the instructor is often asked to unlock the book cabinet before unlocking the supply cabinet.

"An art teacher has a special opportunity," Erickson points out, "to reach the unreached. Readers who have lost hope, including those most likely to become dropouts, often sign up for art, driven there by the fear of failing in reading subjects. They hope to find an activity-centered class where reading is not demanded. I try to stimulate their enthusiasm for art, then use this interest to lead them to reading. Some students, for the first time in their lives, find something to value and enjoy between book covers." Mr. Erickson would like to see libraries like his in every classroom in the school—in music, science, industrial arts, physical education, and elsewhere.

In this chapter we present Mr. Erickson's approaches both to reading improvement and the development of the reading habit, as he uses them in his art classes.

Reaching the Unreached—Through Art Class

What can an art teacher contribute to the whole-school reading program? Robert Erickson, University of Chicago Laboratory School art teacher, spells out a practical answer.

All through the class hour, powerful reading stimuli impinge upon the students in art class. Often, when a student needs the answer to an immediate and pressing problem, the teacher suggests a book.

"I'm having trouble drawing the legs of my lion in motion," a student comments. "Do you think this book might help?" the teacher suggests, indicating the profusely illustrated *Animal Drawing* by Knight. "Here are pictures of the external features and of the muscle structure, and on this page the author gives you pointers."

"I don't know how to develop my roll of film."

"Where can I find information on that artist—what's his name—oh, Kandusky?"

"What is a *cliché verre?*"

"How can I take a photo of Jim shaking hands with himself?"

"Where can I find info on geodesic domes?"

There is no period of waiting—no cooling of enthusiasm—while students run to find a book in the regular school library. Instead, they find in their hands an "instant book." As the students discover solutions to many of their problems in books, their instructor's time and energies can be directed elsewhere.

During the class hour a student may hold a dozen attractive books. While the class in discussing, say, twentieth century architecture, the instructor passes around ten or twelve books, with tabs inserted to mark some special reference ("p. 72, see 3"). Students often check out those books and take them home to read that night. Often a bright new book just added to the class library is put in the spotlight through the instructor's enthusiastic thumbnail sketch of its content, then left on the table for anyone to pick up and examine. An intriguing passage read aloud may capture a student. One day when the class was deeply involved discussing the basic question "What is art?" the instructor read aloud from Andreas Feininger's *The Creative Photographer*. A student checked out the book that night.

The *now* problems of young people searching for values in a society in ferment are grist for excited discussions. A thought provoking editorial may touch one off:

> Can a blindly angry young generation with its so-called documentary, protest pictures do much to better things? It is true that such pictures can motivate others to change things, that they are valuable as stark evidence of the neglect, poverty, and cruelty in the world. But will it not take people with a positive view of change, not simply a blindly angry view, to make the improvements that will really alter deplorable conditions? (adapted from Rothchild, 1970, p. 20).

The question "How does this relate to your lives?" recurs from day to day as the teacher taps the strong interest of teen-agers in ideals, values, and life philosophy. One day Mr. Erickson reads aloud from *The Wisdom of Confucius* or from Albert Schweitzer's *Out of My Life and Thought*. On another day he shares with students the vivid, intimate account of an artist's hopes, despairs, and thoughts about life in *The Daybooks of Edward Weston*.

Start with a Handful of Books

The art library started with a handful of books, which barely filled one side of a small bookshelf over the teacher's desk—total cost: ten or fifteen dollars. Shopping with great discrimination, Erickson had scrounged a dozen choice volumes in used-book stores, at sidewalk sales, at rummage sales, and at Salvation Army and Goodwill stores. This small collection he supplemented by bringing in his own personal books from home. Later, funds from the Art Department's budget for supplies (about thirty to fifty dollars each year) financed books for the growing library. Parents and teachers heard about the project and sent books. Windfalls came when school departments changed textbooks and donated what became resource books in science, drafting, or mathematics. In five years, a mere half a bookshelf had grown to quite an extensive collection—so many, in fact, that the books are now processed in the school library but kept on extended loan in the art classroom.

Simple checkout procedures encourage students to do out-of-class reading. Students list in a notebook their names, homeroom, the title of the book, the author, and the date borrowed. When the book comes back next day, the instructor crosses off the notation. So that all the books will be on hand each day for ready use, checkout privileges are offered only for overnight or for the weekend. The outflow to students is constant. The school library, however, is not neglected, for students go there to probe more deeply into special interests that are the outgrowth of their initial reading in art class.

The subjects of the books are as far-ranging as the interests of the students, and these range over much of the field of art. It has been necessary to stock books on many subjects: collage, sculpture, painting techniques, architecture and city planning, drawing, cartooning, art history, product design, creative process, automation, handicrafts, toys and games, printing, typography, lettering, design, invention, structure, modern art trends, photojournalism, photo tricks, procedures in developing, printing and enlarging photographs, movie-making, night photography—and more. Books are selected on the basis of quality of writing, color, printing, layout, and cost. The latest issues of *Craft Horizons* and *Popular Photography* are also on the shelves.

As an aid for the art teacher in matching book and student, the reading consultant once coded the level of reading difficulty in each book. Each year she arms him with a handy score kit containing a card for each student with standardized reading scores and a suggestion of the student's reading grade level. "These cards," Erickson comments, "alert me to readers who may need special assistance. The scores give me some idea, especially during the first few weeks, whether to hand a student a book of sixth-grade difficulty or one on college level. More often, though, I work intuitively by finding material of vital interest and suggesting small segments to be digested."

Can an Art Teacher Teach Reading?

How can an art teacher, with no special expertise in teaching reading, help less verbally oriented students learn from the answers in books? "Students let me know freely," answers Erickson, "when they don't understand a passage. Then I have a number of choices, or combinations of choices:

> 1. The class is often an activity period during which each student is working in a different direction. This gives me a chance to sit down with the student and read the passage. We work our way by small steps through difficult material. Often we read it sentence by sentence, stopping at the end of each and seeing what the student did or did not comprehend. I help clarify terms not understood.
>
> 2. The reading consultant suggested that we strip a long, involved sentence down to its framework. When there are long, complicating subordinate phrases and clauses, we let these go for the moment and look for the main clause, or kernel of meaning. When this framework shows clearly through and we have a firm hold on the main idea or fact, then

we can return and read the material again with all its trimmings to get the full sense (Pauk, 1974, p. 146).

3. I can ask students to read aloud to me. As they read I discover something about reading blocks: Do they give up completely before a word that seems difficult? Guess wildly at words? Should they try harder to figure words out? Should they be helped to work out context strategies? Can they handle the material at all, or is it hopelessly beyond them?

4. If the reading matter clearly exceeds their reach, I can direct them to simpler material.

5. Sometimes I supply a book I hope students can understand and guide them to a small segment—a paragraph or a page related to what they are doing. I make it a point to observe them as they go on with their work. When they seem to be having difficulty, I step in and help, discussing the troublesome part. Sometimes it's enough just to encourage them to persist—to read and reread the segment.

6. When a technical term is sure to overwhelm students, I teach the term before they begin reading. Ted, who was exploring the work of Jackson Pollock, would have been blocked by *abstract expressionist.* So I explained the term *before* he began reading. Students often search out answers for themselves in our well worn classroom copy of *Dictionary of Art and Artists.* A handy general dictionary is also within reach, and students turn to it often.

7. Sometimes other students are a great help in explaining meaning in readings. I often ask students with greater experience and background to help those less competent with the reading material and with the project itself.

Subject teachers are not reading specialists," Erikson goes on. "They are limited in what they can do. As time goes on, though, I notice that some poor readers can now read more difficult books. And I constantly observe how the driving interest of a student helps leap over barriers. When the desire to know is strong enough, the student can often dig the meaning out of difficult bits of material in highly technical books."

If you are interested in techniques for reading expository chapters in art appreciation, art history, architecture, and related fields, you may wish to refer to "You Can Upgrade Students' Textbook Reading," in Chapter 3.

Especially in photography class, students must often read directions, then carry out with the utmost precision the not-to-be-played-with procedures. Mr. Erickson resists spelling out for students exactly what they are to do. Instead, he equips them to read these directions and, in the process, moves them toward independence. He encourages the student about to mix a gallon of photodeveloper with: "Study the directions on the can with extreme care. They must be followed 100 percent in order for you to have a usable product. Overlooking a single direction in fine print may ruin your developer. Make brief jottings in your own words of the steps you're going to take, then check your steps with me before mixing your developer." The reader interested in detailed direction-reading techniques will find easily adaptable suggestions in "Road Signs for Reading Directions" in Chapter 10.

"Problems" Can Help

In problem-centered art courses, the students are often caught up with exciting problems. Mr. Erickson frequently personalizes the problems, brings them close to the lives of his students; then these problems trigger the drive to read.

> Learn about the artist whose work most closely resembles your own.
>
> Investigate your own nationalistic, racial, or religious roots through art forms.
>
> Try to discover the work of some artist whose point of view most closely parallels your own. Point out the similarities.

Now reading skills for problem solving are germane to the art class. Acquiring these does not drain away time—many such skills can be taught in minutes. Student and instructor now narrow problems to manageable proportions and plan how to organize material better. Doors are opened to rich reading resources in art of which the student has been unaware. As a student holds a promising book in hand, he or she may learn to use the index as an aid to quick finding of what is wanted from among the thousands of words in the book. The student may learn to scan pages and columns for information related to a problem, speeding right past unpromising paragraph headings, then slowing down to examine a promising paragraph. He or she is likely to leave art class with more expertise for exploring problems in the field of art and for continuing art education after the course is over. Skills essential for students in solving problems through reading are found in Chapter 5.

Students Become Lifetime Readers

Students possessed with interest in problems in art are often led to rewarding experiences with reading. Erickson gives some examples:

One day Ricky, a not-so-eager reader, expressed an interest in architecture. I asked, "Do you know the work of Frank Lloyd Wright? Eero Saarinen? Antonio Gaudi?" We went to the bookcase together, looked through some choice books on architecture, and Ricky was attracted to Saarinen. We sat down together at a table with the book, talked over some of the descriptive material. During the course I saw Ricky turn to that book often—and then to others. He probably digested every book on architecture on the shelf. Later he talked about his life choice—and architecture seems to be the direction he has chosen.

Mary, a below-average reader caught up with science, wanted to photograph under the microscope tiny living things in a drop of water. Knowing nothing about taking photomicrographs, she now had a driving reason for reading. I suppose I might have *shown* her how to take these pictures. Instead I suggested, "Here's an explanation in *The Focal Encyclopedia of Photography*. Ask questions about any part you don't understand." Slowly digesting each paragraph and asking frequent questions, she read for four consecutive class sessions. At the end of the fourth day, Mary borrowed a microscope from the science lab and a 35-mm reflex camera from me and began her experimentation. The results were some good color photographs of tiny-celled creatures—and a greater potential for Mary in finding things out for herself.

Carl, a black student who had a reading problem, expressed interest in his own heritage in art. I directed him to books on tribes and forms of African art. He spent a good deal of time studying the illustrations and reading about his ancestral people. We discussed the characteristics of the various tribal examples and together formulated some creative examples that challenged him and enabled him to depart from—yet use— material he had studied. A year later, Carl still drops by the art room, browses through the books for hours, selects some to read, and takes time to talk over what he is reading.

Often students begin their own private library collections as a result of reading successes in the art classroom. Judy, a sophomore, in response to the assignment to find the work of some artist whose work most closely resembled her own, wrote a paper on her reactions to Picasso's work and brought in a new book on Picasso for me to see and to use as I marked her report. She commented, "The best thing about the assignment was that I added this book to my own collection!"

Charles, both reluctant and retarded as a reader, had great successes in art class but failures everywhere else in school. I encouraged him to look at work by other artists in our books. He started to look at slides and at color reproductions in the books, but he didn't read—at first. I read aloud, though, to his class, and he became curious about the ideas expressed by artists. He began to read small bits of information related to the artists whose work he admired. Later he joined an art book club and began to build up his own home art library. As each new book arrived, he would bring the precious volume to me so that I could share his newly found joys. He even selected books for me to read. I felt some real success with Charles.

It Doesn't Take with Every Student

"Reading doesn't take with every student," Erickson found. "Some are not reached at all. They are not anxious to read but only to *do*. They avoid reading suggestions and reading assignments. They take a grade of *F* on an assignment that involves reading rather than meet the requirement. And there is another problem—the problem of thefts. My classroom library used to be in the next room where students could quietly go and do research, browse, read, or just relax with a book. Many fine volumes were stolen, particularly those dealing with nudes, anatomy, and photo techniques, and those dealing with Dada and surrealist art. Such volumes are now kept out of reach in locked cabinets. These may be signed out only for use during the class period. I have moved the art library into both the art and photo classrooms where I can constantly check the volumes. Thefts are less frequent, but they still occur. I hate to think of keeping the books locked up. I would rather take the attitude that the gains for students through having books easily accessible outweigh the losses. However, the books I bring from my own home are used only by the period. I do not loan them for overnight use."

Dividends from Operation Reading

Staggering sums are required to reclaim students who leave school without reading power and without earning power. The sum expended to finance an art class library is an investment in *prevention*.

1. A student's strong interest in art related subjects can help remove psychological blocks to reading progress.

2. The world of words has never been the world of poor readers. When a teacher guides them to a book right in difficulty and

interest, they may, for the first time, spend many hours in the world of printed words. They meet words repeatedly in similar and different settings, often with a little increment of meaning at each encounter, and they gradually incorporate new words into their vocabulary. Their reading practice tends to strengthen comprehension.

3. An impelling interest in some aspect of art may enable poor readers to handle "far too difficult" books and to extend their reading power.

4. They may do an about-face in attitudes toward books. Though the printed page has held little appeal for them, they may now view it as a possible source of solutions to in-class and out-of-class problems.

5. The presence of the classroom collection daily builds toward voluntary and habitual reading.

6. Inviting do-it-yourself projects often leads to home hobbies, especially when the student has the ability to read and follow simple directions. Some simple photo and art materials at home—a simple camera, a few pieces of charcoal, some stencils for lettering, a brush or two and some paints—can involve teen-agers in constructive hobbies and can help to keep them off the streets.

7. A student's self-concept determines much of his or her behavior, including reading behavior. A young person who views herself or himself as an individual who cannot read tends to fulfill these expectations. A damaging self-concept may be altered by successful reading experiences in art class and elsewhere. Success through and with reading sometimes helps a discouraged reader take hold, renew efforts, and succeed better in the broader school situation.

References

Erickson, Robert. "Art Class Book Collection Promotes Better Reading." *Journal of Reading*, 11, no. 5 (February 1968): 333–336.

Erickson, Robert. "The Art Room Book Collection." In *Fusing Reading Skills and Content*, edited by H. Alan Robinson and Ellen Lamar Thomas. Newark, Del.: International Reading Association, 1969, pp. 89–96. Paper presented to the 1969 International Reading Association Convention, Kansas City.

Pauk, Walter. *How to Study in College*, 2nd ed. Boston: Houghton Mifflin Company, 1974.

Rothchild, Norman. "Offbeat." *Popular Photography*, 66, no. 6 (June 1970).

17

PHYSICAL EDUCATION

The development of lifetime readers is an obligation as well as an enjoyable responsibility of all teachers. Skill in reading without the concomitant use of the skills for a multitude of purposes selected by the reader is of questionable virtue.

In many classes, such as physical education, the actual teaching of reading skills has little or no place. But the physical education instructor has as much of a responsibility as any other teacher (perhaps more) for helping students make use of reading materials related to the field. In fact, the physical education instructor has a remarkable *opportunity* for helping students turn to reading they will enjoy without bothering them about whether or not their reading skills are adequate.

Too often, the words in the opening paragraph above become educational lingo, often stated and infrequently followed. Throughout this volume, however, you meet teachers who *really believe* in the development of lifetime reading habits and who have worked out procedures for doing something about them.

In this chapter you meet a physical education instructor and coach, Sanford Patlak, who is dedicated to the development of lifetime readers. We try to show here (a difficult job without the enthusiasm and spontaneity of Coach Patlak himself) the specific techniques he uses for getting all students, and particularly reluctant readers, to turn to books about sports—fiction, nonfiction, biography, autobiography, reference materials. Some specific book titles are referred to, but the reader should realize that they do not remain static; Coach Patlak adds new titles as he finds materials he feels will be exciting, valid, and pertinent. His most recent bibliography of books for easy reading is a good starting list for teachers who want to get their physical education students to read (Patlak, 1969).

Coaches Can Get Students "Hooked on Books"

Sanford Patlak, whose part in his school's reading program is reported here, is basketball coach and physical education instructor at the University of Chicago Laboratory School. Coach Patlak sees opportunities in schools, particularly inner-city schools, for coaches to help prospective dropouts. He catches his readers young.*

"If you can get the coach to play a part in your reading program, you've got one of the best guys in the school on your team," comments basketball coach "Sandy" Patlak. The status a coach's recommendation to read books has with students can change their attitudes toward reading. Now reading becomes respected instead of "square."†

"There are opportunities," Coach Patlak points out, "with boys in depressed neighborhoods. Sports rate high in these areas. Suppose a boy thinks the coach is great. The coach might say, 'Jim, come into my office—I have this book. Can you look it over and see how you like it?' You just might give him a reading interest—a habit, maybe. You might help keep him off the streets. It just might work."

Students can improve their athletic techniques through books. Publishers are offering outstanding how-to-do-its on every sport. By pushing these books a coach can have more playing power on the team. Television is bringing sports events to millions, many of whom are ill-informed. Through books, students can broaden their backgrounds and add to their enjoyment as spectators.

---

* Coach Patlak's work with students was reported in an article, "Books Are the Greatest," by Ellen Lamar Thomas, *Journal of Reading*, 12 (November 1968): 119–124. Parts are reprinted here with permission. Although "Sandy" works with boys, obviously much of what he reports can be accomplished with girls in physical education classes.

† Mrs. Lois Osberg helped Coach Patlak start his project when she was interning as a reading consultant in the University of Chicago Laboratory School. The reports of some of the coach's reading sessions are drawn from her notes. Mrs. Osberg is now Director of Reading, Duneland School Corporation, Chesterton, Indiana.

The Sports Library—The Busiest Spot

At times Coach Patlak's library of sports books is the busiest spot in the gym. Comments the coach, "It's where sports books belong." A traffic-stopping red and white highway sign invites students to STOP at the coach's bookshelves. A poster headed *"Have you read this?"* displays colorful dustjackets high in sports appeal—*Football Fury, Go Team Go,* and *Baseball Sparkplug.*

A Coach Can Start a Library with Pennies and an Orange Crate

Coach Patlak started his library with little time and less money:

> Someone was getting rid of some bookshelves. I set them on an old training table. My first books were second-hand—had a lot of mileage on them. I asked my varsity boys and the boys in my classes to bring in old books. Mothers and dads heard about it and sent me books. The response was tremendous. And I bought books for pennies at rummage sales.
>
> You can start with a handful of books and an orange crate for a shelf. You can have a plush library—rows of clean, expensive books—but without someone's interest, boys may not reach for one. My library wasn't big, but it did the job.

Later the school's reading consultant paid for the coach's book orders by selling packets of locally made instructional materials to visitors. Hearing about the project, the school's director made a sum available. In other schools, a coach might interest a school service club or a leader of the PTA. School libraries often lend books for classroom collections. The possibility of federal or state funds can be investigated through the school librarian.

Sports Books Invite the Reluctant Reader

Coach Patlak's collection ranges over the entire field of sports. To help him select books, the reading consultant supplied book lists, which offered capsule summaries, interest levels, and reading difficulty levels. On the coach's shelves are action-packed fiction and how-to-do-it books on the major sports as well as on judo, camping out, lifesaving, scuba diving, fishing, and drag racing. There are colorful, attractive paperbacks, slim and trim enough to invite the hand of a reluctant reader. The books span a broad range of difficulty levels from grade four through college. The coach knows his books. He reads the how-to-do-its, skims the fiction, and makes it a point to remember student comments.

You Can Do Your Selling Job in Minutes

Coach Patlak talks up books on the playing field, on the edge of the swimming pool, in the gym with students sitting around him on tumbling mats. "It takes hardly any time," he comments. "You can do your selling job in a few minutes at the beginning of the period." He pushes books hard with younger readers: "Catch kids young—before they lag behind."

He "sells" books to seventh-graders lined up on benches alongside the swimming pool. He pulls books out of a carton, holds up each one, and keeps up a running sales talk. He paces back and forth around the circle, showing a bright paperback, *The Kid Comes Back*. "This is about a fellow who was captured after his plane crashed in wartime. He kept longing to play ball again. It tells how he escaped and became a big league player. It's a tremendous book!"

He reaches into the carton for *How to Star in Track and Field* and waves it before the class. "We'll be starting track soon. This one's topnotch. It shows you how to pace yourself, work up to distance running, improve your starts. A tip you pick up here may make you a better competitor. Sports and books on how to improve your skills go hand in hand. You can learn in your own room. Is it easy? Right! You don't have to worry about hard words. Books are the greatest!"

Out of the carton comes *Strike*, a how-to-do-it book on bowling. "This is for a guy like you, Andy. Bowling is your thing. You'll learn how to have the right stance, how to pick up the ball the right way from the rack. *See* how to bowl. Are there good pictures! One picture may give you a pointer."

Last, he waves *Basketball Rules*. "You might want this one, Don. You're a good ballplayer, but there's a lot to learn about the rules. You can't play—you can't even *watch* intelligently—if you don't know the rules. Read just as much as you want to, maybe just ten or fifteen minutes. You don't have to read all of it, just the parts you're interested in. We've got a good deal going in these books. They're in the locker room with the balls. If you want one, just check it out after class."

Checking Out Books Is Simple

Students, showered and dressed, wait in line by the door for the passing bell, close to the locker room library—its door wide open. "Just take the card out of the book and write your name," suggests the coach, "then put it in the box on my desk." (Books can be processed with cards and pockets by student assistants.)

Star athletes sometimes start runs on books: "Sometimes a school hero carries a book out under his or her arm, and the lowerclassmen say, 'I want that book next time! Wow, I've got to have that book!' After that, I just can't keep that book—it goes out with one student after another."

Operation Match-Up Guides
Students to Books

"Give a kid a book beyond his reach," Coach Patlak comments, "and you'll lose him." The level of difficulty has been color-coded in each book by the reading consultant. "Property of Coach Patlak" is entered in red for a difficulty level around grade 4, green for grade 6, blue for grade 8, and so on. In schools with no consultant, librarians can appraise difficulty.

"I know where the kids stand in reading," the coach explains. "The reading consultant gives me the scores. All the time it's going through my mind. 'You're a poor reader.' 'You're a good reader.' I cover up my intent. If I hand out books during class, the first one goes to a top reader. But later I maneuver so that the right book goes to the one who can't read well."

The coach has in mind sequences of books of increasing difficulty and likes to advance a pupil through a series on some compelling interest like football or scuba diving. A student possessed with such an interest can sometimes handle "far too difficult" books. It's great to see a reader "graduate" from extremely easy books to books that stretch his reading power. Top readers, too, crowd the library, often taking home a book from the coach's own professional collection.

Book Reporting Starts Run on Books

Teen-agers respect a book tip from someone their own age. They sometimes trade tips out on the soccer field, sitting in a circle on the grass.

Coach. I'd like to talk with you a minute about the books you've been reading. Mark, you took one out the other day. Are you through with it? What was it about?

Mark. It was about football. The name of it was *The Keeper Play.*

Coach. Were there some exciting spots?

Mark. Yes. It was cool when they were doing this special play called "the keeper play."

Coach. Hold it! That's the whole thing—that special play! Don't tell about it. Let them read it and find out!

Coach. Do you think someone else here would like your book, Bob?

Bob. I think so. It's *How to Play Baseball*. It showed things you really need to know.

Coach. Did you like anything especially?

Bob. It showed me how to throw a curve ball.

Coach. Who in the class would like it?

Bob. I'd give it to Ron. He wants to be a pitcher.

Coach. Was it hard to read—hard words?

Bob. No, sir. It was OK.

Books Can Help Mixed-Up Students

In the library is an article, "What Man Can Be," by Bob Richards, clipped from *Guideposts* (October 1968) and supplied with bright construction paper cover. "When a kid gets hurt and is feeling low because he or she can't play again," observes the coach, "this one might be just right to talk about. Here you learn about stars who had setbacks. Take Bob Mathias. That guy really had heart. His foot was badly torn. Later it became his take-off foot in jumping. You learn about how great champs started up the ladder again. When a kid has a problem, I try to find a book about the same problem. I can talk up the book walking with the student down the hall."

Sports Page Can Grab Athletes

Coach Patlak rides the crests of sports enthusiasms—the surge of interest as a season approaches, the wave of excitement when a school team is having a winning streak, when the local pros are front-runners. "I catch the kids when they're geared up with a certain interest. Before class starts, I ask a question, "What's the big sports headline today?' That starts a chain reaction: 'Did you see that article about so-and-so who was traded to so-and-so?' 'How did Wimbledon come out?' 'Is the Cubs' streak still alive?' 'Try to look over the sports page Sunday and remember the highlights. We'll have a little rundown Monday.'

"These questions take about a minute. It doesn't take much time to sell reading. I get my regular job done."

The Bulletin Board Can Help Too

The bulletin board "grabs" students as they enter the gym. A large placard spot-lights the local "Players of the Week" and announces the reason these athletes were selected. A series of pictures, with captions, on how to make a free throw invites reading. Displayed on large laminated cards are the Athlete's Creed, the Code of Sportsmanship of a nearby college, and the coach's Thought for the Week: "When the going gets tough, the tough get going."

A Coach Can "Sell" Library Cards

The coach gives vacation reading a sendoff: "We don't want the kids to stop reading when they leave in June. I take five minutes near the end of school and say, 'Soon you're going home for vacation, and I know you're all interested in reading some more books. How many of you have library cards?' Those who have no cards are given applications. They fill these in at home and then bring them back to gym class. The last day of class in June I give out the cards to every-one personally. A student can do the leg work—get the application forms from the library, return these to the library, and bring me the cards."

Coach and Reading Teacher Work Together

Sometimes the coach and the reading teacher talk over under-par readers. One of these was Don—in school a poor reader, out of school an "I won't" reader. The coach reports: "Last week Don broke a record getting dressed to be the first in line for a book. He walked out of the gym with that book under his coat. Today he told me about it. Maybe I've changed an attitude, created an interest. That's all I wanted to do—just create an interest. You reading teachers won't go out and think you can coach basketball. And I don't want you to think that I'm a reading teacher. But working together, we can do the job."

"The coach," Coach Patlak sums it up, "is a seller—he brings in the crowds with his teams. And the coach can be one of the school's best sellers of reading."

Reference

Patlak, Sanford. "Sandy's 99 Sports Books for Reluctant Readers." In *Fusing Reading Skills and Content*, edited by H. Alan Robinson and Ellen Lamar Thomas. Newark, Del.: International Reading Association, 1969, pp. 201–204.

Subject Index

Name Index